Evolution of Government Policy Towards Homosexuality in the US Military

Throughout history, homosexuality has been a complicating factor for men and women electing to serve in the armed forces of the United States. The right to serve became increasingly complicated when the Department of Defense responded to congressional legislation in 1993 by adopting a policy that later became known as *"don't ask, don't tell"* (DADT). DADT permitted homosexual members to serve in the forces, so long as they showed no evidence of homosexual behavior. The compromise policy remained in force until Congress passed the Don't Ask, Don't Tell Repeal Act of 2010 and finally, in September 2011, the ban on gay men and lesbians serving openly in the US armed forces officially came to an end. Reflecting on the 20-year period governed by DADT, this volume explores the history, culture, attitudes and impacts of policy evolution from the mid-20th Century through to the present day. It not only provides insight to the scholarly field of how the most powerful institution in the world has viewed and dealt with homosexuality as it transitioned into the 21st century, but it is also poised to become a seminal collection for researchers in the decades to come.

This book was originally published as a special issue of the *Journal of Homosexuality*.

Jim Parco is an Associate Professor of Economics and Business at Colorado College, USA. He received his Ph.D. from the University of Arizona and an MBA from the College of William & Mary. He previously taught at the Air Command & Staff College, USA, and at the US Air Force Academy. He retired from active-duty in 2011. He has co-authored *The 52nd Floor: Thinking Deeply about Leadership*, *Attitudes Aren't Free: Thinking Deeply about Diversity in the U.S. Armed Forces* and *Echoes of Mind: Thinking Deeply about Humanship*.

David A. Levy is a Professor of Management at the US Air Force Academy. He served on active-duty from 1988-1998 and received his Ph.D. in organizational behavior from Cornell University, USA. He has co-authored *The 52nd Floor: Thinking Deeply about Leadership*, *Attitudes Aren't Free: Thinking Deeply about Diversity in the U.S. Armed Forces* and *Echoes of Mind: Thinking Deeply about Humanship*.

"Parco and Levy have produced a fine edited volume dedicated to deepening our understanding of the federal DADT policy. What has resulted is a deep analysis of the federal policies regarding gays and lesbians in the U.S. military. This volume is filled with rich descriptions and analyses written by the very best thinkers about issues pertaining to gays and lesbians in the U.S. military. Parco and Levy not only offer a comprehensive treatment of DADT, but their book will stand the test of time and spur additional important research about gay, lesbian, bisexual, and queer service members. *The Rise and Fall of DADT* is accessibly written and offers readers a comprehensive understanding of the DADT federal policy and the attendant issues of equity, social justice and ever-changing attitudes about LGBTQ people related to the U.S. military and to the larger American society."

John P. Elia, Ph.D. Editor-in-Chief, Journal of Homosexuality and Professor and Associate Chair of Health Education at San Francisco State University, USA

"As Assistant Secretary of Defense for Public Affairs from 2010 to 2012, and the first openly-gay senior official to serve at the Pentagon, I was witness to and honored to be an active participant in the historic process that led to the ban on discrimination against lesbian and gay service members: men and women who had been hiding in plain sight while risking their lives to serve their country honorably. In this volume, Jim Parco and Dave Levy provide what is perhaps the most comprehensive account to date of the evolution of US government policy regarding LGBT service members. Their study includes outstanding firsthand narratives by many friends who played central roles in the repeal of Don't Ask/Don't tell, including Sue Fulton, Jonathan Lee and former Congressman Patrick Murphy. Parco and Levy provide the opportunity for scholars, experts and ordinary citizens from all walks of life to share in those journeys and in the very positive results that were achieved."

Douglas B. Wilson, former Assistant Secretary of Defense for the United States

Evolution of Government Policy Towards Homosexuality in the US Military
The Rise and Fall of DADT

Edited by
James E. Parco and David A. Levy

Routledge
Taylor & Francis Group

LONDON AND NEW YORK

First published 2014 by Routledge

2 Park Square, Milton Park, Abingdon, Oxfordshire OX14 4RN
711 Third Avenue, New York, NY 10017

Routledge is an imprint of the Taylor & Francis Group, an informa business

First issued in paperback 2018

Copyright © 2014 Taylor & Francis

All rights reserved. No part of this book may be reprinted or reproduced or utilised in any form or by any electronic, mechanical, or other means, now known or hereafter invented, including photocopying and recording, or in any information storage or retrieval system, without permission in writing from the publishers.

Notice:
Product or corporate names may be trademarks or registered trademarks, and are used only for identification and explanation without intent to infringe.

British Library Cataloguing in Publication Data
A catalogue record for this book is available from the British Library

ISBN13: 978-0-415-81603-8 (hbk)
ISBN13: 978-1-138-37768-4 (pbk)

Typeset in Garamond
by Cenveo Publisher Services

Publisher's Note
The publisher accepts responsibility for any inconsistencies that may have arisen during the conversion of this book from journal articles to book chapters, namely the possible inclusion of journal terminology.

Disclaimer
Every effort has been made to contact copyright holders for their permission to reprint material in this book. The publishers would be grateful to hear from any copyright holder who is not here acknowledged and will undertake to rectify any errors or omissions in future editions of this book.

The Views expressed in this volume are expressly those of the authors and do not reflect the official policy of the Department of Defence, U.S. Government or any associated entity.

Contents

Citation Information ix

PREFACE
The Rise and Fall of DADT 1
James E. Parco and David A. Levy

FOREWORD
The Political Battle for Repeal: Personal Reflections from
the Frontlines 7
Patrick J. Murphy

SECTION I
Agents for change 15

1 The President's Pleasant Surprise: How LGBT Advocates Ended
   Don't Ask, Don't Tell 17
   Nathaniel Frank

2 The Politics of Paranoia 73
   Aaron Belkin

3 OutServe: An Underground Network Stands Up 79
   Brenda Sue Fulton

4 The Rise of Repeal: Policy Entrepreneurship and
   Don't Ask, Don't Tell 93
   Christopher L. Neff and Luke R. Edgell

SECTION II
Policy evolution 111

5 From Exclusion to Acceptance: A Case History of Homosexuality
   in the U.S. Court of Military Appeals 113
   Kellie Wilson-Buford

CONTENTS

6   Formalizing the Ban: My Experience in the Reagan Administration   137
Lawrence J. Korb and Alex Rothman

7   The Comprehensive Review Working Group and Don't Ask, Don't Tell Repeal at the Department of Defense   147
Jonathan L. Lee

8   Outing the Costs of Civil Deference to the Military   177
Elizabeth L. Hillman

9   Gays in the U.S. Military: Reviewing the Research and Conceptualizing A Way Forward   193
Armando X. Estrada, Gia A. DiRosa and Arwen H. DeConstanza

SECTION III
Organizational implications   223

10   Policy and Paradox: Grounded Theory at the Moment of DADT Repeal   225
James E. Parco and David A. Levy

11   The Myth of the Warrior: Martial Masculinity and the End of Don't Ask, Don't Tell   251
L. Michael Allsep

12   If We Ask, What They Might Tell: Clinical Assessment Lessons from LGBT Military Personnel Post-DADT   271
Maria Heliana Ramirez, Stephen Joseph Rogers, Harriet Lee Johnson, Jon Banks, Wanda Penny Seay, Billy Lee Tinsley and Andrew Warren Grant

13   Mental Health Characteristics of Sexual Minority Veterans   289
Bryan N. Cochran, Kimberly Balsam, Annesa Flentje, Carol A. Malte and Tracy Simpson

14   Transgender People in the Military: Don't Ask? Don't Tell? Don't Enlist!   307
Adam F. Yerke and Valory Mitchell

15   One Year Out: An Assessment of DADT Repeal's Impact on Military Readiness   329
Aaron Belkin, Morten G. Ender, Nathaniel Frank, Stacie Furia, George R. Lucas, Gary A. Packard, Steven M. Samuels, Tammy S. Schultz, and David R. Segal

APPENDICES 375

Appendix A—Recommendations for post DADT health care systems serving LGBT veterans 377

Appendix B—Standards of Evidence 379

Appendix C—Letter to 553 Retired General and Admirals 381

Appendix D—DADT Repeal Opponents Contacted 383

Appendix E—Watchdog Organizations Contacted 385

Appendix F—Scholars & Experts Interviewed 387

Appendix G—Service Member Interviews 389

Appendix H—Military Times Advertisement 393

Appendix 1: Title 10, Section 654 of the United States Code. "Policy Concerning Homosexuality in the Armed Forces" (1993) 395

Appendix 2: Executive Summary, Report of the Comprehensive Review of the Issues Associated with a Repeal of Don't Ask, Don't Tell 399

Appendix 3: H.R.6520 – Don't Ask, Don't Tell Repeal Act of 2010 417

Index 421

Citation Information

The the following chapters were originally published in the *Journal of Homosexuality*, volume 60, issue 2-3 (March 2013). When citing this material, please use the original page numbering for each article, as follows:

Preface
The Rise and Fall of DADT
James E. Parco and David A. Levy
Journal of Homosexuality, volume 60, issue 2–3 (March 2013) **pp. 1–5**

Foreword
The Political Battle for Repeal: Personal Reflections from the Frontlines
Patrick J. Murphy
Journal of Homosexuality, volume 60, issue 2–3 (March 2013) **pp. 7–13**

Chapter 1
The President's Pleasant Surprise: How LGBT Advocates Ended Don't Ask, Don't Tell
Nathaniel Frank
Journal of Homosexuality, volume 60, issue 2–3 (March 2013) **pp. 17–71**

Chapter 2
The Politics of Paranoia
Aaron Belkin
Journal of Homosexuality, volume 60, issue 2–3 (March 2013) **pp. 73–77**

Chapter 3
OutServe: An Underground Network Stands Up
Brenda Sue Fulton
Journal of Homosexuality, volume 60, issue 2–3 (March 2013) **pp. 79–91**

Chapter 4
The Rise of Repeal: Policy Entrepreneurship and Don't Ask, Don't Tell
Christopher L. Neff and Luke R. Edgell
Journal of Homosexuality, volume 60, issue 2–3 (March 2013) **pp. 93–110**

Chapter 5
From Exclusion to Acceptance: A Case History of Homosexuality in the U.S. Court of Military Appeals
Kellie Wilson-Buford
Journal of Homosexuality, volume 60, issue 2–3 (March 2013) **pp. 113–135**

Chapter 6
Formalizing the Ban: My Experience in the Reagan Administration
Lawrence J. Korb and Alex Rothman
Journal of Homosexuality, volume 60, issue 2–3 (March 2013) **pp. 137–145**

Chapter 7
The Comprehensive Review Working Group and Don't Ask, Don't Tell Repeal at the Department of Defense
Jonathan L. Lee
Journal of Homosexuality, volume 60, issue 2–3 (March 2013) **pp. 147–176**

Chapter 8
Outing the Costs of Civil Deference to the Military
Elizabeth L. Hillman
Journal of Homosexuality, volume 60, issue 2–3 (March 2013) **pp. 177–191**

Chapter 9
Gays in the U.S. Military: Reviewing the Research and Conceptualizing A Way Forward
Armando X. Estrada, Gia A. DiRosa and Arwen H. DeConstanza
Journal of Homosexuality, volume 60, issue 2–3 (March 2013) **pp. 193–221**

Chapter 10
Policy and Paradox: Grounded Theory at the Moment of DADT Repeal
James E. Parco and David A. Levy
Journal of Homosexuality, volume 60, issue 2–3 (March 2013) **pp. 225–249**

Chapter 11
The Myth of the Warrior: Martial Masculinity and the End of Don't Ask, Don't Tell
L. Michael Allsep
Journal of Homosexuality, volume 60, issue 2–3 (March 2013) **pp. 251–270**

Chapter 12
If We Ask, What They Might Tell: Clinical Assessment Lessons from LGBT Military Personnel Post-DADT
Maria Heliana Ramirez, Stephen Joseph Rogers, Harriet Lee Johnson, Jon Banks, Wanda Penny Seay, Billy Lee Tinsley and Andrew Warren Grant
Journal of Homosexuality, volume 60, issue 2–3 (March 2013) **pp. 271–287**

Chapter 13
Mental Health Characteristics of Sexual Minority Veterans
Bryan N. Cochran, Kimberly Balsam, Annesa Flentje, Carol A. Malte and Tracy Simpson
Journal of Homosexuality, volume 60, issue 2–3 (March 2013) **pp. 289–305**

Chapter 14
Transgender People in the Military: Don't Ask? Don't Tell? Don't Enlist!
Adam F. Yerke and Valory Mitchell
Journal of Homosexuality, volume 60, issue 2–3 (March 2013) **pp. 307–328**

PREFACE

The Rise and Fall of DADT

JAMES E. PARCO, PhD

Department of Economics and Business, Colorado College, Colorado Springs, Colorado, USA

DAVID A. LEVY, PhD

Department of Management, United States Air Force Academy, Colorado Springs, Colorado, USA

The repeal of Don't Ask, Don't Tell (DADT) marked the end of another era in the ongoing social evolution of the U.S. armed forces. So, when the editor of the *Journal of Homosexuality*, John Elia, asked us to guest edit a special issue to commemorate it, not only were we honored by the invitation, but we also recognized the importance this issue would likely have for researchers in the decades to come.

We approached our task of creating a definitive collection of leading thought on homosexuality in the U.S. military in much the same way we approached our previous volume, *Attitudes Aren't Free* (Air University Press, 2010) (prior to DADT repeal). In that book, we sought to showcase the complexity of contemporary social issues by bringing the brightest voices from both sides of the debates. Likewise, in this special issue, we have brought together leading advocates, scholars, and experts analyzing the history, context, issues, and challenges that came to define government policies toward gay and lesbian service members during the latter half of the twentieth century up through early post-DADT repeal.

We've organized this issue into three primary sections: "Agents for Change," "Policy Evolution," and "Organizational Implications." In "Agents for Change," we offer key perspectives from some of the most prominent advocates of policy change over the previous decade. As the American political system grappled with the issue of open homosexuality in the U.S. military, these advocates played key roles in the efforts to align government

---

This article is not subject to U.S. copyright law.

policy with evolving societal attitudes and achieve social justice for lesbian, gay, bisexual, and queer (LGBTQ) service members. In the following paragraphs, we provide a brief overview of the articles, authors, and key ideas contained in this special issue.

The lead article in the issue is authored by Nathaniel Frank, acclaimed author and historian. In 2009, he published *Unfriendly Fire* (Thomas Dunne Books, 2009), which has become one of the most definitive and comprehensive historical accounts of DADT. In his article in this issue, "The President's Pleasant Surprise: How LGBT Advocates Ended Don't Ask, Don't Tell," Frank builds on his previous account and extends his historical analysis all the way through DADT repeal. Frank has been a long-time affiliate of the Palm Center, a research institute that has led the scholarly inquiry into DADT. Aaron Belkin, the founding director of the Palm Center and San Francisco State University political science professor, outlines his argument over what DADT had become in his article entitled, "The Politics of Paranoia." Belkin's comments come from a 2010 speech he gave to an audience of 500 U.S. military and international allied officers in a debate with Elaine Donnelly, one of the most vocal antagonists to gays in the military. In his speech, Belkin argues that DADT was never about cohesion, but rather creating political rhetoric reminiscent of McCarthyism of the 1950s rooted in paranoia. As two of the leading scholars in the ongoing dialogue on open homosexuality in the military, it is only fitting that Frank and Belkin set the frame for the rest of the articles that follow.

Brenda Sue Fulton, one of the first women graduates of the U.S. Military Academy and the Executive Director of Knights Out, a West Point LGBTQ alumni organization, is the author of "OutServe: An Underground Network Stands Up," which discusses the emergence of what started as a simple Facebook group. As the Communications Director of OutServe, she chronicles the development of the first social network for LGBTQ active-duty service members and tells the inside story of OutServe's earliest beginnings.

"The Rise of Repeal: Policy Entrepreneurship and Don't Ask, Don't Tell," coauthored by Christopher L. Neff and Luke R. Edgell, looks at the role of policy entrepreneurship in the shift away from DADT. Neff, as the first full-time lobbyist on Capitol Hill dedicated to the repeal of DADT for the Servicemembers Legal Defense Network (SLDN), provides a behind-the-scenes account of the halls within congressional offices during the final years of DADT.

Next, we examine the policy evolution of homosexuality in the military from multiple perspectives. Kellie Wilson-Buford leads the discussion on "Policy Evolution" with her historical account of the seminal cases from the U.S. Court of Military Appeals during the 1950s through the 1970s. In her analysis, she finds that although the appellate court was often used in an attempt to legitimize the policy, in the truest sense of American justice, it paradoxically created a body of case law that ultimately set the groundwork for the full inclusion of openly gay service members.

"Formalizing the Ban: My Experience in the Reagan Administration" captures the personal reflections of a leading figure in the Reagan Administration on the development of policy of homosexuality in the military. In 1981, as former Assistant Secretary of Defense, Lawrence J. Korb was chiefly responsible for writing the directive to implement his predecessor's policy, which declared homosexuality to be incompatible with military service. Korb, writing with Center for American Progress colleague Alexander Rothman, reflects on his personal journey in the policy realm toward gay and lesbian service members over a 30-year span.

In 2010, the U.S. Department of Defense embarked on one of the most comprehensive and extensive studies ever undertaken. Beginning in February of that year, a 68-member team led by Army General Carter Ham and Department of Defense (DoD) General Counsel, Jeh Johnson authored a report that was delivered to Congress 10 months later and found that the risk to the U.S. military of DADT repeal to be low. This report ultimately led to the policy's demise weeks later. In "The Comprehensive Review Working Group and Don't Ask, Don't Tell Repeal at the Department of Defense," Jonathan L. Lee, as a senior DoD official and key member of the Comprehensive Review Working Group, authors an insider's account of how the Comprehensive Review Working Group arrived at the conclusions contained in this historic report. We have included the executive summary of this report as Appendix 2 to this special issue given its seminal importance as primary source document. Likewise, we have also included two other key source documents as appendixes: the text of the law that led to the creation of DADT (10 USC § 654; Appendix 1) as well as the law that repealed it (Public Law 111–321, 124 Stat. 3515; Appendix 3).

In "Outing the Costs of Civil Deference to the Military," Hastings Law School Professor, Elizabeth L. Hillman, offers a unique and competing perspective on the role that the DoD played in DADT repeal. Although she views repeal as a civil rights triumph, she remains critical of the process that manifested. To Hillman, repeal of DADT was inherently a civilian policy decision, and yet she notes the unprecedented deference given to the military establishment by the nation's civilian authorities.

"Gays in the U.S. Military: Reviewing the Research and Conceptualizing a Way Forward," by Armando X. Estrada and colleagues from the U.S. Army's Research Institute for the Behavioral and Social Sciences provide a thorough and thought-provoking review of the contemporary research on gays and lesbians in the U.S. military. They also offer a theoretical framework for participation and inclusion of openly gay service personnel.

The final section of this issue examines some of the most salient organizational implications of homosexuality and military service. Here, we include a study of our own. At the moment of DADT repeal when LGBTQ personnel gained voice for the first time, we captured their narratives. By employing grounded theory techniques, we revealed five irreconcilable contradictions that DADT cast on the organizational realm and the active-duty LGBTQ military members that served under it.

Next, L. Michael Allsep, Jr. contributes a provocative essay on "The Myth of the Warrior: Martial Masculinity and the End of Don't Ask, Don't Tell." In it, he argues that contemporary military culture remains hindered because military leaders continue to treat key events like the integration of women and the repeal of DADT as policy events, not like the calls for culture change that he argues them to be. He notes how technological development and the changing nature of the battlefield have largely been ignored by a revered culture that overemphasizes a martial masculine ethos, which is becoming increasingly irrelevant in today's warfighting environment.

In response to our initial call for papers to the scholarly community, we quickly realized how little research has been conducted on LGBTQ veterans and the issues most pertinent to them. Thus, we decided to include two articles dedicated to veteran-related issues. In the first study presented in "If We Ask, What They Might Tell: Clinical Assessment Lessons From LGBT Military Personnel Post-DADT," Maria Heliana Ramirez and colleagues argue that with upward of a million LGBTQ veterans who could be seeking culturally sensitive heath services in the years to come, a significant strain is about to be placed on the U.S. healthcare systems. Their research team offers insight into the domain of LGBTQ veterans' issues using a community-based participatory approach and provides a series of recommendations for post-DADT healthcare systems improvement.

Likewise, Bryan N. Cochran and colleagues examine the mental health characteristics of LGBTQ veterans in a controlled study. Using the quantitative technique of principal component analysis, they find LGBTQ veterans are more prone to mental health issues due to concealment of LGBTQ identity while in the military, most notably posttraumatic stress disorder and depression.

In the last article, Adam F. Yerke and Valory Mitchell initiate a discussion on what promises to be the next major social challenge to the U.S. armed services: the integration of transgender service members. Noting that 11 countries already allow transgender service within their respective militaries, it is only a matter of time before the U.S. follows suit. Their article, "Transgender People in the Military: Don't Ask? Don't Tell? Don't Enlist!" is a call for action to build on the lessons learned from DADT.

As a postscript to this special issue, we welcome the addition of a Palm Center study entitled "One Year Out" published separately on the first anniversary of DADT repeal. A team of researchers from across military and civilian institutions engaged in an exhaustive study following DADT repeal and found the results to be largely consistent with the experiences of other nations who previously abolished their gay bans. Unfortunately, due to space limitations, we were unable to include this study in the journal version of the special issue, but are pleased to have the opportunity to include it in the book version to be published in August 2013.

We recognize that with any undertaking of this magnitude, some blind spots will inevitably endure. Our attempt with this special issue was never to comprehensively capture every aspect of the evolution of government policy toward gays and lesbians in the military, but instead to commemorate the waypoint between exclusion and inclusion of yet another group of American service members who merely desire to serve their nation.

Finally, we wish to thank all those but for whose efforts, this issue would not have been possible. First and foremost, we want to express our sincere gratitude to the contributors of this issue who have offered profound and original scholarship on a topic of great importance. Moreover, we appreciate your continued diligence to meet deadlines and requests for revision. We also want to thank those authors who submitted articles that were regrettably not included in this issue. With over 60 submissions, we were only able to include the articles that appear in the following pages. Each article submitted went through a rigorous double-blind peer-review process by experts in the field. We are deeply grateful to the two dozen referees who put forth a great deal of time and effort to help us achieve the level of quality desired for this issue. Our board of reviewers included: Aaron Belkin, Fred R. Blass, Lori Bogle, David Boxwell, Morten Ender, Joel England, Nathaniel Frank, Joseph Foster, Daniel Gade, Paula Grant, Kristen Leslie, Julie Manta, Corina McKendry, Gail Murphy-Geiss, Tip Ragan, David Sacko, Steve Samuels, Rachel Sondheimer, Lynn Sylmar, Andrew Wackerfuss, plus several other referees who requested to remain anonymous. We also want to thank Institute for Veterans and Military Families for a grant to help support the administrative aspects of bringing this issue to fruition. A warm and special thanks to the editor of the *Journal of Homosexuality*, John Elia, for putting his trust and faith in us for this project, making it a pleasure at every turn. We also wish to extend our gratitude to Sean Beppler, Emily Ross, and Kimberley Smith at Routledge for their wonderful support, as well as our production editor, Cheryl Zubrzycki, for her outstanding efforts in putting this together.

Last, but certainly not least, we wish to thank the members of the U.S. military not only for their service—past, present, and future—but also for their alacrity in continuing to defend the ideals of our nation so honorably. DADT, rest in peace.

> *I do not pretend to understand the moral universe; the arc is a long one, my eye reaches but little ways; I cannot calculate the curve and complete the figure by the experience of sight; I can divine it by conscience. And from what I see I am sure it bends towards justice.*
> —*Theodore Parker*

FOREWORD

The Political Battle for Repeal: Personal Reflections from the Frontlines

PATRICK J. MURPHY, JD

Former Congressman, Pennsylvania's 8th Congressional District, United States House of Representatives, USA

This article chronicles the story of the author's role as a U.S. Congressman in the effort to repeal the military's Don't Ask, Don't Tell policy. Through a first-hand narrative, it discusses highs and lows in the fight, from President Obama's commitment in his State of the Union Address to lift the ban to Secretary of Defense Robert Gates' plea for Congress to delay a vote, and shares his personal feelings upon achieving victory.

The most insidious element of the odious Don't Ask, Don't Tell (DADT) policy was the forcible silencing of the very people it targeted for unfair treatment. Americans take seriously their right to defend themselves, but here was a law that singled out lesbian, gay, and bisexual (LGB) service members for unequal treatment and made those same people mute when it came to sharing their stories or advocating for themselves and the armed forces they selflessly chose to serve.

That's why I'm so proud to be part of this scholarly assessment of lessons learned from the rise and fall of Don't Ask, Don't Tell. It means replacing silence with facts and with an accounting of what happened and why.

For me, working to end this discriminatory policy was always intensely personal. Many asked why a straight, Irish Catholic from a tough district in Pennsylvania would take on an issue like this. Yet, my answer was always the same: When you see a wrong, and you're a fighter by nature, you have to work to right that wrong. When my daughter is in college 15 years from now and reading this, I want her to be proud of what her daddy fought for when given the responsibility to serve his country in the U.S. Congress.

Long before I entered national politics, I saw firsthand how the military's policy on LGB troops was wrong. In air assault school, I befriended an artillery officer who was the epitome of the great soldier. He was the total package: dedicated, courageous, tough, selfless, and intelligent. He was also gay. When he was discharged for no other reason than his sexual orientation, and our military lost this honorable soldier because of bald prejudice, I came face to face with a policy that was as unjust to patriotic Americans as it was harmful to our nation's defense.

I couldn't remain silent. As a young captain and newly installed professor of constitutional law at the U.S. Military Academy at West Point, I stood in a room with other faculty when a top official in President Bush's administration asked if we had any questions. "I have one," I said. "We're at war. We need all the able-bodied people we can get. So why are we kicking out capable Arabic speakers from the Army just because they're gay?" The official brushed me off, perhaps irritated at this challenge by a young captain, and a few of my colleagues looked on in surprise at my directness.

Joining the House of Representatives from Pennsylvania in 2007 gave me new opportunities to fight for what I thought was right. In 2009, Rep. Ellen Tauscher (D-CA) took over as the leader of the House repeal effort after Rep. Marty Meehan (D-MA) left Congress to become chancellor of the University of Massachusetts, Lowell. Later that year, however, she left Congress to join the State Department. I went to her and asked if I could take the lead on repeal, and she agreed.

When my local newspaper characterized ending the ban a peripheral issue, I was disappointed, but not deterred. This was the only law in the land that punished people for coming out—and not just any people, but folks who volunteered to make the ultimate sacrifice for our country. It was wrong for our LGB troops, wrong for our military and wrong for our country. It wasted talent and taxpayer money. It insulted the dignity of lesbian, gay, and bisexual Americans. It trampled American values. This was about basic justice and fairness, about civil rights, and about national security. It was anything but peripheral.

When I took the lead on repeal, I was the one responsible for leading the fight in the legislative branch of our government. It was an awesome responsibility, which I took very seriously. How did we set out to fight this fight?

First, I had partners who were indispensable. Even before I took over as the leader of repeal in Congress, indeed, before I even was a member of Congress, I met and consulted with researchers from the University of California's Palm Center, who spent a decade conducting studies that helped build a record of facts showing that the policy hurt, rather than helped, unit readiness. Our fight heated up when President Obama—who campaigned on lifting the ban—became president, I met and spoke with leaders at Servicemembers Legal Defense Network (SLDN) and Human Rights

Campaign (HRC) weekly, sometimes daily, for critical discussions of where we were on the vote count and what needed to be done next. Without these crucial allies, we would not have won this fight. I also partnered with the veterans of Servicemembers United (SU), who led a national tour to bring visibility to the harms caused by DADT.

Of course, leading a fight in Congress is ultimately about getting enough votes, and, in this effort, I had enormous support in the House from Speaker Nancy Pelosi (D-CA) and Majority Leader Steny Hoyer (D-MD), who were responsible for setting the Democrats' legislative agenda, and from Rep. Barney Frank (D-MA), Rep. Jared Polis (D-CO), and Rep. Tammy Baldwin (D-WI), the leaders of the LGBT Equality Caucus. On the Senate side, Sen. Carl Levin (D-MI), Chairman of the Armed Services Committee, Majority Leader Harry Reid (D-NV), along with Sens. Joe Lieberman (ID) and Kirsten Gillibrand (D-NY), all made repeal a top priority. Members of my own staff were equally passionate. When I took over as lead, I huddled with my entire office to let the team know what we were taking on, to explain the risks involved, and to make sure they were all onboard for this fight. Not one of them balked; they all dug in their heels and we got to work.

Winning over votes was not easy. I drew on personal relationships I had with other members of Congress. I talked about my own experience serving in Iraq, and how I had seen firsthand that this policy was unfair, unneeded and un-American. During my first term in Congress, I was the only Iraq War veteran in Congress; in my second term there were only four of us. Unlike in the 1970s, when 78% of Congress had served in the military, that figure in 2010 was only 24%. So, the perspective of actual vets mattered.

I spoke with moderates in both parties. I reached out to those who had good records or were known to be open minded on LGB equality, or those who had supported inclusive hate crime legislation or the federal Employment Non-Discrimination Act. I kept notes, including information on who told me privately that they would support repeal when it came to a vote, even if they didn't feel they could state it publicly beforehand. If I needed to, I could draw on these notes to return to their offices and ensure that the members would stand by their word.

I came to these meetings armed with data: about the number of Arabic speakers who had been kicked out under DADT; the dozens of foreign militaries who had lifted their bans amid similar fears that cohesion and recruitment would suffer, only to find that their forces actually strengthened as a result of greater equality; about great military leaders like Gen. John Shalikashvili, the former Chairman of the Joint Chiefs of Staff, who had supported DADT but came to oppose it when he learned about the facts on the ground; about the cost to taxpayers—over $1 billion by some counts—of continuing to enforce a failed policy.

I also came with polling data, sometimes broken down by district, showing that supporting equality in the military was not politically harmful.

I explained that, in fact, repeal had become a winning issue. Members might be criticized by conservatives, but that those critics weren't going to vote for them anyway. Even the Tea Party, which had reenergized the conservative movement, was, at worst, a neutral factor in repeal, with 46% against it and 45% for it.

I told my colleagues that, if they knew in their hearts that ending this policy was the right thing to do, that DADT was wrong morally, militarily, and fiscally, and that supporting repeal would not hurt them politically, then why on earth wouldn't they do the right thing?

At the start of 2010, President Obama said in his State of the Union address that he would work that year with Congress and the Pentagon to end DADT. That was a breakthrough moment in our fight, since the annual speech is considered a key indicator of the White House's agenda for the upcoming year. The president had signaled that lifting the ban was a top priority of his administration, and this really gave us some needed air cover for our battle. The president's announcement was followed by the testimony of Adm. Mike Mullen, the Chairman of the Joint Chiefs of Staff, and Robert Gates, Secretary of Defense, who both offered support for repeal. Adm. Mullen's remarks were particularly heartfelt, as he called repeal the right thing to do and cast the policy as a moral blemish on the integrity of the armed forces.

The support of the White House and Pentagon leadership helped our momentum tremendously. Yet, the forces of opposition were still stacked against us. Our opponents in Congress, with the support of social conservatives and retired military officers, were throwing everything they had at us. Sen. John McCain (R-AZ), a war hero who had said he would listen to the military leadership on this issue, refused to listen when those leaders came out in support of equality. He threatened to filibuster a vote on repeal and repeatedly blocked votes to fund the military because repeal was attached to the overall spending bill.

Some of the support on our side also appeared soft. Secretary Gates announced a 10-month study period at the beginning of 2010 and then urged Congress not to take any action until after the study was complete in December. But the clock was ticking, and we were all too aware that the 112th Congress might not be as open to repeal. In April 2010, Secretary Gates signed a letter to Rep. Ike Skelton (D-MO), the Chairman of the House Armed Services Committee, formally urging Congress to delay action until after the Pentagon's study was complete on December 1—half way through a lame-duck session, which is a historically tough time to pass laws.

The Gates Letter was a low point in our fight, as it gave fence sitters in Congress cover to oppose repeal. We felt we had to push back hard on the letter, coming just weeks before we hoped to vote repeal through in the House. I immediately issued a statement saying the thousands of LGB service members—and those already kicked out—deserved better. "It's either right or it's wrong to discharge service members from the military because of their sexual orientation," said the statement. "No more kicking the can down the road. I will continue fighting for a full repeal this year knowing that we are on the right side of history" (Murphy, 2010). A statement like this can function as a critical message at just the right time, signaling your intention to fight on when a bump forms in the road.

A few weeks later, SLDN, HRC, and SU—my battle buddies—held a lobby day that sent hundreds of veterans to Capitol Hill to push for repeal. We began to work on a new compromise bill that would delay the implementation of repeal until after the Pentagon completed its study and military leaders and the president certified that the force was ready for the change. Despite Gates' letter, we were confident we had the votes in the House, and we were determined to move forward.

By the end of May, just in time for our scheduled House vote, we reached a compromise involving a delayed repeal implementation that earned the blessing of the White House and military leadership. The deal was that we would vote on repeal right away, but its actual implementation would be delayed until the Pentagon had the time it wanted to study and prepare for the change. The House voted the provision into the Defense spending bill by a healthy margin of 40 votes, including five Republicans. The House also passed the overall Defense spending bill that same week, and the Senate Armed Services Committee voted to place repeal into the Senate Defense spending bill. A vote by the full Senate would be the final step.

That vote wouldn't come until the fall, and it failed twice because of a Republican-led filibuster. The GOP chose to oppose the entire bill to fund the military rather than support equal treatment for LGB troops. It was the first time in 48 years the spending bill failed to pass.

The second time the bill was filibustered was on December 9, a month after the midterm election. But at that point, something big had happened: The Pentagon had released its massive study of the likely effects of open service, and found, as decades of research had before it, that the risks would be minimal. As Secretary Gates put it, lifting the ban "would not be the wrenching, traumatic change that many have feared and predicted" (Federal News Service, 2010).

After the second filibuster, I huddled with the Majority Leader Hoyer, to discuss our options. We also consulted with our Senate colleagues, Joe Lieberman and Susan Collins. Our challenge was this: any new bill put forward in the Senate would also require the House, which had already approved repeal, to vote on it again. We simply didn't have time to go through a reconciliation process. With the further cover of the Pentagon study, Sens. Lieberman and Collins decided they could bypass the Senate spending bill as a vehicle for obtaining repeal. The next day, Sens. Lieberman and Collins introduced a stand-alone bill to repeal DADT.

We held a press conference with advocates and Congressional sponsors. The House went first, and again, it approved repeal, passing the stand-alone bill December 15. It was 10 days before Christmas and time was running out for the Senate to act.

All that week, I worked the phones and had countless one-on-one meetings. A Senate vote was set for Saturday, December 18. We knew we had to get this done. I was on the phone late into Friday night. I hadn't seen my wife or children in over a week. I was confident we'd succeed, but the result was in the Senate's hands. As the week ended and I took the train back up to Philadelphia, I knew I'd done all I could.

On Saturday, I tried to relax with our family at the Flyers hockey game, as I awaited the Senate vote. I checked my Blackberry constantly. Then, during the second period, word came that we had the votes. Soon after, we learned that repeal had passed. It passed with 65 votes on our side, 8 from Republicans.

My phone would not stop lighting up. I couldn't answer all the congratulatory calls, but one number showed up on my screen that I had the presence of mind to pick up.

"Is this Murph?" came the voice. "This is Barack." The president congratulated me.

"Mr. President," I said, "Congratulations to you. You led the way when you said repeal was a priority in your State of the Union address."

"Sir," said the president, "it was an honor to work with you on getting this done." It was one of the most emotional moments of my life.

That day, a thought occurred to me: When you take on a fight like this—a fight for basic fairness, for the justice and dignity of all who serve our country—you often have no idea of the lives you're helping. You may never know many of them, but you know you're helping to move forward values you believe in deeply—sticking up for the little guy, giving voice to those who can't use their own, helping to ensure that our country is as strong as it can be—in arms as well as in values. You may never meet that company commander in Afghanistan who is fighting for freedoms that he is denied, but who couldn't be honest about who he is. But you can know that while he's fighting for us on the frontlines, he's a little more hopeful because you're fighting for him back home.

I've always believed our country is great because our country is good. Most folks want to do what's right even in the face of great challenge. But fighting for what's right isn't always easy. This battle was a long, hard slog—far longer for many than for me. And being in a swing district, there were times when I wondered, is this worth it? Aren't there easier fights to take on? Of course, it's easier not to take on a fight at all. But as the West Point cadet prayer says, "Make us to choose the harder right instead of the easier wrong." It's a credo that works in our military, works in politics, and works in life. I'm proud to have been part of this fight, and to have worked with so many others who strive to live their lives by this same noble rule.

REFERENCES

Federal News Service. (2010, December 2). *Hearing of The Senate Armed Services Committee*. [transcript].

Murphy, P. (2010, April 30). *Patrick Murphy statement on secretary Gates' letter calling for delay of Don't Ask Don't Tell repeal*. Retrieved January 14, 2013, from http://72.251.194.213/2010/04/patrick-murphy-statement-on-secretary-gates'-letter-calling-for-delay-of-don't-ask-don't-tell-repeal/

SECTION I
Agents for change

The President's Pleasant Surprise: How LGBT Advocates Ended Don't Ask, Don't Tell

NATHANIEL FRANK, PhD
Center for Gender and Sexuality Law, Columbia Law School, New York, New York, USA

This study assesses the role of LGBT advocates in repealing the military's Don't Ask, Don't Tell policy in the U.S. Congress. It draws on the author's direct involvement with that effort as well as personal interviews and media evidence to consider the contributions of the Obama Administration, members of Congress, the media, and individuals and pressure groups in the repeal process. It argues that repeal succeeded not because of the effective implementation of a White House plan but because the pressure of LGBT advocates ultimately shattered several key obstacles including inadequate messaging and dysfunction and inertia among both politicians and interest groups in Washington. The article offers insight into the role of public pressure in forwarding social change.

KEYWORDS Don't Ask, Don't Tell, DADT, Obama, media, LGBT advocates, Congress, Pentagon, unit cohesion

In a December 2010 interview with *The Advocate* the day he signed the bill to repeal the military's Don't Ask, Don't Tell (DADT) policy, President Obama shared his feelings about the successful effort to lift the ban on openly gay service. "Things don't always go according to your plans," he told the magazine's Washington reporter, Kerry Eleveld. "And so when they do—especially in this town—it's pleasantly surprising" (Eleveld, 2010a).

Ending DADT was a major victory for the Obama Administration, and an important campaign promise kept. But for the purposes of understanding how social movements succeed or languish, the narrative that has emerged in the aftermath of this victory—that the White House had a well-designed plan

---

The author would like to thank Taylor Clarke for her first-rate research assistance on this project, and Columbia Law School's Center for Gender and Sexuality Law.

from the outset that it successfully implemented despite several obstacles along the way—is at best too simple, and at worst wholly incorrect.[1]

In this study, I argue that repeal succeeded not because of the effective implementation of a White House plan but because the pressure of LGBT equality advocates ultimately shattered several key obstacles. These hurdles included inadequate messaging, the de-prioritization of repeal by Washington actors, and a dysfunctional Congress that feared or neglected gay rights. These obstacles were overcome by forces that were uncoordinated and unpredictable, but that were tied together by the theme of public pressure, particularly through savvy use of the media (as well as, of course, a stroke of luck). The story, thus, sheds insight into the role of public pressure in forwarding social change (for how public opinion affects legislation and how media affect public opinion, see Bryant & Zillmann, 2009; Krimmel, Lax, & Phillips, 2012; Page & Shapiro, 1983).

As advocates surmounted the hurdles, sometimes pressuring each other, repeal moved forward. Because of a multiyear reframing campaign, military and elected officials came to see that supporting repeal was not risky or costly and might even be beneficial, both militarily and politically. Because of a specific tactic involving the dissemination of information about the President's legal authority to suspend discharges by executive order, the White House was thrown on the defensive and was compelled to take repeal seriously. Because activists raised a ruckus throughout 2010, Democratic leaders were forced to respect the political prowess of the lesbian, gay, bisexual, and transgender (LGBT) community and were hard pressed to keep their demands off their agenda.

The White House and the Human Rights Campaign (HRC), the nations' largest LGBT rights organization, long assured the LGBT community that there was a plan for victory (e.g., Bellini, 2009; Stolberg, 2009a)—exactly the same thing had happened in 1993 with the White House and insider gay groups, when Bill Clinton's effort to lift the ban collapsed and yielded DADT. The evidence amassed here questions the viability of that plan, and suggests that whatever that plan was relied on the efforts and impatience of many other actors to meet with success. I do not maintain that there was no plan at all to secure repeal, but that what passed for a plan was vague and ineffective, and was not what ultimately secured repeal.

As a candidate, Barack Obama famously said, "I want you to hold our government accountable. I want you to hold me accountable." He was channeling Franklin D. Roosevelt's entreaty to his base, "I agree with you, I want to do it, now make me do it." Likewise, Bill Clinton implored his base to strengthen his hand by applying public pressure on his left (Adair, 2009; Sirota, 2009). Indeed, there is no shame in being pressured by friends to do the right thing. In a sense, the worst that can be said about the President's plan—and any gap between what was planned and what ended up happening—is that it was implemented sooner than the White House thought it would be. That would seem nothing to complain about for repeal advocates. But it leaves the story of how it happened—sooner than planned and, for that matter, at all, still untold.

Here, then, is an attempt to tell the story—at least its first chapter—of how a dedicated group of equality advocates successfully pressed the U.S. government to end one of the last forms of government discrimination against its own people. Because I was one of those advocates, I enjoyed a unique perspective on the story I chronicle here. A participant history has both strengths and limitations. My own participation in the effort allows me to draw on years of research, strategy discussions, meeting minutes, conversations with key players, and notes and emails written to or shared with me.[2] Yet, my involvement at the University of California's Palm Center, a think tank focused on DADT, creates some risk that Palm's role will appear disproportionately in the story. I try to guard against that risk with an historian's commitment to documentable evidence and narrative balance. But, if I fall short, I hope it's some compensation that my personal involvement in both strategizing and chronicling the long-term information campaign I document here allows me the opportunity to share the critical role of research advocacy in forwarding a social movement.

One final note: This is not the story of the Washington lobbying campaign for repeal, which was a critical ingredient in ensuring the ban's end. I do not present this study as the full and definitive history of how repeal was won, a fair account of which will, I think, require an in-depth probe of the private conversations and tactics of lobbyists, legislators, the White House and the Pentagon. Although I include some of that here, I determined that it is too soon to tell that full story with the benefit of both the passage of time and the needed candor of the key players. My focus elsewhere should not be read as taking anything away from the essential role and effectiveness of lobbying in the story of repeal.

But I also don't tell that story because the real story of how DADT was repealed is much broader than the Washington lobbying effort, and started much earlier than the 2008 election of Barack Obama. Thus, the focus of this study is on the social movement developments that made it ripe for Washington actors to press ahead successfully with legislative repeal in 2010. Those developments began years earlier, with the long-term strategic information campaign begun at the moment DADT was born.

THE PUBLIC INFORMATION CAMPAIGN, 1993–2008

SLDN

In 1993, the day after President Bill Clinton announced DADT, a policy that would be codified into law four months later, Michele Benecke and Dixon Osburn founded Servicemembers Legal Defense Network (SLDN).

An outgrowth of the Campaign for Military Service, the short-lived umbrella group formed to advocate for full repeal in 1993, SLDN developed a strategy focusing on legal aid for affected service members, court challenges to the policy, and media attention to help turn opinion against the ban. "The demise of DADT did not occur in isolation or merely as the fulfillment of a presidential campaign promise," Benecke (2011) wrote. "It resulted from a deliberate long-term strategy . . . to put an end to the law by turning public opinion against it" (p. 36).

Benecke argued that SLDN's two-part strategy was to put the military on notice that it was being watched, while bringing national attention to both the suffering and service of gay troops as a way of eroding public support for the policy. SLDN was highly effective at the first goal. Benecke's (2011) article recalls several important actions SLDN took to hold the military accountable in the early years of DADT, when almost no one else was paying attention to the issue of gay and lesbian troops. The group publicized command actions and inactions; it educated military members about their rights under the new policy and represented them when they needed legal aid; it worked to end witch hunts, ensure proper enforcement, and reduce abuse of the policy; it helped challenge downgraded discharge characterizations. The presence of an effective watchdog group, which used public and private pressure to hold officials accountable, helped improve the safety of military members by making clear that the entire chain of command was under scrutiny (Benecke, 2011).

Throughout the 1990s, public support for lifting the ban grew (e.g. Bicknell, 2000; Healy, 1993; Miller, 1994; Zogby International, 2006). Yet, the achievement of SLDN's second goal—eroding support for DADT—was limited by the absence of two critical ingredients in the effort. First, there was little actual research allowing the national debate to trade in hard facts. Other nations had ended their bans with no harm to military effectiveness, and empirical research could allow policymakers to predict the same in the United States—if it existed. This question—the potential impact on national security—would become the sole question that mattered for the military and key senators (and, to a large extent, the courts, which would strike down the ban only if they determined it served no compelling governmental purpose) when they took up the issue in 2010.

The second missing ingredient, then, was a reframing of the public debate to appeal to those whose support was most critical to ultimately winning repeal: cultural, political, and military conservatives who either remained skeptical that the ban could be lifted without harming military effectiveness, or who hid behind that rationale to continue to oppose equality. While support for openly gay service grew in the 1990s, the public dialogue that furthered that support was best suited to winning over the low-hanging fruit of liberal sentiment. Given the respect that the culture and politicians conferred on the military and its leaders, it would be critical to frame the national conversation around the issue of cohesion and security instead of fairness, equality or privacy.[3]

Yet, SLDN's primary frame for indicting the policy—that it treated gay troops unfairly—did not resonate strongly with those who most needed to be convinced to oppose it. In the 1993 debates, wrote Benecke, "there was not yet any national consensus that gay rights issues were civil rights issues. We vowed to change the terms of the debate by putting [LGB] military members front and center . . . This issue simply could not be understood by the courts, Congress, the media and the public without understanding servicemembers' experiences" (2011, p. 41). Typical of the public rhetoric that SLDN used as a result of this framing strategy was Benecke's assertion that "the real issue is that commanders in the field need to know the intent of the policy—that people have a right to privacy," a message that focused not on ending the policy but enforcing it properly, and not on the policy's harm to the military but its impact on the right of gay troops to be left alone (Benecke, 2011; Priest, 1998).

The problem with framing the issue as a violation of gay rights was that it was convincing only to those who already believed that gay rights were civil rights and, even more importantly, only to those who prioritized gay rights over military readiness. Throughout the 1990s and into the next decade, defenders of the ban succeeded at maintaining support for it by suggesting that, no matter how unfair it may seem to gay troops, the ban was necessary to preserve unit cohesion. Military leaders and their political supporters, as well as culturally and politically conservative Americans generally, cared little about the rights of gay people as long as they thought (or could argue) that equal treatment might put the military at risk. As polls showed, there remained a stubborn gulf between the assumptions of liberals about equality and the beliefs of conservatives that lifting the ban threatened national security, and national security trumped fairness.[4]

Palm Center

The Palm Center's research helped fill this gap. An academic policy research organization, Palm was devoted to disseminating facts about the service of LGBT troops, particularly in foreign militaries. But Palm played a highly strategic role in the repeal effort. Its model, pioneered by the center's founding director, Aaron Belkin, was not just to conduct research, but to use research aggressively and repeatedly to earn media attention and reframe the national narrative, beating the ban's champions on their own terms. Palm's status as an academic research center—it was housed at University of California, Santa Barbara, until 2011, and then merged with UCLA School of Law's Williams Institute—bolstered its credibility and visibility with the media and, eventually, with the nation's military and political leadership. Its use of data to attract media attention to an issue that, until 2009, generated little national interest was key, as was its willingness to take the long view and be relentlessly repetitive over time. Its focus on the national security frame instead of the equal rights frame helped orient the national conversation toward the policy's Achilles' Heel—the oft-repeated but never proven assertion that openly gay service harmed unit cohesion, when in fact the policy itself hurt readiness by wasting talent and forcing troops to lie.

In 2000, just after it was founded, Palm released four studies on foreign militaries (in Canada, Israel, Australia, and Britain) showing that when those countries lifted their gay bans, their militaries suffered no harm. Advocates of repeal consistently cited this evidence in the U.S. debate (Blumner, 2003; Gerber, 2003; Martin, 2007; Shalikashvili, 2007). In 2002, Palm worked with SLDN to publicize the stories of clients who were being discharged under the policy. SLDN's quarterly and annual reports contained compelling narratives about the unfairness of the policy, but those stories were not getting the public visibility they deserved. The SLDN strategy of focusing on the privacy rights of gay and lesbian service members, born in the pre-9/11 era, had declining returns, and the post-9/11 era was ripe for tapping into a national security argument about efficacy instead of fairness.

Drawing on SLDN's reports, Palm broke the story of Alastair Gamble, one of seven Arabic language specialists fired for being gay. We built an aggressive media campaign around the story, in which I published a piece in the prestigious *New Republic* magazine to gain visibility with Washington powerbrokers which we then used to secure stories in the Associated Press and on MSNBC, leading to coverage in over 100 newspapers as well as television and radio stations in every major American market. The firing of gay Arabic linguists became a constant trope until the policy's death, with an entire nation lamenting the irrationality of firing capable troops with badly needed skills for reasons having nothing to do with performance or ability.

Increasingly, our national security frame appeared in media stories and editorials of small-town and even conservative newspapers claiming, for instance, that the ban was a stupid waste of critical talent during wartime. The success of the reframing was reflected in polls. By 2003, a Gallup poll put support for openly gay service at 79%, as did a 2005 poll conducted by the University of New Hampshire Survey Center, which also found that even majorities of Republicans and religious people supported repeal. Between 2004 and 2009, support for openly gay service by conservatives and religious people would increase by double digits, moving from under 50% to well over (Belkin, 2008; Greenberger, 2005; Morales, 2009).

In 2005, the Williams Institute, which specialized in LGBT research, began a series of demographic and attitudinal reports on gays in the military that produced sophisticated estimates of the number of gay and lesbian Americans serving in uniform, as well as the number of additional recruits who might join or remain in service if the ban were lifted. The figures were used effectively to combat assertions that the military could lose members who might leave because they opposed open service.

All the while, Palm and other researchers were conducting, compiling, and communicating evidence showing that gay people did not undermine the military, but that discrimination did. We used the research to get media coverage of an issue that otherwise generated little interest, which was critical to maintaining visibility for the issue and keeping pressure on political and military leaders. The research-generated media complemented the media earned by getting coverage for the stories of unfair treatment of gay troops, often clients of SLDN, which generated further media coverage and legal pressure with ongoing court challenges to the law. What all this meant was that, in 2008, when the world finally did turn to this issue because the political stars had aligned, a powerful record of research was available to the powerbrokers who would be pulling key levers.

Military Outreach

In 2006, Palm met with the former Chairman of the Joint Chiefs of Staff, John Shalikashvili, for a conversation set up by a retired gay admiral in the Coast Guard, Al Steinman. Palm asked Gen. Shalikashvili if he would submit an op-ed to *The New York Times*, and he agreed. His piece, "Second Thoughts on Gays in the Military" (Shalikashvili, 2007), said that it was time to "consider the evidence that has emerged over the last 14 years" showing the policy was unnecessary and wasted critical talent during wartime. While he previously supported and indeed oversaw the policy, he cited research, polls and stories that had convinced him that gays and lesbians could now "be accepted by their peers." He wrote that, "I now believe that if gay men and lesbians served openly in the United States military, they would not undermine the efficacy of the armed forces. Our military has been stretched thin by our deployments in the Middle East, and we must welcome the service of any American who is willing and able to do the job."

Gen. Shalikashvili was the most senior retired officer ever to call for repeal, and overnight his op-ed became a news item, with coverage by the Associated Press that was carried in hundreds of newspapers, as well as a CNN story that evening in which former Defense Secretary William Cohen also called for repeal. Gen. Shalikashvili's change of heart became one of the most consistently repeated talking points in the repeal effort and it gave added cover for many other voices to support repeal. Key among them was President Obama, who, along with his press secretary, Robert Gibbs, adopted as a mantra that former members of the Joint Chiefs of Staff believe this policy is not working for our national security. The op-ed also unleashed a steadily rising tide of pro-repeal sentiment by other military members and veterans. Building on the Shalikashvili op-ed, Palm developed a military outreach effort designed to educate retired admirals and generals about DADT, and to collect signatures of those who favored ending it. In November 2008, when that figure crossed one hundred, Palm broke the story in major media outlets including the Associated Press, creating a talking point that over 100 retired generals and admirals now supported repeal.

The year 2008 also saw the release of a Palm Center study authored by a bipartisan group of retired generals and admirals that called for an end to DADT. The report, which subsequently appeared in a major volume published by the military's Air University Press, was based on a year of research including hearings conducted in Washington with an array of experts (Aitken, Alexander, Gard, & Shanahan, 2010). Its initial release was covered in 1,500 media outlets, including over 100 television and radio broadcasts and hundreds of web sources. The report recommended repealing the law and returning authority over the issue to the Pentagon (which, the panel also recommended, should then lift the ban). What they produced was the most far-reaching study calling for repeal by military officers. Their proposal to separate out the repeal of DADT from any new Pentagon policy would ultimately be adopted in 2010.

By the time Barack Obama was elected president, on a platform that included repealing DADT, polls showed that 75% of Americans, including a substantial majority of conservatives, favored repeal. Sentiment within the military was reaching a turning point.

The critical research and advocacy work of groups like Palm, SLDN, and Williams were made possible by another component of the social movement that deserves mention: a funding stream created by the strategic and sustained use of grant making by foundations. In the six years leading up to the 1993 passage of DADT, foundations gave $150,000 to groups working on ending the ban on gay troops. However, starting in 2004, grant-making foundations awarded over $1 million each year to organizations working on repeal, mostly—but not exclusively—foundations whose main mission was LGBT equality. In total, between 1995 and 2009, foundations awarded $10.8 million to the Palm Center and SLDN (Bowen & Lane, 2011).

As part of the long-term information campaign, in the years leading up to repeal, Palm supported the development and publicizing of *Unfriendly Fire: How the Gay Ban Undermines the Military and Weakens America* (Frank, 2009). The book was published in March 2009, on the same day the repeal bill was introduced by the 111th Congress. It brought together decades of evidence against the need for a ban, as well as research showing the costs of the current policy, and the stories of military careers harmed. It ended with a chapter showing how much had changed since 1993, including a long list of military and political officials who had reversed course and now supported repeal.

Throughout 2009 and 2010, the visibility of *Unfriendly Fire* would help put the issue of DADT and its embarrassing failures on the airwaves and pages of major national media, from the "Daily Show with Jon Stewart" and the "Rachel Maddow Show" to National Public Radio, from *The New York Times* to *Newsweek*. Writing in the latter, the columnist Anna Quindlen (2009) noted the oddity that Gen. Shalikashvili had endorsed the book, and hence, "the former chairman of the Joint Chiefs of Staff lauds a book that systematically trashes a policy the general once oversaw." In addition to helping generate public visibility, the book served as a critical blueprint for research by both military officials studying DADT and lawyers challenging it. When the Pentagon created a working group to assess lifting the ban in 2010, *Unfriendly Fire* was widely read within the building, according to a senior Pentagon official, serving as the overview for members of the Pentagon working group, including the most senior officers (senior Pentagon official, personal communication, January 5, 2012). When the Log Cabin Republicans (LCR), a gay Republican group, challenged the policy in federal court, lawyers from White & Case, which represented LCR, said they relied heavily on the book to build their case.[5]

That September, in a stunning rebuke to the policy's rationale, Judge Virginia Phillips ruled it unconstitutional in an 86-page decision that marked the most thorough challenge to the ban ever. Its contents comprised a tour of a decade of research points, citing the loss of critical medical and language skills; the lowering of standards by granting moral waivers; and the blow to the entire rationale by the proof that the Pentagon retained known gay troops during wartime—uncovered by Palm in 2005. The ruling would throw the Pentagon into disarray, suddenly worried about losing control of the repeal process, and, thus, lighting a fire under military leaders to support a legislative repeal that would accommodate the Pentagon's wish to maintain control over the ban's end. The long-term research investment in information about gay service had paid its greatest dividend to date.

LEVERAGING RESEARCH: 2009

Political Logjam

On January 9, 2009, incoming White House Press Secretary, Robert Gibbs, responded in a video to a question about whether the new president would end DADT. The response was as clear as day. "You don't hear politicians give a one-word answer much," Gibbs said on the video. "But it's 'yes'" (Lee, 2009).

Yet, the President and his advisors, many of whom were drawn from the Clinton White House, vividly recalled the firestorm Bill Clinton had encountered when he tried to lift the ban starting in 1992, and the role of that fight in threatening Clinton's domestic agenda and political fortunes. Few aides were likely arguing that lifting DADT should be first out of the gate.

The year 2009 was not 1993. Two wars and a massive recession had replaced an era of peace and prosperity, and attitudes toward homosexuality had liberalized substantially in the intervening sixteen years. Yet, the scars of Clinton's defeat in the last effort to end the gay ban meant that, ironically, the climate in the White House itself was more cautious this time around, despite a social context that was far more pro-gay.

The result was a near-consensus among politicos and advocates that Pentagon buy-in was essential for repeal to succeed. That could take time. On February 1, 2009, *The Boston Globe* reported that Obama aides had told Pentagon officials and gay rights advocates that it would need to study the national security implications of lifting the ban before trying to change the law. A senior officer said that assessment might not begin until 2010. The President was reported to have reservations about asking Congress to make a change before the Pentagon could complete a thorough study of the impact of such a step on military discipline. Only afterward would the President make the case to lawmakers for a legislative change. Indeed, Pentagon officials said they had been told by the White House not to expect the administration to act quickly, and that they had been assured they could conduct their own major study of the impact of repeal before a change would occur (Bender, 2009; Bumiller, 2009a).

The vote count in Congress was, at this early date, uncertain. According to press reports, even many Democratic senators were still undecided, including Sen. Evan Bayh (D-IN), Sen. Claire McCaskill (D-MO), and Sen. Ben Nelson (D-NE). Rep. Ike Skelton (D-MO), the powerful Democratic chairman of the House Armed Services Committee, opposed repeal, but had begun to express openness to holding hearings (Bender, 2009).

Assessing the prospects of repeal in Congress, Aaron Belkin, Palm's director, fretted about how to break the logjam. In early March, he addressed a board meeting of SLDN in a Washington hotel. In laying out the strategy he thought was necessary to see movement toward repeal, he introduced the idea that the White House was the main pressure point. "We have to bash the President," he said, later explaining that "bash" was perhaps too strong a word and he meant nothing personal by it (anonymous, personal communication, January 19, 2012). Members of the board roared their opposition. It was still the first hundred days of the Obama administration, and SLDN was, at that point, still hoping to play an inside game. They believed that pressuring Obama would alienate him and make him less, not more, likely to help. Feelings were so strong at the meeting that tears were shed, and Palm lost a major funder over the idea (Belkin, 2011). That meeting in March marked the start of a tactical disagreement within the movement about where, how, and how much to apply pressure to move repeal forward.

Pentagon Posturing

On March 2, Rep. Ellen Tauscher (D-CA), announced she would introduce legislation to repeal the ban, with 112 cosponsors. Tauscher had first taken on the issue two years before, and she acknowledged a fight to find enough votes to pass it. She called for a commission led by a former military leader such as Gen. Colin Powell. That day, Thomas F. Vietor, a White House spokesman, said in a statement that the President had "begun consulting closely with [Defense] Secretary Gates and Chairman [of the Joint Chiefs of Staff, Adm. Mike] Mullen so that this change is done in a sensible way" (Phillips, 2009).

Yet, by the end of that month, Defense Secretary Gates was stepping on the brakes. On March 29, he responded to a Fox News question about repeal by saying that dialogue within the administration "has really not progressed very far at this point in the administration. I think the [P]resident and I feel like we've got a lot on our plates right now, and let's push that one down the road a little bit" (*Fox News Sunday*, 2009). The following week, Pentagon spokesperson, Cynthia Smith, confirmed there was no ongoing dialogue about the issue between the President and Secretary, saying that Sec. Gates "has had one brief conversation with the President about 'Don't Ask, Don't Tell'" (Beutler, 2009). This statement contradicted the White House assertion that the President was consulting closely with the defense secretary.

Gates continued to indicate a cautious approach to lifting the ban, with *The New York Times* reporting in April that his remarks "suggested that it might not happen at all." "If we do it," he told reporters that month, "it's important that we do it right, and very carefully." He cited President Truman's racial desegregation of the military starting in 1948 and said that process took five years to complete, making some advocates apoplectic about the prospects of imminent repeal (Bumiller, 2009b).

SLDN aired its frustration with the administration's slow pace in a full-page ad in *Roll Call,* and suggested that the President make his intentions clear by including the removal of DADT in his 2010 defense budget. Yet, the White House declined to offer any signal that that might happen, and may have underestimated the negative press that would ensue.

On May 2, the Associated Press described a deliberate strategy by the White House of trying "to hold off debate on contentious social issues such as abortion, immigration and gay rights" for the first year of his presidency, and focus instead on the economy and global events (Babington, 2009). The piece mentioned that liberals had criticized Obama "for postponing efforts to revamp immigration laws, protect access to abortion and allow gays to serve openly in the military" and that "the President has taken the heat from his political base" for avoiding the issues, but that in general, "the strategy has worked so far" (Babington, 2009). The piece said that gay advocates were "unhappy the administration is moving at a snail's pace on efforts" to end DADT and cited a Huffington Post piece which lamented that, "when it comes to actual change in the lives of LGBT people, nothing has been done" (Babington, 2009).

On May 7, Belkin wrote a headline piece for the *Huffington Post* announcing that the first discharge of a gay Arabic linguist under President Obama's watch was set to take place (Belkin, 2009a). Seven weeks earlier, the linguist, Army 1st Lt. Dan Choi, had announced he was gay on MSNBC's Rachel Maddow Show. "I am an infantry platoon leader in the New York Army National Guard," said Choi. "And by saying three words to you today, 'I am gay,' those three words are a violation of Title 10 of the U.S. Code. It's a code that is polluted by the people who want us to lie." Choi said it was an "immoral code" that "goes against every single thing that we were taught at West Point with our honor code" (Wolff, 2009). Choi could be volatile and long-winded, but as an Iraq War combat veteran and West Point graduate, he was also well spoken, passionate, persistent and angry—all of which made for great media.

The Executive Option

Belkin's (2009a) *Huffington Post* piece also announced the impending release of a Palm Center study showing that the President had "statutory, stroke-of-the-pen authority to suspend gay discharges." The study, authored by a team that included top legal and military scholars, explained that President Obama "could simply invoke his authority under federal law (10 USC §12305) to retain any member of the military he believes is essential to national security" (Belkin et al., 2010).[6]

The idea of issuing an executive order suspending the ban, which Palm first mentioned publicly in February was controversial within the repeal movement (Lusero, 2009). While some observers disputed this interpretation of the law, which the Palm legal scholar, Diane Mazur, had noticed and ably defended, no one, including the administration, was able to demonstrate that the statute granting such authority did not apply in the case of DADT. Thus, the debate about whether the President ought to exercise the authority became a political more than a legal one. In addition, many advocates preferred to focus on legislative repeal and worried that executive action would give Congress an excuse for inaction. Jonathan Capehart (2010b) of *The Washington Post* called the executive option a "backdoor maneuver" that would be "the single-most irresponsible action the [P]resident could take." Dixon Osburn (2009), SLDN's former co-director, said an executive order would stand on "shaky legal ground" and would "giv[e] a pass to Congress" by putting the focus on the President. As Belkin had learned firsthand when addressing the SLDN board in March, many activists had little interest at this point in a plan that focused pressure on the President.

Yet, the executive order idea—consistent with Palm's belief that the administration was the critical leverage point in the battle for repeal—was part of a carefully crafted strategy designed not so much to bring about the stop-loss, as to put pressure on the White House to press harder for legislative repeal. Simply circulating the information that the President, personally, had the authority to do more than he was doing, went the thinking, would generate public pressure for repeal, even if the order were never given.

The Palm strategy was one of the most important developments in generating public pressure for repeal because it allowed thousands of voices to demand something that was actually doable—and, therefore, required answers from elected officials, particularly the President, who had made promises to act but appeared to be stalling. Palm created an explosive combination by telling Choi's powerful story, announcing the pending discharge of the first Arabic linguist under Obama, and showing that the President actually had the power to stop this and all discharges with the stroke of a pen. This new meme—that Obama could personally stop discrimination but was choosing not to—spread quickly. LGBT bloggers' anger filtered up to the mainstream media, and Choi himself exploited media interest in his story through flamboyant performance tactics like chaining himself to the White House fence. When activists became a thorn in the side of the administration the next year, their case was made more viable because of Palm's revelation that the President could take specific steps on his own, without waiting on Congress.

A Defensive White House

The circulation of the executive option immediately put the administration on the defensive. When *Newsweek*'s Anna Quindlen (2009), in her write up of *Unfriendly Fire*, called on the President to "immediately issue an executive order suspending this irrational and prejudiced policy," White House press secretary Robert Gibbs demanded a correction from the magazine's editor, Jon Meacham. Quindlen told Meacham that was unacceptable since she had not made a mistake, directing her editor to the legal arguments circulated by Palm's legal experts. An angry White House continued to seek a clarification, but *Newsweek* held firm (A. Quindlen, personal communication, April 5, 2012). It was the start of more than a year of obfuscations and stonewalling in which the administration would find itself compelled to engage as it was continually pressed on why the President wasn't doing all he could to stop the discharges.

The constant appearance of the executive option in mainstream media and public discourse, including an uptick in media discussions of DADT in general, demonstrated the sustained impact of the executive option proposal on the repeal effort. Belkin's (2009a) *Huffington Post* article, announcing the executive order legal analysis to be released four days later, both introduced the idea publicly and began the snowballing buzz about the President's authority. The piece, which was elevated to the top headline, received over 1,800 comments; by comparison, another *Huffington Post* piece (2009) about

Choi that ran on the same day received 9 comments. A Lexis-Nexis print and broadcast media search revealed that discussion of DADT shot up directly following the May 7 revelation: In the 106 days between Obama's inauguration and May 7, 2009, the term was mentioned only 5.6 times per day, while in just the 68 days following May 7, mentions more than tripled to 19.1 times per day (Belkin, 2009b).

The night Belkin's (2009a) piece ran, Rep. Joe Sestak went on *The Rachel Maddow Show* to discuss Choi's impending dismissal. Maddow asked the congressman if, as an "interim step," the President "could order the military to stop investigating whether people are gay, just stop implementing the policy for now?" Sestak demurred, saying, "I'm not sure," and expressing concern about subverting the legal process (Wolff, 2009).

The next day, the *San Francisco Chronicle* ran a story citing Belkin and the Palm Center as "the first to call attention to Choi's case" (Lochhead, 2009). That day, when DNC Chairman Tim Kaine stopped in at a gay and lesbian center in Fort Lauderdale, the local press reported he "got a dose of discontent from gay and lesbian voters concerned over what they see as glacial movement on issues they care about." A leader of the local Democratic gay and lesbian club said of the President, "He can fix these things" but "there needs to be a willingness to do it" (Man, 2009).

The executive option created a particular thorn in the side of Press Secretary Robert Gibbs, who had to fend off an almost obsessive focus by the press on why the President was not using his executive authority to fulfill a campaign promise as discharges—which the White House agreed undercut national security—continued.

Before the circulation of the executive option in May, the media continually reported that only Congress could end the ban (e.g., Turpin, 2009). In the President's first 100 days in office, Gibbs was not asked about DADT even once at the White House daily press briefing. Then, starting on May 12, the day after Palm released its study, reporters began grilling Gibbs on why the President was not doing more to stop the discharges (Belkin et al., 2010). "Even some of the President's friends are now saying that he is hedging on his promises on 'don't ask, don't tell,'" said one reporter to Gibbs, also mentioning the firing of gay Arabic linguists. "But we heard from General Jones saying that 'I don't know' when he was asked when it would be overturned. Some people feel that it's really on the back burner." In his reply, Gibbs said that ending the ban would "require more than the snapping of one's fingers" and that, "to get fundamental reform in this instance requires a legislative vehicle." He reiterated that, like "former members of the Joint Chiefs," the President believed the policy was not serving the national interest and that he was working with the current Joint Chiefs and with Congress to end the ban permanently (State Department Documents and Publications, 2009).

The questioning continued, this time with specific reference to the President's authority to suspend discharges without Congress: "He is the

Commander-in-Chief," said one reporter. "I mean, if the President and the Secretary of Defense can bring about a new leadership in Afghanistan, replace the commanding general there, couldn't the President and the Secretary of Defense delay any more people getting fired under 'don't ask, don't tell?'" (State Department Documents and Publications, 2009).

On May 15, days later, reporters continued to press the issue. The President is "not standing in the way of the ousting of gays in the military, some of whom are interpreters of Arabic," said Jonathan Weisman, then of the *Wall Street Journal*, who wanted to know if "we're seeing a change in attitude toward compromise and a shift toward the middle" since the President's first 100 days in office (The White House, Office of the Press Secretary, 2009). Tommy Christopher (2009), an America Online White House reporter asked Gibbs to "describe the difference between the President's decision to intervene with regard to the abuse photos but not to intervene when it comes to discharging otherwise qualified soldiers because they're gay." Christopher wanted to know why the President couldn't "put a moratorium" on discharges while Congress was deciding whether to act (Christopher, 2009; see also The White House, Office of the Press Secretary, 2009).

With *The Daily Show* skewering DADT by mercilessly mocking Choi's firing as pointless (the segment featured correspondent John Oliver opposing Choi's presence in the military by simply repeating "well, he's gay" as his only argument), *The Advocate* cited a "growing chorus of people" calling for an immediate executive order to halt discharges (Eleveld, 2009a). Knights Out, a group of gay, lesbian and bisexual West Point graduates cofounded by Choi, joined with several other vocal veterans groups including the major Progressive, non-gay veterans group, Vote Vets, to flood White House phones asking to stop Choi's and all future discharges. The California-based online petition group, Courage Campaign, generated over 100,000 signatures calling for a moratorium on firings.

On May 20, Gibbs got it again. Anna Marie Cox of Air America cited three victims of DADT who had all come to the attention of the administration, Dan Choi, Air Force pilot Lt. Col. Victor Fehrenbach and Army 2nd Lt. Sandy Tsao, to whom President Obama wrote a letter saying that Congress must act to stop her discharge. Cox wanted to know, "Is their dismissal a part of his national security strategy or is their dismissal itself a threat to national security? (CQ Transcripts, 2009a).

Then on May 21, Cox asked a series of follow-up questions, marking the fourth time Gibbs faced the issue in 10 days. The tone was becoming increasingly derisive of Gibbs' repetitive responses about a durable solution that must await congressional action. "I wanted to know if there are any other policies that the [P]resident believes to be, as you said yesterday about 'don't ask, don't tell,' not in our national interest, but is content to let Congress take the lead on," said Cox. "And second, President Truman didn't see it necessary to clear desegregation through Congress, so how is this different?" (CQ Transcripts, 2009b). In his reply, Gibbs revealed a lack of familiarity with both the basic historical context of Truman's desegregation order and of the legal basis for an immediate Obama suspension of the gay ban. He said he may have used poor language, but that, again, Congress must act in order to provide a durable solution. "So when can we expect a durable policy on racial desegregation in the military, since that's never gone through Congress?" Gibbs had no answer. Of course, the major difference between DADT and racial segregation was that the military had never been segregated by statute, and, thus, did not require a statutory change to fully and permanently reverse. Gibbs' failure to offer that rather obvious response may reflect either how much the line of questioning had put him on the defensive or how little the administration had really looked into the issue to date. Gibbs' final answer to Cox, who asked if there was legislation pending, suggested the latter. Gibbs' replied, "I don't know what's been introduced in Congress" (CQ Transcripts, 2009b)

Mainstream reporters gave the grilling of the administration broad coverage, casting the White House as on the defensive. *The Wall Street Journal* ran a piece entitled, "Obama Avoids Test on Gays in Military" (Bravin & Meckler, 2009). It reported that the White House was being "pressed to explain whether the administration would intervene to protect Lt. Dan Choi." The piece also noted that some LGBT observers had noticed that the White House website had been changed, with some of the President's promises about LGBT issues edited or removed. Among those that were edited out was the commitment to lifting DADT. White House Spokesperson, Ben LaBolt, said the changes were made simply to "reflect the President's broad agenda," and that those commitments that were no longer being broadcast on the web had not been lessened (Bravin & Meckler, 2009). Following complaints by LGBT bloggers and advocates, the reference to repeal was restored to the website. Yet the restored language still reflected an alteration—from a full "repeal" of DADT to "changing" the policy "in a sensible way" (Bravin & Meckler, 2009) The new language may have been designed to lay the groundwork for what became the administration's interim plan on DADT which was to soften its enforcement rather than repeal it outright.

The Associated Press also cast the administration as on the defensive. Covering Gibbs' press briefing, it ran a piece reporting that the White House "insisted Thursday that officials are working to overturn a policy that bans gays and lesbians from serving openly in the military, pushing back against Pentagon assessments that such efforts were low priorities and Democratic activists' complaint of slow progress." It reported that "The administration has drawn criticism from gay and lesbian activists for not moving quickly enough to repeal the policy." The story then traced the muddled and fitful path of White House and Pentagon responses to queries and criticism about the pace of change, including reversals, back-offs and zig-zags (Elliott, 2009b).

The Seattle Times wrote that the "recent coming out by dozens of gay West Point graduates, including Arabic-language specialist Lt. Daniel Choi, put pressure on Congress and the Obama administration White House to make good on promises to repeal the ban and the 'don't ask' policy." The article paired that analysis with news of the Palm report about Obama's executive authority to stop the discharges (Williams, 2009).

Throughout June, more and more people joined the call for an executive order stopping all discharges, and a constant drumbeat of media coverage reflected growing criticism of White House inaction. On June 4, Joe Solmonese, president of HRC, which worked closely with the White House, endorsed the executive order on television, saying that the President "has the opportunity to do it" and "I don't know why he wouldn't do it." On the same MSNBC broadcast, Lorri Jean, head of the nation's largest gay and lesbian community center, in California, endorsed the option. The host, Chris Matthews, even asked about the executive order, showing how widely the option was being circulated (Nichols, 2009).

On June 8, Rachel Maddow asked Rep. Rush Holt, "What happened to the Barack Obama who ran for president who was so against 'don't ask, don't tell?'" (Wolff, 2009). Holt discussed Dan Choi, and said discharges like his could be halted "on a temporary basis from the White House" but also "on a more permanent basis from Congress." He said that "it would be good to have, you know, a word from leadership, a word from the White House, to move it along." Asked by Maddow whether he'd support a stop-loss order by the President, he said he would.

Maddow summed up the gap between Obama's campaign promises and his achievements on DADT this way: "Since he has been a 'fierce advocate in chief,' has he repealed the 'don't ask, don't tell' policy? No. Has he pushed Congress to repeal the policy? Not really. Has he hit the pause button on investigating members of the military to ferret out who's gay and who's not? No, he has not. Has he used his stop-loss powers to put a hold on dismissals of people under the policy? No. No, he hasn't. In fact, as Commander-in-Chief of the Armed Forces, 'President Fierce Advocate' actively still is firing people from the U.S. military because they're gay" (Wolff, 2009).

Growing Public Pressure

On June 10, *The New York Times* editorial page joined the call, saying that if indeed the President had stop-loss authority, he ought to take that step (*New York Times*, 2009). After publicly criticizing the idea of an executive order as likely to cause an "unnecessary and distracting showdown," Sarvis of SLDN wrote in a letter to *The New York Times* that he now agreed the President should consider an executive order to "kick-start the legislative process" ("Room for Debate" 2009; Sarvis, 2009). Sen. Harry Reid said at a press conference that, while the Senate had no plans to introduce a companion repeal bill since he had not identified any sponsors, "My hope is that it can be done administratively" (Eleveld, 2009b) According to a Washington source, Sen. Reid was pushing the repeal issue back into the President's lap in part out of frustration that the White House was failing to lead on the issue, an approach that dovetailed nicely with Palm's strategy of putting pressure on the administration (anonymous, personal communication, April 5, 2012). At Palm's suggestion, Gen. John Shalikashvili published another op-ed in *The Washington Post* citing the "inevitability of change, whether via executive order or legislative repeal" (Shalikashvili, 2009).

On June 22, 77 House members (including one Republican) signed a letter backing Palm's executive option ("Hastings and 76 Members of Congress," 2009). Urging the President to use his executive authority to halt discharges, the letter cited Choi's pending discharge and asked the President "to exercise the maximum discretion legally possible in administering Don't Ask, Don't Tell until Congress repeals the law." The letter, authored by Rep. Alcee Hastings (D-FL), outlined a "bilateral strategy" that, like Palm's and CAP's proposal, would halt discharges immediately—thereby demonstrating no harm would ensue—which could help grease the wheels for congressional action.

Stars and Stripes ran a story with the subheading, "Obama, Congress and Gates all waiting for the other to make the first move" (Shane, 2009a). The piece said that the "White House and congressional leaders quickly began backing away" from action on repeal, with "each saying they're waiting for the other to take the first step." In what the article described as a "hot-potato game between the White House and Capitol Hill" that was "fueling frustration among gay-rights advocates," Sen. Harry Reid said members of Congress were waiting for the White House to provide a legislative proposal and that Reid was calling for more "presidential leadership and direction" on how to move forward (Shane, 2009a). The White House declined comment, and, at the Pentagon, Sec. Gates said Congress had to act first. Sen. Levin echoed Sen. Reid's call for White House leadership, with *The Hill* reporting that, while supportive of repeal, he was "noncommittal on a repeal being initiated by Congress. Accordingly, he has shifted the burden onto the White House" (Blake & Tiron, 2009). Levin told reporters in late June that any chance of lifting the ban "requires presidential leadership. This cannot be addressed successfully without that kind of leadership" (Blake & Tiron, 2009).

On June 24, Center for American Progress (CAP, 2009) issued a report laying out a path to end the ban. CAP, which was known to work closely with the Obama administration, nevertheless complained about presidential foot-dragging:

> Now is the time for President Obama to fulfill his pledge and begin the process of repealing this outmoded, unfair, unnecessary, and costly law. This is not just a fight about the rights of patriotic American men and women; it is about military readiness as well. Yet, it is puzzling

that there is not a stronger momentum within the administration to begin the process of repealing DADT, given the unacceptable moral and national security implications of DADT, as well as President Obama's stated campaign pledge.

The report went on to detail a plan to end the ban that started with an executive order and continued with legislative repeal (CAP, 2009).

On June 25, several prominent LGBT leaders boycotted an LGBT fundraiser for the DNC in an effort, according to the Associated Press, "to pressure Obama to make good on his promises now" (Elliot, 2009a). Two weeks earlier, the Justice Department had filed a brief defending the Defense of Marriage Act in a legal challenge. While the administration's position, clearly laid out in Obama's campaign, was to oppose DOMA, the Justice Department argued that it was obligated to defend existing laws from legal challenges, except in rare circumstances. Later, the White House would decide this was one of those circumstances, and it, ultimately, stopped defending the law. The brief defending a law the President opposed set off a firestorm in the LGBT community, particularly because its strong wording drew on some of the most offensive ideas about homosexuality, including an apparent comparison of same-sex marriage to incest.

On June 29, the White House hosted a reception marking the 40th anniversary of the Stonewall uprising that marked the birth of the modern gay rights movement. *The New York Times'* coverage of the event noted that LGBT leaders had "grown increasingly impatient and critical" of the President, who had been forced to confront their frustration at the reception. The President, said the article, "directly addressed criticism from gay and lesbian leaders that he had not been a forceful advocate for them," saying, "I know that many in this room don't believe progress has come fast enough," and that he understood their impatience (Stolberg, 2009b).

Referring to repeal of both DADT and DOMA, the piece said the President had been "accused of dragging his feet on both, but especially on 'don't ask, don't tell' because he could use his executive authority to order the military not to enforce the rule." In the Stonewall event, the President again rebuffed that option, saying the best approach was to work with Congress "to see that this change is administered in a practical way and a way that takes over the long term" (Stolberg, 2009b).

Reporters pressed Gibbs several more times as June wound down. On the last day of the month, Gibbs was asked if the President had a timeline on when a plan for repeal would emerge. He did not. It was the twelfth time Gibbs was asked about repeal since the executive order option was circulated on May 7 (CQ Transcripts, 2009c, 2009d).

To be sure, reporters raised many issues at the White House press briefing more often than DADT. For questions about health care, the economy, and foreign policy, a dozen asks in a summer would not be remarkable. But to go from zero to a dozen mentions of an issue that had not otherwise held national interest immediately after a new executive option was made known is strong evidence of its impact on the conversation. This is corroborated by the specific language of the queries, which involved the explicit grilling of the administration on why the President was not using this executive authority to fulfill a campaign promise.

Pentagon Response

On June 30, a week after 77 members of Congress had urged executive action, and following more than six weeks of relentless pressure by LGBT voices, Sec. Gates made an announcement: The Pentagon planned to soften enforcement of DADT for the first time ever. The secretary would not release details until the following spring; but in other countries, such steps had often preceded outright ends to the bans. Gates said the step was intended to make enforcement "more humane" (Shane, 2009b). According to a senior Pentagon official, it was, in part, an effort to placate criticism from those frustrated with the slow pace of change toward the administration's stated goal of repeal. The Pentagon leadership did not believe the ban was going to be lifted and felt pressure to deliver some level of change (senior Pentagon official, personal communication, January 5, 2012). It was the same day that a military board recommended the official discharge of Lt. Dan Choi.

The pressure that was being exerted on political leaders was not only of the short-term variety, and it did not emerge in a vacuum. It was instead a critical turning point in what was actually a decades-long effort by advocates—and ordinary LGBT people—to give respectability to sexual minorities and to make support for their rights a politically advantageous (or at least neutral) position. The recognition by all kinds of national politicians during this period that supporting repeal was not costly and might even be a winning issue for them, while at the same time many of them were coming to see this position personally as morally right, was the essence of that turning point. The progress would be reflected not only in the successful repeal of DADT in 2011, but in a slew of national polls that year finding that, for the first time, a majority of Americans nationwide supported the right of same-sex couples to marry. It would be reflected politically in the administration's decision two months after signing repeal that, seeing negligible political cost from supporting repeal, it would cease defending DOMA in court. In 2012, Obama would finally come out personally in favor of same-sex marriage, citing, as one inspiration, his concern for the plight of gay troops who fought for freedoms they couldn't enjoy.

A New Political Reality

The beginning of that turning point vividly emerged in the press coverage during the summer of 2009. A piece in *Roll Call* (Bendery & Toeplitz, 2009) reflected a new attitude among politicians, which itself reflected growing public irritation with inaction. The piece described a meeting of Democratic House members to chart a course on gay rights, and noted that the "high level huddle" came after Obama "threw a bone" to the gay community with the extension of federal partner benefits, and "as Democratic candidates in left-leaning states have been embracing key aspects of the gay agenda, including supporting gay marriage." Rep. Alcee Hastings, who had spearheaded the congressional letter calling on the President to suspend DADT, said that having openly gay elected officials such as Barney Frank, Jared Polis, and Tammy Baldwin had "added a new tone to the committees that they work on. They have brought their partners to Democratic Caucus meetings and here to meet us. That part of it is softening." He said that more lawmakers were supporting gay rights because of changing public attitudes (Bendery & Toeplitz, 2009).

Barney Frank said that "Democrats are in a very good place" to press ahead with gay rights initiatives, with a pro-gay Democratic President, a strong House vote the previous year on the Employment Non-Discrimination Act (ENDA) and what *Roll Call* paraphrased as "a general shift in public opinion on gay issues" (Bendery & Toeplitz, 2009). The piece said that "public support for gay rights is also becoming politically popular for a few Senate Democrats who might face primary opposition in 2010" and it cited Sen. Kirsten Gillibrand and Roland Burris among its examples (Bendery & Toeplitz, 2009).

The *Roll Call* piece also cited Chris Dodd, who had just changed his position to support same-sex marriage. It quoted a Democratic consultant as saying: "You don't have to be a rocket scientist to figure out that if you're in the political fight of your life, the LGBT community is an excellent community to appeal to the Democratic base of voters" (Bendery & Toeplitz, 2009).The article said that Democrats had begun to "see the power of the gay community's purse," and quoted another consultant calling the gay community a "compelling voting bloc." "They are organized. They work hard. They vote and they have money," the consultant said. "They are a powerful financial institution" (Bendery & Toeplitz 2009).

This was the political context in which Rep. Patrick Murphy (who authored the foreword to this volume) stepped up to take the lead on repeal in the House in July 2009.[7] While Murphy had long opposed DADT as a military officer, he also found repeal to be a politically attractive position. His hometown paper, *The Philadelphia Inquirer,* quoted political analysts who believed that, since his district was moderate on social issues, it was "unlikely his stance will hurt him locally," and one consultant said that, in embracing repeal, "there's only upside" (Farrell, 2009).

When Murphy took over as lead sponsor, the bill was still in subcommittee and had 151 cosponsors. Murphy said he would meet individually with lawmakers to build the support needed to win. "It's not going to happen in a couple days. It's going to be months," he said. "I'm optimistic that we're going to eventually get this done. No one ever said change was easy" (Farrell, 2009).

On July 2, 2009, Murphy, the HRC, and Servicemembers United announced a joint campaign to urge the end of DADT. It was one of many steps that advocates and veterans, including those working with SLDN, took to bring attention to the costs of the policy and to press elected officials to end it. The media coverage they helped generate, along with the presence of a straight veteran taking the lead on repeal in Congress, was a critical piece of the pressure strategy that was missing from the 1993 failed effort to lift the ban (e.g. Couric, 2009; Welna, 2009).

Murphy opted to keep pressure on his fellow members of Congress, and even pushed back against the use of executive authority, supporting the President's preference for Congress to take the lead. "If the Congress passes a law, he will sign it," Murphy said of the President. "Now it's our job in the Congress to put a bill on his desk to overturn this policy" (Farrell, 2009). But between Murphy's efforts, the veterans' media tour, and the lobbying and media efforts of SLDN and HRC, the press kept pressing on, reporting on the sustained anger of the gay community and the failure of the President to exercise his executive options.

In July, the *New Yorker* covered the boycott of the DNC fundraiser with a particularly helpful summary of where things stood, including mention of the reports from Palm and CAP proposing executive action preceding congressional repeal (Hertzberg, 2009). Hendrick Hertzberg's assessment is worth quoting in full, as it encapsulates what the mainstream media was absorbing about the repeal effort. "A fair test of [the President's] commitment," wrote Hertzberg (2009),

> Would be a quick end to the dithering over D.A.D.T. A permanent solution will require an act of Congress, and the Administration is understandably reluctant to seek one at a moment when Congress's plate is already piled to the ceiling. But the President doesn't have to wait. The Palm Center, a public-policy institute at the University of California, Santa Barbara, has made a persuasive case that he can order an immediate halt to involuntary discharges of gay servicemen and servicewomen under the same "stop-loss" law that his predecessor used, less admirably, to force soldiers to extend their enlistments. Last Wednesday, the Center for American Progress, a think tank that has provided many Obama appointees, proposed a plan whereby a stop-loss executive order would be followed by a Presidential panel on implementing repeal and, ultimately, by repeal itself. On Thursday, Robert Gibbs, the White House press secretary, seemed to dismiss the idea ("The Administration believes that this requires a durable legislative solution"), but he also seemed to leave the door ever so slightly ajar ("There could be differences on strategy"). The President should kick that door open, and if he doesn't his

gay supporters and their allies should do a little kicking of their own. The community organizer on Pennsylvania Avenue will get the message.

As Sen. Gillibrand continued courting support from the LGBT community, she began looking for creative ways to push for an end to DADT. She found a warm reception working with gay advocates who felt the current timeline was too slow and risked missing the critical window when Democrats would have the power to get it done. An article in *The Hill* quoted several political analysts saying that supporting gay rights was becoming increasingly important for politicians, especially in Democratic primaries (Blake & Tiron, 2009). "It's not just gay and lesbian and transgender people that are involved," said one. "It's also a lot of people on the left. It's a much bigger audience that cares about all the civil rights issues that gays are involved in" (Blake & Tiron, 2009). It was the start of talk of a so-called enthusiasm gap—disappointment among the liberal base over inadequate progress—that, for the first time, included LGBT equality as a natural metric. Democrats were beginning to have to take notice.

Gillibrand ramped up repeal pressure by proposing legislation to put a moratorium on gay discharges. She dropped the idea when it became clear she didn't have enough votes, but her involvement yielded a commitment from Sen. Carl Levin to hold the first senate hearings on gays in the military since the notorious ones in 1993 that led to the policy in the first place.

HRC was also coming under increasing pressure that summer to push harder for repeal. A number of bloggers and gay activists had been critical of HRC throughout the spring of 2009 for what they saw as an inadequate record of results in the first few months of the Obama Administration. By May, that criticism was spreading. Belkin's (2009a) *Huffington Post* article publicizing the Choi discharge and executive order option had also leveled an accusation at parts of the LGBT movement, saying that "some major gay rights groups are actively lobbying to delay consideration of the issue. They seem to believe that Obama should focus on other gay-rights issues first, and that he shouldn't spend his precious political capital trying to ram a repeal bill through Congress."

LGBT Priorities

In June, an explosive piece in the *Daily Beast* (Bellini, 2009) reported that gay rights leaders in Washington had "made a deal" with members of Congress "to not push for an end to DADT" until 2010 and that HRC instead wanted Congress to focus on its own goals of passing hate crimes and a federal non-discrimination bill. HRC adamantly denied making such a deal, and the allegation, which the *Beast* said came from "congressional sources," was likely an exaggeration: while no proof of such a "deal," or of the power of HRC to make one, surfaced, an array of sources and evidence show that

HRC had prioritized lobbying for a non-discrimination bill over a repeal bill, in part because its own membership ranked the former over the latter in importance (Bellini, 2009). As a result, the White House felt reassured that it did not need to prioritize repeal in order to keep the LGBT community happy. Indeed, citing Sen. Chuck Schumer, the *Beast* reported that HRC had stated that repeal was not a White House priority (anonymous, personal communication, January 6, 2012; Bellini, 2009; Boland, 2011; Signorile, 2009).[8]

In fact, this order of priorities had been the basic plan since before Obama's inauguration, when House Speaker Nancy Pelosi had met with gay groups and agreed to a timeline that put repeal third, after hate crime and workplace non-discrimination legislation. This plan was reiterated in a June 2009 story by *Stars and Stripes* (Shane, 2009a) reporting that "an official with the House Democratic leadership said the House is committed to repealing 'don't ask' but has agreed with civil rights groups to put new hate crime legislation and a workplace nondiscrimination bill on the legislative calendar before taking up the military issue." It was consistent with an August interview with HRC's Joe Solmonese saying, "I see a road map of six-month windows: the hate crimes bill, then the Employment Non-Discrimination Act, then don't ask, don't tell" (Gilgoff, 2009). It was also consistent with reports that the Pentagon was preparing to back a plan that used 2010 to study the issue and did not move to a vote until 2011, and that Adm. Mullen's lawyers had advised him in a Pentagon memo to delay repeal until at least 2011 (Ambinder, 2010; Shane, 2009a; Gearan, 2010).

There was a logic to putting repeal as the last priority: Both repeal advocates and politicians and their staff generally believed that Pentagon buy-in was needed to ensure enough votes for repeal in Congress, and that building that support would take time and the obligatory study for ground cover. Why not pass other gay rights legislation, some thought, in the meantime? Yet, it was also possible to use that thinking, and the study itself, as a rationalization for inaction on something that was gaining momentum in the public eye, in part because of pressure by advocates who did prioritize repeal. Failing to start—and complete—the obligatory Pentagon study sooner likely meant pushing repeal further and further back, and if the Democrats lost control of the House or a filibuster-proof margin in the Senate (both of which they did), that could mean delaying congressional repeal for years.

The day the *Beast* report came out, HRC requested an interview with the popular gay rights radio host, Michelangelo Signorile, who had, until that day, complained that HRC's director, Joe Solmonese, had "seemingly gone underground" and rebuffed interview requests. The sudden outreach appears to have been an effort to reassure the LGBT community that HRC was with them, and was not advocating against their interests in order to maintain its ties to the White House. Signorile argued that HRC was trying to avoid seeming "irrelevant" as powerful and vocal new LGBT rights organizations were forming, including the American Foundation for Equal Rights, which was bringing a lawsuit against California's Proposition 8, banning same-sex marriage. (Interestingly, its founder, Chad Griffin, would become the executive director of HRC in 2012.) Signorile also cited calls by new and outsider activist voices for a march on Washington as a show of frustration with the pace of change (Signorile, 2009).

Following the criticism leveled in May and June, HRC also began working with gay veterans, including Servicemembers United, both by helping launch the Voices of Honor tour and by hiring Jarrod Chlapowski, a gay former Army linguist, as a veteran spokesman and advocate. According to several sources, the move was intended, in part, to mollify the criticism that HRC was not doing enough to press for repeal (anonymous, personal communication, December 13, 2011, January 6, 2012).

If the move helped, it didn't help enough. In late July, Andrew Sullivan (2009), a longtime HRC critic whose enormously popular blog President Obama had cited as one of his favorite reads (Korblut & Fletcher, 2010), slammed HRC for hypocrisy. In a post entitled, "HRC And The Stop-Loss Option," he complained bitterly about HRC, saying the group was claiming publicly that it was pressuring the White House for repeal but was privately doing nothing or worse. He suggested people give to other groups who cared more about achieving equality: "They write to say that they are publicly backing it. Joe Solmonese backed it on MSNBC, David Smith did so in the *Washington Blade* and that is their formal position. What they tell administration and congressional Democrats privately is another matter. But read the *Blade* story closely and you begin to see why Aaron Belkin is pissed. It seems to me that the gay rights groups that actually want to change the laws should stop expecting anything from HRC; and that gay donors should contribute to SLDN or Immigration Equality or groups that care more about civil rights" (Sullivan, 2009). By the end of the summer, it was increasingly clear not only to HRC but to the Pentagon, the White House and congressional Democrats, that repeal was gaining momentum and that ignoring it would be politically costly.

On September 24, Sen. Reid sent letters to President Obama and Sec. Gates asking for their views on repeal and reiterating his and Levin's July calls for greater input from the administration (Zimmermann, 2009). "As Congress considers future legislative action, we believe it would be helpful to hear your views on the policy," Reid wrote. "Your leadership in this matter is greatly appreciated and needed at this time." Just before the annual HRC Washington dinner in October, SLDN's Sarvis made his own appeal for stronger political leadership, saying in a press release, "We've seen no action and the clock is ticking. A clear timeline from this White House and Congress is urgently needed" (Servicemembers Legal Defense Network, 2009). At the HRC dinner, President Obama reiterated that, "I will end 'don't ask, don't tell'" (Zimmermann, 2009).

On October 15, Sen. Mark Udall (2009) wrote a letter to the President praising him for his stance at the dinner while pressing him on the "urgency" of action by the administration, and specifically by the Pentagon leadership. "I am now awaiting the Admiral's views," Udall wrote of Admiral Mullen's promise to comment on repeal. "I respectfully request, Mr. President, that you consider asking Secretary Gates and Admiral Mullen to send their views within the next thirty days." That day, Rep. Murphy announced he'd amassed 180 cosponsors for repeal, 31 more than the previous high of 149. He had collected nearly 40 new cosponsors under his leadership in total.

By November, the senate hearings secured by Sen. Gillibrand were being delayed, but still appeared to be imminent. Aware that he would soon be asked to state his views publicly, Adm. Mullen formed a research group that included representatives from each of the service chiefs' offices. He wanted to amass all the available research on DADT and the likely impact of getting rid of it. Mullen had spoken with pro-gay veterans in a meeting set up by SLDN, in which he heard firsthand about the costs to integrity of DADT, but he needed to be assured that resolving the integrity issue would not create a readiness issue (Ambinder, 2010; Hirshman, 2012).

In November, *The Hill* reported that both Pelosi and President Obama backed a strategy of repealing the ban as part of the 2010 Defense Authorization Bill, citing a Barney Frank aide (Zimmermann, 2009). It also said that Barney Frank had told *The Advocate* that repeal would be included in the next year's Defense spending bill. "Military issues are always done as part of the overall authorization bill," Frank said in the story. "'Don't ask, don't tell' was always going to be part of the military authorization." *The Hill* reported 183 cosponsors (Zimmermann, 2009).

As it became increasingly clear that ENDA was not going to get through Congress, and, as the clamoring from the LGBT community continued unabated, both HRC and the White House, along with congressional Democrats, began to understand that a win on a gay rights bill was likely to be helpful, rather than neutral or harmful, to their own fortunes. Political science professors, for instance, noted that Sen. Gillibrand's adoption of gay rights as a top priority was "good politics, good policy," and that she was "Exhibit A" of a new kind of Democratic politician who believed they could build support with their base by embracing LGBT equality (Brune, 2009; see also Blake & Tiron, 2009; Gerstein, 2010).

Yet, it was not until the end of 2009 that HRC made repeal a top priority. In December, Solmonese met with Sen. Joseph Lieberman's office to discuss strategy (HRC background brief, [available from author], December 2011; Boland, 2011). Sen. Lieberman, who had left the Democratic Party to become an Independent, had also become convinced of the benefit of taking the lead on senate repeal, which could help his reputation among liberals and moderates. Lieberman had begun talks in October with the White House, which appeared to want the senator's centrist credentials helping them make the lift. By year's end, Lieberman had decided to sponsor a Senate repeal bill, which, with continued prodding by Sen. Gillibrand, he would introduce in March (Hirshman, 2012; Johnson, 2010).

FINISHING THE JOB: 2010

HRC Shifts

Politicians' newly positive orientation toward gay rights was also reflected in, and shaped by, polls, public remarks, and media commentary. Growing political support for gay rights issues was, in part, a product of advocates placing the numbers in politicians' laps. A January 2010 Greenberg Quinlan Rosner (2010) poll commissioned by CAP of likely voters showed that support for repeal was "no longer a significant political liability." In one key question, respondents were asked if they would be more or less likely to vote for a politician who supported repeal—regardless of their own position. The poll showed that respondents would be no less likely to vote for congressional supporters of repeal, and the largest category of respondents was "no difference" (Greenberg Quinlan Rosner 2010). As part of its lobbying and pressure strategy, HRC hired the personal pollsters of some of the wavering senators, most of whom found the same results, and were, thus, able to assure the senators that supporting repeal would not hurt them politically.

By the beginning of 2010, HRC was engaged in what its fundraising staff called "a shift of the organizational resources" to focus on repeal. A membership operations staffer told *Fundraising Success Magazine* (Boland, 2011) that in 2010 HRC "just moved a lot of what we might normally be working on and made [repeal] an all hands on deck effort." The magazine, which honored HRC in 2011 as its "Nonprofit Organization of the Year" for its success in repealing DADT, described the quandary HRC faced in 2010, "when something incredibly urgent happens that strikes a critical chord with your organization's mission, but may not be the most top of mind for your supporters" (Boland, 2011). Indeed, although vocal LGBT advocates, particularly in the blogosphere, had clamored for repeal throughout 2009, HRC members had rated the issue eighth on their priority list. The article said that repeal became HRC's "No. 1 priority in 2010 after much internal discussion and debate" that partly revolved around whether repeal was a popular enough issue with its membership for HRC to focus on (Boland, 2011). The organization's director of annual giving said it was the "first time that HRC had mounted an effort of this intensity and scope," and described an "unprecedented" effort to focus on repeal across all of HRC's departments (Boland, 2011). "When this strategy was laid out that we were going to focus on the repeal of don't ask, don't tell," she said, "I have to admit there was a lot of concern. Our most popular issue from a fundraising perspective and survey responses is marriage equality," not repeal. They had to make repeal "compelling" to donors and activists, she said (Boland, 2011).

On January 13, 2010, LGBT advocates and funders gathered for a tense meeting at HRC headquarters to discuss the strategy for winning repeal. By then, HRC had received word, according to several people who attended the meeting that the White House was about to tell the groups its plan for repeal. Advocates could be with them or not, but further input—at least on the timeline—was not being invited. Some felt that HRC was trying to get the groups in line to back the White House plan, whatever it was, even if it meant delaying repeal past the timeline that advocates wanted. Little was resolved at the meeting (anonymous, personal communication, December 14, 2011, December 30, 2011).

State of the Union

On January 27, a major part of the administration's plan was revealed. President Obama reiterated his pledge to repeal DADT in one of the most prized pieces of rhetorical real estate: the State of the Union address (Obama, 2010a). "This year, I will work with Congress and our military to finally repeal the law that denies gay Americans the right to serve the country they love because of who they are," he said toward the end of his 70-minute remarks. "It's the right thing to do." Although the remarks were carefully crafted to emphasize the process of working on repeal during 2010, it was widely reported that the President had promised to actually end the ban within the year, and the wording allowed LGBT advocates to hold his feet to the fire.

Following President Obama's promise in the State of the Union address, *The New York Times* (2010) lay the burden at the feet of the President, saying he had to do more to press both military leaders and lawmakers to act: "This is a winnable battle, but it will take committed leadership, starting with Mr. Obama, who until Wednesday was not vocal enough on the subject as President. He should prod the Pentagon to speak out, but the military officers will need strong support in Congress." The *Times* piece also cited research on foreign militaries where open service had been a success: "The policy of drumming gay men and lesbians out of the military is based on prejudice, not performance. Gay people serve openly and effectively in the armies of Britain, Israel, Australia and Canada."

SLDN also amped up its pressure on the President, both praising his words in the speech and again calling for him to include repeal in the Pentagon spending bill. "We applaud the President tonight for his call to Congress to repeal 'don't ask, don't tell' this year," Sarvis said. "We call on the President to repeal the archaic 1993 law in his defense budget currently being drafted; that is probably the only and best moving bill where DADT can be killed this year" (Eleveld, 2010b). The next week, in hearings before the Senate Armed Services Committee, Adm. Mullen became the first sitting Chairman of the Joint Chiefs of Staff to endorse openly gay service. In poignant, forceful language, Mullen said that there were still questions to be answered and that he was not "all-knowing" about the impact repeal would have on the military. But "speaking for myself and myself only, it is my personal belief that allowing gays and lesbians to serve openly would be the right thing to do" (Barnes, 2010).

Sec. Gates was less personal in his remarks but focused on the fact that repeal was the administration's position. "The question before us," he told senators, "is not whether the military prepares to make this change, but how we prepare for it." Gates announced he would appoint a working group to conduct a 45-day review of the policy that would determine ways the Pentagon could soften enforcement without awaiting congressional action—an idea that had been announced amidst pressure in June 2009 but had not yet been implemented. The new enforcement standards would include raising the level of authority of those who could initiate a discharge inquiry, and tightening the standards of evidence that could trigger a discharge. He also announced a much longer review by the Comprehensive Review Working Group (CRWG) that would be due on December 1st, 2010 three weeks after the midterm election.

In an angry response, Sen. McCain, who had previously said he would listen to the advice of the nation's top military leaders, told Sec. Gates he was "deeply disappointed" in his testimony. "Your statement obviously is one which is clearly biased, without the view of Congress being taken into consideration." Vowing to continue what was becoming a crusade to block repeal, he said he was "happy to say that we still have a Congress of the United States that would have to pass a law to repeal 'don't ask, don't tell' despite your efforts to repeal it in many respects by fiat."

Despite the ornery McCain, the moment was a high point for the repeal effort. Yet it was also a low point. The one-two punch of the President's commitment in the State of the Union Address and the supportive testimony of Mullen and Gates buoyed hopes of real progress. Yet the simultaneous announcement that the Pentagon would study the issue for nearly the full year, and only deliver its results in December—half way through a lame duck session of Congress, was a blow to the prospects of getting repeal done this year.

Complicating matters even more, Jim Messina, the President's deputy chief of staff who had been tasked with handling repeal, convened a meeting at the same time with LGBT groups but shut out SLDN because of the fraying relationship between the group and the White House, which was angry at SLDN's public criticism (Naff, 2010). At the meeting, described by one attendee as a "definitive shut-down from Messina," the deputy chief of staff reportedly told them that the President would not put repeal into the Defense Authorization Bill, the most straightforward way to ensure that it was taken up—and passed—by Congress, and a clear signal from the White House that it did not plan to push repeal in 2010. Reports also surfaced that some White

House staff were counseling the President against moving on repeal before 2011, a plan that would be corroborated in complaints by Barney Frank the next month (Eleveld, 2010e).

This was apparently the plan that HRC had told fellow advocates to expect in the January 13 meeting—that 2010 would be spent building Pentagon support for repeal, but that, as part of a deal with Gates, the White House would not press for a congressional vote before 2011, as evidenced by the decision not to put repeal in the 2011 Defense Authorization Bill. Again, there was some logic to the timetable, given the perceived need to build support among the military leadership, but there was equal logic to the alarm bells sounded by advocates warning that pushing repeal beyond 2010 could mean an indefinite delay if the House were to fall into GOP hands or if Democrats were to lose enough seats to make overcoming a filibuster impossible.

LGBT bloggers responded by leading a "blog swarm"—in which numerous bloggers purposely comment on the same story—which focused attention on HRC: "OUR MESSAGE TO HRC IS SIMPLE: Publicly demand that President Obama take the lead in getting DADT repealed this year. 1) That means the President needs to state publicly that he wants Congress to repeal DADT this year; and 2) The President needs to take the lead in working with Congress to make sure the repeal happens" (see http://www.towleroad.com/2010/02/join-our-blog-swarm-call-hrc-today.html).

To be sure, getting the support of Mullen and, especially, Gates was a critical accomplishment for the President. Yet according to *National Journal*'s Marc Ambinder, the President "unexpectedly found that he would have no greater ally than" Mullen, who was, therefore, not a particularly heavy lift. Gates, on the other hand, had to be "courted to stay" on as Defense Secretary from the outset. This meant Obama had to work carefully and slowly to build trust with Gates, a Republican appointee, before asking for his support for repeal, which he reportedly broached in their first meeting after the inauguration (Ambinder).

But in getting Gates onboard, Obama found that the Secretary's support came at the cost of moving repeal on Gates' timeline, which was to spend 2010 building cover through the study, and for Congress not to vote on repeal until 2011.[9] In claiming that the administration had a plan for repeal, according to Ambinder, "the White House had not yet adjusted for the possibility that Democrats might lose control" of Congress, a prospect that both history and advocates had warned of as soon as Obama won the White House—historically the party that controls the White House frequently loses seats in the midterm election, and the growth of the anti-government Tea Party starting in 2009 made this prospect abundantly clear. When Messina was asked by senior staff at HRC and CAP what the White House's plan was to repeal DADT in a Republican House, according to Ambinder, "Messina didn't have a good answer" (Ambinder, 2010).

Messina and other White House staff reportedly thought that the reassurance of Obama, Mullen and Gates in the State of the Union and the Senate hearings would mollify activists who were anxious about an inadequate plan to secure repeal. But the timeline that was revealed by the plan—parking repeal in a ten-month study and the refusal of the President to insert repeal into the base Pentagon spending bill—did no such thing. In fact, the Pentagon reportedly "envisaged a two-year process" with legislation being "introduced in 2011." Advocates, particularly from outside the Beltway, were increasingly convinced either that there was no plan or, if this was the plan, it was a lousy one (Ambinder, 2010).

Indeed, Robert Gibbs had consistently made clear that the White House backed the Pentagon plan to pass repeal in 2011 rather than 2010. When *The Advocate's* Eleveld asked him in February, "Would the [P]resident like to see Congress pass repeal this year?" all Gibbs could muster is, "there is a process that's under way." In politispeak, not saying 'yes' to a simple question like that means saying 'no,' especially for a press secretary who had previously boasted about the rare "one-word answer"—yes—to the question after Obama's election about whether he still planned to lift the ban. Eleveld then pressed Gibbs, expressing advocates' "fear that if it doesn't happen this year, that it very well may not happen throughout the entire first term" because Democrats could lose control of the next Congress ("Federal News Service," 2010b).

Gibbs' response—if taken at face value—was revealing. "I don't think the [P]resident shares that," he said, referring to the view that 2010 is the last possible window in the near future. Citing public polling, the support of Pentagon leaders, and "strong bipartisan support for its repeal," he reiterated that "we think it will become law" ("Federal News Service," 2010b). In April, Eleveld would get further confirmation that the White House was onboard for the Pentagon's 2011 plan. She asked Gibbs if, before the law is changed, the President was committed to "letting the Pentagon work through its working group process until December 1." Gibbs replied, "Yes. The President has set forward a process with the Chair of the Joint Chiefs and with the Secretary of Defense to work through this issue" and that is the process "he believes is the best way forward" in trying to change the law ("State Department Documents," 2010). Could passage in the lame duck have been the plan? If so, it suggests, at best, a very low prioritization of repeal by the administration.

GetEQUAL

On March 18, Dan Choi, whose pending discharge was still not finalized perhaps because the Pentagon did not welcome the publicity that would bring, chained himself to the White House fence in a direct action coordinated by the newly founded GetEQUAL organization. He was arrested and spent the night in jail. Choi was a polarizing figure, but he was becoming the face of repeal, inspiring young people, with college groups paying up to $10,000 to bring him to campus (Wright, 2010), and irritating establishment Washington. As one measure of Choi's influence on the debate, an Army Major pointed out in a *Military Law Review* article that Choi had spoken at over fifty events in 2009 and 2010, had "become the poster-child for repealing DADT," "garnered the support of many influential people in Washington," and that his "defiance marked a new era in DADT reform attempts" (Bunn, 2010).

While many military members regarded Choi's tactics—getting arrested in military uniform—with scorn, they reacted more favorably to the stories of other veteran activists like Mike Almy and Victor Fehrenbach, who were quietly serving their country when they became caught up in the policy's clutches. For the Pentagon and the White House, fielding press inquiries about these service members became harder and harder, as their stories—of selfless patriots needlessly wasted—gained visibility and embarrassed those with the power to make change. The stories of many of these service members were touted in legal challenges brought by SLDN—and eventually LCR—part of their multi-pronged strategy to erode support for the law and overturn it in the courts. According to a senior Pentagon official, leaders at the Pentagon, the White House and in Congress were all feeling the pressure of clamoring by LGBT advocates and media. Increasingly, Pentagon leaders wanted the policy to just go away (senior Pentagon official, personal communication, January 5, 2012).

While the stories of Almy and Fehrenbach were what resonated most in the Pentagon, the tactics of Choi and GetEQUAL, covered widely in the media, were the most provocative. Whatever official Washington said about not responding to public pressure, they were difficult to ignore. Choi's arrest was covered live, and narrated in emotional terms, on CNN: "Look at these pictures," said host Rick Sanchez. "Apparently he's had enough." Sanchez said it was "a difficult story to watch, it's certainly a very emotional one." Gibbs was asked in the briefing room about Choi while he was chained to the fence outside. Early the next morning, White House staff contacted an advisor to GetEQUAL asking for a meeting. At the meeting, the White House staffer and the GetEQUAL advisor agreed, according to the latter, that, in contrast to ENDA, which was expected to be carried forward by Congress, repeal was in the President's court. The White House staffer said he would be talking to others in the administration about what GetEQUAL was demanding, which focused on the President putting repeal in the Defense Authorization Bill. But the administration had already decided not to take that step (GetEQUAL advisor, personal communication, December 14, 2011).

GetEQUAL was not the only group losing patience. SLDN's Sarvis had made clear that the 10-month timeline for the Pentagon study was excessive, and this one-time Beltway insider, who had initially planned to cooperate with an insider strategy for repeal, no longer trusted that repeal would happen without making trouble. On April 19, *Politico* reported that the White House was quietly urging members of Congress to avoid a vote on repeal until 2011. SLDN's Sarvis wrote an angry public letter to the President, saying: "I am very disturbed by multiple reports from Capitol Hill that your congressional liaison team is urging some Members of Congress to avoid a vote on repeal this year. The upcoming House and Senate votes will be close, and very frankly, Mr. President, we need your help now" (Smith, 2010b). At SLDN, staff discussed how to up the ante as they worried repeal could slip away.

That day, hecklers from GetEQUAL disrupted Obama's remarks at a fundraiser for Sen. Barbara Boxer in California, drowning out his desired message of economic repair. The famously calm-tempered President, visibly rattled, was forced to leave the podium to confirm whether Boxer had opposed DADT in 1993 (she had), before returning to his speech to again tell the hecklers he was already with them (see http://www.youtube.com/watch?v=eX9AMRV2ZHw)

According to Ambinder's (2010) interview with Messina, a furious President stepped into his limousine after the event, incredulous about the interruptions. The swearing commander in chief asked Messina, "What is it about what we are doing that they don't get? If they want to protest, they should go protest someone who was against this." The next day, the pressure resumed. Dan Choi and five others in uniform were arrested for again chaining themselves to the White House fence, garnering coverage of that and the Boxer speech disruption as CNN's top prime time political story that night.

Congressional Chatter

At the same time, the insider-outsider game was yielding fruit, at least with allies in Congress. The March 18 GetEQUAL arrests at the White House had been paired with sit-ins at Speaker Pelosi's office, with the goal of pressing her to move forward with an ENDA vote. By April, with clear evidence that ENDA was stalled, lobbying groups met with Pelosi to press for movement on repeal instead. Pelosi agreed to introduce legislation in the House that would adapt Rep. Murphy's bill to include a delayed implementation as an olive branch to the Pentagon. The idea, first crystallized in a memo by Servicemembers United's Alex Nicholson, was to pass legislation that called for repeal but allowed for a delayed implementation to accommodate the Pentagon's timeline involving a months-long study. Rep. Murphy endorsed the idea, arguing—against pushback from the White House and Pentagon—that he saw no reason why Congress couldn't proceed with a repeal vote at the same time as the Pentagon was conducting its study which, after all, was tasked with assessing not whether to lift the ban, but how (Nicholson, 2010; Rushing & Tiron, 2010).

News that the House planned to move forward with a repeal vote angered Rep. Ike Skelton, the Democratic Chairman of the House Armed Services Committee, and presented the White House with a quandary about how to honor its deal with Gates to wait until 2011. The *Denver Post* (Riley, 2010) reported "The White House is facing a budding revolt over its carefully crafted strategy for repeal of the ban on gays serving openly in the military that would have pushed the decision past the November election." Congressional staff, said the piece, which also mentioned the heckling of Obama at the Boxer event, said movement toward a vote was "likely to face opposition from the White House, which in February laid a timetable built around an extensive Pentagon study that won't be completed until Dec. 1st, pushing a final move on the contentious issue past what's expected to be Democrats' toughest election cycle in years" (Riley, 2010).

Although Skelton would agree to hearings, he was unlikely to allow repeal to get voted out of his committee. So, the Pelosi plan was to introduce an amendment in the House that would bypass Skelton's committee. In what appeared to be retaliation, Skelton provoked a public rebuke for the plan from Sec. Gates. As he prepared his Committee to mark up the 2011 Defense spending bill, Skelton asked Gates to share his views on a repeal vote before the Pentagon study was complete in December.

Gates' Letter

Gates' response was unyielding: "I believe in the strongest possible terms that the Department must, prior to any legislative action, be allowed the opportunity to conduct a thorough, objective, and systematic assessment of the impact of such a policy change." If Congress acted before the study came out in December, the letter said, it "would send a very damaging message to our men and women in uniform that in essence their views, concerns and perspectives do not matter." The letter was signed by both Gates and Mullen and was addressed to Rep. Skelton, giving him and other Democrats cover for inaction. "Our military must be afforded the opportunity to inform us of their concerns, insights and suggestions if we are to carry out this change successfully," the letter said (Braiker, 2010).

Gates' letter sparked anger in the LGBT community and created a crisis in the repeal movement that the White House could not avoid, as the administration now seemed to be squarely standing in the way of repeal. SLDN said that "The President of the United States appears to have reversed himself" from his State of the Union commitment and said it strongly "repudiates . . . a delay game plan" (Braiker, 2010). A statement by Speaker Pelosi said she understood the report was in progress, but that "in the meantime, the administration should immediately place a moratorium on dismissals under this policy until the review has been completed and Congress has acted" (Braiker, 2010). Rep. Murphy also released a statement vowing to press on, despite Gates' letter. "No more kicking the can down the road," said the statement (Murphy, 2010).

"All hell broke loose between the gay community and the Obama administration on Friday," wrote *The Washington Post*'s Jonathan Capehart (Capehart, 2010a). Normally an avid defender of the White House, including having repeatedly impugned LGBT advocates for pressuring the President too hard over DADT (see Capehart, 2009, 2010b), even Capehart now wrote that "I can't say that I blame folks on the front lines of the repeal effort" for their anger (Capehart, 2010a). After reassuring those people for months that the White House was doing all it could to ensure repeal by 2010's end (see Capehart, 2009, 2010b), he had noticed "signs of late that Obama might be willing to let that self-imposed deadline slip" (Capehart, 2010a). He admitted to remaining "a little cranky about protesters focusing all of their attention on Obama," but wrote "the Gates letter is a stark reminder for me that pressure on the [P]resident is paramount if the repeal is to get done" (Capehart, 2010a).

On May 2, Dan Choi and five other service members went back to the White House gates and were arrested for cuffing themselves to the fence for a third time. Taking the bullhorn, Choi addressed the President directly to remind him that he had the authority to stop the discharges: "President Obama, you are the Commander in Chief. You have the power to repeal discrimination, you have the power to follow leadership like President Truman's when he desegregated the armed forces racially, you have the power" (Price, 2010).

By spring 2010, Choi had become the face of DADT and the visuals of coverage of the issue had shifted from an impersonal rainbow or dog tag to the iconic image of a uniformed American chained to the White House fence. Images like these and the ongoing anger that caused them were, according to *National Journal* and other sources, taking a toll on the administration. Footage of Choi was "ubiquitous on TV" and served as a relentless reminder that neither the President's State of the Union promise nor the testimony by Gates and Mullen had quelled disaffection among LGBT advocates (Ambinder, 2010).

Despite the President's deal with Gates to delay repeal until after the study was complete, Jim Messina recognized, according to Ambinder (2010), that a course correction was required. The deputy chief of staff called several meetings that May with the numerous parties involved in repeal. They culminated at the end of the month with what journalist Chris Geidner (2010b) has called "the most deft legislative accomplishment of the Obama administration thus far."

As late as May 21, *The Hill* was reporting that Sec. Gates, "backed by the White House, is opposing any efforts to repeal the ban before the Pentagon has the chance to finish its study on the implementation of repeal by the end of 2010" (Tiron, 2010). The Associated Press reported days later that the

"The White House had hoped lawmakers would delay action until Pentagon officials had completed their study so fellow Democrats would not face criticism that they moved too quickly or too far ahead of public opinion in this election year" (Elliott, 2010).

Compromise

On May 24, the White House called advocates to a feverish series of meetings as Democratic congressional staff met simultaneously to hammer out a compromise. That compromise, first circulated by CAP in consultation with Sen. Lieberman's and Rep. Steny Hoyer's office, would allow a crucial vote to repeal DADT before the next Congress was sworn in, but the actual language of the bill would delay the implementation of repeal until the Pentagon had time to complete its study and certify that its force was ready for the change. It was a variation on the Servicemembers United plan to delay implementation but gave the Pentagon the added leverage of deciding when to implement repeal. Some LGBT advocates decried this provision by pointing out that nothing in the bill ensured the Pentagon would ever decide to lift the ban. A final part of the compromise dropped the non-discrimination language that the legislation had contained since it was first introduced in 2005. Both the Pentagon and some senators were said to have opposed the non-discrimination clause, but, while Pentagon support was always considered crucial, it is unclear if dropping the clause, in retrospect, was necessary to secure the needed votes in Congress (Osborne, 2010). Ultimately, the deal was begrudgingly supported by the all-important defense secretary (Flaherty, 2010). It was passed as an amendment to the National Defense Authorization Act, by the full House on May 27, with 234 voting for it, including 5 Republicans, and 194 against. With the newly announced support of Sen. Ben Nelson and of Sen. Susan Collins, the first Republican to support repeal, the Senate Armed Services Committee voted an identical provision out of committee to await a full senate vote (Herszenhorn & Hulse, 2010).

Constitutional Challenge

The summer seemed quiet on the repeal front. Only a few reporters and bloggers showed up in Riverside, California, to cover what turned out to be the policy's gravest test, and one it would miserably fail. In 2004, LCR had filed suit in federal district court challenging the constitutionality of DADT. The suit was delayed for years as the government, first under President Bush and then under President Obama filed motions to dismiss the case—some routine, some rather extraordinary. Finally, in July 2010, the case proceeded to trial.

Less than two months later, on September 9, Judge Virginia Phillips handed down her decision. "The 'don't ask, don't tell' act infringes the fundamental rights of United States service members in many ways," wrote Judge Phillips. "In order to justify the encroachment on these rights, defendants faced the burden at trial of showing the 'don't ask, don't tell' act was necessary to significantly further the government's important interests in military readiness and unit cohesion. Defendants failed to meet that burden." The aggregated evidence, wrote Phillips, "directly undermines any contention that the Act furthers the Government's purpose of military readiness." Not only did the policy fail to protect national security, concluded Phillips, but it actually undercut it. "The testimony of both its lay and expert witnesses," wrote Phillips of the plaintiff, "revealed that the Act not only is unnecessary to further unit cohesion, but also harms the Government's interest" by "impeding the efforts to recruit and retain an all-volunteer military force" and "by causing the discharge of otherwise qualified servicemembers with critical skills" (*Log Cabin Republicans vs. USA and Robert M. Gates, Secretary of Defense*, 2010).

The decision in the LCR case—although it had yet to go through the appeals process—marked the death knell for the ban. For decades, the military and other champions of discrimination had argued that treating gay troops equally would harm readiness, an assertion that bolstered an ingrained cultural narrative that gay people were a threat to American culture. The courts had consistently put their imprimatur on that myth, deferring to military judgment and avoiding a genuine evaluation of what were entirely ungrounded allegations. So long as the military could argue with impunity that open service harmed readiness, the ban was locked into place politically, legally, and culturally. But when provided with rock-solid evidence, in the fact-finding context of a court of law, that the policy did not protect readiness because the presence of gay troops did not harm it—indeed, that the policy itself hurt readiness, it became impossible for the military, cultural conservatives, or Justice Department lawyers to argue that a compelling governmental interest was served by discriminating against gay people. That was the only way that such discrimination could be considered constitutionally valid. In so thoroughly addressing the legal question of the ban's constitutional validity, the court had definitively answered the political and cultural question of the ban's continued justifiability.

The court's momentous decision reflected years of research and debate about the costs, purpose and impact of DADT. Its compelling conclusion that the policy did not further a legitimate governmental purpose crystallized the fruits of a strategic shift in focus by advocates from attacking the ban as a moral violation of fairness to attacking it as a practical violation of national security. It was a conscious move away from using the equal rights lens—that appealed to LGBT and progressive Americans but resonated less with conservative and military audiences—to using the frame of the ban's supporters—military readiness and national security. The new rhetoric turned the old frame on its head: Gay people don't threaten national security; the ban does—and the deployment of this rhetoric by LGBT advocates in the political arena meant, ultimately, enlisting the government in a successful attack against its own policy. Indeed, Judge Phillips quoted President Obama's indictment of the policy in her decision striking it down: "Defendants have admitted that, far from being necessary to further significantly the Government's interest in military readiness, the Don't Ask, Don't Tell Act actually undermines that interest. President Obama, the Commander-in-Chief of the Armed Forces, stated on June 29, 2009: 'Don't Ask, Don't Tell doesn't contribute to our national security. Preventing patriotic Americans from serving their country weakens our national security . . . Reversing this policy [is] the right thing to do [and] is essential for our national security.'" (*Log Cabin Republicans v. USA and Robert M. Gates, Secretary of Defense*, 2010).

While much of the rest of the world coalesced around the court's conclusion that the policy was a failure which must end, the Senate stood firm. On September 21, 2010, in an unexpectedly successful filibuster led by Republicans, the Senate voted to block repeal by opposing the entire Defense spending bill to which it was attached. Repeal was falling victim to traditional politicking, with Republicans adopting a just-say-no strategy of denying the Democratic President a win on anything. *The New York Times* called the vote "more a result of a dispute between Democrats and Republicans over legislative process than a straightforward referendum on whether to" repeal the ban (Herszenhorn, 2010), because Majority Leader Harry Reid chose to attach other provisions to the bill and to limit input by Republicans, which he knew would anger them. Every Republican and two Democrats voted against the bill, which failed 56 to 43. Sen. Susan Collins was among the Republican no votes who some repeal advocates had hoped would vote for the bill. It was the first time in 48 years that the Pentagon spending bill had failed to gain congressional approval.

The court case was exerting enormous pressure on both the White House and the Pentagon to achieve legislative repeal. The White House found it embarrassing to repeatedly have to defend in court a policy that the President had campaigned on eradicating; and the military did not want to be forced to lift the ban by courts under terms it could not control. In October, Judge Phillips issued a worldwide injunction against enforcement of the ban. The ban was lifted for the first time ever. The injunction lasted only eight days until it was stayed by an appeals court. Nevertheless, the suspension showed the world that no harm resulted from a military without DADT.

The court's injunction created a major headache for the Pentagon. *The New York Times* described October's events as a "series of court decisions [that] whipsawed the Pentagon into suspending and then resuming enforcement of the law over the course of little more than a week, creating bewilderment at recruiting stations and confusion among Defense Department lawyers" (Bumiller, 2010a). Jeh Johnson, the Defense Department's general counsel and co-chair of the 2010 CRWG, complained to the Senate that "in the space of eight days we had to shift course on the worldwide enforcement of the law twice, and in the space of a month faced the possibility of shifting course four different times" (Bumiller, 2010a). He later recalled that "the LCR case sent us into, frankly, a real panic." The last thing the military wanted was to have to tell two million people to stop following the law one day, then start the next, then stop and start again. "That had a real impact on Secretary Gates," said Johnson (Bailey & Barbato, 2011).

Indeed, Gates reacted to the legal developments with increasing alarm, reiterating that the pressure was on Congress to make a decision, but continuing, at least initially, to ask that lawmakers wait until the December 1 study was out before voting on a change. By November, Gates had taken the next step, saying for the first time that he actually backed legislation to lift the ban so as to ward off a court mandate. "I would like to see the repeal of 'don't ask, don't tell,'" he said, "but I'm not sure what the prospects for that are" (Keyes, 2010). On November 10, three weeks before it was due, a draft of the Pentagon study was leaked to *The Washington Post*, which reported that the authors had concluded the ban could be lifted without great risk to the military (O'Keefe & Jaffe, 2010). If authorized by top officials, the leak may have been an effort by the Pentagon to push repeal forward.

The White House also used the occasion of the court case for both tough talk and a reiteration of support for the slow roll through Congress: "Time is running out on the policy of 'don't ask, don't tell,'" said Press Sec. Gibbs, while also saying that the legislative branch should lead the process of change: "The best way to end it is for the Senate to follow the lead of the House of Representatives so that that end can be implemented in a fashion that is consistent with our obligations in fighting two wars." Yet he also implied the White House had not ruled out the use of other executive actions, which could have referred to a stop-loss order or a decision not to appeal the California court ruling. "Absent that action," Gibbs said about congressional repeal, "the [P]resident has again set up a process to end this policy" (Richardson, 2010).

Just a week before the midterm election, facing headlines like "Obama's Go-Slow 'Don't Ask, Don't Tell' Plan Backfires" (Gerstein, 2010), the White House invited a group of gay advocates and a group of gay and progressive bloggers to meet with the President.[10] The meetings were unusual in that the President himself sat down with activists in the Roosevelt Room for an extended conversation. The blogger meeting was unprecedented. Both were widely seen as efforts by the White House to burnish its bona fides with its base as the growing enthusiasm gap—disaffection with the Obama achievement record among one-time supporters—threatened to bog

Democrats down in the midterm elections. Among the bloggers invited was Joe Sudbay of AMERICAblog, one of the administration's loudest progressive critics, particularly on its record on LGBT rights. The very fact of the meetings suggests the White House took seriously this new breed of progressive writer advocates, and sought to use them as mouthpieces to get its message out: "We hear you and are working on issues you care about." The meeting with gay advocates, which was specifically to discuss the repeal strategy, also may have suggested both that the White House knew how important repeal was to the progressive base, and that it doubted it was going to be able to deliver repeal. At least, the meeting would show, they tried.

Lame Duck

On election day, the Democrats lost control of the House in a wave election that yielded 63 seats to the GOP.

On November 15, a dozen activists including Dan Choi got arrested once again for chaining themselves to the White House fence. The media coverage was intense (e.g., "'Don't Ask, Don't Tell' Arrest Outside White House," 2010; Malveaux, 2010; O'Keefe, 2010; Smith, 2010a). As a gridlocked Congress squabbled, with antics that were bringing its approval numbers toward single digits (Jones, 2010), uniformed Americans were pleading to be able to serve their country at the gate of a President who was refusing to sign a paper halting the discriminatory firings.

On November 30, 2010—one day early—the Pentagon released its nine-month-long comprehensive report on repeal. Symbolic though it may have been, the fact that Sec. Gates allowed the release of the report one day before originally scheduled (and may have authorized the leaking of the report to *The Washington Post*) suggests he was doing his part to move repeal along, as any additional hours could only help in a crowded lame duck session. The report concluded that "the risk of repeal of Don't Ask, Don't Tell to overall military effectiveness is low," and that the military could lift the ban without harming readiness (U.S. Department of Defense, 2010). It cited "a widespread attitude among a solid majority of service members that repeal of Don't Ask, Don't Tell will not have a negative impact on their ability to conduct their military mission." The report discussed the experiences of foreign militaries as well as surveys indicating that most U.S. troops already knew of gay peers in their units—all data points and frames that research advocates like the Palm Center had expressed for years (U.S. Department of Defense, 2010).

President Obama released a statement (2010b) hailing the study and "call[ing] on the Senate to act as soon as possible so I can sign this repeal into law this year." It said the report "confirms that, by every measure—from unit cohesion to recruitment and retention to family readiness—we can transition to a new policy in a responsible manner that ensures our military strength and national security. And for the first time since this law was enacted seventeen years ago today, both the Secretary of Defense and the Chairman of the Joint Chiefs of Staff have publicly endorsed ending this policy."

Addressing the Senate following the report's release, Sec. Gates said that repeal "would not be the wrenching, traumatic change that many have feared and predicted [. . .] Now that we have completed this review," he said, "I strongly urge the Senate to pass this legislation" (Federal News Service, 2010a). For Gates, legislative repeal had become "a matter of some urgency because, as we have seen this past year, the judicial branch is becoming involved in this issue, and it is only a matter of time before the federal courts are drawn once more into the fray. Should this happen, there is the very real possibility that this change would be imposed immediately by judicial fiat, by far the most disruptive and damaging scenario I can imagine" (Pellerin, 2010). The irony was not lost on some observers that Gates, who said a week later that he "would hope that [Congress] would" vote for repeal but he was "not particularly optimistic," was largely responsible for holding back a vote until it was all but too late to have one.

If passing repeal in the lame duck session was part of the Democrats' repeal plan, that was far from clear in the public record. When Wolf Blitzer asked senior White House advisor Valerie Jarrett, "Will you push for repealing 'don't ask, don't tell' during the lame duck session?" she merely replied that "the [P]resident has said he wants it repealed as quickly as possible," that most Americans favor repeal, and that "we do fully intend to push forward" (Blitzer, 2010). Throughout November, the White House continued to back the Pentagon's timeline of awaiting a vote until after it released its report the last day of that month. In early December, Sen. Majority Leader Reid rattled off the priorities he hoped the Senate would address in the rapidly dwindling days of the session including tax cuts, funding the government, renewing the Strategic Arms Reduction Treaty (START), and immigration reform. "That's the plan; we hope we can execute it," he said, in time to adjourn the week before Christmas. Only when Sen. Carl Levin murmured in his ear that he should "say something about the Defense bill," did Sen. Reid add that item, which was to include repeal (Eleveld, 2010c).

While the President had worked with the Pentagon since 2009 to line up the support of Sec. Gates and Adm. Mullen, there was little evidence that he was personally involved in whipping up senate votes.[11] That changed in December 2010, when Obama became increasingly involved in the fight for repeal. Obama called both the service chiefs and repeal advocates to White House meetings as soon as the report was released and made clear he did not want to trade repeal for any other administration initiatives (Bumiller, 2010b; O'Keefe & Rucker, 2010). *The Washington Post* reported that President Obama called several senators in December to urge them to support repeal (O'Keefe & Kane, 2010).

Still, even at this late date, according to both White House staff and lawmakers, the START treaty was a higher priority for the administration, which pressed senators to pass that over DADT repeal. Barney Frank said Hoyer was pressured not to push repeal as a stand-alone because it could threaten passage of START (R. Berman, 2010; O'Keefe & Whitlock, 2010).

Lobbying and mobilization efforts by advocates, including HRC, SLDN, Servicemembers United, CAP Action Fund, and Log Cabin Republicans, were intense. HRC took out full-page advertisements in major papers, used telemarketing and social media, launched field campaigns focusing on states with persuadable senators, created Spanish-language outreach efforts, identified hundreds of pro-repeal veterans to meet with senators, and generated thousands of constituent contacts. In 2010, the group sent 19 million e-mails to members and supporters and 625,000 e-mails to members of Congress. SLDN had recruited Lady Gaga to the cause, deploying her to reach out to her 7 million Twitter followers and help generate additional media for her efforts (Boland, 2011).

Yet, on Thursday, December 9, the Senate again filibustered repeal, failing by three votes to move the measure forward. The newly elected Sen. Joe Manchin (D-WV) was the only Democrat to vote against it. Republicans continued their just-say-no strategy to defeat any goal embraced by Democrats—just as they had sought to do with a healthcare reform plan that was first proposed by Republicans—and were holding any sort of progress hostage to their demands for tax cuts. *The Washington Post* reported that the no vote had "thwarted a months-long push by President Obama and the Democratic leadership to force a vote on the issue" (O'Keefe & Kane, 2010). The President issued a statement saying, "Despite having the bipartisan support of a clear majority of senators, a minority of senators are standing in the way of the funding upon which our troops, veterans and military families depend" (O'Keefe & Kane, 2010).

HRC sent out an e-mail the day of the vote failure pronouncing repeal dead. "The United States Senate has failed our military and failed the American people," it said. "It appears Congress won't repeal the law this year" and that the fate of gay troops "now rests in President Obama's hands" (Aravosis, 2011). Executive action, said Joe Solmonese, is now "imperative in order for him to fulfill his State of the Union promise" to end the ban (O'Keefe & Kane, 2010).

Death of DADT

Yet, Sens. Lieberman and Collins were already holding a press conference the afternoon of the vote failure promising to introduce a stand-alone bill that was the last chance to get repeal through the Senate. Lieberman, with a major assist from Rep. Steny Hoyer, along with repeal groups, had begun to devise an alternate plan to passing repeal through the Defense Authorization

Act. It involved a stand-alone bill that, contrary to conventional wisdom, might end up the cleaner and more viable path to victory. Hoyer had conversations with five key Republican senators, four of whom committed to supporting the stand-alone bill. He then worked with Pelosi and Murphy to convince his House colleagues to endure another vote on repeal—this time on a stand-alone bill to match the one that Lieberman and Collins would introduce in the Senate. He told Reid of the plan, who said he would try to make time for another repeal vote, which he had the power to expedite using his leadership privileges. The House passed the stand-alone repeal bill, introduced by Hoyer and Murphy just a day before, on December 15. With a tax stand-off resolved, and the repeal measure separated out from the larger defense spending bill, the Senate followed suit on December 18, passing a bill introduced by Lieberman and Collins in a 65-31 vote that included support by eight Republicans. President Obama signed the measure into law on December 22, and the military would eventually implement the repeal on September 20, 2011 (R. Berman, 2010; O'Keefe & Whitlock, 2010; Steinhauer, 2010).

CONCLUSION

How did repeal happen? Did it indeed go all according to a much-discussed but scarcely revealed plan that the White House and HRC devised and implemented? Or did the President refer to the pleasantly surprising success of repeal because he, along with so many others, was aware that there was no plan that was likely to carry repeal across the finish line? Clearly credit for repeal is due to the powerful lobbying and mobilizing efforts of Washington's LGBT advocacy groups and veterans; to the leadership of Sens. Lieberman, Reid, Levin, Gillibrand, Udall, and—eventually—Collins, and of Speaker Pelosi and Reps. Murphy, Frank, and Hoyer; to the good faith effort by the Pentagon to assess the impact of repeal, read the political tea leaves, and get on the right side of history; and to a President and his staff who believed that repeal was the right thing to do and increasingly saw that it was worth spending political capital to achieve.

But all of this was dependent on a long-term public information campaign that expanded support for repeal into areas that once seemed impenetrable, and a pressure campaign by advocates that moved the ball perpetually forward. The strategic, research-based and media-driven reframing of the national dialogue from one of equal rights to one of the efficacy of the policy and its impact on the nation was critical to this effort. In particular, the Palm Center's focus on the national security frame helped reach moderates and conservatives on their own terms and also insisted that the debate be rooted in facts—never sexy, never sufficient to win a debate, but, ultimately, essential to winning in spheres ranging from the court of law to the court of public and military opinion. This consistent and strategic presentation of fact was an essential complement to the emotional and political pressure that veterans and groups like SLDN and HRC exerted, often by sharing soldiers' stories on the airwaves, at the Capitol, and in the courts.

The pressure campaign became increasingly strident, broad-based and vocal in 2009 and 2010. In the latter year, it became clear that ENDA was stalled and that hate crime legislation was not enough of a delivery for President Obama, and that not only LGBT Americans but many in Obama's progressive base found it unacceptable not to chalk up a win on ending DADT. This was made even plainer with the December 9 failure to secure repeal as part of the defense spending bill, and when the President cut a deal with congressional Republicans to extend the Bush tax cuts, which further angered his liberal base, now clamoring for a progressive win (A. Berman, 2011).

The tactics deployed by GetEQUAL in March 2010 started months of direct action meant to pressure the White House and congressional Democrats to ensure the timely passage of repeal. The tactics, and their impact, have been debated since they began, as has the role of outsider disruptions in social movements throughout history. It would be impossible to conclude definitively that these tactics were responsible for moving repeal across the finish line in December 2010, and in the view of White House and HRC officials, a sound plan to secure repeal had been in place long before any of the outsider tactics raised their irritating voices.

What we do know, however, as laid out in these pages, strongly suggests a critical role for these pressure tactics. While the White House and its allies claimed the administration and others in Washington did not respond to pressure, White House staff routinely reached out to groups small and large when those groups became, or threatened to become, a nuisance.[12] The President, himself, was personally irked by the disruptions at his speaking events, which pressed him to raise questions to his senior staff about his approach to the issue and to gay voters. The President's deputy chief of staff, Jim Messina, was increasingly frustrated by his collapsing relations with LGBT groups and worried about alienating a vocal constituency, particularly since he hoped to run Obama's reelection campaign (Ambinder, 2010). HRC was concerned by the criticism it was taking from the LGBT community and decided late in 2009 to abruptly switch its lobbying and public education priorities to focus on repeal (Boland, 2011). The Pentagon, according to a senior official there, was feeling pressure from the media chorus of complaints, as well as legal challenges staring them down, and felt compelled to deliver some tangible progress toward softening or ending the ban. Finally, the White House called in gay groups and gay and progressive bloggers for a rare meeting with the President a week before the 2010 midterm elections, a time when the President has no time for anything that is not directly election-related. It was a strong signal that the administration had become highly concerned by an enthusiasm gap among its base, and was persuaded that a victory on a gay issue was not only beneficial, but essential.

Neither the administration nor HRC ever publicly stated what the plan was, first promised in 2009, to ensure repeal before a GOP House takeover took it off the table indefinitely. But it seems certain what the plan was not: to accept a timetable dictated by the Pentagon that created a study group to give cover to moderate lawmakers that would be due in the final weeks of a lame-duck session of Congress; to back Sec. Gates' wish to delay a vote until then; to reverse that plan six months early amid pressure by Democratic congressional leaders and LGBT advocates by orchestrating a House vote well before the working group released its study; to lose twice on a cloture vote in the Senate that fall; to introduce an immediate stand-alone bill the next day using a rarely invoked tactic to bypass the regular debate process with days to go in the congressional session; and to drag repeal across the finish line the week before Christmas in a lame-duck session of nearly unprecedented legislative productivity (Franke-Ruta, 2010). That was not the plan.[13] As the President had said, success was a pleasant surprise, and it was one made possible by an unprecedented collective campaign of public pressure that held the government accountable to the people it serves.

NOTES

1. Looking back through the lens of President Obama's dramatic 2012 announcement that he favored same-sex marriage, the gay blogger, Andrew Sullivan (2012), praised the President's evolutionary approach, expressing remorse for his own part in hazing the White House for its slow pace on ending DADT. "We were wrong," he wrote. The President made "the brilliant calculation" to move slowly and ultimately "outmaneuvered Republicans" to clinch victory just before the clock ran.

2. I also draw on 15 background interviews with key players who participated in the repeal effort. I guaranteed them confidentiality so they would feel free, at this early date, to share with me information they felt was critical to the story but that they might not be at liberty to discuss publicly.

3. Lt. Col. Allen Bishop, USA (ret.; 2010), names me as the figure who "perhaps began this line of reasoning" around 2004, referring to casting the argument for repeal in terms of efficacy rather than justice (p. 120). In singling me out, Bishop surely gives me too much credit; but he is correct that the framing was a conscious strategic decision (by me and others) in the years following the 2001 terrorist attacks (see Belkin, 2011).

4. In 1996, one poll found that 91% of liberals favored allowing gays to serve, while only 57% of conservatives did. A 2004 poll put the spread at 83% to 46% (Morales, 2009; Yang, 1999).

5. I served as an expert witness in the case. The other expert witnesses were Aaron Belkin, Elizabeth Hillman, Larry Korb, Robert MacCoun, Alan Okros, and Melissa Sheridan Embser-Herbert.

6. Note that it was not the don't ask, don't tell statute that granted this authority but 10 USC § 12305, a separate statute that overrides any mandate to discharge service members, saying, "Notwithstanding any other provision of law, during any period members of a reserve component are serving on active duty . . ., the President may suspend any provision of law relating to promotion, retirement, or separation applicable to any member of the armed forces who the President determines is essential to the national security of the United States." See 10 USC § 12305, Authority of President to Suspend Certain Laws Relating to Promotion, Retirement, and Separation.

7. Disclosure: I helped organize a fundraiser for Patrick Murphy's first Primary contest.

8. The charge against HRC was echoed in a piece by Michelangelo Signorile (2009) in which Aaron Belkin cited "many offices" on Capitol Hill claiming that gay rights groups were "lobbying against consideration" of repeal at this time.

9. Six sources among my background interviews cited Sec. Gates as the figure who was in control of the timeline through his leverage as head of the Pentagon, whose support most advocates and politicians believed was crucial for repeal.

10. I was among those meeting with the President on October 26, 2010.

11. Organizing for America, the administration's outfit for mobilizing support for its legislative agenda, had swung into action for repeal only around Thanksgiving of 2010 (Geidner, 2010a). The White House said the President telephoned Sen. Carl Levin in November to discuss passing the National Defense Authorization Act with don't ask, don't tell repeal attached, at which point it had the opportunity to recount additional phone calls (Eleveld, 2010d).

12. In addition to GetEQUAL, other repeal advocates received White House emails at key moments in their public advocacy asking about their concerns and sometimes asking them to hold their fire.

13. SLDN's Aubrey Sarvis said in a 2011 interview, "I don't care what anyone says, no one had a secret plan to have two votes in the lame-duck session after the Democrats have lost control of the House." He believed a number of the President's advisers were content to delay repeal beyond 2010, a point corroborated by a Senate staffer who recalls that "The White House staff had to be dragged kicking and screaming the whole way toward repeal" (Hirshman, 2012).

REFERENCES

Adair, B. (2009). Editor's note: Introducing the Obameter. *PolitiFact.com*. Retrieved from http://www.politifact.com/truth-o-meter/article/2009/jan/14/editors-note-introducing-obameter/

Aitken, H., Alexander, M., Gard, R., & Shanahan, J. (2010). Report of the General/Flag Officers' Study Group. In J. E. Parco & D. A. Levy (Eds.), *Attitudes aren't free: Thinking deeply about diversity in the U.S. armed forces* (pp. 139–159). Maxwell Air Force Base, AL: Air University Press.

Ambinder, M. 2010, December 20). Outing the debate: An inside account of the struggle to end "don't ask, don't tell." *National Journal*. Retrieved from http://www.nationaljournal.com/magazine/the-battle-to-end-don-t-ask-don-t-tell--20101209

Aravosis, J. (2011, February 15). Obama rewrites a wee bit of history on DADT repeal [Web log]. Retrieved from http://gay.americablog.com/2011/02/obama-rewrites-wee-bit-of-history-on.html

Babington, C. (2009, May 2). Analysis: New justice may re-ignite social issues. Associated Press. Retrieved from http://www.realclearpolitics.com/news/ap/politics/2009/May/02/analysis__new_justice_may_re_ignite_social_issues.html

Bailey, F., & Barbato, R. (Directors). (2011). *The strange history of "don't ask, don't tell"* [Film]. Los Angeles, CA: World of Wonder Productions/HBO.

Barnes, J. (2010, February 2). Joint chiefs chairman Mullen supports right of gays to serve in military. *Los Angeles Times*. Retrieved from http://articles.latimes.com/2010/feb/02/nation/la-na-gays-military3-2010feb03

Belkin, A. (2008). 'Don't Ask, don't tell': Does the gay ban undermine the military's reputation? *Armed Forces and Society, 34*, 276–291.

Belkin, A. (2009a, May 7). Obama to fire his first gay Arabic linguist. *Huffington Post*. Retrieved from http://www.huffingtonpost.com/aaron-belkin/obama-to-fire-his-first-g_b_199070.html

Belkin, A. (2009b, July 27). Self-inflicted wound: How and why gays give the White House a free pass on "don't ask, don't tell. *Palm Center Report*, 8.

Belkin, A. (2011). *How we won: Progressive lessons from the repeal of "don't ask, don't tell."* New York, NY: Huffington Post Media Group.

Belkin, A., Frank, N., Herek, G, Hillman, E., Mazur, D., & Wilson, B. (2010). How to end 'don't ask, don't tell': A roadmap of political, legal, regulatory, and organizational steps to equal treatment. In J. Parco and D. Levy (Eds.), *Attitudes aren't free: thinking deeply about diversity in the U.S. armed forces* (pp. 199–232). Maxwell Air Force Base, AL: Air University Press.

Bellini, J. (2009, June 4). The surprising holdouts on don't ask don't tell. *The Daily Beast*. Retrieved from http://www.thedailybeast.com/articles/2009/06/04/the-surprising-holdouts-on-dont-ask-dont-tell.html

Bender, B. (2009, February 1). Obama seeks assessment on gays in military: No rush to repeal "don't ask, don't tell." *Boston Globe*. Retrieved from http://www.boston.com/news/nation/washington/articles/2009/02/01/obama_seeks_assessment_on_gays_in_military/?page=full

Bendery, J, & Toeplitz, S. (2009, June 25). House leaders plot gay rights agenda. *Roll Call*. Retrieved from http://www.rollcall.com/issues/54_152/-36273-1.html

Benecke, M. (2011, Fall). Turning points: Challenges and successes in ending don't ask, don't tell. *William & Mary Journal of Women and the Law, 18*, 35–86.

Berman, A. (2011, March 30). Jim Messina, Obama's enforcer. *The Nation*. Retrieved from http://www.thenation.com/article/159577/jim-messina-obamas-enforcer

Berman, R. (2010, December 21). Gay-rights advocates say Dem leader Hoyer saved "don't ask" repeal. *The Hill*. Retrieved from http://thehill.com/homenews/campaign/134763-gay-rights-advocates-say-hoyer-saveddont-ask-repeal

Beutler, B. (2009, April 2). Gates: We've only spoken to obama about don't ask, don't tell one time. *Talking Points Memo*. Retrieved from http://tpmdc.talkingpointsmemo.com/2009/04/gates-weve-only-spoken-to-obama-about-dont-ask-dont-tell-one-time.php

Bicknell, Jr., J. W. (2000, March). Study of Naval officers' attitudes toward homosexuals in the military. (Master's thesis). Naval Postgraduate School, Monterey, CA.

Bishop, Lt. Col., A., USA (ret.). (2010, March-April). Efficacy or justice: Overturning the ban. *Military Review*, 117–120.

Blake, A., & Tiron, R. (2009, July 13). Gillibrand mulls move left on gays in military. *The Hill*. Retrieved from http://thehill.com/homenews/senate/50115-gillibrand-mulls-move-left-on-gays-in-military

Blitzer, W. [anchorman]. (2010, October 23). The situation room. [Television program]. CNN. Washington, DC.

Blumner, R. (2003, April 27). "Don't ask, don't tell" rules don't make sense. *St. Petersburg Times*. Retrieved from http://www.sptimes.com/2003/04/27/Columns/_Don_t_ask__don_t_tel.shtml

Boland, J. (2011, August 18). Case study: Human Rights Campaign don't ask, don't tell repeal. *Fundraising Success Magazine*. Retrieved from http://www.fundraisingsuccessmag.com/article/case-study-human-rights-campaign-dont-ask-dont-tell-repeal-part-1/1#utm_source=fundraisingsuccessmag.com&utm_medium=search_results_page&utm_campaign=search_result

Bowen, A., & Lane, A. (2011, July 26). End of "don't ask, don't tell" is a victory for philanthropy. *The Chronicle of Philanthropy*. Retrieved from http://philanthropy.com/article/Philanthropys-Military/128431/

Braiker, B. (2010, April 30). Gates letter not to repeal DADT draws fire. *ABC News* [web blog]. Retrieved from http://abcnews.go.com/blogs/politics/2010/04/gates-letter-not-to-repeal-dadt-draws-fire/

Bravin, J., & Meckler, L. (2009, May 19). Obama avoids test on gays in military. *Wall Street Journal*. Retrieved from http://online.wsj.com/article/SB124268952606832391.html

Brune, T. (2009, July 27). Gillibrand wins Senate hearing on military policy on gays. *Newsday*. Retrieved from http://www.newsday.com/news/nation/gillibrand-wins-senate-hearing-on-military-policy-on-gays-1.1330782

Bryant, J. & Zillmann, D. (2009). A restropective and prospective look at media effects. In R. Nai & M. Oliver (Eds.), *The Sage handbook of media processes and effects* (pp. 9–18). Thousand Oaks, CA: Sage.

Bumiller, E. (2009a, January 30). After campaign push, Obama cultivates military. *The New York Times*, A14.

Bumiller, E. (2009b, April 16). Gates cautious on repeal of ban on gays in military. *New York Times Blog*. Retrieved from http://thecaucus.blogs.nytimes.com/2009/04/16/gates-cautious-on-repeal-of-ban-on-gays-in-military/

Bumiller, E. (2010a, December 5). For pentagon lawyer who co-wrote report on gays, military bias hits home. *New York Times*, A32.

Bumiller, E. (2010b, December 1). Pentagon sees little risk in allowing gay men and women to serve openly. *The New York Times*, A 21.

Bunn, S. (2010, Spring). Straight talk: The implications of repealing "don't ask, don't tell" and the rationale for preserving aspects of the current policy. *Military Law Review, 203*, 207–283.

Capehart, J. (2009, June 21). For Obama, a hit and a miss on gay rights. *The Washington Post*. Retrieved from http://www.washingtonpost.com/wp-dyn/content/article/2009/06/19/AR2009061902746.html

Capehart, J. (2010a, May 4). Justified anger over Sec. Gates' letter on don't ask don't tell. *The Washington Post*. Retrieved from http://voices.washingtonpost.com/postpartisan/2010/05/justified_anger_over_sec_gates.html

Capehart, J. (2010b, October 18). Obama is right on don't ask don't tell. *The Washington Post*. Retrieved from http://voices.washingtonpost.com/postpartisan/2010/10/obama_is_right_on_dont_ask_don.html

Center for American Progress. (2009, June 24). Ending 'don't ask, don't tell': Practical steps to repeal the ban on openly gay men and women in the U.S. military [report]. Retrieved from http://www.americanprogress.org/issues/lgbt/report/2009/06/24/6296/ending-dont-ask-dont-tell/

Christopher, T. (2009, May 15). President Obama exercises authority on detainee photos but not gay soldiers. *Politics Daily*. Retrieved from http://www.politicsdaily.com/2009/05/15/president-obama-exercises-authority-on-detainee-photos-but-not/

Couric, K. [Anchorwoman]. (2009, August 20). Katie Couric on SU's "Voices of honor" tour. [Television broadcast episode]. *CBS Evening News*. New York, NY: CBS. Retrieved from http://www.youtube.com/watch?v=VZLxF2Pgg5s

CQ Transcripts. (2009a, May 20). White House Press Secretary Robert Gibbs Holds White House Regular News Briefing. [Transcript].

CQ Transcripts. (2009b, May 21). White House Press Secretary Robert Gibbs Holds White House Regular News Briefing. [Transcript].

CQ Transcripts. (2009c, June 29). White House Press Secretary Robert Gibbs Holds White House Regular News Briefing. [Transcript].

CQ Transcripts. (2009d, June 30). White House Press Secretary Robert Gibbs Holds White House Regular News Briefing. [Transcript].

"Don't ask, don't tell" arrest outside White House. (2010, November 16). *Fox News*. Retrieved from http://nation.foxnews.com/dont-ask/2010/11/16/dont-ask-dont-tell-arrest-outside-white-house

Eleveld, K. (2009a, May 18). DNC chair asked about ending DADT. *The Advocate*. Retrieved from http://www.advocate.com/News/Daily_News/2009/05/18/DNC_Chair_Asked_About_Ending_DADT/

Eleveld, K. (2010a, December 22). Obama: "Prepared to implement." *The Advocate*. Retrieved from http://www.advocate.com/news/news-features/2010/12/22/exclusive-interview-president-barack-obama-dadt

Eleveld, K. (2010b, January 27). Obama re-pledges DADT repeal. *The Advocate*. Retrieved from http://www.advocate.com/printArticle.aspx?id=106066

Eleveld, K. (2010c, December 6). View from Washington. *The Advocate*. Retrieved from http://www.advocate.com/news/2010/12/06/view-washington-dadt-dead-duck

Eleveld, K. (2010d, November 22). White House lame duck line up. *The Advocate*. Retrieved from http://www.advocate.com/news/daily-news/2010/11/22/white-house-lines-lame-duck-bills

Eleveld, K. (2010e, April 21). White House sends mixed messages on DADT. *The Advocate*. Retrieved from http://www.advocate.com/news/daily-news/2010/04/21/white-house-sends-mixed-messages-dadt

Elliott, P. (2009a, June 26). Gays bemoan White House go-slow approach. *Associated Press*, Retrieved from http://www.ohio.com/news/gays-bemoan-white-house-go-slow-approach-1.126959

Elliott, P. (2009b, May 21.) White House says 'don't ask' policy under review. *The Associated Press*.

Elliott, P. (2010, May 24). White House eyes a compromise on gays in military. *Associated Press*.

Farrell, J. (2009, July 8). Murphy takes up overturn of "don't ask, don't tell." *The Philadelphia Inquirer*. Retrieved from http://www.pewforum.org/Religion-News/Murphy-takes-up-overturn-of-dont-ask-dont-tell.aspx

Federal News Service. (2010a, December 2). *Hearing of the senate armed services committee*. [Transcript].

Federal News Service. (2010b, February 22). The White House regular briefing. [Transcript].

Flaherty, A. (2010, May 25). Proposal to lift ban on gays in military in doubt. Associated Press. Retrieved from http://dailycaller.com/2010/05/25/gates-agrees-to-proposal-to-repeal-gay-ban/

FOX News Sunday with Chris Wallace. (2009, March 29). [Television broadcast episode]. Washington, DC: Fox Broadcasting Company. Retrieved from http://www.foxnews.com/story/0,2933,511368,00.html

Frank, N. (2009). *Unfriendly fire: How the gay ban undermines the military and weakens America*. New York, NY: St. Martin's Press.

Franke-Ruta, G. (2010, December 22). The most productive lame duck since WWII—and maybe ever. *The Atlantic*. Retrieved from http://www.theatlantic.com/politics/archive/2010/12/the-most-productive-lame-duck-since-wwii-and-maybe-ever/68442/

Gearan, A. (2010, January 14). Military lawyers advise wait to lift gay ban. Associated Press. Retrieved from http://www.kxan.com/dpps/military/Lawyers-advise-wait-to-lift-gay-ban_3187920

Geidner, C. (2010a, December 2.) DNC's LGBT lead talks about DADT repeal efforts. *Metroweekly*. Retrieved from http://www.metroweekly.com/poliglot/2010/12/dncs-lgbt-lead-talks-about-dad.html

Geidner, C. (2010b, June 2). News analysis: Four days that shook DADT. *Metroweekly*. Retrieved from http://www.metroweekly.com/news/?ak=5262

Gerber, R. (2003, November 26). End decade-old 'don't ask' policy. *USA Today*. Retrieved from http://usatoday30.usatoday.com/news/opinion/editorials/2003-11-25-gerber-edit_x.htm

Gerstein, J. (2010, October 17). Obama's Go-slow "don't ask, don't tell" plan backfires. *Politico*. Retrieved from http://www.politico.com/news/stories/1010/43708.html

Gilgoff, D. (2009, August 7). Why gays can trust Obama. *U.S. News and World Report*. Retrieved from http://www.usnews.com/news/religion/articles/2009/08/07/why-gays-can-trust-obama

Greenberg Quinlan Rosner Research. (2010, February). Ending don't ask, don't tell. Center for American Progress.

Greenberger, S. S. (2005, May 15). One year later, nation divided on gay marriage. *Boston Globe*. Retrieved from http://www.boston.com/news/specials/gay_marriage/articles/2005/05/15/one_year_later_nation_divided_on_gay_marriage/

Hastings and 76 members of congress urge President Obama to suspend "don't ask, don't tell" and initiate bilateral repeal process. (2009, June 9). U. S. Congressman Alcee L. Hastings. Retrieved from http://www.alceehastings.house.gov/index.php?option=com_content&task=view&id=336&Itemid=98

Healy, M. (1993, February 28). *The Times* poll: 74% of military enlistees oppose lifting gay ban. *Los Angeles Times*. Retrieved from http://articles.latimes.com/1993-02-28/news/mn-410_1_times-poll

Herszenhorn, D. (2010, September 22). Move to end 'don't ask, don't tell' stalls in senate. *New York Times*, A1.

Herszenhorn, D. M., & Hulse, C. (2010, May 28). House votes to allow repeal of "don't ask, don't tell" law. *The New York Times*, A1.

Hertzberg, H. (2009, July 6). Stonewall plus forty. *New Yorker*. Retrieved from http://www.newyorker.com/talk/comment/2009/07/06/090706taco_talk_hertzberg

Hirshman, L. (2012). *Victory: The triumphant gay revolution*. New York, NY: HarperCollins.

Huffington Post. (2009, May 7). Dan Choi, fired gay Arabic-speaking linguist, speaks to Rachel Maddow. *Huffington Post*. Retrieved from http://www.huffingtonpost.com/2009/05/07/dan-choi-fired-gay-arabic_n_199592.html

Johnson, C. (2010, March 3). Lieberman unveils Senate "don't ask" repeal legislation. *Washington Blade*. Retrieved from http://www.washingtonblade.com/2010/03/03/lieberman-introduces-bill-to-repeal-dont-ask/

Jones, J. (2010, December 15). Congress' job approval rating worst in Gallup history; Thirteen percent approve of the way Congress is handling its job. *Gallup.com*. Retrieved from http://www.gallup.com/poll/145238/congress-job-approval-rating-worst-gallup-history.aspx.

Keyes, C. (2010, November 8). Signs of trouble for Dems who want to repeal 'don't ask, don't tell.' *CNN.COM*. Retrieved from http://articles.cnn.com/2010-11-08/politics/dems.dont.ask.dont.tell_1_repeal-don-t-dadt-military-families?_s=PM:POLITICS

Kornblut, A. E., & Fletcher, M. A. (2010, January 25). In Obama's decision-making, a wide range of influences. *The Washington Post*. Retrieved from http://www.washingtonpost.com/wp-dyn/content/article/2010/01/24/AR2010012403014.html

Krimmel, K. L., Lax, J. R., & Phillips, J. H. (2012, April 13). Gay rights in Congress: Public opinion and (mis)representation. Proceedings from Midwest Political Science Association's Annual National Conference. Chicago, IL. [Working Paper].

Lee, J. (2009, January 9). *Open for Questions—Response*. CHANGE.GOV. Retrieved from http://change.gov/newsroom/entry/open_for_questions_round_2_response/

Lochhead, C. (2009, May 8). 'Don't ask' repeal losing momentum. *San Francisco Chronicle*, A16.

Log Cabin Republicans v. USA and Robert M. Gates, Secretary of Defense. (2010, September 9). United States District Court, Central District of California. Case No. CV 04-08425-VAP (Ex), Memorandum Opinion.

Lusero, I. (2009, February 3). Marine general questions obama plan to study gay ban. *Palm Center News Release*. Retrieved from http://www.palmcenter.org/press/dadt/releases/Marine%20General%20Questions%20Obama%20Plan

Malveaux, S. (2010, November 15). Gay rights protesters demand Obama help end "don't ask, don't tell." *CNN*. Retrieved from http://articles.cnn.com/2010-11-15/politics/dadt.protesters_1_gay-rights-gay-service-members-gay-advocates?_s=PM:POLITICS

Man, A. (2009, May 9). Gay, lesbian voters express frustration. *Sun Sentinel*. Retrieved from http://articles.sun-sentinel.com/2009-05-09/news/0905080235_1_gay-marriage-lesbian-community-center-same-sex-couples

Martin, S. (2007, January 8). Will Israeli Army success sway U.S. policy on gays? *St. Petersburg Times*, 1A.

Miller, L. L. (1994). Fighting for a just cause: Soldiers' views on gays in the military. In W. J. Scott & S. C. Stanley (Eds.), *Gays and lesbians in the military: Issues, concerns and contrasts* (pp. 69–85). New York, NY: Aldine de Bruyter.

Morales, L. (2009, June 5). Conservatives shift in favor of openly gay service members. *Gallup*. Retrieved from http://www.gallup.com/poll/120764/conservatives-shift-favor-openly-gay-service-members.aspx

Murphy, P. (2010, April 30). Rep. Murphy statement on secretary Gates' letter calling for delay of don't ask don't tell repeal [statement]. Washington, DC: State News Service.

Naff, K. (2010, April 23). HRC, Solmonese in the hot seat. *Washington Blade*. Retrieved from http://www.washingtonblade.com/2010/04/23/hrc-solmonese-in-the-hot-seat/

New York Times. (2009, June 10). The ban on gays in the military [Editorial]. *New York Times*, A28.

New York Times. (2010, January 29). Ending 'don't ask, don't tell' [Editorial]. *The New York Times*, 26.

Nichols, J. (Producer). (2009, June 8). *Hardball with Chris Matthews* [Television broadcast]. Washington, DC: MSNBC.

Nicholson, A. (2010, February 10). A plan for DADT repeal in 2010. *Huffington Post*. Retrieved from http://www.huffingtonpost.com/alexander-nicholson/a-plan-for-dadt-repeal-in_b_457793.html

Obama, B. (2010a, January 27). *Remarks by the President in the State of the Union address*. Washington, DC: The White House, Office of the Press Secretary. Retrieved from http://www.whitehouse.gov/the-press-office/remarks-president-state-union-address

Obama, B. (2010b, November 30). Obama: 'Don't ask' report confirms nation is ready for change [statement]. *American Forces Press Service*. Retrieved from http://www.defense.gov/news/newsarticle.aspx?id=61898

O'Keefe, E. (2010, November 15)."Don't ask, don't tell" splitting gay rights groups. *The Washington Post*. Retrieved from http://voices.washingtonpost.com/federal-eye/2010/11/dont_ask_dont_tell_splitting_g.html

O'Keefe, E., & Jaffe, G. (2010, November 11). Sources: Pentagon Group finds there is minimal risk to lifting gay ban during war. *The Washington Post*. Retrieved from http://voices.washingtonpost.com/federal-eye/2010/11/sources_pentagon_group_finds_t.html

O'Keefe, E. & Kane, P. (2010, December 10). Senate delivers potentially fatal blow to 'don't ask, don't tell' repeal efforts. *Washington Post*, Retreived from http://www.washingtonpost.com/wp-dyn/content/article/2010/12/09/AR2010120906555.html

O'Keefe, E., & Rucker, P. (2010, December 5). Repeal of 'don't ask' is far from certain. *The Washington Post*. Retrieved from http://www.washingtonpost.com/wp-dyn/content/article/2010/12/04/AR2010120403468.html

O'Keefe, E., & Whitlock, C. (2010, December 11). New bill introduced to end "don't ask, don't tell." *The Washington Post*. Retrieved from http://www.washingtonpost.com/wp-dyn/content/article/2010/12/10/AR2010121007163.html

Osborne, D. (2009, July 10). Views split on don't ask. *Gay City News*. Retrieved at http://www.chelseanow.com/articles/2009/07/29/gay_city_news/news/doc4a5667c79b8a5082116155.txt

Osborne, D. (2010, May 26). Don't ask amendment carefully vetted. *Gay City News*. Retrieved from http://www.chelseanow.com/articles/2010/06/18/gay_city_news/news/doc4bfda3364b504269302388.txt

Page, B., & Shapiro, R. (1983, March). Effects of public opinion on policy. *American Political Science Review*, 77, 175–190.

Pellerin, C. (2010, December 2). Gates, Mullen Urge congress to repeal "don't ask" law. *American Forces Press Service*. Retrieved from http://www.defense.gov/news/newsarticle.aspx?id=61924

Phillips, K. (2009, March 2). Repeal sought again of 'don't ask, don't tell' law. *New York Times Blog*. Retrieved from http://thecaucus.blogs.nytimes.com/2009/03/02/repeal-sought-again-of-dont-ask-dont-tell-law/

Price, A. Y.-L. (2010, July-August). The transformative promise of queer politics. *Tikkun, 24*, 52–55, 71–72.

Priest, D. (1998, April 7). Most Gays Used Declaration to Win Independence, Pentagon Study Says. *Washington Post*, A11.

Quindlen, A. (2009, April 3). The end of an error. *Newsweek*. Retrieved from http://www.thedailybeast.com/newsweek/2009/04/03/the-end-of-an-error.html

Richardson, V. (2010, October 14). Military gay ban best left to Congress, Gates says. *The Washington Times*, A4.

Riley, M. (2010, April 21). Dems in Congress unwilling to wait on lengthy repeal of military "don't ask, don't tell." *Denver Post*. Retrieved from http://www.denverpost.com/news/ci_14925042

Room for debate. (2009, May 3). In the barracks, out of the closet. *The New York Times*. Retrieved from http://roomfordebate.blogs.nytimes.com/2009/05/03/in-the-barracks-out-of-the-closet/

Rushing, J. T., & Tiron, R. (2010, March 4). "Don't ask, don't tell" repeal begins. *The Hill*, 3.

Sarvis, A. (2009, June 16). Letting gays serve openly. *The New York Times* (Letters), A 20.

Servicemembers Legal Defense Network. (2009, October 9). SLDN calls on President Obama to address urgency of DADT repeal at HRC dinner [news release]. Washington, DC: PR Newswire.

Shalikashvili, J. (2007, January 2). Second thoughts on gays in the military. *The New York Times*. Retrieved from http://www.nytimes.com/2007/01/02/opinion/02shalikashvili.html?_r=0

Shalikashvili, J. (2009, June 19). Gays in the military: Let the evidence speak. *The Washington Post*. Retrieved from http://www.washingtonpost.com/wp-dyn/content/article/2009/06/18/AR2009061803497.html

Shane, III, L. (2009a, June 22). 'Don't ask, don't tell' in limbo for now; Obama, Congress and Gates all waiting for the other to make the first move. *Stars and Stripes*. Retrieved from http://www.stripes.com/news/don-t-ask-don-t-tell-in-limbo-for-now-1.92676

Shane, III, L. (2009b, July 1). Gates: Pentagon seeking 'more humane' use of 'don't ask, don't tell.' *Stars and Stripes*. Retrieved from http://www.stripes.com/news/gates-pentagon-seeking-more-humane-use-of-don-t-ask-don-t-tell-1.93028

Signorile, M. (2009, June 4). Joe Solmonese interview: Discusses Obama, responds to critics. *The Gist*. Retrieved from http://www.signorile.com/2009/06/joe-solmonese-interview-discusses-obama.html

Sirota, D. (2009). The 'make him do it' dynamic. *Huffington Post*. Retrieved from http://www.huffingtonpost.com/david-sirota/the-make-him-do-it-dynami_b_162599.html

Smith, B. (2010a, November 16). 'Don't ask' protesters target WH outreach. *Politico*. Retrieved from http://www.politico.com/blogs/bensmith/1110/Dont_Ask_protesters_target_WH_outreach.html

Smith, B. (2010b, April 19). Group: White House delaying "don't ask" repeal. *Politico*. Retrieved from http://www.politico.com/blogs/bensmith/0410/Group_White_House_delaying_Dont_Ask_repeal_.html?showall

Solmonese, J. (2010, December 22). The many lessons of DADT repeal. *Huffington Post*. Retrieved from http://www.huffingtonpost.com/joe-solmonese/the-many-lessons-of-dadt-_b_800314.html

State Department Documents and Publications.(2009, May 12). White House Press Briefing by Robert Gibbs. [Transcript].

State Department Documents and Publications. (2010, April 21). Press Secretary Robert Gibbs Briefs Reporters in Washington. [Transcript].

Steinhauer, J. (2010, December 15). House votes to repeal "don't ask, don't tell." *The New York Times*, A27.

Stolberg, S. G. (2009a, May 6). As gay issues arise, Obama is pressed to engage. *The New York Times*, A1.

Stolberg, S. (2009b, June 29). On gay issues, Obama asks to be judged on vows kept. *New York Times*. Retrieved from http://www.nytimes.com/2009/06/30/us/politics/30obama.html

Sullivan, A. (2009, July 28). HRC and the stop-loss option. *The Atlantic Online/Daily Dish*. Retrieved from http://www.theatlantic.com/daily-dish/archive/2009/07/hrc-and-the-stop-loss-option/198260/

Sullivan, A. (2012, May 13). Andrew Sullivan on Barack Obama: The first gay president. *Newsweek*. Retrieved from http://www.thedailybeast.com/newsweek/2012/05/13/andrew-sullivan-on-barack-obama-s-gay-marriage-evolution.html

Tiron, R. (2010, May 21). Pelosi Push on 'don't ask, don't tell' puts panel chairman in a tough spot. *The Hill*, 3.

Turpin, C. [Executive Producer]. (2009, February 24). *All things considered*. [Radio broadcast]. Washington, DC: NPR.

Udall, M. (2009, October 15). Letter to the President of the United States. Retrieved from http://extras.mnginteractive.com/live/media/site36/2009/1015/20091015_052938_DADTObamaletter.pdf

U.S. Department of Defense. (2010). *Report of the comprehensive review of the issues associated with the repeal of "don't ask, don't tell."* Washington, DC.

Welna, D. [Contributor]. (2009, July 9). *Morning Edition*. [Radio broadcast]. Washington, DC: NPR. Retrieved from http://www.npr.org/templates/story/story.php?storyId=106409760

The White House, Office of the Press Secretary. (2009, May 15). Press Briefing by Press Secretary Robert Gibbs. [Transcript].

Williams, C. (2009, May 23). Slow going on gays-in-military issue. *Seattle Times*. Retrieved from http://seattletimes.nwsource.com/html/politics/2009253656_milgays23.html

Wolff, B. (Producer). (2009, March 19). *The Rachel Maddow Show* [Television broadcast]. New York, NY: MSNBC.

Wright, J. (2010, October 27). Lt. Dan Choi talks about Grindr, responds to criticism that his speaking fee is way too high. *Dallas Voice*. Retrieved from http://www.dallasvoice.com/lt-dan-choi-talks-grindr-responds-criticism-speaking-fee-high-1049894.html

Yang, A. S. (1999). From wrongs to rights: Public opinion on gay and lesbian Americans moves toward equality. *National Gay and Lesbian Task Force, Policy Institute*, 1–31.

Zimmermann, E. (2009, November 12). Leaders fix on strategy for "don't ask, don't tell" repeal. *The Hill*, 1.

Zogby International. (2006, December). Opinions of military personnel on sexual minorities in the military. Retrieved from http://www.palmcenter.org/files/active/1/ZogbyReport.pdf

The Politics of Paranoia

AARON BELKIN, PhD
*Department of Political Science, San Francisco State University,
San Francisco, California, USA*

For almost 20 years, gay rights advocates and defenders of military anti-gay discrimination engaged in a phony debate about whether allowing open service would undermine unit cohesion. To be sure, a preponderance of evidence showed that open service would not undermine cohesion, and the repeal of don't ask, don't tell (DADT) required advocates to prevail on that point in the court of public opinion. But concerns about cohesion were never the basis of opposition to open service. Rather, opposition was a modern incarnation of the politics of paranoia, a dangerous tradition in American history. Acknowledging that DADT had nothing to do with cohesion and that military leaders allowed the armed forces to be implicated in the politics of paranoia could facilitate disabling paranoia as the basis for other political projects such as anti-immigrant xenophobia. For a video on DADT and paranoia, search for "Donnelly Belkin DADT" on YoutTube.

This speech was given at the Air Command and Staff College at Maxwell Air Force Base, Montgomery, Alabama on Wednesday, May 26, 2010, where I was an invited guest on a panel discussion on "Gays in the Military." I thank Jim Parco for his generous friendship, his incredible work on this project, and his brave and relentless pursuit of equality for those who haven't achieved it. The full debate is available at http://www.youtube.com/watch?v=v4s_kkmwEJY

Thank you so much for the hospitality and generous introduction. I have to tell you that I'm missing my dance class in San Francisco this morning. I go about five times per week, and I can't tell you how many times the dance class has consisted of me and forty-five other women. Once, I asked the teacher, "Where are all the other gay guys?" This is a true story by the way. He answered, "Well, you know, they attend sometimes but they don't like getting their asses kicked by the suburban heterosexual women." And I said, "I'm comfortable here because that's the story of my life." So we'll see how the debate goes today.

It's a big honor to be here with my distinguished colleagues, Michael Allsep and Elaine Donnelly. Elaine Donnelly and I disagree on many issues (turning to the panel) but I respect very much your passion and your fighting for your values and it's an honor to share this stage with you. So I'm very glad to be here.

I only want to make three points today. The first point I want to make is that don't ask, don't tell is gone. Repeal is a done deal. It actually might happen tomorrow when the Senate Armed Services Committee marks up this year's defense authorization bill. It might happen next year. It might happen in two years. The timing is indeterminate, but the policy is gone. The majority of the American people, including Republicans, want it gone. The Chairman of the Joint Chiefs of Staff wants it gone. The Commander in Chief wants it gone. The Secretary of Defense wants it gone. It's gone. So, you can think that's a good thing, or you can think that's a bad thing. You can think that's going to harm unit cohesion. You can think that's going to help unit cohesion. But the main thing that I want to say today is that this policy's demise is inevitable, so we as a community need to think about how to deal with that and how to plan for that day, whether the day is in the immediate future or slightly beyond that.

Now there will be pressure once don't ask, don't tell goes away to pretend that it never happened, and to smile and to say, "Well, that was a part of our history and we've moved on as a culture. We've moved on as a military. And now, after don't ask, don't tell, we're an inclusive force and were going to get along just fine." But, I actually think there's a little bit of a danger when historical memory works like that.

So, for the second of my three points—and again, I only make three points today—I want to meditate for a minute about what I think don't ask, don't tell has been about. I think there is a danger in forgetting what this policy has really meant to the military and to the culture. I want to argue that don't ask, don't tell is an example of the politics of paranoia. I take this from a fantastic, classic book by Richard Hofstadter (1965), *The Paranoid Style in American Politics*. Hofstadter finds paranoia on the American right and the American left, so this is not a phenomenon that's unique to one side of the aisle or the other. But, in this case I want to make the claim that don't ask, don't tell is a classic example of what Hofstadter is talking about.

So, how do you know the politics of paranoia when you see it? How do you know what the politics of paranoia is? Well, Hofstadter gives us three different ways to know when we're looking at the politics of paranoia, and I want to go through each of those three elements and talk about the resonance with don't ask, don't tell. So, I'm going to read—and I know it's horrible to be read to—but I'm going to read a very brief passage. Regarding the first of three elements that make up the politics of paranoia, Hofstadter says:

> The central image [of the politics of paranoia] is that of a vast and sinister conspiracy, a gigantic yet subtle machinery of influence set in motion to undermine and destroy a way of life. (p. 29)

That is the most important element of the politics of paranoia. If you look at the rhetoric in the conversation about don't ask, don't tell among the people that defend anti-gay discrimination, you will see that that is exactly their mentality. They believe that a gay agenda is taking over this country, destroying our way of life, and that we have to draw the line in the sand at gays in the military. I'll read one or two passages to you. Here's one from Ronald Ray, former Deputy Assistant Secretary of Defense:

> Citizens must make an effort to understand how the elite . . . are working together to establish an entirely new morality. The morality of the New World Order. The new morality seeks to "free" people including our children from any moral limits on commonsense right and wrong. Good and decent people must see that the opening up of the military to homosexuals (right on the heels of allowing women to serve in combat) is simply the latest step in an agenda that has at its end the complete transformation of the nation's moral and spiritual being (Britt & Dickinson, 2006).

And here is Elaine Donnelly on the radio:

> If this kind of [homosexual] agenda is forced upon the Marine Corps, if it's okay for the Marines, then why is it not okay for the local school, the local marriage bureau. Ultimately, all of civilian life would be affected (Corley, 2010).

So, this first element of the politics of paranoia is the idea that there is a great conspiracy out there to change the country and undermine the country, and this is a classic element of don't ask, don't tell and the politics of paranoia.

A second element of the politics of paranoia has to do with sexual deviance and sexual power. Again, I read to you briefly from Hofstadter. In the political paranoid mind,

> sexual freedom [is] often attributed to him [the enemy], his lack of moral inhibition, his possession of especially effective techniques for fulfilling his desires, give exponents of the paranoid style an opportunity to . . . express unacceptable aspects of their own minds. (p. 34)

Now, I'm not going to go on at great length about this second element of the politics of paranoia. I think we know it when we see it. But I will tell you based on my reading of the literature that if you look at the defense of anti-gay discrimination and its history, you will find that literature littered with claims about gays as predators, gays as rapists, gays as people who drink each other's urine, gays as people who ingest each other's feces, and on and on and on. This is a classic element of the politics of paranoia.

A third and final element of the politics of paranoia that maps perfectly onto don't ask, don't tell has to do with the relationship to fact. Here, again, is Richard Hofstadter:

> What distinguishes the paranoid style is not, then, the absence of verifiable facts . . . but rather the curious leap in imagination that is always made at some critical point in the recital of events. (p. 37)

So, how does that map onto don't ask, don't tell? Well, the examples are all over the debate, all over the literature, but I'll give you two recent examples of that curious leap between the tiny little fact that may actually be accurate and the consequences of that fact. General Sheehan, a retired, four-star Marine general, recently testified in the Senate and went so far as to tell Senator Levin during his testimony that the 1995 Srebrenica Massacre, the worst massacre in the history of Europe since the second World War, in which 8,000 Bosniaks, mostly men and children were killed, was the responsibility of gay soldiers in the Dutch armed forces. That it was because the Dutch included gays and lesbians in their armed forces that the Srebrenica Massacre happened, because the Dutch couldn't be effective peacekeepers. Now, this caused such a firestorm in the Netherlands that the general was forced to retract his remarks. But you get the picture. Or, consider the one thousand generals who recently signed a statement, urging President Obama not to repeal don't ask, don't tell, that said if don't ask, don't tell is repealed, this will "break the All-Volunteer Force" (Center for Military Readiness, 2009). It will break the all-volunteer force. Really?

This is the worst tradition of American politics, the politics of paranoia. We see it in McCarthyism. We see it in the Korematsu ruling. It's divide-and-conquer politics. It's the politics of divisiveness.

And you might ask yourself, "But isn't don't ask, don't tell about unit cohesion? Isn't it about military readiness? Is it really about the politics of paranoia?" I'm glad to have a debate with you about unit cohesion. I've been having it for the past decade, and it's certainly true that the preponderance of evidence shows that the repeal of don't ask, don't tell will not undermine unit cohesion. But don't ask, don't tell has never been about unit cohesion. Peter Pace, former Chairman of the Joint Chiefs of Staff, was honest enough several years ago to say at an editorial board meeting of the *Chicago Tribune* that the reason we have don't ask, don't tell is because homosexual conduct is immoral (Shanker, 2007). He was also forced to retract his remarks, but what I told the media at that time was that I was probably the only gay person in the country who was happy that he had finally been honest. Someone defending the policy had finally been honest about the real reason for the policy. It's not unit cohesion. It's morality. And I am glad to have that moral conversation.

Now to my third point, my conclusion. If I asked you to name the military's proudest moment, some of you might vote for Gettysburg. Some of you might have another moment that you'd point to, but in my mind, the military's proudest moment was the 1954 Army-McCarthy hearings. Because during the 1954 Army-McCarthy hearings, the military finally stood up and said to Senator McCarthy "Enough. Enough." Senator McCarthy, consistent with Richard Hofstadter's views, actually did have some facts on his side. It turns out, as the decryption of Soviet cables shows, that there actually were some Communists in government. It's not clear that they were doing any harm, but there were some Communists in government, and Senator McCarthy's politics ripped the country apart. It was the politics of paranoia in perhaps their most extreme manifestation, and the military was the only organization capable of standing up to him.

In my opinion, civilian control is not just about having a nonpartisan military. It's not just about having an officer corps that stays out of politics. It also depends, more institutionally and organizationally, on the military's ability and willingness to avoid the temptation to get dragged into the politics of paranoia. On don't ask, don't tell, not only did you allow yourself to get dragged into the politics of paranoia, but frankly, your leaders did not tell the truth. They were not honest about the real source of their opposition to gays in the military—the moral basis of their opposition—and so they made up these arguments about unit cohesion. As don't ask, don't tell fades into the dustbin of history, that's what we must remember.

REFERENCES

Britt, T. W., & Dickinson, J. M. (2006). Morale during military operations: A positive psychology approach. In Britt, Thomas W., Castro, Carl, & Adler, Amy B. (eds.). *Military life: The psychology of serving in peace and combat, 1*. Westport, CT: Praeger.

Center for Military Readiness. (2009). *Flag & General Officers for the Military*. Retrieved from http://www.flagandgeneralofficersforthemilitary.com/.

Corley, M. (2010, January 27). *Top DADT Advocate says Abu Ghraib abuses happened because women are allowed in the military*. Retrieved from http://thinkprogress.org/politics/2010/01/27/79060/donnelly-abu-ghraib/?mobile=nc

Hofstadter, R. (1965). *The paranoid style in American politics*. New York, NY: Alfred A. Knopf.

Shanker, T. (2007, March 14). Top general explains remarks on gays. *New York Times*.

OutServe: An Underground Network Stands Up

BRENDA SUE FULTON, BS
Board Member, OutServe-SLDN, Washington, DC, USA

From the perspective of an insider, this article explains how an underground network of actively-serving lesbian, gay, bisexual, and transgender (LGBT) military members was formed, and able to engage in the fight against the Don't Ask, Don't Tell policy. By providing the means to connect with one another within the constraints of the law, OutServe enabled the voices of gay and lesbian active military personnel to be heard. This new visibility informed the political debate surrounding the policy and played a role in the final days of Don't Ask, Don't Tell.

BEGINNINGS

The idea of OutServe grew out of a crisis. A young Air Force lieutenant, Josh Seefried, was blackmailed by a civilian instructor who threatened to out him if he refused to have sex with him. Seefried, a 2009 graduate of the U.S. Air Force Academy, managed to avoid being discharged under Don't Ask, Don't Tell (DADT) when he reported the incident and was investigated. But Lt. Seefried was outraged, and vowed to do all he could to prevent others from falling into the same situation. DADT meant that, regardless of what might have been learned in basic training, the chain of command could not be relied on to support gay and lesbian service members. They needed to support each other, and that support network became Seefried's mission.

With his good friend and civilian information technology expert, Ty Walrod, he created an underground social networking site that linked gay friends and colleagues from the U.S. military, mostly Air Force officers. Cautious about identifying too publicly as active duty military, they named the group Citizens for Repeal of Don't Ask, Don't Tell (later shortened to Citizens for Repeal, then to just CFR). Walrod recalls:

> I was a little naïve about the problems associated with DADT—but it was clear that Josh was being treated unfairly. The two of us decided we had to do something about it. Josh [Seefried] had his own network of gay friends from USAFA, and that formed the core of the underground network. About the same time, his situation was so outrageous that we decided to take a more public stand—we decided to create a Facebook fan page called Citizens for Repeal of DADT. We bought a website—citizensforrepeal.com—where we would post stories of service members affected by DADT. When SUNY Oswego invited Josh to speak [under the pseudonym "JD Smith," May 5, 2010], that's when we started to get traction. No media, no photography, no cell phones, but that event had a profound effect, building awareness on college campuses. That sealed the deal for us in being a legitimate organization.

In June, 2010, CFR made the front page of the *Denver Post* on June 9, 2010 (Riley, 2010), with an open letter to the Secretary of Defense: "Secretary Gates, we need to talk"—and Walrod and Seefried knew they needed to take their group bigger.

This article outlines a rough history of the group that grew out of those beginnings. I am neither a social scientist nor historian, but played an active role in the emergence of the OutServe organization. This is an attempt to capture how the group formed and grew, based on personal experience, and supported by the author's personal notes and collected email. What follows is a discussion of how members were added; how Knights Out and Dan Choi influenced OutServe's public advocacy; how a secret group developed a public face and identity; the impact of *OutServe Magazine*; and the public introduction of OutServe members with the end of DADT.

WHY IT WORKED

The first key to the group was an ability to communicate freely in secret. The hidden Facebook group fit the bill: Members could only be added by the creators of the page and their designees, and others viewing one's Facebook profile would not see his or her membership unless they, too, were members. Second, CFR's commitment to keeping the organization exclusively for active-duty military (later expanded to actively serving military, to include mobilized Reserve and National Guard members) was essential to its uniqueness. Unlike other organizations, CFR (and later OutServe) would be composed, not of veterans or activists, but LGBT people currently serving in the military. That meant growing carefully—adding only those who had been vetted to ensure they were both a) active military and b) lesbian, gay, bisexual, or transgender.

BECOMING ACTIVISTS: THE INFLUENCE OF KNIGHTS OUT

Other gay military social networks existed, including the Service Academy Gay and Lesbian Association (SAGALA) and Servicemembers United, but the members of CFR were motivated to create something different. Seefried's experience made him want more than a safe social network, and he was used to leading. At the Air Force Academy, he served on the wing staff with other top-ranking cadets. He wanted to make sure that no other gay service member ever faced what he had faced: He wanted to see DADT ended. Walrod shared that goal.

CFR connected with veterans at Servicemembers Legal Defense Network (SLDN), the most respected, visible, and effective organization supporting LGBT service members. Retired Navy Commander Zoe Dunning, one of SLDN's board leaders, introduced them to fellow Naval Academy graduate, former Marine Capt. Tom Carpenter. Together, they encouraged Seefried to follow his instincts, and connected him with other organizations, including a group of West Point LGBT alumni called Knights Out.

Knights Out had made a splash when it launched in 2009 with Lt. Dan Choi as a spokesperson. The last of the Academy LGBT alumni groups to be created (after USNA Out in 2003 and the Air Force Academy's Blue Alliance in 2007), Knights Out took on a more activist role than the Air Force and Navy groups. Formed after the election of President Obama, the Knights Out board chose to take on repeal of DADT as a mission, co-equal with their stated mission to "support West Point in preparing cadets to lead an Army that includes LGBT soldiers." Lt. Choi proved to be a charismatic and effective speaker, and the public was galvanized by his credentials as a West Point graduate, Infantry officer, and Iraq War veteran. By coming out publicly while still active in the New York National Guard, he triggered the DADT provision that resulted in his notice of discharge, which created a media firestorm.

Choi and Knights Out were disciplined in their messaging from the beginning. Eschewing discussion of civil rights and the fairness of DADT, they emphasized the idea that DADT is bad for the Army. From their original message points, published verbatim in an early news release:

> **"Don't Ask, Don't Tell" compromises unit cohesion.** Forcing soldiers to lie about who they are, and who their families are, tears down trust, and erodes the bonds that make military units strong.
>
> **"Don't Ask, Don't Tell" is dishonorable.** Integrity and honor are, and should be, central to our military code. The "Don't Ask, Don't Tell" policy forces soldiers to choose between their honor and their military duty. (Knights Out, 2009)

Choi—and former U.S. Army captains, Becky Kanis and myself—referenced West Point's honor code ("A Cadet will not lie, cheat, steal, or tolerate those who do"), and how DADT forced soldiers to lie (West Point Association of Graduates, 2007). The focus on integrity was central to the story. Others had tried to change the conversation in this way, but it was in 2009 that the popular discussion finally shifted. The impact of this came clear months later, when Chairman of the Joint Chiefs of Staff Adm. Mike Mullen testified before Congress, saying this in support of repealing DADT:

> For me, personally, it comes down to integrity. No matter how I look at the issue . . . I cannot escape being troubled by the fact that we have in place a policy which forces young men and women to lie about who they are in order to defend their fellow citizens . . . for me, personally, it comes down to integrity: theirs as individuals, and ours as an institution." (Montopoli, 2010)

The integrity message resonated with Seefried as a service academy graduate. Looking for help with media and communications, he and Walrod reached out to me as the Knights Out communications director through Tom Carpenter. Choi had already left his role at Knights Out to engage in direct action. The West Point group remained active, but behind the scenes, in Pentagon and administration meetings. I eagerly agreed to serve voluntarily at CFR as communications director (while maintaining my volunteer position at Knights Out). During the summer of 2010, we wrestled with how to re-brand CFR and go public as an exclusively actively serving LGBT military organization. At the end of July, with the support of Aaron Belkin and the Palm Center, OutServe officially launched.

Only Ty Walrod and I could be public, however. None of the other members, including Seefried, could speak openly to the media, the Pentagon, or other administration officials without violating DADT. Seefried took on the pseudonym JD Smith in all press releases and print interviews. OutServe needed to find a few more people—ideally recent veterans—to serve as the public face of a necessarily invisible organization. Fortunately, the timing was perfect to bring on two: Jonathan Hopkins and Katherine Miller.

THE FACES OF OUTSERVE

Fourth in his class at West Point, Jonathan Hopkins joined the Infantry and was deployed three times to Iraq and Afghanistan, earning three Bronze Stars, including one for valor. As an Infantry lieutenant, he led his platoon in a combat parachute jump into Northern Iraq during the start of Operation Iraqi Freedom in 2003. Following a successful deployment to Afghanistan as a planning and operations officer, Hopkins returned to Iraq as an Infantry company commander. Outed as gay by a fellow officer, his career was ended under the so-called Don't Ask, Don't Tell policy. During months of discussions with Knights Out, Hopkins weighed coming out before his discharge, but finally decided to delay. Now that his discharge was coming through, he wanted to be involved in ending DADT. He was ready to tell his story.

Cadet Katherine Miller, a brilliant scholar and superb athlete, ranked ninth in her West Point class. During her time at the Academy, dealing with the realities of the Don't Ask, Don't Tell policy, Miller had focused her sociological scholarship on understanding the roots of the military's anti-gay prejudice. Her work, supported by her instructors (particularly in the Academy's Behavioral Sciences and Leadership Department), and hours of self-reflection led to the difficult decision to leave West Point at the beginning of her third year, before she would incur a postgraduation five-year service obligation. Many cadets leave at this point, but Miller's case was unusual; she loved West Point, looked forward to being an officer, and was by any measure a successful cadet. However, she could not square her personal integrity with the daily half-truths required by the Don't Ask, Don't Tell policy. She not only decided to leave, but made the controversial decision to go public. As Miller recalls:

> When deciding whether or not I would go public with my story, I always thought back to the same lesbian cadet I knew and looked up to when I was a sophomore. She resigned at the beginning of her junior year due to DADT but had avoided stating her rationale explicitly. I understand that she was scared to reveal the actual reasons why she would be leaving the military, but her silence failed to evoke change. Her silence failed to make the academy and the army a better place for the people she left behind, like me. I cared about making the military and the lives of my friends better. I would go public; I regarded it as my duty. (Personal communication)

The *Rachel Maddow Show* on MSNBC had done an extraordinary job presenting the issues around DADT to the public. Profiles of Maddow referenced her interest in issues of military readiness and defense policy (Steinberg, 2008). In addition to detailed coverage of the U.S. military in Iraq and Afghanistan, Maddow had allowed gay and lesbian veterans to tell their stories on her show, including Air Force Lt. Col. Victor Fehrenbach and Major Mike Almy as well as Dan Choi. So, when Miller's resignation coincided with Hopkins's discharge in one August week, I approached the producers at *The Rachel Maddow Show*. With the opportunity to break both their stories (along with news of Fehrenbach's lawsuit), Maddow and her staff chose to devote an entire one-hour show to DADT on August 11, 2010, telling all three stories in a dramatic illustration of the policy's destructive impact. It was dicey for Miller—she had not been fully out-processed from West Point and could not leave Academy grounds—so she did the interview via Skype from her barracks room (Seefried, 2011). But the poise gained from years at West Point served both Miller and Hopkins well. Their accomplishments were undeniable, and they spoke eloquently with impressive calmness, hitting their key points in an effective rebuttal to the underlying concept of DADT (Wolff, 2010d).

Both Hopkins and Miller agreed to join the OutServe Board, representing those in the service they had so recently left. Hopkins soon moved to Washington, DC, and became not only national spokesperson, but a regular visitor to the Pentagon. Hopkins's combat credentials and scholarly demeanor made him more effective behind the scenes, hashing out issues with the Department of Defense's Comprehensive Review Working Group and later the Repeal Implementation Team, than in a media spotlight better suited to the drama and rhetorical fireworks of a Dan Choi.

CHAPTER FORMATION

Hopkins and Miller continued to appear in national media representing OutServe, debating repeal opponents, and making the case that DADT was disrupting military readiness. Interviewers responded positively to them, and there was keen interest in the actively serving group they represented. As media coverage grew, service members found OutServe and joined. No longer could they allow any member to vet a new member; nor could just a few people handle the volume of requests. Membership jumped from the initial 450 (at the July 2010 launch) to more than 1,200 by the end of November. The solution was to form chapters.

OutServe Chapters started in locations where a trusted leader would be responsible for checking potential members for eligibility. Long-standing members reinforced a culture of self-policing: If you had any doubt about another online member, you raised it in the group, and impostors were quickly identified. Members were invested in the integrity of the group; after all, your own career was on the line if someone's civilian friend saw your name on the discussion and carelessly outed you to the wrong person.

One of the earliest conflicts arose when members left the military and had to give up that Facebook connection with other OutServe members. Hard as it was, most understood that the identification of the group as actively serving only was important. The board created an OutServe Vets & Allies page, which mollified some.

Additional pages were created: OutServe Marines (and Army, Navy, Air Force, Coast Guard); OutServe Women; OutServe Service Academies (for cadets and midshipmen only); OutServe Trans (reserved for transgender members); and others. Discussions ran the gamut, mostly a mix of news clips on gay rights; advice about professional issues; advice about relationships; "can you believe what happened at work today?"; and "who wants to go out tonight?" As always, new members frequently expressed their joy at being able to connect with others in a safe space.

The organization remained flat, with a working (rather than a fundraising) board, and chapter leaders all on an equal footing. Over 30 chapter leaders led 40 location-based chapters (some doubling up) as well as taking administrative responsibility for the non-location-based Facebook groups like OutServe Army. Some chapters organized social events so that members could meet in person; still others took on charitable work, like OutServe Hawaii's support of local gay-straight associations and the AIDS charity, Life Foundation.

The OutServe Board included Seefried, Walrod, Fulton, Hopkins, and Miller as its directors, and kept this flat, loose governing structure until the fall of 2011, when an Actively Serving Leadership group was created to oversee chapter activities.

ACTIVE DUTY VOICES

During the final months of 2010, DADT repeal remained a contentious issue, as Congress wrestled with a repeal clause in the National Defense Authorization bill. For OutServe, the main opportunity was connecting active duty gay and lesbian service members with key decision makers, but it was a risky proposition. As eager as the Obama Administration might have been to speak with actual service members affected by the policy, DADT presented significant legal hurdles for service members to talk about being gay in the military to anyone in a position of responsibility. This created an apparently untenable situation: administration officials were unable to gather information about the impact of their policies directly from those affected by the policy without violating the law. DADT prevented members of the military from telling the simple truth about their lives and experiences to the Commander in Chief.

In the end, the legal issues were sorted out, and OutServe was allowed to send four military members to speak with a senior official. Three members were chosen by the OutServe Board, and vetted to join Seefried: a soft-spoken African American Navy lieutenant commander (name withheld), bound for seminary after his military obligation; Army Maj. Casey Moes, a West Point graduate (of German descent) and highly decorated military policewoman; and Marine Sgt. Edgar Luna, a Latino headed for commissioning as an officer in the Marine Corps. All had deployed; all had experienced heartbreak and sacrificed relationships and integrity to pursue the careers they loved.

The participants were characteristically humble, despite their combat experience. Maj. Moes reflected:

The meeting was extraordinary because I was able to tell my story to someone who really could make a difference. I served as a company commander in Iraq. The stress of command and combat was magnified when I found out my partner had a terminal illness. I couldn't talk to anyone about it. I didn't want anyone else to have to go through that. I'm proud of my thirteen years in uniform, but the idea that I could play a small part in changing this makes me even more proud. (Personal communication)

Similarly, Marine Sgt. Edgar Luna remarked:

We left the meeting feeling that we had been fortunate to have had an influence, even small, over whether or not repeal was put on a back burner and forgotten for the foreseeable future. (Personal communication)

These few represented the thousands of members of OutServe, and bore witness to the effects of DADT.

PREPARING FOR THE REALITY OF REPEAL

The efforts of so many organizations and individuals came to a surprising and dramatic end in the last few weeks of December 2010. The DADT Repeal clause included in the Defense Authorization bill died when the Senate could not achieve cloture. Through some heroic behind-the-scenes work by advocates and lawmakers (Foley, 2010; and others), a stand-alone bill squeaked through in the lame-duck session and was signed into law by President Obama on December 21, 2011. The bill-signing ceremony was held at an auditorium at the Department of the Interior to accommodate hundreds who had worked to achieve this milestone. The OutServe Board attended, along with four actively serving members – in civilian clothes, protecting their identities while DADT was still in effect.

As many have noted, the ceremony was incredibly emotional (the *Washington Post* used the headline "Obama signs DADT repeal before big, emotional crowd") (Branigan, Wilgoren, & Bacon, 2010). Zoe Dunning, Board Chair of SLDN, and Marine Sgt. Eric Alva, representing the Human Rights Campaign, were onstage with the President, and appropriately recognized for their work. In the President's speech, he also mentioned another veteran. As he told the story of former Army Capt. Jonathan Hopkins, the OutServe members in the audience glowed with pride.

In the months following the signing of the bill, OutServe remained engaged with the Pentagon, working closely with other groups in supporting the work of the DADT Repeal Implementation Team (RIT), and membership continued to boom, passing the 3,000 mark in May 2011, and 4,000 by September 2011, when DADT finally came to an end.

FINAL REPEAL

Repeal certification on July 22, 2011, accelerated preparations for the OutServe Summit. Rather than scheduling events for "Repeal Day"—September 20, 2011—the OutServe Board chose to maintain focus on the summit. Acknowledging that veterans and advocates rightfully deserved to celebrate, the leadership felt it unseemly to promote parties for active-duty military—although OutServe chapters were encouraged to schedule low-key local get togethers. The important messaging was: September 20: Business as usual. Besides, the board of five was plenty busy. With only one paid staff member to coordinate the conference, the still-unpaid board was occupied with planning workshops, panels, and a national dinner. A number of national organizations had accepted invitations to attend—although official Department of Defense representatives clearly would not respond before repeal was finalized—and a good showing was essential for the organization's future. However, there was significant planning for September 20 from a media standpoint. National coverage of the milestone was expected, and OutServe needed to prepare for interviews. Furthermore, the *OutServe Magazine* staff planned to publish their third, and most historic, issue at midnight on that date.

101 FACES OF COURAGE

In conversations with Pentagon officials and OutServe members, many expressed the belief that military members were unlikely to come out in vast numbers immediately after repeal, despite the research showing that coming out is critical to reducing homophobia: those who don't believe they know anyone gay are significantly more likely to harbor negative feelings about gay people (Morales, 2009). OutServe leaders believed that, the longer actively serving military people stayed in the closet, the longer it would take for any remaining homophobia to wane.

With that in mind, *OutServe Magazine* staff set out to find 100 service members willing to have their photos published, along with name, rank, and branch of service, in the September 20, 2011, issue. The hope was that seeing 100 actual gay and lesbian service members, of all ranks, from all branches, would communicate simultaneously the importance and the insignificance of the change reflected by final repeal. They ended up with 101—and the response was overwhelming.

The media outreach was equally successful. In the space of one day, people got to know, not one spokesperson, but many. Seefried was included in an event on Capitol Hill, along with Staff Sgt. Jonathan Mills, executive editor of *OutServe Magazine*, and Marine Capt. Sarah Pezzat, whose video clip of coming out—choking up briefly, then in fine Marine fashion, straightening herself up and saying sharply, "Pardon me" before continuing—was widely rebroadcast (Pezzat, 2011).

Army Lt. Col. Todd Burton approached his public affairs officer (PAO) at the National Guard to inform them that he had agreed to be interviewed on *CBS Evening News*; to his surprise, the PAO responded positively, offering to coordinate the event with leadership and assist in preparations and scheduling to do the filming in their studio (Shevlin, 2011).

Coast Guard Lt. Commander Zac Mathews appeared on *PBS NewsHour* for a thoughtful discussion; Army Chief Warrant Officer Charlie Morgan talked about her wife and daughter with Thomas Roberts on MSNBC. Many more appeared on local television, including chapter leaders Navy Petty Officer Luz Bautista in San Diego (*Yahoo News*), Navy Petty Officer Jeffry Priela in Honolulu (*Hawaii News Now*), and Air Force Major Jeff Mueller in Denver (KOAA).

At long last, OutServe members were able to be seen and heard. Finally, Americans could hear in their own words from gay and lesbian soldiers, sailors, airmen, Marines, and Coast Guardsmen.

GOING FORWARD

At the time of this article's writing, OutServe continues to grow and to develop as an organization. A scholarship foundation is being formed, to provide educational opportunities for spouses and children of LGBT service members. Chapters are evolving, and actively serving leaders are emerging into new roles. The media has mostly moved on from the DADT issue, but a telling sign of how the world has changed happened in December, the one-year anniversary of the bill signing: ABC and NBC each featured a story on the members of OutServe Afghanistan. Gay and lesbian service members have come into their own.

NOTES

1. On methods and sources: Aware of the historic nature of the work to end Don't Ask, Don't Tell, I have been keeping email and filing personal notes since 2009. Where specific external references are not cited, the history in this essay comes from those notes and email.

2. Transgender service members were included in Citizens For Repeal (CFR) from the beginning, and continue to be part of OutServe. However, regulations still prohibit them from serving. In this article,

you will see reference to supporting LGBT service members, but in discussions about public disclosure, only gay, lesbian, and bisexual service members are mentioned due to the existing ban.

3. The following gay veterans and service members appeared on *The Rachel Maddow Show* before the OutServe launch: Army Lt. Dan Choi, March 19, 2009, March 20, 2009, May 7, 2009 (Wolff, 2009); Air Force Lt. Col. Victor Fehrenbach, May 19, 2009, June 21, 2009, June 29, 2009, February 3, 2010, July 7, 2010, July 16, 2010 (Wolff, 2009b, 2009c, 2010a, 2010c); Air Force Maj. Michael Almy, March 3, 2010 (Wolff, 2010b).

REFERENCES

Bowling, K., Firestone, J. M., & Harris, R. J. (2005). Analyzing questions that cannot be asked of respondents who cannot respond. *Armed Forces & Society, 31*, 411–437. Retrieved from http://afs.sagepub.com/content/31/3/411.abstract

Branigan, W., Wilgoren, D., & Bacon, P. (2010, December 22). Obama signs DADT repeal before big, emotional crowd. *The Washington Post*.

Brown, E. (Producer). (2011, December 24). "Out" on the front lines: Troops reflect on "Don't Ask, Don't Tell. *ABC World News with Diane Sawyer* [Television broadcast]. New York, NY: American Broadcasting Company.

Burkey, P. (Producer). (2011, December 21). No incidents reported since DADT repealed. *NBC Nightly News* [Television broadcast]. New York, NY: National Broadcasting Company.

Burns, R. (2010, September 20). Repeal of gay ban causing few waves in military. *Yahoo! News*. Retrieved from http://news.yahoo.com/repeal-gay-ban-causing-few-waves-military-070236711.html

Foley, E. (2010, December 18). "Don't ask, don't tell" repeal passes Senate 65-31. *Huffington Post*. Retrieved from http://www.huffingtonpost.com/2010/12/18/dont-ask-dont-tell-repeal_5_n_798636.html

Garamone, J. (2011, July 22). Pentagon officials explain repeal implementation. *American Forces Press Service*. Retrieved from http://www.defense.gov/news/newsarticle.aspx?id=64782

Goldstein, K. (2011, September 20). There's something I need to tell you, sarge ... *Slate*. Retrieved from http://www.slate.com/articles/news_and_politics/politics/2011/09/theres_something_i_need_to_tell_you_sarge_.html

Groom, D. J. (2010, May 4). Oswego State speaker wants repeal of "don't ask, don't tell." *The Post-Standard*. Retrieved from http://www.syracuse.com/news/index.ssf/2010/05/post_220.html

Hopkins, J. (2010, September 13). Don't Ask, don't tell, don't be all you can be. *The New York Times Blogs: At War*. Retrieved from http://atwar.blogs.nytimes.com/2010/09/13/dont-ask-dont-tell-dont-be-all-you-can-be/

Kirmani, I. (Producer). (2010, November 29). Former Army Capt. Jonathan Hopkins. *MSNBC News Nation* [Television broadcast]. New York, NY: MSNBC.

Knights Out. (2009). Knights out calls for president to issue stop-loss order (Press Release). Retrieved from http://www.knightsout.org/articles/press_release_knights_out_calls_for_president/

Kruzel, J. (2010, February 2). Gates appoints panel for potential end of "don't ask, don't tell." *American Forces Press Service*. Retrieved from http://www.defense.gov/News/NewsArticle.aspx?ID=57835

Lee, J. (2010, December 22). The president signs repeal of "don't ask, don't tell": "Out of many, we are one." *The White House Blog*. Retrieved from http://www.whitehouse.gov/blog/2010/12/22/president-signs-repeal-dont-ask-dont-tell-out-many-we-are-one

Miller, J. (2010, August 11). Idaho aviator sues to block DADT. *Associated Press*. Retrieved from http://www.sldn.org/news/archives/associated-press-idaho-aviator-sues-to-block-dadt/

Montopoli, B. (2010, February 2). Mullen: Ending don't ask, don't tell "right thing to do." *CBS News Political HotSheet*. Retrieved from http://www.cbsnews.com/8301-503544_162-6166493-503544.html

Morales, L. (2009). Knowing someone gay/lesbian affects views of gay issues. *Gallup*. Retrieved from http://www.gallup.com/poll/118931/knowing-someone-gay-lesbian-affects-views-gay-issues.aspx

Noren, Nicole. (Producer). (2010, October 17). Don't ask, don't tell. *ESPN Outside the Lines* [Television broadcast]. New York, NY: ESPN, Inc.

Ocamb, K. (2011, October 14). OutServe conference opens in las vegas. *LGBT POV*. Retrieved from http://lgbtpov.frontiersla.com/2011/10/14/outserve-conference-opens-in-las-vegas/

Okita, T. (2011, September 20). Historic day: Don't ask, don't tell ends. *Hawaii News Now*. Retrieved from http://www.hawaiinewsnow.com/story/15519133/its-a-historic-day-for-the-us-military-after-years-of-debate-the-dont-ask-dont-tell-policy-for-gay-actively-serving-troops-is-over

Palm Center. (2010). Active duty gay troops helping Pentagon prepare life after "don't ask, don't tell" (Press release). Retrieved from http://www.palmcenter.org/press/dadt/releases/active_duty_gay_troops_helping_pentagon_prepare_life_after_%E2%80%98don%E2%80%99t_ask_don%E2%80%99t_tell%E2%80%99

Pezzat, S. [sbpezzat]. (2011, September 20). *Capt Pezzat on DADT Repeal* [Video file]. Retrieved from http://www.youtube.com/watch?v=zaueVZ0Qq_U

Riley, M. (2010, June 9). Pentagon's "don't ask, don't tell" study draws fire from advocates, gay soldiers. *The Denver Post*. Retrieved from http://www.denverpost.com/frontpage/ci_15256223

Romero, J. (2011, September 20). Serviceman reacts to "don't ask, don't tell" repeal. *KOAA.com*. Retrieved from http://www.koaa.com/news/serviceman-reacts-to-don-t-ask-don-t-tell-repeal/

Seefried, J. (2011). *Our time: Breaking the silence of "don't ask, don't tell."* New York, NY: The Penguin Press.

Shane, L. (2011, October 17). Don't ask, don't tell: Summit celebrates gains, focuses on work still ahead for gay troops. *Stars & Stripes*.

Shevlin, P. (Producer). (2011, September 20). *CBS evening news* [Television broadcast]. New York, NY: Columbia Broadcasting Service.

Steinberg, J. (2008, July 7). MSNBC has its eye on Rachel Maddow. *The New York Times*. Retrieved from http://www.nytimes.com/2008/07/17/arts/television/17madd.html?scp=6&sq=rachel%20maddow&st=cse

Stone, A. (2011, October 16). OutServe summit ends with high hopes and many challenges ahead. *Huffington Post*. Retrieved from http://www.huffingtonpost.com/2011/10/16/outserve-summit-ends-with_n_1014265.html

Thompson, O. (Producer). (2011, September 20). Army officer declares she's a lesbian on air. *MSNBC Live with Thomas Roberts* [Television broadcast]. New York, NY: MSNBC.

Werner, D. (Producer). (2011, September 20). *PBS Newshour* [Television broadcast]. New York, NY: Corporation for Public Broadcasting.

West Point Association of Graduates. (2007). *Cadet honor code and system.* Retrieved from http://www.westpointaog.org/netcommunity/document.doc?id=621

Wolff, B. (Producer). (2009a, March 19-20). Lt. Dan Choi and Knights Out. *The Rachel Maddow Show* [Television broadcast]. New York, NY: MSNBC.

Wolff, B. (Producer). (2009b, May 19). Lt. Col. Victor Fehrenbach. *The Rachel Maddow Show* [Television broadcast]. New York, NY: MSNBC.

Wolff, B. (Producer). (2009c, June 21). Lt. Col. Victor Fehrenbach. *The Rachel Maddow Show* [Television broadcast]. New York, NY: MSNBC.

Wolff, B. (Producer). (2010a, February 3). Lt. Col. Victor Fehrenbach. *The Rachel Maddow Show* [Television broadcast]. New York, NY: MSNBC.

Wolff, B. (Producer). (2010b, March 3). Air Force Major Michael Almy. *The Rachel Maddow Show* [Television broadcast]. New York, NY: MSNBC.

Wolff, B. (Producer). (2010c, July 7). Lt. Col. Victor Fehrenbach. *The Rachel Maddow Show* [Television broadcast]. New York, NY: MSNBC.

Wolff, B. (Producer). (2010d, August 11). Right to serve. *The Rachel Maddow Show* [Television broadcast]. New York, NY: MSNBC.

Wolff, B. (Producer). (2010e, September 13). Former Cadet Katie Miller. *The Rachel Maddow Show* [Television broadcast]. New York, NY: MSNBC.

The Rise of Repeal: Policy Entrepreneurship and Don't Ask, Don't Tell

CHRISTOPHER L. NEFF, MPP
Department of Government and International Relations, University of Sydney, Sydney, Australia

LUKE R. EDGELL, BLAS
Department of Gender and Cultural Studies, University of Sydney, Sydney, Australia

We report on policy entrepreneurship by Servicemembers Legal Defense Network (SLDN) and how its legislative strategies used mini-windows of opportunity to shift Capitol Hill perspectives of Don't Ask, Don't Tell (DADT) from political plutonium to an emerging issue requiring a second look. Four phases in the legislative history of DADT are identified: radioactive, contested, emerging, and viable. In all, this article argues that SLDN's entrepreneurship focused on contesting congressional sensibilities to wait or defer on repeal, maintained that every discharge was damaging and transitioned toward a post-repeal mind set. Finally, we illustrate the importance of these transitions by comparing SLDN's 2004 estimated vote count for the introduction of the Military Readiness Enhancement Act with the final 2010 voting results on the Don't Ask, Don't Tell Repeal Act.

KEYWORDS Don't Ask, Don't Tell, agenda setting, policy entrepreneur, gay rights

---

The authors wish to thank the University of Sydney Faculty of Arts and Social Sciences and the Faculty of Science as well as several individuals for their leadership and support, including: Aaron Belkin, Denise Riordan, Dixon Osburn, Sharra Greer, Kathi Westcott, Jeff Cleghorn, Sharon Alexander-Debbage, Alec Papazian, and Nathaniel Frank. Special thanks to Megan Mackenzie and the reviewers for their comments on previous versions.

Address correspondence to Christopher L. Neff, Department of Government and International Relations, Room 269, Merewether Building (H04), The University of Sydney, NSW, 2042, Australia. E-mail: Christopher.neff@sydney.edu.au

The dramatic shift in the policy direction of Don't Ask, Don't Tell (DADT) between 1993 and 2011 offers an important case study for the gay rights movement and policy change researchers. This paper provides a first-hand account of how the issue of gays in the military[1] reemerged in Congress and how repeal legislation was introduced in the House of Representatives in 2005.[2] We report on policy entrepreneurship by Servicemembers Legal Defense Network (SLDN) and how their legislative strategies used mini-windows of opportunity to shift Capitol Hill perspectives of DADT from political plutonium to an emerging issue requiring a second look. SLDN did this by mobilizing around three unforeseen events: first, they reengaged the Senate on the issue by opposing President George W. Bush's 2002 nomination of Maj. Gen. Robert Clark. Second, staff built a coalition of congressional offices and organized for legislative action following the 2002 discharge of gay Arabic linguists. Lastly, SLDN recruited supportive offices and exercised a test run for the introduction of repeal legislation during House Republican's 2004 fight over ROTC university restrictions.

Critical to these actions were the congressional contexts. Four phases in the legislative history of DADT are identified: radioactive, contested, emerging, and viable. In the radioactive phase (1993–2002), Congress was overwhelmingly hostile to this issue; in the contested phase (2002–2005), opposing arguments gained new traction; during the emerging period (2005–2009), arguments and political structures aligned to challenge repeal; and, most recently, a viable phase (2009–2010) saw the alignment of political arguments, structures, and leadership to make repeal success possible. In all, this article argues that SLDN's entrepreneurship focused on contesting congressional sensibilities to wait or defer on repeal, maintained that every discharge was damaging and transitioned toward a post-repeal mind set. Finally, we illustrate the importance of these transitions through a comparison of a 2004 vote count used to prepare for introduction of the Military Readiness Enhancement Act with the final 2010 voting results on the Don't Ask, Don't Tell Repeal Act.

POLICY ENTREPRENEURSHIP

Policy entrepreneurs are experts in a field that dedicate their time and resources to brokering desired outcomes (Kingdon, 1984). They can include issue specialists, congressional staff, or elected officials (Mackenzie, 2004; Walker, 1977; Weiss, 1989). David Rochefort and Roger Cobb (1994) explain the role of these entrepreneurs as policy actors who strategically cultivate issues through problem definitions, that reframe otherwise normal events as problems that government needs to solve. Policy space is created for issues by highlighting their severity and proximity. These qualities of savvy, compromise, and access are unique and can be seen in individual policy entrepreneurs or teams.

The gay rights movement is replete with examples of powerful policy entrepreneurship from individuals and advocacy groups. Harry Hay, Franklin Kameny, Barbara Giddings, Harvey Milk, and Larry Kramer begin a long list of notable actors who (both as individuals and in teams) accumulated the necessary expertise, skills, and networks to advocate for their issues. A key feature of policy entrepreneurship is patience. It takes time to be positioned appropriately within the system, to wait for policy windows, or engineer opportunities. If the political terrain is not favorable, these actors will cross to other jurisdictions or venues to pursue their goal (Mackenzie, 2004; Mintrom & Norman, 2009). In short, policy entrepreneurship involves being a *skilled hunter* that seeks openings and a savvy *outcome broker* when these moments arise.

The study of teams within organizations has been an underresearched component of policy entrepreneurship as well as gay studies. The Mattachine Society, Daughters of Bilitis, Gay Activist Alliance (of New York and Washington, DC), as well as the Campaign for Military Service and Human Rights Campaign (HRC) have all included committees, departments, and teams of entrepreneurs. Building strong coalitions is an essential component for policy actors (Mintrom & Norman, 2009). Their goal is to marshal enough force (of ideas, people, symbols, rhetoric, and resources) to play a pivotal role in establishing political inertia for their intended change. This high level of expertise, ambition and access allows policy entrepreneurs to advocate for their outcome by identifying the failings of the present system, the dangers of alternatives and the security and feasibility of their position. The staff of SLDN, of which I (C. L. Neff) was a member, provides an example of policy entrepreneurship on DADT between 2002 and 2005 because it was the only organization working fulltime on the issue following the passage of the law.

SLDN was founded in 1993 by attorneys Dixon Osburn and Michelle Benecke and financed through private contributions. Its chief role was to provide free legal services to service members affected by the law, but also included assisting in federal court challenges and regulatory oversight. In the early days of DADT, the hope was that the law would be declared unconstitutional by the courts or that the Clinton Administration would balance the rights of gay troops with the limitations of the law. Neither occurred and Congress was loathe to promote openly gay anything.

THE ENTREPRENEURIAL TEAM

I was part of the entrepreneurial team at SLDN along with attorneys Kathi Westcott, Sharra Greer, Sharon Alexander, and Jeff Cleghorn. Kathi Westcott also had experience in policy issues during her previous work for People for the American Way and Sharon Alexander had worked for HRC. I had previously worked for Sen. Harry Reid (D-NV) and Sen. John Warner (R-VA), and was responsible for developing and implementing the legislative repeal introduction strategy; yet, this was—from beginning to end—a team endeavor. Kathi Wescott and I attended many meetings together, Jeff Cleghorn was instrumental in the Arabic linguists story, and Sharon Alexander was central to the drafting of legislation. As Department Head for Law and Policy, Sharra Greer oversaw our team.

Additionally, coalition allies were critical to these efforts including Christopher Labonte at HRC, Tanya Clay at People for the American Way, Christopher Barron at Log Cabin Republicans, Aaron Belkin at the (then) Center for the Study of Sexual Minorities in the Military, and Eric Stern at the Democratic National Committee. However, in 2002, the issue of openly gay military service was in the political wasteland of loser issues and it would be three years before any legislative action took place.

DADT REPEAL AS RADIOACTIVE (1993–2002)

The issue of gays in the military became legislatively radioactive as the painful political process of what became known as the Don't Ask, Don't Tell policy took shape (U.S. Code, Title 10S654). Nine hearings were held in the Senate and five in the House in 1993. Sen. Sam Nunn (D-GA) chaired the Senate Armed Services Committee and led the effort to enact the ban. Attempts by Sen. Barbara Boxer (D-CA) and Cong. Marty Meehan (D-MA) to delete the prohibition on openly gay service failed (Congressional Record, 1993, House Amendment 316). In addition, the President's losses mounted as his efforts at healthcare reform went down and the Democratic Party lost its majority in Congress in the historic 1994 electoral defeat.

Republican members in the new majority attempted to capitalize on the weak political support for gays in the military. In 1996, Cong. Bob Dornan (R-CA) successfully led an effort to pass an anti-gay ban or expulsion provision on active duty service members who were diagnosed with HIV. This legislative rider passed both chambers and was signed into law in February 1996 before later being repealed the following April. In July 1996, Cong. Duncan Hunter (R-CA) won passage of a repeal of DADT in the House, to reinstate previous restrictions, but his bill failed in the Senate. The collective political trauma experienced by Democrats around DADT meant that phrases like "ill-fated" (Brewer, 2008, p. 70) and "expending precious political capital" (Siciliano, 1994) still echoed through Congress on this issue in 2002. I had been told repeatedly by congressional staff in 2002 that the pitfalls from the events of 1993, 1994, and 1996 had cemented for congressional survivors the belief that these issues were political plutonium and should be left alone.

The homophobia-related murder of Private First Class (PFC) Barry Winchell in 1999, while asleep on base at Fort Campbell, KY, reinforced a hands-off approach by Congress. The murder, by fellow soldiers, was framed as a Department of Defense issue. President Clinton stated that the policy was "out of whack" (Richter, 1999) and in December, 1999, "Secretary Cohen ordered an Inspector General survey to assess anti-gay harassment" (Sobel, Westcott, Benecke, Osburn, & Cleghorn, 2000, p. iv). No effort was made to legislatively change the law, with the focus on Pentagon anti-harassment measures. This period of congressional dormancy changed in 2002 with President Bush's nomination for promotion of then Maj. Gen. Robert Clark, the former Commanding General at Fort Campbell.

DADT REPEAL AS CONTESTED (2002–2005)

Clark Nomination

President Bush's October 2002 nomination of Maj. Gen. Robert Clark to the rank of lieutenant general provided the first mini-window for SLDN policy entrepreneurs to hunt for new openings in DADT. First, SLDN hired staff to establish a legislative agenda that would later include repeal. Second, PFC Winchell's parents worked with SLDN to contest the success of DADT and offered a tragic example of its policy failures. Third, senators were engaged personally on the issue of gays in the military creating space for a renewed debate. In particular, Sen. Kennedy led a challenge to the law on the Senate floor based on moral grounds.

Since 1999, SLDN had been involved in the investigation of the murder of PFC Barry Winchell. Attorney Kathi Westcott had worked closely with Barry's parents, Patricia (Pat) and Wallace (Wally) Kutteles. It was clear to her and SLDN staff that Maj. Gen. Clark had tolerated an anti-gay climate that contributed to his death. Following Clark's nomination for promotion, she and fellow attorney Jeff Cleghorn recognized that opposing the nomination would require the organization to dedicate new resources and staff up. I initially joined the team as a policy associate, and, in November 2002, our work began. SLDN was joined by People for the American Way and the National Organization for Women (NOW) in opposing the nomination, which was referred to the Senate Armed Services Committee (NOW, 2002).

SLDN staff worked closely with the Kutteles to discuss the nomination with key senators. Sen. Kennedy was particularly concerned. To him, it was clear that there had been problems at the base and the murder was a tragic indicator of a massive policy failure. Nominations for senior military officer promotions are handled confidentially by senators and involve private but routine executive sessions that often result in uncontroversial approvals. So, it came as a surprise to many, when Senate Armed Services Committee Chairman Carl Levin (D-MI) adjourned consideration of the Maj. Gen. Clark nomination without a vote in 2002. The congressional term had ended and with that all nominations would need to be resubmitted. This move facilitated a nomination fight that would continue for the next 14 months.

A change in the Senate's majority in 2003 made Sen. Warner the Chairman of the Armed Services Committee. As expected, President Bush renominated Maj. Gen. Clark in March. Part of our job was to assist in setting up key Senate meetings. Between October 28, 2002, and December 18, 2002, SLDN held 9 Senate meetings, while in 2003, the Kutteles and SLDN collectively attended 56 meetings ahead of the Maj. Gen. Clark nomination. Broken down by party, SLDN increased meetings in Democratic Senate offices to its highest level ever (37). They also increased the number of meetings with Republican Senate offices to 19. Some meetings were held with staff, while others were one-on-one meetings with senators.

In one instance, we called Sen. Warner's office and asked for a professional committee staffer to meet with PFC Winchell's parents. I was told "under no circumstances will I meet with you or them" (C. Neff, personal communication, April, 2003). This hostility motivated SLDN and the Kutteles to reach out to Sen. Warner himself and a meeting was set up between the Kutteles, Sen. Warner, and Sen. Levin on May 14, 2003. Just before this meeting, the Kutteles and SLDN staff met with Sen. Kennedy. Pat and Wally told him of their family's commitment and service in the military. Wally had served in Korea and they had another son in the Armed Services. Senator Kennedy said that he was moved that a family that had lost their son so tragically remained pro-military. The meeting ended and Sen. Kennedy said that he hoped the upcoming discussion with Sen. Warner would be positive. Wally would later recount that before the formalities began with Sens. Warner and Levin, Warner leaned forward and said to him, "I hear that you served in Korea" (C. Neff, personal communication, May 14, 2003).

Pat and Wally Kutteles also attended one-on-one meetings with Sen. Hillary Clinton (D-NY), Sen. Mark Dayton (D-MN), Sen. Susan Collins (R-ME), Sen. James Talent (R-MO), Sen. Saxby Chambliss (R-GA), and Sen. Daniel Akaka (D-HI). Importantly, the increased attention by senators themselves, not just staff, who were handling the confidential aspects of the nomination, demonstrated who future allies on DADT repeal may be. Sen. Collins discussed the nomination on *NBC Nightly News* announcing that, "there is compelling evidence that there were problems at this base" (Schindler, 2003). With bipartisan attention, a new frame emerged around DADT and Barry Winchell's mother was the leading messenger. Pat Kutteles put forward a moral argument against the policy, telling the *San Antonio Current*, "'Don't ask, don't tell' creates an atmosphere of violence and . . . the military is the biggest discriminator in the country. We hope it will change as another generation comes in that isn't as biased" (Sorg, 2003).

One additional anecdote captures the personal nature of this nomination fight. On the day of the second private executive session between senators and Maj. Gen. Clark himself, I was standing outside Sen. Warner's office. There had been a chance that following the session there would be an immediate vote on the Senate floor. I was holding position to see how things transpired when Maj. Gen. Clark and his eight Pentagon staff arrived in the hallway, standing across from me. As we stood on either side of the long marble hallway, Sen. Warner emerged from a committee meeting room. He looked at Maj. Gen. Clark and his entourage and then walked up to me. He said, "Hello Chris, we are going to take a break for 10 minutes for a vote on the floor and then we'll be back up here. Okay?" I said, "Okay." The Senator walked off without speaking to the General or his surprised staff.

The executive session took place, but the final vote did not. A hold was placed on Maj. Gen. Clark's nomination that blocked it from final consideration. We called Senate Democratic offices to see which office had placed the hold, but no one knew. Several days passed and Kathi, Sharra, Sharon, and I went as a team to the National Gay and Lesbian Task Force's "Creating Change Conference" in Miami, FL. On the final day, we were packing up our display table in the conference lobby when we received word that Sen. Jim Bunning (R-KY) had retaliated with a counter-hold of his own, to force a vote on the Maj. Gen. Clark nomination. Sen. Bunning was now blocking all Department of Defense nominations, in every service, from approval (Maze, 2003).

The SLDN team stepped outside the hotel, to the swimming pool, to discuss this latest twist in events. We noted that no general officer could now allow harassment of gay troops at their base and feel impervious. It was at this moment, sitting together, that we made a collective decision: the time had come to draft and introduce legislation to end DADT. This mini-window in the Senate had been made larger and it taught us that there was more room to navigate politically on DADT. As a team, we could do this. We now had the experience to take this step and believed that above all, gay service members had waited long enough. The law would be contested on legislative grounds and the work would begin immediately.

The nomination fight ended on November 18, 2003 (Files, 2003). A compromise was reached by Majority Leader Tom Daschle (D-SD), Sen. Bunning and the mystery hold in which the nomination would come to a vote, but only after two hours of floor debate (Congressional Record, 2003, S15029). This was the longest debate on gays in the military since 1993 and 10 senators would participate. Sens. Kennedy, Frank Lautenberg (D-NJ), and Dayton spoke against the promotion and Sens. Warner, Levin, Bill Frist (R-TN), John Cornyn (R-TX), Jeff Sessions (R-MS), Chambliss, and Bunning spoke in favor (Congressional Record, 2003, S15029).

Sen. Kennedy challenged the morality of DADT and stated that, "such a crime sends the poisonous message that some members of the community deserve to be victimized solely because of who they are" (Congressional Record, 2003, S15029). He added that of all the Army's 271 DADT discharges in 1999, 120 were from Fort Campbell, compared with six the year before. The nature of DADT had affected the whole base. Sen. Dayton echoed this sentiment stating, "I am not proud of an Army, or any other institution in this country, that permits discrimination against men and women because of their sexual preference." He added, "The military system that allowed that atrocity to occur remains" (Congressional Record, 2003, S15038).

Sens. Russ Feingold (D-WI), John Kerry (D-MA), and Akaka also added their comments to the record. Sen. Feingold noted that, "the unusually lengthy and controversial nomination of Gen. Clark has, once again, brought attention to the failure of the Pentagon's policy towards gay service members." He concluded, "I fear that this policy may have been a contributing factor in the June 5, 1999, brutal murder of PVT Barry Winchell . . . "The 'Don't Ask, Don't Tell' policy has failed" (Congressional Record, 2003, S15042).

SLDN had jump started political operations, worked with the Kutteles to reach Senators and been inspired to introduce repeal legislation. The debate over gays in the military had begun again in the Senate, yet, the Senate as a repeal venue remained inhospitable because bipartisan support was elusive. SLDN would turn to the House as the legislative battleground for DADT repeal.

Arabic Linguist Discharges

Stories of gay Arabic linguists being fired under DADT turned out to be a game changer for repeal. On November 18, 2002, Nathaniel Frank (2002) published an article in the *New Republic,* telling the story of seven gay Arabic linguists who were discharged in two months from the Defense Language Institute. This event created a second mini-window of opportunity that shifted the legislative ground in Congress in several ways. First, congressional offices became interested in legislation that would protect gay Arabic linguists from discharge. Second, this provided a critical pressure point to contest every discharge under the law. Third, it highlighted a salient national frame where DADT was counterproductive at best and undermined military readiness at worst.

SLDN's increased presence on the Hill was central to capitalizing on this political opening. The team began widespread meetings with House offices to reintroduce the issue. To our surprise, a number of congressional offices expressed interest in introducing legislative carve outs to exempt gay service members with language training from DADT discharges. This attention increased over the coming months in both the House and the Senate. At SLDN, it emphasized the need for a strategic legislative plan. We had hunted for an opening and now new policy space was being presented. But it was crucial to use our expertise to broker the best outcome for all troops. We believed that a quick fix to the Arabic linguist story would play into

Republicans' hands and remove an essential argument to total repeal: that this was emblematic of a wide-spread policy failure. Yet, there was a real chance that an office may go rogue and introduce legislation on their own at any time. As a result, SLDN began a two-pronged strategy: first, to establish the congressional leader on the issue of gays in the military in the House and, second, to bring all interested offices together in a core group that would keep them in the loop and build a strategy that was on the same page.

The lead office in the House was Rep. Marty Meehan (D-MA). Cong. Meehan's first bill as a freshman in 1993 was an amendment to cut DADT language from the 1994 Defense Authorization Bill and he had remained supportive of openly gay service ever since. SLDN and Cong. Meehan worked together to raise awareness of DADT-related issues in the LGBT community and in Congress. Meehan served as the keynote for SLDN's June 2003 (and first) Lobby Day and we coordinated the start of DADT core group meetings in the House on July 14, 2003. This partnership was managed between myself and Meehan's legislative assistant for military issues, Lauren Briggerman.

The primary issues being addressed by House offices were how to capitalize on the policy failures raised by the Arabic linguist discharges. The conclusion reached was that more data was needed to expand the scope of the harm caused by DADT. Government sources were emphasized given the need to contest DADT in a way that gave cover to frightened Representatives (from the radioactive period) and provided hard evidence to undermine existing rationales. As a result, we sought information on the financial and military readiness costs of DADT in a joint letter to the Government Accountability Office (GAO), signed by 22 members of Congress. The letter to the GAO (2005) was broad and asked for data related to "the separation of service members with critical occupations" (p. 2). Our strategy was to gather data that would allow us to contest every discharge under DADT and to ascribe a political penalty for supporters of the current law. This was an important lesson of the linguist issue. Previously, discharges had been perceived as a measure of success; however, we determined that (with data) each discharge could represent measure of policy failure.

In this stage of the contesting process, it was important to both cut into DADT and build a long-term coalition. SLDN believed that promoting small successful projects would help offices feel more comfortable on the issue and play an additional role in making DADT less radioactive politically. It was not enough to look for easy entry points to make a statement. We knew that how repeal was contested needed to be situated in a manner that would make it approachable, and shift it from a loser issue to one that provided future political gain. The hope was that these actions would build support for cosponsors of future repeal legislation. In addition to the letter to the GAO, the core group send a joint letter from twenty-two offices to the Pentagon pressing them for greater action on the military's anti-harassment action plan and sent a joint letter requesting an updated report on DADT from the

Congressional Research Service. Indeed, an internal SLDN memo drafted by the author in 2004 noted, "SLDN's current model for core group meetings is the foundation of its repeal efforts. Core group attendees are the front line offices for SLDN and represent the number of immediate co-sponsors SLDN should expect once legislation is introduced."

The increase in core group activity reflected an increase in overall House meetings. The biggest increase was among Democratic offices where meetings jumped from 7 in the House in 2002, to 46 in 2003, and 65 in 2004 (see Figure 1). SLDN mobilized grassroots members and held annual lobby days in 2003 and 2004 that boosted congressional staff contacts in offices and intelligence on their DADT position.

The legislative context; however, did not exist in a vacuum. The years 2002–2004 were important as the movement collectively challenged norms around gay rights in a number of venues. The court case *Lawrence v. Texas* (June 2003) fundamentally changed the legal status of gay Americans. The coming out of retired flag and general officers was historic as Brig. Gen. Keith Kerr, Brig. Gen. Virgil Richard, and RADM Alan Steinman (December 2003) appeared in *People Magazine*. In addition, direct challenges to DADT took place in federal court filings by the Log Cabin Republicans in *LCR v. Rumsfeld* (October, 2004) and SLDN's *Cook v. Rumsfeld* (December 2006). All of these actions reveal the crucial role of allied organizations and think tanks, such as the Palm Center, whose research on foreign militaries provided key information throughout this period. SLDN's role as a policy entrepreneur required balancing these elements. By working with House

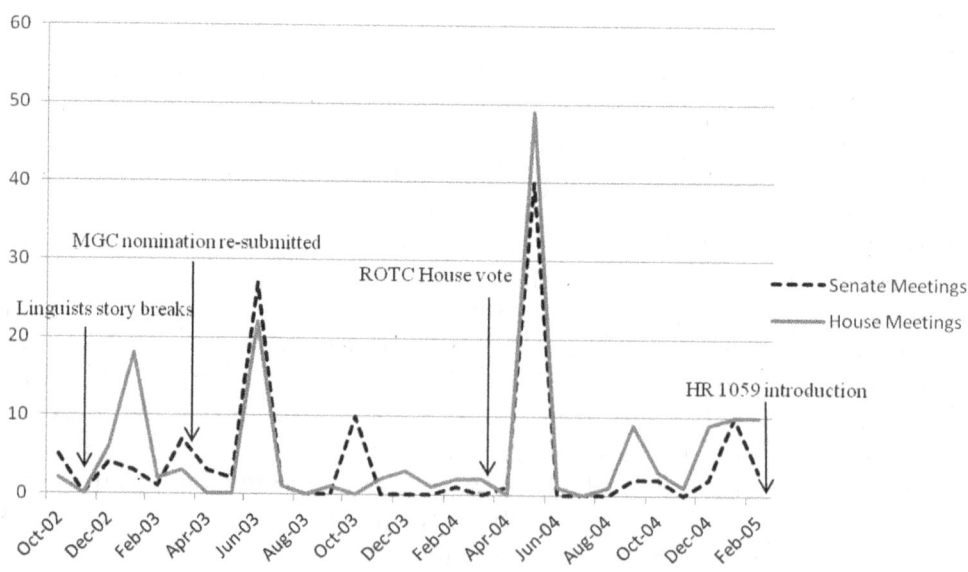

FIGURE 1 SLDN Senate and House Meetings from October 2002 to March 2005.

members in drafting legislative language, we were able to form monthly coalition roundtable meetings and manage the introduction strategy. What was unknown at the time was that Republican opposition to an ROTC campus-access issue would help SLDN and House offices to prepare for the introduction of repeal by demonstrating that DADT was a contested issue with potential.

Republican Opposition to University ROTC Policies

The House Republican's March 2004 debate on the Military Recruiter Equal Access to Campus Act provided the third mini-window of opportunity for SLDN. This debate assisted SLDN and Cong. Meehan's office in gaining new members of the core group, and provided an important tool that could help predict the future vote count for repeal (Congressional Record, 2004, H1695-701). At issue for Republicans and universities was the continued strength of the Solomon Amendment, a provision that banned federal funding for colleges and universities who prohibited ROTC on campus (based on a college's nondiscrimination policies). While the Republican majority was assured a victory on any floor vote, the debate was used as a mobilizing opportunity. SLDN provided talking points to offices to support them and reinforce the momentum built by the core group. Republicans would debate ROTC recruiter access and Democrats would debate DADT.

Remarks were offered by nineteen members of Congress during this floor debate, the longest discussion of gays in the military since 1993. Speakers included Reps. John Boehner (R-OH), Eric Cantor (R-VA), Ike Skelton (D-MO), Buck McKeon (R-CA), and Meehan. Talking points were not needed; however, for Cong. Barney Frank (D-MA), who set the tone for all Democrats. He stated, "we have fewer Arabic-speaking translators in the military today because of the policy which kicked out a number of people at the Army language school because they were discovered to be gay. These were people who would, if they had not been kicked out some time ago, been available today to do that important job of translation" (Congressional Record 2004, H1699). The linguist argument was shared by Cong. Sam Farr (D-CA) who stated, "Equality was not a concern for the military in 2002 when they discharged sixteen Arabic linguists from the Defense Language Institute in my district" (Congressional Record 2004, H1710). Finally, Rep. Pete Stark (D-CA) offered a solution stating, "we ought to be voting today to overturn the military's don't ask don't tell policy and instituting a policy that prohibits discrimination based on sexual orientation" (Congressional Record 2004, H1710).

The debate concluded on an amendment that passed the House 343-81 on March 30, 2004 (Congressional Record, 2003, H1695-701). With these votes in hand, Lauren Briggerman and I set out to contact those offices who opposed the amendment and were not part of the core group. Offices were also micro-targeted during SLDN's 2004 Lobby Day in May and asked if they would join the group. In addition, the debate was revealing because no response had come to the pro-repeal arguments presented. Following nearly two years of contesting DADT, there was no politically damaging response. The new frame for DADT repeal consideration in Congress was coined by Kathi Westcott, who titled our drafted legislation the "Military Readiness Enhancement Act." A careful political orchestration would now move to repeal introduction. DADT was now more than a contested issue, repeal was emerging.

DADT REPEAL AS AN EMERGING ISSUE (2005–2008)

SLDN's legislative plan was outlined in a memo drafted by C. L. Neff for the introduction of DADT repeal in December 2004. It noted attention to the "pre-introduction strategy, introduction strategy, and post introduction strategy" (SLDN, 2004). The pre-introduction steps were in place, with core group offices lined up to be cosponsors. In particular, the memo noted that "SLDN has met with over 200 congressional offices since November 2002." Offices and allies had agreed upon SLDN and Cong. Meehan's legislative language. The Military Readiness Enhancement Act was written in a way that transitioned the issue to an emerging status by offering a picture of what openly gay service looked like.

The repeal language included three pillars that had been constructed by SLDN, congressional offices and the law firm Wilmer Cutler Pickering. First, the ban would be eliminated. Second, DADT would be replaced with an affirmative non-discrimination policy and the right to open service in the military. Finally, service members who had been discharged under the policy would have the opportunity to be considered for reenlistment. These were intended as starting points, the beginning of a process to derail DADT. In an outcome broker role, SLDN's goal was to establish a high bar within the legislative language for congressional support of openly gay service, so that the management of this bill and any future legislation would be more workable.

Ensuring that introduction went smoothly and with few surprises was a chief concern that required months of planning. SLDN viewed this as a crucial test of its role as both experts on DADT and a political organization leading repeal. The 2004 SLDN memorandum noted these concerns stating:

> Between the release of an impending GAO Report and SLDN's DADT litigation, there are few scenarios under which legislation regarding "Don't Ask, Don't Tell" won't be introduced in the first session of the 109th Congress. The only questions are whether it will be opposition legislation or helpful legislation and whether it will be SLDN's legislation or a rogue introduction.

To address this issue, Lauren Briggerman and I attended 28 meetings between January 1 and March 2, 2005. SLDN prepared to play both offense and defense at the same time and adopted a Powell doctrine for DADT introduction, to introduce the bill with overwhelming force. Our target was 50 bipartisan cosponsors at introduction. We believed that this would present a strong, active front and limit any potential Republican backlash. In addition, we had discussed the need to place a Senate hold on any anti-gay legislation if Republicans responded, and our experience with the Clark nomination gave us confidence that this was possible. With a defensive plan in place, SLDN assumed an aggressive stance awaiting the introduction, which would be triggered by the long-awaited GAO report. We expected that this report would present a new picture of DADT as a national failure and the introduction of repeal legislation presented the solution to this problem.

On February 23, 2005, the GAO released the most complete review on the military readiness costs of Don't Ask, Don't Tell. It found that 757 service members were discharged from critical occupations and specialties, including 300 foreign language specialists (GAO, 2005). After the report was made public, Cong. Meehan told the *Boston Globe*, "the conventional justification for Don't Ask, Don't Tell has been that allowing gays to serve undermines military readiness. Now we have the numbers to prove that the policy itself is undermining our military readiness" (Bender, 2005) As planned, the Military Readiness Enhancement Act was introduced on March 2, and this included 57 cosponsors, a bipartisan bill including Rep. Christopher Shays (R-CT; Congressional Record, 2005, H.R.1059). With the original cosponsors onboard, the bill would attain 107 total cosponsors by the end of the year. The issue of openly gay service had again returned to the congressional legislative agenda.

SLDN's responses to the small windows of opportunity illustrated our role as policy entrepreneurs. We expanded the scope of our work, built a strong coalition of offices, and transitioned the issue from a status of radioactive isolation to a problem that could attract broad congressional support. Following the emergence of repeal, it is instructive to look at the final transition toward a viable period that fulfilled this goal of open service in 2010.

The factors that moved DADT from an emerging status to a viable status included structural changes based on electoral shifts, the change in political benefits versus costs and leadership from President Obama. For instance, DADT repeal was not viable in 2007 and 2008 due to a lack of support (and likely veto) by the Bush Administration, even with Democratic majorities in the House and Senate. The comparison below highlights the ways in which this viable stage can be analyzed using the 2004 SLDN estimated vote count and the 2010 actual (final) votes on repeal in the House and Senate.

Comparing 2004's Vote Count to 2010's Results

A key tool in the lead up to legislative introduction in 2005 was a matrix created in 2004 that predicted how members of the House and Senate would likely vote in favor of DADT repeal if the vote was held at that time. This estimated vote count was used as a planning tool to prioritize outreach for cosponsors and to identify offices that may be movable on the issue. This analysis looks at the final overall results and then reviews how these indicate a transition to the viability phase. Tables 1 and 2 compare the projected 2004 vote counts in the House and Senate with the actual final vote counts, across six estimated categories: yes, leaning yes, undecided, no, leaning no, and unknown (based on being new to Congress). This measurement can only reflect on elected members who were in Congress in 2004 and also voted on the Don't Ask, Don't Tell Repeal Act in 2010.

The estimated House vote count (see Table 1) notes the predicted positions on repeal in 2004, which calculated that there were 106 estimated yes votes, 55 leaning yes votes, 25 undecided, 15 leaning no, 194 no, and 40 members identified as new to Congress. We then asked, of these predictions, which members were still in Congress in 2010 and how did they vote on repeal? This section notes that overall 70% of members remained in Congress for the 2010 vote in the House; however, the change in party majority in 2008 is a significant event. Finally, Table 1 illustrates the tally of actual yes and no votes among the members who were still in Congress in 2010 and notes the percentage that was estimated accurately. The number of unaccounted members was attributed to those who were no longer in Congress.

The results of the comparison show that of those who were predicted to vote yes or leaning yes, most did. However, two members who were predicted as leaning yes voted no: Rep. Gerlach (R-MD) and Rep. Frelinghuysen (R-NJ). In addition, 9.2% of the estimated no votes (11 members) from 2004 voted in favor of repeal in 2010. These included

TABLE 1 House Comparison of 2004 Estimate Vote Count and 2010 Final Vote

Predicted positions on repeal in 2004	Total members still in Congress in 2010	Voted for repeal in 2010	Voted against repeal in 2010	Did not vote in 2010	No longer in Congress	Percentage predicted correctly
Yes (106)	86 (80%)	85	0	1	20	98.8%
Leaning Yes (55)	43 (78%)	39	2	2	12	90.7%
Undecided (25)	19 (76%)	14	4	1	6	73.7% for yes 21.1% for no
Leaning No (15)	8 (53%)	2	6	0	7	75%
No (194)	119 (61%)	11	106	2	75	89.1%
Unknown (40)	30 (75%)	14	15	1	10	46% for yes; 50% for no
Total: 435	305 (70%)	165	133	7	130	

TABLE 2 Senate Comparison of 2004 Estimate Vote Count and 2010 Final Vote

Predicted position on repeal in 2004	Total members left in 2010	Voted for repeal in 2010	Voted against repeal in 2010	Did not vote in 2010	No longer in Congress	Percentage predicted correctly
Yes (29)	21 (72.4%)	21	0	0	8	100%
Leaning yes (12)	9 (75%)	9	0	0	3	100%
Undecided (13)	10 (76.9%)	9	1	0	3	90% for yes; 10% for no
Leaning No (5)	3 (60%)	1	2	0	2	67%
No (41)	26 (63.4%)	1	22	3	15	84.6%
Total: 100	69 (69%)	41	25	3	31	

Reps. Boucher (D-VA), Boyd (D-FL), Costello (D-IL), Dreier (R-CA), Edwards (D-TX), Ehlers (R-MI), Flake (R-AZ), Gordon (D-TN), Holden (D-PA), Paul (R-TX), and Platts (R-PA).

In the Senate, 69% of members from 2004 were still in the Senate for the repeal vote in 2010. Of those predicted to vote yes or leaning yes, 100% voted in favor while 89.1% of predicted no votes voted against repeal in 2010. This shift from expected to actual votes by Sen. Voinovich (R-OH) and Sen. Burr (R-NC) support the conclusion that a new phase of political viability was present during this period of DADT repeal consideration.

The role of electoral viability can best be seen by first looking at the change in electoral majority of those whose vote moved from undecided to yes. Of the House members who were undecided in 2004, 73.7% voted for repeal and 92.9% of these were Democrats. Among Senators who were undecided on repeal in 2004, 90% voted in favor of repeal in 2010 and 77.8% of these were Democrats. The seven predicted undecided Democratic Senators included Max Baucus (D-MT), Kent Conrad (D-ND), Herb Kohl (D-WI), Bill Nelson (D-FL), Mark Pryor (D-AR), Jay Rockefeller (D-WV), and Arlen Specter (D-PA). The electoral change can also be seen in the shift between the predicted no and yes categories with six Democratic Representatives ultimately voting yes on repeal. In total, 20 Democrats in the House voted in favor of repeal after having been predicted as undecided, leaning no, or no.

The second issue of viability relates to a change in the costs or penalties in supporting repeal as well as the political benefits of being supportive of a historic vote for equality. We argue that this is reflected in the shift between a number of predicted and actual Republican votes. Four Senate Republicans varied from their undecided, leaning no, and no predictions to vote yes in favor of repeal. There are a number of potential reasons for these movements by Republicans. The first is that the vote count was intentionally written to be cautious and conservative, so this may be an internal bias. Any offices that were not confirmed as being pro-repeal were kept in these other categories. In addition, some members appear to have been pro-repeal (such as Cong. Drier) but refused meetings with SLDN or refused to state their position. Other Republican members seem to have been on the fence and ultimately voted for repeal after passage was already assured in each Chamber. For instance, Sens. John Ensign (R-NV) and Senator Burr voted for repeal after the cloture vote (filibuster) was overridden. The total number of Republicans in the Senate voting for repeal also seems to have provided cover for others. Last, it should also be recognized that leadership by President Obama, the Department of Defense's Working Group Report, and leadership by Defense Secretary Gates and Admiral Mullen provided additional impetus for pro-repeal votes (Montopoli, 2010). In this case, the Pentagon report in 2010 functioned in the same way as the GAO report in 2005.

A number of points can be drawn when comparing the predicted and actual votes. First, while the issue was largely the same, these were two different pieces of legislation. A number of amendments on the Senate side may have influenced swing votes by members. Second, the 30% difference in membership for both chambers in 2010 largely reflected a decline in the number of Republicans following the Democrats 2009 takeover of the House. This data suggests that electoral changes between 2004 and 2010 proved to be a crucial factor that led to repeal. In addition, it is important to note the significant role of gay advocates, organizations, and allies who a) educated House and Senate members to impact their votes, b) educated the public, and c) maintained political pressure to achieve final repeal success. This article is premised on the substantial role of entrepreneurs during each phase of the repeal process and encourages further research on this issue.

CONCLUSION

We reported on the role of SLDN in using mini-windows of opportunity to reframe DADT as a legislative issue; build a consensus for action in Congress; and draft and manage the introduction of repeal legislation with House allies. While DADT may now be recognized as an issue whose time had come, there were many battles on that path (and many more than documented in this article). We argue that the period before an issue reaches consensus is often left to the policy entrepreneurs. How these actors manage planned and unplanned events is an understudied area of policy change research and deserves greater attention.

A number of conclusions are demonstrated in this review. First, President George W. Bush can be credited for escalating the repeal of DADT. His nomination of Maj. Gen. Clark for promotion following PFC Winchell's murder galvanized the team at SLDN. Second, the discharge of gay Arabic linguists served to mobilize the effort further by involving key House offices.

Third, Republican attacks on colleges and universities' ROTC programs provided an organizing moment and test run for a redefined repeal argument. Finally, SLDN staff used these events as opportunities to hasten and engineer the introduction of repeal legislation by changing perceptions of the issue from radioactive to contested, and, finally, to an emerging issue in Congress.

NOTES

1. The authors wish to highlight that the use of the term "gay" is intended to reflect all members of the LGBTQI community, including lesbian, bisexual, transgender, intersex, and queer-identified individuals.

2. This research is based on participant-observation and supporting documentation. Data for this analysis relies on publicly available sources, work documents, personal communications, and firsthand meetings. The limitations of confirming firsthand knowledge are supported by independent sources where possible, including organizational memorandum, newspaper reports, and the Congressional Record. The vote count document was prepared with assistance from SLDN interns. It was determined through a review of previous congressional votes and any additional information from meetings with offices.

REFERENCES

Bender, B. (2005, February 24). Gays' ouster seen leaving gap in military. *Boston Globe*. Retrieved from http://www.boston.com/news/articles/2005/02/24/gays_ouster_seen_leaving_gap_in_military/

Brewer, P. (2008). *Value war: Public opinion and the politics of gay rights*. Lanham, MD: Rowman & Littlefield.

Congressional Record. (1993, September 28). House Amendment 316. Retrieved from http://www.govtrack.us/congress/vote.xpd?vote=h1993-460

Congressional Record. (2003, November 18). Retrieved from http://www.gpo.gov/fdsys/pkg/CREC-2003-11-18/pdf/CREC-2003-11-18-pt1-PgS15029-2.pdf#page=1

Congressional Record. (2004, March 30). Retrieved from http://www.gpo.gov/fdsys/pkg/CREC-2004-03-30-pt1-PgH1695.htm

Congressional Record. (2005, March 2). Retrieved from http://thomas.loc.gov/cgi-bin/bdquery/D?d109:69:./temp/~bdPRA8::

Cook v. Rumsfeld. (2006). 429 F. Supp. 2d 385 (D. Mass.).

Frank, N. (2002, November 18). Perverse: "don't ask, don't tell" v. the war on terrorism. *The New Republic*. Retrieved from http://www.tnr.com/article/politics/perverse

Files, J. (2003, November 19). Washington: General's delayed promotion. *The New York Times*. Retrieved from http://www.nytimes.com/2003/11/19/us/national-briefing-washington-general-s-delayed-promotion.html?ref=barrywinchell

General Accountability Office. (2005, February) U.S. Government Accountability Office report to congressional requesters: GAO-05-299. *Military personnel: Financial costs and loss of critical skills due to DoD's homosexuality conduct policy cannot be completely estimated*. Retrieved from www.gao.gov/new.items/d05299.pdf

Kingdon, J. W. (1984). *Agendas, alternatives and public policies.* Boston, MA: Little Brown.

Lawrence v. Texas. (2003). 539 U.S. 558.

Log Cabin Republicans v. United States. (2004, October 12). No. CV 04-8425 GPS (ex) (C.D. Cal.)

Mackenzie, C. (2004). Policy entrepreneurship in Australia: A conceptual review and application. *Australian Journal of Political Science 39*, 367–386.

Maze, R. (2003, December 3). Robert Clark gets controversial third star. *Army Times.* Retrieved December 28, 2011 from http://www.armytimes.com/legacy/new/0-ARMYPAPER-2409591.php

Mintrom, M., & Norman, P. (2009) Policy entrepreneurship and policy change. *Policy Studies Journal 37*, 649–667.

Montopoli, B. (2010, February 2). Mullen: Ending don't ask, don't tell "right thing to do." *CBS News.* Retrieved from http://www.cbsnews.com/8301-503544_162-6166493-503544.html

National Organization for Women. (2002, October 10). *Oppose Promotion of Major General Robert T. Clark to Lieutenant General.* Press Release. Retrieved from http://www2.now.org/issues/military/alerts/101002clark.html?printable

People Magazine. (2003, January 14). Military secrets. *People, 61.*

Richter, P. (1999, December 28). Few are happy with 'don't ask' policy. *Los Angeles Times.* Retrieved from http://articles.latimes.com/1999/dec/28/news/mn-48378

Rochefort, D., & Cobb, R. (Eds.). (1994). *The politics of problem definition: Shaping the policy agenda,* Lawrence, KS: University Press of Kansas

Schindler, P. (2003, June 20–26). New hurdles for General Clark. *Gay City News.* Retrieved from http://204.2.109.187/gcn225/newhurdles.html

Servicemembers Legal Defense Network. (2004, December 14). Memorandum drafted by C. Neff: SLDN legislative plan 2005."

Siciliano, C. (1994, May 10). Uncivil religion. *NewsDay.*

Sobel, S., Westcott, K., Benecke, M., Osburn, D., & Cleghorn, J. (2000, March 9). Conduct unbecoming: The sixth annual report on "don't ask, don't tell, don't pursue, don't harass." Servicemembers Legal Defense Network. Retrieved from http://dont.stanford.edu/commentary/conduct6.pdf

Sorg, L. (2003, March 27). Boys don't ask, don't tell, don't cry. *San Antonio Current.* Retrieved from http://www2.sacurrent..com/printStory.asp?id=56851

U.S. Federal Code. (1993). U.S. House of Representatives. armed forces, general military law, personnel. Retrieved from http://uscode.house.gov/download/pls/10C37.txt

Walker, J. L. (1977). Setting the agenda in the U.S. Senate: A theory of problem selection. *British Journal of Political Science,* 7, 423–445.

Weiss, J. A. (1989). The powers of problem definition: The case of government paperwork. *Policy Sciences, 22,* 97–121.

SECTION II
Policy evolution

From Exclusion to Acceptance: A Case History of Homosexuality in the U.S. Court of Military Appeals

KELLIE WILSON-BUFORD, MA
Department of History, University of Nebraska-Lincoln, Lincoln, Nebraska, USA

Policing the legality and normalcy of service members' sexual lives was a contentious process for military courts throughout the 1950s, 1960s, and early 1970s that resulted in the inconsistent enforcement of the homosexual exclusion policy. Military personnel of all ranks and occupations harbored a variety of attitudes and beliefs about homosexuality that challenged the legitimacy and uniformity of the military's legal assault on sexual deviance. Over half of the active duty personnel originally accused of homosexual tendencies received either sentence reductions or sentence reversals as a result of this highly contested process by which official military policy was translated into practice via courts-martial. Paradoxically, the very policies that discriminated against alleged homosexual service members generated legal avenues through which gays and lesbians exercised their rights to due process, and, ultimately, their rights as American citizens embodied in the repeal of the Don't Ask, Don't Tell policy. Rather than being an ideologically homophobic monolith, the Cold War American military rocked with contestation over an exclusion policy that attempted—unsuccessfully—to eliminate all gay and lesbian service members.

The author would like to thank her doctoral mentor, Margaret D. Jacobs, for her unwavering guidance without which this and numerous other works would not have come to fruition; anonymous readers and editors, Jim Parco and Dave Levy, whose invaluable suggestions transformed the essay into one of publishable quality; and, her husband, Petree V. Buford, for his unyielding support and encouragement.

> The seduction of our young men in the service by the homosexual is a singularly detestable and reprehensible crime. It is apparently a growing evil, or else it is more noticeable now than ever before. The evil corrupts; it can destroy those it touches. It should be wiped out. But it must be wiped out in a manner consistent with the protection of our Constitution. (Albrink & Jones, as cited in *United States v. Hillan*, 1957)

The two decades after World War II were of critical importance in establishing the legal and civil rights of homosexual service members embodied in the recent repeal of the Don't Ask, Don't Tell policy (DADT), although scholars have generally glossed over this period as one that simply witnessed the intensification of military homophobia. A typical example of this trend in historiography is that of G.D. Sinclair (2009), who summarizes the period from the end of World War II to the mid-1970s in a single sentence: "Although the discrimination of both gay men and lesbians continued, both in and out of the military, a new social movement was emerging in the United States that was beginning to call for civil rights for gays and lesbians" (. 40). In Sinclair's estimation, it was not until the 1970s that Leonard Matlovich and others unsuccessfully challenged the military's anti-homosexual policy. Similarly, Elizabeth Lutes Hillman (2005) argued that the extremely homophobic culture of the Cold War military made it nearly impossible for alleged homosexual service members to receive impartial trials at courts-martial, resulting in appellate reversals of guilty sentences. According to this common declension narrative, discrimination against homosexuals in the services steadily increased as the twentieth century progressed.

In reality, decades before the gay liberation movement targeted the military's exclusion regulations as a civil rights violation, service members within the military justice system were debating the purpose, legality, legitimacy, and effectiveness of the service-wide homosexual exclusion policy. The confusion the disposition regulations generated over what constituted homosexual behavior and orientation created space for service personnel and legal officials to challenge the military's exclusionary logic. Excluding alleged homosexuals from the American military in the decades following World War II was just one aspect of the military's broader, service-wide assault on all forms of sexual deviance from the established heterosexual, monogamous, and consensual norm. By criminalizing behaviors such as fornication, oral and anal sodomy, adultery, bigamy, indecent exposure, prostitution and pandering, the viewing of pornography, rape, child sexual abuse, and abortion, the Uniform Code of Military Justice (UCMJ) granted military courts wide-ranging authority to police the sexual lives of all service members and their families rather than just suspected homosexuals. Courts-martial for sexually deviant acts far outnumbered same-sex sodomy cases, illustrating that homosexuality was just one of many forms of sexual deviance that military courts sought to punish. Alongside the thoroughly documented legal prosecution of homosexual service members in the postwar American military ran a parallel, although less visible, pattern of legal protection that laid the groundwork for the repeal of DADT. The Court of Military Appeals (CMA), created in 1951 as the postwar military's supreme appellate authority and tasked with enforcing the new UCMJ, played a crucial role in the decades-long build-up to the creation and repeal of DADT by recognizing homosexual service members as legitimate individuals worthy of legal rights to due process. Upholding their rights to impartial trials and protection from double jeopardy, undue command influence, and entrapment at courts-martial for same-sex sodomy in the 1950s, 1960s, and early 1970s, the CMA established a powerful precedent of sexual nondiscrimination in the military justice system that resulted in the retention of countless allegedly homosexual service members. These legal victories were not widely publicized, however, because their precedents of legal protection challenged the legitimacy of the military's exclusionary logic by acknowledging that service personnel's sexual relationships and preferences had no bearing on their job performance or troop morale. Neither punishments nor protections were applied universally to alleged homosexual service members, just as troops did not universally agree on the nature and application of the service-wide exclusion policy. Both existed in tandem and detailed a rich and complex history of activism on behalf of allegedly homosexual military personnel who utilized the appeals process to challenge violations of their constitutional and UCMJ rights to due process in the military justice system. By acknowledging homosexuals as troops worthy of the same legal safeguards that heterosexuals enjoyed from the early 1950s onward, the CMA's precedent-setting cases of the post-World War II years paved the way for service members like Leonard Matlovich to openly challenge the military's exclusion policies into the twenty-first century with the confidence that they would receive fair treatment at courts-martial.

POLICIES OF EXCLUSION

Creation of the UCMJ made the postwar military justice system ripe for legal reform because it streamlined the services' diverse policies and procedures for criminalizing and punishing sexual deviance. The CMA, in turn, was vested with supreme authority to interpret the provisions of the UCMJ in a manner that protected the rights of all service members to due process in the military justice system (Lurie, 2001). Service members accused of Article 125 violations often contested unfair trial proceedings and sentences by appealing to the CMA, which had the power to reverse, reduce, or dismiss court-martial sentences.

The postwar military justice system's prosecution of sodomy mirrored American states' legal efforts to curtail non-procreative sexual relations throughout American history (Eskridge, 2008). Like its counterparts in civil law, Article 125 of the UCMJ criminalized both consensual and forcible sodomy, and penalized consenting adults with a maximum punishment of five years confinement at hard labor, total forfeitures, and dishonorable discharge. Defining sodomy as the unnatural copulation between two persons of the same or opposite sex or between a person and an animal, the UCMJ and *Manual for Courts-Martial* (1951) did not linguistically discriminate between homosexuals and heterosexuals. Because military courts interpreted Article 125 to include consensual acts of oral and anal penetration, heterosexuals (even married couples) who engaged in non-procreative sexual relations could also be and occasionally were court-martialed for their sexually deviant activities. CMA Judge Kilday (*United States v. Goodman*, 1963) castigated the act of sodomy as "a degradation of the virile organ" and the most "vicious insult to manhood," which should elicit no less than feelings of "outrage" and "revulsion" among heterosexual male victims. Sodomites were supposedly the most dangerous variants of sexual deviates in the military because their unnatural sexual behavior violated both religious and secular tenants of moral decency. By criminalizing sodomy as the "infamous crime against nature," the UCMJ established heterosexual, procreative marital sex as the normative standard against which deviant sexuality was measured. Although Article 125 criminalized both heterosexual and homosexual consensual acts of sodomy equally however, the postwar courts-martial overwhelmingly targeted alleged homosexuals, in effect homosexualizing the crime of sodomy. What Article 125 did not specify was how convicted sodomites should be prosecuted and discharged from the services.

The Navy established the first exclusionary regulations pertaining to alleged Navy and Marine Corps homosexuals on December 10, 1949. Secretary of the Navy (SECNAV) Directive 1620.1 (*United States v. Betts*, 1961, p. 213), established in 1949, argued that homosexuals were liabilities to the service and must be discharged. Employing the same logic of liability, the Army followed suit with Army Regulation (AR) 635-443 on January 12, 1950 (later superseded by AR 600-443, AR 635-89, AR 635-212, and AR 635-100) (*United States v. Goins*, 1956, pp. 543–544), and the Air Force implemented Air Force Regulation (AFR) 35-66 on January 12, 1951 (revised on May 31, 1954) (*United States v. Adams*, 1956, pp. 739–740). Similar in content and form in spite of dozens of revisions, these regulations dictated the convoluted process by which homosexuals were to be prosecuted and discharged under Article 125.

To determine the type of discharge and punishment appropriate for convicted sodomites, the regulations created a classification system defining different levels of homosexuals into military law. Class I homosexuals were considered the most dangerous to moral codes of decency because their perversity involved assaulting or coercing unwilling victims into homosexual acts, even minor children under age sixteen. Class II suspects included overt, confirmed homosexuals whose participation in at least one consensual act of same-sex sodomy could be proven beyond a reasonable doubt. The regulations defined consensual acts of Class II homosexuals broadly however, prosecuting proposals, solicitations, and attempts at sodomy as equally criminal as committing the consensual act of same-sex sodomy itself and making no distinction between active and passive participants. Class III homosexuals consisted of those service members whose degree of latent homosexual tendencies (as determined by military psychiatrists) rendered them unsuitable for service, even though they either had never engaged in same-sex sodomy, or had refrained from doing so since entering the military.

The process for discharge differed according to the legal class military officials assigned to alleged homosexuals. Deemed deserving of punishment for having uncontrollable, perverse urges, those service members categorized as Class I homosexuals were automatically prosecuted by courts-martial, and if found guilty, imprisoned and discharged. Class II and III homosexuals, although subject to trial by court-martial, were given the choice to by-pass courts-martial hearings and accept an undesirable administrative discharge in order to decrease the length and cost of the legal prosecution mounted against them.

According to AFR 35-66 (1951), alleged homosexuals were offered the chance to convene a hearing before a board of officers who would determine if the facts of the case warranted administrative discharge or retention in the service, and then make a recommendation for action to the Secretary of the Air Force Personnel Council. Personnel could refuse the board hearing and voluntarily agree to accept an administrative discharge, but the officer exercising general court-martial jurisdiction over the accused ultimately determined and recommended to the Air Force Personnel Council whether administrative discharge or disciplinary action was warranted. Even if the record disclosed that the accused committed a punishable offense, the officer could still recommend administrative discharge without punishment. The Secretary of the Air Force retained ultimate authority to approve the sentence upon the recommendation of the Air Force Personnel Council. Accused personnel who refused to accept either a board hearing or separation from the services under dishonorable conditions were court-martialed to establish the facts of their cases and to determine their guilt or innocence and their usefulness to the services.

Service members charged with sexual abuse of minor males were usually ranked as Class I homosexuals because the extent of their sexual perversion was supposedly so uncontrollable that they preyed on innocent children. The publicity these cases received in military news media made homosexuality synonymous with perversion and pedophilia—a stereotype that proved exceedingly difficult, although not impossible thanks to the appellate process instituted by the UCMJ for precisely these reasons, for convicted service members to overcome at courts-martial. But Class I was the least ambiguous tier of the homosexual classification system because it involved only cases of nonconsensual coercion. Classes II and III, on the other hand, generated extensive debate among legal officials over what behaviors and mannerisms counted as evidence of homosexuality because the regulations neither defined the behavior that constituted so-called homosexual tendencies, nor explained which tendencies (and to what degree a person exhibited these tendencies) rendered individuals unsuitable for military service. For example, AR 635-89 (1955) dictated that individuals should be court-martialed who possessed "homosexual tendencies to such a degree as to render them unsuitable for military service," yet conversely held that those service members who "profess homosexual tendencies should normally be retained in service" (*United States v. Goins*, 1956, pp. 543–544). Without any instruction on how to determine an individual's degree of homosexual tendencies, legal officials faced same-sex sodomy courts-martial ill-equipped to enforce the exclusion regulations with any degree of consistency.

AMBIGUOUS DEFINITIONS

Navy Fireman William Adkins' case illustrates how the vague definitions of homosexual behavior in the service disposition regulations nurtured irrational speculation about homosexuals (*United States v. Adkins*, 1955). Adkins was charged with sodomy while stationed on the island of Guam, and originally sentenced to a bad conduct discharge, total forfeitures of pay and allowances, and hard labor confinement for 18 months in spite of numerous recommendations testifying that Adkins was an honest and moral person. Sandoval, Adkins' consensual partner, confirmed that he was indeed a homosexual who accepted Adkins' sexual advances. The prosecution presented the testimony of a Naval Intelligence agent, Mr. Kinniry, whose claim to have investigated roughly 400 homosexuality cases over a decade made him an expert on homosexuals in the court members' eyes. Kinniry made a number of general remarks that cast Adkins in a guilty light, including that it was his experience that "birds of a feather flock together," that in all the cases he investigated he has "never known a confirmed homosexual to intentionally name and falsely accuse the wrong person and stick to it," that homosexuals were "products of broken homes," and that homosexuals typically came from large families where three to four children slept together in one bed" (*United States v. Adkins*, 1955, p. 120).

Adkins appealed his case to the U.S. Court of Military Appeals on the grounds that his right to a fair and impartial trial was compromised when the judge presiding over his trial admitted Kinniry's testimony as expert testimony. The CMA reviewed Adkins' case and reversed his guilty sentence on the grounds that Adkins' right to an impartial trial was, in fact, prejudiced by Kinniry's testimony because Kinniry's lack of official medical or psychiatric training reduced his opinions to non-expert personal observation. The judges questioned Kinniry's credibility by highlighting that his assertion that active homosexuals were always truthful about the persons with whom they had sex was unverifiable with concrete evidence. This concrete evidence was impossible to provide, in the judges' estimation, because consensual sodomy was rarely performed in public as it was a felony in both civil and military law. The elements of Adkins' case were common among courts-martial for same-sex sodomy in the postwar years: Alleged sodomites were often subject to irrational and incriminating speculation about the nature and veracity of homosexuals because service regulations provided no clear definitions of what constituted homosexual behavior. Such speculation often benefitted the accused because the CMA consistently stepped in to protect their UCMJ-mandated rights to fair and impartial trials.

If the ambiguous language of the classification regulations left room for multiple interpretations of what constituted homosexual behavior, contradictions complicated the regulations' linguistic imprecision. AR 635-89 (1955), for instance, categorized service members who had engaged in provable consensual homosexual acts as Class II homosexuals, but conversely defined Class II homosexual acts as "overt acts, active and passive in nature, and proposals, solicitations, or attempts to perform any homosexual act *even though no overt act is committed*" (italics added, *United States v. Goins*, 1956, pp. 543-544). Thus, Class II homosexuals could be categorized as such based on acts and attempts to act that could be provable. Without criteria for what constituted provable behavior however, legal officials were often at odds over what counted as proof because witnesses' testimonies of the facts were almost always at odds. At sodomy trials especially, often what was provable depended on who legal officials chose to believe because such intimate encounters rarely occurred in the presence of an audience whose testimony could tip the scales toward guilt or innocence.

LINGUISTIC IMPRECISION LEADS TO DEBATE

Airman Third Class Nathaniel Smith's case offers an excellent illustration of how confusion over how to prove a person's homosexuality led to disagreement and debate among judicial officials at courts-martial (*United States v. Smith*, 1959). Smith was charged with committing sodomy against a fellow airman at Nousseur Air Base's military stockade in Morocco in 1959. The presiding judge initially recommended Smith for clemency, restoring him to active duty status in the Air Force. He later withdrew his clemency recommendation however, because Smith's falsetto voice and effeminate manner made it more likely that he committed the crime at hand. Unsure how to pinpoint Smith's sexual orientation, the judge altered his recommendation for restoration in the Air Force based largely on Smith's effeminate characteristics. The review board, the intermediate appellate authority over general courts-martial trials, reversed Smith's guilty sentence on the grounds that the judge's withdrawal of his clemency recommendation for rehabilitation was "hasty, ill-advised, and almost injudicious because it was based on no more than flimsy information pertaining to physical characteristics of the accused which were deemed to lend substance to the report that he had committed a homosexual act" (*United States v. Smith*, 1959). Protecting Smith's right to a fair trial, in his case a trial free from prejudicial error, the officers sitting on the review board condemned the indictment of an alleged homosexual based on physical characteristics alone. Although the Smith case provided some clarity on the confusing issue of how to prove a person's sexual orientation, legal officials continued to struggle with the ill-defined classifications of the service disposition regulations into the 1990s after DADT went into effect.

Categorizing service members into Class III of the homosexuality tier was an equally contentious task because the regulations failed to dictate how an individual's sexual orientation should be confirmed. If Class III homosexuals were persons who had not engaged in homosexual activities since their entry into the services, then on what basis, if not sexual activity, was sexual orientation confirmed? Class III was especially controversial because the logic suggested that a person's gender-coded mannerisms or character traits, rather than specific sexual behaviors, indicated his or her sexual orientation. But if mannerisms such as an effeminate gate and falsetto voice equated to homosexual tendencies, nowhere did the UCMJ specifically authorize legal authorities to punish service members for such traits. Article 125 criminalized the action of sodomy alone, not mannerisms or sexual orientation. However, commanders could, and often did, prosecute suspected homosexuals with violations of the general articles, Articles 133 and 134, because their linguistic imprecision allowed commanders the leeway to criminalize any action or mannerism that threatened the heterosexual masculine normative behavioral standard that ordered the social conduct of post-World War II service members.

Both homosexuals and heterosexuals could be prosecuted under the UCMJ's Articles 133 and 134. Article 133 criminalized any public or private behavior or action that constituted conduct "unbecoming an officer and a gentleman," while Article 134 sanctioned assault with the intent to commit sodomy, indecent assault, and indecent acts, and prohibited all conduct "to the prejudice of good order and discipline in the armed forces." The vague language of Articles 133 and 134 made them extremely elastic and applicable in many cases where homosexuality was suspected but could not be proven with a sodomy conviction. Because the UCMJ and the *Manual for Courts-Martial* did not define specific behaviors that were considered "indecent" or unbecoming of an officer and a gentleman, military courts were charged with the fraught task of criminalizing gendered behaviors of service members that threatened normative standards of moral and sexual decency at courts-martial (para. 213a). By criminalizing both sexual and non-sexual acts that violated vague standards of conduct, the UCMJ, ultimately, granted military courts wide-ranging jurisdiction over service members' intimate lives. This authority often benefitted convicted homosexuals by enabling them to appeal their cases to the CMA.

ARMY VERSUS AIR FORCE DISPUTE OVER HOMOSEXUAL EXCLUSION POLICIES

The case of Army Pvt. Earnest Rudolph Goins illustrates how linguistic vagueness incited debate over the nature and legality of the services' exclusion regulations (*United States v. Goins*, 1956). Court-martialed for two charges of homosexual sodomy with other soldiers at Ft. Knox, Kentucky in 1956, Goins pleaded guilty and received the maximum sentence of dishonorable discharge, total forfeiture of pay and allowances, and confinement at hard labor for five years. Prior to the sentence, however, military psychiatrist Maj. Murray Finn examined Goins and testified that since he fell under Class II as a confirmed homosexual, he should be given the choice to accept an administrative discharge or to resist discharge and face a court-martial in accordance with AR 635-89. Goins did not resist discharge because he was never afforded the opportunity to do so. The Army Review Board reversed Goins' sentence on the grounds that Goins' rights were substantially prejudiced when he was not given the opportunity afforded to him under AR 635-89 to accept an undesirable discharge in lieu of trial by court-martial.

The issue at hand was whether AR 635-89 constituted a mandate that all Class II homosexuals be afforded the opportunity to accept an undesirable discharge in lieu of trial by court-martial, or whether the regulation gave the accused's commander the discretion to withhold this opportunity. In a surprising assertion of Class II homosexuals' right to choose how they would be separated from the services, Army officials on the review board interpreted AR 635-89 as a mandate granting Class II homosexuals the opportunity to accept an administrative discharge to avoid court-martial as a matter of right. Only by resisting administrative discharge, the Board interpreted, should Class II homosexuals be tried by court-martial. The irony of Goins' case was that the very regulation that defined him as a criminal in military law also established his right as a soldier to choose the method of his own discharge. Certainly, AR 635-89 was designed to entice confirmed homosexuals to choose the cheaper and quicker administrative discharge in exchange for escaping punishment, but Class II homosexuals often resisted discharge because courts-martial offered the possibility of innocence, clemency, and the chance to continue serving their country.

An Air Force Review Board flatly disagreed with the Army Review Board's interpretation of the regulation as a mandate of accused rights in *Goins*. In 1960, TSgt. William K. Sheehan appealed his sodomy conviction on the grounds that he, like Goins, was not given the choice of administrative separation prior to trial by court-martial (*United States v. Sheehan*, 1960). The Air Force Review Board interpreted AFR 35-36 not as a mandate asserting alleged homosexuals' rights to choose the method of their discharge as had Goins' review board, but rather as a guideline for how the administrative elimination of homosexuals were to proceed if the presiding officer chose this option over the court-martial. Because the Army's ruling in *Goins* divested commanders of their decision-making powers by reserving the right of choice to accused service members, Air Force officials ruled that the Army's decision simply did not apply to Air Force officers. Rather, Air Force officials protected officers' decision-making authority by arguing that the disposition regulations could not place presiding officials in a "mental straight jacket" denying them freedom of choice over how to conduct same-sex sodomy cases (*United States v. Sheehan*, 1960). Where the Army interpreted the regulation as a mandate of rights of the accused, the Air Force interpreted the regulation as mere guidance for an officer if he chose the route of administrative discharge over trial by court-martial. Because presiding officials interpreted AFR 35-36 as a procedural guideline for officers rather than a mandate of Sheehan's right to choose his method of discharge, they confirmed Sheehan's sentence of dishonorable discharge, total forfeitures, confinement at hard labor for one year, and reduction to the grade of airman basic.

In addition to debating the nature of the regulations as mandates of rights of the accused or as procedural guidelines for officers, judicial personnel questioned the legality of AR 635-89, AFR 35-36, and SECNAV 1620.1. Army Pvt. Vernon B. Green's case illustrates this trend clearly (*United States v. Green*, 1957). Green pleaded not guilty to one charge of sodomy, and was found guilty of the lesser offense of a violation of Article 134, namely, committing an "indecent, lewd, and lascivious act with another" (*United States v. Green*, 1957). He was sentenced to a dishonorable discharge, total forfeitures, and confinement at hard labor for three years. The convening authority reduced Green's sentence to two years but otherwise approved it. Green's attorney challenged the sentence arguing that AR 635-89 improperly influenced" the officers presiding over Green's trial. The Staff Judge Advocate wrote a letter to Green's commander, Col. Dawson, stating that AR 635-89 was a directive of "doubtful legality" because it tended to directly control the judicial process. Because of its' questionable legality, the Staff Judge Advocate requested that Col. Dawson reconsider Green's sentence, with specific disregard for the directive provisions of paragraph 6b(1)(b) of AR 635-89.After considering the Staff Judge Advocate's request for reconsideration, Col. Dawson recommended to the convening authority that the charges against Green be dropped completely and that he simply be reassigned to a different command.

To justify his change of heart, Dawson invoked paragraph two of AR 635-89, arguing that Green's case should be dismissed because it represented a single homosexual instance where excessive intoxication overpowered his ability to adhere to reason. Paragraph two of AR 635-89 expressly referenced cases such as Green's, dictating that accused homosexuals should be retained in the services where they had committed a single homosexual act under the influence of alcohol, and where psychiatric evaluations revealed that they were neither confirmed homosexuals nor possessed strong homosexual tendencies. Because there was no evidence of actual penetration, Dawson reasoned, it was impossible to confirm the permanency, and, hence, liability, of Green's homosexual orientation. The convening authority, in spite of Dawson's recommendation for Green's charges to be dropped, referred the charges to a general court-martial for trial.

Green rejected administrative discharge and opted instead for trial by court-martial, but Capt. Pilon, Green's immediate commander who filed the charges against him in the first place, testified in an out-of-court hearing that he felt a general court-martial was unwarranted since the only reason he recommended court-martial in the first place was AR 635-89. Green's attorney argued that the Department of the Army subjected Capt. Pilon to undue command influence through AR 635-89, preventing Pilon from freely exercising his discretion guaranteed in the UCMJ and *Manual for Courts-Martial*. The Army Review Board disagreed, however, and upheld Green's guilt with a reduced confinement period of six months. In Green's case, as in those of Goins and Sheehan, court officials debated the intentions of the service regulations that codified homosexuals into military law. Army officials in *Green* and *Goins* debated AR 635-89 as both a mandate of accused rights and as a directive of doubtful legality, while Air Force officials debated AFR 35-36 as a procedural outline that did not prevent officers from freely exercising their professional discretion in homosexual sodomy cases. SECNAV 1620.1 was no less controversial in Navy and Marine Corps courts-martial, as exemplified by the courts-martial of Betts and Rivera, especially after the Crittenden Report was released in 1957 (*United States v. Betts*, 1961; *United States v. Rivera*, 1961).

CHALLENGING THE LOGIC: POLICY CONTRADICTIONS

Contradictions within the disposition regulations were mirrored by contradictions between official policies and reports. The Crittenden Report, released by the Navy in 1957, challenged the exclusionary logic of SECNAV 1620.1 by arguing that homosexuals showed no difference in job performance or ability than heterosexuals (Gibson, 1978). If "gay men posed no great national security risk in terms of susceptibility to extortion," then under what conditions were alleged homosexuals liabilities to the services according to the logic of SECNAV 1620.1 (D'Amico, 1996)? The report's findings startled military officials and created an atmosphere of apprehension and denial. To quell any potential uprisings from within the ranks over the irrationality of the service-wide exclusion policy, the Navy hid the report for 32 years until it was ordered by a federal court to release it to the public in 1989, generating a public discussion of the military's exclusion regulations that led to the creation of DADT (D'Amico, 1996). The Crittenden Report's revolutionary potential was not service-specific to the Navy and Marine Corps. Because the Army and Air Force adopted the same exclusionary logic and classification system for defining homosexuals, courts-martial for homosexual sodomy in the Army and Air Force had equally revolutionary potential to create new masculinities that were conducive to military service.

But, even before the Crittenden Report caused a firestorm of controversy over the military's exclusion policy in 1957, military officials at courts-martial were questioning the validity of the military's policy that homosexuals were liabilities to the military's mission and must be eliminated from the ranks. Positive character recommendations from high-ranking officers, for example, challenged the logic of job liability by offering evidence of exemplary job performance. Army 1st Lt. Henry Lawrence Davisson's case exemplifies this trend clearly (*United States v. Davisson*, 1952). Charged with two counts of sodomy with enlisted men at Ft. Benning, Georgia, in 1952, Davisson pleaded guilty and was sentenced to dismissal from the Army. In Davisson's attempt to explain his "unnatural urge" to have sexual relations with men, he testified that he first experienced an attraction to men in 1938, at the same time that he became engaged to a Red Cross nurse (*United States v Davisson*, 1952). After consulting a psychiatrist for eighteen months and feeling "cured," he lived a normal heterosexual life, even after the tragic death of his fiancée in 1944. Since his re-engagement to another woman, Davisson admitted that his unnatural urge had overtaken him the past couple of years. With searing honesty, Davisson went on to explain that he felt responsible for correcting his situation "because of society's attitude toward it," and that he planned to seek the professional help of physicians and psychiatrists to overcome his affliction. The Chief of the Neuropsychiatric Section at Ft. Benning Army Hospital evaluated Davisson and concluded that even though in appearance he was "mildly effeminate," Davisson lacked any permanent characteristics worthy of diagnosis as a sexual deviate. Two Colonels testified on Davisson's behalf, offering evidence of outstanding job performance in spite of Davisson's admission of homosexual sodomy. Lt. Col. Stanislaus J. Codner of the Adjutant General's Corps described Davisson's job performance as being marked by "outstanding efficiency and devotion to duty" and stated that the current proceedings had made no difference in Davisson's exemplary job performance. Codner summarized his feelings toward Davisson by adding that he knew of no other officer in the Adjutant General's Corps in Davisson's grade as exceptional as the young lieutenant, and assured court members that his superior, Col. Shugart, the Adjutant General of the Infantry Center, shared his sentiments about Davisson's stellar work ethic.

Davisson's own admission of both his homosexual urges and actions did not influence the professional testimony in support of his retention in the Army. To the contrary, the Chief psychiatrist's conclusion that Davisson was not a sexual deviate directly negated Davisson's testimony, while Col. Codner's glowing praise of Davisson's job performance did not waiver the least after hearing Davisson admit to homosexual urges and actions. By arguing for Davisson's retention in the service in spite of his sexual urges, Col. Codnar—and by extension his commander Col. Shugart—exposed the flawed logic of the military's exclusion policy. Far from being a liability, Davisson's job performance was so stellar that two Colonels risked their professional reputations on their support of a young officer whose admission of homosexual sodomy defied the military's normative moral standards of conduct. The psychiatrist's conclusion that Davisson was an asset to the military in spite of evidence of homosexual inclinations also countered the exclusionary logic by suggesting that homosexuals could be indispensable to the mission.

As Davisson's case suggests, military officials struggled to confirm service members' sexual orientations in the context of competing evaluations that sometimes contradicted an accused's personal testimony. As early as 1952, high-ranking military officials were challenging the military's exclusionary logic by arguing that service members' private sexual encounters had no bearing on their public duties. Ultimately, the absence of a universal standard of behavior to determine the degree to which homosexual tendencies made personnel unsuitable for military service created a legal climate of possibility for alleged homosexuals to challenge their sentences because military legal personnel rarely agreed on how to interpret the vague and contradictory definitions of the different classes of homosexuals stipulated by these service regulations. In this environment, accused personnel often successfully challenged their criminality by utilizing the appeals process to contest unfair sentences or trial proceedings and to receive sentence reductions, reversals, and re-hearings. Their steady stream of appeals increased the length and cost of prosecution by courts-martial, and contributed to the falling rate of courts-martial for the crime of homosexual sodomy up to the repeal of DADT in 2011.

LAYING THE LEGAL GROUNDWORK FOR DADT REPEAL

Navy Chief Engineman Edward Joseph Knudson was the first of many alleged homosexual service members to achieve the justice commonly afforded to heterosexual service members (*United States v. Knudson*, 1952). Charged with and convicted of sodomy in violation of Article 125 of the UCMJ in 1952, the general court-martial sentenced him to a dishonorable discharge, total forfeiture of all pay and allowances, reduction to the grade of fireman recruit, and confinement at hard labor for one year. Knudson contested being tried by court-martial by petitioning the Secretary of the Navy for relief on the ground that he was tried and acquitted in a California state court on April 4, 1952 for the same offense that initiated the present court-martial. Although Navy policy generally dictated that service members could not be tried at court-martial for the same act for which they were tried in civil court, in effect protecting personnel from double jeopardy, the review board denied Knudson's petition for relief of trial by court-martial on the grounds that the Navy Department policy protecting service members from double jeopardy did not apply to alleged homosexuals. SECNAV 49-882, dated December 10, 1949, waived homosexual service members' rights to protection from double jeopardy in an effort to discharge as many homosexuals as possible.

Knudson also challenged the prejudicial nature of the court-martial proceedings by arguing that the presiding law officer erred when he failed to direct the court to disregard the trial counsel's inflammatory remarks. The sum of these inflammatory remarks, Knudson challenged, prejudiced his right to an impartial jury. The review board agreed with Knudson that the trial counsel's comments were improper, but concluded that such misconduct on trial counsel's part did not substantially prejudice the accused since the facts proved beyond a reasonable doubt that Knudson was guilty of sodomy. In other words, the review board reasoned that the jury would have found Knudson guilty even in the absence of inflammatory remarks because Knudson's guilt was obvious from the evidence alone. The CMA heard the case in 1954 and reversed Knudson's guilty conviction on the grounds that the convening authority's action of interfering with the law officer's decision to grant Knudson's request for a continuance was illegal and violated a substantial right of Knudson to due process. Knudson's case was, ultimately, the first to protect alleged homosexuals from double jeopardy despite regulations exempting them from such protection. As one of the first cases of homosexual sodomy to reach the newly created CMA, Knudson's legal victory in the midst of the McCarthy era "lavender scare" set the tone for the legal victories to follow.

Protections from Unfairly Prejudicial Evidence & Testimony

In addition to protection from double jeopardy, the CMA enforced alleged homosexuals' right to protection from unfairly prejudicial evidence or testimony. Navy Lt. Robert Daniel Warren's case exemplifies this trend (*United States v. Warren*, 1955). In 1955, Warren was charged with two offenses of sodomy and two offenses of taking indecent liberties. His trouble began in March 1952, when he was a university Navy ROTC instructor. Durant, an

ROTC student of Warren's, filed a sexual assault charge against him, claiming that Warren's improper advances after a night of drinking ultimately resulted in the crimes at hand. While Warren was awaiting trial for the Durant charge, seaman Swailes made similar accusations against Warren, claiming that on January 2, 1953, he and Warren "occupied the same bed" at Kip and Jerry's house in South Carolina where sodomy and other "immoral acts" occurred (*United States v. Warren*, 1955). At the court martial, a prosecution witness, Cisa, attested that he knew Kip and Jerry to have lived together in numerous apartments and that he had seen Warren frequent their various residences. On one occasion, in 1949 or 1950, Cisa observed Warren impersonating a woman and claimed that Warren acted like a homosexual by dancing, making jokes with, and embracing Kip and Jerry in a romantic manner. Another prosecution witness, Hoblitzell, testified that he met Warren in Charleston in 1949, and on an automobile ride Warren "fondled" his private parts. Although Hoblitzell admitted that he was intoxicated during this automobile ride, he presumed that he and Warren probably committed an act of sodomy with each other.

Warren testified on his own behalf, corroborating many of the facts stated by Cisa and Hoblitzell, but denying all facts of an incriminating nature. He challenged the general court-martial's ruling of guilty on the grounds that the law officer presiding over the court martial admitted prejudicial evidence against him, which negatively influenced the trial outcome. The CMA heard Warren's appeal in 1955, and ruled that the "damning nature" of the evidence impaired Warren's credibility in the eyes of the court members. Since the evidence was essentially deduced to the prosecution witnesses' word against Warren's, the court-martial's findings of guilty stemmed from court members' disbelief of his testimony. Because the CMA judges were convinced of the irreparable damage to Warren's credibility, they dismissed his charges and ordered a re-hearing of the entire case.

The CMA reasoned that the testimony given by Swaines and Cisa was unfairly prejudicial because the acts of sexual misconduct described were completely unrelated to Durant's charge. Whether or not Warren impersonated a woman, embraced a man, or fondled Hoblitzell in an automobile was irrelevant to the charges of sodomy committed with Durant because Warren was under no obligation to disclose to the court his sexual history unrelated to the present charge. Summarily, the prosecution's key witness testimony was struck from the appellate record because it was both irrelevant and unfairly incriminating.

The CMA, ultimately, protected Warren from unfairly prejudicial testimony by ruling that evidence in sexual perversion cases was only admissible if it proved that acts of prior sexual misconduct were between the accused and the victim in the present case. In ruling that testimony of past homosexual tendencies did not presume Warren's guilt in the present charges of sodomy, the CMA clarified the blurry distinction between homosexual acts and homosexual tendencies that service regulations muddied during the Cold War. By banning all third-party testimony unrelated to the incident between Durant and Warren, the CMA sent a strong message to military courts that alleged homosexuals' past intimate relationships unrelated to the present court-martial were not open to legal interrogation and interpretation.

Protections from Accusatory Questioning and Innuendos

Accusatory questions and suggestive innuendos also posed formidable barriers to homosexuals' rights to a fair trial. In Army Sergeant First Class Richard Bird's case, the review board reversed the court-martial and convening authority's finding of guilty and ordered a re-hearing of the case to assert Bird's right to unbiased, objective questioning by trial counsel (*United States v. Bird*, 1957). Tried by general court-martial in Stuttgart-Moehringen, Germany in 1957, the court found Bird guilty of attempted sodomy with Pvts. Greene and Murphy. Bird denied the charges and offered good character evidence by Col. Kunzig, but was subjected to a lengthy cross-examination during which the prosecution attorney asked Bird such questions as, "Back in 1954, did you ever fondle anybody's legs—male legs?" "Have you ever given anybody in your company, Headquarters Company, any reason to feel that you were queer?" and, "Do you have a bad character when it comes to homosexual tendencies?" (United States v. Bird, 1957, 448-49).

The review board ruled that these questions were unfairly prejudicial because they insinuated Bird's guilt and deprived him of his right to a fair trial by jeopardizing Bird's credibility in the eyes of the court members. Reasoning that the prosecuting attorney could not employ tactics that convicted the accused of a crime which the evidence does not prove, Lancefield and Howell, Bird's appellate counsel, protected Bird's right to impartial cross-examinations and established a precedent of enforcing alleged homosexuals' rights to fair trials in future sodomy cases. Bird's case illustrates a noteworthy trend in military justice during the Cold War, namely that the CMA was not the only court that protected alleged homosexuals from injustice. At intermediate levels within the military justice system, review boards often upheld alleged homosexuals' rights to due process.

Protections from Command Influence

Unfairly prejudicial evidence and accusatory questioning were not the only ways service members' rights to a fair trial were jeopardized. Impartiality of court members on the issue of homosexuality and proper punishment also threatened service members' rights to a fair hearing and sentence, especially when the court members were high ranking officers or commanders who used their rank superiority to sway the actions and opinions of lower ranking court members. Both the CMA and military review boards asserted alleged homosexuals' rights to trials free of command control—the age-old habit of commanders and high-ranking officers abusing their rank privilege to their own benefit. Trials for homosexual sodomy during the Cold War were especially vulnerable to command influence because homosexuality evoked extremely strong opinions from service personnel about morality and religion. Court members ranged in rank from the lowest to the highest grades, and officers often presided over trials as presidents, giving them wide-ranging authority to dictate the circumstances of the trials. It was not uncommon for presiding officials to wield the power of their ranks to influence court members' decisions about an accused's guilt or innocence.

Army Pvt. Carl Lackey's case illustrates this trend. In 1956, Lackey was court-martialed for a sodomy offense (*United States v. Lackey*, 1956). Pleading guilty to the charge, he received a dishonorable discharge, total forfeiture of pay and allowances, and confinement at hard labor for two years. The convening authority reduced the length of confinement to one year, but the military review board, ultimately, dismissed the charges because the president's abuse of rank deprived Lackey of his Sixth Amendment right to an impartial trial. On voir dire examination by the defense counsel, who was a first lieutenant, the president of the court, Col. Hollis, expressed dissatisfaction with the declining severity in punishments for guilty soldiers. Because voir dire examination was a procedural safeguard of the UCMJ, Lackey's defense counsel was required to question all court members about their biases toward issues related to homosexuality before trial to insure the impartiality of court members. Court members who were found to harbor prejudice about homosexuality that would bias their judgment against the accused, like Col. Hollis, were replaced. Col. Hollis' statements indicated that he felt courts should impose severe sentences since higher authorities could reduce extreme punishments. When Lackey's attorney challenged Hollis on the ground that his beliefs prevented him from fairly and impartially considering the issue of appropriate punishment, Hollis interpreted the challenge as a personal attack on his professional competence and responded in a patronizing manner that emphasized the colonel's superiority in rank and matters of judicial competence over the first lieutenant. Lackey's counsel withdrew his challenge of Hollis' impartiality after Hollis' tirade ended.

Arguing that Col. Hollis' argumentative remarks probably persuaded the defense counsel to withdraw his challenge, judges Lancefield and Ayars asserted Lackey's right to counsel who were free to perform their duties fully. Reprimanding Hollis' overt display of command influence as an embarrassing attempt to discredit a young lieutenant who was trying to perform his duty in representing an accused, the judges asserted Lackey's right to impartial court members.

The CMA faced a similar command influence case in 1957, condemning it as a "discredit to military law," and moved swiftly to protect the accused's right to impartiality of the court members. In what the judges termed an "unparalleled situation," a law officer persuaded the staff judge advocate and the convening authority to influence a guilty conviction (*United States v. Kennedy*, 1957). The accused, Army Pvt. Joe Kennedy, was found guilty of assault with intent to commit sodomy and given the maximum punishment of five years confinement at hard labor, total forfeitures of pay and allowances, and a dishonorable discharge despite the fact that the victim of Kennedy's assault refused to acknowledge that Kennedy attacked him. In an extremely rare circumstance, the convening authority approved the maximum punishment (normally convening authorities reduced sentences), although the majority of service members found guilty of homosexual sodomy during the Cold War received much more lenient sentences.

Kennedy appealed to the CMA on the grounds that he was denied a fair and impartial trial by inappropriate influence of the law officer and other personnel unrelated to the trial. In an effort to reinforce the absolute necessity of remaining neutral to all judicial officials, judges Quinn and Ferguson dismissed Kennedy's case entirely, reasoning that supporting a finding of guilty would essentially condone the use of command influence in future courts-martial. Had Kennedy not appealed to the CMA, he would have spent five years in military prison and the remainder of his life struggling to overcome the stigma of a dishonorable discharge for a crime that the prosecution could not prove. By protecting Kennedy's right to an impartial trial by court-martial, a right granted to all American citizens under the Constitution, the CMA refused to allow military courts to trample service personnel's rights to due process regardless of their alleged criminality or sexual orientation.

The cases of Lackey and Kennedy were monumental legal victories for homosexual service members in the postwar American military because they established that alleged homosexuals would not be excluded from the Constitution's basic protections under military law. Foreshadowing the repeal of DADT, the outcomes of Kennedy and Lackey's cases established a counter logic to that of homosexual exclusion by requiring that service members, regardless of sexual orientation or activities, be included among those heterosexuals who enjoyed basic constitutionally and UCMJ-mandated rights to due process. The repeal of DADT echoed this early logic of inclusion by establishing a policy of acceptance toward service members who identified as gay and lesbian.

Protections from Government Entrapment

In addition to protection from double jeopardy, unfairly prejudicial evidence, and biased court members, the CMA asserted homosexuals' rights to immunity and protection from government entrapment. Airman First Class Cyrus Haynes' case exemplifies this trend (*United States v. Haynes*, 1957).

In 1957, Haynes was tried by general court-martial for charges of sodomy, attempted sodomy, and extortion. Air Force Office of Special Investigations (AFOSI) agents brought the charges against Haynes after he made questionable admissions of homosexual tendencies. The record established that Haynes underwent extensive questioning and polygraph testing by various AFOSI agents in an effort to receive a security clearance. The agents told him that the sole purpose of the testing was to ensure that he was qualified to receive a top-secret security clearance and that everything he said would be confidential. Despite the agents' assurances that the extensive testing was solely for determining Haynes' eligibility for a security clearance, they used his answers as evidence of his homosexual acts. The review board dismissed Haynes' claim that he was unfairly denied a grant of immunity by ruling that the AFOSI agents did not have the power to grant such immunity in the first place. The review board also denied the defenses' challenge for cause after the voir doir examination revealed that one of the court members had participated in the administrative disposition of homosexual service members and was thus not impartial in determining Haynes' guilt or innocence.

Haynes appealed to the CMA on the grounds that the AFOSI agents did not uphold their promise of confidentiality and that he had been entrapped through deceitful means. The CMA reversed Haynes' guilty sentence in 1958 on numerous grounds, including that of inadmissible evidence. Ruling that the prosecution's evidence was inadmissible because it was obtained deceitfully under the promise of confidentiality, the CMA upheld Haynes' right to protection from entrapment. Mirroring the logic of a similar case in civil court, the CMA refused to convict Haynes because the methods employed by the AFOSI agents to bring about conviction were manipulative, deceitful, and illegal. Although shut down by the review board, Haynes' attorney claimed he could prove that Haynes' experience was shared be countless alleged homosexual service members. Recognizing the likelihood that the AFOSI employed similar deceitful tactics to weed out other alleged homosexual service members, the CMA wielded its appellate authority to prevent OSI agents from trampling alleged homosexuals' rights to confidentiality and protection from entrapment.

Protections from Unreasonable Searches

Service members suspected of homosexuality in the 1950s and 1960s often had their rights to privacy violated during investigators' attempts to prove their sexual perversion by finding evidence in their private quarters. Navy Radarman Clifford C. Hillan became the poster boy for this issue in 1957, when he was court-martialed for homosexual sodomy (*United States v. Hillan*, 1957). The evidence prosecution witnesses offered as the basis for

Hillan's homosexuality was obtained unconstitutionally. A shore patrol officer at a YMCA in Norfolk, Virginia, entered Hillan's room without a warrant after hearing the bedsprings creaking. The officer caught Hillan and another man engaged in anal sodomy. The prosecution justified Hillan's guilt based on what the patrol officer saw after he entered the room unannounced, but the military review board invalidated such justification because the patrol officer's entry without a warrant, regardless of what he saw after he entered the room, violated Hillan's Fourth Amendment right to protection from unreasonable searches and seizures. Condemning the patrol officer's unannounced entry into Hillan's room on the grounds that no reasonable cause existed to support the officer's action, the review board (*United States v. Hillan*, 1957) invalidated the prosecution's circular logic by reasoning that, "if the noise incident to a YMCA bed be sufficient to establish 'unusual circumstances,' then every squeaking bed in every hostelry would be grounds for search." In a striking admission that service members, regardless of sexual orientation, were citizens first and service members second, Judge Tyson remarked:

> . . . it is only these rights and privileges, that make up the Bill of Rights, which stand between the citizens of this great country and the Police State—a phenomenon not unknown to today's world. The greatest, most impressive and solemn duty of the courts is to zealously guard and preserve these rights. In guarding these rights courts are not concerned with the guilt or innocence of a particular accused, for our system of justice—the system that has given this country strength, courage, and preserved independence—provides that no man may be convicted except by due process of law. (*United States v. Hillan*, 1957, p. 805)

The CMA echoed the review board's protection of Hillan's right to reasonable searches and seizures in the 1963 court-martial of Navy dental officer Charles Battista (*United States v. Battista*, 1963). Battista was charged with sodomy and inducing seamen who were under the influence of drugs to pose for nude photographs. As in Hillan's case, the prosecution's evidence was obtained in violation of Battista's Fourth Amendment protection from searches without probable cause. After a dental patient complained to the Office of Naval Investigations agents that Battista engaged in an act of sodomy with him while he was semiconscious from drugs purportedly administered for medical purposes, the Office of Naval Investigations agents searched Battista's office to find incriminating evidence. Although they found the photographs to which the victim alluded, the CMA ruled these photographs were inadmissible in Battista's trial because the agents' reasons for the search were purely intuitive. Despite photographs that proved Battista's guilt, because the search was exploratory in nature and made for the sole purpose of finding incriminating evidence against Battista, the CMA ruled that the search was unconstitutional.

CONCLUSION

By 1972, military judges were questioning the UCMJ's criminalization of sodomy altogether. In the only case where military courts prosecuted a female service member for same-sex sodomy between 1950 and 1975, that of WAC Private Carmen Ortega (*United States v. Ortega*, 1972), legal officials debated the limits of regulating adults' sexual lives. It was into this context of legal debate over the extent to which the military justice system should regulate service members' sexualities that Leonard Matlovich stepped in the mid-1970s to challenge the exclusion policy in the public spotlight. Summarily, the history of courts-martial for same-sex sodomy illustrates that homophobia was neither uniform nor inevitable in the Cold War American military justice system. To the contrary, in a stunning admission that homosexual service members were worthy of legal protections from tyranny, the CMA and select review boards dismissed, overturned or reduced roughly half of alleged homosexuals' guilty sentences in the midst of a nationwide epidemic of extreme homophobia in the 1950s and 1960s that left homosexual service members' civilian counterparts bereft of legal recourse to challenge the daily discrimination they faced. Their legal victories at courts-martial laid the conceptual groundwork for the repeal of DADT by acknowledging, on a fundamental level, that homosexuals were human beings equally deserving of the due process rights that heterosexuals enjoyed. By challenging the logic of liability in an era during which most people assumed without question that a person's sexuality could undermine their job competency and character, military courts, ultimately, planted the seed for the idea of homosexual inclusion in the services that came to full fruition with the repeal of DADT.

But even though DADT's repeal was, according to Servicemembers Legal Defense Network (Standifer, 2012), "a significant step toward equality for all who want to serve their country in uniform," its implications for the future face of military justice remain uncertain. Because Article 125 of the UCMJ has been neither revised to accommodate the repeal of DADT nor deleted in its entirety, military courts still retain the authority to prosecute service members who engage in acts of consensual sodomy, although none have occurred since repeal. Nor have the general articles, Articles 133 and 134, been revised to specify what behaviors and mannerisms (effeminate gait, falsetto voice, etc.) constitute conduct deemed "unbecoming" to officers and prejudicial to "good order and discipline," although military members have been briefed on what behaviors are acceptable and unacceptable in the post-DADT services (MCM, Article 133, para. 212, p. 380; Article 134, para. 213, p. 381. The historical trajectory of military courts' prosecution of consensual heterosexual sodomy (even among married couples) is promising in that prosecutions for this offense were extremely rare and limited to those cases where the sexual act was performed in public to the disgrace of the armed forces. Theoretically, if military courts hold openly gay and lesbian service members to the same standards to which they have historically held heterosexual personnel, then same-sex couples will have the freedom to engage in whatever sexual activity they choose so long as it remains private. Whatever the outcome, the continued existence of Article 125 is a telling indication that the surveillance of service members' sexual activities will continue into the twenty-first century, though with a major break from historic trends. Where legal officials of the Cold War era wielded Article 125 primarily as a tool to indict suspected homosexuals, legal officials of the post-DADT future will likely continue to utilize Article 125 for the sole purpose of prosecuting incidents of nonconsensual sexual assault leading to violent acts of sodomy on unwilling victims.

REFERENCES

D'Amico, F. (1996). Race-ing and gendering the military closet. In C. A. Rimmerman (Ed.). *Gay rights, military wrongs: Political perspectives on lesbians and gays in the military* (pp. 3–46). New York, NY: Garland Publishing.

Gibson, E. L. (1978). Crittenden Report (Appendix E). In E. L. Gibson, Get *off my ship: Ensign Bern v. The U.S. Navy*. New York, NY: Avon.

Eskridge, W. N. (2008). *Dishonorable passions: Sodomy laws in America, 1861-2003*. New York, NY: Viking Adult.

Hillman, E. L. (2005). *Defending America: Military culture and the Cold War court-martial*. Princeton, NJ: Princeton University Press.

Lurie, J. (2001). *Military justice in America: The U.S. Court of Appeals for the armed forces, 1775-1980*. Lawrence, KS: University Press of Kansas.

Manual for Courts-Martial (MCM). (1951).

Sinclair, G. D. (2009). Homosexuality and the military: A review of the literature. *Journal of Homosexuality, 56*, 701–718.

Standifer, C. (2012). DADT repeal has less impact than expected, survey shows. *Air Force Times*, 11–12.

United States v. Adams, 21 C.M.R. 733 (A.F.B.R. 1956).

United States v. Adkins, 18 C.M.R. 116 (1955).

United States v. Battista, 33 C.M.R. 282 (1963).

United States v. Betts, 30 C.M.R. 214 (1961).

United States v. Bird, 24 C.M.R. 447 (A.B.R. 1957).

United States v. Davisson, 6 C.M.R. 174 (A.B.R. 1952).

United States v. Goins, 23 C.M.R. 542 (A.B.R. 1956).

United States v. Goodman, 33 C.M.R. 195 (1963).

United States v. Green, 24 C.M.R. 369 (A.B.R. 1957).

United States v. Haynes, 24 C.M.R. 881 (A.B.R. 1957).

United States v. Hillan, 26 C.M.R. 771 (N.B.R. 1957).

United States v. Kennedy, 24 C.M.R. 61 (1957).

United States v. Knudson, 7 C.M.R. 438 (N.B.R 1952).

United States v. Lackey, 22 C.M.R. 384 (A.B.R. 1956).

United States v. Ortega, 45 C.M.R. 576 (1972).
United States v. Rivera, 31 C.M.R. 93 (1961).
United States v. Sheehan, 29 C.M.R. 887 (A.F.B.R. 1960).
United States v. Smith, 28 C.M.R. 782 (A.F.B.R. 1959).
United States v. Warren, 20 C.M.R. 135 (1955).

Formalizing the Ban: My Experience in the Reagan Administration

LAWRENCE J. KORB, PhD and ALEXANDER ROTHMAN, BA
Center for American Progress, Washington, DC, USA

The repeal of Don't Ask, Don't Tell (DADT) is a success story. As of September 20, 2011, one of the most egregious cases of modern day government-sanctioned discrimination has been overturned. But my (Lawrence Korb) involvement with military policy toward gays and lesbians began early in our country's journey toward open service—18 years before the creation of DADT and 30 years before the Obama Administration successfully opened the armed forces to gay and lesbian service members. In 1981, I joined the Pentagon shortly after the Carter administration announced a new Pentagon policy stating that "homosexuality is incompatible with military service" (U.S. Naval Institute [USNI], 2011). As Assistant Secretary of Defense for Manpower, Reserve Affairs, Installations, and Logistics, the responsibility of writing the directive to implement this ban fell to my office. In this article, I detail my recollections from this period in American military history: the codification of the gay ban in U.S. Department of Defense policy.

The repeal of Don't Ask, Don't Tell (DADT) is a success story. As of September 20, 2011, one of the most egregious cases of modern day government-sanctioned discrimination has been overturned. Today, gays and lesbians can serve our country proudly and openly. Not only do our armed forces remain the mightiest in the world, they are stronger due to their diversity.

But as detailed in the pages throughout this volume, the road to open service was long and winding, with many setbacks along the way. To look at the problem from an international perspective, the United States was the 36th country to allow gays and lesbians to serve in the military and the 26th of the 28 NATO member states to do so (U.S. Department of Defense [DoD], 2010). It lagged behind virtually all of its closest allies, including the United Kingdom, France, Israel, Japan, Germany, and Canada (McPherson, 2011). In short, the United States—a country that champions the values of liberty and equality and prides itself on the strength of its military—was among the last in the developed world to accept gays and lesbians into its armed forces.

My (Lawrence Korb) involvement with military policy toward gays and lesbians began early in our country's journey toward open service—18 years before the creation of DADT and 30 years before the Obama Administration successfully opened the armed forces to gay and lesbian service members.

In 1981, I joined the Pentagon as a member of the Reagan Administration. I assumed office shortly after the outgoing deputy Secretary of Defense, Graham Claytor of the Carter Administration, announced a new Pentagon policy stating that "homosexuality is incompatible with military service" (U.S. Naval Institute [USNI], 2011).

As Assistant Secretary of Defense for Manpower, Reserve Affairs, Installations, and Logistics, the responsibility of writing the directive to implement Claytor's gay ban fell to my office. In the following paragraphs, I detail my recollections from this period in American military history: the codification of the gay ban in DoD policy.

BEFORE THE BAN: PENTAGON POLICY TOWARD HOMOSEXUALS

Prior to 1981, the U.S. military did not have a consistent policy banning gays and lesbians from serving. Rather, while service members could be discharged on the basis of their sexual orientation or sexual behavior, the final decision on separation was left to the discretion of their individual commander (USNI, 2011).

This policy resulted in an informal and inconsistently applied ban on homosexuals. For example, discharge rates were high during the relatively peaceful 1950s but dropped significantly during the Vietnam War, when the military's need for manpower reached its highest point since the end of World War II (Manegold, 1993).

By the late 1970s, however, such inconsistencies began to cause problems in the courts. In the years before I joined the Pentagon, DoD suffered two high profile setbacks in judicial challenges to its ban on gays in the military. The first was the case of Technical Sergeant Leonard Matlovich.

In 1975, Matlovich deliberately revealed his homosexuality to his supervisor in protest of the gay ban (Oelsner, 1993). He was discharged later that year. As a Vietnam veteran, recipient of the Purple Heart, and owner of an exemplary record of 12 years of service, Matlovich was an ideal individual to showcase the flaws in the military's rejection of homosexual service members, and his story received significant news coverage.

In 1978, a U.S. Court of Appeals ruled that Technical Sergeant Leonard Matlovich had been wrongly dismissed from the military due to his sexual orientation (Sulzberger, 1998). In its ruling, the court explicitly criticized the inconsistencies in DoD policy toward gays and lesbians, writing:

> But what disturbs us is that it is impossible to tell what grounds the Service refused to make an exception or how it distinguished his case from the ones in which homosexuals had been retained. (*Matlovich v. Thorgersen*, 1978)

While Matlovich was never able to resume his military career, the Pentagon was forced to offer a generous out-of court-settlement in order end the prolonged court battle. In 1980, Matlovich agreed to drop his case against the Air Force as part of a settlement which earned him $160,000 (nearly $500,000 when adjusted for inflation in 2012 dollars; "U.S. to Pay $160,000," 1980). In explaining the settlement, Air Force Secretary Hans Mark revealed the Pentagon's own lack of confidence that it would prevail in the courts, explaining "the Air Force agreed to the settlement because we continue to regard homosexuality as fundamentally inconsistent with military service and wanted to avoid returning Matlovich to active duty" ("U.S. to Pay $160,000," 1980).

The Pentagon fared even worse in its case against Sergeant Miriam Ben-Shalom. In 1975, after her graduation from drill sergeant school, Ben-Shalom told a reporter that she was a lesbian and was subsequently discharged from the military ("Lesbian Struggles to Serve," 1989). But in 1980, a district court ruled that discharging Ben-Shalom on her statements alone was a violation of her right to free speech and ordered her reinstated. Ben-Shalom returned to military service in 1987.

1981: FORMALIZING THE BAN

On January 16, 1981, four days before the Carter Administration left office, then-Deputy Secretary of Defense, Graham Claytor, announced a new Pentagon policy toward gays and lesbians. Exclaiming that "homosexuality is incompatible with military service," Claytor's policy mandated that any service member who "engaged in, has attempted to engage in, or has solicited another to engage in a homosexual act" be discharged (USNI, 2011).

As shown by the Matlovich and Ben-Shalom cases, the military's existing policy prior to 1981 was difficult to defend. As a result, Claytor's explicit ban was intended to comply with the Justice Department request that the Pentagon have a consistent policy toward individuals who admitted or were found to be gay or lesbian. By switching to a policy of immediately discharging all gay service members, the Pentagon hoped that the Justice Department's lawyers would better be able to defend the government's interests in future cases regarding gay service members.

As Assistant Secretary of Defense for Manpower, Reserve Affairs, Installations, and Readiness, the responsibility of overseeing the drafting of the directive fell to me. Over the next year, my office worked on the language formalizing the gay ban into policy. The directive was issued on January 28, 1982 (DoD, 1982). It would stand without successful pushback from any branch of the civilian government for the next 12 years.

The Directive

The DoD (1982) directive justified the gay ban on the premise that the presence of gays and lesbians would undermine military readiness, stating:

> The presence of [homosexuals] adversely affects the ability of the Military Services to maintain discipline, good order, and morale; to foster mutual trust and confidence among servicemembers, to ensure the integrity of the system of rank and command; to facilitate assignment and worldwide deployment of servicemembers who frequently must live and work under close conditions affording minimal privacy: to recruit and retain members of the Military Services; to maintain the public acceptability of military service; and to prevent breaches of security.

It should be noted that numerous government reports dating back to the 1950s confirmed that the presence of gays and lesbians in the military did not undermine unit effectiveness or cohesion (Korb et al., 2010). In fact, according to the Palm Center at the University of California-Santa Barbara, "no reputable or peer-reviewed study has ever shown that allowing service by openly gay personnel will compromise military effectiveness" (Belkin, 2009)

As I will discuss later, however, the discriminatory beliefs codified in the directive were widely accepted by the American public, government, and civil society in the early 1980s. As a result, the directive required a mandatory discharge for military personnel who engage, had engaged, or attempted to engage in homosexual behavior (USNI, 2011). Interestingly enough, it also included a provision intended to discourage heterosexual men and women from feigning homosexual relationships in order to avoid military service (USNI, 2011).

An Honorable Discharge

Homophobia remained so widely accepted throughout the government, military, and society that I was forced to intervene personally to ensure that service members discharged for their sexual orientation could receive an honorable discharge, rather than dishonorable discharge, as recommended by the Joint Chiefs of Staff.

The original draft implementing the Claytor policy mandated that anyone in the service found to be gay would receive a dishonorable discharge. Because eligibility for most veteran's benefits is based on discharge status, such a provision would have denied benefits to service members discharged under the gay ban, regardless of how long or well they had served their country ("Veteran Benefits Explained," n.d.). I refused to support such a policy since these men and women were discharged not for what they did but who they were. Consequently, under my directive, people discharged under the Claytor policy could receive an honorable discharge and be eligible to receive veterans' benefits. Nevertheless, even this was a compromise: my intervention ensured that gays and lesbians could receive an honorable discharge while the Joint Chiefs successfully preserved the potential for a less-than-honorable discharge. Ultimately, service members discharged under DADT most commonly received an honorable discharge while those gays and lesbians in the pre-DADT era were mostly likely to be discharged under "other than honorable" conditions ("Discharge Upgrades," 2011).

A Widespread Acceptance of Homophobia

In hindsight, what remains most striking to me about my work on the directive was the complete lack of opposition to the policy shift. No one in the military services or the Office of the Secretary of Defense privately or openly challenged the essence of the Claytor directive that homosexuality was incompatible with military service. With the Carter Administration having left office, my bosses, Secretary of Defense Caspar Weinberger and his deputy Frank Carlucci, had the authority to modify Claytor's ban or define a new policy toward homosexuals. Neither showed any interest in deviating from the Carter policy. Similarly, there was no opposition to the gay ban on Capitol Hill or in the Reagan White House. When I met with representatives of the American Civil Liberties Union (ACLU) to discuss the separate issue of draft registration, even they remained silent about the gay ban.

In fact, during my time at the Pentagon, only one issue directly involving the implementation of the gay ban came to my attention: the case of Army Sergeant Perry Watkins. Watkins admitted to being gay in his military physical examination when he was drafted during the Vietnam War and was allowed to reenlist several times as an openly gay man (Bernstein, 1988). Looking back on the incident, journalist Randy Shiltz hypothesized that the doctor who cleared Watkins for service assumed he "would be drafted, go to Vietnam, get killed, and nobody would ever hear about it again" (Dunlap, 1996).

Instead, Watkins survived the war, served for 16 years and consistently received outstanding reviews in his evaluations. Yet in 1984, the Army chose not only to throw Watkins out under the new policy, but also deny him his retirement benefits.[1] The Department of Justice, which had asked the DoD to develop a consistent policy, felt that they had to support this policy and defend the Army's position. The Army itself felt that under the Claytor policy it had no choice but to refuse to let Sergeant Watkins reenlist. Our own DoD general counsel supported both the Army and the Department of Justice on these issues. Subsequently, my office could not offer any support on this issue.

Watkins' case went all the way to the Supreme Court and in 1990, Watkins prevailed, receiving all back pay and retirement benefits (Dunlap, 1996).

LEAVING THE BAN BEHIND

The tide began to change in summer of 1985 when it was discovered that two government civilians and one military member were spying for foreign countries. Because all three individuals had a top secret clearance, I was part of a group asked to review the process of granting these clearances. As part of our review, we asked the Defense Manpower Center (DMC) to analyze the issue. By the time DMC finished their analysis, the H.W. Bush Administration had come to power. One of the DMC findings held that being gay not only posed no security risk, but also that homosexuals yielded lower security risks than their heterosexual counterparts. Subsequently, the Bush Administration attempted to suppress the study by stamping it as a draft (Sciolino, 1989).

Nevertheless, the study made its way to members of Congress, and the issue came to the public's attention. Given my official position, I found myself engaged in debate with the likes of former Rep. Robert Dornan (R-CA) and Sen. Dan Coats (R-ID).

Both Dornan and Coats vehemently supported the Claytor policy and argued that allowing gays and lesbians to come in or remain in the military would completely undermine unit cohesion. Dornan was particularly outspoken, arguing that dropping the ban in any way, shape, or form would be Armageddon. Fortunately, he and I were in separate studios during a particular debate on *Nightline*.

Once I left office, I testified in the court martials of several individuals who were being discharged under the Claytor policy. My most memorable military court appearance occurred at Fort Lewis in Washington when testifying for Army Colonel Margarethe Cammermeyer, a Vietnam veteran who served for 27 years before being discharged under the gay ban. Cammermeyer's sexual orientation became public when she was asked about it and answered honestly during a routine background check to update her security clearance. Her commander famously wept when he was forced to dismiss her (Egan, 1992). A federal judge ultimately ruled her discharge was based "solely on prejudice" and ordered her reinstated (Schmitt, 1994).

Even more important than the outcome of the case was Cammermeyer's question to then-Governor Bill Clinton about the Claytor policy during a town hall meeting during the 1992 campaign. Clinton answered that if elected he would repeal the policy and it became a campaign promise he tried to keep leading to the creation of DADT.

CONCLUSION

The 1981 military ban on homosexuals was a product of two presidential administrations from both sides of the aisle. The Carter Administration announced the policy change and the Reagan Administration implemented it. Moreover, the policy went unchallenged by Congress, the courts, and outside groups like the ACLU for an extended period. In 1981, there was no appetite, inside or outside of government, to take on the military's ban or defend the rights of gay men and women in the service. Thus, it went unchallenged because it was largely in line with the views held by civilian government and society at the time.

Thirty years later, the repeal of DADT is a success story. A success for those who served for years in silence; a success for those who championed equal rights; a success for President Obama and a success for our country. This unjust and unwise policy is now relegated to the history books.

Beginning with my time in the Reagan Administration and continuing through my participation in court cases like that of Greta Cammermeyer and the Log Cabin Republicans, I have had the opportunity to witness our national journey toward open service. From my positions inside and outside of government, I have witnessed the principle of civilian control over the military, messy though it may be, work effectively in the modern American political system.

The struggle for equality in the armed forces is far from over. The 1996 Defense of Marriage Act, or DOMA, bars the federal government from recognizing the marriages of same-sex couples. As a result, because many military benefits are reserved only for married troops, same-sex couples in the armed services and their families are deprived of critical support systems intended to take care of our military families. Additionally, women are still not allowed to serve in ground combat, a restriction that makes it much more difficult for them to achieve the same rank and influence as their male counterparts. But for these two movements, the repeal of DADT provides a clear blue print for success: Win the American public, and the civilian government and, finally, the military will fall in line.

NOTE

1. While Watkins was discharged during my time at the Pentagon, my office was not involved in his case.

REFERENCES

U.S. to pay $160,000 in homosexual's suit on air force ousting. (1980, November 25). *The New York Times*. Retrieved from http://query.nytimes.com/mem/archive/pdf?res=F4081EF6385410728DDDAC0A94D9415B8084F1D3

Belkin, A. (2009). *How to end "don't ask, don't tell."* Retrieved from http://www.palmcenter.org/files/active/0/Executive%20Order%20on%20Gay%20Troops%20-%20final.pdf

Bernstein, R. (1988, August 8). A bad deal for a good soldier. *The New York Times*. Retrieved from http://www.nytimes.com/1988/08/08/opinion/a-bad-deal-for-a-good-soldier.html

Defense of Marriage Act. (1996, January 3). Washington, DC: U.S. Government Printing Office. Retrieved from http://www.gpo.gov/fdsys/pkg/BILLS-104hr3396enr/pdf/BILLS-104hr3396enr.pdf.

Discharge upgrades. (2011). *Servicemembers Legal Defense Network*. Retrieved from http://www.sldn.org/pages/discharge-upgrades

Dunlap, D. (1996, March 21). Perry Watkins, 48, gay sergeant won court battle with army. *The New York Times*. Retrieved from http://www.nytimes.com/1996/03/21/nyregion/perry-watkins-48-gay-sergeant-won-court-battle-with-army.html

Egan, T. (1992, May 31). Dismissed from army as lesbian, colonel will fight homosexual ban. *The New York Times*. Retrieved from http://www.nytimes.com/1992/05/31/us/dismissed-from-army-as-lesbian-colonel-will-fight-homosexual-ban.html?pagewanted=all&src=pm

Korb, L., Duggan, S., Conley, L, & Center for American Progress. (2010). *Implementing the repeal of 'don't ask, don't tell' in the U.S. armed forces*. Retrieved http://www.americanprogress.org/issues/2010/03/pdf/dadt_repeal.pdf

Leonard P. Matlovich v. Secretary of the Air Force and Colonel Alton J. Thorgersen, 591 F.2d 852 (D.C. Cir., 1978).

Lesbian struggles to serve in army. (1989, August 10). *The New York Times*. Retrieved from http://www.nytimes.com/1989/08/10/us/lesbian-struggles-to-serve-in-army.html

Manegold, C. (1993, April 18). The odd place of homosexuality in the military. *The New York Times*. Retrieved from http://www.nytimes.com/1993/04/18/weekinreview/the-odd-place-of-homosexuality-in-the-military.html?pagewanted=all

McPherson, S. (2011, September 26). Map: Which countries enlist gay soldiers. Advocate.com. Retrieved from http://www.advocate.com/news/2011/09/22/map-which-countries-enlist-gay-soldiers

Oelsner, L. (1975, May 26). Homosexual is fighting military ouster. *The New York Times*, p. 24.

Schmitt, E. (1994, June 2). Pentagon ordered to reinstate nurse forced out as a lesbian. *The New York Times*. Retrieved from http://www.nytimes.com/1994/06/02/us/pentagon-ordered-to-reinstate-nurse-forced-out-as-a-lesbian.html?pagewanted=all&src=pm

Sciolino, E. (1989, October 22). Report urging end of homosexual ban rejected by military. *The New York Times*. Retrieved from http://www.nytimes.com/1989/10/22/us/report-urging-end-of-homosexual-ban-rejected-by-military.html?pagewanted=all&src=pm

Sulzberger, A. O. (1978, December 7). Court says 2 homosexuals were wrongly dismissed from the military. *The New York Times*. Retrieved from http://query.nytimes.com/mem/archive/pdf?res=FA0A10F73A5413728DDDAE0894DA415B888BF1D3

Veteran's benefits explained. (n.d.). Military.com. Retrieved from http://www.military.com/benefits/content/veteran-benefits/veterans-benefits-explained.html#1

U.S. Department of Defense. (2010). *Report of the comprehensive review of the issues associated with a repeal of "don't ask, don't tell."* Retrieved from website: http://www.defense.gov/home/features/2010/0610_dadt/DADTReport_FINAL_20101130%28secure-hires%29.pdf

U.S. Department of Defense Directive 1332.14. (1982). Retrieved fromhttp://dont.stanford.edu/regulations/regulation41.pdf

U.S. Naval Institute. (2011). *DADT timeline: Key dates in U.S. policy on gay men and women in military service*. Retrieved from http://www.usni.org/news-and-features/dont-ask-dont-tell/timeline

The Comprehensive Review Working Group and Don't Ask, Don't Tell Repeal at the Department of Defense

JONATHAN L. LEE, JD
Washington, DC, USA

In February 2010, Secretary of Defense Robert Gates and Chairman of the Joint Chiefs of Staff Adm. Michael Mullen established the Comprehensive Review Working Group (CRWG) to conduct a comprehensive review of the issues associated with a repeal of Don't Ask, Don't Tell (DADT). Over the next 10 months, the CRWG undertook one of the most extensive studies of a personnel issue in the history of the U.S. military. This article describes the work and the findings of the CRWG (on which the author served) in the context of the activities within the Department of Defense (DoD) following President Obama's call for DADT repeal in his January 2010 State of the Union Address and leading up to the passage of the Don't Ask, Don't Tell Repeal Act in December 2010. It argues that the CRWG served a number of important functions in the DADT repeal process, particularly that it a) provided a rigorous, fact-based assessment of the impacts of repeal from which DoD senior leaders and Congress could base their views; b) developed a road map for a smooth and orderly implementation of repeal; and c) opened a conversation among military service members about what repeal would really mean to them. In doing so, the CRWG contributed to what has been a largely incident-free and successful transition to a post-DADT military.

This article is not subject to U.S. copyright law.
The views expressed in this article do not necessarily reflect the views of the Department of Defense or of the United States Government.

Within the U.S. Department of Defense (DoD) in 2010, efforts and attention regarding the possible repeal of Don't Ask, Don't Tell (DADT) centered on an extensive nine-month study. Secretary of Defense Robert Gates and Chairman of the Joint Chiefs of Staff Adm. Michael Mullen announced that the DoD would undertake this high-level comprehensive review in their testimony before the Senate Armed Services Committee on February 2, 2010, six days after President Obama called for repeal in his first State of the Union Address. Sec. Gates and Adm. Mullen selected two senior DoD officials—DoD's General Counsel, Jeh Charles Johnson, and the Commander of U.S. Army Europe, Gen. Carter F. Ham—to lead the review and to report back with their findings and conclusions. Johnson and Ham's 68-person team, which took on the nondescript name Comprehensive Review Working Group (CRWG), proceeded over the next nine months to undertake what many considered to be one of the most extensive studies of a personnel issue in the history of the U.S. military.

Sec. Gates charged the CRWG with a three-fold task. First, it was to assess the impact of repeal of the DADT law[1] on six criteria: military readiness, military effectiveness, unit cohesion, recruiting, retention, and family readiness. Second, it was to develop recommendations for how best to implement repeal, should Congress in fact repeal the law. And, third, in undertaking this work, it was to "systematically engage the force"—both service members and their families" (Gates, 2010, p. 1).

The end product of the comprehensive review was a 151-page report, accompanied by an 87-page implementation plan, which the CRWG completed and the DoD released publicly on November 30, 2010.[2] Two days later, Sec. Gates and Adm. Mullen once again appeared before the Senate Armed Service Committee to present the findings of the review and to provide their own recommendations to Congress about DADT repeal. In the three weeks after that, both houses of Congress passed the Don't Ask, Don't Tell Repeal Act of 2010 (DADT Repeal Act), and President Obama signed it into law.

In this article, I describe the formation, structure and composition, and lines of effort of the CRWG, the contents and conclusions of its report, and the events surrounding the report's release. I served on the CRWG in my position at the time as Special Assistant to the DoD General Counsel, Jeh Johnson. In that capacity, I participated in many of the CRWG's activities, including the engagement of the force, the development of policy recommendations, and the preparation and writing of the final report.

Based on my experience on the CRWG, I also offer some thoughts on the functions the CRWG served in the repeal process. First, the CRWG helped DoD senior leaders and Congress answer the question of whether repeal could occur without unacceptable effects on the military and provided a common set of facts from which they could formulate their views about repeal. Second, the CRWG laid the groundwork for the repeal implementation process and for the policies that have been instituted since repeal came into effect. Finally, through its "systematic engagement of the force" (Ham & Johnson, 2010a, p. 33), the CRWG not only obtained information about service members' views and attitudes, but also, and perhaps more importantly, encouraged the military to engage in a conversation with itself about what it would mean for gays and lesbians to serve without having to hide their identity. In all, the CRWG's efforts, and particularly the internal conversation it helped spark among the force about what repeal would really mean to them, were part of a healthy process that contributed to a largely successful and incident-free transition to a post-DADT military.

FORMATION

State of the Union and Senate Hearing

DADT repeal captured the close attention of senior leaders within the DoD when President Obama addressed the issue in his first State of the Union address, on January 27, 2010. President Obama had consistently advocated for repeal of DADT during his presidential campaign and from his first days in office; in his 2010 State of Union address he marked the issue as one of his policy priorities and publicly articulated his method for achieving it. The President's call for repeal came in the form of just two sentences: he said, "This year I will work with Congress and our military to finally repeal the law that denies gay Americans the right to serve the country they love because of who they are. It's the right thing to do" (Obama, 2010). In those sentences were embedded several key features of his administration's approach to ending DADT. First, it would involve working with the Congress to repeal the DADT statute—something that could not be done by executive action alone. Second, it would involve working closely with the military. Third, the work would begin that year.

Six days later, on February 2, 2010, Sec. Gates and Adm. Mullen appeared before the Senate Armed Services Committee to announce how the DoD would work with the Congress and the White House in support of President Obama's call for repeal (Military Posture and to Receive Testimony Relating to the "Don't Ask, Don't Tell" Policy, 2010). That hearing is best remembered for Adm. Mullen's eloquent and emphatic testimony in which, for the first time, the senior-most military officer in the United States spoke out in favor of DADT repeal. In a dramatic moment in a full hearing chamber, Adm. Mullen addressed the panel and said:

> Speaking for myself and myself only, it is my personal belief that allowing gays and lesbians to serve openly would be the right thing to do. No matter how I look at this issue, I cannot escape being troubled by the fact that we have in place a policy which forces young men and women

to lie about who they are in order to defend their fellow citizens. For me personally, it comes down to integrity—theirs as individuals and ours as an institution. (p. 86)

Adm. Mullen's testimony came just after that of Sec. Gates, who, in his statement, explained to the committee that the President had "directed the Department of Defense to begin the preparations necessary for a repeal of the current law and policy" (Military Posture, 2010, p. 82). Gates continued to say, "I fully support the President's decision. The question before us is not whether the military prepares to make this change, but how we best prepare for it" (p. 82).

Gates then announced that, "to ensure that DoD is prepared should the law be changed," he was establishing a "high-level working group" within DoD to conduct "a review of the issues associated with properly implementing a repeal of the 'Don't Ask, Don't Tell' policy" and to "thoroughly, objectively and methodically examine all aspects of this question" (Military Posture, 2010, p. 82). Gates explained that this working group "will reach out to the force to authoritatively understand their views and attitudes about the impact of repeal" because "an important part of this process is to engage our men and women in uniform and their families over this period, since, after all, they will ultimately determine whether or not we make this transition successfully" (pp. 82–83). Because of the importance of this issue to the DoD, he said that both he and Mullen believed the review needed to be led by "the highest level officials," and that he had therefore selected the DoD's General Counsel, Jeh Johnson, and the Commander of U.S. Army Europe, General Carter Ham, as co-chairs of the effort (p. 83).

In his testimony immediately following, Adm. Mullen expressed his support for the review process. Even as he so emphatically stated his personal view that the law should be repealed, he noted that he could not yet provide his professional view—the "best military advice" (Military Posture, 2010, p. 85) that he and the other members of the Joint Chiefs of Staff are obligated to provide to the Secretary of Defense and the President—about the impacts of a repeal of the law, and the manner in which it should be implemented.

Adm. Mullen elaborated, explaining that:

I also believe that the great young men and women of our military can and would accommodate such a change. I never underestimate their ability to adapt. But I do not know this for a fact, nor do I know for a fact how we would best make such a major policy change in a time of two wars. That there will be some disruption in the force I cannot deny. That there will be legal, social, and perhaps even infrastructure changes to be made certainly seem plausible. We would all like to have a better handle on these types of concerns, and this is what our review will offer. (p. 86)

With that testimony of the two senior-most officials in the DoD, efforts to support the President's call for repeal were underway.

Terms of Reference

Sec. Gates formally established the CRWG on March 2, 2010, in a memorandum to Johnson and Ham titled "Comprehensive Review on the Implementation of a Repeal of 10 U.S.C. §654" (Gates, 2010). The memorandum instructed them to "stand up an intra-Department, inter-Service working group to conduct a comprehensive review of the issues associated with a repeal of the law" (p. 1). Attached to the memorandum was the "terms of reference" (pp. 3–4)—a two-page document that described the objectives, scope, methodology, and deliverables for the review. Issuing a terms of reference document is a standard practice for DoD studies, the purpose being to set forth in writing what the official commissioning the study—in this case, the Secretary of Defense—expects out of the review group: what issues it is to address, how it is to go about its work, and what it is to deliver.

Specifically, the terms of reference signed out by Sec. Gates tasked the CRWG to:

1. Determine any impacts to military readiness, military effectiveness and unit cohesion, recruiting/retention, and family readiness that may result from repeal of the law and recommend any actions that should be taken in light of such impacts.
2. Determine leadership, guidance, and training on standards of conduct and new policies.
3. Determine appropriate changes to existing policies and regulations, including but not limited to issues regarding personnel management, leadership and training, facilities, investigations, and benefits.
4. Recommend appropriate changes (if any) to the Uniform Code of Military Justice.
5. Monitor and evaluate existing legislative proposals to repeal 10 U.S.C §654 and proposals that may be introduced in the Congress during the period of the review.
6. Assure appropriate ways to monitor the workforce climate and military effectiveness that support successful follow-through on implementation.
7. Evaluate the issues raised in ongoing litigation involving 10 U.S.C §654 (Gates, 2010, p. 3).

The terms of reference instructed the CRWG to utilize a variety of methods in accomplishing its work, including, in particular, the "systematic engagement of all levels of the force and their families" (Gates, 2010, p. 4). As Sec. Gates explained in his tasking memorandum, "To effectively accomplish this assessment, I believe it is essential that the working group systematically engage the force. The participation of a range of age, rank and warfare communities in this study including families, in addition to active outreach across the force is a critical aspect that will undoubtedly lead to insights and recommendations essential to the Department's implementation of any change" (p. 1).

The end product was to be "a Report . . . delivered to the Secretary of Defense not later than December 1, 2010," and "a plan of action to support the implementation of a repeal of the law" (Gates, 2010, p. 4).

In essence, the CRWG's charge was three-fold: first, to provide an assessment of the impacts of repeal; second, to provide recommendations on how repeal should be implemented, should it in fact occur; and third, to "systematically engage" the force (Gates, 2010, p. 1). The assessment was to address the impact of repeal on six key factors: military readiness, military effectiveness, unit cohesion, recruiting, retention, and family readiness. The recommendations were to cover any new or revised policies, regulations, guidance, and training that should be put in place in the event of repeal. And, the systematic engagement of the force was to involve an extensive outreach to service members, their families, and others in the military community on the issue of DADT repeal.

The tasking memorandum and terms of reference Sec. Gates provided to the CRWG proved very important over the course of the review period. These documents, which the DoD released publicly, provided a set of written materials to which the CRWG could turn whenever the question arose—be it internally within the CRWG or DoD, or externally among Congress, the media, and interested organizations—as to what it was the CRWG was supposed to do. In this vein, the terms of reference helped the CRWG navigate between competing visions of the CRWG's proper purpose. On the one hand were some who perceived that the CRWG was only to come up with an implementation plan for repeal; these claims were often linked to Sec. Gates' statement in his testimony that "The question before us is not whether the military prepares to make this change, but how we best prepare for it" (Military Posture, 2010, p. 82). On the other hand were those who claimed the CRWG needed to address the question of whether the law should be repealed in the first place. The answer provided by the terms of reference was, in a sense, neither and both. The terms of reference charged the CRWG to provide an assessment of the impacts of repeal, thus addressing the question of whether repeal *could* occur without unacceptable impacts on the military, but leaving the broader question of whether repeal *should* occur to the nation's political leadership. The terms of reference also required the CRWG to provide an implementation plan that accounted for the impacts, if any, on the DoD, thus addressing the question of how to best implement repeal, if Congress did in fact repeal the law.

Additionally, the tasking memorandum and terms of reference provided helpful language for the CRWG to use in steering clear of the charge of presuming the outcome of the repeal debate. There was an inherent awkwardness in assessing the impacts of, and doing implementation planning for, a change that was not assured of happening and that would be the Congress's decision to make. To account for this, the CRWG became adept in the use of the subjunctive mood and regularly drew on two particular formulations used in the tasking memorandum and terms of reference—adding the indefinite article "a" before the word "repeal" ("implementation of *a* repeal of 10 U.S.C. §654"; Gates, 2010, p. 1; emphasis added) or adding "should it occur" afterwards ("The Review will examine the issues associated with repeal of the law *should it occur*"; Gates, 2010, p. 3; emphasis added).

STRUCTURE AND COMPOSITION

Sec. Gates and Adm. Mullen's selection of Jeh Johnson and General Carter Ham as the CRWG co-chairs was in keeping with common practice within the DoD to have both civilian and military leadership on such high-profile reviews. Both co-chairs brought unique perspectives to the CRWG, based on their respective positions—Johnson as a senior administration official and the DoD's top lawyer, and Ham as a four-star military officer and the top U.S. Army commander in Europe. Both had the trust and confidence of Sec. Gates and Adm. Mullen to address this issue thoroughly and professionally, and to exercise sound judgment in making their assessment and recommendations.

In the days immediately following the announcement at the Senate Armed Service Committee hearing—as a week of record snowstorms brought much of the rest of Washington, DC, to a near halt—Johnson and Ham began mapping out the structure and composition of their working group. They established four functional teams, each led by two or three senior officials from the DoD personnel and legal communities—two- and three-star generals and admirals, and equivalent-level civilians (both Senate confirmed and from the Senior Executive Service). The Survey Team was responsible for overseeing the engagement of the force through various means; the Policy Team examined the policies that were implicated, either directly or indirectly, by repeal; the Legislative, Regulatory, and Legal Team analyzed relevant laws and regulations and monitored the legal landscape; and the Education and Training Team developed training principles and materials. There were nine such team leads in all, selected to provide broad representation, both military and civilian, from the military services and the Office of the Secretary of Defense.

To manage the day-to-day operations, and to integrate the activities of the four teams, the co-chairs appointed a Chief of Staff for the CRWG, Air Force Maj. Gen. Gregory Biscone. A small staff directly supported the co-chairs and the chief of staff, and included legal, public affairs, outreach, and legislative advisors. (I was part of this direct support staff for the co-chairs.) Navy Fleet Master Chief Scott Benning served as Senior Enlisted Advisor to the co-chairs—a vital role, given that enlisted personnel constitute over 80% of the military. In all, the CRWG constituted 68 people from across the DoD and each of the military services—Army, Navy, Air Force, Marine Corps, and Coast Guard—of which 49 were military (both officer and enlisted) and 19 were civilians.

Johnson and Ham also routinely sought the advice of an executive committee, consisting of the under secretaries and vice chiefs of staff of the military services, as well as the Under Secretary of Defense for Personnel and Readiness, and a senior enlisted leader from each military service. The executive committee provided input to, and received regular reports from, the CRWG. Given the central role the military service chiefs would play, both in the debate about DADT repeal and in its ultimate implementation, the executive committee served as an important additional link to the senior leadership of the military services, as well as to the other entities within the DoD.

Although not officially designated as such in its chartering documents, the CRWG took on its name in reference to its tasking from the Secretary of Defense to undertake a comprehensive review of the issues associated with a repeal of DADT. This nondescript name came into being after unsuccessful attempts to incorporate the words "repeal" or "Don't Ask, Don't Tell" in a way that effectively captured the group's multifaceted mission and the still-undetermined outcome of the repeal debate.

LINES OF EFFORT

Over the course of the spring and summer of 2010, the CRWG conducted the bulk of its work compiling the information and materials upon which the co-chairs' assessment, recommendations, and implementation plan would be based. The major lines of effort of the CRWG broke down roughly according to the four teams: engagement of the force (Survey Team), legal and policy review (Policy Team and Legislative, Regulatory, and Legal Team), and leadership, education, and training (Education and Training Team).

In addition, the CRWG engaged in various other information gathering and analytical activities to support the co-chairs. The CRWG collected information on the experiences of foreign militaries and other domestic organizations integrating gay and lesbian personnel, examined other historical experiences in the U.S. military with racial and gender integration, and engaged the RAND Corporation to update its 1993 study "Sexual Orientation and U.S. Military Personnel Policy" (National Defense Research Institute,

1993). The CRWG met with various advocacy organizations both for and against repeal and with veteran and military service organizations to obtain their input. In late summer, a small team of CRWG members and internal DoD experts undertook a risk-based "panel assessment" to assist the co-chairs in formulating their assessment of the impacts of repeal.

Engagement of the Force

To meet Sec. Gates's instruction to systematically engage the force, the CRWG, led by the Survey Team, devised a variety of means to reach out to service members and their families to solicit their views.

Information Exchange Forums

The CRWG visited military installations, both in the United States and overseas, to interact face-to-face with service members and their families. At these base visits, the CRWG conducted a series of large-group sessions, termed "information exchange forums," or IEFs. The IEFs were, in essence, town hall meetings that consisted of a large group of service members, typically between 150 and 300, engaging in a question-and-answer-style discussion with two or three senior members of the CRWG.

In addition to the service member IEFs, the CRWG conducted a number of smaller sessions for spouses and military family members. At the direction of Sec. Gates, the CRWG did not conduct base visits or hold IEFs in Iraq or Afghanistan, to avoid interference with the missions there. But, of course, the IEF attendees at the bases the CRWG visited did include many service members who had deployed, or who were preparing to deploy, to Iraq, Afghanistan, and elsewhere.

In all, from April to August 2010, the CRWG conducted 95 such IEFs at 51 military installations and in the process interacted with over 24,000 service members. The CRWG co-chairs themselves led a number of the IEFs personally, and, as they wrote in their report, "With very few exceptions, we found the discussion at IEFs to be lively, frank, candid, and at times emotional, but always civil" (Ham & Johnson, 2010a, p. 33). I observed many of these sessions myself and found them to be remarkable opportunities to witness the military community openly and candidly discuss a significant social issue within the force, and within society at large. The discussions varied both across and within sessions, with service members expressing views both in favor of repeal, and in favor of keeping the existing policy. As reflected in the final report, several issues were repeatedly raised, specifically a) benefits (e.g., would same-sex partners get benefits?); b) personal privacy (e.g., would we create separate bathrooms and showers for gays and lesbians?); c) standards of conduct (e.g., would we change the military's behavioral standards?); and d) religious and moral concerns. The results of these IEFs highlighted some of the issues that the CRWG would need to address in its assessment of impacts and policy recommendations. In addition, the IEFs served to give service members an opportunity to communicate face-to-face with senior leaders in the DoD, and to see that these senior leaders were listening to them and taking what they had to say seriously.

Focus Groups

At the base visits, typically as a follow-on session to the IEFs, the CRWG conducted smaller focus groups with service members, as well as with spouses and family members. These sessions were facilitated by a professional discussion leader brought in by the CRWG and generally were held in groups of around 10. The purpose of the focus groups was to allow for more informal conversations among service members and military family members than was possible in the large-group setting of the IEFs. The focus groups also allowed for more targeted and tailored discussions of particular topics. The CRWG conducted 140 focus group sessions.

Online Inbox

The CRWG set up an online tool, termed the "Online Inbox," through which service members could anonymously submit their views on DADT repeal to the CRWG. The Online Inbox was, in essence, a web page with an open-entry comment box in which service members could type their views. These submissions were anonymous—service members were asked to list their rank and their branch of service, but the CRWG received no other identifying information. The CRWG received a total of 72,384 entries to the Online Inbox.

Like many such open-entry online comment portals, the inputs varied in their tone, content, and level of thoughtfulness—from short assertions of opinion to more extensive mini-essays on the merits or drawbacks of repeal. As with the IEFs and focus groups, service members did not necessarily limit their inputs to the impacts of, and issues associated with, a repeal of DADT—the subjects the CRWG nominally asked of them. In many cases, they also offered their views on the broader question of whether they thought the policy should be lifted or kept in place, and, at times, about homosexuality more generally.

Surveys

The most extensive information-collecting exercise that the CRWG undertook was a large-scale survey provided to approximately 400,000 service members. Of the various engagement methods used by the CRWG, the survey was the only one intended to obtain statistically valid results suitable for quantitative analysis.

To administer the survey, the CRWG contracted with Westat, a research and statistical survey organization with significant experience serving government and private-sector clients. The survey consisted of 103 questions, which representatives from the CRWG, Westat, and internal DoD social science experts jointly developed. Because of the importance the survey would play in the assessment, the CRWG co-chairs personally reviewed and approved the survey questions and provided the questions to the military service chiefs, Sec. Gates, and Adm. Mullen to personally review as well.

The bulk of the survey questions attempted to gauge service members' views about the impact of a repeal of DADT on the various factors the CRWG was charged to evaluate: military effectiveness, military readiness, unit cohesion, recruiting, retention and family readiness. For instance, Question 68a—designed to assess impacts on unit cohesion—asked "If Don't Ask, Don't Tell is repealed and you are working with a service member in your immediate unit who has said he or she is gay or lesbian, how would it affect how service members in your immediate unit work together to get the job done?" (Ham & Johnson, 2010a, p. 197). Similarly, Question 71b was one of a host of questions designed to address impacts on military effectiveness, and did so by asking how this same scenario would affect "your immediate unit's effectiveness at completing its mission when a crisis or negative event happens that affects your immediate unit" (p. 202). The CRWG chose to frame many of these questions in terms of perceived impacts on a service member's immediate unit, as opposed to the military more generally or some hypothesized unit. One of the primary purposes in doing so was to get service members to base predictions on their actual experiences working within their unit, and less on generalized notions of what it would mean to have gays and lesbians serve openly in the military, or of how they expected others might react.

One question the survey did not ask was whether service members thought the law *should* be repealed. This was a purposeful decision by the co-chairs, as Sec. Gates had made clear that he did not intend for the survey to be a referendum of service members. This decision not to ask service members their opinion about whether DADT should stay or go was a point that critics of the CRWG repeatedly raised. In response, however, the co-chairs—and Sec. Gates himself—regularly pointed to the fact that the DoD does not make policy decisions via referendum of service members. The purpose of the survey was to assist the co-chairs, and other senior leaders, in understanding the potential impacts a repeal of DADT might have on military effectiveness, military readiness, unit cohesion, recruiting, retention and family readiness. The CRWG, therefore, wrote the survey questions to focus on those topics.

The survey also contained questions on various topics (e.g., personal privacy, participation in military social activities) that had repeatedly been raised at the IEFs and focus groups and through the Online Inbox. There was some reluctance within the CRWG to include these types of questions, especially to the extent that they appeared to be based on, or reinforced, negative stereotypes of gays and lesbians. The CRWG chose to approach these questions by asking service members to frame their answers in terms of their own expected actions. For example, Question 90 asked, "If Don't Ask, Don't Tell is repealed and you are assigned to bathroom facilities with an open bay shower that someone you believe to be a gay or lesbian service member also used, what are you most likely to do?" (Ham & Johnson, 2010a, p. 228). Similarly, Question 93 addressed social functions by asking service members what they were most likely to do if "a gay or lesbian Service member attended a military social function with a same-sex partner" (p. 230).

The survey also included various background and demographic questions (e.g., occupational specialty, recent deployment history, marital status), baselining questions about service members' views on their current unit's performance and morale, and questions about their experiences serving with someone they believed to be gay or lesbian. These questions were included to enable more detailed analysis of the survey results.

The survey was launched on July 7, 2010, and was available for service members to complete through August 15, 2010. Initially, the CRWG intended to make the survey available to 200,000 service members; at the direction of Sec. Gates, this number was increased to 400,000. The survey participants were selected at random based on standard sampling methods employed by the Defense Manpower Data Center to achieve adequate representation along various characteristics (e.g., branch of service, rank and pay grade, military occupational specialty, gender). The survey itself was administered online and was accessed via a unique personal identification number provided to each randomly selected service member. The survey responses were anonymous, and the CRWG did not have access to information linking individual responses to the identity of the respondent (other than basic demographic information for analytical purposes). In all, 115,052 service members submitted responses to the survey, a number more than sufficient to ensure statistically significant answers to all of the survey questions. The 28% response rate was in line with other surveys of this type within the military.

In addition, the CRWG administered a paper-based survey to 150,000 randomly selected military spouses. The spouse survey consisted of 43 questions, taken mainly from the service member survey and existing DoD family readiness surveys, plus other questions based on issues raised at family IEFs and focus groups. The spouse survey was mailed to selected recipients on August 13, 2010, and responses were accepted until September 26, 2010. There were 44,266 responses received for the spouse survey, a response rate of over 30% and again more than sufficient to obtain statistically significant results.

A team of analysts, including social science experts from Westat, the Defense Manpower Data Center, and the CRWG, analyzed the survey results. Westat published its findings in a 161–page report, with 38 appendices spanning over 1,600 pages (Westat, 2010). In addition, the CRWG provided a small team of analysts from each of the military services with access to survey data to analyze service-specific results and to report back to their respective service secretaries and chiefs. The CRWG co-chairs otherwise restricted access to the survey data during this period to a limited number of working group members and senior DoD officials to avoid leaks prior to the completion and publication of the final report.

Confidential Communications Mechanism

As a means of obtaining input from currently serving gay and lesbian service members without putting them in a position where they might reveal their sexual orientation to DoD personnel, the CRWG engaged Westat to administer confidential online dialogues with service members. This online chat portal, termed the "Confidential Communications Mechanism," was made available to all service members during the same period that the service member survey was active, from July 7, 2010, through August 15, 2010. Among the questions Westat moderators would ask was whether the service member identified as gay, lesbian, or bisexual (this question was not asked by the CRWG in any of its other engagement methods). 2,691 service members engaged in these online dialogues through the Confidential Communications Mechanism, of which 296 self-identified as gay, lesbian, or bisexual (Ham & Johnson, 2010a, p. 39).

More generally, while the CRWG recognized the importance of obtaining the views of currently serving gay and lesbian service members, it was constrained in its ability to actually do so. Because of the way in which the DADT law and policy functioned, gay and lesbian service members could not identify themselves as such to the CRWG without putting themselves at risk of discharge under DADT. This was an issue the CRWG struggled with, and while there was no perfect approach, it employed a variety of methods to attempt to obtain the candid views of gay and lesbian service members. The Confidential Communications Mechanism was one such method. Another approach the CRWG took was to meet with gay and lesbian former service members—including some who had been discharged under DADT, and others who had not—as well as with spouses and partners of currently serving gay and lesbian service members. In addition, RAND, during the course of its work to update its 1993 study, conducted a limited survey designed to assess the extent to which gay and lesbian personnel would make their sexual orientation known post-repeal. This survey obtained responses from 208 current service members who self-identified as gay, lesbian, or bisexual.

Policy and Legal Review

The CRWG identified a set of policy and legal issue areas that related, directly or indirectly, to gays and lesbians serving in the military and that merited a more extensive review. The 11 issue areas considered by the CRWG, and for which the CRWG developed recommendations, were:

a. standards of conduct;
b. moral and religious concerns;
c. equal opportunity;
d. collection and retention of sexual orientation data;
e. Uniform Code of Military Justice;
f. privacy and cohabitation;
g. benefits;
h. duty assignments;
i. medical;
j. re-accession; and
k. release from service commitments.

These issues came from a variety of places: some were specifically called out in the terms of reference (e.g., personnel management, benefits, Uniform Code of Military Justice); others were raised by service members at IEFs, through focus groups, and the Online Inbox (e.g., will gays and lesbians have separate bathrooms?; will I be able to get out of the military if I oppose serving with someone who is gay or lesbian?; how will my religious opposition to homosexuality be accommodated?); others still came up through discussion among the policy and legal experts on the CRWG (e.g., how would we treat people who apply to rejoin to the military after having been discharged under DADT?; should we collect and maintain data on a service member's sexual orientation?).

For each of these issue areas, the CRWG, led by the Policy Team and the Legislative, Regulatory, and Legal Team, examined relevant laws, regulations, and policies, and developed proposals for how these issues should be addressed in the event of repeal.

Discussions of these policy proposals among the CRWG team leads and the executive committee members were in depth, and at times intense. To some extent, they were also educational, as the senior military and civilian leadership delved into a set of issues that had been taken for granted, or had simply not come up, in an environment in which gay, lesbian, and bisexual personnel were prohibited from engaging in so-called homosexual conduct and required to keep their sexual orientation a secret. These senior leaders grappled with sometimes competing considerations as they searched for optimal policy solutions for a post-repeal environment. Among the considerations that figured most prominently in the policy debates were fair and equal treatment, both for gay and lesbian service members and their heterosexual counterparts; maintaining standards of military readiness and effectiveness; and ensuring a successful transition to a post-repeal environment.

Two of the more complicated issues with which the CRWG dealt were the provision of benefits for partners of gay and lesbian service members and the treatment of sexual orientation under the military equal opportunity policy.

The benefits issue proved particularly difficult because it was not possible, under existing federal law, to resolve it in a manner consistent with the principle of fair and equal treatment for all service members, regardless of sexual orientation. Many benefits, including dependent health care and augmented housing stipends (so-called basic allowance for housing at the with-dependent rate), are provided, based on statutory provisions, only to a service member's "spouse," which the Defense of Marriage Act (DOMA, 1996) defines to refer "only to a person of the opposite sex who is a husband or a wife." Thus, without a change to the DOMA statute or to other underlying statutes defining the categories of beneficiaries, it was not possible to give gay and lesbian service members—even those legally married in one of the jurisdictions that permits same-sex marriage—the same array of spousal benefits as their heterosexual counterparts. The CRWG did not consider it within its charge to assess the validity of, or recommend changes to, DOMA or other related statutes. As such, finding viable policy solutions on the benefits issue that were fair to all service members, administrable to the millions of beneficiaries, and legal under DOMA proved challenging. This subject consumed many hours of debate among the CRWG policy experts, team leads, and the executive committee, without clear resolution—as ultimately reflected in the final report.

Discussion on the subject of equal opportunity centered around how to ensure that gay and lesbian service members were treated the same as their heterosexual counterparts after repeal, and how to provide appropriate means for redressing cases of unfair treatment. The DoD military equal opportunity directive states that it is DoD policy to "[p]romote an environment free from personal, social, or institutional barriers that prevent service members from rising to the highest level of responsibility possible. Service members shall be evaluated only on individual merit, fitness, and capability" (DoD Directive, 2003, para. 4.2). In addition to this general statement, the military equal opportunity policy also prohibits "unlawful discrimination," which is defined with reference to five specific classes: race, color, religion, sex, and national origin (para. 4.2). The CRWG extensively debated whether to add sexual orientation to this list of so-called protected classes, thereby allowing service members to pursue complaints of discrimination on the basis of sexual orientation through the resources of the military equal opportunity program—that is, outside the chain of command—and establishing sexual orientation as a category for various diversity programs. This debate centered on whether doing so would help ensure the fair and equal treatment of gay and lesbian service members, or whether, on the other hand, it might counterproductively lead—rightly or wrongly—to the perception that they were receiving some form of special treatment.

Leadership, Education, and Training

The CRWG developed leadership guidance, an education and training framework, and a set of tools that could be used to train the force in the event of repeal. Early on, the CRWG became aware that this effort would be one of the most important to successful implementation of a repeal. As the CRWG increasingly came to the conclusion that existing policies were adequate and did not need to be changed to accommodate repeal, the need to educate service members about those policies—and to clear up their misunderstandings of how the policies would be applied in a post-repeal environment—became all the more important.

The CRWG's Education and Training Team led the effort to develop the leadership, education, and training guidance, framework, and tools, working in close consultation with training experts in the military services, the service academies, and the Defense Equal Opportunity Management Institute. The leadership guidance consisted of a set of principles describing what leaders at various levels should do to ensure successful implementation of repeal (e.g., "leaders reinforce standards of conduct and expectations for exemplary conduct of all service members"; Ham & Johnson, 2010b, p. 46)). The framework involved a sequenced, three-tiered approach to providing training to the force: the first two tiers would consist of more detailed information for senior leaders, commanders, and legal and personnel specialists, while the third tier would be the mandatory training administered to the entire force. The training tools consisted of recommended talking points leaders could use in explaining repeal to service members, as well as a set of frequently asked questions and vignettes.

Other Research

The CRWG undertook a variety of other research efforts to inform the co-chairs' assessment and recommendations. These efforts included an examination of three past instances of organizational change that were potentially analogous to DADT repeal: 1) the experiences of foreign militaries integrating gay and lesbian personnel, 2) the experiences of other state and federal organizations in the United States integrating gay and lesbian personnel, and 3) the historical experiences in the U.S. military with racial and gender integration. For each of these, the CRWG recognized that the comparisons were imperfect, but each could provide lessons about accommodating institutional change that could be relevant to DADT repeal.

To obtain information about foreign militaries' policies and their views and experiences on integrating gay and lesbian personnel, the CRWG engaged directly with representatives of the militaries of various partner nations. The DoD Historical Office conducted much of the research on racial and gender integration in the military, while RAND provided the bulk of the research on domestic institutions, as well as additional information on foreign militaries.

RAND's research came in the context of a broader update to its 1993 study "Sexual Orientation and U.S. Military Personnel Policy" (National Defense Research Institute, 1993; 2010). Sec. Gates directed the CRWG to engage RAND to conduct this update in response to a previous request from the Senate Armed Service Committee. In 1993, RAND's study, which famously concluded that sexual orientation was not germane to military service, played an important role in the debates that led to the creation of DADT. Its conclusions and recommendations stood in stark contrast to findings by an internal DoD working group during this same period, which concluded that homosexuality was inconsistent with military service (Office of the Secretary of Defense, 1993). Not wanting to create another situation where there was a potential for conflicting reports from RAND and from the DoD, the CRWG was careful to structure its requested update from RAND to be a source of additional input and information to inform the CRWG's own assessment and recommendations, and not a separate, stand-alone assessment by RAND. The RAND study update also included, among other things, a small survey with currently serving gay and lesbian service members, an analysis of possible impacts of repeal on recruiting and retention, and updated research on the circumstances in which gay and lesbian individuals may choose to reveal their sexual orientation to others.

The CRWG also met with a number of internal and external experts on issues of relevance to the CRWG, including organizational change management, military personnel policy, public health, and religious and moral concerns. For example, to assist in the assessment of medical issues, the CRWG met with the surgeon general of each of the military services. Because of the frequency with which moral and religious issues were raised at IEFs and through the Online Inbox, and the opposition to repeal and concerns about impacts on the chaplain corps publicly expressed by many religious organizations, the CRWG felt it particularly important also to directly engage the military religious community. The CRWG co-chairs met with the senior chaplain of each of the military services, and, through the Armed Forces

Chaplain's Board, the CRWG requested information from the 202 religious organizations that serve as endorsing agencies for military chaplains.

Engagements With Outside Groups

The CRWG met on a number of occasions, over its first several months of operation, with a variety of external organizations interested in DADT and its potential repeal. The meetings served as an opportunity to obtain these groups' input on the issues associated with repeal of DADT, as well as to explain the CRWG's mission, as set out in the terms of reference, and socialize the CRWG's approach and methods.

Among the external groups with which the CRWG met were advocacy organizations both for and against repeal. To maximize the extent to which the CRWG could receive information from the advocacy groups—as opposed to generating cross-talk among the groups themselves—the CRWG structured these meetings into separate sessions, one with the groups favoring repeal of DADT, and another with the groups opposing repeal. Several of the pro-repeal groups also helped facilitate sessions between CRWG members and gay and lesbian veterans, as well as partners of currently serving gay and lesbian service members. As discussed above, these meetings were among the methods the CRWG employed to obtain the views of gay and lesbian service members, with whom the CRWG could not engage directly in candid discussion.

The CRWG also met with military and veteran service organizations; these organizations by and large did not present formal positions to the CRWG in favor of or in opposition to repeal.

Panel Assessment

In September 2010, the CRWG co-chairs convened a panel of subject matter experts to undertake a risk-based assessment of repeal, based on all the information collected by the CRWG. Panel members were drawn from within the CRWG and elsewhere in the DoD, representing a wide range of service affiliations, ranks, and military specialties, including combat arms. The panel utilized a standard decision support process utilized by the Force Structure, Resources, and Assessment (J-8) division of the Joint Staff.

The panel began by constructing a model that defined the relationships of the six assessment areas specified in the CRWG's terms of reference—military effectiveness, military readiness, unit cohesion, recruiting, retention, and family readiness. The panel then divided each of these areas into component subareas and weighted them by relative importance—for instance, unit cohesion divided into task cohesion (weighted at 84%) and social cohesion (weighted at 16%). The panel then consolidated and reviewed the material collected by the CRWG pertinent to these areas, and rated the level of risk on a 9-point scale. The panel undertook this process twice: first, assuming no risk mitigation measures (e.g., policies, training, leadership guidance) were in place, and then, again, assuming risk mitigation measures had been implemented. The end result yielded a set of numerical scores indicating estimated risk levels for each of the areas and sub-areas being studied by the CRWG.

The panel assessment exercise intended to assist—not supplant—the co-chairs' assessment of the impacts of repeal. It did so by providing them with additional analysis derived from a structured process that had been used in other circumstances by the DoD. To that end, the panel did not directly estimate risk for military effectiveness—which, according to their model, was the overarching concept into which the other areas fit—but left that overall assessment to the co-chairs.

REPORT

The CRWG compiled its report during October and November of 2010, as the various inputs from the engagement of the force, the policy and legal review, the other research and information collection efforts, and the panel assessment became available. A small writing team produced initial drafts, and the co-chairs drafted and edited much of the text of the final version themselves, in addition to personally reviewing and approving the entirety of the report. Because of the sensitivity of the report and its contents, the co-chairs restricted access to the document only to the writing team and a limited number of their immediate staff on the CRWG. In early November, the co-chairs invited the team leads to a weekend session to review a late-stage draft of the report. Several days later, they provided the senior military and civilian leadership of the military services—the service secretaries and chiefs—with copies of the report for their review and comment. Even then, each copy of the report was individually tracked and hand-delivered in sealed packages, marked "eyes only." These senior officials provided comments on the report, which the co-chairs carefully considered and which, in some cases, resulted in revisions to the final report. The CRWG writing team spent Thanksgiving week and weekend finalizing the report, and it was signed by the two co-chairs and publicly released on November 30, 2010—one day before the December 1 deadline set by Sec. Gates nine months prior.

The "Report of the Comprehensive Review of the Issues Associated with Repeal of 'Don't Ask, Don't Tell'" (Ham & Johnson, 2010a) ran 151 pages, divided into an extended executive summary and 12 body chapters. An additional 104 pages of materials, including question-by-question results of the service member and spouse surveys, were included as an appendix. The body of the report began with the background of the DADT law and policy, the status of pending litigation and legislation on the issue,[3] the mission and structure of the CRWG, and the work it undertook over the previous nine months. It continued with a summary of what the CRWG heard through its qualitative engagements with the force and families—IEFs, focus groups, the Online Inbox, and the Confidential Communications Mechanism—followed by a detailed account of the quantitative results of the service member and spouse surveys. The report then described lessons learned from the racial and gender integration of the U.S. military, and from the experiences of foreign militaries and other domestic organizations with integrating gay and lesbian personnel.

In the final two chapters, the co-chairs addressed the two analytical tasks given to them by Sec. Gates: 1) to assess the impacts of repeal on military effectiveness, military readiness, unit cohesion, recruiting, retention, and family readiness, and 2) to provide recommendations for how repeal should be implemented, should it in fact occur.

The report, while based on the work undertaken by the CRWG, was the product of the two co-chairs themselves, Jeh Johnson and General Carter Ham. They wrote it in the first person—wherever the word "we" appears in the report, it refers to the two of them specifically—and signed their names to it. Thus, the assessment of the impacts of repeal was *their* assessment, and the recommendations on how to implement were *their* recommendations. As such, the report did not necessarily represent the consensus opinion of the CRWG, nor was it the corporate position of the DoD or the military services, but of these two senior officials whom the Secretary of Defense and the Chairman of the Joint Chiefs of Staff had selected for the task.

Assessment

The co-chairs' assessment of the impacts of repeal was encapsulated in one paragraph on the third page of the report's executive summary, which appeared again in the opening of the assessment chapter in the main body of the report. It reads, in full:

> Based on all we saw and heard, our assessment is that, when coupled with the prompt implementation of the recommendations we offer below, the risk of repeal of Don't Ask, Don't Tell to overall military effectiveness is low. We conclude that, while a repeal of Don't Ask, Don't Tell will likely, in the short term, bring about some limited and isolated disruption to unit cohesion and retention, we do not believe this disruption will be widespread or long-lasting, and can be adequately addressed by the recommendations we offer below. Longer term, with a continued and sustained commitment to core values of leadership, professionalism, and respect for all, we are convinced that the U.S. military can adjust and accommodate this change, just as it has others in history. (Ham & Johnson, 2010a, pp. 3, 119)

In the subsequent pages, the co-chairs explained the basis for their assessment. They paid particular attention to the results of the service member survey, as it was the only quantifiable and statistically valid indicator of service member views. They noted responses to particular questions related to military effectiveness, military readiness, unit cohesion, and recruiting and retention. They cited that, overall, across a variety of questions, 50–55% of service members predicted repeal would have mixed or no impact, 15–20% predicted positive impacts, and 30% predicted negative impacts. They also noted that, among survey respondents who reported that they were currently serving with someone they believed to be gay or lesbian, predictions about negative impacts of repeal were lower.

The co-chairs proceeded to explain other factors underlying their assessment. They described what they termed a "perceptions gap" (p. 122) between service members' *actual* experiences working with fellow military members they knew or believed to be gay or lesbian, and the more negative views about what they thought it would be like to serve alongside an imagined openly gay or lesbian service member. To account for the survey data showing that those in war-fighting and combat arms units were more likely to predict negative impacts of repeal than the force overall, the co-chairs again turned to this perceptions gap, noting that a smaller percentage of service members in combat arms units reported that they had served with someone they believed to be gay or lesbian. But, as with the rest of the force, those in combat arms units who did have experience serving with gays and lesbians were less likely to predict that repeal would have negative effects. The co-chairs also noted that, when asked to predict the effect on their unit's effectiveness during an intense combat situation, the number of service members—including those in combat arms units—predicting negative effects was lower.

The co-chairs observed that, with racial and gender integration in the U.S. military, predictions about the impacts of these changes were generally much more negative than what was borne out in reality. They noted that in foreign militaries, as well as in domestic institutions, the integration of gay and lesbian personnel had by and large occurred without incident. They also cited the work of the risk assessment panel, which had evaluated the risks to the key areas of military readiness, unit effectiveness, and unit cohesion to be low, and the risks to all other areas examined to be either low or moderate.

Based on these findings, the co-chairs concluded that the risk of repeal to overall military effectiveness was low.

Recommendations

The co-chairs offered a set of recommendations for how they believed repeal should be implemented, organized around the 11 issue areas considered through the policy and legal review. They began with an overarching recommendation about the importance of leadership, training, and education: "First and foremost," they wrote, "successful implementation of a repeal of DADT requires strong leadership, a clear message, and proactive training and education" (Ham & Johnson, 2010a, p. 132).

The recommendations in the 11 issue areas were reflective of the policy discussions within the CRWG and at the meetings of the executive committee. Generally speaking, the co-chairs' recommendations coalesced around the principle of equal treatment of all service members, regardless of sexual orientation. As the co-chairs wrote:

> Motivating many of our recommendations is the conclusion, based on our numerous engagements with the force, that repeal would work best if it is accompanied by a message and policies that promote fair and equal treatment of all Service members, minimize differences among Service members based on sexual orientation, and disabuse Service members of any notion that, with repeal, gay and lesbian Service members will be afforded some type of special treatment. (p. 131)

Thus, the co-chairs concluded that, in most instances, existing policies were adequate to accommodate repeal and should be left in place. Instead of formulating new policies specific to gay and lesbian service members or to a post-repeal environment, the DoD should educate service members on how existing policies and regulations would, in the event of repeal, continue to be applied equally to all service members in a sexual orientation-neutral manner.

On the subject of benefits, the co-chairs noted the impossibility under current law of full benefit parity. They recommended, for the more limited set of benefits for which the statutory categories of beneficiaries were more flexible, that the DoD review whether such benefits could be extended to partners of gay and lesbian service members, and also potentially to unmarried opposite-sex partners of heterosexual service members, in light of "policy, fiscal, and feasibility considerations" (p. 145). Recognizing the ongoing debate about same-sex marriage in this country, and the pending litigation about the constitutionality of DOMA, the co-chairs also recommended that the DoD revisit this issue at a later date.

On the subject of equal opportunity policy, the co-chairs wrote that the general military equal opportunity policy to "promote an environment free from personal, social, or institutional barriers that prevent service members from rising to the highest level of responsibility possible" would apply to gay and lesbian service members (p. 136). They also recommended that, should repeal occur, the DoD should make clear that sexual orientation may not "be a factor in accession, promotion, or other personnel decision-making" (p. 138). However, the co-chairs recommended that sexual orientation *not* be specifically listed alongside race, color, sex, religion or national origin as a protected class, and that complaints of discrimination on the basis of sexual orientation be dealt with predominantly through the chain of command, as opposed to being automatically eligible for resolution through the military equal opportunity program.

The co-chairs also made particular mention, in response to concerns expressed by some service members, that repeal of DADT would not mean that individuals would have to change firmly held moral and religious beliefs. They wrote:

> In the event of repeal, we cannot and should not expect individual Service members to change their personal religious or moral beliefs about homosexuality, but we do expect every Service member to treat all others with dignity and respect, consistent with the core values that already exist in each Service. These are not new concepts for the U.S. military, given the wide variety of views, races, and religions that already exist within the force. (p. 10)

Overall, for each of the issue areas addressed, the co-chairs provided a description of their recommendations, how the issue related (directly or indirectly) to repeal, and the rationale for their recommendations. Further detail on the concrete steps that would need to be taken to implement these recommendations in the event of repeal, along with the education and training approach and materials developed by the CRWG, was included in the 87-page "Support Plan for Implementation" (Ham & Johnson, 2010b) accompanying the co-chairs' report.

SUBSEQUENT ACTIVITY

Senate Hearings

On December 2, 2010, two days after the CRWG's report was publicly released, the Senate Armed Services Committee convened a hearing to hear from the CRWG's co-chairs, as well as from Sec. Gates and Adm. Mullen (The Report of the Department of Defense Working Group, 2010). At this tense hearing, Sec. Gates and Adm. Mullen spoke to the co-chairs' assessment and recommendations and once again provided their views on repeal, informed now by the CRWG's report.

Sec. Gates began by expressing that repeal is something the U.S. military can do. He said:

> In my view, the concerns of combat troops as expressed in the survey do not present an insurmountable barrier to a successful repeal of "Don't Ask, Don't Tell." This can be done and it should be done without posing a serious risk to military readiness. However, these findings do lead me to conclude that an abundance of care and preparation is required if

we are to avoid a disruptive and potentially dangerous impact on the performance of those who are serving at the tip of the spear in America's wars. (The Report of the Department of Defense Working Group, 2010, p. 7)

Sec. Gates went on to recommend that Congress "pass this legislation [repealing DADT] and send it to the President for signature before the end of the year" (p. 7). In making this recommendation, Gates emphasized the risk that DADT could be overturned in the courts. Over an eight-day period from October 12–20, 2010, Sec. Gates had witnessed the DADT policy be, in essence, turned off and then back on again as the result of federal court decisions in the *Log Cabin Republicans* case (*Log Cabin Republicans v. United States*, 2010). This was a particularly disruptive experience that ran counter to his vision of the orderly and well-planned manner in which repeal should occur. Recognizing that the legal future of DADT was still in question, and that other similar court orders could be forthcoming, Gates told the panel that he considered Congressional action on repeal to be "a matter of some urgency" (p. 8).

Adm. Mullen followed, and forcefully reiterated his view that DADT should be repealed, explaining that this opinion was now based not only on his personal belief but on the information contained in the CRWG's report. He said:

> My personal views on this issue remain unchanged. I'm convinced that repeal of the law governing "Don't Ask, Don't Tell" is the right thing to do. Back in February when I testified to this sentiment, I also said that I believed the men and women of the armed forces could accommodate such a change, but I did not know it for a fact.
>
> Now I do. So what was my personal opinion is now my professional opinion. Repeal of the law will not prove an unacceptable risk to military readiness. Unit cohesion will not suffer if our units are well led. And families will not encourage their loved ones to leave the service in droves. (The Report of the Department of Defense Working Group, 2010, p. 9)

The following day, on December 3, 2010, the Senate Armed Service Committee continued its examination of DADT repeal, this time with the five military service chiefs—Army Chief of Staff Gen. George Casey, Chief of Naval Operations Adm. Gary Roughead, Air Force Chief of Staff Gen. Norton Schwartz, Commandant of the Marine Corps Gen. James Amos, and Commandant of the Coast Guard Adm. Robert Papp—as well as Vice Chairman of the Joint Chiefs of Staff Gen. James Cartwright. The service chiefs were, as Sec. Gates had testified the prior day, generally "less sanguine than the Working Group about the level of risk of repeal with regard to combat readiness" (The Report of the Department of Defense Working

Group, 2010, p. 7), and this hearing was the venue for them to publicly advise the Congress of their views.

The chiefs varied in their views, with, generally speaking, the Vice Chairman of the Joint Chiefs of Staff, the Chief of Naval Operations, and the Commandant of the Coast Guard in favor of repeal, and the Chiefs of Staff of the Army and Air Force and the Commandant of the Marine Corps not in favor of repeal at this time. But all agreed that the CRWG had done a thorough and commendable job, that the information collected through the CRWG process helped inform their position on the issue, and that the implementation approach the CRWG had developed was a sensible way to go about this, should Congress decide to repeal the law.

With those two days of hearings complete, the DoD had completed its task of providing Congress with the views of the senior civilian and military leadership on repeal of DADT, fully informed by the work of CRWG.

Legislative Action

Congress absorbed, debated, and acted on this information over a tumultuous three-week period following the Senate Armed Services Committee hearings. On December 9, 2010, the Senate moved to bring forward the National Defense Authorization Act (NDAA) for Fiscal Year 2011, which included the provision to repeal DADT that had been added by the Senate Armed Services Committee in May (NDAA for Fiscal Year 2011, S. 3454, 2010) and that had previously passed the House of Representatives (NDAA for Fiscal Year 2011, H.R. 5136, 2010). But, in a 57–40 vote, this measure fell three votes shy of the necessary 60 votes to proceed to debate on the bill. Six days later, on December 15, 2010, the House of Representatives brought to the floor the Don't Ask, Don't Tell (DADT) Repeal Act of 2010, a stand-alone piece of legislation incorporating word-for-word the repeal provision that had been part of the National Defense Authorization Act. That bill passed by a vote of 250–175, and, three days later, on December 18, 2010, in a dramatic vote on the Senate floor, the Senate passed this same bill by a vote of 65–31. Four days later, on December 22, 2010, the President signed the DADT Repeal Act into law.

Certification and Implementation

Under the terms of the DADT Repeal Act, actual repeal of the DADT law, and the end of the associated DoD policies, would not take effect until 60 days after the President, Secretary of Defense, and Chairman of the Joint Chiefs of Staff certified that various factors had been met. These factors were a) that they had received and considered the CRWG's report; b) that the DoD had "prepared the necessary policies and regulations" to implement repeal; and, c) that implementation of those policies and regulations was "consistent with the standards of military readiness, military effectiveness, unit cohesion, and recruiting and retention of the Armed Forces" (§ 2(b); DADT Repeal Act of 2010, 2010).

In the seven months following the signing of the DADT Repeal Act, the DoD and the military services drafted the necessary policies and regulations, and developed and delivered training for the force on serving in a post-repeal environment. These policies and regulations, by and large, were based on the recommendations provided by the CRWG co-chairs in their report and the Support Plan for Implementation. For example, the co-chairs recommended that service members previously separated under DADT be permitted to apply for re-entry to the military under the same criteria as other prior service members. To execute this, each of the services developed procedures for how to address the fact that the re-enlistment code on these service members' discharge paperwork would otherwise preclude them from being considered for re-entry. Because the majority of the co-chairs' recommendations were that existing policies were adequate, so long as service members were sufficiently trained on their application post-repeal, the bulk of the regulatory changes in the implementation process involved removing references to homosexuality and homosexual conduct in existing regulations.

Similarly, the training approach and materials developed and executed by the military services built on what had been developed by the CRWG's Education and Training Team and included in the Support Plan for Implementation. In all, much of the time and energy spent in the implementation process came in delivering the training to the over two million members of the military, a logistically involved undertaking.

On July 22, 2011, after the preparation of these policies and regulations was complete and nearly all of the force had received the repeal-related training, and after each of the service secretaries and chiefs and the combatant commanders had communicated that their services and commands were prepared for repeal, Adm. Mullen, the Secretary of Defense, Leon Panetta (who had succeeded Sec. Gates on July 1, 2010), and President Obama signed the certification and transmitted it to Congress. Sixty days later, on September 20, 2011, nearly 19 months after President Obama's call for repeal in his 2010 State of the Union Address, DADT was officially ended.

CONCLUDING THOUGHTS: PURPOSE AND FUNCTION

The DoD's comprehensive review process was one that, for all the time it took, helped ensure that the DoD was able to go about DADT repeal in an orderly and effective way. When Sec. Gates laid out the rationale for the comprehensive review in his testimony before the Senate Armed Service Committee in February 2010, he remarked that "our approach may cause some to wonder why it will take the better part of a year to accomplish this task" (Military Posture, 2010, p. 83). Nevertheless, he said he supported this careful and deliberate approach because of the imperative "to get this right and minimize disruption to a force that is actively fighting two wars" (p. 83).

The CRWG accomplished the tasks set before it—assessment of impacts, recommendations on implementation, and systematic engagement of the force—and in doing so, helped facilitate a DADT repeal process that met the President's and the Secretary of Defense's vision of the right way to accomplish this change.

First, through its assessment, the CRWG helped provide an answer to the question of whether DADT could be repealed without unacceptable impacts on the military—information that proved important to Congress as it made its decision as to whether DADT should be repealed. This assessment was by no means a fait accompli, but came through the CRWG's serious engagement with the survey data and the other information it collected. It also reflected the thoughtful and considered judgment of the two co-chairs, who engaged personally and deeply on the issue. More generally, the information compiled by the CRWG, and summarized in its report, served as a commonly agreed-upon set of facts from which senior leaders in the DoD, as well as members of Congress, could base their positions about repeal. Prior to this, no widely accepted data on service member attitudes existed, nor did any definitive study of the impacts of repeal. The CRWG's service member survey provided this information about attitudes, and the co-chairs' assessment provided a thorough and careful account of the impacts. Adm. Mullen summed up this contribution of the CRWG best when he said in his December testimony, "Back in February when I testified to this sentiment [that DADT should be repealed], I also said that I believed the men and women of the armed forces could accommodate such a change, but I did not know it for a fact. Now I do" (The Report of the Department of Defense Working Group, 2010, p. 9). Similarly, within the Congress, many cited the CRWG data, and the co-chairs' assessment, as providing them with the facts they needed to make up their mind on how to vote on the repeal legislation.

Second, through its recommendations and its Support Plan for Implementation, the CRWG provided the DoD with a clear roadmap for how to effectively implement repeal after the President signed the repeal legislation into law. Over the course of many hours of discussion and deliberation, the CRWG developed post-repeal policies that, by and large, are now in effect across the military. The education and training framework and materials that the CRWG developed helped the military services effectively train over two million service members in seven months.

Finally, through its systematic engagement of the force, the CRWG ensured that service members themselves were part of the repeal process. The various engagement mechanisms the CRWG developed enabled the DoD to obtain the input of service members regarding the impacts of repeal—input that proved very important to the co-chairs, DoD senior leaders, and the Congress in formulating their own views about repeal. Additionally, and perhaps most importantly, the systematic engagement of the force not only served as means for the CRWG to receive information from service members, but also facilitated a conversation within the force itself. The first-order effect of the DADT law and policy was to prohibit gay and lesbian service members from revealing their sexual orientation, but it also had the second-order effect of stifling conversation about the policy itself and the underlying issue of what it would mean for gays and lesbians to serve openly in the military. Through the CRWG process, senior DoD leaders, beginning with the Secretary of Defense and Chairman of the Joint Chiefs of Staff, encouraged service members to express their views about DADT. In doing so, they not only demonstrated to the force that their views would be listened to, but they also encouraged service members to talk amongst themselves. This internal conversation within the force, which took place not only through the formal mechanisms established by the CRWG, but also in the everyday discussions and interactions among service members and their families, helped service members better come to terms with what repeal would really mean to them. It also helped relieve some of the pressure that had built up over the years within the military on this emotionally charged issue.

By the counts of those that relied on the work done by the CRWG—most notably Sec. Gates, Adm. Mullen, and the military service chiefs, as well as many members of Congress—the CRWG accomplished its mission capably. From my vantage point within the CRWG, I witnessed the seriousness with which the CRWG members—from the co-chairs to the team leads to the most junior members—approached the issue of repeal, and did so in an open, honest, and unbiased manner. In all, the CRWG addressed a complex and charged issue in a careful, methodical, and professional way. By providing a rigorous, fact-based assessment of the impacts of repeal, by providing a road map for a smooth and orderly implementation, and by opening a conversation within the force about what repeal would really mean to them, the comprehensive review that the CRWG undertook proved a healthy and productive process that helped engender what has been, by nearly all accounts, a largely incident-free and successful transition to a post-DADT military.

NOTES

1. This law, which was passed by Congress in 1993, was codified at Section 654 of Title 10 of the United States Code and titled "Policy Concerning Homosexuality in the Armed Forces." Collectively, this law, and DoD policies implementing it, were what was commonly referred to as Don't Ask, Don't Tell.

2. The executive summary of the CRWG report can be found as Appendix 2 to this special issue.

3. In the time between creation of the CRWG and the publication of its report, two significant legislative and legal developments had taken place regarding DADT. On the legislative side, the House of Representatives on May 28, 2010, passed its version of the National Defense Authorization Act (NDAA) For Fiscal Year 2011, which contained a provision that would have allowed for the repeal of the DADT law (NDAA for Fiscal Year 2011, H.R. 5136, 2010). That same day, the Senate Armed Services Committee voted to include an identical provision in the version of the NDAA it reported to the full Senate (NDAA

for Fiscal Year 2011, S. 3454, 2010). On the legal side, in September 2010, a federal judge in the Central District of California ruled in the case *Log Cabin Republicans v. United States* (2010) that DADT was unconstitutional. On October 12, 2010, the judge issued an injunction prohibiting DoD from enforcing DADT, with immediate effect. Eight days later, the Ninth Circuit Court of Appeals stayed this injunction. At the time of the publication of the CRWG's report in November 2010, the NDAA containing the repeal provision had not been brought to a vote in the full Senate, and the government's appeal in the *Log Cabin Republicans* case was still pending.

REFERENCES

Defense of Marriage Act, 1 U.S.C § 7 (1996).

Don't Ask, Don't Tell Repeal Act of 2010, Pub. L. No. 111-321, 124 Stat. 3515 (2010).

Gates, R. (2010, March 2). Memorandum from the Secretary of Defense to the General Counsel of the Department of Defense and the Commander, U.S. Army Europe, "Comprehensive review on the implementation of a repeal of 10 U.S.C. § 654." Retrieved from http://www.defense.gov/news/CRTOR.pdf.

Ham, C. & Johnson, J. (2010a). *Report of the comprehensive review of the issues associated with a repeal of "don't ask, don't tell."* Retrieved from http://www.defense.gov/home/features/2010/0610_dadt/DADTReport_FINAL_20101130(secure-hires).pdf.

Ham, C. & Johnson, J. (2010b). *Report of the comprehensive review of the issues associated with a repeal of "don't ask, don't tell": Support plan for implementation.* Retrieved from http://www.defense.gov/home/features/2010/0610_dadt/DADTReport-SPI_FINAL_20101130(secure-hires).pdf.

Log Cabin Republicans v. United States, 716 F.Supp.2d 884 (C.D.Cal. 2010).

Military Posture and to receive testimony relating to the "don't ask, don't tell" policy: Hearing on S. 3454, Department of Defense authorization for appropriations for fiscal year 2011 before the S. Comm. on Armed Services, 111th Cong. 1 (Feb. 2, 2010).

National Defense Authorization Act for Fiscal Year 2011, H.R. 5136, 111th Cong. (as passed by House of Representatives, May 28, 2010).

National Defense Authorization Act for Fiscal Year 2011, S. 3454, 111th Cong. (as reported by S. Comm. on Armed Services, May 28, 2010).

National Defense Research Institute (1993). *Sexual orientation and U.S. military personnel policy: Options and assessment.* Prepared for the Office of the Secretary of Defense (MR-323-OSD). RAND.

National Defense Research Institute (2010). *Sexual orientation and U.S. military personnel policy: An update of RAND's 1993 study.* Prepared for the Office of the Secretary of Defense (MG-1056-OSD). RAND.

Obama, B. (2010, Jan. 27). The White House, Office of the Press Secretary. Remarks by the president in state of union address, Washington, DC. Retrieved from http://www.whitehouse.gov/the-press-office/remarks-president-state-union-address

Office of the Secretary of Defense (1993). *Summary report of the Military Working Group.* Retrieved from http://dont.law.stanford.edu/wp-content/uploads/2010/11/militaryworkinggroupJul1993.pdf

Policy Concerning Homosexuality in the Armed Forces, 10 U.S.C. § 654 (repealed 2011).

The report of the Department of Defense Working Group that conducted a comprehensive review of the issues associated with a repeal of Section 654 of Title 10, U.S.C., "Policy concerning homosexuality in the Armed Forces": Hearings before the S. Comm. on Armed Services, 111th Cong. 1 (December 2–3, 2010).

U.S. Department of Defense Directive 1350.2, Department of Defense Military Equal Opportunity (MEO) Program (2003).

Westat. (2010). *Support to the DoD comprehensive review working group analyzing the impact of repealing "don't ask, don't tell"* (vol. 1). Prepared for Department of Defense Comprehensive Review Working Group.

Outing the Costs of Civil Deference to the Military

ELIZABETH L. HILLMAN, JD, PhD

Hastings College of the Law, University of California, San Francisco, California, USA

Placing the costs and process of repeal into the framework of U.S. civil governance and military power reveals the faltering state of civilian control over, and understanding of, contemporary military institutions. The excessive delays, repetitive studies, and lack of judicial oversight that characterized the process of repeal expose a military unmoored from the constitutional and democratic constraints of civilian control. The end of Don't Ask, Don't Tell is more than a civil rights triumph. It is also a lesson in the steep costs and troubling consequences of excessive civilian deference to the armed forces.

Like President Truman's order for equality of treatment across race lines in 1948 and the lifting of the 2% ceiling on women in the ranks in 1974, the repeal of Don't Ask, Don't Tell (DADT) in 2011 was a historic step toward fair treatment of a disfavored minority of military personnel (Belkin, 2011; Hillman, 2005). Repeal signaled a major shift toward official tolerance of sexual minorities in the U. S. Armed Forces. Military discrimination on the basis of sexual orientation did not end, of course. Federal law provides greater pay and benefits to service members whose families include opposite-sex rather

---

I am grateful for the superb research assistance of Jonathan Estes, UC Hastings Class of 2012, and extremely helpful comments of Aaron Belkin, Eugene R. Fidell, Diane Mazur, Bridget Wilson, Dan Woods, Jean Marie Lutes, and the anonymous reviewers for the *Journal of Homosexuality*. Thanks, too, to Jim Parco for his encouragement. All errors that remain are my own.

than same-sex spouses, and social and cultural discrimination against sexual minorities continues to harm lesbian and gay service members (Walters, 2011). Despite those limitations, the end of the official exclusion of lesbian and gay service members was greeted as a major victory by civil rights advocates (Benecke, 2011). It triggered joy and relief among lesbian and gay personnel, rhetorical flourishes by politicians, and a host of powerful images, including a photo of a female petty officer kissing her girlfriend when the *U.S.S. Oak Hill* returned to Virginia Beach after 80 days at sea (Barnard, 2011; "Sailor's Gay Kiss," 2011).

As warranted as the celebrations that accompanied the repeal of DADT were, they should not obscure what the end of this misbegotten law can teach us about the decay of civil governance over the contemporary armed forces. For the first time in the history of U.S. civil rights, a federal law ending official discrimination was allowed to take effect only after the military agreed to its terms (Don't Ask Don't Tell Repeal Act of 2010). In the past, progress toward integrating racial minorities and women into the military was sometimes halting and uneven, slowed by cultural resistance and institutional inertia (Bailey, 2009; Hillman, 2005; Nalty, 1986). But in the past, executive orders and legislative acts that reformed military rules and regulations did not require the acquiescence of military leaders before they became law. The repeal of DADT required that the President, the Secretary of Defense, and the Chairman of the Joint Chiefs of Staff certify that repeal was "consistent with the standards of military readiness, military effectiveness, unit cohesion, and recruiting and retention of the Armed Forces" before the law could become effective (Don't Ask, Don't Tell Repeal Act of 2010). Thus, DADT, even after being denounced by the President and declared unconstitutional by a federal court, could come to an end only if a uniformed military officer, the Chairman of the JCS, certified that it was a good idea. This is a powerful example of the extent to which Congress now defers to the military—or more precisely, to a set of assumptions about what military leaders need in order to be effective during a time of great operational stress and multiple deployments.

DADT lasted eighteen years partly because of the declining efficacy of civil governance over the U.S. military. Most of the U.S.'s allies left their own versions of a gay and lesbian exclusion policy behind long ago, as civilian and judicial oversight prevailed over the opinions of military leaders (Belkin & Embser-Herbert, 2007; Hillman, 2012; RAND, 2010). The United States is now exceptional not only in the power that it claims for its military, but in the structural deference that military receives from all branches of civil government (Bacevich, 2008). Political reverence for the all-volunteer military constrains debate and criticism of military policies and practices (Bacevich, 2010). Judicial deference to military decision-making prevents courts from enforcing constitutional rights within the armed forces (Mazur, 2010). Perhaps most troubling, given the role the Constitution assigns Congress with respect to war and military oversight, the absence of congressional engagement with internal military affairs has often left little real debate over military issues as critical as whether wars ought to be fought, and who ought to fight them (Fidell, 2010). The Constitution explicitly restricts the autonomy of the military by requiring that Congress declare war and authorize military expenditures and that the President act as Commander-in-Chief of the armed forces (Kohn, 1991). The agonizingly slow fade of DADT, and the extraordinary costs it imposed, reflect the extent to which the U.S. civil government no longer exercises the control over its armed forces that the Constitution demands.

Placing the costs and process of repeal into the framework of U.S. civil governance and military power reveals the faltering state of civilian control over, and understanding of, contemporary military institutions. Even the high cost of repeal pales in comparison to the systemic costs of a military unmoored from the constitutional and democratic constraints of civilian control (Bacevich, 2008; Kohn, 1991; Mazur, 2010). The end of DADT is more than a civil rights triumph. It is also a lesson in the steep costs and troubling consequences of excessive civilian deference to the armed forces.

THE DEPARTMENT OF DEFENSE'S SELF-STUDY: NEEDLESS REPETITION

President Obama brought the political will to end de jure discrimination against gay and lesbian service members into office with him in 2009. His decision to oppose the DADT statute was supported by extensive empirical analysis by U.S., foreign, and international academic and government researchers into the impact of ending sexual orientation discrimination within the military (Belkin, 2011). This data had consistently led researchers to conclude that sexual orientation had no relevance to individuals' capacity to serve in the military, and that open service by gay men and lesbians was likely to have little impact on military effectiveness (Frank, 2009). Official reports included the U.S. Navy's 1957 Crittenden Report, which found that gay men and lesbians were not a risk to national security; the Pentagon's 1987–1989 Personnel Security Research and Education Center (PERSEREC) Report, which concluded that a policy excluding lesbians and gay men was unnecessary and perhaps harmful; and the 1993 RAND study, which concluded that sexual orientation was not germane to service members' ability to contribute to military missions (Frank, 2010). For more than five decades, government studies that found little to justify the exclusion of lesbians and gay men from the military.

Much like the work of social scientists who studied military policies about sexual orientation, scholars whose work focused on the culture of military institutions more broadly also considered the repeal of DADT a virtual non-event. Historian Robert L. Goldich (2011) predicted that the end of the ban on open service by gays and lesbians would make little difference to military effectiveness or culture. In fact, Goldich characterized American military culture as almost entirely unchanged by the integration of various minorities since World War II, pointing out that previously excluded groups "have done nothing to change the austere, isolate, self-referential, traditional masculinity of the force" (p. 68). During the Cold War, the army, the largest of the services and the only to fill its ranks with large numbers of conscripts, was "centralized, impersonal, and bureaucratic" (Bacevich, 1986, p. 119), characteristics that persisted into the all-volunteer army that followed the end of the draft. A change in the personnel rules regarding sexual orientation put none of the essentials of military culture at risk.

The all-volunteer force, however, did put civil governance of military forces at risk. Kohn and Feaver's (2001) pioneering studies on the growing gap between soldiers and civilians in the late twentieth century reached troubling conclusions about the impact of that gap on national security. This separation between military and civilian society served to justify deference to what some civilian leaders assumed the military must want even when the armed forces themselves asserted contrary interests. Mazur (2010) analyzes an especially telling example in her study of judicial deference. She points out that in 1981, the Supreme Court rejected a constitutional challenge to male-only selective service registration by ignoring the military's stated need during times of war for qualified personnel, including female conscripts, in favor of an unproven assumption that only combat-ready male conscripts would be useful if the draft were reinstated. As civil society's familiarity with military affairs lessened, it became easier for assumptions about what constituted military priorities to take hold, even when those assumptions—whether about women or sexual minorities—did not reflect the actual perceptions of either military leaders or the rank and file.

Despite both President Obama's resolve and definitive social science and government research establishing that repeal would have little impact on military effectiveness, in 2010 the President and the Secretary of Defense ordered a massive military self-study, the Comprehensive Review Working Group (CRWG), to assess how open service by gays and lesbians might affect the armed forces (U.S. Department of Defense [U.S. DoD], 2010). Military insiders were appointed to lead the effort, presumably because only military personnel were deemed able to make decisions about military policy, a baseline premise of the exaggerated form of civilian deference to the military that dominates U.S. political culture. As a result, the United States invested tremendous resources so that its military could study an issue that involved neither weapons, threats, strategies, or training, but rather personnel policy and civil rights, political and legal realms outside the military's traditional core of expertise.

The self-study by the CRWG went well beyond what might have constituted a reasonable inquiry into the potential impact of a statutory change on morale and readiness. Its timing, since it was to be completed before any legal change was endorsed, prioritized the preservation of existing military culture and demographics over the imperative to protect civil rights, including the rights of lesbian and gay service members who were serving in the ongoing post-9/11 wars in Iraq and Afghanistan. The CRWG was ordered to evaluate the likely impact of DADT repeal on "military readiness, military effectiveness, unit cohesion, recruiting, retention, and family readiness" (U.S. DoD, 2010, p. 1) and to make policy recommendations related to implementing repeal. The self-study team, heavily weighted toward the senior-most officials in the DoD and branches of service, interpreted this charge as a mandate to poll service members regarding their attitudes toward open service by lesbians and gay men. Due diligence regarding the implementation of a new personnel policy is undeniably both prudent and squarely within military leaders' competence. Considering potential reactions of current service members to potential policy changes was a reasonable undertaking for military and civilian officials. But requiring such a massive, multi-faceted inquiry to precede legal reform—which itself included additional implementation delays in deference to concerns about military readiness—turns upside down the constitutional mandate for civilian control of the military.

The final report of the CRWG itself acknowledges the monumental nature of its work: "[O]ur nine-month review and engagement of the force was the largest and most comprehensive in the history of the U.S. military, on any personnel-related matter" (DoD, 2010, p. 3). The CRWG team grew to include 68 people under the direction of two top officials: Jeh Charles Johnson, General Counsel of the DoD and the government's top non-uniformed military lawyer, and Carter F. Ham, a four-star army general and one of only 11 such officers holding that highest of all possible army grades at the time (Department of Defense Active Duty Military Personnel by Rank/Grade, 2010). The senior enlisted advisor, Scott A. Benning, was a fleet master chief, one of only four such positions in the navy, holding a grade just below that of the most senior enlisted person in the entire navy. The members of the working group were nine top-level military and civilian leaders, the equivalent of two- and three-star flag officers, with an air force two-star general assigned as chief of staff (Department of Defense Active Duty Military Personnel by Rank/Grade, 2010). A navy captain and senior civilian official were placed in two staff leadership positions and led a production team of seven writers, two editors, and four designers. They produced a glossy 260-page final report with four appendices, plus a 95-page supplemental "Support Plan for Implementation" (U.S. DoD, 2010).

The CRWG awarded a contract of $4.4 million to Westat, a Maryland firm with extensive experience in military-funded studies, to run a survey using information provided by the Defense Manpower Data Center (Bender,

2010; Westat, 2012). More than 100 questions were sent to 400,000 service members, an effort modestly described in the final report as "one of the largest surveys in the history of the U.S. military" (U.S. DoD, 2010, p. 3). The working group also solicited the views of 150,000 spouses, collected 72,384 entries from an online inbox for service members and families, held 95 face-to-face meetings at 51 bases and posts around the world involving some 24,000 service members, convened 140 smaller focus group sessions, and solicited the views of senior military leaders, members of Congress, service chiefs, and external groups such as foreign allies, veterans groups, and advocacy organizations (U.S. DoD, 2010). The Secretary of Defense and the Senate Armed Services Committee also asked RAND, an independent research agency that frequently studies military policy, to update its exhaustive $1.3 million 1993 study, in which 75 researchers had concluded there was no correlation between sexual orientation and military effectiveness (Frank, 2009; RAND, 1993). It did so with an impressively researched, comprehensive 444-page report prepared by a 36-member research team (RAND, 2010). Each of these efforts confirmed what was clear from earlier official studies, from the experiences of other military forces, and from existing non-defense related social science scholarship: Open service by lesbians and gay men was unlikely to have much impact on the armed forces.

Even in the data-heavy atmosphere of military social science, the DADT self-study was remarkable. Military leaders in the late-twentieth century sometimes benefited from social science studies about racial and gender integration when implementing changes in personnel policies. But mass surveys of the force were not part of the decisions to integrate the military after World War II or the Vietnam War. For example, surveys about attitudes toward racial integration were undertaken at various historical junctures, such as the army's 1951 "Project Clear," which collected and analyzed information to support racial desegregation (Bogart, 1992). Similarly, in the early 1970s, racial disparities in military justice triggered widespread concern, investigations, and reports (DoD, 1972). Compared to these earlier efforts, the depth and breadth of the CWRG was unprecedented.

In the CWRG survey alone, hundreds of thousands of service members were asked to answer more than 100 questions (U.S. DoD, 2010, Appendix C). These included some 37 questions about whether the respondent had ever served with a person "believed to be homosexual" and, if so, what impact that belief had on 43 questions, many of which invited them to air their discomfort with lesbians and gay men (U.S. DoD, 2010, pp. 180–194). These included questions about whether they would attend fewer informal social functions if a gay or lesbian service member attended with a same-sex partner, and whether they would try to move out of on-base housing if an openly gay or lesbian service member were living nearby (U.S. DoD, 2010, Appendix D). The surveys tilted toward venting of potential grievances rather than preparing service members and their families for a change in the civil law governing the military. No questions, for instance, were asked about the status of sexual orientation discrimination in international human rights or U.S. constitutional law, about evolving notions of equality and capability, or about respect for civilian governance of the military.

Other recent data collection efforts confirm the extraordinary scope of the CWRG's self-study even in a new era of data aggregation and analysis. In 2011, to study the grave problem of sexual assault at the U.S. national service academies, a research team convened 27 focus groups (Defense Manpower Data Center, 2011b). To collect data on the impact of repealing DADT, the CWRG convened 140 focus groups on bases and posts around the world (U.S. DoD, 2010). Ninety thousand service members were surveyed in the most recent official study of sexual assault across the armed forces (Defense Manpower Data Center, 2011b). The DADT self-study surveyed more than half a million service members and military spouses (U.S. DoD, 2010). Sixty eight people were assigned to the DADT study, close to the 80 people working for the 9/11 Commission at its peak strength, when that commission's massive inquiry into pressing, complex matters of national security resulted in public hearings and relied on worldwide research (A. Felzenberg, personal communication, March 15, 2012; Ferrara, 2004; 9/11 Commission, 2004). The sheer size and scale of the DoD self-study, ordered after the President declared DADT contrary to national security interests and years after the Supreme Court first struck down a statute because of sexual orientation discrimination, defies common sense.

THE GOVERNMENT'S RESPONSE TO LITIGATION: OBSTRUCTION AND DELAY

Whatever the total cost of the DoD's comprehensive, nine-month investigation into the possible consequences of repeal, it was dwarfed by the resources poured into litigating the constitutionality of DADT. From a pure economics perspective, this may be the most compelling argument for the costs, whatever they might have been, of the CWRG's massive study. The study did lead to repeal, after all, which finally drained at least part of the expensive legal marsh of DADT. During its 18-year life, DADT led to thousands of discharges, hundreds of law suits, and dozens of judicial opinions (Benecke, 2011). The high legal costs of allowing, and in some instances requiring, that the military separate suspected lesbians and gay men from service were exposed as extremely expensive in studies as early as 1971 (Williams & Weinberg, 1971). After DADT was enacted in 1993, challenges to the law flourished, with varying degrees of success, and the costs of litigation grew quickly as federal and military law regarding sexual orientation discrimination matured.

Once the Supreme Court struck down an amendment to Colorado's constitution that denied any legal protections to lesbians and gay men in 1996, the military practice of banning open service by gays and lesbians seemed a constitutional violation ripe for challenge (*Romer v. Evans*, 1996). Yet, DADT and its implementing regime was defended by the U.S. government and upheld in cases that reached the Fourth and Eighth Circuit Courts of Appeal in 1996 (*Richenberg v. Perry*, 1996; *Thomasson v. Perry*, 1996) and the Second Circuit in 1998 (*Able v. United States*, 1998). Even after the Supreme Court struck down sodomy laws as unconstitutional in 2003 (*Lawrence v. Texas*, 2003), DADT continued to survive against challenges, including in the U.S. Court of Federal Claims in 2005 (*Loomis v. United States*, 2005) and the First Circuit Court of Appeals in 2008 (*Cook v. Gates*, 2008). In *Cook v. Gates*, the Servicemembers Legal Defense Network (SLDN) represented 12 service members in a carefully constructed challenge that was dismissed on the government's motion for summary judgment. The dismissal was based not on new evidence, but on the rationale for DADT that appeared in Congressional findings in the 1993 enactment of the statute itself. Each of these appeals, of course, required extensive briefing and consumed significant government resources.

In 2008, legal resources continued to sink into the DADT marsh, but the tide began to turn in terms of outcomes. The same year that the First Circuit rejected SLDN's challenge, the Ninth Circuit ruled in favor of an Air Force major who challenged her DADT discharge (*Witt v. Department of the Air Force*, 2008). Upon remand to the district court, Major Witt won again when the government failed to prove that its enforcement of DADT served an important government interest. The law was held unconstitutional as applied, since Witt's discharge did not serve the interests of unit cohesion or military readiness (*Witt v. U.S. Department of the Air Force*, 2010). The costs of government ligation related to DADT continued to accumulate, but the statute remained in effect.

The case that eventually led to a federal district court striking down the statute, if only for a few days, began in 2005 and was not resolved until 2012. After a two-week trial at which the plaintiffs put on extensive evidence about the irrationality of the law while the government relied only on the 1993 Congressional findings, the district court found that DADT violated the Constitution. The court issued an immediate injunction to prevent continued enforcement of the law (*Log Cabin Republicans v. United States*, 2010).

For eight days in October of 2010, the district court's injunction effectively lifted the ban on open service by gays and lesbians. Then, the government requested an emergency stay, which was granted by the Ninth Circuit, notwithstanding the absence of demonstrated harm to military readiness under the injunction. In July 2011, the Ninth Circuit lifted the stay on the injunction for a few days before reinstating a different restriction that prohibited the government from "investigating, penalizing or discharging anyone" under the statute (*Log Cabin Republicans v. United States*, 2011). That order remained in effect until September 20, 2011, when the legislative repeal took effect. On September 29, 2011, the Ninth Circuit vacated the district court's holding and held it moot (*Log Cabin Republicans v. United States*, 2011), thus removing from the record the only broad-gauge legal challenge to DADT that actually went to trial and built a full evidentiary record.

The Log Cabin Republicans' case, taken by itself, imposed great costs on government lawyers and resources. It required extensive pre-trial motions, deposition of witnesses, and other preparation for trial, involved two full weeks of actual trial, and triggered multiple appeals. After the trial, the government filed no less than fourteen motions or briefs before the Ninth Circuit, all of which were written after the President had gone on record opposing the policy and after the district court had declared the statute itself unconstitutional based on a full record (U.S. Court of Appeals for the Ninth Circuit, 2011). As for the plaintiffs' costs, $550,000 was recouped through the government's settlement of a motion for fees filed under the Equal Access to Justice Act (EAJA; Woods, 2012). If the government's legal argument in a suit is not "substantially justified," the EAJA permits a prevailing party to recover attorney's fees (Woods, 2012, p. 6). Because the government's defense of DADT was so weak, the United States ended up paying not only its own costs, but also a substantial fraction of the plaintiffs' costs (Bronstad, 2012). Half a million dollars, however, does not come close to covering the actual costs of bringing the case, which was six years in the making. Dan Woods, now a partner at Musick, Peeler & Garrett LLP, but previously a partner at White & Case LLP, the global law firm that represented the plaintiffs during this litigation, led a team of eight attorneys whose estimated fees and costs, even at a discounted rate, came in at more than $3.5 million for nearly 17,000 hours of preparation (Woods, 2012). A full accounting of the expenses the government incurred while defending DADT not only against the successful Log Cabin Republicans' challenge, but through nearly two decades of legal challenges, is beyond the scope of this article. But there is no doubt that it consumed significant military and civilian government resources that could have been otherwise deployed.

Civilian deference to the military thus helped to handcuff not only the executive, but also the judiciary from exercising control over the armed forces. The executive's decision to defend a statute with which the President disagrees is more art than science, but once the district court had ruled DADT unconstitutional, only political, not legal, obstacles prevented the executive from allowing the district court's ruling to stand (Meltzer, 2012). Once the full record had been created in the Log Cabin Republicans case, there was no longer any need for the executive to continue to appeal the court's ruling. The executive's obligation to defend an act of Congress does not require neverending appeals of legal judgments. As Judge Virginia Philips held in ruling that the government's defense of the statute was unreasonable: "In opposing the lift of the stay [which prevented enforcement of the order to suspend enforcement of the statute], Defendants advocated for continued enforcement of Don't Ask, Don't Tell, even though Congress had passed the Repeal Act and Defendants no longer defended Don't Ask, Don't Tell as constitutional" (as cited in Bronstad, 2012). Political theater does not get much more absurd than the government appealing a court ruling that would have ended a legal regime that both the President and military leaders were already on record as opposing. The dismantling of DADT arrived in this halting, expensive fashion partly because of the peculiar type of judicial deference to the military that prevented all but Judge Phillips from getting to the merits of DADT itself.

THE COSTS OF DEFERENCE

The full costs of DADT run well beyond the expenses of litigation (which continue apace as gay and lesbian service members and their families sue for benefits that they are denied under the Defense of Marriage Act) and a redundant DoD self-study. Many of those costs are difficult or perhaps impossible to quantify, including the cost of replacing the labor and skills of persons discharged or voluntarily separated because of the law; the costs of investigating, prosecuting, and separating those suspected to be gay or lesbian; the costs of injustice and infidelity to the honor and higher purpose that service members are encouraged to embrace. One study established a $363 million price tag for ten years of discharging and replacing service members under DADT (Blue Ribbon, 2006). Costs estimates are made more tenuous because of the government practice of limiting disclosures, especially for military expenditures, rather than allowing full transparency (Fidell, 2010; Goitein & Shapiro, 2011). Despite those accounting barriers, future studies will no doubt be able to sketch a more accurate picture of the resources lost to enforcing, defending, and ending DADT.

The costs of civilian deference to the military are likewise far greater than those imposed by DADT. The extent of civil government's deference to military judgment, or perceived military judgment, has grown alongside the maturation of the all-volunteer, permanent, professionalized armed forces. The "uncritical deference" to military assertions adopted by then-Justice Rehnquist in the 1980s trumped alternative approaches, including the "careful, nondoctrinaire approach" of Justice Stevens, who, like Rehnquist, was a military veteran (Fidell, 2010, p.1000). The escalation of judicial deference to military decision-making in the late-twentieth century had a resounding impact on civil governance of the military. It preserved the all-male selective service system, exempted the military from the constitutionalization of criminal procedure, and widened the gap between civil and military cultures (Mazur, 2010).

Since the end of the draft in 1973, the United States has become accustomed to an exceedingly active military force (Bacevich, 2010) composed only of volunteers (Rostker, 2006), many of whom appear frustrated at the moral shortcomings of U.S. society (Goldich, 2011). Critics of the demographics of the volunteer force point out that the burdens of wartime losses now fall not on the families of the U.S. elite nor across the full spectrum of U.S. society, but instead disproportionately on middle-class families, many of whom have sent children into the armed forces because of the economic opportunity the military provides (Bacevich, 1998; Roth-Douquet & Schaeffer, 2006). Defenders of the volunteer military stress both that volunteers bring higher morale and better skills to military service and that conscription is an historical anomaly that the United States has practiced only during relatively brief periods of extended fighting (Bicksler, Gilroy, & Warner, 2004; Rostker, 2006).

The convergence of trends toward civilian deference to the military, an all-volunteer force, and expanding use of military force has pushed military culture to adopt an ever more resentful posture toward civilian authority (Mazur, 2010, 2012). Goldich points out that service members in the twenty-first century military are "people who accept the social legitimacy of violence" during an era in which civil society increasingly recognizes the universality of human rights and abhors physical coercion (Goldich, 2011, p. 62). He argues that U.S. military has become a force of "internal immigrants," persons who leave their families for a challenging life that requires "moral and physical courage" that civil society seems to neither require nor value (p. 67). A sense of superiority pervades military culture, rooted in a conviction that soldiers are better than those who remain civilians because of their intrinsic qualities as well as their military training and experience. The notion that soldiers are superior to civilians was not, of course, invented in the late twentieth century. But the dynamics of an all-volunteer force, coupled with increasing reliance on the use of military force to protect national interests, have exacerbated this aspect of military culture. In Bacevich's (2010) terms, these relatively new "warrior-professional[s]" stand above, not with, their civilian counterparts; they are no longer "citizen-protector[s] of the nation" but have become instead legionnaires of the U.S. empire (p. 240). Civilian deference to military institutions, and a related desire to preserve the good will and continued support of those who serve within them, helps explain why the government appeared so unsure in taking a step toward civil and political equity that struck so many, in and outside of military service, as either inevitable or insignificant. The very tentativeness of the repeal process might well have undermined its legitimacy among service members who see civil society as lacking moral courage and a commitment to principles.

Not all deference is equal, of course. Mazur's (2012) work reveals the high costs of civilian deference to military institutions while accepting the necessity for "professional military expertise" to guide key decisions of civilian government officials related to military matters (p. 156). She considers military professionalism a prized public good and marvels at the extent to which civilian deference has undermined the constitutional dimensions of that professionalism (Mazur, 2012). Rather than blame military leaders for short-sightedness or self-interest, she argues that the absence of effective civilian control of the military is the primary source of the contemporary imbalance in civil-military affairs. Similarly, historian Brian Linn casts the structure and governance of military institutions as contributing to the tendency of "war intellectuals," civilian and military alike, to recycle old dogma rather than embrace hard-won insights into military effectiveness (Linn, 2011, p. 34). He also points out that touting the U.S. military as the best in the world, a frequent statement of both civilian and military leaders, is but a mantra that should not be confused with a strategy (Linn, 2011). Strategic concerns, including decisions about when to use military force and how to meet the personnel needs of the services, belong in the hands of civilians, no matter how powerful and respected the members of the U.S. Armed Forces might be. The decision to end DADT ought to have been made by civilians, whether sitting on a federal bench, in the U.S. Capitol, or in the White House. Giving military leaders an apparent veto over civil law serves neither the interests of the armed forces or the nation.

The operation of civilian deference can, however, allow a political minority to exploit the genuine gratitude and respect that the public feels toward the members of the armed forces who shoulder the burdens of wartime service. Perhaps DADT lasted so long, and was protected so carefully and expensively by a government no longer convinced of its efficacy, because of the influence of a powerful conservative minority of civilian political leaders. Perhaps those leaders opposed open service by lesbians and gay men so tenaciously that only extraordinary measures could lead to eventual reform (Frank, 2009). If so, civilian deference to military institutions was a potent tool used to great effect in prolonging the death of DADT.

REFERENCES

Able v. United States, 155 F.3d 628 (1998).
Bacevich, A. J. (1986). *The pentomic era: The U.S. Army between Korea and Vietnam*. Washington, DC: National Defense University Press.
Bacevich, A. J. (1998). Who will serve? *The Wilson Quarterly, 22*(3), 80–91.
Bacevich, A. J. (2008). *The limits of power: The end of American exceptionalism*. New York, NY: Metropolitan Books, Henry Holt & Co.
Bacevich, A. J. (2010). *Washington rules: America's path to permanent war*. New York, NY: Metropolitan Books, Henry Holt & Co.

Bailey, B. (2009). *America's army: Making the all-volunteer force*. Cambridge, MA: Belknap Press of Harvard University Press.

Barnard, J. W. (2011). Introduction. *William and Mary Journal of Women and the Law, 18*. 1–4.

Belkin, A. (2011). *How we won: Progressive lessons from the repeal of don't ask/don't tell*. Huffington Post. eBook. Retrieved from http://howwewon.com/

Belkin, A., & Embser-Herbert, M. S. (2007). The international perspective. In M. S. Embser-Herbert (Ed.), *The U.S. military's "don't ask, don't tell" policy: A reference handbook* (pp. 59–80). Westport, CT: Praeger Security International.

Bender, B. (2010). Troops to weigh in on 'don't ask' policy. *Boston Globe*. Retrieved from http://www.boston.com/news/nation/washington/articles/2010/05/20/troops_to_weigh_in_on_dont_ask_policy/

Benecke, M. 2011. Turning points: Challenges and successes in ending don't ask, don't tell. *William and Mary Journal of Women and the Law, 18*, 35–84.

Bicksler, B. A., Gilroy, C. L. and Warner, J. T., eds. (2004). *The all-volunteer force: Thirty years of service*. Dulles, VA: Brassey's Inc.

Blue Ribbon Commission. (2006). *Financial analysis of "don't ask/don't tell."* Retrieved from http://www.palmcenter.org/publications/dadt/financial_analysis_of_dont_ask_dont_tell_how_much_does_the_gay_ban_cost

Bogart, L. (Ed.). (1992). *Project clear: Social research and the desegregation of the United States Army*. New Brunswick, NJ: Transaction Press.

Bronstad, A. (2012, March 16). Log Cabin Republicans win attorney fees in DADT case. *National Law Journal*. Retrieved from http://www.law.com/jsp/nlj/PubArticleNLJ.jsp?id=1202546014981&Log_Cabin_Republicans_win_attorney_fees_in_DADT_case_&slreturn=20130006195357

Cook v. Gates, 528 F.3d 42 (2008).

Defense Manpower Data Center. (2011a). *2011 Gender relations focus groups report*. Retrieved from http://www.sapr.mil/index.php/research

Defense Manpower Data Center. (2011b). *2010 workplace and gender relations survey of active duty service members overview report on sexual assault*. Retrieved from http://www.sapr.mil/index.php/research

Department of Defense active duty military personnel by rank/grade. (2010, March). Retrieved from http://siadapp.dmdc.osd.mil/personnel/MILITARY/miltop.htm

Don't Ask, Don't Tell Repeal Act of 2010, Pub. L. No. 111–321, 124 Stat. 3515 (2010).

Ferrara, J. (2004). That September day . . . [Review of *The 9/11 Commission Report*]. *Georgetown Public Policy Review, 10*, 163–168.

Fidell, E. R. (2010). Justice John Paul Stevens and judicial deference in military matters. *University of California Davis Law Review, 43*, 999–1020.

Frank, N. (2009). *Unfriendly fire: How the gay ban undermines the military and weakens America*. New York, NY: John Dunne.

Goitein, E., & Shapiro, D. M. (2011). *Reducing overclassification through accountability*. New York, NY: Brennan Center for Justice.

Goldich, R. L. (2011). American military culture from colony to empire. *Daedalus, 140*(3), 58–74.

Hillman, E. L. (2005). *Defending America: Military culture and the Cold War court-martial*. Princeton, NJ: Princeton University Press.

Hillman, E. L. (2012). Sexual violence in state militaries. In Morten Bergsmo, Alf Butenschøn Skre, & Elisabeth J. Wood (Eds.), *Understanding and proving international sex crimes* (pp. 421–435). Brussels, Belgium: Forum for International Criminal and Humanitarian Law.

Kohn, R. H., & Feaver, P.D. (Eds.). (2001). *The civil-military gap and American national security*. Cambridge, MA: MIT Press.

Kohn, R. H. (Ed.). (1991). *The United States military under the Constitution of the United States, 1789–1989*. New York, NY: New York University Press.

Lawrence v. Texas, 539 U.S. 558 (2003).

Linn, B. M. (2011). The U.S. armed forces' view of war. *Daedalus, 140*(3), 33–44.

Log Cabin Republicans v. United States, 658 F.3d 1162 (9th Cir. 2011).

Log Cabin Republicans v. United States, 716 F. Supp. 2d 884, 927 (C.D. Cal. 2010).

Loomis v. United States, 68 Fed. Cl. 503 (2005).

Mazur, D. H. (2012). The constitutional bond in military professionalism: A reply to Professor Deborah Pearlstein. *Texas Law Review, 90*(4), 145–156.

Mazur, D. H. (2010). *A more perfect military: How the Constitution can make our military stronger*. New York, NY: Oxford University Press.

Meltzer, D. J. (2012). Executive defense of congressional acts. *Duke Law Journal, 61*, 1183–1235.

Nalty, B. (1986). *Strength for the fight: A history of Black Americans in the military*. New York, NY: The Free Press.

9/11 Commission. (2004). Retrieved from http://www.gpo.gov/fdsys/pkg/GPO-911REPORT/pdf/GPO-911REPORT.pdf

RAND. (1993). *Sexual orientation and U.S. military personnel policy*. Santa Monica, CA: National Defense Research Institute.

RAND. (2010). *Sexual orientation and U.S. military personnel policy: An update of RAND's 1993 study*. Washington, DC: National Defense Research Institute.

Richenberg v. Perry, 97 F.3d 256 (1996).

Romer v. Evans, 517 U.S. 620 (1996).

Rostker, B. R. (2006). *I want you! The evolution of the all-volunteer force*. Santa Monica, CA: RAND.

Roth-Douquet, K., & Schaeffer, F. (2006). *AWOL: The unexcused absence of America's upper classes from our military—And how it hurts our country*. New York, NY: HarperCollins.

Sailor's gay kiss is a milepost on a long road of change. (2011, December 24). *L.A. Times* [Editorial]. Retrieved from http://articles.latimes.com/2011/dec/23/opinion/la-ed-army-20111223

Thomasson v. Perry, 80 F.3d 915 (1996).

U.S. Department of Defense. (1972). *Report of the Task Force on the Administration of Justice within the Armed Forces*. Washington, DC.

U.S. Department of Defense. (2010). *Report of the comprehensive review of the issues associated with "don't ask, don't tell."* Retrieved from http://www.defense.gov/home/features/2010/0610_dadt/DADTReport_FINAL_20101130(secure-hires).pdf

Walters, S. D. (2011). The few, the proud, the gay: Don't ask, don't tell and the trap of tolerance. *William and Mary Journal of Women and the Law, 18*, 87–114.

Westat. (2012). *Military and veterans*. Retrieved from http://www.westat.com/Westat/expertise/military_and_veterans/index.cfm

Williams, C., & Weinberg, M. (1971). *Homosexuals and the military*. New York, NY: Harper & Row.

Witt v. Department of the Air Force, 527 F.3d 806 (9th Cir., 2008).

Witt v. U.S. Department of the Air Force, 739 F. Supp. 2d 1308, 1316 (W.D. Wash., 2010).

Woods, D. (2012). *Motion for award of attorneys' fees and expenses pursuant to (1) The Equal Access to Justice Act (28 U.S.C. § 2412) and (2) Fed. R. Civ. P. 37; memorandum of points and authorities in support thereof*. [On file with the author, with email update re settlement dated May 30, 2012].

U.S. Court of Appeals for the Ninth Circuit. (2011). Retrieved from http://www.ca9.uscourts.gov/content/view.php?pk_id=0000000492

Gays in the U.S. Military: Reviewing the Research and Conceptualizing a Way Forward

ARMANDO X. ESTRADA, PhD, GIA A. DIROSA, MS, and ARWEN H. DECOSTANZA, PhD

U.S. Army Research Institute for the Behavioral and Social Sciences, Aberdeen Proving Grounds, Maryland, USA

This article contributes to ongoing discussions related to the challenges and opportunities associated with the participation and inclusion of openly gay service personnel within the U.S. military. The article reviews research related to sexual orientation and military service and outlines a theory of the antecedents and outcomes of open integration of gays in the military environment. We discuss implications of this theory for future research in this area.

Gay service personnel[1] have served honorably in the U.S. military in just about every major conflict and war dating back to the American Revolutionary War (Berube, 1990; Shilts, 1993). However, they have had to remain silent and even lie about their sexual orientation because exclusionary policies did not allow them to be open and honest about their sexual orientation (10 U.S.C. § 654). Gay service personnel were often discriminated against, systematically persecuted, and promptly separated from the military whenever their sexual orientation became public (Chauncey, 1989; Haggerty, 2003; Murphy, 1988; Shilts, 1993). This situation changed on December 22, 2010, when President Barack Obama signed the Don't

---

This article is not subject to U.S. copyright law.

All authors are part of the Foundational Science Research Unit at Aberdeen Proving Grounds, Maryland. The views expressed in this article are those of the authors and do not necessarily reflect the official policy or position of the Department of the Army, the Department of Defense or the U.S. Government.

Ask, Don't Tell Repeal Act of 2010, which effectively eliminated all restrictions prohibiting gay individuals from serving openly in the U.S. military (HR 2965; S4023).

This article is intended to contribute to ongoing discussions related to the challenges and opportunities associated with the participation and inclusion of openly gay service personnel within the U.S. military. We review empirical research on sexual orientation and military service and outline a theory of the antecedents and outcomes of the participation and inclusion of gay service personnel within the military environment. The theory specifies individual, occupational-organizational, and societal factors that are posited to influence the participation and inclusion of openly gay service personnel within the military environment (Estrada, 2012). The theory also specifies individual, group/unit, and organizational outcomes associated with the participation and inclusion of openly gay service personnel within the military environment. We conclude with a discussion of the implications of the proposed theory for future research involving the integration of gay service personnel within the military environment.

CONTEMPORARY RESEARCH ON GAYS IN THE U.S. MILITARY

Research on gay service personnel within the U.S. military is quite limited and narrowly focused on issues involving the acceptance of gay individuals; the compatibility of gay individuals with the organizational culture and values of the U.S. military; and the perceived impact that the integration of gay service personnel may have on unit cohesion, readiness, and effectiveness.

Acceptance of Gay Service Personnel

Issues concerning the acceptance of gay service personnel within the U.S. military have been addressed in a various public and military opinion polls (see Tables 1 and 2). Data from public opinion polls indicate that a majority of Americans are in favor of allowing gay individuals to serve in the U.S. Armed Forces (U.S. Department of Defense [DoD], 2010a; National Defense Research Institute [NDRI], 1993, 2010; Torres-Reyna & Shapiro, 2002; Yang, 1997). Examples can be gleaned from public opinion polls conducted by the Gallup Organization (1977–2001) showing that 50–70% of Americans believe that homosexuals should be hired for the armed forces (Torres-Reyna & Shapiro, 2002; Yang, 1997); and in public opinion polls conducted between 1994 and 2010 by the Pew Center for the People and the Press (2010) showing that 50–60% of Americans favor allowing gay and lesbians to serve openly in the U.S. military (Pew Center for the People and the Press, 2010). While it is clear that a majority of Americans appear to support gays in the military (see Table 1), support for gays in the military tends to be higher

TABLE 1 Public Opinion Polls on Gays in the Military

Source	Sample size	Survey question	Result
ABC News/Washington Post (1993)	549	Do you think homosexuals should or should not be allowed to serve in the military?	47% should, 47% should not
American National Election Studies (NES) (1993)	750	Do you think homosexuals should be allowed to serve in the United States Armed Forces, or don't you think so?	59% should, 36% should not
CBS News/The New York Times (1993)	1,179	Do you favor or oppose permitting homosexuals to serve in the military?	42% favor, 48% oppose
Gallup (1993)	1,011	Is [DADT] a plan you would support or oppose?	58% support, 37% oppose
LA Times (1993)	1,474	Do you approve is disapprove of allowing openly homosexual men and women to serve in the armed forces of the United States?	41% approve, 52% disapprove
NBC News/The Wall St. Journal (1993)	751	Do you think homosexuals should or should not be hired for . . . the armed forces?	47% should, 43% should not
	1,502	Do you favor or oppose permitting openly gays or lesbians to serve in the military?	43% favor, 49% oppose
Princeton Survey Research Associates (PSRA) for Newsweek (1993)	750	Do you think homosexuals should or should not be able to serve in the armed forces?	48% should, 43% should not
Yankelovich Partners (1993)	1,800	Do you favor or oppose Bill Clinton's plan to allow gays and lesbians to serve in the United States military?	43% favor, 48% oppose
Gallup (1994)	1,013	Is [DADT] a plan you would support or oppose?	60% support, 36% oppose
Princeton (1994)	750	Do you think homosexuals should or should not be hired for . . . the armed forces?	58% should, 35% should not
Yankelovich, Skelly, & White (1994)	800	Do you favor or oppose permitting openly gays or lesbians to serve in the military?	53% favor, 41% oppose
Gallup (1996)	1,003	Do you think homosexuals should or should not be hired for . . . the armed forces?	65% should, 29% should not
NES (1996)	1,534	Do you think homosexuals should be allowed to serve in the United States Armed Forces, or don't you think so?	66% should, 30% should not
PSRA/Newsweek (1998)	602	Please tell me if you think gays and lesbians should or should not be hired for . . . the armed forces?	66% should, 30% should not

(Continued)

TABLE 1 (Continued)

Source	Sample size	Survey question	Result
Yankelovich, Skelly, & White (1998)	1,036	Do you favor or oppose permitting openly gays or lesbians to serve in the military?	52% favor, 39% oppose
Gallup (1999)	1,054	Do you think homosexuals should or should not be hired for . . . the armed forces?	70% should, 26% should not
ABC/WP (2000)	1,007	Do you think homosexuals should or should not be allowed to serve in the military?	67% should, 29% should not
PSRA/Newsweek (2000)	803	Please tell me if you think gays and lesbians should or should not be hired for . . . the armed forces?	69% should, 25% should not
Gallup (2001)	1,012	Should homosexuals be employed in . . . the armed forces?	72% should
Fox News (2003)	900	Do you favor or oppose . . . allowing gays and lesbians to serve openly in the military?	64% favor, 25% oppose
Gallup (2003)	1,014	Do you think homosexuals should or should not be hired for . . . the armed forces?	80% should
Gallup (2004)	1,015	Do you favor or oppose allowing openly gay men and lesbian women to serve in the military?	63% favor
Boston Globe (2005)	760	Do you think gays and lesbians should be allowed to serve openly in the United States military?	79% yes, 18% no
Gallup (2005)	1,005	Should homosexuals be hired for . . . the armed forces?	76% yes, 22% no
Pew Research Center (2006)	695	Please tell me whether you strongly favor, favor, oppose, or strongly oppose allowing gays to serve openly in the military	60% favor, 32% oppose
CNN (2007)	1,029	Do you favor or oppose the plan in which the U.S. military does not ask new recruits whether they are homosexual, but would still prohibit homosexuals from serving if they reveal their sexual orientation?	38% favor, 57% oppose
	1,028	Do you think people who are openly gay or homosexual should or should not be allowed to serve in the U.S. military?	79% should, 18% should not

Newsweek (2007)	1,001	Do you think gays and lesbians should or should NOT be able to serve openly in the military?	63% should, 28% should not
ABC/WP (2008)	1,119	Do you think homosexuals who do NOT publicly disclose their sexual orientation should be allowed to serve in the military or not?	78% yes, 18% no
		Do you think homosexuals who DO publicly disclose their sexual orientation should be allowed to serve in the military or not?	75% yes, 22% no
CNN (2008)	1,013	Do you think people who are openly gay or homosexual should or should not be allowed to serve in the U.S. military?	81% should, 17% should not
Newsweek (2008)	1,006	Do you think there should or should NOT be gays and lesbians serving openly in the military?	66% should, 29% should not
CNN (2009)	1,014	Do you favor, or oppose the policy sometimes called "Don't Ask, Don't Tell" in which the U.S. military does not ask new recruits whether they are gay or lesbian, but prohibits gays and lesbians from serving in the military if they reveal their sexual orientation?	48% favor, 47% oppose
Democracy Corps (2009)	847	Federal law currently prohibits openly gay men and women from serving in the military. Do you think this law should be repealed or not?	55% yes, 35% no
Gallup (2009)	1,015	Do you favor or oppose allowing openly gay men and lesbian women to serve in the military	69% favor
Quinnipiac (2009)	2,041	Federal law currently prohibits openly gay men and women from serving in the military. Do you think this law should be repealed or not?	56% yes, 37% no
ABC/WP (2010)	1,004	Do you think homosexuals who do NOT publicly disclose their sexual orientation should be allowed to serve in the military or not?	83% yes, 15% no
		Do you think homosexuals who DO publicly disclose their sexual orientation should be allowed to serve in the military or not?	75% yes, 24% no
CBS/The New York Times (2010)	1,084	Do you favor or oppose homosexuals serving in the military?	59% favor, 29% oppose

(Continued)

TABLE 1 (Continued)

Source	Sample size	Survey question	Result
CNN (2010)	1,023	Should homosexuals be allowed to serve *openly* in the military?	44% favor, 42% oppose
Fox News (2010)	900	Do you favor or oppose permitting people who are openly gay or lesbian to serve in the military?	69% favor, 27% oppose
Gallup (2010)	1,029	Do you favor or oppose allowing gays and lesbians to serve openly in the military?	61% favor, 30% oppose
McClatchy-Marist (2010)	810 adults	Do you favor or oppose allowing openly gay men and lesbian women to serve in the military	70% favor, 25% oppose
		Do you think the current Democratic Congress should repeal the "Don't Ask, Don't Tell" policy, and allow gay men and women to serve openly in the military or do you think they should not repeal it so they continue to serve but not openly?	47% should repeal, 48% should not
NBC/WSJ (2010)	1,000	Let me read you three statements about gay men and women serving in the military, and please tell me which one comes closest to your point of view.	50% favor allowing to serve, 38% favor under DADT policy, 10% oppose allowing to serve
Pew Research Center (2010)	1,500	Do you strongly favor, favor, oppose, or strongly oppose allowing gays and lesbians to serve openly in the military?	59% favor, 24% oppose
Quinnipiac University (2010)	2,424	Federal law currently prohibits openly gay men and women from serving in the military. Do you think this law should be repealed or not?	58% should be repealed, 34% should not be repealed
CBS News (2011)	1,012	Should gays and lesbians be able to serve openly in the military?	68% favor, 22% oppose

TABLE 2 Military Opinion Polls on Gays in the Military

Source	Sample	Survey Question	Result
Healy (1993)	2,346 Enlisted Men/Women	How do you feel about lifting the ban on gays in the armed forces?	74% oppose 76% men/55% women
Miller (1994)	1943 Male Army Soldiers 1606 Female Army Soldiers	Gay and Lesbians should be allowed to enter and remain in the military.	75% men oppose 43% women oppose
U.S. Air Force Poll (Miller, 1994)	800 Enlisted Air Force Personnel	How do you feel about the current policy of separating known homosexuals or discharging people who state they are homosexuals?	67% support policy
Cleveland & Ohl (1994)	605 Naval Officers	Homosexuals should not be restricted from serving anywhere in the Navy.	75% favor restriction
Friery (1997)	298 Naval Officers	Homosexuals should not be restricted from serving anywhere in the Navy.	66% favor restriction
Estrada & Weiss (1999)	72 Marine Reservists	I feel that the ban on homosexuals in the armed forces should be lifted.	75% favor ban
Triangle Institute for Security Studies 1998–1999 (Miller & Williams, 2001)	2,901 Officers	Do you think gay men and lesbians should be allowed to serve in the military?	73% favor restrictions
Annenberg Public Policy Center (2004)	655 Service Personnel/Family Member on Active Duty from February—October 2004	Should gays and lesbians be allowed to serve openly in the military or shouldn't they be allowed to serve openly?	50% of active duty oppose Open Service 57% of Reserve/Guard opposed open service
Rodgers (2006)	545 U.S. Service Members	Do you agree or disagree with allowing gays and lesbians to serve openly in the military?	37% oppose open service
McGarry (2010)	3,000 Active Duty Personnel	Do you favor or oppose allowing gays to serve openly in military?	51% oppose open service
Navy Postgraduate School (2010)	383 Naval Officers, 91 Marine Corps Officers	Gays and lesbians should be allowed to serve openly in our military.	40% of Navy officers disagree; 54% of Marine officers disagree
Vet Voice Foundation (2010)	510 Iraq/Afghanistan Veterans	Do you favor or oppose allowing openly gay men and lesbian women to serve in the military?	36% oppose

Note. Data compiled from Estrada, 2012.

when polls ask whether gays should be allowed to serve versus whether gays should be allowed to serve openly (DoD, 2010a; NDRI, 2010).

Data from military opinion polls on gays in the military is quite limited and not as methodologically sophisticated as those from public opinion polls (DoD, 2010a; Sinclair, 2009). Surveys conducted in the 1990s reveal that large percentages of military respondents expressed disapproval or opposition toward removing the ban on homosexuals in the armed forces (see Table 2). Illustrative examples of this finding can be observed in studies reported by Miller (1994) where 75% of male soldiers and 43% of female soldiers disagreed or strongly disagreed with the statement that "gays and lesbians should be allowed to enter and remain in the military" (p. 70); Cleveland and Ohls (1994, p. 88) and Friery (1997, p. 74), where 60–70% of Naval officers disagreed/strongly disagreed that "homosexuals should not be restricted from serving anywhere in the Navy;" and Estrada and Weiss (1999), where 72% of Marine reservists disagreed/strongly disagreed with the statement that "I feel that the ban on homosexuals in the armed forces should be lifted" (p. 89).

However, studies conducted in the 2000s reveal that 40–60% of military respondent's disapprove or oppose allowing gays in the military as compared with 60–70% who expressed such views in the 1990s (see Table 2). Illustrative examples of this finding can be observed in studies conducted by the Annenberg Public Policy Center (2004), where 50% of active duty and 57% of Reserve and National Guard respondents thought gays and lesbians should not be allowed to serve openly; Zogby International (Rodgers, 2006) where 37% of military respondents disagreed or strongly disagreed that gays and lesbians be allowed to serve openly in the military; and the *Military Times* (McGarry, 2010), where 51% of military respondents opposed or strongly opposed allowing gays to serve openly in the military. While it is important to acknowledge that none of these studies include data from large probability based samples that are representative of the U.S. military population (DoD, 2010a; Sinclair, 2009), the converging evidence does suggest that military opinion appears to be more tolerant today than it was in the 1990s (see Table 2).

Research on the correlates of military personnel's attitudes toward gays in the military has shown that negative attitudes appear to be associated with certain demographic (e.g., gender, race and ethnicity, religious and political ideology, interpersonal contact) and military characteristics (e.g., rank, years of service, military occupation). Specifically, research shows that male military personnel tend to disapprove or oppose gays in the military to a greater extent than female military personnel (Healy, 1993; Miller, 1994; Moradi & Miller, 2010; Rodgers, 2006); that military personnel of White or Latino background tend to disapprove or oppose gays in the military to a greater extent than African Americans (Healy, 1993; Rodgers, 2006); that military personnel with more conservative political and religious views tend disapprove or oppose gays in the military to a greater extent than those holding less conservative political and religious views (Estrada & Weiss, 1999; Moradi & Miller, 2010); that military personnel who have not had interpersonal contact with gay service personnel tend to disapprove or oppose gays in the military to a greater extent than military personnel with such interpersonal experiences (Estrada & Weiss, 1999; Moradi & Miller, 2010); that military personnel with more time in service as well as those with higher rank tend to disapprove or oppose gays in the military to a greater extent than individuals with less time in service and of lower rank (Moradi & Miller, 2010; Rodgers, 2006); and that military personnel in the combat arms tend to disapprove or oppose gays in the military to a greater extent than military personnel in either combat support, or combat service support (DoD, 2010a; Healy, 1993).

Compatibility of Gay Service Personnel

Concerns regarding the compatibility of gay individuals and military service have centered on issues involving personal privacy in berthing and billeting of service personnel; self-disclosure of sexual orientation among gay personnel; and perceived conflict with military and family values of the U.S. military institution.

Personal Privacy

Privacy concerns are important when considering any policy affecting military personnel. However, personal privacy in the military is often subjugated to the needs of the military mission. A number of studies involving military respondents who served in a unit with a person who they believed (or knew) to be gay have found few, if any, problems concerning privacy violations involving gay service personnel (DoD, 2010a; McGarry, 2010; Moradi & Miller, 2010; NDRI, 2010; Rodgers, 2006). DoD's Comprehensive Review Working Group (CRWG) found that if the law was repealed, 29.4% military respondents said they would do nothing different when it came to showering, 11% would discuss behavioral expectations with gays service personnel, 25.8% would shower at a different time and 17.7% of military respondents would talk to a leader to see if they had other options (DoD, 2010a). The study also found that if military personnel were assigned to share a room, berth, or field tent with gay service member, 26.7% would do nothing, 24.3% would have a discussion about expectations, 2.4% would seek advice from others and 28.1% would talk to their leader and seek an alternative option (DoD, 2010a).

Disclosure of Sexual Orientation

Until recently, U.S. law required that sexual orientation and sexual behavior remain a personal and private matter within the military environment (10

U.S.C. § 654). When an individual's sexual orientation or behavior became public, the law required the military services to separate individuals because homosexuality was presumed to create an unacceptable risk to the high standards of morale, good order and discipline, and unit cohesion of the U.S. military (Aspin, 1995; Otjen et al., 1993). This prohibition notwithstanding, it is clear that the sexual orientation and sexual behavior of gay service personnel, at times, became public with little (if any) risks to the functioning or performance of military units (DoD, 2010a; NDRI, 2010). In fact, the CRWG found that "when Service members had the actual experience of serving with someone they believe to be gay, in general, unit performance was not affected negatively" (DoD, 2010a, p.4). Moreover, the CRWG found that when the repeal of the law would be implemented, only 15% of gay service personnel indicated that they would mainly be open about their orientation with other service personnel in their units (DoD, 2010a; NDRI, 2010).

Military and Family Values

Military institutions differ from civilian institutions in many respects, not the least of which involve the culture and its accompanying rules, customs, values, and traditions (Otjen et al., 1993). Military culture is characterized by the organized use of legitimate violence (Janowitz, 1971); bureaucratic control (Elron, Shamir, & Ben Ari, 1999); task oriented missions (Dunivin, 1994); a professional ethos that places high regard on discipline, obedience, courage, trust, self-sacrifice, and emphasizes the primacy of the group over the individual (Collins, 1998; Hillen, 1999; Townshend, 1993); and a masculine-warrior image that identifies and extols military service in terms of masculine norms (Dunivin, 1994). Although these organizational culture differences do matter, it is important to note that gay individuals who volunteer for military service are likely to do so with the understanding that the military, like the rest of society, has yet to come to terms with how to successfully manage the integration of gay individuals in the workplace. Moreover, openly gay service personnel, like their heterosexual counterparts, are likely to adapt their behaviors in order to minimize the potential for negative effects for themselves or their unit and perform their duties within the confines of the military culture (Belkin & Ember-Herbert, 2002; Goffman, 1963; Herek, 1993; Herek & Belkin, 2005; NDRI, 2010; Shawyer, 1987, 1995). With regard to family concerns, evidence from recent surveys of military spouses suggests that removal of the ban on gays in the military would have no impact on family readiness (77.2%), nor affect participation in military social events (72%), deployment support activities (76.4%), or family support programs (75.1%; Westat, 2010). Moreover, 43% of spouses did not think any special activities or communications would be necessary to prepare or assist spouses in understanding the new policy if the ban on gays in the military was removed. In fact, 44% of service members and 63% of spouses indicated that if they lived on base with a gay or lesbian service member and partner as neighbors they would get to know the gay or lesbian service member like any other neighbor (DoD, 2010a; Westat, 2010).

Perceived Impact of Gay Service Personnel

Concerns regarding the perceived impact of integrating gay service personnel have centered on issues involving unit cohesion, military readiness, and unit effectiveness (DoD, 2010a; Otjen et al., 1993).

UNIT COHESION

U.S. military policies note that performance and effectiveness in combat is influenced by a wide variety of factors (DoD, 1992; NDRI, 2010). However, high combat effectiveness is premised on "a synergistic mix that can be best expressed as the product of unit cohesion and readiness" (Otjen et al., 1993, p. 162). Cohesion reflects the "bonding together of members of a unit in such a way as to sustain their will and commitment to each other, their unit, and the mission" (Johns et al., 1984, p. ix). Research indicates that unit cohesion can influence both individual and group performance (see Table 3; Beal et al., 2003; Chicchio & Essiembre, 2009; Mullen & Cooper, 1994). However, other research suggests that there are structural (e.g., size, proximity, interdependence, interpersonal contact) and situational (e.g., leadership style, command climate, threat or challenge conditions) factors that may play a larger role in understanding the complex relationships among cohesion, effectiveness, and performance than either sexual orientation, or sexual behavior of gay service personnel (Beal et al., 2005; Chicchio & Essiembre, 2009; Estrada, 2012; Mullen & Cooper, 1994; NDRI, 1993, 2010). In fact, the DoD's CRWG found that large percentages of military personnel reported that removal of the ban on gays in the military would have a positive, a mixed, or no effect on aspects of task cohesion (70–76%), and social cohesion (67–78%; DoD, 2010a).

MILITARY READINESS

Readiness refers to the ability of forces or units to deliver the outputs for which they were designed, including the ability to deploy and employ without unacceptable delays, to provide capabilities required by the combatant commander, and to fight and meet the demands of the National Military Strategy (DoD, 2012). Military readiness is influenced by many factors that include organizational, training, and equipment-related variables. Among organizational variables, recruitment, retention, and medical wellbeing figure most prominently in discussions involving the inclusion of openly gay service personnel (Otjen et al., 1993). With regard to recruitment and retention, it

TABLE 3 Summary of Meta-Analytical Findings Involving Cohesion and Performance

Source	Overall cohesion	Task	Social	Group identity
Evans & Dion (1991)	.419	—	—	—
Gully, Whitney, & Devine (1995)	.199	—	—	—
Individual performance	.228	—	—	—
Group performance	.317	—	—	—
Mullen & Copper (1994)		—	—	—
Experimental studies	.223	.428	.271	.403
Correlational studies	.252	.249	−.132	.084
Oliver, Harman, Hoover, Hayes, & Pandhi (1999)				
Individual performance[a]	.196	—	—	—
Group performance[a]	.400	—	—	—
Individual performance[b]	.310	—	—	—
Group performance[b]	.331	—	—	—
Beal, Cohen, Burke & McLendon (2003)		.278	.199	.261
Behavioral performance	.301	.302	.315	—
Outcome performance	.168	.273	.139	—
Effectiveness	.175	.232	.148	—
Efficiency	.310	.343	.284	—
Chiocchio & Essiembre (2009)	—	—	—	—
Behavioral performance	—	.359	.485	—
Outcome performance	—	.346	.201	—

Notes. All correlation coefficients are corrected for attenuation and sample size.
[a]Correlations are weighted by number of participants.
[b]Correlations are weighted by number of groups.
— correlations not reported.

has been argued that youth's propensity to enlist in the military would be lowered because the military image would be tarnished and that significant numbers of service members would not re-enlist if openly gay individuals were allowed to serve in the military (Otjen et al., 1993). Although the logic of this rationale appears straightforward, research shows that there are a host of different variables, besides sexual orientation, that influence the process of recruiting and retaining qualified personnel (e.g., academic background, socioeconomic status, social and political attitudes; Faris, 1984; Griffith, 2005; Hosek et al., 1989; Kleycamp, 2006; Moore, 2002; NDRI, 1993, 2010; National Research Council, 2003; Stewart & Firestone, 1992; Warner & Asch, 1995). In fact, the CRWG found that a 60% majority of military respondents indicated that their career plans would not change if restrictions on gays in the military were repealed; 11% would consider leaving sooner than planned; and 13% would definitely leave sooner than planned (DoD, 2010a).

With regard to medical wellbeing, recent advances in the testing, treatment, and prevention of illness have improved considerably, enabling the military to exercise significant control over the medical wellbeing of the force. New recruits undergo extensive medical screens to assess their suitability for service, and service members receive routine physicals, and medical treatment periodically, as well as before and after a deployment (DoD, 2010a). For example, service personnel are tested for HIV at least every two years, on the advice of a doctor, or upon request (DoD, 2010a; NDRI, 2010). The efficacy of these procedures led the Surgeons General of the Army, Navy, and Air Force to conclude that medical procedures to prevent the spread of HIV and secure the blood supply of the military were sufficient to protect the health of the force (DoD, 2010a).

Unit effectiveness

A unit's effectiveness reflects its ability to accomplish assigned tasks or missions and is determined by structural and situational factors that may be internal or external to the unit (DoD, 2010a, 2010b). It has been argued that the presence of openly gay service personnel could affect cohesion by straining social relations among unit members, which in turn would impair a unit's ability to accomplish tasks or missions, that is, unit effectiveness; and that the presence of openly gay service personnel could affect retention of military personnel by affecting military personnel's decision to remain in the military, leading to personnel shortfalls that would in turn impair a unit's ability to accomplish tasks or missions, that is, unit effectiveness. These concerns notwithstanding, research points to other factors, besides sexual orientation, that are far more important in fostering cohesion and retention among military personnel (see preceding section on cohesion and retention). According to the CRWG, large percentages of military respondents (50–80%) indicated that the presence of openly gay service personnel would not uniformly impact unit effectiveness (DoD 2010a).

To summarize, data from both public and military opinion polls indicate that large percentages of Americans now favor allowing gay individuals to serve in the U.S. Armed Forces (DoD, 2010a; NDRI, 1993, 2010; Torres-Reyna & Shapiro, 2002; Yang, 1997). Research on the correlates of these attitudes points to the importance of demographic (e.g., gender, race or ethnicity, religious and political ideology, interpersonal contact) and military characteristics (e.g., rank, years of service, military occupation) as predictors of military personnel's acceptance of gay service personnel within the military environment. Research also demonstrates that while disclosure of sexual orientation has been prohibited by law (10 U.S.C. § 654), sexual orientation or behavior of gay service personnel, at times, became public with little (if any) risks to the personal privacy of military personnel (DoD, 2010a; McGarry, 2010; Moradi & Miller, 2010; NDRI, 2010; Rodgers, 2006), their personal values and the values of the military institution (DoD, 2010a; NDRI, 2010), or the cohesiveness, readiness, and combat effectiveness of military units (DoD, 2010a; NDRI, 2010).

A FRAMEWORK FOR INTEGRATING OPENLY GAY SERVICE PERSONNEL IN THE U.S. MILITARY

We have learned a great deal about the challenges and opportunities associated with the inclusion of openly gay service personnel in the U.S. military in the past three decades (DoD, 2010a, 2010b; NDRI, 1993, 2010; Westat, 2010). However, much of this research has been guided by pragmatic concerns related to the acceptance, compatibility, and perceived impact that openly gay individuals may have on the U.S. military (DoD, 2010a; NDRI, 1993, 2010; Otjen et al., 1993). Given recent changes in U.S. law, it is critical to develop conceptual frameworks to inform efforts to implement Don't Ask, Don't Tell Repeal Act of 2010 and ensure the successful integration of openly gay service personnel within the military environment. Accordingly, we propose a theoretical framework of the antecedents and outcomes of participation and inclusion of gay service personnel within the military environment. Our theory incorporates individual, occupational-organizational and societal antecedents proposed by Estrada (2012). Additionally, we specify individual, group or unit, and organizational outcomes associated with the participation and inclusion of openly gay service personnel within the military environment. Figure 1 displays the proposed theoretical framework of antecedents and outcomes of participation and inclusion of gay service personnel within the U.S. military.

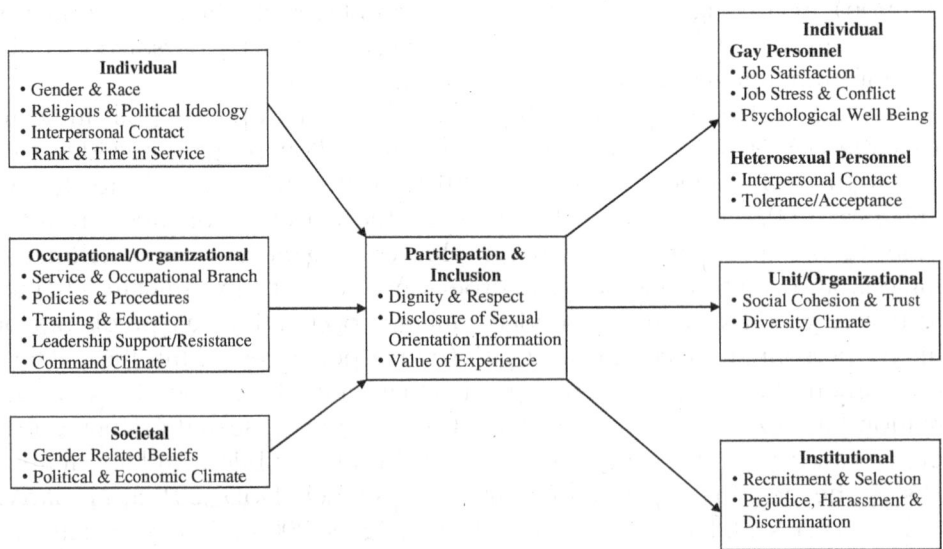

FIGURE 1 Antecedents and consequences of participants and inclusion of openly gay service personnel in the U.S. military.

Antecedents of Participation and Inclusion

Three classes of variables are posited to play a role in the participation and inclusion of openly gay service personnel within the U.S. military (see Figure 1). Individual variables include demographic background, religious and political ideology, interpersonal contact experiences, and military characteristics. Occupational and organizational variables include service and occupational branch, policies and procedures, training and education, leadership support or resistance, and command climate. Societal variables include gender-related beliefs and political and economic climate.

INDIVIDUAL VARIABLES

Past research shows that less tolerance of gays in the military tends to be expressed by male individuals of White or Latino backgrounds (Healy, 1993; Miller, 1994; Moradi & Miller, 2010; Rodgers, 2006), as well as among individuals espousing conservative political and religious views (Estrada & Weiss, 1999; Moradi & Miller, 2010) and those with limited interpersonal contact with gay service personnel (DoD, 2010a; Estrada & Weiss, 1999; Moradi & Miller, 2010). Other research also shows that less tolerance for gays in the military tends to be expressed by military personnel with more time in service as well as those of higher rank (Moradi & Miller, 2010; Rodgers, 2006). Accordingly, Estrada (2012) proposed that:

Proposition 1: Gender, ethnicity, religious and political views as well as interpersonal contact with gay service personnel will influence the participation and inclusion of openly gay service personnel.

Proposition 2: Rank and time in service will influence the participation and inclusion of openly gay service personnel.

OCCUPATIONAL AND ORGANIZATIONAL VARIABLES

Past research shows that less tolerance of gays in the military tends to be expressed by service members from the Marine Corps and Army as compared with individuals from the Navy or Air Force (Annenberg Public Policy Center, 2004; DoD, 2010a; Healy, 1993; McGarry, 2010; Rodgers, 2006; Westat, 2010); and among military personnel in the combat arms (DoD, 2010a; Healy, 1993; Westat, 2010). Accordingly, Estrada (2012) proposed that:

Proposition 3: Service and occupational branch will influence the participation and inclusion of openly gay service personnel.

Previous research has noted the importance of having clear policies and procedures as well as proper training and education for the successful integration of openly gay service personnel in the U.S. military (DoD, 2010a, 2010b; Estrada & Laurence, 2009; NDRI, 1993, 2010; Zellman, 1996). Accordingly, Estrada (2012) proposed that:

Proposition 4: Organizational policies and procedures as well as training and education will influence the participation and inclusion of openly gay service personnel.

Research suggests that gay service personnel consider many factors before deciding to disclose their sexual orientation to other military personnel (DoD, 2010a; NDRI, 2010). These factors include perceived organizational, supervisory, and peer support—that is, leadership support or resistance (Chrobot-Mason, Button, & DiClementi, 2001; Driscoll et al., 1996; Griffith & Hebl, 2002; Ragins, Singh, & Cornwell, 2007); as well as the command's climate for diversity (Claire, Beatty, & Maclean, 2005). Accordingly, Estrada (2012) proposed that:

Proposition 5: Leadership support or resistance and command climate will influence the participation and inclusion of openly gay service personnel.

CULTURAL AND SOCIETAL VARIABLES

Research shows that individuals (Glick & Fiske, 1996, 1999; Spence & Hahn, 1997; Twenge, 1997) and societies (Glick & Fiske, 2001; Glick et al., 2000; Hofstede, 2001; Schwartz, 1994) differ in their tolerance of violations for proscribed behaviors of men and women. Estrada (2012) suggested that individuals with more traditional gender role beliefs may be less likely to tolerate behaviors that violate these norms, and be more likely to enforce sanctions against individuals who violate these norms (e.g., Pryor, Giedd, & Williams, 1995; Pryor & Whalen, 1997). For example, heterosexual service personnel with more traditional gender-related beliefs may view openly gay service personnel as violating societal gender norms, and, thus, be motivated to enforce sanctions against gay personnel to address perceived violations. The enforcement of sanctions by heterosexual service personnel could therefore influence the participation and inclusion of gay service personnel within the military environment. Accordingly, Estrada (2012) proposed that:

Proposition 6: Gender-related beliefs will influence the participation and inclusion of openly gay service personnel.

Estrada (2012) noted that the political and economic climate of the United States affects the armed forces in several ways. The U.S. military is generally favored when the preponderance of elected officials tend to favor and pursue politically conservative policies. As an example, DoD Directives 1332.14 and 1332.30 were developed when the executive branch was occupied by a politically conservative administration, and passage of 10 USC § 654 occurred when the legislative branch was dominated by a politically conservative electorate. In contrast, repeal of 10 USC § 654 occurred when the executive and legislative branches of government were dominated by a politically liberal electorate. Accordingly, Estrada (2012) suggested that the participation and inclusion of openly gay service personnel may be affected by the political climate of the country. He proposed that:

Proposition 7: Political climate will influence the participation and inclusion of openly gay service personnel.

With regard to the economic climate, Estrada (2012) noted that past research indicated that the state of the civilian economy can influence the military's ability to recruit and retain individuals into military service (e.g., Asch & Warner, 1994; Faris, 1984; Goldberg, 2001; Hosek et al., 1989; Warner & Asch, 1995). During economically prosperous times, opportunities for employment are greater, and military recruitment is more difficult. Conversely, during economically impoverished times, less opportunities for employment exist, and the military has more opportunities to recruit qualified personnel from a larger pool of applicants. Accordingly, Estrada (2012) reasoned that the participation and inclusion of openly gay service personnel is likely to be affected by the economic climate of the country because higher numbers of individuals, to include gay individuals, may be motivated and qualified for military service during periods of economic scarcity. Estrada (2012) proposed that:

Proposition 8: Economic climate will influence the participation and inclusion of openly gay service personnel.

Participation and Inclusion of Openly Gay Service Personnel

Participation and inclusion of openly gay service personnel can be manifested in many ways. However, we posit that an inclusive military environment is one in which openly gay service personnel a) are treated with dignity and respect; b) feel free to share information about their sexual orientation and their personal lives without fear of reprisals; and where c) their unique experiences, as members of a sexual minority group, are valued and leveraged to enhance both individual and unit functioning. From this perspective, greater participation of openly gay service personnel in work (e.g., special or high-visibility assignments) and non-work activities (e.g., attendance to social events sponsored by their military chain of command) may be indicative of an inclusive military environment.

Outcomes of Participation and Inclusion

The participation and inclusion of openly gay service personnel within the U.S. military is posited to influence three classes of variables including individual, unit or organizational, and institutional (see Figure 1). Individual variables include job-related as well as psychological and health outcomes for gay service personnel, and interpersonal contact and attitudinal variables for heterosexual personnel. Unit and organizational variables include social cohesion, trust, unit conflict, as well as command climate. Institutional variables include prejudice, harassment and discrimination, recruitment and selection, and cultural change.

Individual Variables

The participation and inclusion of openly gay service personnel is posited to influence individual level variables for both gay and heterosexual service personnel (see Figure 1). As noted above, inclusion of openly gay service personnel may be manifested in terms of dignity and respect, disclosure of sexual orientation, and value of sexual minority experiences. Past research suggests that disclosure of sexual orientation among gays in the workplace has been associated with improved interpersonal relations (Beals & Peplau, 2006; Collins & Miller, 1994), increased job satisfaction (Griffith & Hebl, 2002), better psychological health (Meyer, 2003; Morris, Waldo, & Rothblum, 2001); less conflict between work and family life (Day & Schoenrade, 1997). Accordingly, we posit that the participation and inclusion of openly gay service personnel (as evidenced by disclosure of sexual orientation information) is likely to yield positive job, health, and psychological outcomes for gay personnel. Therefore, we propose that:

Proposition 9: Increased participation and inclusion of openly gay service personnel within the military environment will influence job satisfaction, job stress and conflict, and psychological wellbeing of openly gay service personnel.

Participation and inclusion of openly gay service personnel is also likely to increase opportunities for positive interpersonal contact experiences among gay and heterosexual service personnel. Past research shows that interpersonal contact with members of an outgroup is likely to bring about positive changes in attitudes and behaviors of ingroup members toward outgroup members (Pettigrew & Troop, 2006; Smith, Axelton, & Saucier,

2009). Accordingly, we propose that increased participation and inclusion of openly gay service personnel within the military environment may bring about increased tolerance and acceptance of gays in the military among heterosexual personnel over time (Estrada & Weiss, 1999; Herek, 1996; Herek & Capitanio, 1996; Herek & Glunt, 1993; Moradi & Miller, 2010). Therefore, we propose that:

Proposition 10: Increased participation and inclusion of openly gay service personnel within the military environment will be associated with greater tolerance and acceptance of gays in the military among heterosexual service personnel.

Unit or Organizational Variables

We propose that increased participation and inclusion of openly gay service personnel within the military environment may have a number of positive unit and organizational effects to include cohesion, trust, and command climate for diversity (see Figure 1). Unit cohesion is thought to result from "controlled, interactive forces that lead to solidarity within military units [which] direct soldiers toward common goals—i.e., *task cohesion* . . . [and foster] commitment to [individuals]—i.e., *social or interpersonal cohesion* . . . and to the unit as a whole"—that is, group identity or pride and esprit de corps (emphasis added; Headquarters Department of the Army, 1986, p. 204). As noted previously, unit cohesion is important because it has been linked to group performance (e.g., Beal et al., 2003; Chicchio & Essiembre, 2009; Mullen & Cooper, 1994). Although military perspectives on the topic of gays in the military allude to a negative relationship between participation and inclusion of openly gay service personnel and unit cohesion (Otjen et al., 1993), empirical evidence in support of this relationship is nonexistent. Thus, we propose an alternative viewpoint. Specifically, we suggest that the participation and inclusion of openly gay service personnel may have the potential to positively impact interpersonal relations (i.e., social cohesion) among unit members within the military environment. Empirical support for this proposition comes from research showing that mere exposure to target stimuli can, in and of itself, produce greater liking for a target (Bornstein, 1989; Harmon-Jones & Allen, 2001; Lee, 2001; Zajonc, 1968) and from research showing that interpersonal contact with members of an outgroup is likely to bring about positive changes in attitudes and behaviors of ingroup members toward outgroup members (Allport, 1954; Pettigrew & Troop, 2006, 2008; Smith et al., 2009). Based on this research, we reason that increased exposure and interpersonal contact with openly gay service personnel is likely to influence interpersonal relations among member of unit such that interpersonal bonds among openly gay and heterosexual member of unit will be strengthened (i.e., social cohesion) and greater trust among unit members will result. Therefore, we propose that:

Proposition 11: Increased participation and inclusion of openly gay service personnel within the military environment will be associated with greater levels of social cohesion among unit members.

Proposition 12: Increased participation and inclusion of openly gay service personnel within the military environment will be associated with greater levels of trust among unit members.

Furthermore, we reason that increased exposure and interpersonal contact with openly gay service personnel may also lead to changes in the unit or organization's climate for diversity. Support for this proposition comes from research showing that mere exposure and interpersonal contact with members of an outgroup is likely to bring about positive changes in attitudes and behaviors of ingroup members toward outgroup members (e.g., Allport, 1954; Bornstein, 1989; Pettigrew & Troop, 2006, 2008; Zajonc, 1968) and from research showing that spending time with and self-disclosing to members of an outgroup can result in more positive perceptions toward other groups by members of the ingroup (Davies, Tropp, Aron, Pettigrew, & Wright, 2011; Davies, Wright, & Aron, 2011; Pettigrew & Troop, 2006, 2008). Based on this research, we argue that increased participation and inclusion of openly gay service personnel may lead heterosexual and openly gay service personnel alike to perceive that the unit or organization is more tolerant and or accepting of individuals from other socially recognized or legally protected groups (e.g., race, color, national origin, sex, religion, age, or disability; DoD, 2009). Therefore, we propose that:

Proposition 13: Increased participation and inclusion of openly gay service personnel within the military environment will be associated with more positive perceptions of the unit and organizational climate for diversity.

INSTITUTIONAL VARIABLES

We propose that increased participation and inclusion of openly gay service personnel within the military environment may influence recruitment and selection among gay applicants for military service and influence prejudice, harassment and discrimination toward gay service personnel (see Figure 1). Past research indicates that there are a wide range of factors that influence recruitment and selection of qualified applicants for military service (Faris, 1984; Griffith, 2005; Hosek et al., 1989; Kleycamp, 2006; Moore, 2002; NDRI, 1993, 2010; National Research Council, 2003; Stewart & Firestone, 1992; Warner & Asch, 1995). Although research indicates that educational and economic factors play a significant role in both recruitment and selection of service personnel (Asch et al., 2010; Asch & Warner, 1994, Bicksler & Nolan, 2009; Goldberg, 2001; Kilburn & Klerman, 1999; Warner & Asch, 1995), we propose that the participation and inclusion of openly gay service personnel may also serve to positively influence these processes. Specifically, we argue that the participation and inclusion of openly gay service personnel within the military environment may function to convey that the military environment is both tolerant and accepting of gay individuals within its ranks. As such, this may lead to increased propensity for military service among gay individuals who would ultimately be eligible for recruitment and selection into military service. Therefore, we propose that:

Proposition 14: Increased participation and inclusion of openly gay service personnel within the military environment will be associated with greater propensity for service among gay individuals and lead to higher recruitment and selection of gay individual for military service.

Additionally, increased participation and inclusion of openly gay service personnel within the military environment is also likely to be associated with lower instances of prejudice, harassment, and discrimination toward gays in the military. Research suggests that prejudice, harassment, and discriminatory behaviors are less likely to occur within work environments that are perceived to be intolerant of these behaviors (Chan et al., 2008; Estrada, 2012; Estrada & Harbke 2008; Estrada & Laurence, 2009; Hulin, 1993; Hulin et al., 1997; Willness et al., 2007). Other research also shows that gay individuals report higher levels of discrimination within work environments that lack policies and support systems to prevent such behaviors toward gays in the workplace (Griffith & Hebl, 2002; Ragins & Cornwell, 2000; Ragins et al., 2007). Therefore, we posit that increased participation and inclusion of openly gay service personnel within the military environment is likely to signal to both gay and heterosexual personnel that prejudice, harassment, and discriminatory behaviors are not tolerated; that gay service personnel can feel free to report such behaviors when they occur; and that perpetrators will be punished for enacting such behaviors because they are contrary to good order and discipline required of the professional military. Therefore, we propose that

Proposition 15: Increased participation and inclusion of openly gay service personnel within the military environment will influence prejudice, harassment and discrimination toward gay service personnel.

This section outlined a conceptual framework of antecedents and outcomes of the participation and inclusion of openly gay individuals within the military environment. Fifteen empirical propositions were derived and posited to explain the interrelationships among the variables contained within the proposed framework. The proposed framework is meant to inform ongoing discussion and help to guide future research related to the management, participation, and inclusion of gay service personnel within the U.S. military.

CONCLUSIONS AND IMPLICATIONS FOR FUTURE RESEARCH

We have learned about the many challenges and opportunities associated with the integration of openly gay service personnel within the military environment. However, it is important to note that much of what we know is guided by pragmatic concerns that are not necessarily informed by either relevant psychological theory or empirical research. Thus, there is a need for theoretically informed studies that incorporate relevant psychological research on this topic. Such approaches are particularly important since they can provide concrete guidance on how to manage the integration of openly gay individuals into the military environment. Such approaches can also inform the military's efforts to anticipate, prevent and curtail problems associated with the integration of openly gay service personnel within the military environment before they occur (e.g., Office of the Inspector General, 2000). The synthesis presented in the preceding section of this article represents an attempt to build a conceptual framework of antecedents and outcomes of participation and inclusion of openly gay service personnel within the military environment. This framework represents but one approach by which to incorporate relevant empirical research to uncover factors influencing the integration of gays in the military. Other examples can be observed in the work of Estrada and Laurence (2009) who evaluated a heuristic framework that examined how training related to the DADT policy influenced participant's reactions, learning and cognitive outcomes and behavioral and organization outcomes; and Probst, Estrada, and Brown (2008), who developed a framework of prevention strategies used to address harassment, violence, and hate crimes in the workplace. While these examples are far from comprehensive, they provide exemplars on how to integrate relevant theory and empirical research to inform future studies on issues related to the integration of gays in the military. This article was intended to contribute to ongoing discussions on the participation and inclusion of openly gay service personnel within the U.S. military. It is hoped that the review of the scientific record serves to inform the military's efforts to implement the new policy and inform future research on the successful integration of openly gay service personnel within the U.S. military environment.

NOTE

1. We use the term "gay service personnel" to refer to lesbians, gay, bisexual, and transgender (LGBT) individuals.

REFERENCES

Allport, G. W. (1954). *The nature of prejudice*. Reading, MA. Addison-Wesley.

Annenberg Public Policy Center. (2004). *National Annenberg election survey 2004*. University of Pennsylvania. Retrieved from http://www.annenbergpublicpolicycenter.org/Downloads/Political_Communication/naes/2004_03_2military-data_10-16_pr.pdf

Asch, B. J., Heaton, P., Hosek, J., Martorell, F., Simon, C., & Warner, J. T. (2010). *Cash incentives and military enlistment, attrition and reenlistment* (MG-950-OSD). Santa Monica, CA. RAND. Retrieved from http://www.rand.org/pubs/monographs/MG950/

Asch, B. J., & Warner, J. T. (1994). *A theory of military compensation and personnel policy* (MR-439-OSD). Santa Monica, CA. RAND. Retrieved from http://www.rand.org/pubs/monograph_reports/MR439/

Aspin, L. (1995). Policy on homosexual conduct in the Armed Forces. In R. M. Baird, & M. K. Baird, *Homosexuality: Debating the issues* (pp. 155–157). Amherst, NY: Prometheus Books.

Beals, D. J., Cohen, R. R., Burke, M. J., & McLendon, C. L. (2003). Cohesion and performance in groups: A meta-analytic clarification of construct relations. *Journal of Applied Psychology, 88*, 989–1004.

Beals, K. P., & Peplau, L. A. (2006). Disclosure patterns within social networks of gay men and lesbians. *Journal of Homosexuality, 51*, 101–120.

Belkin, A., & Embser-Herbert, M. S. (2002). A modest proposal: Privacy as a flawed rationale for the exclusion of gays and lesbians from the U.S. military. *International Security, 27*, 178–197.

Berube, A. (1990). *Coming out under fire: The history of gay men and women in World War II*. New York, NY: Free Press.

Bicksler, B. A., & Nolan, L. G. (2009). *Recruiting an all-volunteer force: The need for sustained investment in recruiting resources—An update*. Arlington, VA. Strategic Analysis, Inc.

Bornstein, R. F. (1989). Exposure and affect: Overview and meta-analysis of research 1968–1987. *Psychological Bulletin, 106*, 263–289.

Chan, D. K.-S., Lam, C. B., Chow, S. Y., & Cheung, S. F. (2008). Examining the job-related, psychological and physical outcomes of workplace sexual harassment: A meta-analytic review. *Psychological of Women Quarterly, 32*, 362–376.

Chauncey, G., Jr. (1989). Christian brotherhood or sexual perversion? Homosexual identities and the construction of sexual boundaries in World War I era. In M. B. Duberman, M.Vicinius, & G. Chauncey (Eds.), *Hidden from history: Reclaiming the gay and lesbian past* (pp. 294–317). New York, NY: New American Library.

Chiocchio, F., & Essiembre, H. (2009). Cohesion and performance: A meta-analytic review of disparities between project teams, production teams and service teams. *Small Group Research, 40*, 382–420.

Chrobot-Mason, D., Button, S. B., DiClementi, J. D. (2001). Sexual identity management strategies: An exploration of antecedents and consequences. *Sex Roles, 45*, 321–336.

Claire, J. A., Beatty, J. E., & Maclean, T. L. (2005). Out of sight but not out of mind: Managing invisible social identities in the workplace. *Academy of Management Review, 30*, 78–95.

Cleveland, F. E., & Ohl, M. A. (1994). *"Don't ask, don't tell" policy analysis and interpretation*. (Unpublished master's thesis). Naval Postgraduate School, Monterey, CA.

Collins, J. J. (1998). The complex context of American military culture: A practitioner's view. *Washington Quarterly, 21*, 213–228.

Collins, N. L., & Miller, L. C. (1994). Self disclosure and liking: A meta-analytic review. *Psychological Bulletin, 116*, 457–475.

Davies, K. Tropp, L. R., Aron, A., Pettigrew, T. F., & Wright, S. C. (2011). Cross-group friendship and intergroup attitudes: A meta-analytic review. *Personality and Social Psychology Review, 15*, 332–351.

Davies, K., Wright, S. C., & Aron, A. (2011). Intergroup friendships: How interpersonal connectedness encourage positive intergroup attitudes. In L. R. Tropp & R. K. Mallett (Eds.), *Moving beyond prejudice reduction: Pathways to positive intergroup relations* (pp. 119–138). Washington, DC. American Psychological Association.

Day, N. E., & Schoenrade, P. (1997). Staying in the closet vs. coming out: Relationships between communication about sexual orientation and work attitudes. *Personnel Psychology, 50*, 147–163.

Department of Defense. (1992, June 3). *Directive 7730.65: Department of Defense readiness reporting system (DRRS)*. Washington, DC: Author.

Department of Defense. (2009, February 5). *Directive 1020.02: Diversity Management and Equal Opportunity (EO) in the Department of Defense*. Washington, DC: Author.

Department of Defense. (2010a, March 29). *Directive 1332.14: Enlisted administrative separations*. Washington, DC: Author.

Department of Defense. (2010b, March 29). *Directive 1332.30: Separation of regular and reserve commissioned officers*. Washington, DC: Author.

Don't Ask, Don't Tell Repeal Act. (2010a). S4023. Retrieved from http://thomas.loc.gov/cgi-bin/query/z?c111:S.4023

Don't Ask, Don't Tell Repeal Act. (2010b). HR2965. Retrieved from http://www.gpo.gov/fdsys/pkg/BILLS-111hr2965enr/pdf/BILLS-111hr2965enr.pdf

Driscoll, J. M., Kelley, F. A., & Fassinger, R. E. (1996). Lesbian identity and disclosure in the workplace: Relation to occupational stress and satisfaction. *Journal of Vocational Behavior, 48*, 229–242.

Dunivin, K. O. (1994). Military culture: Change and continuity. *Armed Forces & Society, 20*, 531–547.

Elron, E., Shamir, B., & Ben-Ari, E. (1999). Why don't they fight each other? Cultural diversity and operational unity in multinational forces. *Armed Forces & Society, 26(1)*, 73–98.

Estrada, A. X. (2012). Gay service personnel in the U.S. military: History, progress and a way forward. In J. H. Laurence, & M. D. Matthews (Eds.), *Handbook of Military Psychology*. (pp. 344–364). New York, NY: Oxford University Press.

Estrada, A. X. & Harbke, C. R. (2008) Ethnic differences in the perception of equal opportunity climate among military reservist. *International Journal Intercultural Relations, 32,* 466–478.

Estrada, A. X., & Laurence, J. H. (2009). The impact of training on the don't ask, don't tell, don't pursue policy. *Military Psychology, 21,* 62–80.

Estrada, A. X., & Weiss, D. J. (1999). Attitudes of military personnel toward homosexuals. *Journal of Homosexuality, 37,* 83–97.

Evans, C. R., & Dion, K. L. (1991). Group cohesion and performance: A meta-analysis. *Small Group Research, 22,* 175–186.

Faris, J. H. (1984). Economic and noneconomic factors of personnel recruitment and retention in the all volunteer force. *Armed Forces & Society, 10,* 251–275.

Friery, M. R. (1997). *Trends in Navy officer attitudes toward the "don't ask, don't tell" policy.* (Unpublished master's thesis). Naval Postgraduate School, Monterey, CA.

Glick, P., & Fiske, S. T. (1996). The ambivalent sexism inventory: Differentiating hostile and benevolent sexism. *Journal of Personality and Social Psychology, 70,* 491–512.

Glick, P., & Fiske, S. T. (1999). Sexism and other "isms": The interdependence, status, and the ambivalent content of stereotypes. In W. B. Swan, Jr., J. H. Langlois, & L. A. Gilbert (Eds.), *Sexism and stereotypes in modern society: The gender science of Janet Taylor Spence* (pp. 193–221). Washington, DC: American Psychological Association.

Glick, P., & Fiske, S. T. (2001). An ambivalent alliance: Hostile and benevolent sexism as complementary justifications for gender inequality. *American Psychologist, 56,* 109–118.

Glick, P., Fiske, S. T., Mladinic, A., Saiz, J. L., Abrams, D., Masser, B., et al. (2000). Beyond prejudice as simple antipathy: Hostile and benevolent sexism across cultures. *Journal of Personality and Social Psychology, 79,* 763–775.

Goffman, E. (1963). *Behavior in public places: Notes on the social organization of gatherings.* New York, NY: Free Press.

Goldberg, M. S. (2001). *A survey of enlisted retention: Models and findings* (CRM D0004085.A2/Final). Center for Naval Analyses, Alexandria, VA.

Griffith, J. (2005). Will citizens be soldiers? Examining retention of reserve component soldiers. *Armed Forces & Society, 31,* 353–383.

Griffith, K. H., & Hebl, M. R. (2002). The disclosure dilemma for gay men and lesbians: "Coming out" at work. *Journal of Applied Psychology, 87,* 1191–1199.

Gully, S. M., Whitney, D. J., & Devine, D. J. (1995). A meta-analysis of cohesion and performance: Effects of level of analysis and task interdependence. *Small Group Research, 26,* 497–520.

Haggerty, T. (2003). History repeating itself: A historical overview of gay and lesbians in the military before "don't ask, don't tell." In A. Belkin & G. Bateman (Eds.), *Don't ask, don't tell: Debating the gay ban in the military* (pp. 9–42). Boulder, CO: Lynn Rienner Publishers.

Harmon-Jones, E., & Allen, J. J. B. (2011). The role of affect in the mere exposure effect: Evidence from physiological and individual differences approaches. *Personality and Social Psychology Bulletin, 27,* 889–898.

Headquarters Department of the Army. (1983, October 15). *Dictionary of United States Army terms: AR 310-25.* Washington, DC: Author.

Headquarters Department of the Army. (1986). *Dictionary of United States Army terms: AR 310-25*. Washington, DC. Author.

Healy, M. (1993, February 28). The times polls: 74% of military enlistees oppose lifting gay ban. *Los Angeles Times*, p. A1.

Herek, G. M. (1993). Sexual orientation and military service: A social science perspective. *American Psychologist, 48*, 538–549.

Herek, G. M. (1996). Why tell if you're not asked? Self-disclosure, intergroup contact and heterosexuals' attitudes toward lesbians and gay men. In G. M. Herek, J. B. Jobe, & R. M. Carney (Eds.), *Out in force: Sexual orientation and the military* (pp. 197–225). Chicago, IL: University of Chicago Press.

Herek, G. M., & Belkin, A. (2005) Sexual orientation and military service: Prospects for organizational and individual change in the United States. In T. W. Britt, A. B. Adler, & C. A. Castro (Eds.), *Military life: The psychology of serving in peace and combat* (Vol. 4, pp. 119–142). Westport, CT. Praeger Security International.

Herek, G. M., & Capitanio, J. P. (1996). Some of my best friends: Intergroup contact, concealable stigma, and heterosexuals' attitudes toward gay men and lesbians. *Personality and Social Psychology Bulletin, 22*, 412–424.

Herek, G., & Glunt, E. K. (1993). Interpersonal contact and heterosexuals' attitudes toward gay men: Results from a national survey. *Journal of Sex Research, 30*, 239–244.

Hillen, J. (1999). Must U.S. military culture reform? *Orbis, 43*, 43–57.

Hofstede, G. (2001). *Culture's consequences: Comparing values, behaviors, institutions, and organizations across nations* (2nd ed.). Beverly Hills, CA: Sage.

Hosek, J. R., Antel, J., & Peterson, C. E. (1989). Who stays who leaves? Attrition among first term enlistees. *Armed Forces & Society, 15*, 389–409.

Hulin, C. L. (1993, April). *A framework for the study of sexual harassment in organizations: Climate, stressors, and patterned responses*. Paper presented at the Society for Industrial and Organizational Psychology, San Francisco, CA.

Hulin, C. L., Fitzgerald, L. F., & Drasgow, F. (1997). Organizational influences on sexual harassment. In M. S. Stockdale (Ed.), *Sexual harassment in the workplace: Perspectives, frontiers and responsestrategies* (pp. 127–150). Thousand Oaks, CA: Sage.

Janowitz, M. (1971). *The professional soldier: A social and political portrait*. New York, NY: Free Press.

Johns, J. H., Bickel, M. D., Blades, A. C., Creel, J. B., Gatling, W. S., Hinkle, J. M., et al. (1985). *Cohesion in the U.S. military*. Washington, DC: National Defense University Press.

Kilburn, R. M., & Klerman, J. A. (1999). *Enlistment decisions in the 1990s: Evidence from individual-level data* (MR-944-OSD/A). Santa Monica, CA. RAND Corporation. Retrieved from http://www.rand.org/pubs/monograph_reports/MR944/.

Kleycamp, M. A. (2006). College jobs or the military? Enlistment during a time of war. *Social Science Quarterly, 87*, 272–290.

Lee, A. Y. (2001). The mere exposure effect: An uncertainty reduction explanation revisited. *Personality and Social Psychology Bulletin, 27*, 1255–1266.

McGarry, B. (2010, February 5). "Don't ask" survey published. *Military Times*. Retrieved from http://www.militarytimes.com/news/2010/02/military_dontask_survey_020510w/?loc=interstitialskip.

Meyer, I. H. (2003). Prejudice, social stress and mental health in lesbian, gay, and bisexual populations: Conceptual issues and research evidence. *Psychological Bulletin, 129*, 674–697.

Miller, L. (1994). Fighting for a just cause: Soldiers' view on gays in the military. In W. Scott, & S. Stanley (Eds.), *Gays and lesbians in the military: Issues, concerns, and contrasts* (pp. 69–85). New York: Aldine De Gruyter.

Miller, L., & Williams, J. A. (2001). Civil rights vs. combat effectiveness? Military policies on gender and sexuality. In P. D. Feaver & R. H. Kohn (Eds.), *Soldiers and civilians: The civil-military gap and American national security* (pp. 361–402). Cambridge, MA: MIT Press.

Moore, B. L. (2002). The propensity of junior enlisted to remain in today's military. *Armed Forces & Society, 28*, 257–278.

Moradi, B., & Miller, L. (2010). Attitudes of Iraq and Afghanistan war veterans toward gay and lesbian service members. *Armed Forces & Society, 36*, 397–419.

Morris, J. F., Waldo, C. R., & Rothblum, E. D. (2001). A model of predictors and outcomes of outness among lesbian and bisexual women. *American Journal of Orthopsychiatry, 71*, 61–71.

Mullen, B., & Copper, C. (1994). The relation between group cohesiveness and performance: An integration. *Psychological Bulletin, 115*, 210–227.

Murphy, L. R. (1988). *Perverts by official order: The campaign against homosexuals in the United States Navy*. New York: Haworth Press.

National Defense Authorization Act, 10 USC § 654 (1994). Retrieved from http://law.justia.com/U.S./codes/title10/10usc654.html.

National Defense Research Institute. (1993). *Sexual orientation and U.S. military personnel policy*. Santa Monica, CA. RAND

National Defense Research Institute. (2010). *Sexual orientation and U.S. military personnel policy: An update of RAND's 1993 study*. Santa Monica, CA. RAND.

National Research Council. (2003). *Attitudes, aptitudes and aspiration of American youth: Implications for military recruitment*. Washington, DC: Committee on Youth Population and Military Recruitment.

Office of the Inspector General. (2000). *Evaluation report: Military environment with respect to the homosexual conduct policy* (Report Number D-2000-101). Washington, DC. Department of Defense.

Oliver, L. W., Harman, J., Hoover, E., Hayes, S. M., & Pandhi, N. A. (1999). A quantitative integration of the military cohesion literature. *Military Psychology, 11*, 57–83.

Otjen, J. P., Davitte, W. B., Miller, G. L., Redd, J. S., & Loy J. M. (1993). Summary report of the military working group on recommended Department of Defense homosexual policy. Washington, DC. U.S. Department of Defense. (Reprinted from *Homosexuality: Debating the issues*, pp. 158–270, R. M. Baird & M. K. Baird, 1995, Amherst, NY: Prometheus Books.

Pettigrew, T. F., & Tropp, L. R. (2006). A meta-analytic test of intergroup contact theory. *Journal of Personality and Social Psychology, 90*, 751–783.

Pettigrew, T. F., & Tropp, L. R. (2008). How does intergroup contact reduce prejudice? Meta-analytic test of three mediators. *European Journal of Social Psychology, 38*, 922–934.

Pew Center for the People and the Press. (2010, November). *Most continue to favor gays serving openly in military*. Retrieved from http://pewresearch.org/pubs/1812/dont-ask-dont-tell-repeal-public-supports-gays-serve-openly-in-military.

Probst, T. M., Estrada, A. X., & Brown, J. (2008). Harassment, violence and hate crimes in the workplace. In K. M. Thomas (Ed). *Diversity resistance: Manifestation and solutions* (pp. 93–125). New York, NY: Erlbaum.

Pryor, J. B., Giedd, J. L., & Williams, K. B. (1995). A social psychological model for predicting harassment. *Journal of Social Issues, 51*, 69–84.

Pryor, J. B., & Whalen, N. (1997). A typology of sexual harassment: Characteristics of harassers and the social circumstances under which harassment occurs. In W. O'Donohue (Ed.), *Sexual harassment: Theory, research and treatment* (pp. 129–152). Boston, MA: Allyn and Bacon.

Ragins, B. R., & Cornwell, J. M. (2000). Pink triangles: Antecedents and consequences of perceived workplace discrimination against gay and lesbian employees. *Journal of Applied Psychology, 86*, 1244–1261.

Ragins, B. R., Singh, R., & Cornwell, J. M. (2007). Making the invisible visible: Fear and disclosure of sexual orientation at work. *Journal of Applied Psychology, 92*, 1103–1118.

Rodgers, S. (2006). *Opinions of military personnel on sexual minorities in the military*. Zogby International. Retrieved from http://www.palmcenter.org/files/active/0/ZogbyReport.pdf.

Shilts, R. (1993). *Conduct unbecoming: Gays and lesbians in the U.S. military*. New York, NY: St. Martin's Press.

Schwartz, S. H. (1994). Beyond individualism/collectivism: New cultural dimensions of values. In U. Kim, H. C. Triandis, C. Kagitcibasi, S.-C. Choi, & G. Yoon (Eds.), *Individualism and collectivism: Theory, method and applications* (pp. 85–119). Thousand Oaks, CA: Sage.

Shawver, L. (1987). On the question of having women guards in male prisons. *Corrective and Social Psychiatry, 33*, 154–159.

Shawver, L. (1995). *And the flag was still there: Straight people, gay people and sexuality in the U.S. military*. New York, NY: Harrington Park Press.

Sinclair, G. D. (2009). Homosexuality and the military. A review of the literature. *Journal of Homosexuality, 56*, 701–718.

Smith, S. J., Axelton, A. M., & Saucier, D. A. (2009). The effects of contact on sexual prejudice: A meta-analysis. *Sex Roles, 61*, 178–191.

Spence, J. T., & Hahn, E. D. (1997). The attitudes toward women scale and attitude change in college students. *Psychology of Women Quarterly, 21*, 17–34.

Stewart, J. B., & Firestone, J. M. (1992). Looking for a few good men. *American Journal of Economics and Sociology, 51*, 435–458.

Torres-Reyna, O., & Shapiro, R. Y. (2002). The polls-trends: Women and sexual orientation in the military. *Public Opinion Quarterly, 66*, 618–632.

Townsend, C. (1993). Militarism and modern society. *Wilson Quarterly, 17*, 71–82.

Twenge, J. M. (1997). Attitudes toward women, 1970–1995: A meta-analysis. *Psychology of Women Quarterly, 21*, 35–51.

U.S. Department of Defense. (2010a). *Report of the comprehensive review of the issues associated with the repeal of "don't ask, don't tell."* Washington, DC. Author.

U.S. Department of Defense. (2010b). *Report of the comprehensive review of the issues associated with the repeal of "don't ask, don't tell": Support plan for implementation.* Washington, DC. Author.

U.S. Department of Defense. (2012). *Joint Publication 1-02: Department of Defense dictionary of military and associated terms 08 November 2010* (as amended through 15 March 2012). Retrieved from http://www.dtic.mil/doctrine/dod_dictionary/

Warner, J. T., & Asch, B. J. (1995). The economics of military manpower. In K. Hartley & T. Sandler (Eds.), *Handbook of Defense Economics* (pp. 347–398). Amsterdam, the Netherlands: Elsevier.

Westat. (2010, November). *Support to the DoD comprehensive review working group analyzing the impact of repealing "don't ask, don't tell" Volume 1: Findings from the surveys.* Rockville, MD. Author.

Willness, C. R., Steel, P., & Lee, K. (2007). A meta-analysis of the antecedents and consequences of workplace sexual harassment. *Personnel Psychology, 60,* 127–162.

Yang, A. S. (1997). Trends: Attitudes toward homosexuality. *Public Opinion Quarterly, 61,* 477–507.

Zajonc, R. B. (1968). Attitudinal effects of mere exposure. *Journal of Personality and Social Psychology, 9*(Monograph Suppl. 2), 1–27.

Zellman, G. L. (1996). Implementing policy changes in large organizations: The case of gays and lesbians in the military. In G. M. Herek, J. B. Jobe, & R. M. Carney (Eds.), *Out in force: Sexual orientation in the military* (pp. 266–289). Chicago, IL: University of Chicago Press.

SECTION III
Organizational implications

Policy and Paradox: Grounded Theory at the Moment of DADT Repeal

JAMES E. PARCO, PhD
Department of Economics and Business, Colorado College, Colorado Springs, Colorado, USA

DAVID A. LEVY, PhD
Department of Management, United States Air Force Academy, Colorado Springs, Colorado, USA

Through a mixed-methods approach of oral history and grounded theory, we report on a study investigating the effects of the U.S. military's Don't Ask, Don't Tell policy on active-duty service members at the moment of transition to open service. A stratified, snowball sample of lesbian, gay, bisexual, and queer (LGBQ) service members (n = 17) from across all branches of the armed services were interviewed within two weeks of repeal (September 20, 2011). We find evidence that DADT was implicated in the structuring of military culture in terms of five irreconcilable contradictions: values, heroism, wartime, control, and silence. Military culture had moved in the direction of acceptance of LGBQ service members long before repeal, without the recognition of many leaders who had entered military service decades earlier.

This article is not subject to U.S. copyright law.

We wish to thank Aaron Belkin, Nathaniel Frank, and Andy Armacost for reviewing earlier versions of this article; Melodie Crummett for her impeccable efforts in transcript preparation; and Noah Schroeder (CC '12) for his outstanding research assistance in coding them. We also want to thank the anonymous participants in this study who remain unknown to us. Although many of the details of your individual stories don't appear here, each and every one was instrumental in furthering our understanding to arrive at the conclusions herein. Your stories were exceedingly inspirational and we thank you all for your continued service. Finally, we must note that the views expressed in this article are ours alone and do not necessarily reflect the official policy or position of the U.S. Air Force Academy, the U.S. Air Force, the Department of Defense, or the U.S. Government.

GOVERNMENT POLICY TOWARDS HOMOSEXUALITY IN THE US MILITARY

INTRODUCTION

The history of gays and lesbians serving in the United States military has been well-documented (Belkin, 2011; Bérubé, 1990; Burg, 2002; Frank, 2009; Haggerty, 2003; Herek & Belkin, 2006; Lehring, 2003; Meyer, 1998; Murphy, 1988; Shilts, 2005) The public debate that emerged in the 1980s over the efficacy of a policy that would allow gays to serve openly turned out to be a latent referendum on the morality of homosexuality (Frank, 2009; Levy & Parco, 2010). The result of that debate shrouded in the arguments of unit cohesion, military effectiveness, morale, good order and discipline manifested in a codification which later became known as Don't Ask, Don't Tell (DADT) (Pub. L. 103-160, 1993).

In 1993, only 40% of Americans supported the idea of gays and lesbians serving openly in the U.S. military (Burrelli & Dale, 2006). Key senior military leaders also shared these negative attitudes. In a 1993, Senate Armed Services Committee testimony, retired Army Gen. Norman Schwartzkopf testified that ". . . in my years of military service, I've experienced the fact that the introduction of an open homosexual into a small unit immediately polarizes that unit and destroys the very bonding that is so important for the unit's survival in time of war" (Healy, 1993). He also warned of the dangers that open homosexuality posed to heterosexuals when he stated on the record that "I am aware of instances where heterosexuals have been solicited to commit homosexual acts, and, even more traumatic emotionally, physically coerced to engage in such acts" (Belkin & Embser-Herbert, 2002). In line with a thin majority of public opinion, some of America's most recognizable military leaders went on record strongly advocating for an exclusionary policy, in cloaked opposition to civilian authority (Kirchick, 2008). Yet, despite a near crisis in civilian-military relations (Hillman, 2013), the debate ebbed with America finding itself in a strange space between the evolving cultural attitudes within society and a military policy that fomented an organization of silence.

By the mid-1990s, the debates in other Western nations across the globe began moving toward more inclusive approaches to open homosexuality, both within their societies and within their militaries (Frank et al., 2010; Gade, Segal, & Johnson, 1996). Studies of the Australian, Canadian, and Israeli experience (Belkin, 2003; Belkin & Levitt, 2001; Belkin & McNichol, 2000a, 2000b; Frank et al., 2010; Walzer, 2000) concluded negligible negative effects of repeal in any of the respective countries. Meanwhile, the United States and Britain remained the most notable exceptions and continued to ban openly gay service. In 2000, the United Kingdom repealed its ban and within nine months, the British Ministry of Defense reported policy implementation to be better than anticipated "with fewer problems than might have been expected" (British Ministry of Defense, 2000). The British government stated "no reported difficulties of note concerning homophobic behavior amongst Service Personnel" and concluded their report noting "a marked lack of reaction" to the change.

As evidence continued to mount against the hypothesized threats to unit cohesion (Bateman & Dalvi, 2004; Belkin, 2003; Belkin & Canaday, 2010; Belkin & Evans, 2000; British Ministry of Defense, 2000; Frank et al., 2010; Kaplan & Rosenmann, 2010), military effectiveness (Belkin, 2003, 2008; Kier, 1998), and morale (Belkin & Canaday, 2010; Belkin & Evans, 2000; Belkin & Levitt, 2001; Belkin & McNichol, 2000a), public attitudes in the United States continued to evolve (Estrada & Weiss, 1999). By 2008, in stark contrast to 1993, the trend among public opinion polls showed that a significant majority of Americans supported a move to repeal DADT. Belkin (2008) writes:

> [B]etween 58 and 79 percent of the public believes that gays and lesbians should be allowed to serve openly. Even the conservative Fox News polling organization found that 64 percent of the public, including 55 percent of Republicans, believe that gays and lesbians should be allowed to serve openly. Gallup found that 91 percent of young adults believe that gays and lesbians should be allowed to serve openly, and the polls show that solid majorities of people who attend church on a regular basis and people who hold negative attitudes about homosexuality believe that gays and lesbians should be allowed to serve openly in the military. Regardless of which of these eight polls most accurately captures the public's attitudes, it seems quite clear that "don't ask, don't tell" is inconsistent with public opinion . . .

As a result, on December 22, 2011, President Barack Obama signed the Don't Ask, Don't Tell Repeal Act of 2010 (Pub.L. 111-321, 2011). Seven months later, the U.S. military certified to Congress that it was ready to implement policy repeal, and, on September 20, 2011, DADT was relegated to the policy dustbins of history.

During the period of DADT, a great deal of research had been accomplished on the hypothesized impacts of policy repeal, but because of the policy limitations, little to no research was possible into the impact on those the policy affected most: lesbian, gay, bisexual, and queer (LGBQ) service members. Since repeal, there have been a significant number of stories told, chronicling the experiences of LGBQ service members who served under DADT (Huffman & Schultz, 2012; Seefried, 2011). Although many of the reports are compelling, empirical studies using narratives from LGBQ service members are scant.

OVERVIEW

We report on a study that investigated the policy impacts on LGBQ service members at the moment of repeal. Such studies of minority integration in the U.S. military have largely been impractical in the past. For example, due to the suddenness that President Harry Truman integrated ethnic minorities into the military by Executive Order 9981 in 1948, systematic studies did not emerge until months and years later (Binkin & Eitelberg, 1982). Likewise, when Congress began gender integration of the military academies, narrative analyis was also problematic at the moment of integration because it happened over a prolonged period (Segal, 1986). In the case of DADT repeal, the situation was markedly different because there were many months between policy change and implementation of that change.

Previous studies have documented stories of LGBQ service members pre-repeal, and in the future, it is likely that more studies will engage LGBQ service members post-repeal. However, a significant gap remains in the literature with no recorded scholarship on narrative analysis of LGBQ service members' stories at the moment of repeal. The present study aims to address this gap.

In the pages to follow, we report on an investigation that capitalized on the profound opportunity to analyze previously unheard voices of LGBQ service members at the moment of DADT repeal. Our research design uniquely captures the data without the confounding effect of time delay. We argue the present study is important for several reasons:

1. Any analysis prior to DADT repeal was constrained legally, and had a distorting and limiting effect under a policy that had been designed to eliminate voice of any kind.
2. Future analysis about the moment of repeal will unavoidably be subject to hindsight bias and other methodological problems (i.e., typical problem of forgetting).
3. Narrative analysis at the micro-level (individual) at the moment of repeal provides insight at a period of transition at the macro-level (organizational, institutional, and policy level).

With the unique design of the present study, we captured an oral history snapshot of active-duty service members' narratives at an otherwise fleeting moment. In the following sections, we employ a grounded theory approach that analyzes these captured narratives and formulates a conceptual framework of the impacts of DADT on an individual, interpersonal, and organizational level.

METHODS

This study used a two-stage protocol that combined oral history methods (Thomson, 1998; Doel, 2003; Leavy, 2011) for data-collection followed by grounded theory methods (Strauss & Coribin, 1998; Glaser & Strauss, 1967) for data analysis. Through anonymous oral interviews, we documented the attitudes, opinions, perceptions and stories of lesbian, gay, bisexual, and queer (LGBQ) men and women who served on active-duty in the various branches of the U.S. armed forces prior to DADT repeal on September 20, 2011.

Oral history was befitting as the first-stage of this study because of the nature of the data sources. Until DADT repeal, active-duty service members could have been discharged for homosexual behavior or a propensity to engage in such (DADT; Pub. L. 103–160, 1993), and, thus, gay service members remained without voice to express the impacts of the policy. Once DADT was repealed, these voices were restored, allowing us to pursue oral history as a primary data source to investigate DADT's impacts on the gay service member.

When analyzed collectively, oral histories can provide insights beyond traditional interview summaries (Thomson, 1998). This qualitative method allows interview subjects an opportunity to not only address the historical record directly by clarifying misconceptions in third-person accounts, but also to discuss their own reflections, motives, analysis—and most significantly, to provide a personal assessment of the significance of the events in which they took part. Employing an oral history method can capture a far richer context leading to a more refined understanding of both the intent of the participants and the events themselves.

SAMPLE

The Don't Ask, Don't Tell Repeal Act of 2010 (Pub. L. 111-321, 2010) was certified by the President and Joint Chiefs of Staff as ready for implementation on July 22, 2011. Subsequently, in accordance with the law, the repeal went into effect on September 20, 2011. Within four weeks of repeal, we interviewed a cross-sectional sample of active-duty military members using a snowball sampling technique. By the completion of the study, 27 telephone-recorded interviews yielded 862 minutes of data. Interview duration ranged from 20 to 58 minutes in length. On average, interviews lasted approximately 34 minutes.

Of the 32 initial volunteers who contacted us for this study, only 17 were willing to follow through with the interview at the moment of repeal, for a response rate of 53%. Whereas 38% of recruited Air Force subjects declined, 50% of Army subjects, and 66% of Navy subjects declined, respectively.

During August 2012, just prior to the one-year anniversary of repeal, we conducted follow up interviews with as many subjects as possible ($n = 10$), although due to the anonymity inherent in the protocol, we had no way to follow up with subjects who had abandoned the anonymous email account initially established for this study.

SUBJECTS

Respondents were 59% male and 41% female. Eighty-two percent self-identified as either lesbian or gay, whereas 18% identified as either bisexual or queer. The youngest interview subject was 19 years old, while the oldest was 43 years of age. Although we strived to have equal representation within the sample of enlisted, cadet, and officer subjects, the resultant sample was officer-biased at 47%, compared to 30% enlisted and 23% cadet. Each of the uniformed services was represented in the sample (Army, Navy, Marines, Air Force, and Coast Guard) to include the three service academies. (We included at least one cadet from West Point, Annapolis, and the Air Force Academy.) Approximately half of the sample identified as White or Caucasian with the other half identifying as African American (12%), Asian (18%), or Hispanic (12%). All subjects were active duty service members during the moment of repeal with the exception of two reservists. One reservist indicated she had recently transitioned to the reserves in order to remain co-located with her partner at an overseas assignment. The other reservist had been initially commissioned in the reserves 14 years previously but had served as a full-time reservist immediately prior to, and during the moment of DADT repeal.

PROCEDURE

Recruiting proved to be one of the most challenging aspects of this study since all recruiting had to be accomplished prior to the repeal of 10 USC § 654 to begin interviews immediately thereafter. Because of the potential risks faced by volunteers to speak openly about their homosexual identity, the Colorado College Institutional Research Board (IRB) mandated a procedure to elicit volunteers with complete anonymity. Using this procedure, we solicited volunteer participation through the OutServe Facebook group (http://www.facebook.com/OutServe) in July 2011 inviting potential participants to create an anonymous email account (such as Yahoo, Hotmail, or Gmail) and using a fictitious name. At the time, there were approximately 3,500 members of the group. Through this recruiting method, we received only one response. We then implemented a snowball sampling technique asking trusted agents to reach out to gay and lesbian members which resulted in 32 volunteers who responded to an anonymous online survey in a manner in which they could not be identified since the DADT policy was in effect during the period of recruitment.

Interviewing Technique

After recording volunteers' (fictitious) names and (anonymous) e-mail addresses in a database, letters were sent out electronically to participants approximately two to four weeks in advance of the anticipated interview welcoming him or her to the study. In the introductory letter, the purpose and process of the study was explained. Additionally, the following eight questions were posed for subjects to ponder:

1. Can you recall any incidents that made you feel uncomfortable as a gay service member?
2. Have you faced integrity issues as a gay service member while living under DADT?
3. Were your peers aware of your sexual orientation? What about your superiors? Can you recall any stories of how others viewed homosexuality (yours or in general?)
4. Why did you join the military, and why have you remained on active duty?
5. How did "don't ask, don't tell" affect you?
6. Now that DADT is gone, how might you imagine things will be different for you?
7. If there is one thing you'd like the world to know about what life was like as a gay service member, what would that be?
8. There are people who believe that homosexuality is a choice. What would you like these people to understand about homosexuality from your perspective?

The questions were not intended as directive, but merely to catalyze subjects to reflect.

After scheduling a mutually acceptable time by email, electronic invitations were emailed to participants with a phone number and secure passcode. After obtaining affirmative consent, as required by the IRB, and gaining the subjects' express consent to have the interview recorded, the lead interviewer engaged in several minutes of conversation to put the subject at ease and then turned the interview over to the subject asking them to share any stories that came to mind as they thought about the interview.

All interviews were conducted over a recorded telephone line using a WebEx conferencing system. Both coauthors participated in each interview with one person conducting the interview and remaining fully present and engaged with the subject, with the other person taking notes of key themes, events, and concepts. Immediately following the interview, the coauthors held a private conference to discuss and record any other observations and capture real-time analysis and thematic connections.

All interviews were recorded and held in a secure electronic storage location. A professional transcriptionist transcribed each interview, word for word, identifying each interview by page and line number to facilitate coding. Three paper copies of each interview were produced and separately coded by each coauthor (following a grounded theory coding methodology) in addition to a research assistant hired specifically for this task.

Analysis

The data collected from the oral history interviews became the basis for qualitative data analysis using grounded theory protocols (Corbin & Strauss, 2008; Glaser & Strauss, 1967). The earliest phase of analysis occurred during and immediately after each interview with one of the two researchers responsible for memoing. This memoing process became invaluable during the initial coding process where all transcripts were open coded. Open coding was initially accomplished by each of the coauthors independently to identify the most salient themes: both those themes that emerged from the initial memoing process and those themes that emerged from a second pass through the data. This process allowed us to configure the emergent conceptualizations into integrated patterns, which are denoted by categories and their properties (Glaser, 1998). The emergent categories included values, self-preservation tactics, relationships, emotions and organizational context, which became the basis for the axial codes, which appear in Figure 1 and were used in the second phase of transcript coding (Kelle, 2005). These axial codes involved the context, interactional strategies and consequences inherent in the data (Strauss & Corbin, 1990). In the case of our data, we also discovered that interactions occurred on three distinct levels: the individual, the interpersonal, and the institutional.

Coding worksheets were prepared from the axial codes and used to independently recode each transcript (by three independent coders) in an effort to bolster analysis validity and between-rater reliability.

The final stage of coding involved memoing and sorting. Memoing is often regarded as the "core of grounded theory methodology" (Glaser, 1998). It involves recoding all transcripts, but this time through a holistic perspective conceptualizing the critical incidents in the oral history data. When complete, we had created approximately 40 pages of memos. Once the second phase

Individual	Interpersonal	Institutional
Emotional	Relationships: On-duty/Off-duty	Cultural acceptance/nonacceptance
Forced reflectiveness	Networks	Influence of war
Personal identity	Attitudes of others	Data-driven knowledge
Individual values	Values of others	Institutional values
←	Values	→

FIGURE 1 Axial codes.

of memoing had been completed, we sorted the memos and identified the most critical incidents, which appeared in two or more independent observations. These critical incidents included career limitations, attempted suicide, rape, fake marriages, alcohol problems, depression and PTSD symptoms, blackmail, and coercion. We include examples of these incidents in later paragraphs.

Comparing the themes from the memoing analysis and with integrated coding worksheets around the axial codes, we recategorized the data into blocks around the holistic themes and axial codes into a tentative core. The tentative core which integrated the entirety of the oral history data revealed two primary categories: 1) military leadership; and 2) military culture. Based on this core, we developed a grounded theory of contradiction as the core of the study that largely explained the variation in the data as incongruence of values at the individual, interpersonal, and institutional levels across organizational contexts.

THEORETICAL RESULTS

We propose a grounded theory of contradiction as the core integrating the axial codes identified in Figure 1, which formed a tentative core around the concepts of leadership and culture. By continually asking the question, "What's going on?" we arrived at the following five irreconcilable contradictions inherent in the implementation of DADT. In the paragraphs that follow, we articulate a grounded theory that most aptly captures the variance in the oral history data of our subject population ($n = 17$) of active-duty LGBQ service members who served under the policy.

Values Contradiction

> And I've commanded twice, both at the rank of captain. And in both situations, I was interviewed. Usually when you get to the question about, you know, for some odd reason we'll go over whatever is on my officer record brief; we'll talk about the experiences that I've had; we'll talk about, you know, my officer evaluation reports. At the end of the interview, we'll start talking about personal life, personal goals, family, et cetera. Right around that question, "Well, are you married?" "No, I'm not married yet." "Oh, well, what are you waiting on?" "I'm not waiting on anything. Just not married yet, sir." "Oh, okay. Well, do you have kids at least?" "No, I don't have any kids." And, you know, maybe it was my imagination, but it was almost as if—well, it wasn't almost as if. I found myself bracing on either occasion, waiting for the lieutenant colonel or the colonel that was interviewing me at the time, you know, just waiting for that question, either "Are you gay?" or "Do you not like women?" And

there was at least one time in particular I thought that I wasn't going to get the command, because I felt like the commander had that raised eyebrow and sort of had that question in the back of his head. But luckily it didn't turn out that way. (Troy, p. 10)

At an organizational level, desired values are manifest in the institutionally articulated core values held by each service. Analysis of the various branches core values across the services revealed the fundamental core value explicitly common to every military service as one of integrity. As stated in the core value statement for the Army, "Integrity is a quality you develop by adhering to moral principles. It requires that you do and say nothing that deceives others" (Army; http://www.goarmy.com/soldier-life/being-a-soldier/living-the-army-values.html). The Navy defines integrity as a form of honor and instructs its sailors to "Abide by an uncompromising code of integrity, taking responsibility for [your] actions and keeping [your] word (Navy; http://www.navy.mil/navydata/navy_legacy_hr.asp?id=193). The Marine Corps most explicitly defined the expected behaviors, "exemplify the ultimate in ethical and moral behavior; to never lie cheat or steal; to abide by an uncompromising code of integrity; respect human dignity; and respect others (Marines; http://www.usmarines.com/core-values.html). Both the Coast Guard and Air Force list integrity as their respective first core value: "Integrity First" (http://www.airforce.com/learn-about/our-values/), and "Integrity is our standard. We demonstrate uncompromising ethical conduct and moral behavior in all our personal actions" (Coast Guard; http://www.uscga.edu/display.aspx?id=339). Yet, the very organization demanding integrity from their organizational members was paradoxically the very same institution, which systemically prevented it through policy enforcement, to maintain institutional integrity.

At an individual level of analysis, we initially hypothesized that sacrifice was a necessary burden of an LGBQ service member who elected to serve under DADT, as pointed out by Adm. Mullen in February 2010, that sacrifice was one's integrity (Barnes, 2010). Indeed, this finding was among the most robust in our data with every subject revealing some pattern of deceit, avoidance, and misrepresentation. For example:

I made a conscious decision to marry one of my friends, a gay man, before I came into the Air Force. So, I came into the Air Force as a married woman and have remained a married woman. So, even though it gets a little hard to explain why I don't live with my husband, because we're constantly apart, it does provide me a huge amount of protection, because with that wedding ring on I am just assumed to be an outspoken, sometimes liberal, tough lawyer instead of assumed to be a lesbian. (Jaws, p. 5)

> I mean, I found myself at times lying and making up a girlfriend, you know. And I flat out, you know—I would just make up stories that didn't exist. I mean, it's very, very uncomfortable. (Josh, p. 5)

> I'm so used to not being able to trust anybody that I just automatically—you know, your first instinct is to lie, whether it's a friend or foe. (Coastie, p. 11)

What we had not hypothesized was the integrity dilemma DADT created at an interpersonal level, particularly for military members who were opposed to gays in the military. Supervisors with strong religious convictions often wanted to reach out to suspected gay service members in order to help or fix them. According to one subject:

> I remember one commander asked whether he could meet with my client. I said, "Why did you want to do that?" He said, "You know, I want to tell him about Jesus." I said, "Sir, what do you mean by that?" "Well, you know, I believe that God can deliver him, and you know, if he's being discharged for"—he had made an outing statement. He's like, "I'd really like to talk to him about how his mother feels about that, how his mother feels about the fact that he's gay, whether he's tried reparative therapy." (Josh, p. 7)

For those with religious beliefs that compelled them to reach out and "help" LGBQ service members to become more moral individuals, DADT ran counter to their value system because they couldn't. Because of this, integrity was not an option for these service members either.

Even supervisors and commanders that were against an exclusionary policy who did all they could to maintain the highest levels of mental health and wellness were forced to turn their heads to issues with their LGBQ subordinates when homosexual relationships were involved. Moreover, when these commanders became aware of impermissible conduct under DADT and were forced to separate their troops, they too, had to sacrifice their values. The letter of the law left them no choice, and when they turned their heads and followed their consciences, again, they were forced to sacrifice their values of obedience and loyalty to the institution when they failed to do their legally required duty. The policy created a significant conflict for commanders who tried to maintain the integrity of the institution and simultaneously preserve their own:

> So, there's that scripted speech that the commanders all have to give about Don't-Ask-Don't-Tell, and there's part of it that talks about the Defense of Marriage Act—I think it does—maybe my [commander] just added that part, I don't know. But during that part he kind of like stopped the speech and was like, "You know, this is"—he's kind of the swearing

type—"this is bullshit. It's like we're telling gay people we will treat you like—treat you equally some of the time, but not all the time." He went on to explain that because of the Defense of Marriage Act, that gay couples in the military still couldn't get any benefits and stuff. He was just angry about that. And while he was giving the speech, he was looking right at me the whole time. It was like he was staring me down. It was like "This is bullshit that this is what's going on." It was sort of a really awesome experience there with him and with my squadron in general. They were all so supportive. If someone had tried to like turn me in or get me in trouble because of Don't-Ask-Don't-Tell, my squad would have definitely turned on them, like they wouldn't have been able to really do anything, which just meant a lot to me, because I was very worried about it before, you know, that someone would turn me in and stuff. (Walt, p. 14)

10 USC § 654 made it explicitly clear in the letter of the law that sacrifice was the price of service in the armed forces:

10 USC § 654 (a)(5): The conduct of military operations requires members of the armed forces to make extraordinary sacrifices . . .

Yet, despite the intent of DADT, everyone was placed in a position of having to sacrifice his or her values. Regardless of one's position on the policy, gay, and heterosexual alike—a contradiction of values emerged from DADT implementation.

Wartime Contradiction

In 1993, after a prolonged period free from any major national conflict (notwithstanding the 43 days of Operation Desert Storm), no one balked at the preamble of 10 USC § 654, section (a)(6) that held "Success in combat requires military units that are characterized by high morale, good order and discipline, and unit cohesion." It was generally believed that military units must be appropriately structured to allow the nation to most effectively fight its wars. Opponents of gays in the military successfully argued their presence degraded America's ability to fight wars for reasons stated in the law. However, following the events of 2001, America's status returned to a nation at war providing an unexpected test of the efficacy of DADT's assumptions. Empirically, the very presence of gays in the military showcased the most salient factors of what really mattered in wartime.

Due to extensive press coverage of discharged Arabic linguists in 2004 (Frank, 2009), Americans realized that the military was discharging service members with critical skills when the country needed them the most, simply because they were gay. Many commanders had great difficulty willfully parting with critically needed resources. This pattern was also identified in multiple cases throughout our data. We found significant evidence at the institutional level of bold and defiant commanders who put the mission first by refusing to discharge openly gay personnel in their units. One subject remarked:

> One of the younger females from a different division went to her leading petty officer and told her that I was gay, and her leading petty officer sent it up to my master chief. My master chief actually told her to go away and to mind her own business, because she had better things to do than to kick someone out of the Navy during a time of war for, you know, liking girls. So, I—that actually made me feel pretty good, because I knew at that point that I had the support of my leadership. (Carolyn, p. 5)

Deeper still, the question regarding gays in the military revolved around war fighting capability and whether or not openly gay service would have an adverse effect on it. An exclusionary policy remained in place for so long because arguments of hypothesized negative impact of openly gay service persisted by tenacity, despite an absence of evidence. When data became available as America transitioned to a wartime nation, the empirical results supported the opposite case. Many commanders refused to discharge gay troops because they were needed immediately in order to preserve combat capability. This aspect was observed by gay troops, for example:

> Most of the people are generally accepting of it so long as you don't do anything else to damage—so long as you do your job, your mission, you do it well, you do it right, you do it on time, they're not going to have a problem with you. (Joe, p. 5)

10 USC § 654 made it explicitly clear that homosexuals would pose an unacceptable risk to military capability:

> **10 USC § 654 (a)(14)&(15):** The armed forces must maintain personnel policies that exclude persons whose presence in the armed forces would create an unacceptable risk to the armed forces' high standards of morale, good order and discipline, and unit cohesion that are the essence of military capability. The presence in the armed forces of persons who demonstrate a propensity or intent to engage in homosexual acts would create an unacceptable risk to the high standards of morale, good order and discipline, and unit cohesion that are the essence of military capability.

But when put to the test, known gays not only didn't harm military capability, they enhanced it when the nation needed its servants' expertise most when it came to fighting its wars (Frank, 2009). When military performance in combat finally mattered, gay was okay.

Heroism Contradiction

> All the years that I've been in, you see all the "Support the troops" stuff, little yellow ribbons, in my mind and in the minds of a lot of other gay people, there's always been a little invisible asterisk there that says "except for the gays." (Coastie, p. 11)

As America waged war in Iraq and Afghanistan, its citizens reflected on the price paid by its service members to seek revenge on those who would do them harm. "Thank you for your service" became a mantra within American culture, a sharp departure from the post-Vietnam era. America's military men and women became its heroes.

Nearly all of the participants in the study acknowledged they had joined their respective branch of the service for patriotic reasons. However, we captured the personal histories of several participants who joined the military to fix themselves. They aspired to be the heroes most Americans view every soldier, sailor, airman, and Marine to be. On one level, many of these participants served and behaved in a truly heroic fashion, earning decorations and medals to prove it. They displayed no outward ego, they asked for no special attention, and they sought no further reward or payment. By most common definitions, they were, indeed, heroes. Unfortunately, with DADT, because they were lesbian, gay, or bisexual, they also received another message from the very organization that made them heroes. The message from DOD was very clear: "If you are gay, you cannot be a hero, even if you were, and if we find out about it, we will throw you out of our ranks." One subject remarked:

> And that was kind of a reality check right there, because I knew that if I were to tell anyone or if anyone were to find out, I had the chance of getting kicked out. And I had only ever wanted to serve the military—or serve my country as far as I can remember. Since the second grade, I had wanted to go to the Naval Academy and, you know, just serve my country. (Carolyn, p. 4)

As was suggested by a majority of the our study participants, it can be argued that the patriotism demonstrated by gay service members was, in some ways, more noble than their straight counterparts because of the additional sacrifices they were willing to endure in order to serve.

> And in a way for the gay, lesbian, bisexual—for the queer folks who did choose to do the military service, you could characterize them as potentially more patriotic than your regular straight ones, because they chose—it was that important to them to serve their country, they chose to endure having these limitations placed on them for, you know, acting—being able to just lead a healthy lifestyle. (Leona, p. 15)

The irony was profound. The very individuals who were hailed as heroes by the citizens they served could be immediately regarded as outcasts if deemed to be in the best interests of the organizations that made them heroes in the first place, because DADT required it:

> **10 USC § 654 (b)(1)(d):** A member of the armed forces shall be separated from the armed forces under regulations prescribed by the Secretary of Defense if, under the particular circumstances of the case, the member's continued [homosexual] presence in the armed forces is consistent with the interests of the armed forces . . .

Control Contradiction

No one has articulated the paradoxical nature of behavioral control and the chain of command more eloquently than the senior officer portrayed in the 1992 movie, *A Few Good Men*. At the conclusion of the movie, Col. Nathan R. Jessup is questioned on the witness stand for the death of one of his Marines, at the hands of his own Marines. He's caught in a logic trap after affirming that all Marines follow his orders, and he ordered that the private be left alone, and, yet, he is beaten to death by the hand of his fellow Marines. The question posed to Col. Jessup is whether or not he was in control. Either he wasn't, and his Marines disobeyed him, or he was, and he was, ultimately, responsible for ordering a murder.

That very same year that *A Few Good Men* debuted, the highest ranking officer in the U.S. military, Gen. Colin Powell, gave sanction to the policy that would eventually become DADT in a letter to Rep. Patricia Schroeder of the House Armed Services Committee stating:

> Skin color is a benign nonbehavioral characteristic. Sexual orientation is perhaps the most profound of human behavioral characteristics. Comparison of the two is a convenient but invalid argument. (Powell, 1992)

Like the mythical Col. Jessup, the very real Gen. Powell communicated to everyone in the clearest manner of a supremely confident military commander. Powell believed that unlike skin color, being gay was different because of its implied behavioral impact. Although Powell's argument carried the day in 1992, the irony of his latent behavioral argument was befuddling. Known for its insistence on discipline, the military is well versed in controlling behavior. Absent any empirical evidence from and American military context to the contrary, it seemed ironic at the time to hear an argument that the integration of openly gay service members would somehow threaten the military's ability to control their behavior.

Then, 17 years later, the repeal of DADT went off without a hitch because of the same overwhelming hierarchical control that defines the very nature of military bureaucracy. As it turned out, Powell was exactly right, but on a different level. Military leaders could not control what was happening in their own organizations, but it had nothing to do with fantasized behavior of LGBQ service members at an individual level. Instead, the more meaningful change was transpiring at the organizational level—the culture was changing. Senior military leaders focused on the wrong level. Despite their most ardent desire to control every aspect of the military, senior leaders who led the resistance to DADT repeal could not control the one aspect that mattered most, and of which they remained largely unaware. Their own organizational culture had changed without them. At the lower organizational levels, things had changed, despite the persistence of DADT remaining in place:

> Everywhere I seemed to go, no one cared if you were gay. Even the leadership was like "I'm not wasting my time doing a bunch of paperwork and kicking some sailor out just because they're a homosexual. It's a waste of time. It's a waste of money. It's a waste of resources. You know, the Navy trained—spends so much money to train someone to get in the fight, to lead and protect our country, and we want to kick them out because they're gay?" "No, it's stupid. We're just going to turn the other cheek and, you know say, 'I don't know what you're talking about.'" (Carolyn, p. 9)

Advocates of banning gays and lesbians in 1993 argued that the chain of command would be threatened if gays were allowed to serve openly, however, when repealed in 2011, the end of DADT resulted with no observable impacts, in large part, because of the tremendous control the military has over its personnel. Evidence following the first anniversary of repeal supports this finding (Belkin et al., 2012).

> **10 USC § 654 (a)(7):** One of the most critical elements in combat capability is unit cohesion, that is, the bonds of trust among individual service members that make the combat effectiveness of a military unit greater than the sum of the combat effectiveness of the individual unit members.

Silence Contradiction

Arguments against allowing gays to serve openly in the military tended to revolve around the notion that gays would have a negative impact on unit cohesion, which is vital to military effectiveness. Under DADT, it looked like the policy worked to a non-astute observer. Gays were able to serve and unit cohesion appeared to be unaffected. Straight service members did not feel threatened, partly due to the fact that those with homophobic biases tended to not see gays among the ranks. Gay service members didn't complain either, primarily because their voices were silenced by the policy that promised expulsion if they were to speak.

Even though DADT may have seemed like a viable political compromise in 1993, it turned out to be a policy that could never work because it took voice away from everyone. Gays couldn't speak out to seek help for the harms they endured, for fear of being discharged. Those in positions of authority who recognized the perils of DADT were unable to speak out either because they were forced to process discharges for openly gay service members. Even those opposed to openly gay service were silenced because the policy seemingly appeased them on this one issue. DADT didn't work, and, yet, it continued to perpetuate a self-sustaining illusion for nearly two decades by suppressing the very voices that could invalidate it from within.

Beyond not working, however, DADT also fostered an operational environment conducive to mental and physical injury of LGBQ service members. In our very small sample ($n = 17$) of what was likely thousands of active-duty LGBQ members in September 2011, we discovered multiple occurrences of physical harm (suicide attempts, rape, alcohol abuse), psychological harm (depression, PTSD, harassment), and damage to one's career (blackmail, coercion, adverse personnel action). Nearly every subject in our study provided one or more examples of harm as a direct result of DADT. Below are a series of quotes as representative examples of critical incident that illustrate some of the more disconcerting ways of how DADT impacted the lives of LBGQ service members.

Isolation

I was raped about two years ago back when I was in Monterey, California. And it was by a guy. And I wasn't really sure what to do. And I went for a week without telling anybody, because I didn't know who [sic] to tell. I wasn't sure how to handle this. (Pedro, p. 15)

Fake Marriages

There was one person that did know, that I ended up telling, who later on ended up telling everybody else. When she started telling people and the flight chief actually got involved and said, "I'm hearing some things about you. It needs to stop." And out of left field, I said, "Well, sir, I'm actually engaged. I don't know what she's talking about." So, I actually ended up getting married while I was in, full well knowing that I was a lesbian; full well knowing that this guy was gay, which was perfect for me because I didn't have to perform in any way. But it was—he was able to come to functions with me and it made it look legit. (Beth, p. 7)

Suffering in silence

And then just times where I was just mad at the military in general—like when a boyfriend of mine died unexpectedly who was also in the military. It really was tough trying to fake my emotions about why I was upset and trying to act like I wasn't as upset as I was, because nobody knew about us. I wanted to talk to his family and I just couldn't because I was afraid that the military would find out and I would lose my job. And it just really hurt, having no one to talk to at the time, and then seeing this whole situation where people have died and they get to go home and time off for grieving. I just had to sit there at my own desk and deal with it alone. (Coastie, p. 14)

Sexual assault

An army O-5 at one point during my deployment raped me at gunpoint. I'd been a cop in a previous life, dealt with plenty of cases dealing with rape victims, prosecuted and defended numerous rape cases, and still never thought it would happen to me, but it did. At the time he told me that he would kill me if I told anyone. The fact that he was pointing a gun at my head sort of made me believe that threat. And he was in a particular position in that deployment where he controlled who went out on convoys and who didn't. So, it wasn't a very happy time in Afghanistan. (Jaws, p. 12)

Inability to seek help

I had to go to mental health and get counseling, and—because for me realizing and understanding what I was and who I was came at a horrible time. I think it's a horrible time to have to go through that at [a military academy] because it just exacerbates the problem, but in counseling I couldn't really—because it was a military counselor, I couldn't say how I felt, I couldn't say what I was going through. I couldn't bring a huge factor of the problems I was having into the conversation to get help. And that's what I was there for, to get help. (Susan, p. 7)

GOVERNMENT POLICY TOWARDS HOMOSEXUALITY IN THE US MILITARY

BLACKMAIL

There were straight cadets that found out I was gay. I think one found out because of another gay cadet was pissed off at me, so he went around telling people I was gay, which didn't really make any sense. So he went and told a couple of straight cadets that I was gay and then they kept trying to have me basically help them out with homework and stuff like that. I don't want to get too much into that, but basically they were—I don't want to say that they were blackmailing me or threatening me, but they were kind of holding it over my head, like "Hey, we're not going to keep spreading these rumors as long as you keep helping us out." That was a lot freshman and sophomore year. (Jake, p. 14)

CAREER HINDRANCE

And I was told, "You've given a great interview and I would recommend you. However, I'm not going to be able to, because your detachment command does not support it." And the reason why is he told me he believes that you lead an alternative lifestyle, and he's therefore—and that you would be, you know—you would leave a black mark on the Air Force if put out there into the public eye to try and represent the Air Force and recruit; that it would send the wrong message to the public . . . As a result, I reassigned to the reserves, so I could stay close, you know, for my father's final months. So, that's how I started my career. So, Don't-Ask-Don't-Tell and specific discrimination and harassment really shaped the start of my career. (Leona, p. 7)

DOUBLE LIFE

There's this entire part of your life that they either don't know about or you have to lie about. You have to make it up as you go along, because if you're not with a guy or you're not sleeping with somebody, eventually it starts, "Well, what are you, gay?" And it's like, "No, no, no, of course not." "Okay, so maybe there is somebody." It's very hard. So there's always this factor in your mind that you can get as close to a person as you want, but you have to have this wall up, and then either not say anything or lie. It just—it's awful and it messes with your integrity and it messes with you as a human being and who you are. (Beth, p. 4)

FEIGNED INTENT

And I definitely felt pressure. People would set you up with friends, being a single guy, a pilot, available—people want to set you up with people.

So, I would always go on a first date and then never let it go beyond that or try to never let it go too far, only because I knew that in my heart that it wasn't right. I didn't want to be wasting anybody's time. And I guess that really was a little bit selfish of me, but you know, in the light of self preservation, I kind of did it anyway. (Tom, p. 8)

Depression

It got to the point where I was diagnosed with depression. I was drinking too much. I'd never had a drink in my life. I was a Christian person. I was taught alcohol was evil. I started to drink. You know, I got depressed. Not until I started talking with my counselor did I realize all this surrounded how I view myself as a gay person. I had a low self-esteem, and that—I may perform highly at my profession and I may be able to keep a lot of friends, but I have a terrible view of one's self, and DADT fed into that. I mean, it basically was a policy that reconfirmed what I struggled with, which is that I was a bad person. I mean, why else would the government fire me, if I wasn't bad. I mean, they would fire me for no other reason other than I'm gay, if they found out that I'm gay. That's pretty serious in 2011 to lose your job over something that quite frankly has no impact on my job. (Josh, p. 15)

In summary, despite the harms imposed on LGBQ service members by DADT, it remained a viable policy because it's very structure defied assessment of any kind. It outwardly appeared to work because nothing, and no one, could contest it.

CONCLUSIONS

10 USC § 654 (a)(8): Military life is fundamentally different from civilian life in that—
   (A) the extraordinary responsibilities of the armed forces, the unique conditions of military service, and the critical role of unit cohesion, require that the military community, while subject to civilian control, exist as a specialized society; and
   (B) the military society is characterized by its own laws, rules, customs, and traditions, including numerous restrictions on personal behavior, that would not be acceptable in civilian society.

10 USC § 654 was a statement of culture by the 103rd Congress that open homosexuality was incompatible with military service. Policy makers excluded open lesbian and gay service members because it was then culturally acceptable to do so. However, as the empirical data that gay

(1) The Values Contradiction — "Integrity is not an option"

All were forced to sacrifice their values under DADT: those that supported LGBQ service members, those that opposed them, and the LGBQ service members themselves.

(2) The Wartime Contradiction — "It doesn't matter when it matters"

The presence of LGBQ service members was inconsistent with combat capability until the nation went to war, and then it didn't matter.

(3) The Heroism Contradiction — "Yellow ribbon, no rainbow"

The very individuals who were hailed as heroes by the citizens they served could be immediately regarded as outcasts if deemed to be in the best interests of the organizations that made them heroes in the first place.

(4) The Control Contradiction — "We can't control them unless we need to"

Military leaders argued that behavioral control would be threatened if LGBQ service members were allowed to serve openly, and yet when DADT was finally repealed, it happened without issue because of the tremendous control military leaders have over their personnel, both gay and straight, who tend to behave anyway.

(5) The Silence Contradiction — "Don't ask, don't tell, don't know"

DADT persisted as a viable policy because it allowed no mechanism to assess the effectiveness of the policy's impact on military effectiveness, cohesion or morale.

FIGURE 2 A grounded theory of contradiction (Parco & Levy, 2012).

service—open or not—was never the threat that was claimed, society's understanding changed. It took the 111th Congress to close the increasing gap between societal attitudes and military policy. As societal attitudes evolved, so did the attitudes of the majority of citizen-soldiers who comprised the military. Years before DADT repeal, military culture had moved in the direction of acceptance of LGBQ service members. However, many leaders who had entered the military decades earlier failed to recognize that their organizational cultures had changed without them.

Increased divergence between societal attitudes and military policy toward LGBQ service members created a system of irreconcilable contradiction that drove the evolution of military culture. As shown in Figure 2, the oral history data gathered in this study found evidence of five contradictions—values, heroism, wartime, control, and silence—that confounded cultural convergence toward acceptance of openly gay service members. The most resilient finding, across every narrative analyzed was contradiction of values. Individual LGBQ service members tended to live double lives, suffered from depression and harassment, with some enduring career limitations as a direct result of DADT.

Overall, this study concluded at a macro level, that while the core of military culture had remained resilient throughout the tenure of DADT, it converged toward greater acceptance of suspected gay service members years before repeal. More remarkably, this cultural shift happened unbeknownst to the senior leaders who continued to rally behind the rhetoric of 10 USC § 654 as a justification of the policy.

In the end, DADT worked for the same reason DADT repeal worked. Military leaders declared how things were to be done in accordance with society's mandates, and that is precisely what happened. Despite the negative impacts fostered by DADT during its tenure, military leaders held to the unwavering virtue of obedience to their civilian masters, and implemented the will of the people once more.

REFERENCES

Barnes, J. (2010, February 2). Joint Chiefs Chairman Mullen supports right of gays to serve in military. *Los Angeles Times*. Retrieved from http://articles.latimes.com/2010/feb/02/nation/la-na-gays-military3-2010feb03

Bateman, G., & Dalvi, S. (2004). *Multinational military units and homosexual personnel*. Center for the Study of Sexual Minorities in the Military, University of California, Santa Barbara. Retrieved from http://www.palmcenter.org/publications/dadt/multinational_military_units_and_homosexual_personnel

Belkin, A. (2003). Don't ask, don't tell: Is the gay ban based on military necessity? *Parameters, 33,* 108–119. Retrieved from http://www.palmcenter.org/node/617

Belkin, A. (2008). Don't Ask, Don't Tell': Does the gay ban undermine the military's reputation? *Armed Forces & Society, 34,* 276–291. Retrieved from http://www.palmcenter.org/publications/dadt/dont_ask_dont_tell_does_the_gay_ban_undermine_the_militarys_reputation

Belkin, A. (2011). *How we won: Progressive lessons from the repeal of "don't ask, don't tell."* The Huffington Post Media Group. [Amazon Kindle ed.]

Belkin, A., & Canaday, M. (2010). Assessing the integration of gays and lesbians: Into the South African National Defence Force. *Scientia Militaria, 38,* 1–21. Retrieved from http://www.palmcenter.org/publications/dadt/assessing_integration_gays_and_lesbians_south_african_national_defence_force

Belkin, A., & Embser-Herbert, M. S. (2002). A modest proposal: Privacy as a flawed rationale for the exclusion of gays and lesbians from the U.S. military. *International Security, 27,* 178–197. Retrieved from http://www.palmcenter.org/publications/dadt/a_modest_proposal

Belkin, A., Ender, M. G., Furia, S., Packard, G. A., Lucas, G. R., Schultz, T. S., Samuels, S. M., & Segal, D. R. (2012). One year out: An assessment of DADT repeal's impact on military readiness. In J. E. Parco & D. A. Levy (Eds.), *Evolution of government policy towards homosexuality in the US military: The rise and fall of DADT*. New York, NY: Routledge, forthcoming. Retrieved from http://www.palmcenter.org/publications/dadt/one_year_out

Belkin, A., & Evans, R. L. (2000). The effects of including gay and lesbian soldiers in the British armed forces. Unpublished manuscript, Palm Center, University of California, Santa Barbara. Retrieved from http://www.palmcenter.org/publications/dadt/british_soldier_motivation

Belkin, A., & Levitt, M. (2001). Homosexuality and the Israel Defense Forces. *Armed Forces & Society, 27*, 541–565. Retrieved from http://afs.sagepub.com/content/27/4/541.full.pdf+html

Belkin, A., & McNichol, J. (2000a). Effects of the 1992 lifting of restrictions on gay and lesbian service in the Canadian forces. Unpublished manuscript, Palm Center, University of California, Santa Barbara. Retrieved from http://www.palmcenter.org/publications/dadt/effects_of_the_1992_lifting_of_restrictions_on_gay_and_lesbian_service_in_the_canadian_forces_appraising_the_e

Belkin, A., & McNichol, J. (2000b). The effects of including gay and lesbian soldiers in the Australian Defence Forces: Appraising the evidence. Unpublished manuscript, Palm Center, University of California, Santa Barbara. Retrieved from http://www.palmcenter.org/publications/dadt/the_effects_of_including_gay_and_lesbian_soldiers_in_the_australian_defence_forces_appraising_the_evidence

Bérubé, A. (1990). *Coming out under fire: The history of gay men and women in World War Two*. New York, NY: The Free Press.

Binkn, M., & Eitelburg, M. J. (1982). *Blacks in the military*. Washington, DC: Brookings Institute.

British Ministry of Defense. (2000). A review of the armed forces policy on homosexuality. Unpublished manuscript. British Ministry of Defence, London, UK.

Burg, B. R. (2002). *Gay warriors: A documentary history from the ancient world to the present*. New York, NY: New York University Press.

Corbin, J., & Strauss, A.L. (2008). *Basics of qualitative research: Grounded theory procedures and techniques* (3rd ed.). New York, NY: Sage.

Doel, R. E. (2003). Oral history of American science: A forty-year review. *History of Science, 41*, 349–378.

Don't Ask, Don't Tell Repeal Act of 2010, Pub. L. No. 111-321, 124 Stat. 3515 (2010). Retrieved from www.gpo.gov/fdsys/pkg/PLAW.../pdf/PLAW-111publ321.pdf

Estrada, A. X., & Weiss, D. J. (1999). Attitudes of military personnel toward homosexuals. *Journal of Homosexuality, 37*, 83–97.

Frank, N. (2009). *Unfriendly fire: How the gay ban undermines the military and weakens America*. New York, NY: Thomas Dunne Books.

Frank, N., Basham, V., Bateman, G., Belkin, A., Canaday, M., Okros, A., & Scott, D. (2010). Gays in foreign militaries: A Global Primer. Unpublished manuscript, Palm Center, University of California, Santa Barbara.

Gade, P. A., Segal, D. R., & Johnson, E. M. (1996). The experience of foreign militaries. In G. M. Herek, J. B. Jobe, & R. Carney (Eds.), *Out in force: Sexual orientation and the* military (pp. 106–130). Chicago, IL: University of Chicago Press.

Glaser, B. G. (1998). *Doing grounded theory: Issues and discussions*. Mill Valley, CA: Sociology Press.

Glaser, B. G., & Strauss, A. L. (1967). *The discovery of grounded theory: Strategies for qualitative research*. Chicago, IL: Aldine Transaction.

Healy, M. (1993, May 12). Schwarzkopf: "A 2nd-class force" if gay ban ends. *Los Angeles Times*. Retrieved from http://articles.latimes.com/1993-05-12/news/mn-34392_1_armed-force

Herek, G., & Belkin, A. (2006). Sexual orientation and military service: Prospects for organizational and individual change in the United States. In T. W. Britt, A. B. Adler, & C. A. Castro (Eds.), *Military life: The psychology of serving in peace and combat* (Vol 4, Section III). Westport, CT: Greenwood Press. Retrieved from http://www.palmcenter.org/publications/dadt/sexual_orientation_and_military_service_prospects_for_organizational_and_individual_change_in_the_united_state

Hillman, E. L. (2013). Outing the costs of civil deference to the military. *Journal of Homosexuality, 60*, 307–321.

Huffman, J. F., & Schultz, T. S. (2012). *The end of don't ask, don't tell*. Quantico, VA: Marine Corps University Press. Retrieved from http://www.dtic.mil/cgi-bin/GetTRDoc?AD=ADA283762

Kaplan, D., and Rosenmann, A. (2010). *Presence of openly gay soldiers in IDF does not undermine unit social cohesion*. Unpublished manuscript, Palm Center, University of California, Santa Barbara, 1-18. Retrieved from http://www.palmcenter.org/files/KaplanRosenmann_IDFSurveyReport.pdf

Kelle, U. (2005). Emergence vs. forcing of empirical data? A crucial problem of grounded theory reconsidered. *Forum: Qualitative Social Research, 6*(2), 1–23.

Kier, E. (1998). Homosexuals in the U.S. military: Open integration and combat effectiveness. *International Security, 23*(2), 5–39.

Kirchick, J. (2008, August 2). Powell's cautionary tale. *The Atlantic*. http://www.theatlantic.com/magazine/archive/2008/10/powells-cautionary-tale/307099/

Leavy, P (2011). *Oral history: Understanding qualitative research*. New York, NY: Oxford University Press.

Lehring, G. L. (2003). *Officially gay: The political construction of sexuality by the U.S. military*. Philadelphia, PA: Temple University Press.

Levy, D. A., & Parco, J. E. (2010). An elephant named morality: The latent argument over "don't ask, don't tell." *Armed Forces Journal, 9*, 34–37.

Meyer, L. (1998). *Creating GI Jane: Sex and power in the women's army corps during World War II*. New York, NY: Columbia University Press.

Murphy, L. R. (1988). *Perverts by official order: The campaign against homosexuals by the United States Navy*. New York, NY: Routledge.

Policy concerning homosexuals in the armed services [Don't Ask, Don't Tell], Publ. L. 103-160, Title 10, United States Code, § 654. 571, 107 Stat., 1547 (1993). Retrieved from http://www.gpo.gov/fdsys/pkg/STATUTE-107/pdf/STATUTE-107-2-2.pdf

Powell, C. (1992). A personal letter to Congresswoman Patricia Schroeder, May 8, 1992, 28–29. Retrieved from http://dadtarchive.org/wp-content/uploads/2010/02/237.pdf

Seefried, J. (2011). *Our time: Breaking the silence of "don't ask, don't tell."* New York, NY: Penguin Press.

Segal, M. W. (1986). The military and the family as greedy institutions. *Armed Forces & Society Fall, 13*, 9–38.

Shilts, R. (2005). *Conduct unbecoming: Gays and lesbians in the U.S. military*. New York, NY: St. Martin's Griffin.

Strauss, A. L., & Corbin, J. (1990). Grounded theory: An exploration of process and procedure. *Qualitative Health Research, 16*, 547–559.

Strauss, A. L., & Corbin, J. (1998). *Basics of qualitative research: Grounded theory procedures and techniques* (2nd ed.). Thousand Oaks, CA: Sage.

Thomson, A. (1998). Fifty years on: An international perspective on oral history. *Journal of American History, 85*(2), 581–595.

Walzer, L. (2000). *Between Sodom and Eden*, New York, NY: Columbia University Press, 19.

Wolff, T.B. (2004). Political representation and accountability under "don't ask, don't tell." *Iowa Law Review, 89*, 1633.

The Myth of the Warrior: Martial Masculinity and the End of Don't Ask, Don't Tell

L. MICHAEL ALLSEP, JR., JD, PhD
Department of Leadership and Strategy, Air Command and Staff College, Maxwell Air Force Base, Alabama, USA

The image of the male warrior still dominates military culture, to the exclusion of women and homosexuals. Complicating the picture is a technological revolution that promises to widen the current gap between the myth and reality of the modern warrior even further. Nonetheless, despite long arguing that homosexuals were a direct threat to military culture and effectiveness, the Pentagon has largely treated the end of Don't Ask, Don't Tell as a policy matter. The difficulties still experienced by women in the armed services 40 years after they were first incorporated in significant numbers indicates that this response will be insufficient to address the deeper cultural issues. Gender issues implicate deeply held beliefs and values that persist even in the face of years of official admonishment and denial. Unless the military begins to transparently bridge the gap between the myth and reality of the modern warrior, military service without discrimination based on sexual orientation will remain an unachieved goal.

The end of Don't Ask, Don't Tell (DADT) has largely been greeted with a collective shrug of the shoulders. The prediction of many that repeal would be a nonevent after the electronic eye of the media turned away seems to have been accurate. The U.S. Department of Defense has saluted smartly,

---

This article is not subject to U.S. copyright law.

The views expressed here are those of the author and do not necessarily reflect those of Air University, the United States Air Force or the Department of Defense.

changed its policies in conformity with the law, and gone about its business. Yet, history is not so sanguine about the prospects of a military truly free of its homophobic past. Military culture continues to preserve images and meanings hostile to open homosexuality. Unless military culture changes in conformity with the realities of the modern warrior, this superficial image of a military open to gay warriors will merely mask the reality of a culture hostile to the very idea.

War has always been imagined as a physical contest between male warriors. Although technological change long ago ended the era when wars were decided by bodies of men clashing with weapons of slash and bludgeon, the image of the warrior has remained remarkably constant. In the U.S. Armed Forces, the Marines capture this image best. Their most consistent recruiting theme is a small squad of men engaged in military drill, an image as old as the musket and pike, and equally as irrelevant to modern war. (LEAP-USMC Recruiting Commercial [New], 2008) In their most recent commercials, high technology military hardware has its place, but it's the image of armed men running to the sound of the chaos that dominates. ("Toward the Chaos," 2012) In their recruiting, they emphasize the personal over the technological, the physical over the mental. Even in a century that dawned on wars fought by airborne drones remotely controlled from the American heartland firing guided missiles on enemies in South Asia and the Arabian peninsula, Marine recruiting efforts still emphasize the age-old traditions of direct combat. Although the other services place more emphasis on technology, those traditions still dominate the image of the warrior in all the services. Asked to give the keynote address to the Marine Corps Association in 2009, Army General David Petraeus opened his speech with a joke.

> The Marines' sense of toughness permeates the Corps' lore as well as its reality. To recall an illustrative story, a soldier is trudging through the muck in the midst of a downpour with a 60-pound rucksack on his back. "This is tough," he thinks to himself. Just ahead of him trudges an Army Ranger with an 80-pound pack on his back: "This is really tough," he thinks. And ahead of him is a Marine with a 90-pound pack on. And he thinks to himself, "I love how tough this is!" Then, of course, 30,000 feet above them, an Air Force pilot flips aside his ponytail—I'm sorry, I don't know how that got in there, they haven't had ponytails in a year or two—and looks down at them through his cockpit as he flies over. "Boy," he radios his wingman, "It must be tough down there." ("No Joke: Petraeus Apologizes to Schwartz," 2009)

Many in the Air Force community took offense, especially as Petraeus was then the head of U.S. Central Command. Thousands of Airmen were risking their lives daily under his command in Iraq and Afghanistan, many of them doing the essential warfighting that made ground operations in those countries possible. Expressing the wounded sensibilities of many in the Air Force, the Air Force Association's daily newsletter called Petraeus' remarks "beyond outrageous" and said they "belittled the contributions of the Air Force to the joint force" ("Petraeus Zinger Wounds Air Force Egos," 2009) Regardless of changes in the nature of war and the warfighter, even a joking assault on the myth of the warrior stirred anger.

Most writing about war and the military focuses on middling issues—strategy and tactics, the lives of the great commanders, the history of one war or one campaign or one battle, or the anecdotal remembrances of one or more participants. Comparatively, little literature attempts to deal with the fundamentals of war, although the best war writing tries to place a more limited story within that larger context. Among those fundamentals of war is its position in culture. Every warrior is a product of a specific culture, and every war is a clash of cultures. Warrior culture is "a complex amalgam of attitudes and ideas about such things as the heroic, the need for sacrifice, the justness of the cause, the embrace of the aggressive spirit, compassion toward the defeated (to name only a few ingredients in this rich soup), or, indeed, the rejection of all the forgoing" (Stephenson, 2012, p. xiv). While there are common strands of belief and shared values across generations and cultures, each culture and each generation constitutes a unique warrior culture. The U.S. military is one of those unique cultures, and the ending of the DADT policy constituted a major watershed in the continuous development of that culture, as well as a serious challenge to many of its most deeply held beliefs and values. Before all members of the armed forces can serve without fear of discrimination based on their sexual orientation, those cultural beliefs and values will have to change to embrace the image and idea of the gay warrior. As the Petraeus story indicates, a military still struggling to accept pilots as warriors has a long way to go before it embraces gay warriors.

THE WARRIOR IDEAL

The oldest forms of warfare consisted of weapons wielded and propelled by muscle directly into the bodies of the enemy. The development of missile weapons, starting with simple sling-like weapons, introduced a new element. Muscle mass and physical prowess began its long decline in importance. Nonetheless, the heroic in warfare, especially in Europe and those other areas of the planet often termed the Western world, was still embodied in the image of the individual warrior who overcomes his foe in direct combat, the original stand-up fight. The Greeks placed such emphasis on the virtue of face-to-face combat that even fighting on horseback was considered somewhat unseemly (Stephenson, 2012). In medieval warfare, this division was reified in class structure, with aristocratic knights fighting in the same armies, but never the same units, as peasant archers. That the archers were often far more effective, especially in killing the aristocratic warriors in the opposing army, witness the slaughter of French nobility at Crécy by

English peasant longbow men, led the medieval church to issue occasional injunctions against the use of missile weapons as being a threat to the class structure ordained by God (Stephenson, 2012). Even as the modern battlefield emptied of warriors fighting with anything but missile weapons, and increasingly emptied of almost all warriors due to the increasing sophistication and power of those weapons, the warrior culture has held stubbornly to the old, outdated image of the muscled warrior who deals death and achieves honor through direct, physical combat (Hamner, 2011). Hence, the persistence of the Marine's recruiting images and their pride in humping the heaviest pack.

That missile weapons allowed the lowest warriors to kill the highest, the weakest to kill the strongest, or even the worst to kill the best, has long been a battlefield reality that the warrior culture has only reluctantly acknowledged. Training and indoctrination has long emphasized the importance of character and skill in fighting effectively and surviving in combat. Yet, the experienced combat veteran eventually learns a baser truth. On the modern battlefield, character and skill are largely irrelevant in determining survival, and, since only living warriors meaningfully impact outcomes, they are often irrelevant in determining effectiveness as well. This is not to say that a poorly trained army has an equal chance with a better trained one, only that in direct fire combat the larger reality fails to translate into a personal one. As the combat veteran and historian Paul Fussell (1989) observed, even well-trained soldiers who thought their skill and training made them invincible soon learned the value of prudence, and then eventually the reality of chance. Given sufficient exposure to combat, the warrior's confidence gave way to, "the perception that death and injury are matters more of luck than of skill" (Fussell, 1989, p. 282) It was that reluctant truth that produced the famous "thousand-yard stare," signaling a steep decline in combat effectiveness and the onset of posttraumatic stress disorder. Nothing drove this truth home more brutally than an artillery barrage. In its impersonal randomness and lethality, artillery shells seemed to those subject to bombardment, "like the finger of God" (Hamner, 2011, p. 87).

Since it was the job of military culture to motivate warriors to enter this deadly environment with confidence and courage, the truth of combat became increasingly hostile to preparation for it. To convince recruits that combat was survivable meant teaching them that the battlefield was in some ways controllable (Hamner, 2011). The best way to do that was to use the image of the timeless warrior who relied on the ageless advantages of strength, character, and skill to dispatch his foe. In pursuit of that image, the Marines have even resorted to a commercial that features a lone warrior slaying a dragon. (THE BEST–U.S. Marines TV Recruitment Spot–Ever Produced, 2006) That this image was in conflict with the reality that most deaths in modern war are caused by warriors removed from direct contact with their victims, whether those warriors are pulling lanyards, flying planes, setting booby-traps, or pushing buttons, seemed a minor quibble. The values of the warrior ideal seemed beneficial to every man in uniform, besides only a small percentage of those trained for combat ever got anywhere near it, and truth is the first casualty in war.

Consequently close-quarters combat continued to define the true warrior long after it no longer defined the most effective one. This privileging of direct combat was not only useful for training and indoctrination, but it was also an indispensable image for preserving the perception of the heroic in warfare. As one military historian recently observed,

> The bullet or heat-seeking bomb does not give a jot for courage or trial-by-arms; they fly to the heart of the matter with unblinking dispassion. . . . whereas the swordsman and the spearman, the soldier wielding a bayonet, must look into the eye of his fellow warrior, see his fear, hear his cry, smell his blood. And in that contact there is a whole moral world; a world that might be hateful, angry, terrified, disgusted, full of regret, or crazed with exultation -but never dispassionate, never coldly inhuman. (Stephenson, 2012, p. 8)

War is often described as inhuman, yet, it is actually the most human of activities in the sense that warfare is almost unknown anywhere else in the animal kingdom. As the purest expression of the humanness of war, the persistent identification of heroic warriors with close-quarters combat makes sense. As the most graphically and brutally human way of fighting, direct combat seems to preserve the self-sacrificing and heroic in a way that more distant ways of fighting do not. This is especially important in creating remembrance, that essential gift younger generations offer to older ones that is so vital in preserving the warrior culture (Stephenson, 2012). Yet, as the technology of war developed, and as the characteristics of the muscled warrior lost relevance to the smart warrior, the gap widened between the warrior whose efforts actually dominated the battlespace and determined the outcome of the engagement, and the warrior celebrated in military culture.

MARTIAL MASCULINITY

Throughout history men have dominated the ranks of warriors, not only to the almost total exclusion of women, but in open hostility to feminine identity. The advantages of masculinity in the historical arena of physical combat privileged the masculine over the feminine to such an extent that the identity of the warrior was exclusively masculine in almost all cultures. This is not to suggest that homosexual warriors have not been present in war since the beginning. Reviewing the battlefield of Chaeronea in 338 BC, the Macedonian King Philip came across the bodies of the Theban "Sacred Band" of 150 homosexual couples who had died to a man resisting the Macedonian invasion of their homeland. As Plutarch describes it,

> He stopped at the spot where the three hundred lay; all slain where they had met the long spears of the Macedonians. The corpses were still in their armor and mixed up with one another, and so he became amazed when he learned that these were the regiments of lovers and beloved. "May all perish," he said, "who suspect that these men did or suffered anything disgraceful." (Stephenson, 2012, p. 38)

From classic Sparta to public school England, homosexuality has occasionally been institutionalized in a way not inconsistent with the manly virtues of the warrior, but never often enough to constitute more than exceptions to a general rule. More important, in the remembrance of heroic warriors the memory of heroic gay warriors was not only virtually erased, but the homophobic privileging of heterosexual warriors was actively perpetuated.

For as long as armies have battled, masculinity has been the core cultural identity of the warrior class. Despite notable exceptions to this rule, women in combat have been an aberration, and so femininity has been antithetical to the values of the warrior. Despite the diversity in wars and the vast diversity in cultures that engage in warfare, the universal gendering of war until very recently remained nearly absolute. The gender divide at the connection of war and gender, Goldstein (2001) concluded, "is more stable, across cultures and through time, than are either gender roles outside of war or the frequency of war itself" (p. 9). The warrior ethos that this produced became more than a fighting spirit necessary to win wars, it also defined what it meant to be a man. The attributes of the warrior became equated with the attributes of manhood to the extent that participation in the war system, or at least the perception of possessing warrior-like qualities, became part of the rites of passage to manhood. "Being a warrior is a central component of manhood," Goldstein observed, "forged by male initiation rites worldwide" (p. 266).

The universal gendering of war and the correlation of warrior traits with masculinity created a warrior component to culture, a martial masculinity, that extended its influence far beyond the uniformed military, and for men constituted a virtual cradle-to-grave standard of manhood. Martial masculinity can be defined as a culturally constructed identity that gives special privileges to those who can assert it, especially within military institutions and among their supporters, but in larger society as well. It is based on beliefs, values, and basic assumptions many of them unreflectively and unconsciously learned and lived, that are expressed in artifacts, images, bodies, routines, practices, institutions, and other sites of cultural creation and expression (Belkin, 2012; Hull, 2006; Sen, 2007). This martial masculinity was created at the expense of femininity, which was considered the lesser other against which martial masculinity competed.

As the nature of war changed during the industrial era, the connection between masculinity and war also began to change. As Connell (1995) observed, "Violence was now combined with rationality, with bureaucratic techniques of organization and constant technological advance in weaponry and transport" (p. 192). In military terms, this resulted in the first general staffs, increased professionalism, and what Millis (1981) called the "managerial revolution" in warfare (p. 131). In gender terms, it meant a split in hegemonic masculinity between dominance behavior and technical expertise. Dominance behavior had to make room for expertise, which was not only incompatible with traditional notions of dominance masculinity, but also began to undermine the relationship between traditional notions of masculinity and effective warfighting. Neither form of masculinity displaced the other, but their coexistence was uneasy and often competitive, creating a battle between expertise "on tap or on top." (Connell, 1995, p. 192).

The struggle between these competing versions of masculinity threatened traditional gender norms in war as never before. As a result, a form of hegemonic masculinity that privileged direct dominance, excluded women and feminine identity, and felt challenged by expertise claimed the mantle of the warrior with increasing vigor. This close embrace of the warrior myth was inversely related to the continuing vitality of the connection between traditional masculinity and war, but was, nonetheless, a powerful cultural concept. In the face of advancing technology that increasingly made traditional masculinity irrelevant in war, the myth of the warrior sought to protect the privileges of increasingly outdated hegemonic masculinity. What technology challenged, mythology attempted to preserve. A mythic form of martial masculinity emerged from this struggle and took its place at the center of military culture.

THE TECHNOLOGICAL CHALLENGE TO MARTIAL MASCULINITY

That advances in technology continuously alter the nature of war is a truth universally acknowledged, but very seldom recognized is that those technological advances also alter the nature of the warrior. The technological changes that eroded the relationship between masculinity and effectiveness in war did not stop with the recent near-perfection of missile weapons. In his seminal study on the potential impact of the robotics revolution on future warfare, Singer (2009) observed that, "the new technologies of war are changing the experience of war itself" (p. 327). From Odysseus to the grunt who left yesterday for the Hindu Kush, going to war has historically meant a physical remove from the safety of home to the danger of the battlefield. It has largely been this shared experience of danger and deprivation in a distant place that gave combat units their invaluable comradeship. Even support troops and pilots were generally located in the theater of operations, even if their billets were far removed from the world of bunkers and foxholes. It was, in fact, that geographic distance that frontline soldiers often cited to disparage their rear area brethren. The short period of terror and extreme danger faced by an aircrew over enemy territory still didn't seem to compare to weeks and months spent in the muck. Yet, technology has now made it possible for warriors to engage on the battlefield nine to five, then pick up kids and groceries on the way home. A firefight might have to be postponed for an orthodontics appointment. Nor is this reality somewhere in the distant future; it has been lived by warriors in the recent past, and represents the most dynamically growing area of military technology.

The experience of Air Force Col. Gary Fabricious exemplifies these changes and their implications for the warrior. A self-described F-15 fighter jock with the callsign "Fabs," he went kicking and screaming to command the first Predator drone squadron. The warriors in his squadron never left their complex of trailers located on an Air Force base in Nevada, but they engaged 24-hours a day with enemies in Iraq and Afghanistan. Sitting at consoles in the American desert, they not only gathered intelligence from across the battlespace, but they directed deadly missiles at enemy targets and flew the first unmanned air combat missions using Predators armed with Stinger anti-air missiles. Combat actions such as the Marine's assault on Fallujah were made possible by the combat power and real-time intelligence of Fabricious' squadron. Yet, all this was accomplished by fighters who were not only removed from the fight, but who never left home. For these new generation of warriors, going to war was less an odyssey than a commute. As one commander observed, "At the end of the duty day, you walk out of the deployment and walk back into the rest of life in America" (Singer, 2009, pp. 328–330).

Although physically removed from war, these new warriors were not immune from the mental demands and cost of combat. One drone pilot remembered being so intensely involved in the battle that when his drone was about to crash thousands of miles away he instinctively reached for the lever of his ejection seat. Many of these warriors found that physical distance from the battlefield did not remove them from the mental hazards of combat. In fact, using the high-resolution cameras on their drones and missiles, many of these modern warriors got a clearer look at their enemies' deaths than most modern infantrymen, and suffered the resulting mental anguish. One Predator pilot recalled watching in anticipation as the Hellfire missile he had just launched made its way toward an unsuspecting enemy, only to see an innocent old man tottering into his picture. Helplessly he watched in horror as the missile impacted, leaving a burning hulk where the enemy's car had been, but also hurling the old man's body violently into the street. "Those who would call this a Nintendo game had never sat in my seat," he wrote, "Those were real people down there. Real people with real lives" (Martin, 2010, p. 55).

That pain contrasted with the exhultation of having so much power at your fingertips. "Sometimes I felt like God hurling thunderbolts from the sky," remembered that same Predator pilot (Martin, 2010, p. 3). Despite the power they wielded on the battlefield, these new warriors found little acceptance among the fraternity of true warriors. Many people seemed appalled at the very idea of a warrior sitting in safety thousands of miles away watching television and pushing buttons that killed people. "Let me get this right. You're out there on the air force base killing innocent people on the other side of the world while they can't shoot back at you?" was a comment that often confronted them. (Martin, 2010, p. 263) As one special operations officer remarked, "You have some guy sitting at Nellis and he's taking his kid to soccer. It's a strange dichotomy to war. He's disconnected to the enemy he's fighting" (Singer, 2009, p. 331). He went so far as to express more admiration for the warrior bonafides of Abu Musab al-Zarqawi, the leader of al-Qaeda in Iraq, who at least "was right there hanging his balls out on the battlefield." To him the equation was simple, "A warrior has to assume physical risk" (Singer, 2009, p. 331).It's some indication of the power of the warrior myth that sometimes it even trumps national allegiance among the fraternity of warriors.

The conflict between heroism as it is imagined in military culture, and the greater effectiveness of technology that creates more efficient ways of killing is as old as technological innovation itself. The special forces operator who doubts the heroism of drone pilots is himself fighting with a form of technology that was once considered cowardly. As one writer in the 1400s put it, warriors who used gunpowder weapons were "cowards and shirkers who would not dare to look in the face the men they bring down from a distance with their wretched bullets" (Boot, 2006, p. 22). That the warrior of today picks up a gun with no shame is testament to the fact that military culture changed to accept the new technological reality. The implications of modern technology, especially at the emerging margins of such fields as robotics, computer science, and nanotechnology, not only promise to change the nature of war, but the nature of the warrior for those nations able to afford it. The underlying essence of war may remain the same, but the attributes of the effective warrior must adapt. As Singer (2009) observed, the technologies of robotics and microcomputers call for a new look at what courage, comradeship and hierarchy must look like on this new battlefield. Can military culture imagine heroism and self-sacrifice on a battlefield devoid of humans, fought from the comfort of home, and managed in Internet chat rooms where the avatars of colonels look no more scary than those of privates?

LEADERSHIP BY BUMPER STICKER

Compared to this coming challenge to the warrior myth, the integration of gay warriors, many already serving, would appear a minor challenge. Yet, for decades the arguments linking sexual orientation with the warrior ethos have been so wrapped in the rhetoric of unit cohesion, morale, good order and discipline, and plain patriotism that the image of the gay warrior sits uneasily at best on the military mind. Because women and open homosexuals have historically been excluded from the realm of war, the essential military values have been associated with heterosexual men for so long that it requires a major cultural adjustment to separate them. Thus, the persistent attempts to defend the cultural status quo of the military and exclude people who threaten notions of hegemonic masculinity rests not on military necessity, but cultural prejudice. This prejudice is not readily apparent because it comes dressed in the garb of heritage and patriotism, yet beneath the veneer of concern over military effectiveness is the presumed right of the military profession to protect its own culture against what it considers undue and harmful meddling by outsiders. As the self-styled Center for Military Readiness (2012) recently put it,

> As if there were not enough social turmoil in the armed forces, due to Congress' vote to impose the LGBT (lesbian, gay, bisexual, transgendered) agenda on the military, a high-profile advisory panel is calling for the assignment of female soldiers and Marines to all-male close combat units such as the infantry . . . This is not a military commission, it is the civilian EO (equal opportunity) industry trying to create a new power base in the Pentagon, in order to implement and enforce the current administration's plans to put "diversity" above all other considerations. (p. 1)

Despite long arguing that homosexuals were a direct threat to military culture and effectiveness, the Pentagon nonetheless treated the end of DADT as a policy matter, avoiding the fundamental issue of military culture. With the repeal of DADT, the traditionally constructed standards of military culture came in for direct challenge. Martial masculinity, inside and outside the ranks of the military, constituted the primary obstacle to the realization of a military free from discrimination on the basis of sexual orientation. Unfortunately, the military determined to meet this challenge with training oriented toward behavior alone, rather than education targeting the mutual responsibility of all service members to insure that military culture, and especially the cult of martial masculinity, makes room for warriors regardless of their sexual orientation. Despite the long and acrimonious fight waged by many in and out of uniform to preserve discriminatory laws directed at homosexuals, the military response to the repeal of DADT assumes that only conduct needs adjustment.

The military had plenty of warning to prepare itself for the end of DADT, and significant time and effort was expended preparing for the day the law changed. All members of the Air Force, military and civilian, were required to view a PowerPoint presentation addressing the repeal of DADT (Repeal of Don't Ask, Don't Tell, 2012). That presentation derived directly from the Department of Defense Comprehensive Review of the Issues Associated with a Repeal of "Don't Ask, Don't Tell" (U.S. Department of Defense, 2010). Despite a lengthy report, replete with appendixes and take aways, the key implementation message was reduced to "Leadership–Professionalism–Respect." More suitable for a bumper sticker than a plan to change the culture of an organization long hostile to homosexuals, such a superficial and frankly silly approach raises the question of whether the leadership of the military was really that clueless, or whether they were simply adrift trying to maintain the fiction that the end of generations of active hostility to gays could be accomplished through PowerPoint. The report itself belied the notion that the leadership was simply clueless. The use of resources such as Parco and Levy's (2010) excellent, but uneven, *Attitudes Aren't Free: Thinking Deeply about Diversity in the U.S. Military Services* and interaction with the Palm Center Forum on the Experiences of Foreign Militaries, indicated that the Working Group was at least exposed to a variety of viewpoints.

At the same time, the report relied heavily on white papers submitted by the service academies, papers apparently heavy on leadership issues and light on the relevance of culture. Although recognizing the relevance of organizational culture theory, the summary of the white papers provided by the Working Group report evidenced a distinct lack of relevant critical theory, anthropology, sociology, or cultural history. It's as if the past three decades of work in academe hadn't happened. By restricting their literature base to white papers from the service academies and doing little to review relevant work from any of the country's great institutions of higher learning, the Working Group's knowledge base became excessively narrow and entirely too dependent on work produced at undergraduate institutions under military command. In only one line was it recognized that "culture change is a long-term process that will require persistence." The remainder of the paper emphasized the role of leadership and "the importance of initially focusing on behavior rather than attitudes or culture." By advocating a "minimalist approach to change," and focusing "on military readiness, cohesion, and effectiveness and not difficult moral debates on sexual orientation," the Pentagon effectively avoided any need to discuss its own past hostility to homosexuals, much less any confrontation with the continuing hostility many members of the leadership still had to such a dramatic and fundamental assault on what until very recently most of them considered core values based on the integrity of moral and religious precepts.

Despite the fact that the military has long inculcated the belief that non-heterosexuals have no place in the armed forces, the first slide of the presentation emphasized that the purpose of the brief was *not* to change individual beliefs. In blithe and breathtaking denial of the effects of having fostered an anti-gay culture for so long, the military proposed to deal with the repeal of DADT as merely a policy matter. For the lifetime of the entire serving military, and for generations before, the services argued that homosexuals in uniform were a threat so serious as to require separation or even prosecution, yet, only "policy-focused questions" were allowed now. No wonder attendees were cautioned to "maintain a professional demeanor," since the core beliefs of many of them were being turned upside down while they were allowed no means to voice their dismay. That those cautionary words were thought necessary on the very first slide is indicative of the fact that the military knew full well that the repeal of DADT was an issue that went to the heart of military culture, but was unwilling to directly confront the implications.

Nor was the presentation defective only in form, in substance it failed to address the fundamental questions of what it means to be gay in the military, what it means to serve with gay warriors, and what it means to military culture when such a fundamental tenet is overturned? The briefing dealt with moral and religious concerns in an offhand way, repeating the axiom that, "free exercise of religious expression, within law and policy, remains unchanged," and encouraging service members with moral concerns to discuss them with their "commander/chaplain." Sexual orientation was now "a personal and private matter." Everyone was admonished "to treat all with dignity and respect." By providing nothing more than soothing bromides in the wake of a tectonic shift in cultural values, service members who still believed what military culture had long taught were left with no option but to take their anti-gay beliefs and values underground.

A WARNING FROM HISTORY

The fact that the military has struggled for more than four decades to extend equal treatment to women illustrates the depth of the problem. America's sudden entry into World War II motivated the first large-scale attempt to incorporate women into the military. Even in such exigent circumstances, the reaction of some was extreme. "A women's army to defend the United States of America!" one Congressman thundered, "Think of the humiliation. What has become of the manhood of America, that we have to call on our women to do what has ever been the duty of men." (Meyer, 1996, p. 13) The permanent integration of women into the U.S. military in 1948 affected only a small number of billets and was overwhelmed in the public discourse by the integration of Blacks, but the introduction of the all-volunteer force in 1973 forced all the services not only to open opportunities for women, but to actively recruit them for most of their occupational specialties. This challenged the prevailing notion of the male warrior in a substantial way for the first time, even if women were still barred from what were defined as combat roles.

As a young captain fresh from Vietnam, Army Gen. Barry McCaffrey served on the staff of the Modern Volunteer Army initiative. Along with everyone else who worked on the issue, McCaffrey became convinced that only by a dramatic increase in the number of women in the military, concomitant with opening most occupational specialties to women, could the volunteer military concept work (Kitfield, 1995). He knew that most professional military officers opposed the idea, but assumed that they too would recognize its inevitability. Invited to give a talk to the annual gathering of what were called Young Turk officers from all the services at the Air Force Academy in 1973, McCaffrey presented a paper that recommended discontinuing the Women's Army Corp, incorporating women into the regular army, and opening all but combat positions to them. He received enthusiastic applause from the group, but on the plane ride back he was warned by superior officers that he "would be ill-advised to publish that paper" (Kitfield, 1995, p. 133). On returning to his job at West Point, he quickly found himself standing before the superintendent for a dressing down by his furious superior. The paper was conspicuously absent when the conference proceedings were published, and was even denied clearance by the Freedom of Information Office. His own father, a decorated and highly regarded Army general, would hardly speak to him for weeks afterward (Kitfield, 1995). In retrospect, McCaffrey could only marvel at his own naiveté, but in truth nothing about his military education had prepared him to adequately understand the myth of the warrior at the heart of his own service culture, or the ramifications of that myth for women in uniform.

The most sacred bastions of military culture are the service academies. The service academies do more than provide an undergraduate education to a select portion of the officer corps, they are in many ways the institutional heart of their respective services. The Pentagon, which they all must share, is more often thought of as at best the brain of the services, or at worst the site of their most persistent blood feuds. The academies on the other hand represent the heart of the services. They are the places where each service can be entirely itself, and where they preserve their most cherished identities by passing them on to a new generation of believers. It should come as no surprise then that the introduction of women into these hallowed domains initiated some of the fiercest and most agonizing struggles over the place of women in military culture. During Congressional hearings on the admission of women to the academies, Secretary of the Army Howard H. Callaway, a West Point graduate and Korean War combat veteran from Georgia, made the argument that women would destroy "the Spartan atmosphere" that was necessary for producing combat leaders (Hearings Before the Subcommittee No. 2, 1975). His view was echoed in the short statement of a West Point senior who accompanied him to the hearings. "I think by injecting women into this last bastion of military puritanism that West Point truly is, I think you are going to start a weakening process . . . of the Army." He went on to claim that many of the cadets who had not yet incurred their full military commitment would resign rather than continue at a coed West Point. "True, there is a bit of chauvinism in all this," he admitted. "We're just saying that West Point is our school." (Hearings Before the Subcommittee No. 2, 1975)

Vice Adm. William P. Mack, the superintendent of the Naval Academy, offered a different view. After reading a statement opposing admitting women, he testified under questioning that his opposition rested solely on the current exclusion of women from combat. "In my estimation," he testified, "women could serve in any role in the U.S. Navy at any time if this law were changed. They could come to the Naval Academy; they could pass the course in large numbers, and do all that's required of them physically, mentally, professionally, and in any other way, and there would be little requirements for change in our course curriculum, physical facilities, or anything of that sort." "If the law were changed," he concluded, "in my mind, women could do anything that men could do, and in some cases, perhaps even better" (Hearings Before the Subcommittee No. 2, 1975).

Admiral Mack argued that, "having seen summer Olympics on television, having seen Billie Jean King on television, there are many women who can do all sorts of things that they are prepared for, and it would be a question, sir, of taking the training, passing it successfully, and demonstrating that that particular person, man or woman, could do the job" (Hearings Before the Subcommittee No. 2, 1975).

This then was the fundamental clash between those unalterably opposed to women based on cultural prejudice, and those willing to evaluate whether a particular person, man or woman, could do the job. Those whose arguments were grounded in martial masculinity already had all the evidence they needed from military history and tradition; never mind that it was a history that treated women as second-class citizens and denied them opportunities to prove their equal worth. As long as military culture was dominated by men who understood masculinity as a gender reality ultimately determined by nature and confirmed by historical experience, there could be only respect for traditions built on the natural gender order, or a perversion of it. Those who believed that individual women might prove themselves equal to the task if given the chance, but who were opposed to special treatment or a separate track for women, were, whether they recognized it or not, admitting that gender was a social construct. Theirs was a masculinity that respected expertise over direct dominance, and the evidence of their eyes rather than the traditions of their forebears was their standard of reference. The appeal of women to be given an equal chance to succeed or fail was appealing to officers like Mack, partly because they could ultimately judge on the observed evidence, rather than relying on the nostrums of a sacred past. For those whose touchstone was martial masculinity rather than empirical reason, men or women, the call of the sacred past was altogether too strong to be so easily dismissed.

In the shadow of these momentous political battles, women entered military service in large numbers. Very few of them would have self-identified as feminists, as the age-old connection between conservatism and military service holds true as much for women as for men. Moreover, the ignorance of most of these women to the debt they owed to feminism was paralleled by a reticence among movement feminists to see these uniformed women as sisters in the struggle for equality. The desire for feminist liberation seldom sat easily alongside the desire to fly jet fighters or fire an M16 in anger. As Elizabeth Fox-Genovese observed in the late 1990s.

> For several decades, I have called myself a feminist and, like many women of my generation, have been puzzled that so many women reject the term even though they have benefited from the feminist gains of the past thirty years. Hard experience has also taught me that the "official" feminist movement does not have much patience for women who do not support every plank in its increasingly radical platform. And it gradually dawned on me that even when the women whom I interviewed and with whom I had been speaking informally knew little or nothing about feminist positions, they had a gut sense that feminism was not talking about their lives. Worse, they had a sneaking suspicion that feminists do not think that their lives are important. (Fox-Genovese, 1996, p. 2)

Nonetheless, the opponents of this influx of women and the threat they posed to martial masculinity had no problem conflating the two. In the critical fights over women's place in military culture, the efforts of women in uniform, many from families with proud military traditions and lineages, were equated with the goals and objectives of a feminist movement most women in the military barely acknowledged and many opposed. Women in the military thus found themselves largely cutoff from the feminist movement that had been so important in opening doors for them, even as that movement itself was in steep decline. On the other hand, the defenders of martial masculinity were riding a rising political and cultural tide that soon made liberal or feminist terms of derision, as evidenced by the success of radio host Rush Limbaugh's *feminazi* demagoguery.

Women in the military mostly made their way up the ranks on their own efforts and avoided politics, but they could not avoid the backlash their very presence inspired. Unloved by both the liberal left and the conservative right, they were often pawns in the culture wars, especially when they seemed to threaten the warrior myth. One of the first women to graduate the Naval Academy returned to her alma mater for homecoming 16 years later only to discover a new generation of young women still fighting many of the same battles she had thought won long ago. "How could this be?" she wondered. Motivated by that revelation and her own deep love for the Academy, she decided to write a book preserving the history of her fellow women classmates. She found that even among female graduates serving at high rank, the old fears persisted. "Originally there was another main character based on an individual who is still on active duty," she wrote, "When I called her to schedule a final interview, she expressed sincere regret that she could no longer be part of the story. She feared that her career in the navy, which is going well, would be jeopardized. ASso that character was deleted" (Disher, 1998, pp. ix–x). Despite the deep-seated cultural belief that women were incapable of fulfilling the traditional warrior role, women in the U.S. military have proven their ability time and time again, even against substantial hostility amongst their male comrades. After surveying the combat experiences of women warriors fighting the war in Iraq, Kirsten Holmstedt (2007) concluded, "What more evidence do the American people need to prove that the experiment of women in combat has been a success? The military no longer differentiates between male and female convoy commanders. When will the American people stop making a distinction?" (p. 312).

The persistence of cultural beliefs hostile to female warriors despite the military's attempts over several decades to address the issue through behavior alone provides a warning for the long-term difficulties the military faces before it truly embraces the ideals of service without discrimination based on sexual orientation. The history of women in the military makes absurd the notion that the end of DADT requires little more than some training and leadership. As this article was being written, the news media and Internet were alive with fallout from the continuing struggle of women to compete against martial masculinity. Two female airmen awarded Bronze Stars for meritorious service in Afghanistan for their work in support missions came under fierce and personal criticism after the Air Force posted their stories online. Article comments and related blog posts became a free fire zone for sometimes vicious and almost universally anonymous diatribes against the weakening of martial masculinity by the awarding of medals for exemplary service other than in combat. Some of the comments accused the Air Force of giving the award out of favoritism or because the recipient was a female or minority. One story was subsequently pulled from the Web site because of the number of hostile comments posted. "No one deserves that level of criticism for meritorious service in a combat zone," said an Air Force spokesman. He added that at no time during his 47-year career with the Air Force had he ever seen such "hateful rhetoric" ("Tech. Sgts. Take heat after receiving medals," 2012). The fact that the medals were not combat awards, were awarded in an entirely appropriate manner, and had been awarded to countless men for similar conduct without notice, did little to quell the passion of offended warriors.

Within days of that story breaking, *CNN Presents* led off its newsmagazine broadcast with a story about two women at the service academies forced out after making allegations of rape against upperclassmen. Noting that reports of sexual assault at the service academies had risen by almost

60% over the past year, the story also reported that of sixty-five sexual assault cases reported, only one had resulted in a court-martial ("Betrayal of Trust?," 2012) The personal stories of the former cadet and midshipman profiled were tragic, and yet almost banal when put in context with the countless similar stories that have issued in an unbroken stream from the academies since women were first admitted in the summer of 1976. The obstacles to reporting the assaults, the relative lack of concern on the part of the chain of command, the failure to prosecute, the ultimate re-victimization of the women, the overriding concern of the military for the image of the institution, and eventually the righteous response of higher authority promising zero tolerance; the response of the military in 2012 followed on script with all the previous versions of the same tired play.

As these examples illustrate, the front lines of this clash between martial masculinity and femininity run from the aggravating to the criminal. The unexpected blowback from a local effort to encourage breastfeeding by a support group of military women and spouses with the unthreatening name Mom2Mom when they posted a picture of women in uniform breastfeeding might seem superficial, but it shares a cultural link with more dramatic outrages such as the ongoing sexual assault prosecutions at Lackland AFB ("Air Force Relieves Basic Training Commander Over Widening Lackland Sex Scandal," 2012; "Instructor for Air Force is Convicted in Sex Assaults," 2012; "Parental Pride or Indecent Exposure," 2012). Sexual assault is a crime of violence, but it is more likely to occur in a culture where breastfeeding in uniform is compared to defecating or urinating in public ("Military Mom 'Proud' of Breast-Feeding in Uniform, Despite Criticism," 2012). That this article could have been written at almost anytime in the past four decades amid similar stories points to the failure of the military to understand or be competent to deal with the problems created by the clash of martial masculinity and the requirement for equal service regardless of sexual orientation. This ongoing failure of military culture to adapt to women is a warning of the challenges ahead in the wake of the repeal of DADT.

In battlefields with no front lines such as Iraq and Afghanistan, an ill-prepared and sometimes poorly led military found that it often needed women warriors in combat roles, regardless of the legislative prohibition against it. The number of women among the casualties of those wars bears witness to their willingness to serve and sacrifice. Yet, the reality of combat units remains overtly hostile to them. Experiencing that reality in its purest form, a forward combat base in the Korengal Valley in Eastern Afghanistan, Junger (2010) described a world where sex was the greatest deprivation, and yet a constant presence. In the absence of women, soldiers sexualized their language, their weapons and their comrades. New men arrived as cherries, sexy weapons became stand-ins for real sex, and physical contact with fellow soldiers took the place of intimate contact with women. In actual combat the adrenaline rush substituted for sex, but in the long intervals between firefights the sexual world of the modern combat unit at the edge of the American empire could get "weird." In this case, weird meant "strange pantomimed man-rapes and struggles for dominance and grotesque, smoochy come-ons that could only make sense in a place where every other form of amusement had long since been used up" (Junger, 2010, pp. 224–225). At times it was so hypersexual that gender bent in new directions. One soldier even argued that it would be gay not to have sex with another man in such conditions, since the masculine imperative of sex was far more important than the gender of your partner (Junger, 2010). The divide between the culture that sustains that reality and the behavior mandated by the Pentagon is a measure of the distance the military still needs to cover before reality matches it's rhetoric.

THE GAY WARRIOR

What will be the impact of the repeal of DADT on the military culture that underlies and sustains American national defense? While reports from some parts of the military are encouraging, it is still too early to judge. Midshipmen at the Naval Academy report more acceptance and support than overt hostility, but even they worry about what happens after graduation when they join the "real" navy. ("Mids Describe Smooth Transition From 'Don't Ask, Don't Tell,'" 2012) The difficulties still experienced by women in the armed services 40 years after they were first incorporated in significant numbers demonstrates how resilient military culture is when defending what are imagined to be its core values. Policy changes alone are insufficient to change these longstanding cultural images and meanings. Gender issues implicate deeply held beliefs and values that persist even in the face of years of official admonishment and denial. The vertiginous onrush of change has always been a challenge for conservative institutions such as the military, but the combined pressures of cultural shifts in American society and emerging technology that is redefining the attributes of effective warriors imply a coming crisis in military culture. Unless the military begins to transparently bridge the gap between the myth and reality of the modern warrior, military service without discrimination based on sexual orientation will not only remain an unachieved goal, but the ability of the U.S. military to fight and win future wars may hang in the balance.

REFERENCES

Air Force relieves basic training commander over widening Lackland sex scandal. (2012, August 13) *Washington Post*. Retrieved from http://www.washingtonpost.com/national/ap-sources-air-force-relieve...scandal/2012/08/10/2fb434f8-e319-11e1-89f7-76e23a982d06_story.html

Belkin, Aaron. (2012). *Bring me men: Military masculinity and the benign facade of American empire, 1898–2001*. New York, NY: Columbia University Press.

Betrayal of trust? Allegations of rape at West Point, Annapolis. (2012, April 26, 2012). *CNN Justice* online. Retrieved from http://www.cnn.com/2012/04/22/justice/miltary-academy-lawsuit/index.html

Boot, M. (2006). *War made new*. New York, NY: Gotham Books.

Center for Military Readiness. (2012). *New commission wants 'diversity' taken to extremes*. Retrieved January 4, 2013, from http://cmrlink.org/articles/print/34552?author=0&image=0&domain=0

Connell, R. W. (1995). *Masculinities*. Berkeley, CA: University of California Press.

Disher, S. H. (1998). *First class: Women join the ranks at the naval academy*. Annapolis, MD: Naval Institute Press.

Fox-Genovese, E. (1996). *Feminism is not the story of my life: How today's feminist elite has lost touch with the real concerns of women*. New York, NY: Doubleday.

Fussell, P. (1989). *Wartime: Understanding and behavior in the Second World War*. New York, NY: Oxford University Press.

Goldstein, J. S. (2001). *War and gender: How gender shapes the war system and vice versa*. Cambridge, UK: Cambridge University Press.

Hamner, C. H. (2011). *Enduring battle: American soldiers in three wars, 1776–1945*. Lawrence, KS: University Press of Kansas.

Hearings Before the Subcommittee No. 2 of the Committee on Armed Services, House of Representatives, Ninety-third Congress, Second Session on H.R. 9832 to Eliminate Discrimination Based on Sex with Respect to the Appointment and Admission of Persons to the Service Academies and H.R. 10705, H.R. 11267, H.R. 11268, H.R. 11711, and H.R. 13729 to Insure that Each Admission to the Service Academies Shall Be Made Without Regard to a Candidates Sex, Race, Color, or Religious Beliefs, (1975). Washington, DC: Superintendent of Documents, U.S. Government Printing Office.

Holmstedt, K. (2007). *Band of sisters: American women at war in Iraq*. Mechanicsburg, PA: Stackpole Books.

Hull, I. V. (2006). *Absolute destruction: Military culture and the practices of war in imperial Germany*. New York, NY: Cornell University Press.

Instructor for Air Force is convicted in sex assaults. (2012, July 20) *The New York Times*. Retrieved from http://www.nytimes.com/2012/07/21/us/lackland-air-force-base-instructor-guilty-of-sex-assaults.html?_r=1&pagewanted=all

Junger, S. (2010). *War*. New York, NY: Twelve.

Kitfield, J. (1995). *Prodigal soldiers: How the generation of officers born of Vietnam revolutionized the American style of war*. Washington, DC: Potomac Books.

LEAP-USMC recruiting commercial (New). (2008, August 25). You Tube. Retrieved from http://www.youtube.com/watch?v=UhiErlxpGJA

Martin, M. J., with C. W. Sasser. (2010). *Predator: The remote-control air war over Iraq and Afghanistan; A pilot's story*. Minneapolis, MN: Zenith Press.

Meyer, L. D. (1996). *Creating GI Jane: Sexuality and power in the women's army corps during World War II*. New York, NY: Columbia University Press.

Mids describe smooth transition from 'don't ask, don't tell, (2012, May 21). mcall.com. Retrieved from https://www.mcall.com/news/breaking/bs-md-naval-academy-gay-20120519,0,2273092.story?page=2

Military mom 'proud' of breast-feeding in uniform, despite criticism. (2012, May 30). *Today Moms*. Retrieved from http://moms.today.msnbc.msn.com/_news/2012/05/30/11955844-military-mom-proud-of-breast-feeding-in-uniform-despite-criticism?lite

Millis, W. (1981). *Arms and men: A study in American military history*. New Brunswick, NJ: Rutgers University Press.

No joke: Petraeus apologizes to Schwartz. (2009, August 28). *Air Force Times*. Retrieved from http://www.airforcetimes.com/news/2009/08/airforce_petraeus_joke_082809w/

Parco, J. E., & Levy, D. A. (Eds.). (2010). *Attitudes aren't free: Thinking deeply about diversity in the U.S. armed forces*. Maxwell AFB, AL: Air University Press.

Parental pride or indecent exposure: Photos of military women breastfeeding in uniform stirs controversy. (2012, May 31) *Fox News*. Retrieved from http://www.foxnews.com/us/2012/05/31/parental-pride-or-indecent-exposure-photos-military-women-breastfeeding-in/

Petraeus zinger wounds Air Force egos. (2009, August 21). *Time U.S.* Retrieved from http://www.time.com/time/nation/article/0,8599,1917841,00.html

Repeal of don't ask, don't tell (DADT). (2012). United States Air Force [Online learning PowerPoint presentation]. U.S. Department of the Air Force, Department of Defense.

Sen, A. (2007). *Identity and violence: The illusion of destiny*. New York, NY: Norton.

Singer, P. W. (2009). *Wired for war: The robotics revolution and conflict in the 21st century*. New York, NY: Penguin Books.

Stephenson, M. (2012). *The last full measure: How soldiers die in battle*. New York, NY: Crown.

Tech. sgts. take heat after receiving medals. (2012, April 16). *Air Force Times*. Retrieved from http://www.airforcetimes.com/news/2012/04/air-force-tech-sergeants-take-heat-bronze-stars-041612/

THE BEST–U.S. Marines TV recruitment Spot–ever produced. (2006). You Tube. Retrieved from http://www.youtube.com/watch?v=62tnJtLBQzQ

Toward the chaos. (2012). U.S. Marine Corps. Retrieved from http://www.marines.com/videos/-/video-library/detail/VIDEO_TV_SPOT_TOWARD_SOUND_OF_CHAOS

U.S. Department of Defense. (2010). *Report of the comprehensive review of the issues associated with the repeal of "don't ask, don't tell": Support plan for implementation*. Washington, DC. Author.

If We Ask, What They Might Tell: Clinical Assessment Lessons from LGBT Military Personnel Post-DADT

MARIA HELIANA RAMIREZ, MSW
School of Social Welfare, University of California, Berkeley, Berkeley, California, USA; VA Palo Alto Health Care System, Palo Alto, California, USA

STEPHEN JOSEPH ROGERS, MSW and
HARRIET LEE JOHNSON, AA
VA Palo Alto Health Care System, Palo Alto, California, USA

JON BANKS, MBA, WANDA PENNY SEAY, BILLY LEE TINSLEY, and ANDREW WARREN GRANT

Following repeal of the Don't Ask Don't Tell Policy, nearly one million lesbian, gay, and bisexual veterans and service members may increasingly seek access to Veterans Affairs services (G. Gates, 2004; G. J. Gates, 2010). Limited data exist regarding lesbian, gay,

---

Special thanks for editing assistance to Joe David Ramirez, PhD, Dawn Marcia Wilson, Catherine Baker, and Kevin Rocap, and support from Cary Cook, LCSW, and Steve Finkelman, LCSW. Special thanks also for contributions to this article by Bernard Young, Peni Bethel, Homerina Bond, Lani Yoshimoto, Dorian Banks, and Caroline Buster. This article was authored according to the principles of Community Based Participatory Research (CBPR; Israel et al., 2008), with all coauthors intimately involved in every aspect of the research process including problem formulation, literature review, data collection, and analysis and manuscript generation. CBPR principles were chosen to inform this article's methodology, as one outcome of institutionalized homophobia in anti-gay military policies like DADT is that "socially and economically marginalized communities often have not had the power to name or define their own experience" (Israel et al., 2008, p. 50) and because marginalized communities have expert knowledge often unavailable to researchers who are not members of the community (Clements-Noelle & Bachrach, 2008; Jones, Koegel, & Wells, 2008; and Chavez, Duran, Baker, Avila, & Wallerstein, 2008). CBPR principles create collaborative and equitable partnerships between traditional researchers and marginalized communities based on shared power and decision making (Minkler & Wallerstein, 2008), which is critical to the generation of knowledge about this relatively invisible population given the void of empirical data on LGBT veteran experiences (Burks, 2011).

bisexual, transgender (LGBT) military personnel posing a unique challenge to clinicians and healthcare systems serving veterans with evidence-based and culturally relevant practice. In an effort to fill this information void, participatory program evaluation is used to inform recommendations for LGBT-affirmative health care systems change in a post-DADT world.

In the United States, an estimated 71,000 active duty service members, reservists and retired reserve force members are lesbian, gay and bisexual (Gates, 2010) while an additional 870,000 veterans are assumed to be lesbian or gay (Gates, 2004).[1] With an end to the Don't Ask Don't Tell Policy (DADT), close to one million (941,000) lesbian, gay, and bisexual (LGB) service members and veterans may eventually seek culturally sensitive services[2] from the U.S. Department of Veterans Affairs (VA). At present, federal courts are considering the legality of differential access to family benefits based on veterans' sexual orientation in a case brought by the Servicemembers Legal Defense Network (SLDN-OutServe) against the VA and Veterans Health Administration (VHA) in *McLaughlin v. Panetta* (2011). In addition, the VHA National Leadership Council has adopted recommendations from a work group on lesbian, gay, bisexual, and transgender (LGBT) veteran care to "take immediate, coordinated action to advance the health and wellbeing of lesbian, gay, bisexual and transgender veterans" (p. 1) in part by:

> [C]reating a welcoming environment that allows all Veterans to recognize themselves in the policies, practices, clinical expertise and culture of the facility (which) helps to remove barriers so that LGBT Veterans can be confident that they will receive the high quality care that they deserve. (U.S. Department of Veterans Affairs [VHA], 2012, p. 2)

Established as a compromise, DADT resulted in significant barriers to LGB service members' participation in social science research (Frank, 2004; Trivette, 2010). As exemplified in the DADT-era article title, "Asking Questions that Cannot be Asked of Respondents Who Cannot Respond," (Bowling, Firestone, & Harris, 2005), DADT resulted in scant research on LGB service members and veterans (Burks, 2011), which is sorely needed by practitioners if they are to provide culturally sensitive, evidence-based practice.

This article documents the design, launch, and lessons learned from the VA Palo Alto Health Care System's (VAPAHCS) Living Out Loud/Laughing Out Loud (LOL) support group as an example of an evidence-based intervention for LGBT veterans in a post-DADT world, in spite of limited empirical hard data.

CLINICAL ASSESSMENT

The LOL model is informed by data collected from participants on intake and six-week follow-up clinical assessments, which are used to inform the group intervention. Assessment outcomes are periodically examined to identify LOL participants' evolving physical and mental health needs and their recommendations for effective services, exemplifying that evidence-based practice refers both to the creation of interventions based on empirical research in the literature and using data from ongoing clinical assessments, to inform the design and ongoing evaluation of the intervention's cultural relevance and clinical efficacy. In addition to clinical assessments, the LOL model is also informed by an extensive literature review. This literature review (1981–2011) explored research on LGBT physical and mental health in the civilian population (233 articles) and DADT-related research on LGBT military (39 articles). Written by one of the LOL group facilitators, the literature review was discussed with self-selected LOL participants and formed the basis to the forgoing discussion of LOL. Participant reviewers described the process of community based participatory review of the social science literature as increasing their awareness of health care needs and experiences among LGBT people in general, themselves in particular and an increased sense of agency to request culturally responsive services in the VA health care system.

Comprised of 38 LGBT veterans and service members, LOL met weekly. On average, 13 veterans attended each group session from a variety of racial and ethnic, gender, and class backgrounds. Two licensed clinical social workers (one gay, Native American male, and one pansexual, Chicana female) with a combined 28 years of experience serving LGBT individuals facilitated the group at one of VAPAHC's five campuses in the San Francisco Bay area. Facilitators' identities are noted in lieu of research suggesting higher rates of participation among minority clients with practitioners' whose lived experiences result in increased cultural awareness and whose minority statuses result in less racial bias toward and, thus, increased trust from minority clients (Dovidio et al., 2008).

Special care was taken to increase veterans' comfort attending group given the deleterious impacts of DADT on LGB service members' access to and damaging experiences with mental health and chaplains' military services (Benecke & Dodge, 1990; Damiano, 1998–1999; Bowling et al., 2005; Katz, 2010; Moradi, 2009; Terman, 2004) and historical experiences of prejudice in the fields of psychology and psychiatry (Davison, 2005; Herek, 2010; Maher et. al., 2009). Considering historical injuries incurred from military and civilian mental health services, LGBT veterans may face unique barriers to group attendance such as hyper-vigilance to maintain secrecy of one's sexual orientation or gender identity (i.e., being closeted). For example, two LGBT veteran support groups other than LOL have been attempted at a VA campus in the greater Bay Area however due to lack of participation, both were discontinued. LOL participants speculate that the other groups' time and location may have resulted in less privacy and, thus, low participation rates, suggesting that LOL's theoretical orientation of culturally sensitive practice was an essential ingredient to attracting and retaining LGBT veterans in a public support group environment.

Data Summary

The following data from LOL clinical assessments are presented as a unique glimpse into the relatively unknown experiences, strengths, and health care needs of LGBT veterans. Assessment responses were changed where necessary to protect the confidentiality of group members. Barriers to LOL participation identified through LOL Intake assessments included: "protecting my ability to complete my tour of duty" (i.e., not being outed while on active duty), conflicts with group meeting time, "issues with my PTSD," and transportation barriers. Based on this feedback, group facilitators employed a variety of culturally sensitive strategies to support diverse participation. To accommodate concerns of being outed, the group was held in the early evening when most people had left the campus. In addition, the room location was not publicly advertised as a means of protecting group members' confidentiality and to deter potential interruptions from people with views hostile toward LGBT veterans. Charting in veterans' medical records was written with discretion to maintain confidentiality of participants to other VA providers (e.g., a note in a veteran's chart would read, "The group discussed family issues" instead of "The group discussed coming out to parents"). Finally, due to safety concerns of meeting, when few staff were on campus and the highly charged nature of LGBT military service during the pre-DADT repeal period, emergency call buttons were placed in the meeting location and VA police officers would patrol the area upon facilitators' request. While these security measures may have seemed extreme, they were critical to mediating DADT-related fear and hyper-vigilance following DADT investigations (Estes, 2005; Frank, 2004; Katz, 2010; Wescott & Sawyer, 2010). Participants reported that such efforts to create a secure environment, increased group members' sense of comfort and ease, making LOL meetings the most comfortable clinical space at VAPAHCS.

LOL Group Meetings and Discussion Topics

As noted, creating an evidence-based practice when there is limited available research to inform intervention development, can be accomplished through ongoing clinical assessment and careful attention to issues raised in group. LOL's initial groups discussed local opportunities to meet other LGBT individuals. This topic was chosen based on elevated rates of depression and social exclusion among LGBT people (Cochran & Mays, 2009; Hammack & Cohler, 2011) and isolation among LGBT service members from DADT (Frank, 2004; Trivette, 2010). Of note, LOL intake assessments revealed a similar trend of loneliness and longing for social engagement as 46.4% of LOL participants reported interest in discussing leisure activities and 40% reported interest in discussing ways to overcome isolation. Subsequent groups addressed discussion topics rated highest by group members on the LOL intake assessment forms, with the exception of weeks including notable holidays. Additionally, LOL participants requested facilitators teach stress management skills which resulted in the creation of a stress management session (i.e., this need was not identified on the clinical assessment forms but rather through group discussion). This psycho-education module was periodically revisited in part or in whole, depending on influxes of LOL participants from post-traumatic stress disorder (PTSD) programs, stressfulness of the day's discussion topic, and upon veteran request.

In LOL's second month, members completed six-week follow-up clinical assessments. Additional group topics were selected based on incoming intake and six-week assessments thereafter. This strategy for identifying group topics based on periodic review of assessments, not only allowed LOL to be participant centered, but also enabled the group to adjust to new and core group members' changing goals, interests and needs over time. One challenge, however, was that six-week assessments were collected on a rolling basis according to when veterans joined LOL making impossible, the comparison of all intake and follow-up assessments at any given time. For example, open enrollment meant that, for LOL in week 20, 6-week assessment forms had only been collected from eight participants with facilitators waiting for six previously distributed forms to be returned, as the remaining 19 LOL members had yet to complete a sixth week of group session.

Perhaps because LOL's core group was eager to meet other LGBT veterans (in fact, the number one goal for group participation reported on intake assessments was connecting with other LGBT veterans), new group members had settled into LOL without major disruptions to group dynamics (a risk for groups using an open enrollment model). One LOL group member remarked, "When someone (new) walks in, they may not know what to ask for but we know what they're there for." Responses to the intake assessment question "What do you hope to get from this group?" describe interest in developing new connections with peers through sharing their unique yet commonly recognizable, experiences as LGBT veterans.

At the first LOL meeting, one member recalled feeling relief when she realized "there's other people (like me), I'm not alone anymore," which resulted from "hearing other people's stories and (realizing) they actually relate to you." Described as *nonverbal knowing*, LOL members stated that when they share their stories of being LGBT veterans, others were comforted in the recognition of knowing that story in their own lives. This sense of personal reflection in peers' lives was extremely important to LGBT veterans who were isolated from LGBT peers in the military. By preventing LGBT service members from knowing who among their colleagues are LGBT (Estes, 2005), DADT barred access to critical ingredients in the formation of a coherent sense of self and community, two key aspects of LGBT identity development (Appleby & Anastas, 1998). One LOL participant exemplified the importance of the sense of self in relation to others,[3] stating "Before (LOL) I didn't have any connection to others, now LOL is like family." For this reason, LOL hosted a holiday celebration at group members' requests for an event to which they could bring loved ones to meet the people "my wife notices I smile about on Thursday mornings."

Introduction to LOL Group Members

LOL group members who attended regularly (i.e., on average attend two to four groups per month), formed a core group of 22 veterans. In the first months of LOL, members and group facilitators regularly shared snacks and celebrated significant events (e.g., the repeal of DADT). The importance and role of sharing food and celebrating holidays (such as Veterans Day) cannot be overstated to the development of group cohesion among LOL participants. This sentiment is reflected in group members' assessment responses to the question "What do you find helpful about LOL?" with the following comments: "Being with people who have the same experience," "The beautiful spirits that give life to me by opening up themselves," "knowing that I am not the only gay veteran," and "having an outlet and being connected with other queer folks listening to others and identifying with them."

LOL was described as "uplifting and refreshing," because "LGBT issues are discussed here that can't be brought up with everyone in the VA." Additionally LOL has had a "positive" impact on one veteran who "knew a few transgender people before this group (but not other LGB people) and now I know gay and lesbian veterans too." Finally, another group member remarked "I've learned so much about other things here (due to the variety of personalities and life experiences among group members), who knows what one person will say or the insights of another. While we are really different, we all relate (to one another)."

LOL participants' were highly skilled in intergroup dynamics, due in part to their previous experience in group therapy and milieu environments where they developed skills helpful to group participation such as thought checking, common in cognitive behavioral therapy (Wenzel Brown, & Karlin, 2011). This LOL community strength may be particular to groups recruiting members from treatment programs using cognitive behavioral therapy like the VAPAHCS Trauma Recovery Program. Additionally, group members were highly empathic toward one another and routinely extended warmth and compassion to new LOL members with applause and other gestures of interpersonal generosity at new members' initial meetings. LOL members also expressed appreciation for LOL with comments including disbelief they were finally able to be completely honest about who they were in a VA support group. For most, this was the first time they felt understood by others in terms of being both a veteran and an LGBT person. Veterans explained discomfort accessing VA services was due in part to a "lack of trust because some staff fear broaching sexual orientation and gender identity," sending an implicit message that these aspects of their lives were not appropriate discussion topics at the VA. Tears and riotous laughter were both common occurrences at LOL meetings. Additionally, group members established online chat rooms for peer support outside of LOL meetings.

Outreach Strategies

Staff initiating LGBT veteran groups are encouraged to utilize diverse outreach strategies as veterans learned about LOL through paper flyers (35.7%), VA staff referral (25%), friends (17.8%), Facebook or Twitter (10.7%), e-mails (7.1%), and LGBT community center staff referral (3.5%). Group eligibility screenings were completed by facilitators via a phone interview and chart review to assess appropriateness of fit and ability to tolerate an active support group environment (i.e., ability to tolerate direct questions and challenging of ideas by peers and group facilitators and ability to follow group ground rules). Due to disproportionately high rates of substance abuse, physical and mental health challenges in LGBT populations (Addis, Davies, Greene, MacBride-Stewart, & Shepherd, 2009; Austin et al., 2009; Bryant & Schilt, 2008; Conron, Mimiaga, & Landers, 2010; Dilley, Simmons, Boysun, Pizacani, & Stark, 2010; Eady, Dobinson, & Ross, 2011 Feldman & Meyer, 2011; Pizacani et al., 2009), LOL group eligibility was based in a harm reduction approach to both substance use and psychiatric diagnosis to allow the greatest amount of participation while maintaining group safety. Veterans were not required to be abstinent in order to attend the group but were asked to leave if unable to participate due to substance use (e.g., aggressive toward others or self, passing out). Psychiatric diagnoses did not prevent group attendance however people living with serious mental health challenges were required to have a primary mental health provider. To accommodate PTSD-related challenges to group participation, facilitators taught grounding exercises, coordinated care with inpatient PTSD staff, and checked in with group members about PTSD-related symptoms during meetings and field trips. Group facilitators were available as needed for individual support and the Veteran's Crisis Line and National LGBT Mental Health Line numbers were printed on group meeting agendas.

Veterans reported that while the phone screen was uncomfortable as they were coming out to an unknown VA provider, the discomfort was worth it. It may be that getting through the discomfort of the phone screen became a psychological and emotional investment, increasing the likelihood that veterans continued attending group sessions. Variations in group attendance appeared to follow changes in weather, holidays, and the price of gas as veterans traveled up to fifty miles round trip to attend LOL. For privacy purposes, some veterans preferred attending an LGBT veterans' meeting on a VA campus where they did not receive primary medical care. As such, LOL's success may be due in part to its central location among VA campuses.

Participant Demographics

LOL Group members' ages ranged from 26 to 66 years old, with an average age of 51 years. The closest markers to class on the intake assessment revealed that in terms of employment two weeks prior to attending LOL, 46.4% of group members had not worked at all and wanted to be working more. These data suggest that employment resources may be of particular interest to LGBT veterans. LOL group discussions included issues noted in the social science literature regarding LGBT work-related dynamics such as managing homophobia at work, passing as heterosexual, coming out at work, and the residual impacts of DADT on LOL group members' hyper-vigilance to maintain the secrecy of their sexual orientations and gender identities at work and the VA, even decades after military discharge (Huffman, Watrous-Rodriguez, & King, 2009; King et al., 2009; McDermott, 2006; Raggins, Singh, & Cornwell, 2008).

In terms of isolation versus social engagement, 35.7% of LOL group members reported wanting to spend less time alone and 64.2% wanting to spend more time with friends. In the six-week follow-up assessments ($n = 8$), four veterans said they wanted to spend more time with friends, while the other four reported satisfaction with the amount of time spent with friends. One group member described LOL as the only place where she engages socially with friends during the week while another group member described LOL as being "kind of like our own fraternity."

Health Needs and Challenges

Consistent with higher prevalence rates of depression, anxiety, substance abuse, physical health problems, and victimization in the literature (Boehmer

& Case, 2006; Burkalter et al., 2011; Conron, et al., 2010; Jabson, Donatelle, & Bowen, 2011; Kelly, Izienicki, Bimbi, & Parsons, 2011; Lehavot & Simoni, 2011; Lewis et al., 2009; McCabe et. al., 2010; McNair & Hegarty, 2011; Meyer, Dietrich, & Schwartz, 2009; Roberts, Austin, Corliss, Vandermorris, & Koenen, 2010; Sanchez, Halipern, & Calderon, 2007), LOL members reported the following issues as personally challenging when they entered the group: twelve people described mental health concerns of isolation, depression, anxiety, PTSD, and victimization. Additionally, 10 people reported medical concerns including HIV, diabetes, being overweight, gender reassignment surgery, hormone replacement therapy, high blood pressure, Lupus, and fibromyalgia. One respondent wrote, "physically I am fine but mentally I am detached, so sometimes its hard because I don't feel close to anyone" while another respondent wrote, "HIV Poz but in a study of sero-conversion back to HIV neg. Major health risk however (sic.)." Veterans described mental health challenges ranging from managing symptoms like PTSD flashbacks to various interpersonal challenges with schizoid affective disorder. Transgender LOL members reported challenges with "getting my body ready for eight to ten hours under anesthesia and knife" and "transitioning through current changes." Veterans' psychosocial concerns included, "impending death of a family member," "feeling angry and deeply hurting inside," and "I am currently in an unhealthy living environment and need housing at a shelter or couch on the VA grounds."

Group members identified the following experiences they sought from LOL participation: 16 respondents wanted social support from peers with a majority of them identifying the building of new friendships and social contacts as the desired goal. Additionally, numerous people wanted to give support to others by sharing their own experiences with coming out and gender transitioning. Another major theme was acceptance (from others and

TABLE 1 Sexual Orientation/Gender Identity

Sexual orientation	No.	Gender identity	No.
Gay (male)	14	Transgender male	3
Lesbian (female)	10	Transgender female	6
Bisexual	7	Non-transgender male	13
Queer	2	Non-transgender female	14
Pansexual	1	Intersexed	1
Heterosexual transgender female	1	Gender (queer)	1
Heterosexual transgender male	1		
Other[a]	2		

[a]While LOL participants were asked to describe their sexual orientation, which is different than gender identity, some people listed transgender as their sexual orientation (which as noted, typically refers to gender identity). Thus, the number of transgendered people in the Table 1 appears smaller than the number of transgendered people in the Table 2 because some transgender people answered the question about their sexual orientation as gay, lesbian, or bisexual and did not label their sexual orientation as transgender.

self-acceptance) as exemplified by responses like, "Shared stories of degree of support, general acceptance from the greater community. Outreach to people who were still working on coming out," "support, self-acceptance, to help me figure out my boundaries of how out I want to be," "understanding of myself and better understanding of other sexualities other than straight," and "I want to feel comfortable in my own skin." Finally, LOL participants also reported interest in developing self-advocacy skills to get their needs met at the VA and community-based resources.

Group members' rated their interest in discussion topics as indicated in Table 3.

TABLE 2 Ethnicity/Military Branch

Ethnicity	No.	Military branch	Percentage
Caucasian	14	Army	35.7%
African-American	7	Navy	21.4%
Mixed race	5	Air Force	21.4%
Native American	4	Marines	14.2%
Hispanic/Latino	3	Other	7.1%
Chose not to answer	3		
Asian and Pacific Islander	4		

TABLE 3 Discussion Topics/Percentage of Interest by Topic

Discussion topics	Percentage of interest
Leisure activities	48.1%
Coming out	40.7%
Isolation	
Employment	
Body image issues	
Mental health issues	37%
VA benefits	
Romantic relationships	33.3%
Family issues	29.6%
Physical health issues	25.9%
PTSD	22.2%
Legal issues	
Sexual health issues	18.5%
Access to medical care	
Housing	
Suicide	14.8%
Discharge Issues	11.1%
Violence	
Education	
OEF/OIF benefits	
Community organizing	
DADT	7.4%
Gambling	3.7%

Coping Strategies and Stress Mediators

Due to high lifetime rates of minority stress resulting from discrimination, it is essential that LGBT veterans' strengths are identified and reinforced. Additionally, the deleterious physical and mental health impacts of internalized homophobia (Newcomb & Mustanski, 2011; Szymanski, Kashubeck, & Meyer, 2009),[4] can be mediated by focus on and development of LGBT individuals' pride in their personal qualities and abilities. LOL members answered the question "Please describe any talents, hobbies, positive characteristics or strengths that you bring to group," as follows: three people reported sobriety and seven people noted decades of experience in individual and group therapy, peer mentoring and religious/spiritual support. Additionally, four people reported culinary skills and two people noted humor as qualities they contribute to LOL. The following quotes reflect the diversity of talents among LOL participants: "Twenty-two years sobriety, easy to talk to regarding sensitive issues, open minded," "I love to play video games, work out, and study the supernatural which means I love seeing things from different angles, regardless if I agree with it or not," "Co-chair of an LGBT-related organization, experienced in workplace transition," "successful at symptom management, peer mentor," and "meditation and reiki." Assessments of LGBT veterans' strengths can help practitioners unlearn their own biases as responses contradict stereotypes about LGBT people and can help facilitators build effective and vibrant groups fortified by a wide variety of personal abilities and interpersonal assets among group members.

INDICATORS OF SUCCESS

Group attendance rates suggested that LOL was successful in engaging and retaining participation among LGBT veterans as the majority (35 of 38), had attended more than two groups. In terms of reduced isolation, members reported having discussed critical experiences in group that they had not previously disclosed to others which were key to integrating social identities (e.g., sexual orientation, veteran status) and socialize together outside of group.

Lessons Learned

Maintaining a core group of diverse participants requires constant attention to group dynamics. Group ground rules identified by LOL members, ensured that participants treated each other with respect, and accepted one another's right to self-definition and determination and their own personal responsibility for group dynamics. These rules sought to maintain LOL as a safe space for all members, a lofty goal among veterans whose PTSD, depression, and hyper vigilance from having served under DADT was magnified by peers who share racial, ethnic, or gender characteristics of people they lost, loved, or were sexually victimized by in the military.

Creating and maintaining safe space, did not mean that people's feelings weren't hurt by comments made in group, but rather that group members looked honestly at situations where they offended others and acted in a respectful manner toward individual experiences. Creating safe space involved facilitators posing critical justice-oriented questions following prejudicial comments. For example, when a group member stated she did not go to Oakland due to violence on the news, a group facilitator asked if the statement could be interpreted as a racially laden comment and that violent crimes tend to increase in neighborhoods with fewer jobs. Similarly, comments harmful to transgender people were also addressed directly. For example, when a new transgender veteran introduced herself to LOL, she was asked if she is pre- or postoperation (referring to sex reassignment surgery), to which a group co-facilitator interrupted by asking if people introduce themselves to non-transgender people by inquiring about their genitalia, suggesting it is inappropriate to talk about anyone's private anatomy without their invitation (even in an LGBT support group). This type of question (depending on the intent and context) can also be perceived as reducing transgendered identity to body modification. This type of reductionism is objectionable because the umbrella term transgender describes a variety of gender variant experiences, including people who do not seek sex reassignment surgery.

LOL's diverse members had a range of life experiences that were not as similar as the term LGBT might imply. Regarding the issue of coming out, variations in the importance, meaning and risk involved in choosing to disclose LGBT identities differed in LOL across sexual orientation and gender identity. For example, gay and lesbian veterans described the importance of coming out as a means of avoiding double lives. Conversely, one transgender man in LOL did not come out as a means of preventing potential harassment from the men with whom he enjoyed rural hunting trips, while for some transgender women, physical characteristics such as height or tone of voice, preclude their having a choice in coming out. Diversity among LGBT people can impact HIV prevention education with different psychological implications for LGB people as compared to transgender people. Additionally, the meaning and implications of coming out can vary across racial and ethnic cultures and socioeconomic status.

CONCLUSION

Disparities in LGBT health suggest affected service members and veterans may benefit from culturally relevant and responsive practice including targeted outreach and intervention strategies. Lessons learned from LOL suggest there is great diversity among LGBT veterans resulting in unique assets and barriers according to race, class, gender, and such. Additional research is needed to serve LGBT military personnel with evidence-based practice that addresses minority stressors while also building upon unique forms of LGBT cultural strength and resilience. Recommendations for LGBT-affirmative health care systems change are offered in Appendix A for practitioners and hospital administrators in a post-DADT world.

NOTES

1. Gates' (2010) estimate of 71,000 LGB service members is calculated with the Bayes' Rule using estimates of the size of the LGB community from the 2008 General Social Survey (Davis & Smith, 2009), estimates of LGB service members from the 2008 American Community Survey, estimates of the size of active duty personnel from the U.S. Department of Defense personnel and procurement statistic (September 2008), and estimates of the size of the guard and ready reserve from the U.S. Census Bureau's 2010 Statistical Abstract. Gate's (2004) estimate of 870,221 lesbian and gay veterans is calculated from Census 2000 data, by estimating the proportion of lesbians and gay men by state which is then used to estimate the proportion of gay and lesbian veterans by state. These estimates differ from those identified by RAND (2010) based on the longitudinal Add Health Survey, indicating that in 2008, 26,000 men and 21,000 women "might identify themselves as gay, lesbian, or bisexual" with an additional 15,000 men and 16,000 women reservists potentially identifying as lesbian, gay or bisexual (p. 101). Totaling 78,000 LGB service members, RAND's estimates are greater than Gate's estimate of 71,000.

2. Culturally sensitive healthcare refers to services tailored to meet the unique needs and strengths of minority communities (Maguen, Shipherd, & Harris, 2005; Witten, 2007). Repeal of DADT does not affect transgender servicemembers who remain ineligible for military service due to the psychiatric diagnosis of gender identity disorder, which renders a medical discharge (Kerrigan, 2011). Transgender veterans are included in this article as they are participants in LOL and VHA is creating services and patient protections tailored to the unique experiences of transgender veterans (VHA Directive 2011-024 Transgender/Intersex Care).

3. This is especially crucial to LGBT people who experience parental and community rejection (Appleby & Anastas, 1998).

4. Internalized homophobia is the acceptance of negative views about one's minority sexual orientation (Herek, Norton, Allen, & Sims, 2009).

REFERENCES

Addis, S., Davies, M., Greene, G., MacBride-Stewart, S., & Shepherd, M. (2009). The health, social care and housing needs of lesbian, gay, bisexual and transgender older people: a review of the literature. *Health & Social Care in the Community, 17*, 6.

Appleby, G. A., & Anastas, J. W. (1998). *Not just a passing phase: Social work with gay, lesbian, and bisexual people*. New York, NY: Columbia University Press.

Austin, S. B., Ziyadeh, N. J., Corliss, H. L., Rosario, M., Wypij, D., Haines, J., ... Field, A. E. (2009). Sexual orientation disparities in purging and binge eating from early to late adolescence. *Journal of Adolescent Health, 45*, 3.

Benecke, M., & Dodge, K. S. (1990). Military women in nontraditional job fields: Casualties of the armed force's war on homosexuals. *Harvard Women's Law Review, 13*, 215–250.

Boehmer, U. & Case P. (2006). Sexual minority women's interactions with breast cancer providers. *Women Health, 44*(2), 41–58.

Bowling, K. L., Firestone, J. M., & Haris, R. J. (2005). Asking questions that cannot be asked of respondents who cannot respond. *Armed Forces & Society, 31*, 411–437.

Bryant, K., & Schilt, K. (2008). *Transgender people in the U.S. military: Summary and analysis of the 2008 Transgender American Veterans Association survey*. Palm Center. Retrieved from http://www.palmcenter.org/node/1137

Burkhalter, J. E., Hay, J. L., Coups, E., Warren, B., Li, Y. L., & Ostroff, J. S. (2011). Perceived risk for cancer in an urban sexual minority. *Journal of Behavioral Medicine, 34*, 3.

Burks, D. J. (2011). Lesbian, gay, and bisexual victimization in the military: An unintended consequence of "don't ask, don't tell." *American Psychologist, 66*, 604–613.

Chavez, V., Duran, B., Baker, Q. E., Avila, M. M., & Wallerstein, N. (2008). The dance of race and privilege in CBPR. In M. Minkler & N. Wallerstein (Eds.), *Community-based participatory research for health* (2nd ed., pp. 91–106). San Francisco, CA: Jossey-Bass.

Clements-Noelle, K., & Bachrach, A. M. (2008). CBPR with a hidden population: The transgender community health project a decade later. In M. Minkler & N. Wallerstein (Eds.), *Community-based participatory research for health* (2nd ed., pp. 137–152). San Francisco, CA: Jossey-Bass.

Cochran, S. D., & Mays, V. M. (2009). Burden of psychiatric morbidity among lesbian, gay, and bisexual individuals in the California Quality of Life Survey. *Journal of Abnormal Psychology, 118*, 3.

Conron, K. J., Mimiaga, M. J., & Landers, S. J. (2010). A population-based study of sexual orientation identity and gender differences in adult health. *American Journal of Public Health, 100*, 10.

Damiano, C. M. (1998–1999). Lesbian baiting in the military: Institutionalized sexual harassment under "don't ask, don't tell, don't pursue." *Journal of Gender, Social Policy & the Law, 7*, 499–503.

Davis, J. A. & Smith, T. W. (2009). *General social surveys 2008*. Storrs, CT: The Roper Center for Public Opinion Research, University of Connecticut.

Davison, G. (2005). Issues and nonissues in the gay-affirmative treatment of patients who are gay, lesbian or bisexual. *Clinical Psychology, 12*, 25–28.

Dilley, J. A., Simmons, K. W., Boysun, M. J., Pizacani, B. A., & Stark, M. J. (2010). Demonstrating the importance and feasibility of including sexual orientation in public health surveys: Health disparities in the Pacific Northwest. *American Journal of Public Health, 100*, 3.

Dovidio, J. F., Penner, L. A., Albrecht, T. L., Norton, W. E., Gaertner, S. L., & Shelton, J. N. (2008). Disparities and distrust: The implications of psychological processes for understanding racial disparities in health and healthcare. *Social Science & Medicine, 67*, 478–486.

Eady, A., Dobinson, C., & Ross, L. E. (2011). Bisexual people's experiences with mental health services: A qualitative investigation. *Community Mental Health Journal, 47*, 4.

Estes, S. (2005). Ask and tell: Gay veterans, identity and oral history on a civil rights frontier. *The Oral History Review, 32*(2), 21–47.

Feldman, M. B., & Meyer, I. H. (2011). Comorbidity and age of onset of eating disorders in gay men, lesbians, and bisexuals. *Psychiatry Research, 180*, 2–3.

Frank, N. (2004). *Gays and lesbians at war: Military service in Iraq and Afghanistan under "don't ask, don't tell."* Center for the Study of Sexual Minorities in the Military, Institute for Social, Behavioral, and Economic Research, UC Santa Barbara.

Gates, G. J. (2010). *Lesbian, gay and bisexual men and women in the US military: Updated estimates.* The Williams Institute, UCLA School of Law. Retrieved from http://escholarship.org/uc/item/0gn4t6t3

Gates, G. (2004). *Gay men and lesbians in the US military: Estimates from census 2000.* The Urban Institute. Retrieved from http://proquest.umi.com/pqdweb?index=0&did=2304769401&SrchMode=1&sid=1&Fmt=6&VInst=PROD&VType=PQD&RQT=309&VName=PQD&TS=1329161603&clientId=51532

Hammack, P. L., & Cohler B. J. (2011). Narrative, identity, and the politics of exclusion: Social change and the gay and lesbian life course. *Sexuality Research and Social Policy, 8*, 3.

Herek, G. M. (2010). Sexual orientation differences as deficits: Science and stigma in the history of American psychology. *Perspectives on Psychological Science, 5*, 6.

Herek, G. M., Norton, A. T., Allen, T. J., & Sims, C. L. (2010). Demographic, psychological, and social characteristics of self-identified lesbian, gay, and bisexual adults in a US probability sample. *Sex Research Social Policy, 7*, 176–200.

Huffman, A. H., Watrous-Rodriguez, K. M., & King, E. B. (2009). Supporting a diverse workforce: What type of support is most meaningful for lesbian and gay employees?. *Human Resource Management, 47*, 2.

Israel, B. A., Schulz, A. J., Parker, E. A., Becker, A. B., Allen, A. J., & Guzman, J. R. (2008). Critical issues in developing and following CBPR principles. In M. Minkler & N. Wallerstein (Eds.), *Community-based participatory research for health* (2nd ed., pp. 47–66). San Francisco, CA: Jossey-Bass.

Jabson, J. M., Donatelle, R. J., & Bowen, D. (2011). Breast cancer survivorship: The role of perceived discrimination and sexual orientation. *Journal of Cancer Survivorship-Research and Practice, 5*, 1.

Jones, L., Koegel, P., & Wells, K. B. (2008). Bringing experimental design to community-partnered participatory research. In M. Minkler & N. Wallerstein (Eds.), *Community-based participatory research for health* (2nd ed., pp. 67–90). San Francisco, CA: Jossey-Bass.

Katz, K. A. (2010). Health hazards of "don't ask, don't tell." *New England Journal of Medicine, 363*, 2380–2381.

Kelly, B. C., Izienicki, H., Bimbi, D. S., & Parsons, J. T. (2011). The intersection of mutual partner violence and substance use among urban gays, lesbians, and bisexuals. *Deviant Behavior, 32*, 5.

Kerrigan, M. K. (2011). Transgender discrimination in the military: The new don't ask don't tell. *Psychology, Public Policy and Law, 18*(8), 1–17. doi:10.1037/a0025771

King, M., Semlyen, J., Tai, S. S., Killaspy, H., Osborn, D., Popelyuk, D., & Nazareth, I. (2009). A systematic review of mental disorder, suicide, and deliberate self harm in lesbian, gay and bisexual people. *BMC Psychiatry, 8AR70*.

Lehavot, K., & Simoni, J. M. (2011). The impact of minority stress on mental health and substance use among sexual minority women. *Journal of Counseling and Clinical Psychology, 79*, 2.

Lewis, R. J., Derlega, V. J., Brown, D., Rose, S., & Henson, J. M. (2009). Sexual minority stress, depressive symptoms, and sexual orientation conflict: Focus on the experiences of bisexuals. *Journal of Social and Clinical Psychology, 28*, 8.

Maguen, S., Shipherd, J. C., & Harris, H. N. (2005). Culturally sensitive care for trangender patients. *Cognitive and Behavioral Practice 12*, 479–490.

Maher, M., Landini, K., Emano, D. M., Kinght, A. M., Lantz, G. D., Parrie, M., . . . Sever, L. M. (2009). Hirschfield to Hooker to Herek to high school: A study of history and development of GLBT empirical research, institutional policies, and the relationship between the two. *Journal of Homosexuality, 56*, 921–958. doi:10.1080/00918360903187861.

McCabe, S. E., Bostwick, W. B., Hughes, T. L., West, B. T., & Boyd, C. J. (2010). The relationship between discrimination and substance use disorders among lesbian, gay, and bisexual adults in the United States. *American Journal of Public Health, 100*, 10.

McDermott, E. (2006). Surviving in dangerous places: Lesbian identity performances in the workplace, social class and psychological health. *Feminism and Psychology, 16*, 193–211.

McLuaghlin et al v Panetta et al. (2011). 28:1331. U.S.1.

McNair, R. P., & Hegarty, K. (2011). Guidelines for the primary care of lesbian, gay, and bisexual people: A systematic review. *Annals of Family Medicine, 8*, 6.

Meyer, I. H., Dietrich, J., & Schwartz, S. (2009). Lifetime prevalence of mental disorders and suicide attempts in diverse lesbian, gay, and bisexual populations. *American Journal of Public Health, 98*, 6.

Minkler, M., & Wallerstein, N. (2008). Introduction to CBPR: New issues and emphasis. In M. Minkler & N. Wallerstein (Eds.), *Community-based participatory research for health* (2nd ed., pp. 5–24). San Francisco, CA: Jossey-Bass.

Moradi, B. (2009). Sexual orientation disclosure, concealment, harassment, and military cohesion: Perceptions of LGBT military veterans. *Military Psychology, 21*, 513–533.

Moradi, B., Mohr, J., Worthington, R., & Fassinger, R. (2009). Counseling psychology research on sexual (orientation) minority issues: Conceptual and methodological challenges and opportunities. *Journal of Counseling Psychology, 5*, 5–22.

Newcomb, M. E., & Mustanski, B. (2011). Internalized homophobia and internalizing mental health problems: A meta-analytic review. *Clinical Psychology Review, 30*, 8.

Pizacani, B. A., Rohde, K., Bushore, C., Stark, M. J., Maher, J. E., Dilley, J. A., & Boysun, M. J. (2009). Smoking-related knowledge, attitudes and behaviors in the lesbian, gay and bisexual community: A population-based study from the US Pacific Northwest. *Preventive Medicine, 48*, 6.

RAND. (2010). *Sexual orientation and US Military personnel policy: An update of RAND's 1993 study*. National Defense Research Institute. Prepared for the Office of the Secretary of Defense, Santa Monica, CA.

Ragins, B. R., Singh, R., & Cornwell, J. M. (2008). Making the invisible visible: Fear and disclosure of sexual orientation at work. *Journal of Applied Psychology, 92*, 4.

Roberts, A. L., Austin, S. B., Corliss, H. L., Vandermorris, A. K., & Koenen, K. C.(2010). Pervasive trauma exposure among US sexual orientation minority adults and risk of posttraumatic stress disorder. *American Journal of Public Health, 100*, 12.

Sanchez, J. P., Halipern, S. C., & Calderon, Y. (2007). Factors associated with emergency department utilization by urban lesbian, gay, and bisexual individuals. *Journal of Community Health, 32*, 2.

Szymanski, D. M., Kashubeck, S., & Meyer, J. (2009). Internalized heterosexism—Measurement, psychosocial correlates, and research directions. *Counseling Psychologist, 36*, 4.

Terman, S. (2004). *The practical and conceptual problems with regulating harassment in a discriminatory institution*. Center for the Study of Sexual Minorities in the Military, Institute for Social, Behavioral, and Economic Research, UC Santa Barbara. Retrieved from http:/www.echolarship.org/uc/item/5n9649fm

Trivette, S. A. (2010). Secret handshakes and decoder rings: The queer space of don't ask don't tell. *Sex Research and Social Policy, 7*, 214–228.

U.S. Department of Veterans Affairs. (2012, July 18). Participation in the Health Care Equality Index. Memorandum from the Principal Deputy Undersecretary for Health and Deputy Undersecretary for Health for Operations and Management.

Wenzel, A., Brown, G. K., & Karlin, B. E. (2011). *Cognitive behavioral therapy for depression in veterans and military servicemembers: Therapist manual*. Washington, DC: U.S. Department of Veterans Affairs.

Westcott, K., & Sawyer, R. (2007). Silent sacrifices: The impact of "don't ask, don't tell" on lesbian and gay military families. *Duke Journal of Gender Law & Policy, 14*, 1121–1139.

Witten, T. M. (2007). *Gender identity and the military: Transgender, transsexual, and intersex-identified individuals in the U.S. armed forces*. Palm Center. Retrieved http://www.palmcenter.org/files/active/0/TransMilitary2007.pdf

Mental Health Characteristics of Sexual Minority Veterans

BRYAN N. COCHRAN, PhD
Department of Psychology, University of Montana, Missoula, Montana, USA

KIMBERLY BALSAM, PhD
Pacific Graduate School of Psychology, Palo Alto University, Palo Alto, California, USA

ANNESA FLENTJE, MA, MS
Department of Psychology, University of Montana, Missoula, Montana, USA

CAROL A. MALTE, MSW and TRACY SIMPSON, PhD
Puget Sound Health Care System, United States Veterans Administration, Seattle, Washington, USA

This study examines the mental health characteristics of sexual minority (lesbian, gay, and bisexual, or LGB) veterans, compared these characteristics to those of an existing Veterans Affairs (VA) sample, and examined the relationship between mental health and anxiety around concealment of LGB identity while in the military. Data regarding LGB veterans' (n = 409) military experiences and current mental health were collected via an online survey; comparison data (n = 15,000) were retrieved from a VA data warehouse. LGB veterans were more likely to screen positive for posttraumatic stress disorder (PTSD), depression, and alcohol problems than the comparison sample. Anxiety around concealment of one's sexual orientation while in the service was related to current depression and PTSD symptoms.

This research was funded in part by a grant from the Palm Center at the University of Santa Barbara, California.

Despite significant political and media attention regarding the issue of lesbian, gay, and bisexual (LGB) service personnel in the U.S. military, little data have been available to guide policy decisions. The U.S. military's long-standing ban on gay and lesbian service members was modified with the National Defense Authorization Act of 1994, commonly known as Don't Ask, Don't Tell (DADT; see Sinclair, 2009, for a review). DADT changed the policy toward LGB service members from expulsion on the basis of sexual orientation to expulsion on the basis of sexual behavior; this compromise was the subject of much controversy between activists on both sides of the issue. Under DADT, the military stated that it would not ask about sexual orientation during the enlistment process, and it prohibited service members from openly revealing their sexual orientation. Despite this policy, discharges on the basis of same-sex sexual behavior continued until 2011, when DADT was repealed.

Critics of DADT maintained that it did little more than silence LGB service members with regard to their identities, while reinforcing the fear that revelation of one's sexual orientation will result in expulsion and the loss of veterans' benefits. For LGB service members serving under DADT, the policy often created unique stressors including, but not limited to, needing to conceal important personal information, enduring harassment, and facing discharge or fear of discharge. The DADT policy was repealed on September 20, 2011, with a subsequent change that month deleting homosexual conduct as grounds for discharge. To date, however, there is no empirical research examining the extent to which DADT and prior policies may have impacted LGB veterans after leaving the military.

It is important to note that the DADT policy and its later repeal do not specifically address transgender individuals, although transgender military personnel may be discriminated against on the basis that their transgender status may be treated as a mental illness such as transvestitism, transsexualism, or gender identity disorder by the military, which are medical exclusions according to standards of medical fitness for service (Army, Medical Services, 2007). Additionally, a transgender individual serving under DADT could have been expelled for same-sex behavior; for example, a female-to-male transgender individual's trans identity would not have been acknowledged by the service, and this person could have been discharged for sexual behavior with a female. Concealment of one's transgender identity, similar to the concealment of one's same-sex attractions and behavior, may have resulted in similar experiences for transgender and LGB service members.

Few researchers have studied the impact of military service on LGB individuals, who under the DADT policy had to conceal their sexual orientation to remain in the service. This process of concealment, along with the experience of anti-LGB harassment, discrimination, and/or victimization, may have taken a negative psychological toll on LGB service members (Burks, 2011; Pachankis, 2007). The purpose of this study was to investigate the mental health status of LGB veterans and to examine the extent to which current mental health is associated with concealment of one's identity while in the military.

MENTAL HEALTH CHARACTERISTICS OF VETERAN POPULATIONS

The extensive literature base on the mental health of veteran populations has documented elevated risks for a number of conditions among veterans as a group. Given that many veterans are exposed to combat, war zone stressors, and/or military sexual trauma (MST) during their military service, it is not surprising that veterans are at an increased risk for posttraumatic stress disorder (PTSD; Eisen et al., 2004; Magruder & Yeager, 2009; Surís & Lind, 2008; Thomas et al., 2010). A recent meta-analysis indicated that deployment was associated with 1.5 to 3.5 times greater likelihood of veterans developing PTSD, regardless of the cohort studied (Magruder & Yeager, 2009). At the time of that investigation, the odds ratios were highest for Vietnam era veterans, followed by Persian Gulf era veterans, and the lowest odds ratios were for the OIF/OEF cohort (Operation Iraqi Freedom and Operation Enduring Freedom). With regard to MST, Street, Gradus, Stafford, and Kelly (2007) found that in a survey of former reservists, 8.8% of females and 1.0% of males experienced someone attempting to have sex with them against their will. Overall odds ratios for females experiencing sexual coercion indicated 10 times the risk than for males; for all participants, experiences of sexual harassment were related to depression, PTSD, and general mental health symptoms.

Other mental health diagnoses including depressive disorders, substance abuse disorders, and anxiety disorders are also overrepresented among veteran populations (Hankin, Spiro, Miller, & Kazis, 1999; Liu, Campbell, Chaney, Li, McDonell, & Fihn, 2006). Comorbidity, or presence of multiple diagnoses, is also quite common, with one study finding that 36% of depressed patients receiving care through the Veterans Affairs (VA) system also screened positive for PTSD (Campbell et al., 2007). One recent investigation of OIF/OEF veterans examined rates of substance misuse among these veterans at the time of their first use of VA services; this study found overall rates of 10% for alcohol use disorders, 5% for drug use disorders, and 3% for both (Seal et al., 2011). Exposure to combat related traumas has also been found to compromise health-related quality of life among veterans (Gade & Wenger, 2011), as has exposure to MST (Surís, Lind, Kashner, & Borman, 2007).

Finally, suicidality, which is commonly associated with a variety of mental health diagnoses, is an area of significant concern regarding both active duty personnel and military veterans (Ilgen et al., 2010). Bossarte, Claassen, and Knox (2010) have pointed out that, although rates of completed suicide in the Army have historically been lower than in the civilian population, in 2008, this trend was reversed for the first time on record. Taken together, these studies all point to elevated rates of mental health diagnoses among veterans, with these rates explained by exposure to combat, MST, and other stressors involved in a military career.

MENTAL HEALTH CHARACTERISTICS OF LGB POPULATIONS

Over the past few decades, several population-based studies have established that LGB individuals are at significantly elevated risk for mental health disorders including depressive, anxiety, and substance use disorders (Cochran, 2001). This risk has been explained by the minority stress hypothesis (Meyer, 2003), which posits that living as a member of a stigmatized group in society leads to increased exposure to stressful life events such as discrimination and victimization, which, in turn, have an impact on mental health and wellbeing. Indeed, research has demonstrated elevated lifetime risk of physical and sexual abuse (Balsam, Rothblum, & Beauchaine, 2005) and discrimination (Mays & Cochran, 2001) among sexual minorities compared to their heterosexual peers. A recent prospective study (Hatzenbuehler, McLaughlin, Keyes, & Hasin, 2010) found that the mental health of LGB individuals in U.S. states that instituted a ban on same-sex marriage was significantly worse than in states where such a ban was not enacted, providing further support for the link between institutionalized discrimination and minority stress.

In summary, there is strong research evidence that both veteran and LGB populations experience elevated risk for mental health and substance use problems. However, to date, no empirical research has examined the mental health of those individuals who are both veterans and LGB. A recent study indicated an association between concealment of sexual orientation and diminished unit social cohesion, though the impact on mental health was not ascertained (Moradi, 2009). Given the sociohistorical context of military policies concerning sexual orientation, it is likely that LGB veterans experience unique stressors compared to both the general veteran population and the general LGB population. For example, in society at large, greater degrees of outness or open disclosure of sexual orientation have been linked to better mental health and psychosocial functioning (e.g., Balsam & Mohr, 2007). This may not be the case for LGB individuals serving in the military. Although concealing one's identity may be a risk factor for psychological problems, being out while in the military carries with it a host of other associated difficulties, including overt discrimination and, in the past, possible discharge from the service.

Because no previous studies have inquired about experiences of LGB veterans when we initiated the current study, we developed a new measure based on consultation with LGB veterans to explore correlates of mental health functioning for this population. This new measure is comprised of LGB-related beliefs and experiences associated with military service. We sought to examine the extent to which concealment of one's sexual orientation was related to current mental health functioning for LGB veterans. Additionally, we compared our LGB veteran sample to a large sample of veterans seeking care in the northwest region of the United States on several key mental health indicators.

HYPOTHESES

For this study, we had two primary research goals. The first goal was to provide preliminary data characterizing the mental health of LGB veterans. The corresponding hypothesis was that LGB veterans would fare worse than veterans in the VA comparison group in terms of mental health status. The second goal was to examine the extent to which stressful experiences during military service associated with sexual orientation were related to current mental health functioning. Based on previous literature with veteran and LGB populations, we predicted that negative experiences related to being LGB during military service would be associated with poorer current mental health functioning.

METHODS

Study Design and Procedures

Participants were recruited through advertisements in national and regional LGBT publications and postings on LGBT e-mail listservs. The advertisement stated that the research was intended for LGBT veterans of the U.S. Armed Forces. Those who were interested in the study accessed a secure Web site where they were given information about the purpose of the study and were offered the option of giving their implied consent via continuation with the survey. The survey consisted of over 300 questions, with the actual number of questions per participant varying based on previous responses (e.g., those who did not endorse using VA services skipped follow-up questions). No compensation was given to participants. At the end of the survey, a debriefing form provided participants with resources they could contact in the event that their participation caused lingering feelings of distress. Data were anonymously collected from May 2004 until January 2005, and no HIPAA identifiers were collected. All procedures were approved by the University of Washington Institutional Review Board (IRB).

Participant Characteristics

Four hundred forty five participants completed the survey. The participants were 64.7% male, 27.2% female, and 8.1% transgender or other. Because the military's DADT policy specifically addressed sexual orientation, but not gender identity, the 36 participants who identified as transgender were excluded from analyses in this article, although a report of their experiences is currently in preparation. Thus, the total sample for these analyses was 409.

The mean age was 45.0 ($sd = 13.4$) years (range 19–83). Regarding sexual orientation, 93.2% of participants identified as lesbian or gay, 5.7% of participants identified as bisexual, 0.3% of participants identified as heterosexual, and 0.8% of participants identified as other. The participant who identified as heterosexual later in the survey identified that he was gay, but not open about his sexual orientation to others, and as such was included in the analyses.

In reporting ethnicity. 87.3% of participants identified themselves as European American or White, 4.4% identified as multiracial or other, 3.7% identified as Latino or Hispanic, 2.2% identified as African American or Black, 1.0% identified as Native American or American Indian, and 1.2% identified as Asian American or Pacific Islander.

Measures

Demographics and military service

Participants answered demographic questions and questions regarding service history and branch. Because it was possible for participants to have re-enlisted, we asked about their years of service for up to three periods of military service. They were also asked about their reasons for leaving the service and were given eight options, including "my tour of duty ended and I wanted to pursue civilian career options," "I retired," "I was forced to leave by the military because of sexual orientation issues," and "other;" they could select more than one option, if applicable.

PTSD

PTSD was assessed using the PTSD Checklist-Civilian Version (PCL-C, Weathers et al., 1993). The PCL-C is a 17-item measure which is based on the diagnostic criteria for PTSD (Weathers, Litz, Herman, Huska, & Keane, 1993). Cronbach's alpha for the PCL-C was 0.95 within this sample.

Depression and suicidality

Participants' current level of depression was assessed using the Patient Health Questionnaire-9 (PHQ-9), which consists of nine items that assess symptoms on a scale ranging from zero (indicating the absence of a symptom of depression) to three (indicating the persistent presence of a symptom of depression; Kroenke, Spitzer, & Williams, 2001). Cronbach's alpha for the PHQ-9 was 0.94 in the present sample. Participants were also questioned about past history of suicidal behaviors, including whether they had had past suicidal ideation or a serious suicide attempt using questions from Savin-Williams (2001).

Alcohol Misuse

Problematic alcohol use was assessed using the Alcohol Use Disorders Identification Test (AUDIT; Babor, Higgins-Biddle, Saunders, & Monteiro, 2001). The AUDIT queries severity and frequency of alcohol use with 10 items and the AUDIT-C (Bush, Kivlahan, McDonell, Fihn, & Bradley, 1998) is a modified version of the AUDIT which uses 3 items from the AUDIT to assess potentially problematic drinking. The AUDIT and AUDIT-C items are scored on a 5-point scale (0–4, with higher numbers corresponding with greater levels of drinking and drinking-related problems). Within this sample, Cronbach's alpha for the AUDIT was 0.80.

Military Experiences Related to Sexual Orientation

A new measure was created in order to assess participants' beliefs, attitudes, and experiences specifically related to sexual orientation. This measure consists of 26 items and contains items such as "I initially joined the military with hopes of 'overcoming' my sexual orientation," which the participant rated his/her level of agreement on a six-point scale (see Table 1 for the full measure).

A principal components analysis conducted on this measure using varimax rotation identified four components that accounted for 42% of the total variance. We elected to use the first component, labeled "anxiety around concealment," solely for future analyses. This component included items such as "In the service, I was constantly trying to conceal my sexual orientation," and "I overheard homophobic statements while I was in the service" and had a Cronbach's alpha of 0.73. The remaining components had values below $\alpha = 0.70$, and, therefore, were considered to have insufficient internal consistency for further analysis. Complete items and component loadings are included in Table 1.

For the purpose of analyses involving our second hypothesis, scores for the first component were computed, yielding subscale scores. Items that loaded negatively on each component were reverse-scored before computing subscale values for each participant. The resultant possible range for the anxiety around concealment subscale was 6 to 48, with higher scores indicating greater anxiety.

TABLE 1 Items from the Military Experiences of LGBT Veterans Scale[a] Listed by Component with Component Loadings

Item		1[b]	2	3	4
3.	I overheard homophobic statements while I was in the service.	**.401**	.149	−.085	.166
4.	If I had let people in the service know of my sexual orientation, I probably would have been harmed physically.	**.510**	−.148	.071	−.286
5.	I initially joined the military with hopes of 'overcoming' my sexual orientation.	**.371**	−.132	.021	−.159
7.	In the service, I was constantly trying to conceal my sexual orientation.	**.747**	.023	−.005	−.021
8.	In the service, I experienced a great deal of fear and anxiety about my sexual orientation being revealed to others.	**.781**	−.104	−.034	.021
9.	I probably had a much more difficult time in the service than my heterosexual peers.	**.704**	−.212	.068	.208
10.	I left the military because I realized that I could not express my sexuality in that environment.	**.405**	−.213	.000	.395
12.	While in the military, I purposely dated people of the opposite sex in order to make others think that I was heterosexual.	**.543**	−.021	−.193	−.190
17.	I initially had difficulty finding work after leaving the military.	.270	**−.623**	−.134	.130
18.	At times, I have been able to keep civilian jobs (or a job) for at least several years.	.164	**.485**	.071	.221
19.	The initial transition to civilian life was easy for me.	−.162	**.679**	.290	−.116
20.	I feel that my current adjustment to civilian life is good.	−.051	**.716**	.268	.113
21.	I initially had difficulty finding supportive GLBT people in the civilian community because of my veteran status.	.092	**−.555**	.010	.014
22.	I currently have some supportive GLBT non-military friends who know that I am a veteran.	.161	**.382**	.221	.358
11.	It was in the military that I first became aware of my sexual orientation.	.154	−.122	**−.323**	−.017
16.	I wanted to be 'career military.'	.327	.054	**−.592**	.162
23.	When I first left the military, I liked the freedom and lack of structure of civilian life.	.033	.122	**.742**	.018
24.	Now I like the freedom and lack of structure of civilian life.	.201	.192	**.744**	.096
25.	I regret my decision to leave the military.	.081	−.287	**−.600**	.170
26.	I look back on my time in the military fondly.	−.069	.411	**−.482**	.324

(Continued)

TABLE 1 (Continued)

Item		1^b	2	3	4
1.	For a lot of other soldiers, I was probably the first gay/lesbian/bisexual/transgender person they knew.	.012	−.303	.224	**.352**
2.	I never told anyone about my sexual orientation while I was in the service.	.297	.032	.121	**−.611**
13.	There were other soldiers around me who supported me regardless of my sexual orientation.	−.282	.157	−.019	**.644**
14.	I had same-sex sexual experiences while I was in the military.	.124	−.014	−.073	**.639**
15.	I did not know any other gay, lesbian, bisexual, or transgender people who were in the service at the same time as me.	.073	−.069	.073	**−.621**
6.	I had opposite-sex sexual experiences while I was in the military.^{c}	.240	.022	−.046	−.073

^{a}Response options include: 1 = *strongly agree*; 2 = *agree somewhat*; 3 = *neutral*; 4 = *disagree somewhat*; 5 = *strongly disagree*; and 6 = *not applicable*.
^{b}This component, labeled "anxiety around concealment," was the only one of the four components identified that was used for subsequent analyses.
^{c}This item was not included in any subscale due to its incongruence with the other components.

Method for Finding Comparable Comparison Means

In order to compare the LGB veteran sample to a representative sample of veterans, medical record data for veterans receiving care in VA Northwest Health Network (Alaska, Idaho, Oregon, and Washington) were pulled from the Veteran Integrated Service Network (VISN) 20 Data Warehouse. Although a random sample of veterans from the general U.S. community would have been preferable, such a sample with the relevant mental health information could not be located and the VISN20 sample was the best approximation we could identify. Data included gender, age, and mental health screening results on the Patient Health Questionnaire-2 (PHQ-2), AUDIT-C, and PTSD Screen. Records were included if the three mental health measures were completed within ninety days of each other between October 2006 and October 2008 (these data were not collected reliably prior to 2006). Records of 15,000 veterans were randomly selected from the total sample meeting these criteria.

The PHQ-2 (score range 0–6) consists of the first two questions on the PHQ-9 and is widely used as a screen for depressive disorders within the VA health care system. The AUDIT-C (score range 0–12) contains three questions related to alcohol consumption from the AUDIT; it is a screening tool that can help determine if patients are drinking at hazardous levels or have active alcohol use disorders. The PTSD Screen (score range 0–4) is used within VA to identify patients requiring additional PTSD assessment and assesses four symptom groups: re-experiencing, avoidance, hyperarousal, and detachment. Corresponding PCL-C items were used to calculate a PTSD Screen score for the LGB Veteran sample.

Analyses

Descriptive analyses were run to characterize the mental health profile of the LGB veterans in this sample.

LGB Veteran and VA samples were compared on age and gender using two-sample t tests and Chi-square tests, respectively. Linear regression models adjusted for gender and age were used to compare samples on mean PHQ-2, AUDIT-C, and PTSD Screen scores. Logistic and multinomial logistic regression models, also controlling for age and gender, compared LGB and VA samples on dichotomous (positive screens on the PHQ-2 or PTSD Screen) and categorical (AUDIT-C) outcomes.

Hierarchical regression analyses were used to test the hypothesized relationships between anxiety around concealment while in the military and current mental health functioning. Within these hierarchical regression analyses, gender and age were entered as the first step in order to account for gender and age differences that may exist in mental health functioning. The second step was the calculated variable of anxiety around concealment, derived from the new measure of military experiences related to sexual orientation. For the dependent variables, we tested continuous variables of PTSD symptoms (via the PCL-C full score), alcohol misuse (the AUDIT full scale), and depression (the PHQ-9 score).

RESULTS

Mental Health Findings and Comparisons Between LGB Veterans and VA Sample

Mental health data for the LGB veterans in this study are presented in Table 2; these findings are based on screening and cutoff scores for depression, PTSD, and alcohol misuse.

We also compared the LGB sample and the VA (VISN20) sample on demographic and mental health characteristics (Table 3). Individuals in the LGB sample were significantly younger (mean age ± SD LGB: 45.4 ± 13.5, VA: 55.0 ± 17.2, $p < .001$) and more likely to be female (LGB: 29.6%, VA: 7.8%, $p < .001$) than those in the VA sample. After adjusting for age and gender, the LGB sample scored an estimated 0.3 points higher on the PHQ-2 (95% CI: 0.2–0.5, $p < .001$) than the VA sample but were not more likely have a score >2, which would indicate that additional assessment of depression is warranted. On the AUDIT-C, the LGB sample scored over one point

TABLE 2 Mental Health and Military Experiences Characteristics for LGB Veterans ($N = 409$)

Mental health variables	
Depression	12% screened positive on the PHQ-9
PTSD	18% screened positive on the PCL-C
Suicidal behavior	54.7% endorsed suicidal ideation at some point in their lives
	14.7% reported having had a serious suicide attempt
Alcohol use	11% screened positive for current problems on the AUDIT
Military experiences variables	
Impact of sexual orientation	60.5% thought their experiences had been more difficult than their heterosexual peers
	69.3% experienced fear or anxiety about having their LGB identity revealed
	68.7% reported they were constantly trying to conceal their sexual orientation while in the service
Discharge	19.5% reported that discharge was related to sexual orientation (31.0% Marines, 23.6% Navy, 18.8% Air Force, 15.6% Army, 11.8/% Coast Guard)

higher (β_{adj}=1.1, 95% CI: 0.9–1.4, $p < .001$) than the VA sample. As seen in Table 4, individuals in the LGB sample were over twice as likely to score between 5 and 7 (OR$_{adj}$ = 2.5, 95% CI: 1.9–3.3, $p < .001$), indicating potentially hazardous drinking, or over 8 (OR$_{adj}$ = 2.0, 95% CI: 1.4–2.9, p < .001), indicating a likely alcohol use disorder. Likewise, LGB sample scores were significantly higher (1.6 points, 95% CI: 1.5–1.7, p < .001) on the PTSD Screen, with these individuals being more than five times more likely (OR$_{adj}$ =5.8, 95% CI: 4.6–7.2, p < .001) to score over 2, the cut point for additional PTSD assessment in the VA.

Impact of LGB Identity While in the Military

Military experiences for the LGB veterans are briefly summarized in Table 2. The LGB veterans in our sample reported significant anxiety around having their sexual orientation discovered while they were in the service, and, in fact, 19.5% of these veterans reported that their discharge was due to their sexual orientation.

RELATIONSHIP BETWEEN MILITARY EXPERIENCES AND MENTAL HEALTH STATUS

Hierarchical regressions were conducted entering gender and age as the first step, with anxiety around concealment of sexual orientation while in the military entered in the second step. Results are presented in Tables 5–7 for each of the three mental health domains assessed. Because some participants were missing data and cases were deleted listwise, the sample size for these analyses varies from 372 to 384. In the first step of each of these three analyses, age was significantly related to the outcome variable, but the influence of

TABLE 3 Mean Psychological Functioning in LGB and VA samples

Test	Mean lesbian/bisexual females ± SD ($n = 118$)	Mean VA females ± SD ($n = 1163$)	t test (df)	Mean gay/bisexual males ± SD ($n = 287$)	Mean VA males ± SD ($n = 13837$)	t test (df)
AUDIT-C	2.67 ± 2.34	1.43 ± 1.78	−5.68(134.94)**	3.51 ± 2.47	2.24 ± 2.66	−8.62(297.76)**
PTSD Screen	2.74 ± 1.35	0.87 ± 1.45	−14.31(150.16)**	2.47 ± 1.47	0.81 ± 1.40	−18.85(294.67)**
PHQ-2	1.55 ± 1.78	1.09 ± 1.79	−2.68(142.13)*	1.45 ± 1.70	0.98 ± 1.77	−4.57(299.01)**

*$p < .01$.
**$p < .001$.

TABLE 4 Scores on Psychological Measures in LGB and VA Samples by Gender

Score	Lesbian/bisexual females n (%)	VA female n (%)	Gay/bisexual males n (%)	VA male n (%)
PHQ-2				
0–2	97 (82.2)	960 (82.5)	231 (80.5)	11747 (84.9)
3–4	7 (5.9)	119 (10.2)	35 (12.2)	1019 (7.4)
5–6	14 (11.9)	84 (7.2)	21 (7.3)	1071 (7.7)
PTSD Screen				
0–2	40 (33.1)	947 (81.4)	134 (47.0)	11515 (83.2)
3–4	81 (67.0)	216 (18.6)	151 (53.0)	2322 (16.8)
AUDIT-C				
0–4	100 (82.6)	1095 (94.2)	200 (70.2)	11751 (84.9)
5–7	15 (12.4)	54 (4.6)	56 (19.7)	1255 (9.1)
8–12	6 (5.0)	14 (1.2)	29 (10.2)	831 (6.0)

TABLE 5 Regression Analysis Predicting Depression (PHQ-9) Scores for LGB Veterans ($N = 380$)

Variables entered	B	SE B	β	t	sig.
Step 1 ($\Delta R^2 = .026^{**}$)					
Age	−0.073	0.025	−0.153	−2.941	.003
Gender (1 = female, 2 = male)	−0.363	0.733	−0.026	−0.496	.620
Step 2 ($\Delta R^2 = .017^*$)					
Anxiety around concealment	0.121	0.047	0.133	2.571	.011

*$p < .05$.
**$p < .01$.

TABLE 6 Regression Analysis Predicting PTSD (PCL-C) Scores for LGB Veterans ($N = 372$)

Variables entered	B	SE B	β	t	Sig.
Step 1 ($\Delta R^2 = .017^*$)					
Age	−0.144	0.061	−0.125	−2.361	.019
Gender (1=female, 2=male)	−0.774	1.769	−0.023	−0.437	.662
Step 2 ($\Delta R^2 = .066^{**}$)					
Anxiety around concealment	0.570	0.111	0.262	5.137	<.001

*$p < .05$.
**$p < .01$.

gender was not statistically significant. In the second step, which tested our second hypothesis, anxiety around concealment was a significant predictor of PCL-C (PTSD) scores and PHQ-9 (depression) scores in the hypothesized direction. Anxiety around concealment was related to AUDIT (alcohol misuse) scores in the expected direction, but this association was not statistically significant.

TABLE 7 Regression Analysis Predicting Alcohol Use (AUDIT) Scores for LGB Veterans ($N = 384$)

Variables entered	B	SE B	β	t	sig.
Step 1 ($\Delta R^2 = .035$**)					
Age	−0.061	0.017	−0.189	−3.675	<.001
Gender (1 = female, 2 = male)	0.607	0.484	0.065	1.254	.211
Step 2 ($\Delta R^2 = .004$)					
Anxiety around concealment	0.039	0.031	0.063	1.231	.219

*$p < .05$.
**$p < .01$.

DISCUSSION

The policies of the U.S. military have historically prevented LGB military personnel from disclosing their sexual orientation while in the service. The current study examined how these policies might have impacted the mental health of LGB veterans. We hypothesized that LGB veterans would experience elevated mental health risks when compared to established veteran samples, in terms of depression, PTSD, and alcohol and other substance use. We also hypothesized that stressful experiences while in the military related to sexual orientation would serve as predictors of current mental health functioning, and we conducted analyses to test these key hypotheses.

The first hypothesis was supported: Rates of depression, PTSD, and alcohol use were elevated for LGB veterans in our sample in comparison to the VISN20 recipients of VA care. Participants also reported high rates of suicidal thoughts and behavior. Despite the lack of a comparison veterans sample for data regarding suicidality, the report of a serious suicide attempt by 14.7% of our LGB sample is alarming.

In regard to the second hypothesis, there was support for the notion that negative experiences while in the military, especially those related to concealment of one's LGB identity, were predictive of depression and PTSD symptoms. This relationship did not hold true for alcohol use. The fact that alcohol use was not significantly predicted by military experiences, whereas depression and PTSD were, is somewhat surprising. Generally, high rates of co-occurrence of substance use along with depression and PTSD are a consistent finding in the mental health literature.

Results of this study have several implications for the military and for VA medical centers. First, it is important to recognize that LGB identity, in the context of military service, has posed risks for this particular group of LGB service members. The concealment of LGB identity, in particular, seems to be related to elevated mental health risks following discharge from the service. Mitigating these risks could be accomplished through thoughtfully addressing the recent inclusion of sexual minority service members in the military and ensuring that in addition to the policy change, harassment, or victimization of LGB service members is eliminated. The military could also take active steps toward decreasing victimization of its personnel by adopting nondiscrimination policies regarding sexual orientation and gender identity and by enforcing these policies to protect LGB service members.

The results of this study must be interpreted with a number of limitations in mind. First, the method of data collection, online self-report, suffers from a number of possible biases. The participants must have had access to a computer and an Internet connection in order to complete the survey, and they must have heard about the survey through either a mailing group or advertisement. These factors may have drawn a LGB sample that is different in key characteristics from the LGB veteran population, such as inherent interest in the study or socioeconomic status. The resultant sample may have also been more involved in LGB activism than the general population of LGB veterans, and as such may have experienced greater exposure to, or more awareness of, LGB-related minority stress. It is also possible that LGB veterans who were more distressed, in terms of PTSD, depression, or alcohol misuse, were more likely to respond to the recruitment materials. Second, because the data are self-report, there is no way to verify that these reports are accurate. We were not able to give mental health diagnoses; rather, we reported those who screened positive based on available data. Third, our sample represented multiple cohorts of veterans, and the experiences of LGB service members may have differed greatly based on age, years in the service, branch of the service, or other factors. Although we have controlled for age in the mental health analyses for this article, analyzing each separate cohort or branch would significantly reduce the power to detect important effects on each of the resultant groups. Finally, the use of a VISN20 comparison sample, which was geographically restricted and likely contained LGB veterans as well, is not ideal. Another approach may have been to recruit LGB non-veterans for a comparison sample, a strategy that could be utilized in future studies to verify the findings reported here. Despite these limitations, this study is an initial attempt to reach a population that is difficult to identify and access. Future studies may possibly overcome these limitations by recruiting through VA medical centers, sampling from populations that are underrepresented in this study, utilizing a LGB non-veteran comparison sample, or studying a cohort of service members prospectively as they are leaving the military. In a post-DADT era, it will be important to analyze the effects of the policy change on LGB individuals not only while they are in the service, but also as they become part of the next generation of veterans.

REFERENCES

Army, Medical Services. (2007). *Standards of medical fitness*. Retrieved from http://www.apd.army.mil/pdffiles/r40_501.pdf

Babor, T. F., Higgins-Biddle, J. C., Saunders, J. B., & Monteiro, M. G. (2001). *The alcohol use disorders identification test: Guidelines for use in primary care*

(2nd ed.). World Health Organization. Retrieved http://whqlibdoc.who.int/hq/2001/WHO_MSD_MSB_01.6a.pdf

Balsam, K. F., & Mohr, J. J. (2007). Adaptation to sexual orientation stigma: A comparison of bisexual and lesbian/gay adults. *Journal of Counseling Psychology, 54*, 306–319.

Balsam, K. F., Rothblum, E. D., & Beauchaine, T. P. (2005). Victimization over the life span: A comparison of lesbian, gay, bisexual, and heterosexual siblings. *Journal of Consulting and Clinical Psychology, 73*, 477–487.

Bossarte, R., Claassen, C. A., & Knox, K. (2010). Veterans suicide prevention: Emerging priorities and opportunities for intervention. *Military Medicine, 175*, 461–462.

Burks, D. J. (2011). Lesbian, gay and bisexual victimization in the military: An unintended consequence of "don't ask, don't tell"? *American Psychologist, 66*, 604–613.

Bush, K., Kivlahan, D. R., McDonell, M.B., Fihn, S. D., & Bradley, K. A. (1998). The AUDIT alcohol consumption questions (AUDIT-C): An effective brief screening test for problem drinking. *Archives of Internal Medicine, 58*, 1789–1795.

Campbell, D. G., Felker, B. L., Liu, C., Yano, E. M., Kirchner, J. E., Chan, D., . . . Chaney, E. F. (2007). Prevalence of depression-PTSD comorbidity: Implications for clinical practice guidelines and primary care-based interventions. *Journal of General Internal Medicine, 22*, 711–718.

Cochran, S. D. (2001). Emerging issues in research on lesbians' and gay men's mental health: Does sexual orientation really matter? *American Psychologist, 56*, 931–947.

Eisen, S. A., Griffith, K. H., Xian, H., Scherrer, J. F., Fischer, I. D., Chantarujikapong, S., . . . Tsuang, M. T. (2004). Lifetime and 12-month prevalence of psychiatric disorders in 8,169 male Vietnam War era veterans. *Military Medicine, 169*, 896–902.

Gade, D. M., & Wenger, J. B. (2011). Combat exposure and mental health: the long-term effects among US Vietnam and Gulf war veterans. *Health Economics, 20*, 401–416.

Hankin, C. S., Spiro, A., Miller, D. R., & Kazis, L. (1999) Mental disorders and mental health treatment among U.S. Department Veterans Affairs outpatients: The veterans health study. *American Journal of Psychiatry, 156*, 1924–1930.

Hatzenbuehler, M. L., McLaughlin, K. A., Keyes, K. M., & Hasin, D. S. (2010). The impact of institutional discrimination on psychiatric disorders in lesbian, gay, and bisexual populations: A prospective study. *American Journal of Public Health, 100*; 452–459.

Ilgen, M. A., Bohnert, A. S. B., Ignacio, R. V., McCarthy, J. F., Velenstein, M. M., Kim, H. M., & Blow, F. C. (2010). Psychiatric diagnoses and risk of suicide in veterans. *Archives of General Psychiatry, 67*, 1152–1158.

Kroenke, K., Spitzer, R. L., & Williams, J. B. W. (2001). The PHQ-9: Validity of a brief depression severity measure. *Journal of General Internal Medicine, 16*, 606–613.

Liu, C. F., Campbell, D. G., Chaney, E. F., Li, Y. F., McDonell, M, Fihn, S. D. (2006). Depression diagnosis and antidepressant treatment among depressed VA primary care patients. *Administration and Policy in Mental Health and Mental Health Services Research, 33*(3), 331–341.

Magruder, K. M., & Yeager D. E. (2009). The prevalence of PTSD across war eras and the effect of deployment on PTSD: A systematic review and meta-analysis. *Psychiatric Annals, 39*, 778–788.

Mays, V. M. & Cochran, S. D. (2001). Mental health correlates of perceived discrimination among lesbian, gay, and bisexual adults in the United States. *American Journal of Public Health, 91*, 1869–1876.

Meyer, I. H. (2003). Prejudice, social stress, and mental health in lesbian, gay, and bisexual populations: Conceptual issues and research evidence. *Psychological Bulletin, 129*, 674–697.

Moradi, B. (2009). Sexual orientation disclosure, concealment, harassment, and military cohesion: Perceptions of LGBT military veterans. *Military Psychology, 31*, 513–533.

Pachankis, J. E. (2007). The psychological implications of concealing a stigma: A cognitive-affective-behavioral model. *Psychological Bulletin, 133*, 328–345.

Savin-Williams, R. C. (2001). Suicide attempts among sexual-minority youths: Population and measurement issues. *Journal of Consulting Clinical Psychology, 69*, 983–991.

Seal, K. H., Cohen, G., Waldrop, A., Cohen, B. E., Maguen, S., & Ren, L. (2011). Substance use disorders in Iraq and Afghanistan veterans in VA healthcare, 2001–2010: Implications for screening, diagnosis and treatment. *Drug and Alcohol Dependence, 116*, 93–101.

Sinclair, G. D. (2009). Homosexuality and the military: A review of the literature. *Journal of Homosexuality, 56*, 701–718.

Street, A. E., Gradus, J. L., Stafford, J., & Kelly, K. (2007). Gender differences in experiences of sexual harassment: Data from a male-dominated environment. *Journal of Consulting and Clinical Psychology, 75*, 464–474.

Surís, A., & Lind, L. (2008). Military sexual trauma: A review of prevalence and associated health consequences in veterans. *Trauma, Violence, and Abuse, 9*, 250–269.

Surís, A., Lind, L., Kashner, T. M., & Borman, P. D. (2007). Mental health, quality of life, and health functioning in women veterans: Differential outcomes associated with military and civilian sexual assault. *Journal of Interpersonal Violence, 22*, 179–197.

Thomas, J. L., Wilk, J. E., Riviere, L. A., McGurk, D., Castro, C. A., Hoge, C. W. (2010). Prevalence of mental health problems and functional impairment among active component and National Guard soldiers 3 and 12 months following combat in Iraq. *Archives of General Psychiatry, 67*, 614–623.

Weathers, F. W., Litz, B. T., Herman, D. S., Huska, J. A., & Keane, T. M. (1993). *The PTSD checklist (PCL): Reliability, validity, and diagnostic utility.* Paper presented at the 9th annual conference of the ISTSS, San Antonio, TX.

Transgender People in the Military: Don't Ask? Don't Tell? Don't Enlist!

ADAM F. YERKE, PsyD
Chicago School of Professional Psychology, Chicago, Illinois, USA

VALORY MITCHELL, PhD
California School of Professional Psychology, Alliant International University, San Francisco, California, USA

The repeal of Don't Ask, Don't Tell offered legal equality to sexual minorities in the military. However, this big step forward had no impact on the policy of exclusion and rejection and the fear and secrecy that resulted for transgender people (whether lesbian, gay, bisexual, or heterosexual). In this article, we argue that transgender citizens should have equal opportunity to honorably serve their country, and to be treated with respect and sensitivity as they do so. Many transgender persons may be drawn to military service and its ethos of masculine values. However, they are currently not permitted entry, and, if they are to enter, must remain hidden or face dismissal, leaving them vulnerable to harassment. While they report both positive and negative experiences during their service, research documents discrimination in veterans' healthcare as well as mental health risks resulting from fear and harassment. In contrast to the United States, 11 countries include transgender people in their militaries. Drawing in part from their examples, we end with recommendations for change in the direction of respect and equality of opportunity.

The repeal of Don't Ask, Don't Tell (DADT) was significant for lesbian, gay, and bisexual (LGB) people (and for those who engage in homosexual acts without such an identity) because they could no longer be denied admission into the military and could be discharged as a result of homosexual identity or behavior (U.S. Department of Defense [DOD], 2011b). However, this monumental change did not impact transgender people. The U.S. military continues to discriminate against transgender people by barring them from military service and by discharging anyone who is, or is alleged to be, transgender (Kerrigan, 2011; Witten, 2007).

In this article, we argue that transgender citizens should have equal opportunity to serve their country honorably, and should be treated with respect and sensitivity as they do so. We first review U.S. military policies concerning rejection and exclusion. We explain that transgender people may be particularly drawn to seek military service, and that many transgender people have already served. Autobiographical recollections illustrate some of their experiences. Like all military personnel, transgender people deserve appropriate healthcare. We discuss the mental and physical health and healthcare concerns of this population so that policies can be based in understanding, rather than becoming additional domains of discrimination. Finally, we present information about eleven countries whose militaries include transgender persons, followed by some arguments against inclusion. Using the positive models and considering the negative arguments, we conclude with our recommendations for change.

We focus on one group of transgender people, transsexuals. Transsexuals usually choose to live permanently as the other sex and make physical changes to their bodies with hormone-replacement therapy and surgeries; however, individuals differ in their transition interests, and not all transsexuals seek full physical transition (Lev, 2004; Yerke & Mitchell, 2011). Although our focus is on transsexuals, our observations and conclusions often apply to all people who do not completely identify with their birth sex or assigned gender, including transvestites, cross-dressers, androgynous, intersex, genderqueer or other gender-variant people (Brown & Rounsley, 1996; Israel & Tarver, 1997; Lev, 2004).

CURRENT U. S. MILITARY POLICIES

The military's current policies regarding transgender persons may impact "enlistment, appointment or commissioning into the armed forces, or may arise for personnel already serving in the military" (Servicemembers Legal Defense Network [SLDN], 2011, p. 29). Transgender people may be rejected by invoking medical or psychological rationales (SLDN, 2011a; Witten, 2007), or may simply be rejected for behavior that is deemed to reflect negatively on themselves or the military (Uniform Code of Military Justice [UCMJ], 2010a, 2010b).

Transgender people may be disqualified from joining the military as a result of any type of genital surgery, since this is an area of assessment and examination during the initial medical evaluation (Department of the Army [DOA], 2011; DOD, 2011a). According to the DoD directive (2011a), any individual with a "history of major abnormalities or defects of the genitalia such as change of sex (P64.5) (CPT 55970, 55980), hermaphroditism, pseudohermaphroditism, or pure gonadal dysgenesis (752.7)" is precluded from service for what the military considers to be a medical condition (pp. 26–27). DoD directives apply to all branches of the military, but each branch also has its own guidelines to exclude transgender people from serving. For example, the DoA's (2011) Standards of Medical Fitness use language identical to that quoted above, but add that any person with "dysfunctional residuals from surgical correction of these conditions does not meet the standard [for eligibility to be in the Army]" (p. 11).

Transgender people may also be disqualified for service as a result of being seen as having a "psychological condition" (DoA, 2011; DoD, 2011a). The DoD (2011a) excludes people with "Current or history of psychosexual conditions (302), including but not limited to transsexualism, exhibitionism, transvestism, voyeurism, and other paraphilias" (p. 48). Any person identifying themselves as transgender, or suspected of being transgender, can be labeled with these psychosexual conditions. As they do with the medical exclusions, each branch of the military also has their own regulations restricting transgender people on the basis of psychosexual conditions. For example, the DoA (2011, p. 15) uses identical language to the DoD.

These military policies place transsexualism among the paraphilic disorders (DoA, 2011; DoD, 2011a) even though transsexualism is neither a paraphilia nor a diagnosis in the current *Diagnostic and Statistical Manual of Mental Disorders* (4th ed., text rev; DSM-IV-TR; American Psychiatric Association [APA], 2000). Transsexualism concerns a person's gender identity, while paraphilias describe "recurrent, intense sexual urges, fantasies, or behaviors" (APA, 2000, p. 535). Although the term transsexualism does include "sex" in the term, this is related to biological sex rather than sexuality—a point of confusion for those creating and implementing military policies.

Curiously, the psychiatric diagnosis of gender identity disorder (GID), which is often applied to persons identifying as transgender or transsexual (Lev, 2004), is not mentioned in the DoD or other military policy statements. The GID diagnosis requires that the individual experiences subjective distress or functional impairment (APA, 2000), so some transgender individuals would not meet these criteria. If the military were to use GID as a criterion for rejection of transgender persons, those who do not experience distress or impairment could be exempt, which might force the military to be explicit about the actual basis for their rejection.

Some people, having been allowed to enter military service, may begin to identify as transgender once in the military. If they are suspected of being transgender, they may be discharged (SLDN, 2011a; Witten, 2007) using the medical or psychological exclusion criteria already discussed. In addition, transgender (or allegedly transgender) people may be charged criminally using Articles 133 and 134 of the UCMJ (Kerrigan, 2011):

> 933. ART. 133. CONDUCT UNBECOMING AN OFFICER AND A GENTLEMAN
> Any commissioned officer, cadet, or midshipman who is convicted of conduct unbecoming an officer and a gentleman shall be punished as a court-martial may direct.
>
> 934. ART. 134. GENERAL ARTICLE
> Though not specifically mentioned in this chapter, all disorders and neglects to the prejudice of good order and discipline in the armed forces, all conduct of a nature to bring discredit upon the armed forces, and crimes and offenses not capital, of which persons subject to this chapter may be guilty, shall be taken cognizance of by a general, special or summary court-martial, according to the nature and degree of the offense, and shall be punished at the discretion of that court. (UCMJ, 2010a, 2010b)

Kerrigan (2011) describes Article 134 as "a catch-all method the military could employ to justify punishing or discharging someone for almost any behavior seen as out of the ordinary . . . the broad language means that it could be used against a variety of transgender behaviors and appearances" (pp. 8–9).

Any person displaying gender atypical behaviors can be criminalized and discharged under Article 134; this includes homosexuals and bisexuals (and heterosexuals), who may be discharged for gender atypical behavior (Kerrigan, 2011). LGB people may be particularly at risk because gender role behavior is often more fluid for homosexual or bisexual persons (Dawood, Bailey, & Martin, 2009; Rieger, Linsenmeier, Gygax, & Bailey, 2008), that is, gay men may (but may not) behave more effeminately, and lesbians may (or may not) appear more masculine or butch than heterosexuals. Now that homosexual or bisexual servicemen and women are not disqualified for their sexual orientation, they may still be disqualified or discharged for non-traditional gender traits and behavior.

THE PREVALENCE OF TRANSGENDER PEOPLE IN THE MILITARY

It is particularly important for the military to address its discrimination against transgender persons because of the possibility that there is a higher proportion of transgender people in the military than in the general U.S. population (Brown, 1988; Brown & Rounsley, 1996; Frye, 2004; McDuffie & Brown, 2010; Shipherd, Mizock, Maguen, & Green, 2011). In a recent study

(Shipherd et al., 2011), 30% of the male-to-female (MTF) sample were veterans, a rate that triples the prevalence of veterans in the general population (10.1%). Clinicians specializing in transgender care have reported high rates of military service among MTFs (Brown, 1988; Brown & Rounsley, 1996). For instance, Brown (1988), a psychiatrist, reported that he had met with 11 biological males with GID, and 8 of these had extensive active duty military experience. Brown and Rounsley (1996, as cited in Shipher et al., 2011) indicated that over half of their MTF patients had served in the military. Brown (1988) also pointed to several autobiographies by MTFs who were in the military (Cowell, 1954; Jorgensen, 1967; Morris, 1974; Richards, 1983).

Transgender people may be drawn to the military for some of the same reasons as non-transgender (cisgender) people, such as following a family tradition of military service, needing financial help to gain further training and schooling, seeking adventure and excitement, interest in the opportunity for international travel, and patriotism. The autobiographies of two MTFs who transitioned following their military service cite these reasons for joining the military:

> I signed up in the summer of 1970 with the Royal Engineers. This choice was because my dad had been a Royal Engineer, and so had my uncle and his dad before him, so it was a bit of a family tradition. (Murphy, 2003, p. 163)

> I wanted to be accepted by the army for two reasons. Foremost was my great desire to belong, to be needed, and to join the stream of activities around me like the other young people of my acquaintance who were contributing to the times. Second, I wanted my parents to be proud of me and to be able to say, "My son is also in the service." Although they never mentioned it, I was poignantly aware that Mom and Dad must have felt their child was "different" and, therefore, unwanted. (Jorgensen, 1967, p. 35)

Transgender people may be especially interested in the military because of its emphasis on traditional masculine values (Brown, 1988). Devor (2004, as cited in Shipher, et al., 2011) recognizes identity confusion as a stage in transsexual identity development that may include attempts to repress questions about one's gender identity. MTFs in that confusion stage, long prior to transition, may seek activities that express a traditional masculine, or even hypermasculine, role associated with violence, danger, excitement, and manliness (Mosher & Sirkin, 1984). Joining the military is one way that such people can attempt to become real men (Brown, 1988). McDuffie and Brown (2010) describe this experience:

> Transgendered or transsexual natal males can attempt to purge the desire to become feminine by enlisting in an organization that rewards and cultivates exaggerated masculine behaviors: high-risk taking, stoicism, controlled violence, heterosexuality, athletic prowess, and contempt for physical/emotional weakness. (p. 23)

This psychological effort may be deliberate for some but unconscious for others, and only revealed long after the fact (McDuffie & Brown, 2010). Brown (1988) has seen this "flight into hypermasculinity" as common among MTFs prior to transition (p. 539). Brown and Rounsley (1996) stated:

> Many male-to-female transsexuals seek the most rugged, stereotypically male profession or job they can find . . . .Military service is a route that many male-to-female transsexuals follow in their quest for confirmation of their masculinity. Over half of my male patients served in one of the branches of military. Many transsexuals not only become career military officers but also frequently request the most rigorous or dangerous missions they can find in their desire to exaggerate their gender role. Their bravado . . . provides an excellent cover-up. Nobody would ever suspect that these rugged military men are not what they appear to be. (pp. 79–80)

Anecdotal stories by MTFs include this idea of joining the military for its emphasis on hypermasculinity:

> When I was eighteen . . . I moved in with my cousin, who was kind of macho, and I tried to emulate his behavior. He thought that joining the military would be a way of making me a man. I hoped he might be right, so I went along with that and enlisted in the Marines. I somehow managed to get through it, but it didn't cure my gender problems. The transsexualism was always there; I just worked like the devil to repress it. (Brown & Rounsley, 1996, p. 66)

> [I joined the Navy as] a way to prove my manhood. Hey, I'm a man, aren't I? (Girshick, 2008, p. 92)

Female-to-male (FTM) transgender people who have yet to transition may also be interested in the military for its focus on traditional masculinity or hypermasculinity. The military is one place where women are encouraged and commended for adopting masculine traits. Some FTMs who are still living as women may seek refuge in the military because it is an acceptable place for them to express gender behaviors stereotypical of men, before transitioning (Frye, 2004). Some FTMs may not be aware of their gender identity until they actively take on masculine attributes (Lev, 2004). The military may be a safe way of testing and practicing a partial identity as a man, since it is acceptable for women to behave in more masculine ways in the military than in most other professions.

Transgender people may also be attracted to the military for the risks associated with active military duty (Brown, 1988; Brown & Rounsley, 1996). While transgender people (or others with passive suicidal ideation) may not be aware of the reasons they engage in risky behaviors, there is a higher incidence of these behaviors among people who are depressed and hopeless (Beck, Rush, Shaw, & Gary, 1979; Cleveland Clinic Foundation, 2009). Suicidality has repeatedly been shown to be prominent among transgender people (Brown & Rounsley, 1996; Clements-Noelle, Marx, & Katz, 2006; Grant et al., 2011; Israel & Tarver, 1997; Mathy, 2002; Whittle, Turner, & Al-Alami, 2007). It is possible that some transgender people may (consciously or unconsciously) put themselves in life threatening situations as a result of distress and hopelessness regarding their gender identity; joining the military presents opportunities for this. According to Brown and Rounsley (1996), many transsexuals seek some of the most life-risking pursuits within the military, because " . . . if the mission were to end in death, the transsexual would be permanently freed from a lifetime of gender pain" (pp. 79–80). As one MTF stated: "And I joined the military. I even volunteered to go to Viet Nam to get killed to put me out of my misery" (Girshick, 2008, p. 92).

PHYSICAL AND MENTAL HEALTH CONCERNS

One component of military life is the expectation that personnel can meet their healthcare needs within military facilities. For transgender people to realize this expectation, the U.S. military would need to educate providers and create policies based on an informed understanding of the transgender population. Failing to address the unique needs of this population fuels continued discrimination, as has been identified by research with transgender veterans (Bryant & Schilt, 2008; Shipherd, et al., 2011), and can exacerbate mental health problems.

Most people wait to transition until after they've left military service (e.g., Bryant and Schilt [2008] report that 97% of their sample of transgender veterans transitioned after leaving the military); for this reason, medical care for transgender military people is offered primarily in the context of the Veterans Administration (VA). Prior to the recent release of the *Directive for Providing Health Care for Transgender and Intersex Veterans* (U.S. Department of Veterans Affairs, 2011) there were no policies for transgender veterans. Without policies, many transgender veterans described their treatment at the VA as inconsistent, insensitive, and, at times, prejudiced (Bryant & Schilt, 2008; McDuffie & Brown, 2010). Some veterans report being denied necessary services, such as mammograms for FTMs and prostate exams for MTFs

(Bryant & Schilt, 2008; SLDN, 2011a). One FTM stated, "I was told by a religious clerk that I should just go away because I was an insult to the brave real men who were there for treatment" (Bryant & Schilt, 2008, p. 8). Another reported, "I am asked about my genitals and my plans for SRS regardless of whether or not it has relevance to my treatment" (Bryant & Schilt, 2008, p. 8). One transgender veteran described the varied messages received when seeking information about sex reassignment surgery: "I've gotten mixed responses. One doctor told me it has been done in the past. Most tell me it isn't allowed. One cursed me" (Bryant & Schilt, 2008, p. 8). Another was told, " . . . the VA does not turn men into women" (Bryant & Schilt, 2008, p. 8).

Many transgender veterans do not seek necessary treatment (Stalsburg, 2011), or obtain it elsewhere in order to avoid discrimination, and because of their desire for transgender-competent services (Bryant & Schilt, 2008; McDuffie & Brown, 2010). Shipher et al. (2011) identified two major barriers to accessing treatment among transgender veterans: concern about medical providers' reactions and knowledge of others' negative experiences.

Transgender veterans who access the VA likely have limited options for treatment as a result of being unemployed, underemployed, or living in poverty (Bryant & Schilt, 2008); therefore, they are willing to risk (or experience) discrimination in order to receive services. Shipher et al. (2011) found that transgender veterans utilized VA services at a much higher rate (16.3%) than veterans in the general population (6.2–15.8%), even though only half of their sample of transgender veterans believed they were eligible for care. This greater use of VA medical care may reflect discrimination against transgender people that makes them disproportionately more likely to become poor and/or unemployed.

In June 2011, the Veterans Health Administration (VHA) "issued a Directive to all its facilities establishing a policy of respectful delivery of healthcare to transgender and intersex veterans . . . enrolled in the U.S. Department of Veterans Affairs (VA) healthcare system . . . or eligible for VA care" (National Center for Transgender Equality [NCTE], 2011a, p. 1). This policy document began with a brief overview of terms related to transgender and intersex people, demonstrating the VA's understanding of this population (VA, 2011). The policy specifically identified the healthcare that the VA affords transgender veterans, including "hormonal therapy, mental health care, preoperative evaluation, and medically necessary postoperative and long-term care following sex reassignment surgery" (VA, 2011, p. 2). The only service not covered or performed by the VA is clearly stated: sex reassignment surgery itself. Besides the medical and psychological services offered, the policy also calls for VA staff to address transgender people according to their self-identified gender, even in the case that a person's appearance does not seem to match their self-identified gender (VA, 2011).

The implementation of this policy is a huge step toward providing sensitive services to the transgender population, and can be a model for other healthcare providers, both public and private (NCTE, 2011a). However, the directive does not apply to active duty military, retired military, or military dependents, as the healthcare program for these persons is run by DoD and follows a separate protocol (NCTE, 2011).

Because the VA directive (2011) was released recently, any changes in treatment and provider attitudes have yet to impact the research about transgender veterans' experiences. However, because, unlike the VA, the U.S. military does not have policies in place, transgender personnel seeking healthcare are likely to experience discrimination similar to that reported by veterans before the new VA (2011) directive was implemented.

MENTAL HEALTH ISSUES

Research on the mental health of active transgender military members does not exist because potential research participants risk discrimination and discharge if they identify themselves. Therefore, research describing the mental health of transgender veterans and transsexuals in general will be used to speculate about the mental health issues of transgender people in the military.

Some research indicates that transgender people do not significantly differ from the general population in mental health (Brown et al., 1996; Israel & Tarver, 1997; Shipherd et al., 2011), while others find higher rates of psychological problems among transgender people (Clements-Noelle et al., 2006; Nuttbrock, et al., 2010). Since mental health worsens with experiences of discrimination and victimization (Diaz, Ayala, Bein, Henne, & Marin, 2001; Pascoe, & Richman, 2009; Waldo, 1999), it would not be surprising if psychological problems were elevated in the transgender population, because of pervasive discrimination and victimization against transgender people (Clements-Noelle et al., 2006; Israel & Tarver, 1997; Lombardi, Wilchins, Priesing, & Malouf, 2001). A recent study of transgender veterans (McDuffie & Brown, 2010) identified depression, post traumatic stress disorder (PTSD), and substance use disorders as the most common psychological problems, while Shipherd et al. (2011) found that transgender veterans most often sought VA mental health services for depression, PTSD, and gender identity counseling.

A transgender person may need treatment before, during, or after transition to consider gender-related adaptations. Not only does the military not offer competent transgender-related care, but they discharge the person who seeks it (SLDN, 2011a; 2011b). Since there are transgender people in the military, maybe a relatively high number of them (Brown, 1988; Brown & Rounsley, 1996; Frye, 2004; McDuffie & Brown, 2010; Shipherd et al., 2011), the options available to them are a concern. Continuing to live a false identity when one knows better may have negative effects on one's mental health (Besner & Spungin, 1995; Waldo, 1999). One MTF's account supports this notion:

> After some consultation with the medical officer, I was offered help to stop these feelings of being a woman occurring. I was convinced that there was some kind of treatment that could "normalize" me; after all, I was a deviant, abnormal, loony toon. The psychiatrist I saw told me that it was something he could help with, and so I was sent to a psychiatric hospital where they treated all kinds of disorders, including homosexuality... The army's way of treating sexual deviants was probably in contravention of human rights, but we didn't have such legislation to fall back on at that time, should we find the treatment unacceptable. They used brainwashing techniques to cleanse the mind of all abnormal behavior, but I didn't know at the time that was how it was done. In a few weeks I started to feel different: the treatment was working, but I didn't realize what the doctors had done and what the consequences of their actions would lead to. I was sent back to rejoin my army unit and given a clean bill of health, but within weeks I was back in the hospital after attempting to kill myself when the treatment failed to work as they had hoped. ... There were several suicide attempts to resolve what I saw as a hopeless situation. (Murphy, 2003, pp. 161–164)

Mental health, medical, and substance abuse services obtained outside of the military are supposed to be communicated back to the military, so transgender people who seek these services elsewhere still risk exposure (Witten, 2007). This leads individuals to go without treatment, allowing symptoms to exacerbate, and causing some to treat symptoms with alcohol or drugs, which could lead to substance abuse or dependence. Substance abuse is a prevalent problem for the transgender population (Kreiss & Patterson, 1997; Lombardi and van Servellen, 2000; SAMHSA, 2001; Tayleur, 1994; Xavier, 2000, as cited in Lev, 2004). Transgender people may also resort to self-harming behaviors (e.g. cutting, hitting, or burning themselves), another common problem related to untreated gender dysphoria (Bockting, Knudson, & Goldberg, 2006; Fraser, 2009a; Lev, 2009, as cited in World Professional Association for Transgender Health [WPATH], 2011).

If, in addition to the institutional discrimination they experience from the military, a person is directly discriminated against or victimized for being transgender (or being suspected of being transgender), they may be unable to access services for help because of fear of being discharged.

The failure to provide a safe, confidential setting for treatment sabotages any chance that transgender service personnel will allow themselves the self-disclosure needed to implement useful psychotherapy, whether the treatment needs are for depression, trauma, substance-abuse, or gender-related concerns. As such, they create unequal access to these healthcare resources, based on membership in this stigmatized group.

NON-U.S. MILITARIES: MODELS OF INCLUSION

Several non-U.S. militaries allow lesbian, gay, and bisexual people to serve openly (Human Rights Campaign [HRC], 2011; Kerrigan, 2011) and several of those also include transgender people (Stalsburg, 2011). Eleven countries allow transgender people to serve: Australia, Belgium, Canada, Czech Republic, Israel, the Netherlands, Spain, Sweden, Thailand, United Kingdom (SLDN, 2011a), and Uruguay (HRC, 2011). Some of these countries consider transgender individuals' applications on a case-by-case basis, while others have formal policies (SLDN, 2011a).

The United Kingdom, Israel, Australia, Spain, Uruguay, and Thailand have policies for transgender people serving openly in their militaries (HRC, 2011). These militaries have had to gain an understanding about transgender people; policies can only be effective when there is an accurate understanding of the people to whom they will be applied. By utilizing their nation's resources for this purpose, these countries honor transgender people as citizens who are just as deserving as others, rather than treating them as second-class citizens, as they are usually considered in the United States. These countries' militaries benefit from including competent military personnel who are transgender, rather than excluding or expelling them.

The militaries of these countries provide transgender veterans access to the same services as other military personnel, and even in some cases, offer transgender-related healthcare (Bryant & Schilt, 2008). Transgender veterans are able to access their benefits, whether they were transgender or not at the time of duty.

Tracking armed forces' regulations concerning LGBT people around the world is very difficult; "It is incredibly labor intensive to determine with great accuracy what a country permits or prohibits by law and what really happens on a day-to-day basis" (Belkin & Embser-Herbert, 2009, p. 59). Some regions do not offer specific policies regarding LGBT people because they do not recognize that these persons exist, or because transgender or LGB identities are illegal in these countries; military regulations do not ban what is already prohibited by general laws and customs (Belkin & Embser-Herbert, 2009). In addition, military policies and laws change and the application of these may differ by location and command.

United Kingdom

In 2009, the United Kingdom created the Policy for Recruitment and Management of Transsexual Personnel in the Armed Forces (HRC, 2011).

According to this policy, it is unlawful for the U.K. military to reject a person's application for entry for being transgender (Gender Identity Research and Education Society [GIRES], 2009). Transgender persons, like other persons seeking to serve, are dealt with on a case-by-case basis (GIRES, 2009). There is recognition that transgender people (especially those transitioning) may not be appropriate for certain military roles, such as active duty or extensive travel (GIRES, 2009). At the same time, by adopting a case-by-case approach, the U.K. military recognizes the diversity within the transgender population. Overall, the U.K. military rejects the idea that being transgender in itself makes a person unfit for service, which is the view currently upheld by the U.S. military.

This U.K. document includes incidence data as well as a glossary of terms that highlight the policymakers' understanding of the transgender population (GIRES, 2009). The document correctly delineates the differences between sexual orientation and gender identity, as well as the difference between being transgender, transsexual, and cross-dressing (GIRES, 2009). Also included are resources and referrals for transgender persons, and an example of a name-change form (GIRES, 2009). U.K. military policy allows personnel to re-inscribe and replace medals that no longer reflect a person's legal name (GIRES, 2009). The policy document reports that while there may be a higher incidence of mental health problems for these persons, and that assessment is imperative for this reason, a person should not be referred to a psychiatrist or excluded solely because of being a transsexual (GIRES, 2009).

The U.K. military considers transsexualism a medical condition that should be dealt with similarly to other medical conditions, where the person is provided treatment, and where the kind of military service they do may be based on the limitations of their condition (GIRES, 2009). U.K. policy also includes coverage of transgender-related healthcare (GIRES, 2009). Prescriptions, such as those for hormone therapy, can be prescribed by military physicians, and are covered by the military's budget, just like prescriptions for treatment of any other medical condition (GIRES, 2009). However, surgeries are to be paid for privately or by a non-military source (GIRES, 2009).

Canada

Canada's military not only includes transgender personnel, but sometimes pays for sex-reassignment surgeries for transgender people (Bryant & Schilt, 2008). The Canadian Forces (CF) has established specified policies for its transgender service members. They first began covering sex-reassignment surgery in 1998 and continue to do so, on average, for one to two people per year (Cohen, 2011). According to a spokesperson for the National Defense Department, "The CF is unique in that it must recruit, house, clothe, train and deploy its members. This requires clear direction and standardized instructions to deal with individuals who may not fall into the generally accepted categories" (Cohen, 2011, para. 8).

According to Cohen (2011), the CF policies describe transgender people as having "a psychological need" to live as the opposite sex from which they were born, regardless of their stage of transition. As a result, the policy calls for military personnel to treat transgender people with "the utmost privacy and respect" ("Canadian Military Publishes New Transgender Policy," 2010; Cohen, 2011). The CF also allows transgender people to change their name on military records without having to provide any reason for doing so ("Canadian Military Publishes New Transgender Policy," 2010), and requires that service members dress in uniform according to their self-identified gender, regardless of their stage of transition (Cohen, 2011).

Thailand

The Army in Thailand recently (September 2011) changed the language used to describe transgender people (International Lesbian, Gay, Bisexual, Trans and Intersex Association [ILGA], 2011). Previously, transgender people were identified as "having a permanent mental disorder" ("Court to Thai Military," 2011, para. 2) or "psychological abnormality" and were rejected for enlistment as a result (ILGA, 2011, para. 4). This stigmatizing language asserted that all transgender people suffer from mental illness that made them unfit for service, a view that the United States continues to uphold.

In 2012, the Thai army is inclusive of transgender people. Although this is a significant step forward, there continues to be problems. Young men in Thailand are conscripted at the age of 18, so MTF transgender people may be required to serve as their biological sex ("Court to Thai Military," 2011; ILGA, 2011), which could have ramifications for mental health and potential for victimization. The Thai Army has created three classes of males so that MTF transgender people can be recruited into the military: Type 1 is used for biological men who behave and identify according to their birth sex or assigned gender; type 2 includes MTF transgender persons who have had breast augmentation surgery; and type 3 is reserved for MTFs who have had genital reconstructive surgery (ILGA, 2011). While the Thai Army is inclusive of transgender people, they continue to identify them as men, even when they have identified themselves as women.

Spain

After a post-transition FTM (having undergone hormone treatment and a mastectomy) was rejected by the Spanish Armed Forces (SAF) twice, the military changed its policies ("Transsexual Wins Battle," 2009). Prior to this incident, the SAF excluded any man who did not have a penis; after, it changed its policies to allow for FTMs to be included without any genital reconstructive surgery. In 2009 when this 28-year-old FTM's story made headlines, Spain's Minister of Defense promised to revise legislation concerning medical reasons for exclusion from service, so that transgender people could be provided equal opportunities to serve in the military ("Transsexual Wins Battle," 2009).

Australia

Australia previously had policies restricting transgender people from serving in the military (Dennett, 2010). However, in 2010, the Chief of the Australian Defense Force (ADF) issued an instruction revoking these policies. The Air Chief, Marshall Houston, directed ADF commanders to "manage ADF transgender personnel with fairness, respect and dignity . . . and ensure all personnel are not subjects to unacceptable behavior" (Dennet, 2010, para. 3). As a result, transgender people can now serve for the ADF if they meet all other restrictions.

Uruguay

Some militaries do not have specific policies in place for the inclusion (or exclusion) of transgender people. In Uruguay, for example, a set of laws concerning discrimination have been applied to establish standards of equality for transgender people in the armed forces. The Institutional Relations Secretary of Uruguay has cited a law that "penalizes the commission of acts of violence, humiliation or disrespect against people because of their sexual orientation or gender identity" as well as another law that "declares that the fight against all kinds of discrimination is of national interest" (Frank et al., 2010, p. 139). As a result, the Secretary has stated, "there are no restrictions whatsoever for the participation of gay, lesbian and transgender people in our army" (Frank et al., 2010, p. 139).

Czech Republic

In the Czech Republic, military policy stipulates service "for all citizens of the Czech Republic, regardless of sexual orientation" (Frank et al., 2010, p. 137). This military applies the same standards to transgender people, meaning that all citizens are required to serve, including transgender citizens (SLDN, 2011a). There are no policies in place for including or excluding people on the basis of gender identity or expression (HRC, 2011).

Israel, Netherlands, Sweden, and Belgium

Like the Czech Republic, the Israel Defense Forces (IDF), the Armed Forces of the Netherlands, the Belgian Armed Forces (BAF), and the Swedish military are all inclusive of transgender people (SLDN, 2011a) but do not have policies in place for including them (HRC, 2011).

Israeli (IDF) policy indicates that "homosexuals are entitled to serve in the military as are others," and this policy extends to transgender people, even if not specified (Bronner, 1993, as cited in Frank et al., 2010). An anecdotal account of a FTM serving as a man in the IDF has been documented (Jsybird2532, 2011). According to Manigart (2007), there is one documented case of a MTF transitioning while remaining on active duty in the Belgian military; she remained in her same military position and even had sex reassignment surgery reimbursed by social security. In order to ease her transition and reintegration, her superior informed her colleagues of the change (Manigart, 2007).

U.S. OBJECTIONS

U.S. military policy on transgender people reveals some of the discrimination against them. However, these policies do not explain why transgender people should be excluded or discharged, and few authors have presented these arguments.

Bunn's (2010) explanation emphasizes the cost of presumed extra services. She states "[f]or a majority of transgender persons, simply living a stable life requires extensive medical treatment and clinical assistance" (p. 223). While added cost is a plausible concern, Bunn's fiscal speculations are in marked contrast to Bryant and Schilt (2008), who explain that even funding sex-reassignment surgeries would be "[unlikely to] create a financial burden on the military, as the percentage of people accessing such services would be quite small" (p. 9).

"More importantly" Bunn (2010) suggests, "the emotional highs and lows commonly experienced during the course of one's transition" could interfere with the "well-being" of others "in close physical proximity" (p. 223). The assumption that transgender people are emotionally unstable, or that they can damage the wellbeing of those around them, comes closer to the stereotypes that fuel discrimination. These assertions are reminiscent of those used to justify exclusion of lesbians and gay men, and are equally amenable to being overturned by looking to research on psychological stability in the transgender population.

Finally, Bunn (2010) asserts that even after transgender people have transitioned, they continue to have difficulties as a result of societal discrimination. This is less of an argument against transgender people and more a reason for the military to adopt policies requiring fair and equal treatment of them, just as they do for personnel who have been stigmatized by race, religion, or other dimensions of difference.

In order for transgender people to be included in the military there must be policies to mandate this successful change. However, Bunn (2010) fails to acknowledge the diversity of the transgender population: not all transgender people require mental health treatment or suffer from debilitating psychological issues, and they vary in their interests in seeking physical changes.

We are most concerned by Bunn's (2010) worry that including transgender people will turn the military into a "Petri dish for uninformed social experimentation" (p. 226). This argument has been applied to justify exclusion of people on the basis of race or gender in the past, and it is just as antithetical to equal rights and access now as it has proven to have been in those painful chapters of our nation's history.

RECOMMENDATIONS

Service in the U.S. military is not a guaranteed right for its citizens; everyone is not fit and prepared for such service. However, it is discriminatory to exclude a group on the false assumption that they have a medical or psychological problem that would inhibit their functioning as a service member. This sort of discrimination is not tolerated by several armed forces around the world; however, it continues today in the United States. To rectify this injustice and bring government policy and conduct in line with the values of our nation, we recommend the following:

a. The U.S. military policymakers must become informed about the transgender population. They must learn and recognize that, like all other citizens, transgender people include physically and mentally healthy individuals as well as some with weaknesses and illness. They must become familiar with the differences between sex and gender, since this is a point of confusion in the current documents that exclude transgender people. Just as the United Kingdom has done, we recommend that the United States create policies for transgender service members that include definitions and information about the transgender community and the diversity within it. Policies need to recognize that not all transgender persons hold the same goals for transition. Diversity training should be required at all levels of personnel, and as with other types of diversity training, information, materials, and policies should be reevaluated and updated routinely to insure they accurately represent this community.
b. The U.S. Armed Forces must reverse its policies of refusing entry and discharging currently serving transgender persons, and explicitly issue policies of inclusion for transgender people, in the same way that the Women's Armed Services Integration Act (1948) "authorize[d] the enlistment and appointment of women in the [Military]," and Harry S. Truman

declared "equality of treatment and opportunity for all persons in the armed services without regard to race, color, religion, or national origin" (Executive Order No. 9981, 1948).

It follows from this recommendation that the U.S. military should recognize that transgender people are currently serving and have served, and that these service personnel are equally deserving of benefits, including healthcare.

We recommend that the United States adopt a policy similar to that created by the United Kingdom, which allows the military to determine appropriate duties for each enlistee. That policy deals with transgender people on a case-by-case basis, like any other qualified enlistee who has a medical condition.

c. Branches of the U.S. Armed Forces should cover transgender-related healthcare. Like others in the military, it is important for transgender people to access preventive healthcare; availability of care has fiscal and social ramifications for our society, in addition to benefits for the individual. These healthcare services would include prostate and mammogram exams.

d. Healthcare specifically related to transitioning (such as hormones) should be covered, as it is in the United Kingdom and Canada, and transgender-related surgeries should be provided, as they currently are by such government entities as the City of San Francisco and Canadian Armed Forces.

e. The mental health needs of transgender people should be addressed, just as these needs are addressed for other military personnel. We recommend that the United States adopt the U.K. policy, where people are not referred because they are transgender. However, if there are other concerns, or the person requests services, they should be given care by a provider who is trained and competent to work with such a person. To establish competence among mental health and medical providers, we ask the DoD to employ the Standards of Care (WPATH, 2011) that are used by other professionals worldwide to treat transgender people.

SUMMARY AND CONCLUSIONS

The United States has a stated policy of discrimination against transgender people that leads to their marginalization, induces fear and the need to hide, leaves them unprotected from harassment, and deprives veterans of benefits. Other countries have adopted models of inclusion and sensitivity, and the United States can easily look to these eleven nations to assess the viability of including transgender military personnel. Now is the time to ride atop the moral momentum generated by the new U.S. policy toward sexual minorities and press for similar equal treatment for transgender people who wish to serve their country in the military.

Transgender people may be drawn to military service and are vulnerable to mental health concerns as a result of discrimination, harassment, the need for secrecy, and felt marginality. Current policy leaves transgender people who are now in the military stranded without needed medical and/or psychological services, and without protection. Making these inequities widely visible can launch a groundswell of activism to bring the United States closer to its ideals of justice for all.

REFERENCES

American Psychiatric Association. (2000). Diagnostic and statistical manual of mental disorders (4th ed., text rev.). Washington, DC: Author.

Beck, A. T., Rush, A. J., Shaw, B. F., & Gary, E. (1979). *Cognitive therapy of depression*. New York, NY: Guilford Press.

Belkin, A., & Embser-Herbert, M.S. (2007).The international experience. In M. S. Embser-Herbert (Ed.), *"Don't ask, don't tell" policy: A reference handbook* (pp. 59–80). Westport, CT: Praeger Security International.

Besner, H., & Spungin, C. (1995). *Gay and lesbian students: Understanding their needs*. Washington, DC: Taylor and Francis.

Bockting, W. O., Knudson, G., & Goldberg, J. M. (2006). Counseling and mental health care for transgender adults and loved ones. *International Journal of Transgenderism, 9*(3/4), 35–82. doi:10.1300/J485v09n03_03

Brown, G. R. (1988). Transsexuals in the military: Flight into hypermasculinity. In S. Stryker & S. Whittle (Eds.), *The transgender studies reader* (pp. 537–564). New York, NY: Routledge.

Brown, G. R., Wise, T. N., Costa, P. T., Herbst, J. H., Fagan, P. J., & Schmidt, C.W. (1996). Personality characteristics and sexual functioning of 188 cross-dressing men. *Journal of Nervous and Mental Disease, 184*(5), 265–273.

Brown, M. L., & Rounsley, C. A. (1996). *True selves: Understanding transsexualism—For families, friends, coworkers, and helping professionals*. San Francisco, CA: Jossey-Bass.

Bryant, K., & Schilt, K. (2008, August). *Transgender people in the U.S. military: Summary and analysis of the 2008 transgender American veterans association survey*. The Palm Center, University of California, Santa Barbara. Retrieved from http://www.tavausa.org/Transgender%20People%20in%20the%20U.S.%20Military.pdf

Bunn, S. A. (2010). Straight talk: The implications of repealing "don't ask, don't tell" and the rationale for preserving aspects of the current policy. *Military Law Review, 203*, 207–283.

Canadian Military publishes new transgender policy. (2010, December 10). *PinkNews*. Retrieved from http://www.pinknews.co.uk/2010/12/10/canadian-military-publishes-new-transgender-policy/

Clements-Noelle, K., Marx, R. M., & Katz, M. (2006). Attempted suicide among transgender persons: The influence of gender-based discrimination and victimization. *Journal of homosexuality, 51*(3), 53–69. doi:10.1300J082v51n03_04

Cleveland Clinic Foundation. (2009). *Recognizing suicidal behavior*. Retrieved from http://my.clevelandclinic.org/disorders/suicide/hic_recognizing_suicidal_behavior.aspx

Cohen, K. (2011, January 7). *The Canadian Forces have established rules around uniforms worn by transsexual soldiers*. [Web log comment]. Retrieved from http://outmilitary.com/magazine/read/the-canadian-forces-have-established-rules-around-uniforms-worn-by-transsexual-soldiers_18.html

Court to Thai military: Transsexuals not ill. (2011, September 13). *The Independent*. Retrieved from http://www.independent.co.uk/news/world/asia/court-to-thai-military-transsexuals-not-ill-2354067.html

Cowell, R. (1954). *Roberta Cowell's story*. New York, NY: British Book Centre, Inc.

Dawood, K., Bailey, J. M., & Martin, N. G. (2009). Genetic and environmental influences on sexual orientation. In Y.-K. Kim (Ed.), *Handbook of behavior genetics* (pp. 269–279). New York, NY: Springer.

Dennett, H. (2010, September 15). *Let them serve: Defense drops ban on transgender soldiers*. Crikey. Retrieved from http://www.crikey.com.au/2010/09/15/let-them-serve-defence-drops-ban-on-transgender-soldiers/

Department of the Army. (2011, August 4). *Standards of medical fitness: Rapid action review issue*. Washington, DC. Retrieved from http://www.apd.army.mil/pdffiles/r40_501.pdf

Díaz, R. M., Ayala, G., Bein, E., Henne, J., & Marin, B. V. (2001, June). The impact of homophobia, poverty, and racism on the mental health of gay and bisexual Latino men: Findings from 3 US cities. *American Journal of Public Health, 91*(6), 927–932.

Docter, R. F. (2008). *Becoming a woman: A biography of Christine Jorgensen*. New York, NY: The Haworth Press.

Ettner, R. (1999). *Gender loving care: A guide to counseling gender-variant clients*. New York, NY: W.W. Norton & Company.

Executive Order No. 9981 (1992 comp.). *Establishing the President's committee on equality of treatment and opportunity in the armed forces*.

Frank, N., Basham, V., Bateman, G., Belkin, A., Canaday, M., Okros, A., & Scott, D. (2010, February). *Gays in foreign militaries 2010: Global Primer*. The Palm Center, University of California, Santa Barbara. Retrieved from http://media.washingtonpost.com/wp-srv/politics/documents/GaysinForeignMilitaries2010.pdf

Fraser, L. (2009). Depth psychotherapy with transgender people. *Sexual and Relationship Therapy, 24*(2), 126–142. doi:10.1080/14681990903003878

Frye, P. R. (2004). *Transgendered vet*. Retrieved from http://www.cammermeyer.com/board.htm?step=thread&threadid=244

Gender Identity Research and Education Society. (2009). *Policy for the recruitment and management of transsexual personnel in the armed forces*. Retrieved from www.gires.org.uk/assets/Consultations/MOD-policy.doc

Girshick, L. B. (2008). *Transgender voices: Beyond women and men*. Lebanon, NH: University Press of New England.

Grant, J. M., Mottet, L. A., Tanis, J., Harrison, J., Herman, J. L., & Keisling, M. (2011). *Injustice at every turn: A report of the national transgender discrimination survey*. Washington: National Center for Transgender Equality and National Gay and Lesbian Task Force.

Human Rights Campaign. (2011). *Beyond "don't ask, don't tell" repeal: 5 steps for congressional action*. Retrieved from http://www.hrc.org/files/assets/resources/BeyondDADTRepeal.pdf

International Lesbian, Gay, Bisexual, Trans and Intersex Association. (2011, April 9). *Army renames transgender conscripts*. Retrieved from http://ilga.org/ilga/en/article/n9vvaQy1qW

Israel, G. E., & Tarver, D. E. (1997). *Transgender care: Recommended guidelines, practical information, and personal accounts*. Philadelphia, PA: Temple University Press.

Jorgensen, C. (1967). *Christine Jorgensen: A personal autobiography*. New York, NY: Paul S. Eriksson, Inc.

Jsybird 2532. (2011, June 4). Anyone know anything about the climate for transgender/transsexual individuals in Israel? [Web log comment]. Retrieved from http://www.lauras-playground.com/forums/index.php?showtopic=33724

Kerrigan, M. F. (2011). Transgender discrimination in the military: The new don't ask, don't tell. *Psychology, Public Policy, and Law*. doi:10.1037/a0025771

Kreiss, J. L., & Patterson, D. L. (1997). Psychosocial issues in primary care of lesbian, gay, bisexual, and transgender youth. *Journal of Pediatric Health Care, 11*(6), 266–274.

Lev, A. I. (2004). *Transgender emergence: Therapeutic guidelines for working with gender-variant people and their families*. Binghamton, NY: Haworth Clinical Practice Press.

Lombardi, E. L., & van Servellen, G. (2000). Building culturally sensitive substance use prevention and treatment programs for transgendered populations. *Journal of Substance Abuse Treatment, 19*(3), 291–296.

Lombardi, E. L., Wilchins, R. A., Priesing, D., & Malouf, D. (2001). Gender violence: Transgender experiences with violence and discrimination. *Journal of Homosexuality, 42*, 89–101.

Manigart, P. (2007). Diversity in the Belgian armed forces. In J. Soeters & J. Meulen (Eds.), *Cultural diversity in the armed forces* (pp. 185–199). New York, NY: Routledge.

Mathy, R. M. (2002). Transgender identity and suicidality in a nonclinical sample: Sexual orientation, psychiatric history, and compulsive behaviors. *Journal of Psychology & Human Sexuality, 14*, 47–65.

McDuffie, E., & Brown, G. R. (2010). 70 U.S. Veterans with gender identity disturbances: A descriptive study. *International Journal of Transgenderism, 12*, 21–30. doi:10.1080/15532731003688962

Morris, J. (1974). *Conundrum*. New York, NY: Harcourt Brace Jovanovich, Inc.

Mosher, D. L., & Sirkin, M. (1984). Measuring a macho personality constellation. *Journal of Research in Personality, 18*, 150–163.

Murphy, N. (2003). Dream on, and don't wake up to the nightmare of reality. In T. O'Keefe & K. Fox (Eds.), *Finding the real me* (pp. 158–167). San Francisco, CA: Jossey-Bass.

National Center for Transgender Equality (2011a). *Veterans health administration transgender healthcare directive*. Retrieved from http://transequality.org/PDFs/VHA_Trans_Health.pdf

National Center for Transgender Equality. (2011b). *Veterans and military issues*. Retrieved from http://transequality.org/Issues/military.html

Nuttbrock, L., Hwahng, S., Bockting, W., Rosenblum, A., Mason, M., Macri, M., & Becker, J. (2010). Psychiatric impact of gender-related abuse across the life course of male-to-female transgender persons. *Journal of Sex Research*, *47*(1), 12–23. doi:10.1080/00224490903062258

Pascoe, E. A., & Richman, L. S. (2009). Perceived discrimination and health: A meta-analytic review. *Psychological Bulletin*, *135*, 531–554.

Richards, R. (1983). *Second serve: The Renee Richards story*. New York, NY: Stein and Day Publishers.

Rieger, G., Linsenmeier, J. A. W., Gygax, L., & Bailey, J. M. (2008). Sexual orientation and childhood gender nonconformity: Evidence from home videos. *Developmental Psychology*, *44*(1), 46–58.

Service Members Legal Defense Network. (2011a). *Transgender military service*. Retrieved from http://www.sldn.org/pages/transgender-issues

Service Members Legal Defense Network. (2011b, July 27). *Freedom to serve: The definitive guide to LGBT military service*. Retrieved from http://sldn.3cdn.net/5d4dd958a62981cff8_v5m6bw1gx.pdf

Shipherd, J. C., Mizock, L., Maguen, S., & Green, K. E. (2011, December 7). Male-to-female transgender veterans and VA health care utilization. *International Journal of Sexual Health*. doi:10.1080/19317611.2011.639440

Stalsburg, B. L. (2011). *After repeal: LGBT service members and veterans the facts*. Retrieved from http://servicewomen.org/wp-content/uploads/2011/10/LGBT-Fact-Sheet-091411.pdf

Substance Abuse Mental Health Services Administration: Center for Substance Abuse Treatment (SAMHSA: CSAT) (ed.). (2001). *A provider's introduction to substance abuse treatment for lesbian, gay, bisexual, and transgender individuals*. Washington, DC: SAMHSA: CSAT.

Tayleur, C. (1994). Transsexuals and addiction: The unacknowledged crisis. *Chrysallis: The Journal of Transgressive Gender Identities*, *1*(7), 11–14.

Transsexual wins battle to serve in Spain's Armed Forces. (2009, February 13). PinkNews. Retrieved from http://www.pinknews.co.uk/2009/02/13/transsexual-wins-battle-to-serve-in-spains-armed-forces/

Uniform Code of Military Justice, 10 U.S.C. § 933, Article 133 (2010a).

Uniform Code of Military Justice, 10 U.S.C. § 934, Article 134 (2010b).

U.S. Department of Defense. (2011a, September 13). *Medical standards for appointment, enlistment, or induction in the military services: Incorporating change 1*. Retrieved from http://www.dtic.mil/whs/directives/corres/pdf/613003p.pdf

U.S. Department of Defense. (2011b, September 20). *Repeal day memo*. Retrieved from http://www.defense.gov/home/features/2010/0610_dadt/

U.S. Department of Veterans Affairs. (2011, June 9). *Providing health care for transgender and intersex veterans (VHA Directive 2011-024)*. Retrieved from http://www.va.gov/vhapublications/ViewPublication.asp?pub_ID=2416

Waldo, C. R. (1999). Working in a majority context: A structural model of heterosexism as minority stress in the workplace. *Journal of Counseling Psychology, 46,* 218–232.

Whittle, S., Turner, L., & Al-Alami, M. (2007, February15). Engendered penalties: Transgender and Transsexual people's experiences of inequality and discrimination. *The Equalities Review.* Retrieved from http://www.nmhdu.org.uk/silo/files/the-equalities-review.pdf

Witten, T. M. (2007). *Gender identity and the military: Transgender, transsexual, and intersex-identified individuals in the U.S. armed forces.* The Palm Center, University of California, Santa Barbara. Retrieved from http://www.palmcenter.org/files/active/0/TransMilitary2007.pdf

Women's Armed Forces Integration Act of 1948, ch. 449, 62 Stat. 356 (1948).

World Professional Association for Transgender Health. (2011). *Standards of care for the health of transsexual, transgender, and gender nonconforming people* (7th ver.). Retrieved from http://www.wpath.org/documents/Standards%20of%20Care%20V7%20-%202011%20WPATH.pdf

Yerke, A. F., & Mitchell, V. (2011). Am I man enough yet?: A comparison of the body transition, self-labeling, and sexual orientation of two cohorts of female-to-male transsexuals. *International Journal of Transgenderism, 13,* 64–76.

One Year Out: An Assessment of DADT Repeal's Impact on Military Readiness

AARON BELKIN, PhD
Palm Center

MORTEN G. ENDER, PhD
Department of Behavioral Sciences and Leadership, United States Military Academy

NATHANIEL FRANK, PhD
Center for Gender and Sexuality Law, Columbia Law School

STACIE FURIA, PhD

GEORGE R. LUCAS, PhD
Stockdale Center for Ethical Leadership, United States Naval Academy

GARY A. PACKARD, JR., PhD
Department of Behavioral Sciences and Leadership, United States Air Force Academy

STEVEN M. SAMUELS, PhD
Department of Behavioral Sciences and Leadership, United States Air Force Academy

TAMMY S. SCHULTZ, PhD
National Security and Joint Warfare Program, Marine Corps War College

DAVID R. SEGAL, PhD
Center for Research on Military Organization, University of Maryland

In the years preceding the 2011 repeal of the military's "don't ask, don't tell" (DADT) policy barring open service by lesbian, gay and bisexual (LGB) troops, many observers predicted that the policy change would harm the readiness of the military. This study offers a comprehensive assessment of the accuracy of those predictions. A study team conducted research during a half-year period starting six months after repeal was implemented. The team pursued multiple research strategies that included interviews, survey analysis, field observations, media analysis, longitudinal secondary source analysis and quasi-experimentation. The study concludes

---

The authors thank Indra Lusero, Jeremy Johnson, Lenny Francioni, Corinne Vandagriff and Taylor Clarke for their outstanding assistance in the preparation of this study. The views expressed by faculty at US Government Agencies are those of the individuals and do not necessarily reflect the official policy or position of their respective Service Academies, their Service Branches, the Department of Defense or the Government. Non-military institutional affiliations are listed for identification purposes only and do not convey the institutions' positions.

that, in its first year, DADT repeal had no negative impact on overall military readiness or its component parts (unit cohesion, recruitment, retention, assaults, harassment or morale) and appears to have slightly enhanced the military's ability to do its job by removing obstacles to trust and bonding.

INTRODUCTION

On September 20, 2011, the U.S. military allowed lesbian, gay and bisexual (LGB) service members to serve openly after a protracted political battle to lift the ban on open service known as "don't ask, don't tell" (DADT). Public opinion had changed in the decade leading up to the Congressional repeal of DADT, with polls showing most Americans in favor of ending the ban, but many observers suggested that open service would undermine military readiness. In March 2009, more than 1,000 retired generals and admirals released a statement claiming that DADT repeal "would undermine recruiting and retention, impact leadership at all levels, have adverse effects on the willingness of parents who lend their sons and daughters to military service, and eventually break the All-Volunteer Force" ("Flag and General Officers for the Military," 2009). Such forecasts, if true, would prove devastating to the armed forces, but they have not yet been subject to social scientific analysis. This study is the first scholarly effort to assess the accuracy of predications about the impact of DADT repeal on military readiness.

To do so, our study team conducted research during a half-year period starting six months after repeal and concluding at the one-year mark. We sought to maximize the likelihood of identifying problematic evidence by pursuing ten research strategies, each of which was designed to uncover data showing that repeal undermines the military. Those strategies include: (1) Requesting 553 of the retired generals and admirals who predicted that repeal would undermine the military to participate in semi-structured interviews; (2) Requesting semi-structured interviews with every activist and expert that we could identify—22 in total—who opposed repeal publicly; (3) Requesting semi-structured interviews with representatives of 18 watchdog organizations, including opponents and advocates of repeal, who are known for their ability to monitor Pentagon operations; (4) Survey analysis of active-duty service members including closed and open-ended questions; (5) On-site field observations of four military units; (6) In-depth interviews with 18 scholars; (7) In-depth interviews with 62 active-duty service members, heterosexual and LGB, from every service branch, and representing diverse occupational specialties; (8) Content analysis of relevant media articles published during the research period; (9) Longitudinal secondary source analysis of surveys conducted independently by *Military*

Times and OutServe, and of recruitment and retention data released by the Department of Defense; and (10) Pre-test/post-test quasi-experimentation.

Our conclusion, based on all of the evidence available to us, is that DADT repeal has had no overall negative impact on military readiness or its component dimensions, including cohesion, recruitment, retention, assaults, harassment or morale. Although we identified a few downsides that followed from the policy change, we identified upsides as well, and in no case did negative consequences outweigh benefits. If anything, DADT repeal appears to have enhanced the military's ability to pursue its mission.

In the discussion below, we describe our research methodology, offer a brief history of DADT repeal, explain our findings about military readiness and its component dimensions and comment on the validity of our findings. In the main body of the paper, we begin with a discussion of readiness broadly conceived, and then focus on components of readiness that have been central to the public conversation about DADT and whether open service would harm or help the military. While this study does not address service by transgender troops, we refer sometimes to LGB troops, but also occasionally to LGBT troops, depending on whether we mean to indicate the entire LGBT community or only those lesbian, gay and bisexual service members who were directly identified in the DADT policy and law.

METHODS

Our objective has been to conduct an impartial inquiry, based on social science research methods, that assesses the impact of DADT repeal on military readiness. Thus, we constructed our research design to maximize the likelihood of identifying data suggesting that repeal has compromised the armed forces. We pursued ten different research strategies, all described in this section, and reached our conclusions by using a preponderance-of-evidence standard, meaning that we carefully weighed the quality and quantity of all data we collected, and then determined which findings were best supported by the evidence. Because we are most interested in data suggesting that repeal harmed the military, we include almost all such evidence in our report even if it is of low quality. By contrast, because most of the data we collected suggests that repeal did not harm the military, only a fraction of such evidence appears in the report. Throughout this study, we offer specific explanations for how we interpreted each set of relevant data. Additional commentary on our standards of evidence can be found in Appendix B.

We began our research by contacting 553 of the 1,167 retired generals and admirals who signed a 2009 statement claiming that DADT repeal would "break the All-Volunteer Force." We sent a letter to the 553 signatories for whom we could locate contact information, and received responses from 13 officers, including six brigadier generals, three major generals, three lieutenant generals and one general. We interviewed 11 of those who responded and we received a written statement from two, both of whom declined our request for additional commentary. A copy of the initial letter is provided in Appendix C.

To supplement the perspectives of generals and admirals, we made a vigorous effort to contact known public opponents of DADT repeal, because we reasoned that they would be among the most likely to listen for, hear of and report problems if and when they occurred. We generated a list of known opponents who had spoken about or published their opposition to repeal during the last decade, 22 in total. We emailed each opponent at least twice, and, if needed, followed up with at least two phone calls when phone numbers were available. Out of the 22 opponents on our list, one agreed to an interview, three declined and 18 did not respond to our inquiries. While the response rate to our request for interviews was too low to allow us to draw inferences about the overall perspectives of public opponents or of retired generals and admirals, responses we did receive were consistent with one another and with data derived from our other research strategies. The list of public opponents we contacted is provided in Appendix D.

Participants in the nearly two-decade conversation about DADT included a number of non-profit and advocacy groups that are known for the vigilance with which they monitor and report on day-to-day operations in the U.S. military. Such organizations maintain large formal and informal networks of active-duty personnel and have considerable experience in ferreting out and reporting incidents of abuse and other disciplinary breakdowns. We reasoned that anti-repeal watchdog organizations would be particularly motivated to collect evidence of problems so as to build the case for overturning repeal or to confirm their predictions of disruption. Pro-repeal groups, by contrast, might be less focused on uncovering problems resulting from repeal, but their longstanding interest in protecting LGB service members from harassment would serve as an incentive for collecting data and monitoring the post-repeal environment. Thus, we studied the websites and contacted the senior staff of 18 watchdog organizations, listed in Appendix E, including the most prominent and influential pro- and anti-repeal groups.

Some academic scholars who have developed deep expertise about U.S. military personnel policy have published well-regarded, peer-reviewed studies of DADT, and maintain networks of dozens, and in some cases hundreds, of active-duty contacts. Hence, our research includes in-depth interviews with 18 scholars, listed in Appendix F. To identify them, we began with a Palm Center list and then used snowball sampling to find additional interview subjects. During each interview, we pressed repeatedly for evidence of negative consequences that followed from DADT repeal, and we asked subjects to suggest other scholars whom we could contact for our inquiry.

No one is more qualified to comment on the impact of DADT repeal than active-duty service members, who live their lives and perform their duties in the context of the new policy of open service. Thus, we conducted in-depth interviews with 62 active-duty, reserve and National Guard service members from all branches of the U.S. military, and representing a wide range of occupational specialties.[1] These troops included both LGB as well as heterosexual personnel. We recruited LGB troops by disseminating calls for input through the Facebook network of OutServe, an organization representing more than 5,700 active-duty LGBT troops. Palm Center staff and study co-authors put out additional calls for input, and new interview subjects were identified via friends, acquaintances and peers of initial respondents. From these calls we identified and then conducted in-depth interviews with 37 LGB respondents. The 37 active-duty LGB respondents included six women and 31 men, two of whom identify as transgender. Respondents represented diverse racial and ethnic backgrounds including four Latino/as, one African-American, two Asian-Americans and 30 Caucasians, and their ages ranged from 20 to 54. Within the sample there were 19 officers and 18 enlisted personnel. Twenty-eight of the 37 respondents were currently or had previously been deployed. The sample included personnel representing all branches and components of the U.S. military, including four reservists, one member of the National Guard and 32 active-duty service members.

To identify heterosexual service members, we disseminated calls for participation to personal networks and then tapped friends, acquaintances and other peers of initial respondents. Calls for input were sent through various listservs and Facebook groups, including those of current and previous attendees of war colleges and service academies. From these calls we identified, and then conducted in-depth interviews with, 25 heterosexual respondents. We interviewed six women and 19 men, including six Latino/as, one Asian-American, three African-Americans and 15 Caucasians whose ages ranged from 21 to 50, and who had spent between four and 22 years in the military. They represented all branches and components of the U.S. military and included five reservists, two members of the National Guard, three service academy attendees and 15 active-duty personnel. A list of all respondents is provided in Appendix G.

To broaden the pool of active-duty participants in our study, we placed an advertisement on the website of *Military Times* six months after repeal. Our advertisement requested feedback from anyone willing to discuss the consequences of DADT repeal, and we ran it for 50,000 clicks/page views, which translated into three weeks of appearances on the websites of *Army Times, Navy Times, Air Force Times and Marine Corps Times*. On the survey page, we used question logic to make sure that respondents were at least 18 and were current or former members of the military. Anyone who attempted to take the survey who was younger than 18 or not a member of the military community was redirected to a disqualification page. Qualified subjects were directed to an online survey that included 12 demographic questions, seven closed-ended and matrix questions and six open-ended qualitative questions, primarily related to the impact of DADT repeal on military readiness and its component parts, cohesion, recruitment/retention, assaults/harassment and morale. Other questions tapped respondents' views about repeal and knowledge of disciplinary incidents that may have occurred since repeal was implemented. After three weeks of posting the advertisement, we obtained 14 completed surveys from active-duty respondents representing all four branches of the military. These included 10 heterosexual and four LGB troops. Although the results of our survey are consistent with other data, the low response rate undermines their validity and reliability, and we did not rely on them to reach our conclusions. That said, we do comment on responses to our open-ended questions in the text below. The advertisement we posted on *Military Times* websites is provided in Appendix H.

While in-depth interviews and surveys can provide invaluable data, we wanted to observe and compare entire military units engaged in normal operational activities. Thus, we observed the actions of four units, two of which included openly LGB members, and two of which did not. Our aim was to compare the readiness, cohesion and morale of units with and without LGB members and to identify qualitative differences. The observations included regular unit training activities and events on a military base located in a semi-rural region of the United States and at a service academy. The first observations included a combination of enlisted personnel and officers, while the others focused on interactions among cadets. The observing researcher was not an active participant in unit activities, and observed as an unobtrusive outsider, sitting on the sidelines and recording field notes. The researcher did not interfere with or interrupt training activities and did not interview or interact with individual participants during the observation time frame. All observations were conducted during regular unit activities, with other bystanders present.

Many journalists have followed DADT closely, and we augmented our in-depth interviews, surveys and on-site field observations with a content analysis of media stories about DADT repeal. To do so, we did a LexisNexis Academic database search for items containing the keywords "gay," and "don't ask, don't tell" in the 11 months following the date of repeal, between September 20, 2011 and August 20, 2012. The search returned 462 items, and we reviewed each item to identify evidence of the effects of DADT repeal on the U.S. military. We searched major world publications in the "all news" section of LexisNexis Academic. "All news" includes newspapers, wires, television and radio broadcasts and other sources.

A number of organizations have gathered information related to repeal, and we analyzed data from three such sources, each of which collected evidence prior to and then after DADT repeal. Data include results from three comprehensive surveys administered by *Military Times* and from two OutServe surveys that focused on the experiences of LGBT troops, as well as recruitment and retention reports released by the Defense Department for all active-duty, reserve and National Guard components. In order to assess whether DADT repeal has had an impact over time, we performed a longitudinal analysis of these materials.

Finally, because self-reports about a unit's effectiveness can be subjective and unreliable, we conducted what is known as a pre-test/post-test quasi-experiment of nonequivalent groups to provide an independent means for assessing DADT repeal's impact. The rationale of this approach is to compare the level of an outcome before and after an intervention, so as to determine whether the intervention is associated with any observed change in the outcome. In the case at hand, our aim was to compare the level of readiness and cohesion before and after DADT repeal. To conduct our experiment, we administered a brief survey to LGB troops two months before repeal and then six months after repeal. Our survey instrument posed two demographic questions and then asked respondents to rate the readiness and cohesion of their units.[2] None of the questions referred to DADT or sexual orientation. We received 80 responses to our pre-repeal survey and 120 responses to our post-repeal survey. Comparing average pre- and post-repeal reported levels of readiness and cohesion allowed us to assess whether the change to open service may have influenced either of these two factors. For both the pre- and post-repeal surveys, respondents included members from all branches of the U.S. military who were recruited through the OutServe network.

While no individual research strategy is perfect, the ten research strategies that we pursued provided independent means for assessing the impact of DADT repeal on military readiness, as each strategy allowed us to assess repeal's impact in the context of different types of data. Taken together, and given that the preponderance of evidence generated by each strategy pointed in the same direction, this comprehensive research design allows us to have a high degree of confidence in our conclusion that DADT repeal has had no overall negative impact on military readiness or its component parts, including unit cohesion, recruitment, retention, assaults, harassment or morale.

HISTORICAL CONTEXT

"Don't ask, don't tell" is the common term for the policy and federal statute created under President Bill Clinton in 1993. The policy allowed LGB troops to serve in the military, but only if they kept their sexual orientation secret and refrained from engaging in "homosexual conduct," which was defined to include same-sex sexual activity, attempts to marry someone of the same sex and statements indicating that one was lesbian, gay or bisexual. DADT was the product of a political battle that began in 1992 when Bill Clinton, as a presidential candidate, promised to end the longstanding ban on LGB service but met stiff resistance from social conservatives, military leaders and members of Congress who succeeded in codifying the new version of the ban into statute, making it harder to reverse (Frank, 2009).

In 2010, with the support of the top military leadership, Congress voted to repeal DADT, thus allowing the Pentagon to enact regulations that would permit LGB troops to serve without restriction. The legislation called for a delayed implementation of repeal, which would follow certification by the President, Secretary of Defense and Chairman of the Joint Chiefs of Staff that the military was prepared to lift the ban without harming military readiness. The plan called for repeal to occur 60 days after certification. Upon repeal, LGB service members would no longer be required to conceal their sexual orientation or abide by previous conduct restrictions. Additionally, new recruits would be welcome to apply without restrictions on conduct or speech related to sexuality, and previously-discharged LGB service members would be allowed to apply for re-admission to the military if sexual orientation was the sole reason for their dismissal. Repeal did not change the medical disqualification of transgender people and did not provide LGB troops with equal partner benefits, which are restricted by separate statutes and regulations. Repeal legislation did not contain a specific non-discrimination clause protecting LGB troops from unequal treatment, and it did not include sexual orientation or gender identity as protected statuses under the Defense Department's equal opportunity policy.

On July 22, 2011, the President, Secretary of Defense and Chairman of the Joint Chiefs of Staff certified that the military was ready for repeal, and implementation occurred on September 20, 2011. Since then, LGB Americans have been allowed to serve openly. In the next section of this study, we assess whether DADT repeal had an impact on military readiness and its component dimensions.

RESULTS

Military Readiness

Militaries use the term "readiness" to refer to the quality of their preparedness for engaging in combat, in particular whether they have the capacity to wage war immediately and without warning. More broadly, however, readiness can refer to whether a military force is able to achieve its mission. In this broader understanding of the term, readiness refers to overall military effectiveness and the central question of whether a military organization is able to do its job of winning wars rather than the more narrow, operational aspect of preparedness. While the nearly two-decade public dialogue over DADT included debates over a wide variety of issues, military readiness—broadly conceived—was the central, underlying concern of almost every aspect of the discussion. At issue in debates over unit cohesion, recruitment, retention, assaults, harassment and morale was whether or not DADT repeal would undermine combat effectiveness and the military's ability to fulfill its war-fighting mission.

Concern about readiness served as the most fundamental and significant rationale for barring LGB troops from serving openly. When former President Bill Clinton tried to compel the Pentagon to allow open service, opponents insisted that doing so would compromise readiness. According to an influential 1993 report by a Pentagon-appointed "Military Working Group" comprised of a general or admiral representing each service branch, "the presence in the military of individuals identified as homosexuals would have a significantly adverse effect on ... the readiness of the force ... If identified homosexuals are allowed to serve, they will compromise the high standards of combat effectiveness which must be maintained, impacting on the ability of the Armed Forces to perform its mission." Such concerns dominated Congressional hearings, and when DADT was enacted into law, the statute's authors emphasized the risk that they believed LGB troops would pose to combat effectiveness (Department of Defense, 1993).

More recently, when President Barack Obama advocated for the repeal of DADT, opponents made the same claim. The 1,167 retired generals and admirals who predicted that repeal would "break the All-Volunteer Force" added that "our past experience as military leaders leads us to be greatly concerned about the impact of repeal on ... overall military readiness" ("Flag and General Officers for the Military," 2009). Even the Obama Justice Department, in defending DADT's constitutionality, sought to "ensure that any repeal of DADT does not irreparably harm the government's critical interests in military readiness" (Young, 2010).

Despite such concerns, the evidence suggests that DADT repeal has not undermined readiness. Indeed, none of the individual opponents or watchdog organizations we contacted identified any evidence suggesting that DADT repeal has undermined readiness. None of the heterosexual service members who opposed or who continue to oppose repeal and whom we interviewed or surveyed reported any evidence indicating that the new policy has compromised readiness. Even a well-known opponent of DADT repeal has acknowledged that the new policy has not compromised military readiness. According to Elaine Donnelly: "No one predicted anything would happen immediately, so that prediction is true" (Standifer, 2012).

Among the retired generals who signed the statement predicting that repeal would "break the All-Volunteer Force," one said that "I believe evidence is growing that substantiates my initial concerns," (General (ret.), personal communication, May 1, 2012) but he declined to elaborate or provide details. None of the others reported any evidence suggesting that the new policy has compromised readiness. One retired lieutenant general told us that he "had not heard anything or received anything from anyone about having any problems" (personal communication, May 4, 2012). A retired one-star general said that a friend's son who is a company commander in Afghanistan told him "'I don't pay any attention to it. It's not really an issue'" (Brigadier General (ret.), personal communication, May 15, 2012). Another said that there was no indication of any major impact as of yet: "The general perception is that it seems to be working" (Brigadier General (ret.), personal communication, May 1, 2012). Yet another said that he remains opposed to repeal because "homosexual behavior is abnormal," but he is "not aware of anything positive or negative that has happened" (Major General (ret.), personal communication, May 4, 2012).

None of the heterosexual service members we interviewed or surveyed offered any evidence suggesting that repeal has undermined military readiness. An Army Ranger told us that repealing DADT "didn't change anything … We've got a guy in the unit who is gay. We've been working together for years and everyone knew, but no one ever cared. For us it's all about whether or not you're good at your job … it's all about quiet professionalism, not about your sexual orientation" (Anonymous #54, personal communication, April 11, 2012). An Air Force pilot said he could scarcely assess the impact of repeal because "I know that it has been repealed, but it just hasn't affected me in any way, shape or form … I guess I would have to say it is a success. I say that because I honestly haven't noticed any difference at all from before the repeal to now" (Anonymous #42, personal communication, March 27, 2012). A Navy pilot told us that he thought repeal "went very well" (Anonymous #55, personal communication, April 13, 2012). An Army Sergeant First Class explained that "there's been no real changes" since repeal (Anonymous #38, personal communication, March 2, 2012). A heterosexual naval surface warfare commander said, "I kind of look at it like a non-event. It was like asking, 'did the sun rise this morning?' It went pretty smoothly, like driving over a flat road, you don't even notice a ripple" (Anonymous #51, personal communication, April 9, 2012). That sentiment was echoed by a submariner, who told us that "it was such a non-event, I don't even remember it. Nothing noteworthy has happened." He added that repeal, "is not a big deal; it's going to be business as usual. Really we've been inclusive of these people, they've been serving with us forever, now they are going to be allowed to be more open about it. This doesn't change anything with the crew" (Anonymous #49, personal communication, April 13, 2012).

Even heterosexual service members who oppose DADT repeal acknowledged to us that the new policy has not undermined readiness. According to one currently deployed Army National Guard sergeant who opposes open service, there "was not much of a transition, it's not like people come in with rainbow flags or anything … the funny thing about the military is, people come in and do a job. That's all there is to it" (Anonymous #38, personal communication, March 2, 2012). A Navy SEAL who opposes repeal was nonetheless adamant that the military is a professional force, and that even those who do not agree with particular policies will follow them because that is what they are trained to do: "We're professional; we do what we've done in the past, make the work environment professional" (Anonymous #50, personal communication, April 11, 2012).

None of the scholars we interviewed knew of any evidence suggesting that DADT repeal has harmed military readiness. Dr. Jay Goodwin, a principle author of the Pentagon's 2010 report on DADT repeal, told us that, "in terms of negative impact, I have not heard of any" (personal communication, April 2, 2012). As President of the Inter-University Seminar on Armed Forces and Society, John Allen Williams communicates regularly with numerous scholars and experts who study civil-military relations. Asked about the implementation of DADT repeal, he said that it "appeared to be very smooth and very well-done" and that he was not aware of any negative consequences (personal communication, April 3, 2012). Todd Garth, an openly gay Naval Academy professor, said that before DADT repeal, the sense among his colleagues was that "the change would be a non-event for the most part and I get the sense that that's what people think has happened" (personal communication, March 22, 2012). Stephen J. Gerras, a retired Army colonel who teaches at the U.S. Army War College, was surprised when a gay speaker he invited to address his class failed to spark any controversy, "but maybe that's all part of the storyline, which is, thus far, it seems to be a non-event" (personal communication, February 19, 2012). David Kaiser, a professor at the Naval War College, told us that "today's field-grade officers know the troops don't care, for the most part." He added that, "I haven't seen any indication that anyone's very worried about it. I haven't seen any indication that things are going badly" (personal communication, March 29, 2012). George Reed, a retired Army colonel who served as director of Command and Leadership Studies at the Army War College, told us that "there was a big resounding silence after repeal. There has been very limited if any impact" (personal communication, March 29, 2012). David Levy, an Air Force Academy professor, said that "I knew this was not going to be an issue … but I was somewhat amazed about just how much of a non-issue it was. There was virtually no talk about it whatsoever." He said it was "almost eerie" how little attention the change had garnered. "I just don't see anyone talking about this, and I check with a lot of people about it, in classrooms, and elsewhere," he said (personal communication, March 22, 2012).

Finally, political and military leaders have concluded that DADT repeal has not compromised readiness. In February 2012, President Obama referred to repeal as a non-event and said that while some warned that ending the policy would be a "huge, ugly issue," the result was that "nothing's happened" (Boyer, 2012). Defense Secretary Leon Panetta said in May 2012, based on an unreleased Pentagon report that assessed the first months of the new policy, that repeal is "going very well … It's not impacting on readiness."

Secretary Panetta added that, "very frankly, the military has moved beyond" (Brown, 2012). General Martin Dempsey, Chairman of the Joint Chiefs of Staff, told reporters in May 2012 that, "I have not found any negative effect on good order and discipline." He asked, "what were we afraid of?" and answered that, "we didn't know" how repeal would go, but ultimately "it worked out well" (Mulrine, 2012). Three months after the new policy of open service went into effect, the service chief who was most outspoken against repeal, Marine Corps Commandant James Amos, said he was "very pleased with how it has gone." According to the *Washington Times*, Amos "said he heard little from Marines about serving with openly gay troops." The Commandant noted that "the Marine Corps faithfully and willingly carried out the intent of our commander-in-chief and civilian leadership in preparing for repeal. All Marines, sailors and civilian Marines, regardless of sexual orientation, are Marines first. Every Marine is a valued member of our warfighting team" (Boyer, 2012). In March 2012, Pentagon spokeswoman Eileen Lainez confirmed that the new policy is "proceeding smoothly across the Department of Defense" ("'Don't Ask, Don't Tell' Repeal Going Well," 2012).

Among all of the evidence we uncovered via our ten research strategies, we found only a handful of data points, all of which are addressed in the next few paragraphs, suggesting that DADT repeal has compromised any element of readiness or the military's ability to pursue its mission. During his campaign for the Republican presidential nomination, former Senator Rick Santorum said that "gay soldiers cause problems for people living in close quarters" (Goldman, 2012). And, Center for Military Readiness (CMR) President Elaine Donnelly told the *Washington Times* that the existence of OutServe, the network of 5,700 active-duty LGBT troops, is "inherently divisive" (Boyer, 2012). Neither of these comments indicates that DADT repeal has undermined readiness. Senator Santorum did not provide supporting evidence, and his office did not respond to several requests for explanation. Elaine Donnelly also did not provide evidence of divisiveness and, as noted above, acknowledged elsewhere that repeal has not compromised readiness thus far.

We also question a report by CMR that implies that LGB public displays of affection and gay pride celebrations at service academies have undermined military readiness (CMR, 2012). Several public displays have in fact drawn widespread attention, such as a photograph of Marine Sergeant Brandon Morgan kissing his boyfriend that went viral, with more than 40,000 people clicking "like" and 10,000 offering comments (McAvoy, 2012). While such displays may have lowered the morale of some service members, as we discuss in a subsequent section of this study, they do not constitute evidence that DADT repeal undermined overall readiness. As retired Army Colonel and Army War College Professor Charles Allen explained, although some of the well-publicized homecomings among LGB personnel "raised eyebrows," there was no impact on the "ability of the Army to perform its mission ... I've heard nothing that said they were not able to do the withdrawal from Iraq on schedule, nothing to indicate that performance of duty in Afghanistan in a very tough environment was impacted" by the end of DADT (personal communication, March 19, 2012).

While we are not compelled by the Santorum or Donnelly remarks or the CMR report, another data point appears to constitute more persuasive evidence of a possible decline in readiness. In response to a January 2012 *Military Times* survey of 733 active duty troops and 59 reservists mobilized for active duty, 4.5% indicated that after DADT repeal, their unit was negatively impacted when someone disclosed being gay or bisexual or when an openly gay or bisexual person joined their unit. Of 792 active-duty service members and mobilized reservists who completed the survey, 150 (18.9%) indicated that since DADT was repealed, someone in their unit disclosed being gay or bisexual. Of those, 32 (21.3%) said that the disclosure had a negative impact on their unit. In addition, 36 (4.5%) reported that since DADT was repealed, an openly gay or bisexual person joined their unit. Of those, 12 (33.3%) said that the newcomer had a negative impact on their unit. There was some overlap in that eight respondents reported a negative impact from a disclosure as well as from an LGB newcomer. Therefore, a total of 36 (32+12−8) discrete service members reported a negative impact from either a disclosure or from an LGB newcomer. Thus, 36/792 equals 4.5% of respondents indicated that after DADT repeal, their unit was negatively impacted when someone disclosed being gay or bisexual or when an openly gay or bisexual person joined their unit (*Military Times* Poll, 2012).[3] While 4.5% is a small minority, the data should be taken seriously as the one piece of evidence we uncovered that suggests that DADT repeal may have harmed military effectiveness.

That said, a comparison of 2011 pre-repeal and 2012 post-repeal *Military Times* survey data shows that service members reported approximately the same level of military readiness after DADT repeal as before it. On all four components of readiness measured by *Military Times* surveys (quality of training, officers and enlisted leaders, and whether today's service members are the best ever) the 2012 post-repeal data indicate approximately the same levels as the 2011 pre-repeal data. In response to a question asking, "How would you rate your unit's level of training for its wartime mission?" 57% of 2011 respondents answered that they were very well trained or well trained (29% adequate, 10% poor or very poor, 4% not sure), but 62% of 2012 respondents said that they were very well trained or well trained (27% adequate, 7% poor or very poor, 4% not sure). In response to a question about the overall quality of military officers, 60% of 2011 respondents answered that they were excellent or good (26% average, 14% fair or poor), but 63% of 2012 respondents said that they were excellent or good (24% average, 13% fair or poor). In response to a question about the overall quality of enlisted leaders in the military, 62% of 2011 respondents answered that they were excellent or good (25% average, 13% fair or poor), but 64% of 2012 respondents said that they were excellent or good (24% average, 12% fair or poor). In response to a question asking if "today's service members are better than they have ever been," 61% of 2011 respondents agreed or strongly agreed (28% neutral, 21% disagree or strongly disagree), but 52% of 2012 respondents agreed or strongly agreed (27% neutral, 21% disagree or strongly disagree) (*Military Times* Poll, 2011 and 2012).

As we discuss below, the *Military Times* surveys also indicate that after repeal, service-wide morale remained stable, and service members were as likely to say that they would re-enlist as they were before repeal. If repeal had compromised overall readiness in any discernible way, it is hard to understand why every dimension of readiness assessed by *Military Times* survey respondents remained stable after the new policy of open service went into effect. Moreover, as discussed below, there is reason to believe that claims of unit harm may reflect disapproval of repeal, not actual evidence of a decline in readiness. Thus, even though 4.5% of service members indicated that DADT repeal had negatively impacted their unit, the preponderance of evidence contradicts this contention and suggests that, overall, the policy change did not harm the military.

Contrary to expectations of a post-repeal decline in readiness, we uncovered considerable evidence in our open-ended interviews about ways in which the new policy has enhanced the military's ability to pursue its mission. More specifically, both experts and service members told us that repeal had enhanced military readiness in the areas of discipline, command, family readiness and spirituality. Consider these illustrations:

- *Discipline*: A Navy pilot told us about two gay service members who broke a shipboard rule before DADT repeal. Commanders were not comfortable bringing charges for that low-level transgression because doing so would have required outing the service members as gay. The infraction of which they were guilty was minor and had a very slight penalty associated with it, but the penalty for their being labeled as gay was separation from the military. Because the commanders did not believe that the lower infraction was significant enough to warrant discharge, they declined to charge the pair with the lesser infraction. "This put the leadership in an awkward position," explained the pilot, "and the repeal just takes away that extra hurdle and allows commanders to lead better" (Anonymous #55, personal communication, April 13, 2012).
- *Command*: Another Naval officer told us that prior to repeal, commanders could not assist their sailors in the ways they would like because they could be obligated to discharge them if they knew too much. DADT repeal allowed this officer to better understand the sailors under her command so that she could counsel them and address and resolve their issues. She described a sailor who was having personal issues. "He was a very good

sailor, but started having problems" including anxiety and sleeplessness. "Over time it became clear that the problem was possibly with a relationship, but because [the leadership] believed the relationship was with another man, they couldn't talk with him about it." She said that not being able to deal with the issue directly hindered her ability to help the sailor under her command. With the change in policy "everyone, from leadership down, were relieved that at least the sailor could come talk to them, whether or not they supported [homosexuality] themselves ... There were too many service members who fit in the [LGB] category, which caused additional stress in already stressful situations. That is totally unacceptable. This was a very important change" (Anonymous #56, personal communication, May 7, 2012).

- *Family readiness*: An Air Force non-commissioned officer told us about "an airman who had a partner who was gravely ill who he couldn't take care of because we were being deployed. He couldn't get a hardship waiver because he couldn't tell anyone he was gay and that really affected his ability to serve." The repeal of DADT "opened up more possibilities for [troops] to talk about their lives" when doing so was necessary for resolving personal issues so they could focus on their mission (Anonymous #47, personal communication, May 4, 2012).

- *Spirituality*: A chaplain told us that "the repeal will give me more opportunities to expand my ministry. I can help more people now because they can talk to me openly without fear" (Anonymous #44, personal communication, March 28, 2012).

The evidence we uncovered from our ten research strategies indicates that DADT repeal has not undermined overall readiness, and even well-known opponents of repeal did not identify any persuasive evidence indicating that readiness has declined. We concur with West Point Chief of Staff Colonel Gus Stafford, who said that much of the military community "underestimated the adaptability and capability of our young people to adapt" (personal communication, April 2, 2012). With respect to military readiness, predictions of negative consequences have proven unfounded.

Components of Military Readiness

Unit cohesion

Having addressed repeal's impact on the military's overall capacity to pursue its mission, we now turn to an assessment of four components of readiness that have been emphasized frequently during the nearly two-decade public dialogue about DADT: cohesion, recruitment/retention, assaults/harassment and morale. The first and most prominently discussed component of readiness, unit cohesion, refers to bonds of trust among members of a military unit. Scholars distinguish between two types of cohesion: social cohesion, which refers to the degree of bonding and trust, and task cohesion, which refers to the extent to which group members are committed to a common mission. Although a number of studies indicate that of the two, only task cohesion is related to group effectiveness, we focus exclusively on social cohesion because that was a central focus of the debate over DADT (see MacCoun, Kier, and Belkin, 2006).

The Pentagon's 1993 Military Working Group (MWG) observed that "the essence of unit cohesion is the bonding between members of a unit which holds them together, sustains their will to support each other, and enables them to fight together under the stress and chaos of war. The MWG found that the presence of open homosexuals in a unit would, in general, polarize and fragment the unit and destroy the bonding and singleness of purpose required for effective military operations" (Military Working Group, 1993, p. 5) Vincent Pattavina, a retired Navy officer writing in the *Patriot Ledger*, said in 2003 that, "there are good reasons why the military does not want gays and lesbians in the military. One good reason is their presence destroys military cohesion. When you have to live, sleep and fight at close quarters [with gay people], heterosexuals do not have the team fighting ability (military cohesion) that is necessary to win battles. The units of our best soldiers, Marines and sailors in past wars have had excellent military cohesion, which would have been obviated [sic] by the presence of gays and lesbians." The statute that codified DADT into law ("10 U.S.C. 654," 1993) reflected such concerns, in noting that "the presence in the armed forces of persons who demonstrate a propensity or intent to engage in homosexual acts would create an unacceptable risk to the high standards of morale, good order and discipline, and unit cohesion that are the essence of military capability."

More recently, concerns about unit cohesion played a prominent role in the debate over whether Congress should repeal DADT. Testifying before the House Armed Services Committee in 2008, retired Army officer Brian Jones said that, "as a U.S. Army Ranger, I performed long-range patrols in severe cold weather conditions, in teams of 10, with only mission-essential items on our backs. No comfort items. The only way to keep from freezing at night was to get as close as possible for body heat—which means skin to skin. On several occasions, in the close quarters that a team lives, any attraction to same-sex teammates, real or perceived, would be known and would be a problem. The presence of openly gay men in these situations would elevate tensions and disrupt unit cohesion and morale" (Jones, 2008). General James Amos, Commandant of the Marine Corps, was quoted in an AP piece in 2010 that, "there is nothing more intimate than young men and young women—and when you talk of infantry, we're talking about our young men—laying out, sleeping alongside of one another and sharing death, fear and loss of brothers ... I don't know what the effect of [repeal] will be on cohesion. I mean, that's what we're looking at. It's unit cohesion, it's combat effectiveness."

Despite such concerns, the preponderance of evidence suggests that DADT repeal has not undermined unit cohesion. With two exceptions discussed below, none of the heterosexual troops we interviewed and surveyed offered any evidence suggesting that DADT repeal undermined cohesion. A heterosexual chaplain explained that, during his prior service in the Special Forces, long before the repeal of DADT, he served in a combat unit "where everyone knew who was gay and no one cared. The soldiers figured these guys loved being men so much [that] they loved other men, and that was all there was to it" (Anonymous #45, personal communication, April 2, 2012). A heterosexual Army Ranger told us that repealing DADT "didn't affect cohesion … or how we interact, or force us to change any sort of accommodations for anyone" (Anonymous #54, personal communication, April 11, 2012). A heterosexual Air Force captain and emergency room doctor said that civilians often have "ideas about narrow-mindedness of the members of the military, especially as regards religious or social issues. But that's just not how it works. Individuals may have a problem, but there is no problem with the group opinion" (Anonymous #39, personal communication, March 2, 2012).

None of the LGB service members we interviewed or surveyed reported any decline in unit cohesion following the repeal of DADT. A technical sergeant in the Air Force said that he came out to a handful of people after repeal. "All respected me for telling them and felt honored that I trusted them enough to tell them," he said. "It was refreshing" (Anonymous #24, personal communication, April 26, 2012). An Air Force combat crew evaluator revealed his sexual orientation on Facebook at midnight on the day of repeal, and said the reaction was "universally positive," calling it "hands-down one of the most positive things that's ever happened during my career." He said he "had four people approach me around the building and congratulate me" (Anonymous #27, personal communication, May 12, 2012). An Army mortuary affairs specialist was finally able to use honest pronouns in conversations with coworkers. When she did, "I met no surprise or even second glance from anyone," she said, noting that the policy change for her was "relatively seamless. I have a pretty high level of respect from the people that I currently work with and I generally work with people that have enough experience in the military to know that homosexuality has nothing to do with job performance" (Anonymous #29, personal communication, March 20, 2012). A Navy hospital corpsman added that, "there have been no issues regarding the repeal" in his unit and "no negative changes to unit cohesion" since the policy change. He said his commanding officer gave him strong support when he opted to speak as a representative for "Repeal Day." When he revealed his sexual orientation, he said that too was mostly a "general non-event. There were some looks of surprise, but nobody made a big deal about it." He said his peers "treated it as business as usual. Sure, there were malcontents, but they got over it rather quickly" (Anonymous #26, personal communication, May 2, 2012).

Nor did any of the scholarly experts we interviewed know of any evidence suggesting that repeal has undermined cohesion. Martin Cook, who has served as a professor at the Naval War College, Air Force Academy and Army War College, summarized the apparent position of many of these scholars in noting that arguments stressing possible damage to unit cohesion "were really a smokescreen for other reasons; those were just the only publicly acceptable reasons they could put forward" (personal communication, March 22, 2012).

Finally, top political and military leaders have indicated that DADT repeal did not prompt any decline in cohesion. In February 2012, President Obama said of DADT repeal that "there hasn't been any notion of erosion in unit cohesion" (Johnson, 2012). Defense Secretary Panetta told the press in May 2012 that repeal is "not impacting on unit cohesion." Aside from the one retired general who, as noted in the previous section, said that, "I believe evidence is growing that substantiates my initial concerns," none of the opponents of DADT repeal, including activists, watchdog organizations or retired generals, identified any evidence contradicting senior leadership's contention that repeal has not undermined unit cohesion (Parrish, 2012).

While interviews and surveys that ask subjects to describe the impact of DADT repeal on cohesion can provide valuable information, both methods have limitations, specifically the fact that they require respondents to make an inference about causality. That is, when they report whether they believe that repeal has had an impact on cohesion, respondents must offer a causal interpretation of whether the new policy of open service has caused an increase or decrease in cohesion. As psychologists have demonstrated, however, causal inferences are subject to a host of potential distortions, and this is particularly likely when the wording of a survey or interview question provokes an emotional reaction (see Tetlock and Levi, 1982). Thus, when a respondent reports that repeal has not undermined cohesion, his or her response may be more a reflection of the subject's approval of DADT repeal than an appraisal and explanation of any changes or lack thereof in the level of cohesion. Conversely, when a respondent reports that repeal has undermined cohesion, the response may be reflective of a disapproval of repeal rather than constituting actual evidence of causal harm.

To overcome this limitation and provide an additional, independent means for assessing DADT repeal's impact, we designed an experiment that is known as a pre-test/post-test quasi-experiment of nonequivalent groups. In the case at hand, a large group of service members (N=80) ranked their unit's cohesion on a scale of one to ten two months before DADT repeal, and then another large group of service members (N=120) ranked their unit's cohesion six months after repeal. By comparing the pre- and post-repeal average reported levels of cohesion, we were able to assess whether the new policy of open service was associated with any change. To avoid priming the subjects' emotional feelings about DADT repeal, our survey simply asked each respondent to rank his or her unit's level of cohesion and readiness, and did not mention DADT or sexual orientation.

To rigorously test the hypothesis that repeal has not undermined cohesion, we administered our survey exclusively to active-duty members of OutServe. While it would be unsurprising if units composed exclusively of heterosexual troops maintained a steady rate of cohesion after repeal, units including openly LGB troops should have been the most likely to suffer a drop in cohesion after the policy change. And of all LGB individuals serving in the military, members of OutServe should be among those most likely to reveal their sexual orientation, given their willingness to affiliate with an LGBT organization. Hence, according to the logic of opponents of DADT repeal, units that include OutServe members should be the most likely to experience a decline in cohesion. What we found, however, is that LGB troops reported a slight increase in cohesion after DADT repeal: the average level of unit cohesion for the pre-repeal group was 7.18 while the average post-repeal ranking was 7.65, an increase of 6.5%.[4]

Similar to all research methodologies, our quasi-experiment is not perfect. We would have preferred to measure each unit's cohesion by averaging scores of multiple members of that unit rather than relying on a single unit member to rate his or her unit's cohesion. In addition, any nonequivalent groups design is vulnerable to the criticism that observed differences are the result of the nonequivalence, not the intervention. While this is always a possibility, one advantage of our use of the nonequivalent design is that the post-repeal group had no knowledge of the pre-repeal group's rating of cohesion or readiness, and the pre-repeal group had no knowledge of our plan to collect data post-repeal. While there may have been some overlap among members of the pre- and post-repeal groups, there was little if any opportunity to coordinate any effort to bias results by underestimating cohesion and readiness pre-repeal and then over-estimating them post-repeal.

That said, the strength of the quasi-experiment is that it provided an independent means for overcoming limitations, described above, that are inherent in any effort to ask subjects to describe the impact of DADT repeal on cohesion. The results of our quasi-experiment are consistent with the preponderance of evidence we uncovered, and suggest that even in those units that should have been the most likely to experience a decline in cohesion as a result of repeal, cohesion did not decrease after the new policy of open service was put into place.

In addition to interviews, surveys, content analysis and quasi-experimentation, one study author observed daily operations of multiple military units, and found no major differences between units that included openly LGB troops and those that did not. All service members conducted themselves professionally and interacted with one another as professionals. Interestingly, there were observable differences in the way supervisors and subordinates interacted in the various units, but differences were not related to sexual orientation. In two units, the interactions were familiar and easy, while in the other two, interactions were more formal and rigid. These differences were not related to the presence of LGB troops in that one of the formal units included openly LGB members and the other did not, and one of the informal units included LGB troops while the other did not. The different styles of interaction and levels of formality were more reflective of command climate than the presence or absence of LGB troops. Likewise, cohesion, or how well the unit bonded and meshed, seemed most dependent on the compatibility of unit members' personalities, overall command climate and level of familiarity. The units that were the most cohesive had served together the longest and were the most familiar with one another. Units with a high proportion of new members or high turnover were less likely to be cohesive. The sexual orientation of members did not seem to play a role in the level of cohesion within the units observed.

The only data we collected linking open service to a possible impairment of cohesion were unpersuasive. Of 10 active-duty, heterosexual service members who responded to our *Military Times* advertisement requesting survey participants, two indicated that cohesion declined after the repeal of DADT, one reported that cohesion increased after DADT repeal, and seven said that there were no changes. In response to open-ended questions in the Palm Center survey requesting elaboration, one Army National Guard Specialist said that LGB troops would want special treatment, explaining that "the homosexual males will want to do the female scaled PT test." He added that, "males will only shower with other straight males." Another respondent, a Navy Reserve Petty Officer First Class, said that cohesion will suffer because "by repealing DADT a separate [entitlement] group has been created ... [and] this reduces unit cohesion as sailors will not act freely, afraid that they will upset this new special group." We question whether either of these claims indicates a decline in cohesion because neither respondent was aware of LGB troops serving in his unit. Both also used the future tense in responding to open-ended questions, suggesting that their concerns reflected fears of future deterioration rather than evidence of an actual detriment to cohesion following the repeal of DADT. An article in the *Marine Corps Gazette* made similar predictions and espoused future concerns, but also did not provide evidence that cohesion has suffered (Will, 2012).

Although the preponderance of evidence suggests that repeal has not undermined cohesion, we did identify survey as well as interview data indicating that the new policy of open service has promoted greater honesty which, in turn, has enabled the troops to develop tighter bonds of trust. Published and ongoing longitudinal research at West Point confirms that both military academy and ROTC cadets are increasingly tolerant of gays and lesbians in the military, even more so following repeal of DADT (Ender et al., 2012).[5]

Alongside the longitudinal survey data obtained at West Point, our interview and qualitative survey data suggest that DADT repeal has promoted greater trust. A heterosexual active duty Marine sergeant reported in the qualitative section of the Palm Center survey, that "it's been a lot better since we now know with whom we serve. It's all out in the open and now there is no wondering or guessing. We know. And knowledge is power!" He went on to say that, "we now get along better and we accept our unit members as they are; we do not beat around the bush or sugarcoat anything. It's a lot better now. [We're all] very equal."

A heterosexual Army sergeant said that DADT repeal has allowed straight troops to strengthen their relationships with LGB colleagues, in that it "finally allowed people to have the freedom to be who they are. They still don't have the same rights available to everyone, but the freedom [is now] there." He added that post-repeal, "people are more open with their previous experiences" and more likely to introduce LGB peers to same-sex partners (Anonymous #46, personal communication, April 10, 2012). A heterosexual lieutenant commander in Naval meteorology believes the repeal will bring about positive changes in the overall military culture. "It removed a barrier that was neither necessary nor practical," he said. "It will help facilitate the slow cultural change towards greater acceptance" (Anonymous #48, personal communication, April 6, 2012).

A gay Naval Academy midshipman reported that, after repeal, discussing his sexual orientation was no longer a career-ending offense, and in fact brought out the protective instincts of other midshipmen. The midshipman said that "pretty much everybody in my company knows now" about his sexual orientation and "they actually stand up for me" if they hear anti-gay comments (Brown, 2012). A gay Army social worker told us that he used to have to "avoid my unit like the plague," but repeal changed that. "I kept everything to myself" in the past, he said. "I can be one person now," no longer keeping his work life separate from his personal life. Previously, he said, "I went to painstaking lengths to keep them separate, and I don't do that anymore. I go out with my co-workers. So for me it helps so I'm actually part of the unit where I don't think I was before" (Anonymous #9, personal communication, April 19, 2012).

A Navy commander said that during a course on current events, one of her classmates brought up "a story on NPR about a [male] Marine officer who was coming out, and taking a male to the Marine Corps ball that year." Some of her classmates responded "by wondering, 'why can't they just keep that information to themselves?' But then another classmate asked 'why should they have to hide?'" The commander said that the woman who spoke up went on to question why, given that heterosexual troops talk about their dates, she should have to hide who hers was going to be. The woman had not acknowledged her sexual orientation prior to this discussion, and many of her classmates were shocked. The commander said that "it was a conversation stopper. Those guys hadn't thought of it that way before. I also think they didn't realize they knew someone who was actually gay" (Anonymous #56, personal communication, May 7, 2012).

Professor Garth, the openly gay professor at the Naval Academy, explained that, "one of the things about the ban is that it had basically shut down discussion. There was discussion of homosexuality sometimes but it always had to be very impersonal." Now that has changed, and the improvement appears to apply to the bond between midshipmen and faculty. "As strong as that bond was, this has only enhanced it," he said, suggesting that the new level of openness has permeated relationships at the Naval Academy in general (personal communication, March 22, 2012). An Army captain in administrative law told us that repeal had "enhanced our unit cohesion" as he is more open and honest with peers, as are they with him (Anonymous #17, personal communication, April 27, 2012). And an Army signals analyst said that after repeal, "the unit's cohesion was greatly increased ... People were accepting of those who came out and those who were accepted found a whole new respect from those you had just come out to" (Anonymous #28, personal communication, April 30, 2012).

Despite concerns that DADT repeal would undermine unit cohesion and prevent service members from forming bonds of trust, the preponderance of evidence suggests that the new policy of open service has not compromised cohesion, and that, if anything, greater openness and honesty have promoted increased understanding, respect and even acceptance.

Recruitment and retention

Throughout the nearly two-decade conversation about DADT, Pentagon leaders as well as experts on U.S. military personnel policy claimed that allowing gay men and lesbians to serve openly would compromise recruitment and retention. When former President Bill Clinton tried to compel the military to lift its ban in 1993, participants in the debate expressed concerns about the Pentagon's ability to recruit and retain qualified service members. According to the influential 1993 Military Working Group report cited above, "open homosexuality in the military would likely reduce the propensity of many young men and women to enlist due to parental concerns, peer pressure, and a military image that would be tarnished in the eyes of much of the population from which we recruit" (Military Working Group, 1993, p. 7). Such claims were ubiquitous in the 1993 debate, and appear to have played an influential role in Congress's decision to enact DADT into law.

More recently, the 2009 statement signed by 1,167 retired generals and admirals predicted that repeal "would undermine recruiting and retention [and] have adverse effects on the willingness of parents who lend their sons and daughters to military service" ("Flag and General Officers for the Military," 2009). After Congress authorized DADT repeal in 2010, Frank Gaffney Jr., of the Center for Security Policy, wrote in the *Washington Times* that the new policy of open service could "prove decisive to the viability of the all-volunteer force. That viability may, in turn, determine our ability to avoid in the years ahead—as we have for the past four decades—a return to conscription to meet our requirements for warriors in those conflicts" (2011). Elaine Donnelly, of the Center for Military Readiness, writing in the *National Review Online*, predicted an eventual loss of 500,000 service members as a result of repeal (2009).

By contrast, some scholars expected DADT repeal to enhance recruitment and retention. This expectation was premised on the estimate that each year, DADT caused approximately 4,000 LGB service members to separate from the armed forces earlier than would have been the case if they had been allowed to acknowledge their sexual orientation. In addition, scholars estimated that DADT repeal would expand the annual pool of potential recruits because approximately 41,000 LGB individuals would become eligible for service and because repeal would motivate some heterosexuals who had previously avoided an institution they associated with discrimination to join the armed forces. Finally, some scholars predicted that DADT repeal would encourage some universities to invite Reserve Officer Training Corps programs back to campus (Gates, 2007, 2008; Belkin, 2008).

Although we uncovered some evidence supportive of both pessimistic and optimistic predictions, the preponderance of evidence suggests that DADT repeal has had no impact on recruitment or retention. Before addressing those data, however, we review the evidence that is consistent with pessimistic and optimistic forecasts. In response to a January 2012 *Military Times* survey completed after DADT repeal by 792 active-duty troops and mobilized reservists, 8.4% said that repeal made them less likely to remain in the military. Two out of the ten heterosexual troops whom we surveyed indicated that DADT repeal made them less likely to remain in the service beyond their minimum commitment. And in our in-depth interviews, two active-duty naval officers told us that they considered separating from the armed forces prematurely as a result of repeal. By contrast, 3.3% of *Military Times* respondents said that DADT repeal made them more likely to remain in the military. Moreover, the two naval officers who said that they had considered separating early told us that they decided to remain until retirement, and four heterosexual troops told us during interviews that repeal made them more likely to continue to serve beyond their minimum commitment.

Although a minority of service members report that DADT repeal has had an impact on their likelihood of re-enlisting, with some less likely and others more likely to remain, the preponderance of evidence suggests that repeal has not had any discernible impact, either positive or negative, on recruitment or retention. A comparison of 2011 pre-repeal and 2012 post-repeal *Military Times* surveys shows that after repeal, service members were just as likely to say that they would remain in the military as they were before repeal. In response to a question asking, "If you had to decide today, would you re-enlist or—if an officer—extend your commitment," 70% of 2011 respondents answered yes (17% no, 14% undecided), but 72% of 2012 respondents indicated that they would re-enlist (15% no, 14% undecided).[6] In response to the question, "Do you currently plan to remain in the military for at least 20 years and earn a full retirement package," 84% of 2011 respondents answered yes (5% no, 11% undecided), but 85% of 2012 respondents indicated that they would re-enlist (3% no, 12% undecided). Even though 8.4% of 2012 post-repeal *Military Times* survey respondents said that DADT repeal made them less likely to remain in the military, repeal appears to be a minor if not trivial factor in their decision-making. If repeal were a significant factor in re-enlistment decisions for 8.4% of the force, then it would be hard to understand why, post-repeal, troops were just as likely to say that they would re-enlist as was the case before repeal.

That said, the correlation between re-enlistment intentions and actual re-enlistment is generally low unless intention data are collected shortly before the expiration of terms of service, so it is important to consider actual retention rates. The military has successfully met its recruitment and retention targets in the wake of DADT repeal. According to recruitment and retention numbers released by the Department of Defense on June 29, 2012, more than nine months after DADT repeal went into effect, "all four active services met or exceeded their numerical accession goals for fiscal 2012, through May." The Navy, Marine Corps and Air Force achieved 100% of their goals, while the Army exceeded its goal with an additional 253 recruits, thus reaching 101% of its target. In addition, "the Army, Navy, Marine Corps, and Air Force all exhibited strong retention through the eighth month of fiscal 2012." On the reserve side, "five of the six reserve components met or exceeded their numerical accession goals for fiscal 2012, through May." The Army Reserve exceeded its goal, reaching 104% of its target, and the Marine Corps Reserve also exceeded its goal at 106% of its target. The Navy Reserve, Air Force Reserve and Air National Guard all met their targets at 100%. According to the press release, "all reserve components are on target to achieve their fiscal year attrition goals" (U.S. Department of Defense, 2012).

The Army National Guard (ANG) was the only reserve component that did not meet its recruitment target in 2012, reaching only 95% of its goal. However, trend data suggest that the shortfall had nothing to do with DADT repeal. The ANG's post-repeal recruitment numbers mirrored its pre-repeal totals, indicating that repeal was not a likely factor in its performance. In FY 2011, the ANG was the only reserve component to fail to meet its goal, achieving 96% of its target. And, as was the case in 2012 after DADT repeal went into effect, the data from FY 2011 show that during the last period when DADT was still law, all four active-duty branches met or exceeded recruitment and retention numbers, five out of six reserve component branches met or exceeded recruitment goals and all six reserve component branches met or exceeded retention goals. (U.S. Department of Defense, 2012). We contacted the National Guard Bureau to determine if DADT repeal caused the ANG to fail to meet its recruitment goals, and, if not, why it has not achieved its 2012 target. A Bureau spokesperson told us that DADT repeal had nothing to do with the shortfall, and pointed instead to "challenges associated with recruiting to specialized military occupational skills and a reduced available population who meet military requirements. The entrance standards for military service continue to increase in regard to aptitude, physical fitness, morale and particularly behavioral health" (Rose M. Richeson, personal communication, May 3, 2012).[7] We confirmed that entrance standards for military recruitment have in fact increased over the course of the past year. In addition, the military is accepting fewer behavioral waivers from potential recruits who may have committed minor crimes. A final possible explanation for the ANG's failure to meet its goals is that "the Army is also spending hundreds of thousands of dollars less in bonuses to attract recruits or entice soldiers to remain" (Baldor, 2012).

Even among chaplains, the evidence suggests that DADT repeal has had no measurable impact on retention. Chaplains were thought to be among those most likely to leave the military after DADT repeal, in part because contracts allow them to resign more quickly than other military members, and many threatened to resign if LGB troops were allowed to serve openly (Crary, 2012). Such concerns, however, have proven to be unwarranted. Lieutenant Colonel Lisa H. Tice, a chaplain who serves in the personnel, budget and readiness division of the Air Force Office of the Chief of Chaplains, told us that no Air Force chaplains left the military as a result of DADT repeal. Navy Chaplain Capt. John H. Lea III reported that one Navy chaplain separated because of repeal (Samuel, 2011). Lieutenant Colonel Carleton Birch, a spokesman for the Army Chief of Chaplains, said that in March 2011, one Army chaplain left the military over the pending repeal of DADT (Banks, 2011). But when we called the Army Chief of Chaplains office in June 2012, a spokesperson told us that, "we've had nobody else leave for that stated reason in the Army out of the 3,000 or so full-time and part-time chaplains" and that no endorsing denominations had withdrawn their endorsements as a result of DADT repeal (personal communication, June, 20, 2012). A Chaplaincy Corps training slide also indicated that chaplains "who are unable to reconcile repeal of DADT may request voluntary separation per AR 600-8-20."

Scholars have produced an extensive literature on why some young Americans decide to enlist in the armed forces, and why some service members decide to re-enlist when given the opportunity (see Warner and Asch in Hartley and Sandler, 1995, pp. 348–98 and Orvis and Asch, 2001). None of that literature mentions the presence or absence of a gay ban as a factor that influences enlistment and retention decisions, and the literature's silence on this topic is consistent with data, discussed in a subsequent section of this study, that show that even among service members who oppose DADT repeal, only a small minority feel strongly about the issue. The scholarly literature has found that enlistment and re-enlistment decisions are driven by a host of factors that have nothing to do with the presence or absence of openly-serving LGB colleagues, such as the strength of the economy, individual patriotism and the availability of college scholarships as well as enlistment and re-enlistment bonuses. A spokesperson for the National Guard confirmed that "it is unlikely that any single policy will have a significant effect on recruitment or retention numbers" (a representative at the National Guard Office, personal communication, May 2, 2012).

As discussed, a minority of service members report that DADT repeal has influenced their likelihood of remaining in the military, with some indicating that repeal has made them less likely to re-enlist and others suggesting that they are more likely to remain. What the preponderance of evidence shows, however, is that DADT repeal has not had any measurable impact on recruitment or retention, even among chaplains. It is certainly true that the weak domestic economy and disengagement from two wars have made recruitment and retention easier. But in an era when enlistment standards have tightened, service members were just as likely to say that they plan to re-enlist after DADT repeal as was the case pre-repeal. Every active service branch has met its recruitment and retention goals, five out of six reserve components have reached their recruitment targets and every reserve component has achieved its retention objectives. The one reserve component that did not meet its recruitment target in the aftermath of DADT repeal, the ANG, also failed to meet its goal when DADT was still in effect, and an ANG spokesperson attributes the shortfall to factors that have nothing to do with repeal. DADT repeal, in short, has not impacted recruitment or retention.

Assaults and harassment

Among all the predictions about the consequences of allowing open service, some of the most disturbing referred to violence that was expected to occur among service members. Military leaders and experts have warned that allowing open service would prompt an increase in violence because LGB troops would attack their heterosexual peers. During 1993 Senate testimony, General Norman Schwarzkopf said that "I am aware of instances where heterosexuals have been solicited to commit homosexual acts, and, even more traumatic emotionally, physically coerced to engage in such acts"

(Schwarzkopf, 1993). More recently, in May 2010, the Family Research Council released a report, *Homosexual Assault in the Military*, claiming that "homosexuals in the military are about three times as likely to commit sexual assaults than heterosexuals are, relative to their numbers ... If the law is overturned and open homosexuals are welcomed into the military, the number of homosexuals in the armed forces can only increase—leading to a corresponding increase in same-sex sexual assaults" (Sprigg, 2010).

Parallel to concerns about LGB troops assaulting heterosexuals, observers have warned that heterosexuals would express disdain over the prospect of open service by attacking LGB peers. In 1993 Senate testimony, Colonel Fred Peck said that his gay son "would be at grave risk if he were to follow in my footsteps as an infantry platoon leader or a company commander. I would be very fearful that his life would be in jeopardy from his own troops." In 2012, an Army company commander who flew air assault missions in Iraq told us that, "at the unit level, I do expect to see a few situations of gay bashing or assaults, especially among the lower enlisted soldiers or at basic training. People from areas that are less tolerant and less diverse may be more apt to confronting a homosexual and trying to 'correct the error of their ways' through words or force" (Anonymous #25, personal communication, May 11, 2012).

Despite warnings about an increase in assaults, we did not uncover any evidence suggesting that DADT repeal has led to a rise in violence among service members. With one exception discussed below, none of the service members, scholars or activists we interviewed or surveyed or the media articles that we reviewed reported any violent incidents among troops that resulted from repeal. For example, a cadet at one of the service academies said he was initially concerned about "blowback" that could include violence toward LGB service members, as he and his friends worried that LGB troops could be shunned or denigrated given the military's tradition of "hyper masculinity." When asked what happened after repeal, however, he said that, "it never came up ... It turned out it was a non-issue." He asked many of his lesbian and gay friends and they confirmed that, "it hasn't been an issue for them" (Anonymous #58, personal communication, May 7, 2012). More broadly, a Pentagon spokesperson noted in April 2012 that, "military officials say they're unaware of any discipline issues relating to gays serving openly" (Schofield, 2012). *American Forces Press Service* reported in March 2012 that, according to Chief of Naval Operations Admiral Jonathan Greenert, "the U.S. Navy checks the status of the fleet constantly, but there has been no uptick in conduct incidents since the repeal went into effect" (Garamone, 2012).

Gay rights groups that monitor Pentagon operations confirm the observations of Pentagon spokespersons as well as the experts, activists and service members we interviewed and surveyed. OutServe, the network of 5,700 active-duty LGBT service members, monitors the day-to-day implementation of DADT repeal perhaps more closely than any organization in the world. Lieutenant Josh Seefried, OutServe's Co-Director, communicates regularly with hundreds of OutServe members serving at home and abroad and frequently administers surveys to OutServe's membership. Seefried told us that he has heard of one case in which a gay service member may have been physically attacked since repeal, but that it remains unclear whether the victim was gay and whether the attacker believed that the victim was gay (Alexander, 2012). Servicemembers Legal Defense Network (SLDN), a well-regarded watchdog organization with nearly two decades of experience monitoring the status of LGBT troops, reported in March 2012 that since repeal, its staff has received only "a few minor complaints" (UPI, 2012). SLDN staff confirmed in subsequent correspondence that the complaints were about implementation issues, not assaults (personal correspondence, July 2 and 9, 2012).

In May 2012, the Center for Military Readiness (CMR) released a statement suggesting that DADT repeal has caused an increase in male-male rape among service members. The statement, titled "Early Consequences of Military LGBT Law," cited an April 2012 US Army study that reported an increase in male-male sexual assaults between fiscal year 2006 and fiscal year 2011. Yet the Army collected most of the data for its 2012 study prior to repeal, which occurred on September 20, 2011, just nine days before the end of fiscal year 2011 (Department of the Army, 2012).[8] Indeed, a comparison of pre- and post-repeal *Military Times* surveys suggests that the rate of male-male sexual assault did not increase after DADT repeal went into effect. In response to a July/August 2011 pre-repeal *Military Times* survey, 1.4% of male respondents said that they had been a victim of sexual assault while in the military, compared to 1.1% of male service members who indicated on a January 2012 post-repeal survey that they had been victimized. The pre-repeal percent of men who reported having been sexually assaulted by another man during their military service, in other words, was roughly equivalent to the post-repeal rate. On the 2009/2010 *Military Times* survey, 38 out of 1,680 heterosexual males (2.3%) reported that they were victims of sexual assault at some point during their military careers. On the 2011 survey, 14 of 984 heterosexual men (1.4%) reported victimization, and on the 2012 survey, eight out of 704 (1.1%) reported victimization (*Military Times* Poll, 2009 and 2010). These data call into question any attempt to argue that repeal has led to an increase in assaults.

No other watchdog organization or individual opponent of DADT repeal has reported any case of violence attributable to the new policy of open service. Professor Mackubin Owens, who opposes repeal and who teaches at the Naval War College, acknowledged to us that he is unaware of any violent or disciplinary incidents that can be attributed to repeal. A retired Lieutenant General who opposes repeal told us that he has "friends in the military who are disappointed" that DADT is gone but who "have not reported any specific incidences of problems" (personal correspondence, May 7, 2012). With the exception of the spurious CMR statement as well as the unconfirmed incident conveyed by OutServe's Co-Director, military leaders, opponents of DADT repeal, active-duty personnel, scholars and gay rights organizations all concur that repeal has not led to any increase in assaults. And, they agree that there has been no violence to date specifically associated with the new policy.

By contrast, some evidence suggests that, over time, repeal may lead to a decrease in violence, because DADT encouraged would-be perpetrators by dissuading some LGB victims from reporting assaults. A lesbian sailor who was raped by a fellow sailor prior to DADT repeal was smeared as someone who dressed "in four-inch heels and tight jeans who wanted it." "If I'd said I don't even sleep with men—I'm a lesbian—I'm the one who would have been out" of the military, the victim explained. Instead, the encounter was deemed consensual and the perpetrator went free (Henneberger, 2012). In an anonymous survey conducted by OutServe, another service member reported that, "back in the day 1997 I was harassed and threatened with stake knifes [sic] stabbed in my rack. I could not do or say anything to keep my job. Now I would report it no matter what." To the extent that potential perpetrators realize that LGB victims may be more likely to report assaults than would have been the case prior to repeal, the new policy could have a deterrent effect.

Despite the lack of violence associated with DADT repeal, we did find many instances in which service members expressed anti-LGB sentiment. In some cases, LGB troops took such expressions in stride. "Everyone gets bagged on for everything," according to an Air Force Special Operations navigator. "I don't take offense; I just shoot right back" (Anonymous #5, personal communication, March 22, 2012). An Army company commander who flew air assault missions in Iraq and who now teaches at a service academy said that "the only major change I see within the department is the nature of some jokes," hastening to add that he does "not feel offended at all by any of them" (Anonymous #25, personal communication, May 11, 2012). Similarly, a lesbian Air Force Reserve squadron commander told us that she does not know of "anyone who has had really adverse reactions" to people coming out, though she was aware of some people making inappropriate, "vaguely homophobic comments under their breath" (Anonymous #12, personal communication, April 21, 2012). Colonel Gus Stafford, West Point's Chief of Staff, reports that the Academy has seen "no separations" for unacceptable behavior and "no major disciplinary actions whatsoever." Pressed on whether there had been any disciplinary actions at all, he said that there were some incidents, which he called "minor in nature," involving insensitive behavior by cadets in the presence of gays or lesbians, "something like a cadet telling a gay joke in front of a gay or lesbian cadet." Colonel Stafford said that these incidents were resolved at the lowest level, by asking Respect Program staff to initiate appropriate dialogue, or by leadership correcting the inappropriate remarks on the spot. "In most cases," he said, "the cadet says, 'jeez, I didn't realize I was being insensitive'" (personal communication, April 2, 2012).

In other cases, however, expressions of anti-LGB sentiment were more severe. In response to an open-ended question asking LGBT troops whether they had experienced discrimination after DADT repeal and, if so, to describe it, 11% of respondents mentioned disturbing incidents. The question asked, "Since DADT has been repealed, have you experienced, from your commander or other service member, any forms of discrimination on the basis of sexual orientation? Please explain." OutServe administered the survey in December 2011 and 327 respondents answered the question about discrimination. Approximately 89% said they had not experienced discrimination, declined to answer or indicated that any incidents were minor. The percentages are approximate due to subjectivity in coding. For example, the response "no, one incident of minor taunting but that's it" was counted as a "no."

Some of the most serious responses included: "Every day, on every aspect of everything"; "Yes. Was told not to have any PDA with my partner at my promotion ceremony. A Lt. Col. refused to administer the oath of office at my promotion ceremony. My partner was not welcome at our unit's spouse's club"; "Commander has shown greater distance and discomfort talking to me"; "I haven't come out yet because they talk down about gays all day long ... I'm certain that if I did come out my life would be a lot harder. There is little to no tolerance in my squadron"; "One person in the office called me a 'faggot' in a non-work environment. It made the office very uncomfortable to work in because everyone knew about it and that I was extremely mad about it. The situation has not yet been resolved for three months now"; and "My senior NCO (e-8) has made repeated discriminatory remarks about the LGBT community and at myself though I'm not out" (OutServe, 2011b). In April 2012, a female officer was dancing with her girlfriend, another officer, at a military ball, when a squadron commander told the women to stop. The situation escalated and the Command Sergeant Major swore at the women, called them an "abomination," and shoved one across the floor. Reportedly the squadron commander apologized the next day and expressed support for the women's right to express themselves on equal terms with straight officers (Walkley, 2012).

Harassment, discrimination and bias remain problems in the wake of DADT repeal. That said, with the exception of isolated occurrences such as the April 2012 incident mentioned in the previous paragraph, we found no evidence suggesting that service-wide patterns of harassment are a consequence of repeal. Three points merit consideration. To begin, sexual orientation-based harassment long predated DADT repeal, so its mere existence cannot be attributed to the new policy of open service. In 2000, a Defense Department survey of 71,570 service members found that during the previous year, 37% had "witnessed or experienced an event or behavior toward a Service member that they considered to be harassment based on perceived homosexuality" (OIG, 2000). More recently, on the eve of DADT repeal, a service member reported that, "some of the senior enlisted leaders are extremely homophobic, and harass other gay people in the unit, and me to some extent" (OutServe, 2011a) The question, therefore, is not whether repeal transformed a harassment-free environment into a hostile climate, but whether military culture became more or less hostile as a result of repeal. The mere existence of post-repeal anti-gay harassment and other expressions of bias does not in and of itself indicate that any service-wide patterns of hostility are the result of the new policy.

In addition, the majority of LGB service members report that they have been treated well since DADT repeal. In response to a December 2011 OutServe survey asking how, "Post-repeal, colleagues in your unit have treated gay, lesbian, and bisexual personnel ...," 72.4% of LGBT troops indicated that they have been treated "universally with respect and without discrimination" (29%) or "generally free from discrimination with some minor exceptions" (43.4%). Out of 327 respondents, 17.4% responded "very mixed," 4% said "mostly negatively," and 6.1% did not provide an answer. It is difficult to imagine that such a large majority of LGB troops would report acceptance if DADT repeal had created a more hostile work environment.

Finally, we learned of incidents in which DADT repeal was associated with a leveling off or even a decline in harassment. In some cases LGB troops report that for the first time, they have been able to report and resolve problems openly with peers and commanders, while in other cases, the process of coming out has encouraged heterosexual service members to adjust their behavior toward greater tolerance. An Army social worker taking a class in mental health said that one classmate used anti-gay language, but that after DADT repeal he saw "a huge difference. He went from not wanting to talk to me to partnering with me on projects. He'll ask questions about what he doesn't understand" (Anonymous #9, personal communication, April 19, 2012).

Another soldier told us that in the initial period after repeal, he continued to hear derogatory language by some in his unit. Yet when he confronted them and spoke about their behavior in terms of leadership and professionalism, their conduct improved. "They don't agree, but they were willing to be professional about it," he said, referring to moral opposition to homosexuality. He said that frank discussions, which are now far less risky because of repeal, helped disabuse them of preconceived notions about gay people and that ultimately, problems were "completely resolved" through discussion of the fact that he was respected before he was out, and that nothing had changed by his acknowledgement of his sexual orientation (Anonymous #2, personal communication, April 19, 2012).

A cryptologic technician in the Navy described a scenario during training in which he was able to call someone out on his anti-gay banter, newly liberated by the policy change. "There was a new kid, a young sailor, kind of a loudmouth," he said. "I walked into the auditorium and he was looking through the pamphlet and he made a joke about the DADT policy and he didn't know I was gay so he thought it was okay to make that joke and I snapped at him. I called his name out, and said, 'shut up' and he just sunk down in his chair. I don't think he was meaning to be homophobic, just trying to be funny" (Anonymous #7, personal communication, April 20, 2012).

A Navy supply officer told us that, at her training on DADT repeal in Kuwait, there were "a few negative comments" that she summarized as reflecting "a fear that suddenly gay families would be all over the base." She said she confronted one commenter telling him his remarks were rude, and he quickly backed down (Anonymous #12, personal communication, April 21, 2012).

An enlisted soldier stationed at a military university shared a similar experience. When DADT was in effect, his unit mates often used degrading, anti-gay language, almost absent-mindedly and with little consequence. After repeal, he said, "it was kind of a big deal for two weeks," with people wondering what it would mean for people to be openly gay. But after the transition occurred and the initial questions died down, "people's consideration changed." He said the new attitude seemed to be, "now that I know someone who is [gay], I'm talking about a real person. I'm not just using abstract insults [but words] that actually mean something" (Anonymous #2, personal communication, April 19, 2012).

A chief warrant officer in the Navy said that initially she sensed "an increase of sneering jokes and stupid comments" in the aftermath of repeal, but "they faded away fairly quickly." She described the reaction of her commanding officer when she came out to him by mentioning her partner. "Clearly, he didn't want to know," she said, "but in the end, he actually asked questions and talked to me about her." She does not know how her acknowledgment will ultimately affect their working relationship, but despite some initial signals of minor discomfort, she saw no evidence of a negative impact on him "after he adjusted to the fact that I wasn't going to give him pretend answers" (Anonymous #23, personal communication, May 1, 2012).

In sum, we found no evidence suggesting that repeal has caused any increase in assaults among service members. And with respect to non-violent harassment and other expressions of bias, conclusively determining whether DADT repeal has produced a change in their frequency would require comparing pre- and post-repeal incidence rates, a task which is not possible given available data. That said, a majority of LGB service members surveyed report that they have been well-treated since DADT repeal, and many of those we interviewed believe that repeal has enabled them to resolve problems in ways that were not possible while DADT was in effect. Lawyer and researcher Sharon Terman has argued that organizations that discriminate against particular minority groups cannot eliminate harassment of those groups as long as discriminatory laws and policies remain in effect (Terman, 2004). While anti-gay harassment and bias have not disappeared from military culture, DADT repeal provides an unprecedented opportunity for individual service members as well as the Defense Department more broadly to take steps to minimize their occurrence and severity and to address those incidents that do occur in a serious way.

Morale

Morale is a catch-all term that can refer to esprit de corps, satisfaction, well-being and interpersonal adjustment, and that can be used to characterize an individual, a unit or an entire organization. The authors of a recent review of the literature on military morale define it as "motivation and enthusiasm for accomplishing mission objectives" (Britt and Dickinson, 2006). Throughout the nearly two-decade public conversation about DADT, opponents of repeal have predicted that allowing open service would harm military morale. In 1993, as the Senate debated President Clinton's proposal to allow LGB troops to serve openly, former Senator Sam Nunn said that, "in view of the unique conditions of military service, active and open homosexuality by members of the armed forces would have a very negative effect on military morale and discipline" (Healy and Tumulty, 1993). Elaine Donnelly said during 2008 testimony before the House Armed Services Committee that "introducing erotic factors into that kind of a close combat unit ... would be absolutely devastating to morale because people would have no recourse. They can't leave" (DADT hearing, 2008). Retired Marine Corps General John Sheehan and Family Research Council President Tony Perkins wrote in a 2010 Politico.com opinion piece that "sexual attraction among members of the same sex—living, exercising, fighting and training alongside one another in the closest of quarters—could devastate morale, foster heightened interpersonal tension and lead to division among those who, more than virtually any other group in society, need to act as one" (Perkins and Sheehan, 2010).

Despite such predictions, the preponderance of evidence indicates that DADT repeal produced no overall change in service-wide morale. All three measures of morale recorded on *Military Times* surveys indicate that, service-wide, morale remained constant from 2011 to 2012. Respondents to the January 2012 post-repeal survey reported approximately the same quality of life, job satisfaction and willingness to recommend a military career to someone else as respondents to the July/August 2011 pre-repeal survey. In response to a question about their overall quality of life, 68% of 2011 respondents answered that it was excellent or good (22% average, 11% fair or poor), but 71% of 2012 respondents said that it was excellent or good (20% average, 9% fair or poor). In response to a question about job satisfaction, 79% of 2011 respondents answered that they were completely or somewhat satisfied (20% completely or somewhat dissatisfied), but 87% of 2012 respondents said that they were completely or somewhat satisfied (13% completely or somewhat dissatisfied, 1% no opinion). In response to a question asking whether they would recommend a military career to others, 76% of 2011 respondents said yes (13% no, 10% undecided), but 88% of 2012 respondents said yes (8% no, 4% undecided) (*Military Times* Poll 2011 and 2012).

And, as discussed earlier in this study, post-repeal respondents were as likely to say that they planned to remain in the military for 20 years and that they would re-enlist if offered the opportunity to do so today as were pre-repeal respondents. If DADT repeal compromised morale service-wide, it would be hard to explain why, in comparing pre- and post-repeal service-wide data, quality of life, job satisfaction and willingness to recommend a military career did not decline as the new policy of open service took effect.

Although repeal did not produce any net change in service-wide morale, the new policy did lead to a decrease in personal morale for some service members and an increase for others. According to the January 2012 *Military Times* survey of 751 heterosexual, active duty and mobilized service members, 13.7% report that DADT repeal "had a negative impact on my morale," while 5.8% of all troops (LGB and heterosexual) said that it had a positive impact. A number of corroborating data points suggest that repeal decreased the individual morale of some service members. Data from the same *Military Times* survey indicate that 13.8% of heterosexual service members "continue to personally oppose the change despite my command's adoption of the new policy," and that 30.6% of all troops surveyed (32.0% of heterosexuals) disagree that "openly homosexual people should be allowed to serve in the military." This percentage is lower than in 2011 when 45.2 % of all troops surveyed disagreed with the statement. Additionally, for reasons discussed above, we believe that the 8.4% of service members who told *Military Times* that repeal has made them less likely to remain in the military constitutes evidence of disapproval of the new policy—in other words, a possible decline in morale—as opposed to concrete intentions to separate prematurely.

In our in-depth interviews, we uncovered additional evidence suggesting that DADT repeal has produced a decline in morale for some service members. According to a heterosexual Navy SEAL, "there was definitely disappointment ... we're a professional unit, we follow the Constitution and the officers appointed over us, but honestly I know that morale did go down. The way we were presented it, it was definitely disheartening. It's difficult to engage" (Anonymous #50, personal communication, April 11, 2012). And a naval intelligence officer told us that DADT repeal was "not a unit morale issue, [but] more of a service morale issue. No one blamed or found fault with the leadership at [the unit level]; more found fault with the national-level leadership who made decisions and agreed with the repeal" (Anonymous #52, personal communication, April 24, 2012).

When service members report that they do not like or are morally opposed to the new policy, that they do not believe that LGB troops should serve openly, that they plan to leave the military early, that they experience discomfort as a result of the new policy, that they disapprove of public displays of affection among LGB troops or that they blame national leaders for imposing the policy shift on the armed forces, we interpret such claims as indications that repeal may have decreased the morale of those individuals making them.

Although DADT repeal produced a decline in morale for some service members, it led to an increase for others, and the benefits of the policy shift were quite consequential for some troops, both gay and straight. An Army signals analyst told us that, "after the repeal, it was as if a huge weight was lifted off my shoulders. It was an invigorating feeling knowing that there was nothing left to hide" (Anonymous #28, personal communication, April 30, 2012). A gay enlisted soldier told us that "as far as morale goes, now nobody has to worry about getting kicked out for it, so my morale has gone way up in that aspect" (Anonymous #2, personal communication, April 19, 2012).

Jim Parco, who served in the Air Force for twenty years and taught leadership strategy at the U.S. Air Force Academy and Air Command and Staff College, told us that "the fact that we've actually instilled this new sense of integrity into the service by the repeal of the law has been the biggest impact, but it's completely unobservable unless you actually talk to these individuals who were oppressed one on one. If you ask them, they'll unequivocally tell you that 'absolutely it has fundamentally changed my life, my view of the military, my existence; I just feel like a revived person, something is very, very different.'" Professor Parco added that many LGB troops were surprised about the difference repeal made to them: "Most of the people were shocked that it would actually impact them internally," he said. "Very few realized the kind of internal impact it would have and how they would feel after" the change. "It fundamentally changed their view of how they saw themselves in terms of the organization" (personal communication, March 13, 2012).

Some heterosexual troops have experienced positive improvements to their morale as well, and in some cases the increases have been significant. Repeal brought one heterosexual Navy officer "a sense of relief" because remaining ignorant about a service member's life "affects leadership in a big way" (Anonymous #56, personal communication, May 7, 2012). A gay Navy linguist observed that the new openness was helpful to leaders, saying that, "I think my supervisor really appreciated the candor" (Anonymous #7, personal communication, April 20, 2012). And a gay enlisted soldier explained how repeal lifted a burden off his heterosexual peers. Some of his friends told him that, had they known he was gay while DADT was still in place, they would have kept his secret but that doing so would have caused added stress. "If people had found out, they'd have tried to keep it on the down-low because they don't want to see their buddy get kicked out for something stupid like that," he said. Now, "it's not an issue anymore," he said. "I'm not worried about being open about it, so I think morale overall for everybody has gone up" (Anonymous #2, personal communication, April 19, 2012).

Although the 5.8% of LGB and heterosexual troops who told *Military Times* that repeal had a positive effect on their morale is less than the 13.7% of heterosexuals who reported a decline, evidence suggests that in most cases of decline, the decrease consisted of minor disappointment. As discussed in a subsequent section of this report, even among opponents of DADT repeal, the percent of service members who feel strongly about the issue is low. Among chaplains as well, evidence suggests that any decrease in morale that followed from DADT repeal was minor. Professor George Reed, the former director of Command and Leadership Studies at the Army War College, acknowledges a sense of "simmering out there by fundamentalist religious groups, Evangelical Christians perhaps, that are seeing [DADT repeal] as some sort of continuing moral collapse." That said, when Professor Reed delivered a recent presentation to active-duty chaplains in San Diego, the issue of LGB service "just didn't come up" (personal communication, March 19, 2012). We found no evidence that service members suffered a significant decline in morale in any sustained way due to the policy change.

The new policy of open service produced a decrease in morale for a small minority of service members, and enhanced the morale of an even smaller minority. Yet few of those troops who experienced a decline in morale appear to have suffered any measurable consequences. This should come as no surprise, as the extensive scholarly literature on the determinants of military morale does not mention the presence or absence of LGB colleagues (Britt and Dickinson, DATE, pp 164–73). By contrast, for some of those whose morale improved, a "huge weight was lifted off" their shoulders. And service-wide, time-series data discussed above indicate that morale did not decline as the new policy of open service took effect. In contrast to some media reports during the Iraq War, perceptions of organizational morale were exceptionally high among soldiers in Iraq (see Ender, 2009). Our conclusion is that repeal led to an increase in morale for some service members and a decrease for others, and that because the positive and negative consequences of the policy shift roughly balanced one another, no net service-wide change in morale resulted from repeal.

DISCUSSION

Our findings about DADT repeal are consistent with the extensive literature on the more than two dozen foreign militaries that have allowed LGB troops to serve openly. According to that literature, none of the foreign militaries that has enacted policies of open service have suffered a decline in overall readiness or any of its component dimensions including cohesion, recruitment, retention, assaults, harassment or morale. Studies have been conducted by a wide range of scholars and organizations including the Pentagon's Comprehensive Review Working Group and the Rand Corporation (National Defense Research Institute, 1993, 2010; U.S. Department of Defense, 2010). Since the Dutch military became the first to allow open service in 1974, no scholar has documented any decline in readiness or its component dimensions that could be attributable to the lifting of a ban on LGB troops by any foreign military.[3]

In the U.S. case, the success of DADT repeal most likely should be attributed to the Pentagon's carefully-designed implementation and training process, as well as four additional factors (for details on the implementation and training process, see DOD, 2010). First, there was no wave of mass disclosures after repeal, and only 19.4% of 751 heterosexual service members surveyed by *Military Times* indicated that after repeal, someone in their unit disclosed being LGB or that an LGB service member joined their unit (*Military Times* Poll, 2012). While 51.2% of LGB troops surveyed by OutServe said that they have come out to more people in the military after repeal, LGB service members constitute only 2% of all troops. And in the same survey, only 32.4% of LGB troops said that in the aftermath of repeal, they are now out to most or all of their unit (OutServe, 2011b).

Second, LGB as well as heterosexual troops have continued to emphasize professionalism. Among LGB service members, those who acknowledged their orientation before or after repeal have continued to behave professionally. A Navy supply officer who deployed on a submarine to Afghanistan said that "most gay people handled themselves very professionally. You didn't have people running in the streets in tutus and there was no base-wide fanfare. It [DADT repeal] ended up being like any other day. Most people didn't even realize it was going on that day, unless I told them" (Anonymous #12, personal communication, April 21, 2012). Among heterosexuals, even those service members who oppose repeal have conducted themselves in a professional manner. A heterosexual Army Reserve chaplain noted that "anyone who might have been inclined to have a negative reaction knew it would be bad to express publicly—bad for their career, so now it's not part of their 'official persona.' They keep it professional" (Anonymous #45, personal communication, April 2, 2012). And a gay Air Force combat crew evaluator confirmed that, "I don't doubt that various people disapprove personally, but they don't let it affect their interactions with me. I've been consistently overwhelmed by how little its affected peoples' treatment of me" (Anonymous #27, personal communication, May 12, 2012).

Third, prior to the enactment of the new policy, only a small minority of those who opposed repeal felt strongly about the issue. In 2003, retired General Wesley Clark explained that the "temperature of the issue has changed over the decade. People were much more irate about this issue in the early '90s than I found in the late '90s, for whatever reason, younger people coming in [to the military]. It just didn't seem to be the same emotional hot button issue by '98, '99, that it had been in '92, '93" (*Meet the Press*, 2003). A 2006 Zogby poll of 545 troops who had fought in Iraq and Afghanistan found that 72 percent were personally comfortable interacting with gays, and that of the 20 percent who were uncomfortable, only five percent were "very" uncomfortable. Many of the experts and service members we interviewed and surveyed confirmed that even among those active-duty personnel who oppose DADT repeal, few feel strongly about it. As one heterosexual cadet who had an LGB roommate observed, "people in our generation, when it comes down to the troop level, really don't think it is that big of a deal" (Anonymous #60, personal communication, May 17, 2012).

Fourth, some service members who strongly opposed DADT repeal prior to the enactment of the new policy had never knowingly served alongside LGB peers, and their concerns may have been based, in part, on expectations of what would occur after repeal rather than actual experiences of serving alongside LGB troops. Two of us observed recently that, "for many straight people, the ability to truly get to know the gay men and lesbians in their units was stifled by the secrecy mandated by DADT" (Samuels and Packard, 2012). And, the Pentagon's 2010 report on DADT confirmed that those who believed that there were no LGB service members in their units were the most likely to believe that repeal would undermine readiness (U.S. Department of Defense, 2010, p. 73). When those who opposed repeal and who did not know any LGB peers had a chance to interact knowingly with gays and lesbians after the policy transition, attitudes may have shifted in some cases. Herek and Belkin note that, "knowing an openly gay person is predictive of supportive attitudes even in demographic groups where hostility is the norm ... Thus, negative attitudes toward gay men and lesbians are likely to be reduced to the extent that working relationships develop between heterosexual and gay personnel" (2006, p. 134).

It is likely that these four factors, along with the Pentagon's careful preparation for repeal, help explain why the preponderance of evidence indicates that the new policy of open service has not compromised readiness or its component parts including cohesion, recruitment/retention, assaults/harassment or morale.

VALIDITY

While no research strategy is perfect, our use of multiple methods including in-depth interviews, on-site field observations, surveys, content analysis and quasi-experimentation is both comprehensive as well as consistent with social scientific best practices. Nevertheless, observers have raised two points about the absence of evidence suggesting that repeal has compromised military readiness.

Elaine Donnelly has attributed positive reports about DADT repeal to a gag rule imposed by the Obama administration. She said that many troops oppose working with gay peers "but fear speaking out about it" because of a "zero tolerance" policy "against persons who are not enthusiastic supporters of [the] LGBT law" (UPI, 2012). To the extent that such a gag rule exists, either formally or informally, our results would be biased, according to this critique, by subjects' unwillingness to provide and discuss data indicating that DADT repeal has been problematic. We were not, however, able to find any evidence that such a zero tolerance policy was imposed by the White House, Pentagon or any other government office or official, either formally or informally. To the contrary, service members who opposed repeal or who were disappointed that the change had not gone further in extending equal treatment to LGB troops expressed those sentiments openly on *Military Times* surveys and during our interviews.

Some experts have claimed that insufficient time has passed to assess the impact of DADT repeal. Naval War College Professor Mackuban Owens told us that "it will take some time before we really know what's going on." He added that, "we're not even talking about a year here, and that's just the change in the law. The implementation is going to take much longer, and I think that there is going to be some adjustment period. For better or worse it is going to take some time to see whether the worst-case situation predicted by people like myself, or the less problematic situation is going to be the outcome. We just won't know for a while" (personal communication, April 24, 2012). When asked when he thought the effects of repeal might manifest themselves, he stated, "I think at least a year, but more likely two years. I think especially for male homosexuals they will likely keep it where it is, the same as it was with 'don't ask, don't tell.'" Several other experts expressed similar points of view. Elaine Donnelly said that "it is too soon, however, to draw conclusions about the consequences of the LGBT law and related policies for most people in the military" (Donnelly, 2012). She added that, "I've heard from military people who have no way of registering what they feel about this. They're just quietly leaving, but they're not leaving right away" (Standifer, 2012).

We agree that it is not yet possible to tell the complete story of DADT repeal, as some important issues remain unresolved. If and when the Defense Department allows same-sex partners or spouses to live in on-base housing, for example, some worry that this could incite resentment among heterosexual families. In previous instances of minority integration, problems have emerged long after initial policy transitions. Two decades after President Harry Truman's 1948 order that forced the military to change from a separate-and-unequal to separate-but-equal standard, the armed forces were plagued by violent racial tension during the Vietnam War. Yet two factors distinguish racial integration in previous generations from LGB service today: (1) U.S. troops were already serving alongside LGB colleagues before repeal; (2) comfort levels with LGB people as well as support for openly gay service are far higher today than were comfort levels and support for racial integration during the period from World War II through the Vietnam War. These differences make it highly unlikely that tensions associated with racial integration are the correct model for predicting long-term consequences of DADT repeal.

Yet there is little merit to the claim that insufficient time has passed to assess the impact of DADT repeal. Opponents who predicted that DADT repeal would undermine the military rarely said that time would have to pass before negative consequences would emerge, and usually implied that the onset of at least some dire consequences would be immediate. Now that Pentagon leaders have indicated an absence of difficulties, however, opponents are starting to emphasize the possibility of future, long-term problems that will only emerge in the distant wake of repeal.

If repeal were going to cause adjustment problems, at least some of those problems—or indications of their imminence—should have emerged in the immediate wake of the policy transition, when a culture shock was still possible. With respect to retention, for example, some individuals may plan to leave the military at some future date as a result of DADT repeal, as Donnelly suggests. But if DADT repeal posed a serious threat to retention, the exodus should already be at least somewhat apparent in retention data, as it is unlikely that a retention problem resulting from a policy change would go from negligible to full-throttled overnight, at some point well past the implementation of the change.

As the new, post-repeal policy continues to settle, the logic sustaining concerns about future problems becomes increasingly tenuous. Predictions of immediate problems have not been borne out in the U.S. experience, and readiness was not compromised either in the short term or the long term in foreign militaries that have allowed LGB troops to serve openly. While ongoing monitoring may be warranted, there is no reason to believe that DADT repeal will lead to any future decline in readiness.

CONCLUSION

The release of this study coincides with the one-year anniversary of the repeal of DADT. Based on the substantial evidence we gathered, we conclude that, during this one-year period, DADT repeal has had no negative impact on overall military readiness or its component parts: unit cohesion, recruitment, retention, assaults, harassment or morale. While repeal produced a few downsides for some military members—mostly those who personally opposed the policy change—we identified important upsides as well, and in no case did negative consequences outweigh advantages. On balance, DADT repeal appears to have slightly enhanced the military's ability to do its job by clearing away unnecessary obstacles to the development of trust and bonding.

We base our conclusions on data we uncovered via ten research strategies that we designed to maximize the likelihood of uncovering evidence suggesting that DADT repeal has compromised military readiness. While no research strategy is perfect, our reliance on multiple methods including surveys, in-depth interviews, on-site field observations, content analysis, secondary source analysis and quasi-experimentation is both comprehensive and consistent with social scientific best practices, lending confidence to the validity of our conclusions. Our vigorous effort to collect data from opponents of DADT repeal, including anti-repeal generals and admirals, activists, academic experts, service members and watchdog organizations, should also sustain confidence in the validity and impartiality of our findings.

Although the story of DADT repeal will continue to unfold over time, available evidence indicates that in its first year, DADT repeal has not had any overall negative effect on the armed forces, and that predictions of dire consequences were incorrect.

NOTES

1. To protect respondents' identities and to ensure confidentiality, we do not identify demographic or professional details of any service member.

2. We asked the post-repeal cohort to rank their units' morale, but neglected to ask the pre-repeal cohort to do so.

3. *Military Times* also asked what impact DADT repeal had on respondents' units, and 2.4% indicated a major impact, 9.6% reported some impact, 13.7% said there was a minor impact and 74.3% responded that there was no impact. As explained in our appendix on standards of evidence, we did not focus on these data because the question did not allow respondents to specify whether the impact of DADT repeal was negative or positive.

4. Significance: $p<.01$.

5. Although this paper was completed before repeal, Ender and his colleagues have collected additional data in 2012, and those data confirm that post-repeal, academy as well as ROTC cadets have become more tolerant of LGB peers.

6. Percentages do not add up to 100 due to rounding error.

7. We contacted Ms. Richeson after the release of the March recruiting and retention data, which also indicated that ANG was the only component to miss its accession goals, reaching 95% of its target, as would subsequently be the case in May.

8. The report notes that "victims may be more likely to report sexual offenses in the absence of the former Don't Ask, Don't Tell policy."

REFERENCES

Alexander, Keith. (2012, May 16). Prosecutor Says Marine Fatal Stabbing Was a Hate Crime. *Washington Post*.

Baldor, Lolita. (2012, May 22). US Army More Selective on Recruits, Re-enlistments. *Associated Press*.

Banks, Adelle. (2011, March 25). Army Readies Chaplains Before "Don't Ask" Repeal. *USA Today*.

Belkin, Aaron. (2003, Summer). Don't Ask, Don't Tell: Is the Gay Ban Based on Military Necessity? *Parameters*, Vol. 33, No. 2. 108–119.

Belkin, Aaron. (2008). "Don't Ask, Don't Tell": Does the Gay Ban Undermine the Military's Reputation? *Armed Forces & Society*, Vol. 34, No. 2. 276–291.

Boyer, Dave. (2012, February 10). Public "Readily Accepts" Rights for Gays, Obama Tells Donors. *The Washington Times*.

Boyer, Dave. (2012, February 9). Public "Readily Accepts" Rights for Gays, Obama Tells Donors. *Washington Times*.

Britt, Thomas W., & Dickinson, James M. (2006). Morale during Military Operations: A Positive Psychology Approach. In Thomas W. Britt, Carl Castro & Amy B. Adler (Eds.), *Military Life: The Psychology of Serving in Peace and Combat*, 1. Westport: Praeger.

Brown, Matthew Hay. (2012, May 20). A Smooth Turn from "Don't Ask, Don't Tell." *Baltimore Sun*.

Center for Military Readiness. (2009). Flag & General Officers for the Military. Retrieved from http://www.flagandgeneralofficersforthemilitary.com/.

Center for Military Readiness. (2012, May 16). Early Consequences of Military LGBT Law. Retrieved from http://cmrlink.org/HMilitary.asp?docID=417.

Crary, David. (2012, July 5). Chaplains Adjust to Lifting of Ban on Gays. *Associated Press*.

Donnelly, Elaine. (2009, January 2). Military Times Poll: Troops Oppose Gay Agenda for the Military. *National Review Online*.

Donnelly, Elaine. (2012, May 16). Early Consequences of Military LGBT Law. Weblog. Retrieved from http://www.cmrlink.org/HMilitary.asp?docID=417, accessed August 21, 2012.

Ender, Morten G. (2009). *American Soldiers in Iraq: McSoldiers or Innovative Professionals?* New York: Routledge.

Ender, Morten G., Rohall, David E., Brennan, Andrew J., Matthews, Michael D., & Smith, Irving. (2012, January). Civilian, ROTC, and Military Academy Undergraduate Attitudes toward Homosexuals in the U.S. Military. *Armed Forces & Society*, Vol. 38, No. 1. 164–172.

Frank, Nathaniel, et al. (2010). Gays in foreign militaries 2010: A global primer. *Palm Center*. Retrieved from http://bit.ly/f5JyAb.

Frank, Nathaniel. (2009). *Unfriendly Fire: How the Gay Ban Undermines the Military and Weakens America*. New York: St. Martin's Press.

Gaffney Jr., Frank J. (2011, June 13). Gates' Choice: Defense Secretary Should Not Certify Military Readiness for Homosexuals. *Washington Times*.

Garamone, Jim. (2012, March 16). Navy Leader Calls "Don't Ask" Repeal "Non-story." *American Forces Press Service*.

Gates, Gary J. (2007, March). Retention among Lesbian, Gay, and Bisexual Military Personnel. *The Williams Institute*. Retrieved from http://williamsinstitute.law.ucla.edu/wp-content/uploads/Gates-EffectsOfDontAskDontTellOnRetention-Mar-2007.pdf

General Accounting Office. (1993). Homosexuals in the Military: Policies and Practices of Foreign Countries. Washington: General Accounting Office.

Goldman, Michael. (2012, February 26). Everything's Quite Right with Santorum. *Lowell Sun*.

Headquarters, Department of the Army. (2012). 2020 Generating Health & Discipline in the Force Ahead of the Strategic Reset; Report 2012. 122.

Healy, Melissa, & Tumulty, Karen. (1993, January 28). Aides Say Clinton to End Prosecution of Military's Gays. *Los Angeles Times*.

Henneberger, Melinda. (2012, May 9). Military Assault Victims Find their Voice. *Washington Post*.

Herek, Gregory M. and Belkin, Aaron. (2006). Sexual Orientation and Military Service: Prospects for Organizational and Individual Change in the United States. In Thomas W. Britt, Carl Castro & Amy B. Adler (Eds.), *Military Life: The Psychology of Serving in Peace and Combat,* 4. Westport: Praeger. 134.

Johnson, Chris. (2012, February 9). Obama Raises $1.4 Million at D.C. LGBT Fundraiser. *Washington Blade*.

Kaplan, Danny & Rosenmann, Amir. (2012). Unit Social Cohesion in the Israeli Military as a Case Study of "Don't Ask, Don't Tell." *Political Psychology*, Vol. 33, No. 4, 419–436.

MacCoun, Robert, Kier, Elizabeth, & Belkin, Aaron. (2006). Does Social Cohesion Determine Motivation In Combat? An Old Question with an Old Answer. *Armed Forces & Society*, Vol. 32, No. 4, 646–654.

McAvoy, Audrey. (2012, March 2). Homecoming Marine Wanted to Show Partner His Love. *Associated Press*.

Mulrine, Anna. (2012, May 10). Panetta: No Hitches in Military's Repeal of "Don't Ask, Don't Tell." *Christian Science Monitor*.

National Defense Research Institute. (1993). *Sexual Orientation and U.S. Military Personnel Policy: Options and Assessment*. Santa Monica: RAND. 65–105.

National Defense Research Institute. (2010). *Sexual Orientation and U.S. Military Personnel Policy: An Update of RAND's 1993 Study*. Santa Monica: RAND. 275–320.

Office of the Inspector General, U.S. Department of Defense. (2000, March 16). Military Environment with Respect to the Homosexual Conduct Policy. 4.

Orvis, Bruce R., & Asch, Beth J. (2001). *Military Recruiting: Trends, Outlook, and Implications*. Santa Monica: RAND.

Parrish, Karen. (2012, May 10). Report Shows Success of "Don't Ask, Don't Tell" Repeal. *American Forces Press Service*.

Pattavina, Vincent. (2003, December 30). Retired Navy Officer Opposes Gays in Military. *Patriot Ledger*.

Perkins, Tony, & Sheehan, John. (2010, June 15). A Charade with Consequences. *Politico*.

Policy Concerning Homosexuality in the Armed Forces § 10 U.S.C. 654 (1993). Pub. L. No. 103-160, div. A, title V, Sec. 571(a)(1), Nov. 30, 1993, 107 Stat. 1670 (1993).

Rodgers, Sam. (2006, December). Opinions of Military Personnel on Sexual Minorities in the Military. *Zogby International*. Retrieved from http://www.palmcenter.org/files/active/1/ZogbyReport.pdf.

Russert, Tim [moderator]. (2003, June 15). Meet the Press. [Television broadcast]. *NBC*.

Samuel, Stephanie. (2011, February 17). Military Chaplains: We've Been Counseling Gay Soldiers. *Christian Post Reporter*.

Samuels, Steven M., & Packard, Col. Gary A. (2012, February 6). Repeal of DADT Makes the Military Stronger. *Air Force Times*, Vol. 24.

Schofield, Matthew. (2012, April 3). Impact of Ending Military's "Don't Ask, Don't Tell" Law Negligible. *McClatchy Newpapers*.

Spagat, Elliot. (2010, November 6). Amos: Wrong Time to Overturn DADT. *Associated Press*.

Sprigg, Peter. (2010, May). Homosexual Assault in the Military. *Insight*.

Standifer, Cid. (2012, March 12). Survey: DADT repeal has less impact than expected. *Military Times*.

Standifer, Cid. (2012). Military Times Poll. *Military Times*. Retrieved from http://militarytimes.com/projects/polls/.

Terman, Sharon. (2004, May). The Practical and Conceptual Problems with Regulating Harassment in a Discriminatory Institution. *Palm Center*. Retrieved from http://www.palmcenter.org/files/active/0/200405_Terman.pdf.

Tetlock, Philip E., & Levi, Ariel. (1982, January). Attribution bias: On the Inconclusiveness of the Cognition-Motivation Debate. *Journal of Experimental Social Psychology*, Vol. 18, No. 1, 68–88.

U.S. Department of Defense, Office of the Secretary of Defense. (1993, July 1). Summary Report of the Military Working Group.

U.S. Department of Defense. (2010, November 30). Report of the Comprehensive Review of the Issues Associated with a Repeal of "Don't Ask, Don't Tell."

U.S. Department of Defense. (2010, November 30). Support Plan for Implementation; Report of the Comprehensive Review of the Issues Associated with a Repeal of "Don't Ask, Don't Tell."

U.S. Department of Defense. (2012, June 29). DoD Announces Recruiting and Retention Numbers for Fiscal 2012, through May. Retrieved from http://www.defense.gov/releases/release.aspx?releaseid=15418.

United Press International Staff Writer. (2012, March 20). "Don't Ask, Don't Tell" Repeal Going Well. *United Press International*.

United States. Congress. House of Representatives. Committee on Armed Services, Subcommittee on Personnel. (2008). *Statement of Brian Jones, U.S. House of Representatives, One Hundred Tenth Congress, second session, July 23, 2008*. Washington: Government Printing Office.

United States. Congress. House of Representatives. Committee on Armed Services, Subcommittee on Personnel. (2008). *Testimony of Gary J. Gates, U.S. House of Representatives, One Hundred Tenth Congress, second session, July 18, 2008*. Washington: Government Printing Office.

United States. Congress. Senate. Committee on Armed Services. (1993). *Policy Concerning Homosexuality in the Armed Forces: Hearing Before the Committee on Armed Services, Testimony of Norman Schwarzkopf, U.S. Senate, One Hundred*

Third Congress, second session, May 11, 2008. Washington: Government Printing Office.

United States. Congress. Senate. Committee on Armed Services. (1993). *Policy Concerning Homosexuality in the Armed Forces: Hearing Before the Committee on Armed Services, Testimony of Frederick Peck, U.S. Senate, One Hundred Third Congress, second session, May 11, 2008.* Washington: Government Printing Office.

Walkley, A.J. (2012, April 20). Command Sergeant Major Allegedly Assaults Lesbian Captain at Military Ball. *Huffington Post.*

Warner, John T., & Asch, Beth J. (1995). *The Economics of Military Manpower.* In Keith Hartley and Todd Sandler (Eds.), *Handbook of Defense Economics*, 1. Amsterdam: Elsevier. 348–398.

Will, Alan. (2012, February). DADT and Military Effectiveness: Moving Forward. *Marine Corps Gazette.* 32–37.

Young, Paul. (2010, October 14). Government Asks Judge to Stay Injunction Against "Don't Ask, Don't Tell." *City News Service.*

APPENDICES

APPENDICES

APPENDIX A

Recommendations for post-DADT health care systems serving LGBT veterans

1. Resources for LGBT veterans include:
   a. LGBT local resource binder (decrease isolation and increase community integration);
   b. video and text library (increase knowledge and pride about LGBT vets in history);
   c. safe VA/clinical space campaign (increased engagement in treatment); and
   d. LGBT veteran support groups (decrease isolation, increase community integration).
2. Resources for staff (improved patient and employee satisfaction ratings) include:
   a. training: bio-psychosocial impacts of DADT, upgrading DADT discharges, LGBT-affirmative practice, history and current best practices of LGBT mental health care, minority stress model, LGBT-related VA directives, LGBT veteran culture and sources of resilience, "Get Your Questions Answered About Sexual Orientation and Gender Identity from Colleagues Not Clients";
   b. gay-straight alliance for staff.
3. Nursing patient care recommendations include assessments, discharge planning, engaging care givers, and family members.
4. Create a list of LGBT practitioners throughout VA for LGBT-affirmative "warm hand-off" referrals and role out trainings to key players: Operation Enduring Freedom and Operation Iraqi Freedom [OEF/OIF] case managers, addiction treatment services, trauma recovery program, etc. per prevalence rates in LGBT research (improved continuity of care and clinical outcomes).
5. Support LGBT veteran organic social networks (e.g., online support group and chat rooms) and create an LGBT veteran peer support program.
6. Have flexibility in program policies with substance use and abuse and psychiatric diagnoses due to higher prevalence rates among LGBT people.
7. Refer to veterans and their relations as veterans define themselves (in conversation and charting). Create opportunities for veterans to come out to medical providers whether in medicine or mental health.
8. Provide LGBT-affirmative couples and family counseling. Respect LGBT partners with the full range of accommodations given heterosexual partners in hospital situations.
9. Conduct VA outreach online and at community LGBT Pride and veteran events.

10. Conduct an LGBT-affirmative VA public relations campaign, targeting addiction treatment services, trauma recovery program, and mental health clinics, etc.
11. Review all departments within the healthcare system for unique needs of LGBT veterans (e.g., adult day health care, assisted residential living programs, intensive care units, and emergency departments).
12. Know your environment, if you are concerned that community members may be upset about an LGBT group at the VA, seek support from campus administrators and police to ensure that the group is not interrupted or harassed.
13. Ask participants when and where they would be most comfortable and able to attend group (i.e., in the evenings when they won't be seen by others, off VA grounds, etc.).

APPENDIX B – STANDARDS OF EVIDENCE

We used 11 standards to evaluate the relevance and quality of each piece of data we found, and to decide how much weight (or value) to give it in informing our conclusions. Because we are most interested in data suggesting that repeal has harmed the military, we included almost all such evidence in our report even if it was of low quality. By contrast, because most of the data we collected suggests that repeal did not harm the military, only a fraction of such evidence appears in the report. Because our evidentiary standards are not absolute, they should be thought of as guidelines that help determine how much credibility to attach to each data point, not strict rules. To arrive at our overall findings, we used a preponderance-of-evidence standard, meaning that we weighed the quality and quantity of evidence sustaining each hypothesis before reaching a conclusion.

1) <u>Clarity</u>. We assigned less weight to data whose meaning was unclear, such as results of a *Military Times* survey that asked respondents to indicate whether repeal had an impact on their unit, but did not allow them to say whether the impact was positive or negative.
2) <u>Specificity</u>. We assigned less weight to data whose meaning was vague, such as responses to a *Military Times* survey question that asked whether repeal had a negative impact on respondents, but did not allow them to indicate whether the impact referred to cohesion, morale or other factors.
3) <u>Relevance</u>. We assigned less weight to data whose relevance could not be established, such as the stabbing of a Marine by another Marine, because it was unclear whether the perpetrator perceived the victim to be gay, and if so, if he was motivated by DADT repeal.
4) <u>Source bias</u>. We assigned more weight to assessments of scholarly experts such as Naval War College professor Mackubin Owens than to activists or elected officials.
5) <u>Representativeness</u>. We assigned less weight to data that were unrepresentative of underlying populations, such as responses to a Palm Center survey administered to a sample that had a higher proportion of LGB troops than there are in the overall military population.
6) <u>Logical consistency</u>. We assigned less weight to claims that were logically implausible, such as a Center for Military Readiness suggestion that a reported increase in male-male rape between 2006 and 2011 shows that DADT repeal caused a rise in violence, because the report was based on data collected through September 29, 2011, just nine days after DADT repeal.
7) <u>Temporal consistency</u>. We assigned less weight to claims that were temporally inconsistent, such as reports of a post-repeal decline in cohesion

by some service members who, when asked for clarification, referred to the possibility of future problems.
8) <u>Evidentiary consistency</u>. We assigned more weight to evidence that was consistent with a range of other data points than to outliers.
9) <u>Methodological consistency</u>. We assigned more weight to data derived from multiple methodological approaches, such as interviews, surveys and field observations, than to data emerging from just one approach.
10) <u>Base-rate sensitivity</u>. We assigned more weight to data whose value could be measured and compared before and after DADT repeal.
11) <u>Observer proximity</u>. We assigned more weight to interpretations provided by participants in events than by observers who formed their conclusions on the basis of second-hand information.

APPENDIX C – LETTER TO 553 RETIRED GENERALS AND ADMIRALS

PALM CENTER
BLUEPRINTS FOR SOUND PUBLIC POLICY

[Date]
Dear [Title/Name],

As members of a research team with the Palm Center, a research center at the University of California, Los Angeles, we are writing to you because we have identified you as a retired U.S. military officer who may have input to offer about the repeal of the "don't ask, don't tell" policy.

As you may know, that repeal took effect on September 20, 2011. The Palm Center is now conducting a major study of the impact of the repeal. In order to conduct as broad and as thorough a study as possible on the impact of repeal, we are seeking input from a wide variety of experts and interested parties, and would appreciate your help. We plan to incorporate into our conclusions any verifiable evidence of any impact of repeal on military readiness. We're hoping you might agree to share your thoughts on this matter with our researchers, including knowledge you may have or stories you may have heard that may speak to this issue.

It would be very helpful to us to be able to speak with you, whether or not you are directly aware of evidence about the impact of repeal. If you are willing to talk with our researchers, please **contact Dr. Stacie R. Furia** using any of the contact information listed below. She will set up a brief interview with a member of our research team, which you can expect will take about ten to fifteen minutes.

Thank you for your consideration on this important matter. We are sure you will agree that assessing this significant change in personnel regulations is a worthy subject for academic research, and we sincerely hope you are able to add your voice to this study.

Sincerely,
The "Don't Ask, Don't Tell" Repeal Impact Research Team
Palm Center, UCLA School of Law

APPENDIX D – DADT REPEAL OPPONENTS CONTACTED

Mr. James Bowman, Resident Scholar, Ethics and Public Policy Center

Capt. Chad C. Carter, U.S. Air Force

Lt. Col. Daniel L. Davis, U.S. Army

Elaine Donnelly, President, Center for Military Readiness

Frank J. Gaffney Jr., President, Center for Security Policy

Representative Duncan Hunter (R-CA)

Representative Darrell Issa (R-CA)

SFC Brandon Johnson, U.S. Army

SGM Brian Jones, U.S. Army (ret.)

Maj. Antony Barone Kolenc, U.S. Air Force

Andrea Lafferty, Executive Director, Traditional Values Coalition

Lt. Col. Robert Maginnis, U.S. Army (ret.), Senior Fellow, Family Research Council

Lt. Col. Brian Maue, U.S. Air Force

Senator John McCain (R-AZ)

Professor Eugene Milhizer, Ave Maria School of Law

Professor Mackuban Thomas Owens, Naval War College

Tony Perkins, President, Family Research Council

Col. Ronald Ray, U.S. Army (ret.), former Deputy Assistant Secretary of Defense

Peter Sprigg, Senior Fellow, Family Research Institute

Maj. Melissa Wells-Petry, U.S. Army (ret.)

Capt. Tierney A. Williams, Department of Military Science, Central Michigan University

Professor William A. Woodruff, Campbell University

APPENDIX E – WATCHDOG ORGANIZATIONS CONTACTED

Anti-repeal groups and veterans service organizations

American Legion
AMVETS
Center for Military Readiness
Center for Security Policy
Family Research Council
Military Officers Association of America
Reserve Officers Association
Traditional Values Coalition
Veterans of Foreign Wars

Pro-repeal groups

American Military Partners Association
American Veterans for Equal Rights
Blue Alliance
Knights Out
Military Partners and Families Coalition
OutServe
Servicemembers Legal Defense Network
Servicemembers United
USNA Out

APPENDIX F – SCHOLARS & EXPERTS INTERVIEWED

Col. Charles D. Allen, USA (ret.), U.S. Army War College

Professor John Beckman, United States Naval Academy

Dr. Nora Bensahel, Center for a New American Security

Professor Allyson Booth, United States Naval Academy

Lt. Col David Boxwell, USAF (ret.)

Dr. Martin L. Cook, U.S. Naval War College

Colonel Martin France, U.S. Air Force Academy

Professor Todd S. Garth, United States Naval Academy

Col. Stephen J. Gerras, USA (ret.), U.S. Army War College

Dr. Jay Goodwin, U.S. Army Research Institute

Professor David Kaiser, U.S. Naval War College

Dr. Lawrence Korb, Center for American Progress

Professor David A. Levy, U.S. Air Force Academy

Lt. Col. James E. Parco, USAF (ret.), Colorado College

Col. George Reed, USA (ret.), University of San Diego

Col. Charles Stafford, United States Military Academy

Professor John Allen Williams, Loyola University Chicago

Professor Erik Wingrove-Haugland, United States Coast Guard Academy

APPENDIX G – SERVICE MEMBER INTERVIEWS

	Branch	Rank	Occupation	Sexual Orientation
1	Navy	Petty Officer 1st Class	nuclear technician	LGB
2	Army	Specialist	line medic	LGB
3	Air Force	Technical Sergeant	nuclear weapons	LGB
4	Marines	Captain	logistics officer	LGB
5	Air Force	Captain	navigator	LGB
6	Army	Lieutenant Colonel	public affairs	LGB
7	Navy	Sergeant First Class	linguist/cryptologic	LGB
8	Air Force	Major	political-military affairs	LGB
9	Army	Second Lieutenant	nuclear counterproliferation	LGB
10	Army	Staff Sergeant	nurse	LGB
11	Air Force	Major	force support officer	LGB
12	Navy	Lieutenant	supply officer	LGB
13	Army	Captain	signal officer	LGB
14	Navy	Petty Officer 1st Class	public affairs	LGB
15	Navy	Captain	judge advocate	LGB
16	Navy	Lieutenant Commander	aviator	LGB
17	Army	Captain	administrative law	LGB
18	Air Force	Chief Master Sergeant	medical logistics	LGB
19	Army	Second Lieutenant	military police	LGB
20	Army	Cadet Corporal	cadet	LGB
21	Navy	Captain	aviator	LGB
22	Army	Sergeant First Class	small group instructor	LGB
23	Navy	CW02	special evaluator	LGB
24	Air Force	Technical Sergeant	resource coordinator	LGB

GOVERNMENT POLICY TOWARDS HOMOSEXUALITY IN THE US MILITARY

25	Army	Major	social worker	LGB
26	Navy	Sergeant	hospital corpsman	LGB
27	Air Force	First Lieutenant	combat deputy evaluator	LGB
28	Army	Specialist	signals analyst	LGB
29	Army	Staff Sergeant	mortuary affairs	LGB
30	Air Force	Sergeant First Class	none given	LGB
31	Navy	Lieutenant	intelligence officer	LGB
32	Air Force	Technical Sergeant	intelligence analyst	LGB
33	Air Force	Captain	aerospace engineer	LGB
34	Air Force	Staff Sergeant	aerospace craftsman	LGB
35	Army	Specialist	mechanic	LGB
36	Army	Staff Sergeant	cavalry scout	LGB
37	Air Force	Senior Airman	military police	LGB
38	Army	Sergeant First Class	motor sergeant	Heterosexual
39	Air Force	Captain	doctor	Heterosexual
40	Army	Lieutenant	military police	Heterosexual
41	Army	Second Lieutenant	chemical corps	Heterosexual
42	Air Force	Major	pilot	Heterosexual
43	Army	Major	chaplain	Heterosexual
44	Army	Captain	chaplain	Heterosexual
45	Army	Captain	chaplain	Heterosexual
46	Army	Sergeant/Cadet	military police	Heterosexual
47	Air Force	Captain	none given	Heterosexual
48	Navy	Lieutenant Commander	meteorology/ oceanography	Heterosexual
49	Navy	Lieutenant	submariner	Heterosexual
50	Navy	Lieutenant Commander	SEAL	Heterosexual
51	Navy	Commander	surface warfare	Heterosexual
52	Navy	Lieutenant Commander	intelligence	Heterosexual
53	Navy	Lieutenant Commander	surface warfare	Heterosexual
54	Army	Sergeant	Ranger	Heterosexual
55	Navy	Commander	pilot	Heterosexual

GOVERNMENT POLICY TOWARDS HOMOSEXUALITY IN THE US MILITARY

56	Navy	Lieutenant Commander	flight officer	Heterosexual
57	Army	Second Lieutenant	social worker	Heterosexual
58	Army	Cadet	field artillery	Heterosexual
59	Army	Cadet	military police	Heterosexual
60	Army	Cadet	engineer	Heterosexual
61	Marines	Sergeant	none given	Heterosexual
62	Air Force	Chief Master Sergeant	none given	Heterosexual

APPENDIX H – MILITARY TIMES ADVERTISEMENT

Research on the repeal of Don't Ask, Don't Tell

Researchers from the Palm Center at University of California are studying unit Readiness, Cohesion and Morale since the repeal. CLICK HERE to take our anonymous, confidential survey.

PALM CENTER
BLUEPRINTS FOR SOUND PUBLIC POLICY

To recruit subjects for our survey, we ran this advertisement for three weeks and 50,000 clicks/page views on the websites of *Army Times*, *Navy Times*, *Air Force Times* and *Marine Corps Times*.

APPENDIX 1—TITLE 10 USC § 654

10 USC § 654—Policy concerning homosexuality in the armed forces—Repealed

Section, added Pub. L. 103–160, div. A, title V, § 571(a)(1), Nov. 30, 1993, 107 Stat. 1670, related to policy concerning homosexuality in the armed forces.

(a) **Findings.—** Congress makes the following findings:
  (1) Section 8 of article I of the Constitution of the United States commits exclusively to the Congress the powers to raise and support armies, provide and maintain a Navy, and make rules for the government and regulation of the land and naval forces.
  (2) There is no constitutional right to serve in the armed forces.
  (3) Pursuant to the powers conferred by section 8 of article I of the Constitution of the United States, it lies within the discretion of the Congress to establish qualifications for and conditions of service in the armed forces.
  (4) The primary purpose of the armed forces is to prepare for and to prevail in combat should the need arise.
  (5) The conduct of military operations requires members of the armed forces to make extraordinary sacrifices, including the ultimate sacrifice, in order to provide for the common defense.
  (6) Success in combat requires military units that are characterized by high morale, good order and discipline, and unit cohesion.
  (7) One of the most critical elements in combat capability is unit cohesion, that is, the bonds of trust among individual service members that make the combat effectiveness of a military unit greater than the sum of the combat effectiveness of the individual unit members.
  (8) Military life is fundamentally different from civilian life in that—
    (A) the extraordinary responsibilities of the armed forces, the unique conditions of military service, and the critical role of unit cohesion, require that the military community, while subject to civilian control, exist as a specialized society; and
    (B) the military society is characterized by its own laws, rules, customs, and traditions, including numerous restrictions on personal behavior, that would not be acceptable in civilian society.

These appendixes are not subject to U.S. copyright law.

(9) The standards of conduct for members of the armed forces regulate a member's life for 24 hours each day beginning at the moment the member enters military status and not ending until that person is discharged or otherwise separated from the armed forces.
(10) Those standards of conduct, including the Uniform Code of Military Justice, apply to a member of the armed forces at all times that the member has a military status, whether the member is on base or off base, and whether the member is on duty or off duty.
(11) The pervasive application of the standards of conduct is necessary because members of the armed forces must be ready at all times for worldwide deployment to a combat environment.
(12) The worldwide deployment of United States military forces, the international responsibilities of the United States, and the potential for involvement of the armed forces in actual combat routinely make it necessary for members of the armed forces involuntarily to accept living conditions and working conditions that are often spartan, primitive, and characterized by forced intimacy with little or no privacy.
(13) The prohibition against homosexual conduct is a longstanding element of military law that continues to be necessary in the unique circumstances of military service.
(14) The armed forces must maintain personnel policies that exclude persons whose presence in the armed forces would create an unacceptable risk to the armed forces' high standards of morale, good order and discipline, and unit cohesion that are the essence of military capability.
(15) The presence in the armed forces of persons who demonstrate a propensity or intent to engage in homosexual acts would create an unacceptable risk to the high standards of morale, good order and discipline, and unit cohesion that are the essence of military capability.

(b) **Policy.—** A member of the armed forces shall be separated from the armed forces under regulations prescribed by the Secretary of Defense if one or more of the following findings is made and approved in accordance with procedures set forth in such regulations:
(1) That the member has engaged in, attempted to engage in, or solicited another to engage in a homosexual act or acts unless there are further findings, made and approved in accordance with procedures set forth in such regulations, that the member has demonstrated that—
(A) such conduct is a departure from the member's usual and customary behavior;
(B) such conduct, under all the circumstances, is unlikely to recur;
(C) such conduct was not accomplished by use of force, coercion, or intimidation;
(D) under the particular circumstances of the case, the member's continued presence in the armed forces is consistent with the interests of the armed forces in proper discipline, good order, and morale; and

(E) the member does not have a propensity or intent to engage in homosexual acts.

(2) That the member has stated that he or she is a homosexual or bisexual, or words to that effect, unless there is a further finding, made and approved in accordance with procedures set forth in the regulations, that the member has demonstrated that he or she is not a person who engages in, attempts to engage in, has a propensity to engage in, or intends to engage in homosexual acts.

(3) That the member has married or attempted to marry a person known to be of the same biological sex.

(c) **Entry Standards and Documents.—**

(1) The Secretary of Defense shall ensure that the standards for enlistment and appointment of members of the armed forces reflect the policies set forth in subsection (b).

(2) The documents used to effectuate the enlistment or appointment of a person as a member of the armed forces shall set forth the provisions of subsection (b).

(d) **Required Briefings.—** The briefings that members of the armed forces receive upon entry into the armed forces and periodically thereafter under section 937 of this title (article 137 of the Uniform Code of Military Justice) shall include a detailed explanation of the applicable laws and regulations governing sexual conduct by members of the armed forces, including the policies prescribed under subsection (b).

(e) **Rule of Construction.—** Nothing in subsection (b) shall be construed to require that a member of the armed forces be processed for separation from the armed forces when a determination is made in accordance with regulations prescribed by the Secretary of Defense that—

(1) the member engaged in conduct or made statements for the purpose of avoiding or terminating military service; and

(2) separation of the member would not be in the best interest of the armed forces.

(f) **Definitions.—** In this section:

(1) The term "homosexual" means a person, regardless of sex, who engages in, attempts to engage in, has a propensity to engage in, or intends to engage in homosexual acts, and includes the terms "gay" and "lesbian".

(2) The term "bisexual" means a person who engages in, attempts to engage in, has a propensity to engage in, or intends to engage in homosexual and heterosexual acts.

(3) The term "homosexual act" means—

(A) any bodily contact, actively undertaken or passively permitted, between members of the same sex for the purpose of satisfying sexual desires; and

(B) any bodily contact which a reasonable person would understand to demonstrate a propensity or intent to engage in an act described in subparagraph (A).

APPENDIX 2—EXECUTIVE SUMMARY, CRWG REPORT

Report of the Comprehensive Review of the Issues Associated with a Repeal of Don't Ask, Don't Tell

EXECUTIVE SUMMARY

November 30, 2010

On March 2, 2010, the Secretary of Defense appointed the two of us to co-chair a working group to undertake a comprehensive review of the impacts of repeal, should it occur, of Section 654 of Title 10 of the United States Code, commonly known as the "Don't Ask, Don't Tell" law. In this effort, we were aided by a highly dedicated team of 49 military and 19 civilian personnel from across the Department of Defense and the Military Services.

Our assignment from the Secretary was two-fold: 1) assess the impact of repeal of Don't Ask, Don't Tell on military readiness, military effectiveness, unit cohesion, recruiting, retention, and family readiness; and 2) recommend appropriate changes, if necessary, to existing regulations, policies, and guidance in the event of repeal. The Secretary directed us to deliver our assessment and recommendations to him by December 1, 2010.[1] This document constitutes our report of that assessment and our recommendations. The Secretary also directed us to develop a plan of action to support implementation of a repeal of Don't Ask, Don't Tell. That plan accompanies this report.

At the outset, it is important to note the environment in which we conducted our work: the Nation's military has been at war on several fronts for over 9 years. Much is being demanded from the force. The men and women in uniform who risk their lives to defend our Nation are, along with their families, stretched and stressed, and have faced years of multiple and lengthy deployments to Iraq, Afghanistan, and elsewhere. Some question the wisdom of taking on the emotional and difficult issue of Don't Ask, Don't Tell on top of all else.

For these and other reasons, the Secretary directed that we "thoroughly, objectively and methodically examine all aspects of this question," and include, most importantly, the views of our men and women in uniform. Accordingly, over the last nine months we: solicited the views of nearly 400,000 active duty and reserve component Service members with an extensive and professionally-developed survey, which prompted 115,052 responses—one of the largest surveys in the history of the U.S. military; solicited the views of over 150,000 spouses of active duty and reserve component Service members, because of the influence and importance families play in the lives of Service members and their decisions to join, leave, or stay in the military, and received 44,266 responses; created an online inbox for Service members and their families to offer their views, through which we received a total of 72,384 entries; conducted 95 face-to-face "information exchange forums" at 51 bases and installations around the world, where we interacted with over 24,000 Service members—ranging from soldiers at Fort Hood, Fort Benning, and Fort Bragg, sailors at Norfolk, San Diego, and Pearl Harbor, airmen at Lackland, Langley, and Yokota in Japan, Marines at Camp Lejeune, Camp Pendleton, and Parris Island, cadets and midshipmen at our Service academies, and Coast Guardsmen on Staten Island, New York; conducted 140 smaller focus group sessions with Service members and their families; solicited the views of the Service academy superintendents and faculty, Service chiefs of chaplains, and Service surgeons general; solicited and received the views of various members of Congress; engaged RAND to update its 1993 study, *Sexual Orientation and U.S. Military Personnel Policy*; solicited and received the views of foreign allies, veterans groups, and groups both for and against repeal of the current law and policy; and during a two-week period prior to issuance, solicited and received the comments of the Secretaries of the Army, Navy and Air Force, and the Chiefs of each Service, on this report in draft form.

Finally, we heard the views and experiences of current and former Service members who are gay or lesbian. We knew that their viewpoints would be important, and we made affirmative efforts to reach them, though our ability to do so under the current Don't Ask, Don't Tell law was limited. The two of us personally interviewed former Service members who are gay or lesbian, including those who had been separated under Don't Ask, Don't Tell.

To reach those currently in the military, we hired a private company to administer the survey of Service members and an interactive online confidential communications mechanism. This company was obligated to protect the identity of Service members and did not reveal identifying information to the Working Group. Through the confidential communications mechanism, the private company was able to engage a total of 2,691 Service members, of whom self-identified as gay or lesbian, in interactive online conversations about their experiences.

Our Working Group also reviewed hundreds of relevant laws, regulations, and Department of Defense and Service policies and issuances (directives, instructions, and memoranda) and evaluated various policy options. As discussed in detail in section V, the breadth and depth of the Working Group's work was extensive. To our knowledge, our nine-month review and engagement of the force was the largest and most comprehensive in the history of the U.S. military, on any personnel-related matter.

Based on all we saw and heard, our assessment is that, when coupled with the prompt implementation of the recommendations we offer below, the risk of repeal of Don't Ask, Don't Tell to overall military effectiveness is low. We conclude that, while a repeal of Don't Ask, Don't Tell will likely, in the short term, bring about some limited and isolated disruption to unit cohesion and retention, we do not believe this disruption will be widespread or long lasting, and can be adequately addressed by the recommendations we offer below. Longer term, with a continued and sustained commitment to core values of leadership, professionalism, and respect for all, we are convinced that the U.S. military can adjust and accommodate this change, just as it has others in history.[2]

Significant to our assessment are the following:

The results of the Service member survey reveal a widespread attitude among a solid majority of Service members that repeal of Don't Ask, Don't Tell will not have a negative impact on their ability to conduct their military mission.[3] The survey was conducted by Westat, a research firm with a long track record of conducting surveys for the U.S. military.

The survey was one of the largest in the history of the military. We heard from over 115,000 Service members, or 28% of those solicited. Given the large number of respondents, the margin of error for the results was less than ±1%, and the response rate was average for the U.S. military.

The results of the survey are best represented by the answers to three questions:

When asked about how having a Service member in their immediate unit who said he or she is gay would affect the unit's ability to "work together to get the job done," 70% of Service members predicted it would have a positive, mixed, or no effect.[4]

When asked "in your career, have you ever worked in a unit with a co-worker that you believed to be homosexual," 69% of Service members reported that they had.[5]

When asked about the actual experience of serving in a unit with a co-worker who they believed was gay or lesbian, 92% stated that the unit's "ability to work together" was "very good," "good," or "neither good nor poor."[6]

Consistently, the survey results revealed a large group of around 50–55% of Service members who thought that repeal of Don't Ask, Don't Tell would have mixed or no effect; another 15–20% who said repeal would have a positive effect; and about 30% who said it would have a negative effect.[7] The results of the spouse survey are consistent. When spouses were asked about whether repeal of Don't Ask, Don't Tell would affect their preference for their Service member's future plans to stay in the military, 74% said repeal would have no effect, while only 12% said "I would want my spouse to leave earlier."[8]

To be sure, these survey results reveal a significant minority—around 30% overall (and 40–60% in the Marine Corps and in various combat arms specialties)—who predicted in some form and to some degree negative views or concerns about the impact of a repeal of Don't Ask, Don't Tell.

Any personnel policy change for which a group that size predicts negative consequences must be approached with caution. However, there are a number of other factors that still lead us to conclude that the risk of repeal to overall military effectiveness is low.

The reality is that there are gay men and lesbians already serving in today's U.S. military, and most Service members recognize this. As stated before, 69% of the force recognizes that they have at some point served in a unit with a co-worker they believed to be gay or lesbian.[9] Of those who have actually had this experience in their career, 92% stated that the unit's "ability to work together" was "very good," "good," or "neither good nor poor," while only 8% stated it was "poor" or "very poor."[10] Anecdotally, we also heard a number of Service members tell us about a leader, co-worker, or fellow Service member they greatly liked, trusted, or admired, who they later learned was gay; and how once that person's sexual orientation was revealed to them, it made little or no difference to the relationship.[11] Both the survey results and our own engagement of the force convinced us that when Service members had the actual experience of serving with someone they believe to be gay, in general unit performance was not affected negatively by this added dimension. Yet, a frequent response among Service members at information exchange forums, when asked about the widespread recognition that gay men and lesbians are already in the military, were words to the effect of: "yes, but I don't *know* they are gay." Put another way, the concern with repeal among many is with "open" service.

In the course of our assessment, it became apparent to us that, aside from the moral and religious objections to homosexuality, much of the concern about "open" service is driven by misperceptions and stereotypes about what it would mean if gay Service members were allowed to be "open" about their sexual orientation. Repeatedly, we heard Service members express the view that "open" homosexuality would lead to widespread and overt displays of effeminacy among men, homosexual promiscuity, harassment and unwelcome advances within units, invasions of personal privacy, and an overall erosion of standards of conduct, unit cohesion, and morality. Based on our review, however, we conclude that these concerns about gay and lesbian Service members who are permitted to be "open" about their sexual orientation are exaggerated, and not consistent with the reported experiences of many Service members.

In today's civilian society, where there is no law that requires gay men and lesbians to conceal their sexual orientation in order to keep their job, most gay men and lesbians still tend to be discrete about their personal lives, and guarded about the people with whom they share information about their sexual orientation. We believe that, in the military environment, this would be true even more so. According to a survey conducted by RAND of a limited number of individuals who anonymously self-identified as gay and lesbian Service members, even if Don't Ask, Don't Tell were repealed, only 15% of gay and lesbian Service members would like to have their sexual orientation known to everyone in their unit.[12] This conclusion is also consistent with what we heard from gay Service members in the course of this review:

> *"Personally, I don't feel that this is something I should have to 'disclose.' Straight people don't have to disclose their orientation. I will just be me. I will bring my family to family events. I will put family pictures on my desk. I am not going to go up to people and say, hi there—I'm gay."*[13]

> *"I think a lot of people think there is going to be this big 'outing' and people flaunting their gayness, but they forget that we're in the military. That stuff isn't supposed to be done during duty hours regardless if you're gay or straight."*[14]

If gay and lesbian Service members in today's U.S. military were permitted to make reference to their sexual orientation, while subject to the same standards of conduct as all other Service members, we assess that most would continue to be private and discreet about their personal lives. This discretion would occur for reasons having nothing to do with law, but everything to do with a desire to fit in, co-exist, and succeed in the military environment.

As one gay Service member stated:

> *"I don't think it's going to be such a big, huge, horrible thing that DoD is telling everyone it's going to be. If it is repealed, everyone will look around their spaces to see if anyone speaks up. They'll hear crickets for a while. A few flamboyant guys and tough girls will join to rock the boat and make a scene. Their actions and bad choices will probably get them kicked out. After a little time has gone by, then a few of us will speak up. And instead of a deluge of panic and violence . . . there'll be ripple on the water's surface that dissipates quicker than you can watch."*[15]

In communications with gay and lesbian current and former Service members, we repeatedly heard a patriotic desire to serve and defend the Nation, subject to the same rules as everyone else. In the words of one gay Service member, repeal would simply *"take a knife out of my back. . . . You have no idea what it is like to have to serve in silence."*[16] Most said they did not desire special treatment, to use the military for social experimentation, or to advance a social agenda. Some of those separated under Don't Ask, Don't Tell would welcome the opportunity to rejoin the military if permitted. From them, we heard expressed many of the same values that we heard over and over again from Service members at large—love of country, honor, respect, integrity, and service over self. We simply cannot square the reality of these people with the perceptions about "open" service.

Given that we are in a time of war, the combat arms communities across all Services required special focus and analysis. Though the survey results demonstrate a solid majority of the overall U.S. military who predict mixed, positive or no effect in the event of repeal, these percentages are lower, and the percentage of those who predict negative effects are higher, in combat arms units. For example, in response to question 68a, while the percentage of the overall U.S. military that predicts negative or very negative effects on their unit's ability to "work together to get the job done" is 30%, the percentage is 43% for the Marine Corps, 48% within Army combat arms units, and 58% within Marine combat arms units.[17]

However, while a higher percentage of Service members in warfighting units *predict* negative effects of repeal, the percentage distinctions between warfighting units and the entire military are almost non-existent when asked about the *actual* experience of serving in a unit with someone believed to be gay. For example, when those in the overall military were asked about the experience of working with someone they believed to be gay or lesbian,[18] 92% stated that their unit's "ability to work together," was "very good, "good" or "neither good nor poor.

Meanwhile, in response to the same question, the percentage is 89% for those in Army combat arms units and 84% for those in Marine combat arms units—all very high percentages.[19] Anecdotally, we heard much the same. As one special operations force warfighter told us, "We have a gay guy [in the unit]. He's big, he's mean, and he kills lots of bad guys. No one cared that he was gay."[20] Thus, the survey results reflecting actual experience, our other engagements, and the lessons of history lead us to conclude that the risks of repeal within warfighting units, while higher than the force generally, remain within acceptable levels when coupled with our recommendations for implementation.

The survey results also reveal, within warfighting units, negative predictions about serving alongside gays decrease when in "intense combat situations." In response to question 71a, for example, 67% of those in Marine combat arms units predict working alongside a gay man or lesbian will have a negative effect on their unit's effectiveness in completing its mission "in a field environment or out at sea." By contrast, in response to the same question, but during "an intense combat situation," the percentage drops to 48%.[21] See section VII. While 48% indicates a significant level of concern, the near 20-point difference in these two environments reflects that, in a combat situation, the warfighter appreciates that differences with those within his unit become less important than defeating the common enemy.

Our assessment also took account of the fact that the Nation is at war on several fronts, and, for a period of over nine years, the U.S. military has been fully engaged, and has faced the stress and demands of frequent and lengthy deployments. We conclude that repeal can be implemented now, provided it is done in manner that minimizes the burden on leaders in deployed areas. Our recommended implementation plan does just that, and it is discussed more fully in section XIII of this report and in the accompanying support plan for implementation. The primary concern is for the added requirement that will be created by the training and education associated with repeal. We are cognizant of this concern, but note that during this time of war, the Services have undertaken education and training in deployed areas on a number of important personnel matters. These education and training initiatives have included increased emphasis on sexual assault prevention and response, suicide prevention, and training to detect indications of behavioral health problems. The conduct of these programs in deployed areas indicates that training and education associated with a repeal of Don't Ask, Don't Tell can be accommodated. We assess this to be the case, in large part because our recommendations in this report involve a minimalist approach to changes in policies, and education and training to reiterate existing policies in a sexual orientation-neutral manner.

It is also the case that the results of the survey indicate that, in this wartime environment, a solid majority of Service members believe that repeal will have positive, mixed, or no effect. Most of those surveyed joined our military after September 11, 2001, and have known nothing but a military at war.

Our assessment here is also informed by the lessons of history in this country. Though there are fundamental differences between matters of race, gender, and sexual orientation, we believe the U.S. military's prior experiences with racial and gender integration are relevant. In the late 1940s and early 1950s, our military took on the racial integration of its ranks, *before* the country at large had done so. Our military then was many times larger than it is today, had just returned from World War II, and was in the midst of Cold War tensions and the Korean War. By our assessment, the resistance to change at that time was far more intense: surveys of the military revealed opposition to racial integration of the Services at levels as high as 80–90%.[22] Some of our best-known and most-revered military leaders from the World War II-era voiced opposition to the integration of blacks into the military, making strikingly similar predictions of the negative impact on unit cohesion. But by 1953, 95% of all African American soldiers were serving in racially integrated units, while public buses in Montgomery, Alabama and other cities were still racially segregated.[23] Today, the U.S. military is probably the most racially diverse and integrated institution in the country—one in which an African American rose through the ranks to become the senior-most military officer in the country 20 years before Barack Obama was elected President.

The story is similar when it came to the integration of women into the military. In 1948, women were limited to 2% of active duty personnel in each Service,[24] with significant limitations on the roles they could perform. Currently, women make up 14% of the force,[25] and are permitted to serve in 92% of the occupational specialties.[26] Along the way to gender integration, many of our Nation's military leaders predicted dire consequences for unit cohesion and military effectiveness if women were allowed to serve in large numbers. As with racial integration, this experience has not always been smooth. But, the consensus is the same: the introduction and integration of women into the force has made our military stronger. The general lesson we take from these transformational experiences in history is that in matters of personnel change within the military, predictions and surveys tend to overestimate negative consequences, and underestimate the U.S. military's ability to adapt and incorporate within its ranks the diversity that is reflective of American society at large.

Our conclusions are also informed by the experiences of our foreign allies. To be sure, there is no perfect comparator to the U.S. military, and the cultures and attitudes toward homosexuality vary greatly among nations of the world. However, in recent times a number of other countries have transitioned to policies that permit open military service by gay men and lesbians. These include the United Kingdom, Canada, Australia, Germany, Italy, and Israel.

Significantly, prior to change, surveys of the militaries in Canada and the U.K. indicated much higher levels of resistance than our own survey results—as high as 65% for some areas[27]—but the actual implementation of change in those countries went much more smoothly than expected, with little or no disruption. relevant. These agencies include the CIA, FBI, USAID, and the State Department, who at present have personnel who live and work alongside U.S. military personnel in deployed areas. Reportedly, in those agencies the integration of gay and lesbian personnel did not negatively affect institutional or individual job performance.

Finally, our overall assessment is itself based on a risk assessment conducted by a panel of military and DoD career civilian personnel drawn from across the Services, and included those in combat arms specialties. The panel utilized a standard military decision support process recommended by the J–8 directorate of the Joint Staff. This same process has been used by the Department of Defense to support recent decisions about the new Cyber Command location and authority, and the Afghanistan National Security Force size and mix.

Upon reviewing the survey results and other information gathered by the Working Group, the panel members utilized their own professional judgment to assess the risk of a repeal of Don't Ask, Don't Tell to military readiness, unit effectiveness, unit cohesion, recruiting, retention, and family readiness. The results of that exercise are detailed in section XI.

Informed by the panel's determinations, as the co-chairs of the Working Group the two of us then assessed the risk of repeal to overall "military effectiveness" as low. Figure 1 depicts the panel's ratings, plus our own assessment of risk to overall military effectiveness.

In sum, we are convinced the U.S. military can make this change, even during this time of war. However, this assessment is accompanied by, and depends upon, the recommendations provided in section XIII of this report.

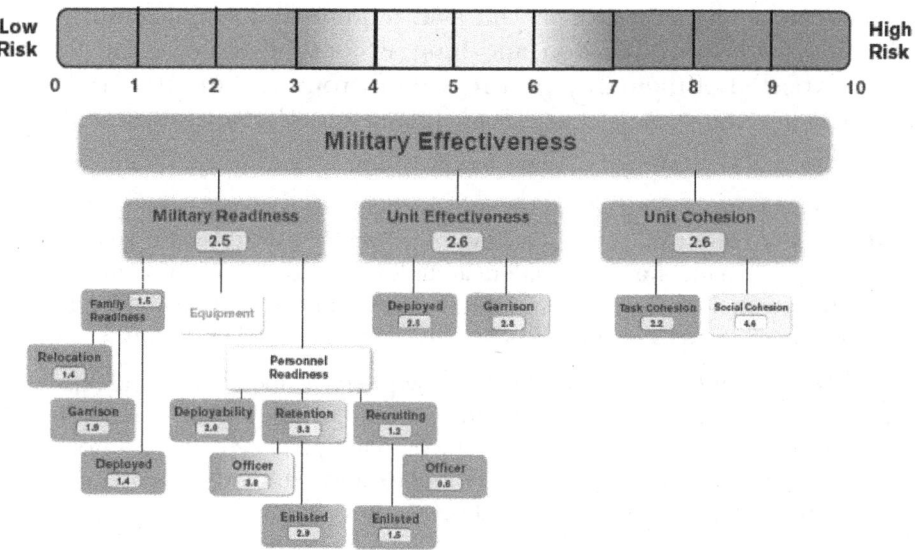

FIGURE 1 Assesment of Impact of a Repeal of Don't Ask, Don't Tell (color figure available online). See http://www.defense.gov/home/features/2010/0610_dadt/DADTReport_final_20101130%28secure-hires%29.pdf, on page 9 of the original report

Motivating many of our recommendations is the conclusion, based on our numerous engagements with the force, that repeal would work best if it is accompanied by a message and policies that promote fair and equal treatment of all Service members, minimize differences among Service members based on sexual orientation, and disabuse Service members of any notion that, with repeal, gay and lesbian Service members will be afforded some type of special treatment.

Included, also, should be a message to those who are opposed to "open" service on well-founded moral or religious grounds, that their views and beliefs are not rejected, and that leaders have not turned their backs on them. In the event of repeal, we cannot and should not expect individual Service members to change their personal religious or moral beliefs about homosexuality, but we do expect every Service member to treat all others with dignity and respect, consistent with the core values that already exist in each Service. These are not new concepts for the U.S. military, given the wide variety of views, races, and religions that already exist within the force.

Our most significant recommendations are as follows:

Leadership, Training, and Education. Successful implementation of repeal of Don't Ask, Don't Tell will depend upon strong leadership, a clear message, and proactive education. Throughout our review, we heard from a number of senior officers and senior enlisted leaders in all the Services words to the effect of "If the law changes, we can do this; just give us the tools to communicate a clear message." This will require us to equip commanders in the field with the education and training tools to educate the force on what is expected of them in a post repeal environment. In our support plan accompanying this report, we set forth this key implementation message for repeal:

> *Leadership.* The clear message from the Working Group's assessment is "leadership matters most." Leaders at all levels of the chain of command set the example for members in the unit and must be fully committed to DoD policy to sustain unit effectiveness, readiness, and cohesion.
>
> *Professionalism.* Leaders must emphasize Service members' fundamental professional obligations and the oath to support and defend the Constitution that is at the core of their military service. In the profession of arms, adherence to military policy and standards of conduct is essential to unit effectiveness, readiness, and cohesion.
>
> *Respect.* Unit strength depends on the strength of each member. We achieve that strength by treating each member with respect.

In our view, the starting point for this message should be a written communication from the leaders of the Department of Defense, including the Secretary of Defense and senior military leaders of each Service, that deliver their expectations in clear and forceful terms.

Standards of Conduct. Throughout our engagement with the force, we heard many concerns expressed by Service members about possible inappropriate conduct that might take place in the event of repeal, including unprofessional relationships between Service members; public displays of affection; inappropriate dress and appearance; and acts of violence, harassment, and disrespect. Many of these concerns were about conduct that is already regulated in the military environment, regardless of the sexual orientation of the persons involved, or whether it involves persons of the same sex or the opposite sex. For instance, military standards of conduct—as reflected in the Uniform Code for Military Justice, Service regulations and policies, and unwritten Service customs and traditions—already prohibit fraternization and unprofessional relationships. They also address various forms of harassment and unprofessional behavior, prescribe appropriate dress and appearance, and provide guidelines on public displays of affection.

We believe that it is not necessary to establish an extensive set of new or revised standards of conduct in the event of repeal. Concerns for standards in the event of repeal can be adequately addressed through training and education about how already existing standards of conduct continue to apply to *all* Service members, regardless of sexual orientation, in a post-repeal environment.

We do recommend, however, that the Department of Defense issue guidance that all standards of conduct apply uniformly, without regard to sexual orientation. We also recommend that the Department of Defense direct the Services to review their current standards to ensure that they are sexual-orientation neutral and that they provide adequate guidance to the extent each Service considers appropriate on unprofessional relationships, harassment, public displays of affection, and dress and appearance. Part of the education process should include a reminder to commanders about the tools they already have in hand to punish and remedy inappropriate conduct that may arise in a post-repeal environment. As a related matter, to address tensions and incidents that may arise between individual Service members in a post-repeal environment, including the Service member who simply refuses to serve alongside a gay person, commanders should be reminded of the enormous latitude and discretion they have, for the sake of unit cohesion, to address any situation concerning Service members who are intolerant or intractable in their behavior toward one another.

Moral and Religious Concerns. In the course of our review, we heard a large number of Service members raise religious and moral objections to homosexuality or to serving alongside someone who is gay. Some feared repeal of Don't Ask, Don't Tell might limit their individual freedom of expression and free exercise of religion, or require them to change their personal beliefs about the morality of homosexuality. The views expressed to us in these terms cannot be downplayed or dismissed. Special attention should also be given to address the concerns of our community of 3,000 military chaplains. Some of the most intense and sharpest divergence of views about Don't Ask, Don't Tell exists among the chaplain corps. A large number of military chaplains (and their followers) believe that homosexuality is a sin and an abomination, and that they are required by God to condemn it as such.

However, the reality is that in today's U.S. military, people of sharply different moral values and religious convictions—including those who believe that abortion is murder and those who do not, and those who believe Jesus Christ is the Son of God and those who do not—and those who have no religious convictions at all, already co-exist, work, live, and fight together on a daily basis. The other reality is that policies regarding Service members' individual expression and free exercise of religion already exist, and we believe they are adequate. Service members will not be required to change their personal views and religious beliefs; they must, however, continue to respect and serve with others who hold different views and beliefs.

Within the chaplain community, the solution to this issue can be found in the existing guidance developed by and for our chaplains, which we believe should be reiterated as part of any education and training concerning repeal. Those regulations strike an appropriate balance between protecting a chaplain's First Amendment freedoms and a chaplain's duty to care for all. Existing regulations state that chaplains "will not be required to perform a religious role . . . in worship services, command ceremonies, or other events, if doing so would be in variance with the tenets or practices of their faith."[28] At the same time, regulations state that "Chaplains care for all Service members, including those who claim no religious faith, facilitate the religious requirements of personnel of all faiths, provide faith-specific ministries, and advise the command."[29]

Privacy and Cohabitation. In the course of our review we heard from a very large number of Service members about their discomfort with sharing bathroom facilities or living quarters with those they know to be gay or lesbian. Some went so far to suggest that a repeal of Don't Ask, Don't Tell may even require separate bathroom and shower facilities for gay men and lesbians. We disagree, and recommend against separate facilities. Though many regard the very discussion of this topic as offensive, given the number of Service members who raised it, we are obliged to address it.

The creation of a third and possibly fourth category of bathroom facilities and living quarters, whether at bases or forward deployed areas, would be a logistical nightmare, expensive, and impossible to administer. And, even if it could be achieved and administered, separate facilities would, in our view, stigmatize gay and lesbian Service members in a manner reminiscent of "separate but equal" facilities for blacks prior to the 1960s. Accordingly, we recommend that the Department of Defense expressly prohibit berthing or billeting assignments or the designation of bathroom facilities based on sexual orientation. At the same time, commanders would retain the authority they currently have to alter berthing or billeting assignments or accommodate privacy concerns on an individualized, case-by-case basis, in the interests of morale, good order and discipline, and consistent with performance of mission.[30] It should also be recognized that commanders already have the tools—from counseling, to non-judicial punishment, to UCMJ prosecution—to deal with misbehavior in either living quarters or showers, whether the person who engages in the misconduct is gay or straight.

Most concerns we heard about showers and bathrooms were based on stereotype—that gay men and lesbians will behave as predators in these situations, or that permitting homosexual and heterosexual people of the same sex to shower together is tantamount to allowing men and women to shower together. However, common sense tells us that a situation in which people of different anatomy shower together is different from a situation in which people of the same anatomy but different sexual orientations shower together.

The former is uncommon and unacceptable to almost everyone in this country; the latter is a situation most in the military have already experienced. Indeed, the survey results indicate 50% of Service members recognize they have already had the experience of sharing bathroom facilities with someone they believed to be gay.[31] This is also a situation resembling what now exists in hundreds of thousands of college dorms, college and high school gyms, professional sports locker rooms, police and fire stations, and athletic clubs around the nation. And, as one gay former Service member told us, to fit in, co-exist, and conform to social norms, gay men have learned to avoid making heterosexuals feel uncomfortable or threatened in these situations.[32]

Equal Opportunity. We recommend that, in a post-repeal environment, gay and lesbian service members be treated under the same general principles of military equal opportunity policy that apply to all Service members. Under the Military Equal Opportunity program, it is DoD policy to "[p]romote an environment free from personal, social, or institutional barriers that prevent Service members from rising to the highest level or responsibility possible.

Service members shall be evaluated only on individual merit, fitness, and capability."[33] This policy goes hand-in-hand with Service-level policies and basic military values that call for treating every military member with dignity and respect. We do *not* recommend that sexual orientation be placed alongside race, color, religion, sex, and national origin, as a class eligible for various diversity programs, tracking initiatives, and complaint resolution processes under the Military Equal Opportunity Program. We believe that doing so could produce a sense, rightly or wrongly, that gay men and lesbians are being elevated to a special status as a "protected class" and will receive special treatment.

In a new environment in which gay and lesbian Service members can be open about their sexual orientation, we believe they will be accepted more readily if the military community understands that they are simply being permitted equal footing with everyone else. In the event of repeal of Don't Ask, Don't Tell, the Department of Defense should make clear that sexual orientation may not, in and of itself, be a factor in accession, promotion, or other personnel decision-making. Gay and lesbian Service members, like all Service members, would be evaluated only on individual merit, fitness, and capability. Likewise, the Department of Defense should make clear that harassment or abuse based on sexual orientation is unacceptable and that all Service members are to treat one another with dignity and respect regardless of sexual orientation. Complaints regarding discrimination, harassment, or abuse based on sexual orientation can be dealt with through existing mechanisms—primarily the chain of command—available for complaints not involving race, color, sex, religion, or national origin.

Benefits. As part of this review, we considered appropriate changes, in the event of repeal, to benefits to be accorded to same-sex partners and families of gay Service members. This issue is itself large and complex, and implicates the ongoing national political and legal debate regarding same-sex relationships. Members of the U.S. military are eligible for and receive a wide array of benefits and support resources, both for themselves and their families. A reality is that, given current law, particularly the Defense of Marriage Act, there are a number of those benefits that cannot legally be extended to gay and lesbian Service members and their same-sex partners, even if they are lawfully married in a state that permits same-sex marriage. An example of this is the Basic Allowance for Housing at the "with-dependent rate." The "with dependent" rate is limited by statute to Service members with "dependents."[34] The word "dependent" is also defined by statute and is limited to the Service member's "spouse" or dependent parents, unmarried children, or certain others under the age of 23 who are placed in the legal custody of the Service member.[35] And, the Defense of Marriage Act limits the definition of the word "spouse" to mean "only a person of the opposite sex who is a husband or wife."[36]

However, there are some benefits that are now, under current law and regulations, fully available to anyone of a Service member's choosing, including a same-sex partner, because they are "member-designated" benefits. Examples here are beneficiaries for Servicemembers' Group Life Insurance and Thrift Savings Plan, missing member notification, and hospital visitation access. If Don't Ask, Don't Tell is repealed, Service members may designate a same-sex partner for these benefits without then having to conceal the nature of the relationship from the military. In the event of repeal, the Department of Defense and the Services should inform Service members about these types of benefits so that they can take advantage of them for their committed same-sex partners should they desire to do so.

A third category of benefits are those that are not statutorily prohibited, but that current regulations do not extend to same-sex partners. With regard to this category, the Department of Defense and the Services have the regulatory flexibility to revise and redefine the eligible beneficiaries to include same-sex partners. Here, we recommend that, where justified from a policy, fiscal, and feasibility standpoint, the benefit be refashioned to become a member-designated one—in other words, to give the Service member, gay or straight, the discretion to designate whomever he or she wants as beneficiary. An example of a benefit in this category is the provision of free legal services by a military legal assistance office, and it may be suitable for this member-designated approach. Military family housing is another prominent benefit in this category. However, we do *not* recommend at this time that military family housing be included in the benefits eligible for this member-designated approach. Permitting a Service member to qualify for military family housing, simply by designating whomever he or she chooses as a "dependent," is problematic. Military family housing is a limited resource and complicated to administer, and a system of member designation would create occasions for abuse and unfairness.[37]

Also, we are *not*, at this time, recommending that the Department of Defense or the Services revise their regulations to specifically add same-sex committed relationships to the definition of "dependent," "family members," or other similar terms in those regulations, for purposes of extending benefits eligibility. We are convinced that, to create an environment in which gay and lesbian Service members can win quick and easy acceptance within the military community, repeal must be understood as an effort to achieve equal treatment for all. If, simultaneous with repeal, the Department of Defense creates a new category of unmarried dependent or family member reserved only for same-sex relationships, the Department of Defense itself would be creating a new inequity—between unmarried, committed same-sex couples and unmarried, committed opposite-sex couples. This new inequity, or the perception of it, runs counter to the military ethic of fair and equal treatment, and resentment at perceived inequities runs deep in military families.

We recommend that the particular issue of a "qualifying relationship" status for couples not in a Federally-recognized marriage be revisited as part of a follow-on review of the implementation of a repeal of Don't Ask, Don't Tell. This will permit the Department of Defense to revisit and reassess the issue as implementation of repeal is underway. It is also in recognition that the national debate on same-sex marriage and partner benefits is ongoing, and that the judicial and legislative landscape on this issue is in a state of flux.

Re-accession. In the event of repeal, we recommend that Service members who have been previously separated under Don't Ask, Don't Tell be permitted to apply for reentry into the military, pursuant to the same criteria as others who seek reentry. The fact that their separation was for homosexual conduct would not be considered as part of the Service member's application for re-accession. For example, a Service member separated under Don't Ask, Don't Tell who received an honorable discharge would be evaluated for re-accession under the same criteria that other Service members who had received honorable discharges would be. Further, consistent with the practice for other Service members who apply for re-accession, we recommend that the Service member who applies for re-accession after having been separated under Don't Ask, Don't Tell not be given any type of credit for the time out of service, subject to any actions a board for the correction of military records may, in its discretion, take.

UCMJ. We support the pre-existing proposals to repeal Article 125 of the Uniform Code of Military Justice and remove private consensual sodomy between adults as a criminal offense. This change in law is warranted irrespective of whether Don't Ask, Don't Tell is repealed, to resolve any constitutional concerns about the provision in light of *Lawrence v. Texas*[38] and *United States v. Marcum*.[39] We also support revising offenses involving sexual conduct or inappropriate relationships to ensure sexual orientation neutral application, consistent with the recommendations of this report. For example, the offense of adultery defined in the *Manual for Courts-Martial* should be revised to apply equally to heterosexual and homosexual sex that is engaged in by or with a married person.

Follow-on Review. Finally, we recommend that one year after any repeal of Don't
 Ask, Don't Tell has been in effect, the Department of Defense conduct a follow-on review to monitor the implementation of repeal and to determine the adequacy of the recommended actions that are adopted. This should include a reassessment of the same-sex partner benefits issues referred to earlier. We are confident in the assessment and recommendations summarized above and detailed in the pages that follow. As stated before, this may have been the most comprehensive and inclusive personnel-related review in the history of the U.S. military. We both personally spent many long hours on this project. Our work was supported by a team of highly-dedicated civilian and military personnel, many of whom are experts in the area of military personnel matters.

Two final points should be made about our mission. In the course of our review, many asked us if the stated positions of the President, the Secretary of Defense, and the Chairman of the Joint Chiefs of Staff in support of repeal in some way influenced, prejudiced, or constrained our review and assessment. This was not the case. The views expressed by Service members and their families in information exchange forums and other engagements were civil and professional, but always frank and diverse and reflected strongly held views both for and against changing the law and policy, without regard to the views expressed by our national leaders.

Next, our mandate was to assess the impact of repeal of Don't Ask, Don't Tell, and how best to implement repeal should it occur; we were not asked to determine *whether* the Don't Ask, Don't Tell law and policy *should* be repealed. However, our engagement of the force was wide-ranging enough that we did answer the question of *whether* the U.S. military *can* implement repeal of Don't Ask, Don't Tell. To be clear, the Service member survey did not ask the broad question whether Don't Ask, Don't Tell should be repealed. This would, in effect, have been a referendum, and it is not the Department of Defense's practice to make military policy decisions by a referendum of Service members. But, among the 103 questions in the Service member survey and the 44 questions in the spouse survey were numerous opportunities to express, in one way or another, support for or opposition to repeal of the current policy. Among the 72,000 online inbox submissions were numerous expressions both for and against the current policy. If the impact of repeal was predominately negative, that would have revealed itself in the course of our review.

Further, as co-chairs, we believe we are both personally required to report our honest and candid assessments to the Secretary—either as the solemn duty of a military officer to his civilian leadership, or because of the fiduciary obligation a lawyer owes his client. Thus, if our assessment was that the risk to military effectiveness of implementing repeal was unacceptable, we both would have been obligated to report that to the Secretary.

We are both convinced that our military can do this, even during this time of war. We do not underestimate the challenges in implementing a change in the law, but neither should we underestimate the ability of our extraordinarily dedicated Service men and women to adapt to such change and continue to provide our Nation with the military capability to accomplish any mission.

Carter F. Ham
General, United States Army

Jeh Charles Johnson
General Counsel, Department of Defense

NOTES

1. During the nine months we conducted our work, the legislative and legal landscape for Don't Ask, Don't Tell changed considerably. In May, efforts in Congress to repeal 10 U.S.C. § 654 gained momentum, and a repeal provision was added to the National Defense Authorization Act (NDAA) for Fiscal Year 2011 in both the House and Senate. The amended NDAA passed the full House, but, as of this writing, has not been voted upon by the full Senate. Also, a federal district court in California declared the Don't Ask, Don't Tell law to be unconstitutional in September, and issued a worldwide injunction immediately prohibiting Don't Ask, Don't Tell enforcement the following month. The decision and injunction were appealed by the Government, and the Court of Appeals for the Ninth Circuit stayed the injunction pending the appeal. As of this writing, the appeal before the Ninth Circuit is still pending. After careful consideration of these legislative and legal developments, we determined they did not alter our assignment in any way.

2. Our assessment is based on conditions we observe in today's U.S. military. It is not meant as commentary on any point prior to today, over the past 17 years since the Don't Ask, Don't Tell law was enacted by Congress. Nothing in this report should be construed as doubt by us about the wisdom of enacting 10 U.S.C. § 654 in 1993, given circumstances that existed then.

3. See Section VII, "The Survey Results."

4. See Appendix C, "Survey Responses: 2010 Department of Defense Survey of Service Members," Question 68a.

5. See Appendix C, Question 36.

6. See Appendix C, Question 47a.

7. See Appendix C, Questions 67–75.

8. See Appendix D, "Survey Responses: 2010 Department of Defense Survey of Spouses," Question 17.

9. See Appendix C, Question 36.

10. See Appendix C, Question 47a.

11. Service members, CRWG Focus Groups, 2010; Service members, Online Inbox, 2010.

12. RAND, *Sexual Orientation and U.S. Military Personnel Policy—An Update of RAND's 1993 Study*, Santa Monica, CA: National Defense Research Institution, November 2010, 27.

13. Service member, Confidential Communication Mechanism, 2010.

14. Service member, Confidential Communication Mechanism, 2010.

15. Service member, Confidential Communication Mechanism, 2010.

16. Service member, Confidential Communication Mechanism, 2010.

17. Westat, *Support to the DoD Comprehensive Review Working Group Analyzing the Impact of Repealing "Don't Ask, Don't Tell,"* vol. 1, Rockville, MD, November 19, 2010, Appendices J and L, Question 68a.

18. See Appendix C, Question 47a.

19. Westat, vol. 1 Appendices J and L, Question 47a.

20. Service member, CRWG Focus Group, 2010.

21. Westat, vol. 1 Appendices J and L, Questions 71a and 71c.

22. Erin R. Mahan, Office of the Secretary of Defense, *Racial and Gender Intergration of the Armed Forces*, August 9, 2010, 5–6.

23. Matthew Cashdollar, "Not Yes or No, But What If: Implications of Open Homosexuality in the Military," in *Attitudes Aren't Free: Thinking Deeply About Diversity in the US Armed Forces*, ed. James Parco and David Levy (Maxwell Air Force Base: Air University Press, 2010), 169.

24. Judith Bellafaire, "America's Military Women—The Journey Continues," accessed November 19, 2010, http://www.womensmemorial.org/Education/WHM982.html.

25. Defense Manpower Data Center, *Female Representation in the Active Component—1980, 1987, & 1990–2009*, Excel spreadsheet.

26. OUSD(P&R), e-mail communication to CRWG, November 12, 2010.

27. United Kingdom Ministry of Defence, *Report of the Homosexuality Policy Assessment Team* (United Kingdom: February 1996); G2–8 and Franklin C. Pinch, *Perspective on Organization Change in Canadian Forces*, January 1994, 22.

28. Department of the Army, AR 165-1, *Army Chaplain Corps Activities*, December 3, 2009, 12.

29. Department of the Navy, SECNAVINST 1730.7D, *Religious Ministry within the Department of the Navy*, August 8, 2008, 5.

30. Each Service has directives on command authority, for example: Department of the Air Force, AFI 51–604, *Assumption of Command*, April 4, 2006; Department of the Army, AR 600–20, *Army Command Policy*, April 27, 2010.

31. See Appendix C, Question 87.

32. Retired Service member, communication to CRWG Co-Chair, May 10, 2010.

33. Department of Defense, DoDD 1350.2, *Department of Defense Military Equal Opportunity (MEO) Program*, August 18, 1995, 2.–3; Department of Defense, DoDD 1020.2, *Diversity Management and Equal Opportunity (EO) in the Department of Defense*, February 5, 2009, 4.

34. 37 U.S.C. § 401.

35. 37 U.S.C. § 401.

36. 1 U.S.C. § 7.

37. Current Service policies state that non-dependents are not allowed to reside in military family housing. We do not recommend any changes to those policies, other than to state that any exception to policy to allow a non-dependent to reside in military family housing, be administered without regard to sexual orientation.

38. 539 US 558 (2003).

39. 60 M.J. 198 (C.A.A.F. 2004).

APPENDIX 3—DADT REPEAL ACT OF 2011

H.R.6520 – Don't Ask, Don't Tell Repeal Act of 2010 (Introduced in House—IH)

HR 6520 IH

111th CONGRESS

2d Session

H. R. 6520

To provide for the repeal of the Department of Defense policy concerning homosexuality in the Armed Forces known as 'Don't Ask, Don't Tell'.

IN THE HOUSE OF REPRESENTATIVES

December 14, 2010

Mr. PATRICK J. MURPHY of Pennsylvania (for himself and Mr. HOYER) introduced the following bill; which was referred to the Committee on Armed Services

---

A BILL

To provide for the repeal of the Department of Defense policy concerning homosexuality in the Armed Forces known as 'Don't Ask, Don't Tell'.

Be it enacted by the Senate and House of Representatives of the United States of America in Congress assembled,

SECTION 1. SHORT TITLE.

This Act may be cited as the 'Don't Ask, Don't Tell Repeal Act of 2010'.

SEC. 2. DEPARTMENT OF DEFENSE POLICY CONCERNING HOMOSEXUALITY IN THE ARMED FORCES.

(a) **Comprehensive Review on the Implementation of a Repeal of 10 U.S.C. 654-**
  (1) IN GENERAL- On March 2, 2010, the Secretary of Defense issued a memorandum directing the Comprehensive Review on the Implementation of a Repeal of 10 U.S.C. 654 (section 654 of title 10, United States Code).
  (2) OBJECTIVES AND SCOPE OF REVIEW- The Terms of Reference accompanying the Secretary's memorandum established the following objectives and scope of the ordered review:

(A) Determine any impacts to military readiness, military effectiveness and unit cohesion, recruiting/retention, and family readiness that may result from repeal of the law and recommend any actions that should be taken in light of such impacts.

(B) Determine leadership, guidance, and training on standards of conduct and new policies.

(C) Determine appropriate changes to existing policies and regulations, including but not limited to issues regarding personnel management, leadership and training, facilities, investigations, and benefits.

(D) Recommend appropriate changes (if any) to the Uniform Code of Military Justice.

(E) Monitor and evaluate existing legislative proposals to repeal 10 U.S.C. 654 and proposals that may be introduced in the Congress during the period of the review.

(F) Assure appropriate ways to monitor the workforce climate and military effectiveness that support successful follow-through on implementation.

(G) Evaluate the issues raised in ongoing litigation involving 10 U.S.C. 654.

(b) **Effective Date**- The amendments made by subsection (f) shall take effect 60 days after the date on which the last of the following occurs:

(1) The Secretary of Defense has received the report required by the memorandum of the Secretary referred to in subsection (a).

(2) The President transmits to the congressional defense committees a written certification, signed by the President, the Secretary of Defense, and the Chairman of the Joint Chiefs of Staff, stating each of the following:

(A) That the President, the Secretary of Defense, and the Chairman of the Joint Chiefs of Staff have considered the recommendations contained in the report and the report's proposed plan of action.

(B) That the Department of Defense has prepared the necessary policies and regulations to exercise the discretion provided by the amendments made by subsection (f).

(C) That the implementation of necessary policies and regulations pursuant to the discretion provided by the amendments made by subsection (f) is consistent with the standards of military readiness, military effectiveness, unit cohesion, and recruiting and retention of the Armed Forces.

(c) **No Immediate Effect on Current Policy**- Section 654 of title 10, United States Code, shall remain in effect until such time that all of the requirements and certifications required by subsection (b) are met. If these requirements and certifications are not met, section 654 of title 10, United States Code, shall remain in effect.

(d) **Benefits**- Nothing in this section, or the amendments made by this section, shall be construed to require the furnishing of benefits in violation of section 7 of title 1, United States Code (relating to the definitions of 'marriage' and 'spouse' and referred to as the Defense of Marriage Act).

(e) **No Private Cause of Action**- Nothing in this section, or the amendments made by this section, shall be construed to create a private cause of action.

(f) **Treatment of 1993 Policy**-
  (1) TITLE 10- Upon the effective date established by subsection (b), chapter 37 of title 10, United States Code, is amended–
    (A) by striking section 654; and
    (B) in the table of sections at the beginning of such chapter, by striking the item relating to section 654.
  (2) CONFORMING AMENDMENT- Upon the effective date established by subsection (b), section 571 of the National Defense Authorization Act for Fiscal Year 1994 (10 U.S.C. 654 note) is amended by striking subsections (b), (c), and (d).

(Repeal effective on the date established by section 2(b) of Pub. L. 111–321. Don't Ask, Don't Tell Repeal Pub. L. 111–321, Dec. 22, 2010, 124 Stat. 3515.)

Index

Adkins, William 118–19
Afghanistan: women warriors 267
alcohol misuse 295
Allsep, L.Michael Jr 4
Almy, Mike 48
ambiguous definitions 118–19
AMERICAblog 56
Arabic linguist discharges 100–3
Army-McCarthy hearings 1954 77
assaults 354–61
Australia: transgender people 320

Belgium: transgender people 320–1
Belkim, Aaron 26–8, 29–30
Benecke, Michele 19–20, 21
Ben-Shaldon, Miriam 139
Bird, Richard 128
blackmail 243
bumper sticker: leadership by 259–62

Cammermayer, Margarethe 142–3
Canada: transgender people 318–19
career hindrance 243
Center for American Progress 34–5
Choi, Dan 81–2, 57, 47–8, 51
Civil deference to the military 177–91; costs of 186–8
Clark nomination 97–100
Class I homosexuals 116–17
Class II homosexuals 116–17
Class III homosexuals 116–17; sexual orientation, and 120
Claytor, Graham 139–40
clinical assessment lessons 271–87
Cochran, Byran N. 4
command 342–3
Comprehensive Review Working Group (CRWG) 147–76; assessment 166–7; certification 171–2; composition 153–4; confidential communications mechanism 159–60; education 162; engagement of the force 155; engagement with outside groups 164; focus groups 156; formation 149–53; function 172–4; implementation, and 171–2; information exchange forums 155–6; leadership 162; legal review 160–2; legislative action, and 171; lines of effort 154–65; military insiders, and 180; Online Inbox 156; panel assessment 164–5; policy 160–2; purpose 172–4; recommendations 167–9; report 165–9; research 162–4; Senate hearings, and 149, 169–71; State of the Union address, and 149; structure 153–4; surveys 156–9; terms of reference 151–3; training 162
CRWG executive summary 399–416; benefits 411–13; cohabitation 410–11; education 407–8; equal opportunity 411; follow on review 414–15; leadership 407–8; moral and religious concerns 409–10; privacy 410–11; re-accession 413; standards of conduct 408–9; training 407–8; UCMJ 413–14
control contradiction 239–40
Cox, Anna Marie 31–2
Crittenden Report 123–4
Czech Republic: transgender people 320

Daily Beast 39–40
Davidson, Henry Lawrence 124–5
Defence Manpower Center 142
Defense Manpower Data Center 181–2
Defense of Marriage Act 1996 143
Department of Defense: self-study 179–83
depression 244, 294–5
discipline 342
DOD Directive 1982 140
Don't ask don't tell (DADT) 1; constitutional challenge 52–6; costs of 186–8; death of 58–9; delayed repeal implementation 11–12; government's response to litigation 183–6; historical context 335–6; laying legal groundwork for repeal 125–32; LGBT advocates, and 17–71; Pentagon report on repeal 56; phases in legislative history 94; political battle for repeal 7–13; public

INDEX

opinion, and 24; repeal as contested 2002–2005 96–104; repeal as radioactive 1993–2002 96–7; repeal, impact of 225–49; rise and fall 1–5; shift in policy 1993–2011 94

Don't ask don't tell Repeal Act 2011 417–19 see also repeal of DADT

double life 243

Edgell, Luke R. 2
Estrada, Armando X 3

fake marriages 241–2
family readiness 343
feigned intent 243–4
Ferenbach, Victor 48
Fox-Genovese, Elizabeth 265–6
Frank, Barney 37
Frank, Nathaniel 2
Fulton, Brenda Sue 2

Gamble, Alastair 22
Gates, Robert 44–6; reaction to legal developments 55; Defense Secretary 27
Gates Letter 10–11, 50–2
gay warrior 268
gays in US military 193–221; acceptance 194; antecedents of participation and inclusion 207–13; compatibility 201; conceptualizing way forward 193–221; contemporary research 194–201; disclosure of sexual orientation 201–2; family values 202; framework for integrating 206–13; implications for future research 214; meta-analytical findings involving cohesion and performance 204; military readiness 203–5; military values 202; perceived impact 203; personal privacy 201; reviewing research 193–221; unit cohesion 203; unit effectiveness 205
Get EQUAL 47–9; tactics 60
Gibbs, Robert 47, 25, 30–1, 32
Gillibrand, Senator 39
Goins, Earnest Ruddolph 121–2
Green, Vernon B. 122–3

harassment 354–61
Haynes, Cyrus 130–1
heroism contradiction 238–9
Hertzberg, Hendrick 38–9
Hillan, Clifford C. 131–2
Hillman, Elizabeth L. 3
homophobia: widespread acceptance 141–2
homosexual exclusion politics: Army versus Air Force disputes 121–3
honourable discharge 140–1

Hopkins, Jonathan 82–3
Human Rights Campaign 18

inability to seek help 242
isolation 241
Israel: transgender people 320–1

Kennedy, Joe 130
Knights Out 81–2
Knudson, Edward Joseph 125–6
Korb, Lawrence J. 3

Lackey, Carl 129
Lee, Jonathan L. 3
Levy, Dave 1–2
LGBT advocates 17–71; blog swarm 46; compromise 52; Congressional chatter 49–50; constitutional challenge 52–6; DADT, and 17–71; defensive White House 29–33; executive option 28–9; finishing the job: 2010 43–59; funding stream 24; growing public pressure 33–6; HRC shifts 43–4; hurdles overcome 18; leveraging research: 2009 25–43; long-term public information campaign 59–60; military outreach 23–5; new political reality, and 36–9; Pentagon, and 26–8; Pentagon response 36; political logjam 35–6; priorities 39–43; State of the Union address 44–7; recommendations for post-DADT health care systems 377–8
Log Cabin Republicans 185
LOL 273–87; composition 273; coping strategies 281; data summary 274; discussion topics 275–6, 280; ethnicity/military branch 280; group meetings 275–6; health needs and challenges 278–80; indicators of success 281–2; introduction to group members 276–7; outreach strategies 277–8; participant demographics 278; sexual orientation/gender identity 279; stress mediators 281
Luna, Sgt Edgar 85–6

Mack, William P. 264
Maddow, Rachel 33, 83
martial masculinity 251–70; technological challenge 257–9
Matlovich, Leonard 138–9
McCaffery, Barry 263
McCain, Senator 45
mental health characteristics of sexual minority veterans 289–305; demographics and military service 294; hypothesis 293; impact of LGB identity while in military 299; limitations of study 303; method for finding comparable comparison

INDEX

means 297; methods 293; military experiences related to sexual orientation 295–7; participant characteristics 294; relationships between military experiences and mental health issues 299–302; research results 298–9; study design and procedures 293

Messina, Jim 45

military readiness 329–73; academic scholars 332; active-duty service members 332–3; concern about 337; DADT repeal opponents contacted 383; impact of DADT repeal 329–73; knowledge of LGB peers 366–7; letter to 553 retired generals and admirals 381; mass disclosures, and 365; meaning 336–7; Military Times advertisements 393; military units, observation of 334; opponents, attitude of 336; pre-test/post-test quasi-experiment 335; professionalism, and 365–6; public opponents of DADT repeal 332; research methods 331–5; research results 336; research strategies 330–1; scholars and experts interviewed 387; service member interviews 389–91; standards of evidence 379–80; validity of research 367–9; watchdog organizations contacted 385

Miller, Katherine 83

Mitchell, Valory 4

morale 361–5

MST 291

Mullen, Admiral 44–5, 149–51

Murphy, Patrick 37–8

myth of the warrior 251–70

Neff, Christopher L. 2

Netherlands: transgender people 320–1

Ortega, Carmen 132

Outserve 79–91; active duty voices 85–6; Board 85; chapter formation 84–5; faces of 82–4; final repeal, and 87; future developments 88; Knights Out, and 81–2; media outreach, and 88; 101 faces of courage 87–8; origins 79; preparing for reality of repeal 86–7; reasons for success 80; secret communications 80

Pentagon: LGBT advocates, and 26–8, 36
Pentagon policy 137–45
Petraeus, David 252–3
Philips, Judge Virginia 25, 53–4
Plutarch 256
policy concerning homosexuality in armed forces 395–7

policy entrepreneurship 93–110; Arabic linguist discharges 100–3; Clark nomination 97–100; comparing 2004's vote count to 2010's results 106–8; DADT repeal as contested 97–104; DADT repeal as emerging issue 103–4; DADT repeal as radioactive 96–7; examples 95; House comparison of 2004 estimate vote count and 2010 final vote 106; period before issue reaches consensus 108; Republican opposition to university RUTC politics 103–4; role 94–5; senate comparison of 2004 estimate vote count and 2010 final vote 107; study of teams within organizations 95; weak political support for gays in military 96

politics of paranoia 73–7; central image 75; conspiracy 75; fact, relationship to 76; sexual deviance 75–6; sexual power 75–6

PTSD 291, 294

public information campaign 1993–2008 19–25

Quindlen, Anna 29

Ramirez, Maria Heliana 4
Reagan administration 137–45
recruitment 350–4
Reid, Senator Harry 34
repeal of DADT, impact of 225–49; interviewing technique 231–2; research analysis 232–3; research methods 228–9; research procedure 230; sample 229; subjects 230; theoretical results 233–44
Republican opposition to university ROTC policies 103–4
retention 350–4
Roll Call 36–7

Seefried, Josh 79–80
service academies 263–7
sexual assault 242
Shalikashvili, General John 23
Signorile, Michelangelo 40–1
silence contradiction 240–1
Skelton, Ike 50
SLDN 19–20; entrepreneurial team 95–6; foundation of 95; policy entrepreneurship, and 93–110; Senate and House meetings October 2002 to March 2005 102
Smith, Nathaniel 119–20
sodomy, definition 116
Spain, transgender people 319–20
spirituality 343
standards of evidence: military readiness 379–80

INDEX

START Treaty 57–8
suffering in silence 242
suicidiality 291–2, 294–5
Sweden: transgender people 320–1

Thailand: transgender people 319
The Hill 42
transgender people 307–28; current US military policies 308–10; mental health issues 315–17; non–US militaries 317–21; physical and mental health concerns 313–15; prevalence in military 310–13; "psychological condition" 309; recommendation 322–3; UCMJ Articles 133 and 134 310; US objections 321–2; vulnerability 324

UCMJ; Article 133 120; Article 134 120; policies of exclusion 115–18; sodomy 116
Udall, Senator Mark 42
Unfriendly Fire 24–5
Uniform Code of Military Justice (UCMJ) 114
unit cohesion 343–50
United Kingdom: transgender people 317–18
University of California: Palm Centre 8–9, 21–3
Uruguay: transgender people 320
US Air Force; exclusionary regulations 116

US Court of Military Appeals 112–35; ambiguous definitions 118–19; case history of homosexuality 112–35; enforcement of UCMJ 115; protection from accusatory questioning and innuendos 128; protection from command influence 128–30; protection from government entrapment 130–1; protection from unfairly prejudicial evidence and testimony 126–8; protection from unreasonable searches 131–2; repeal of DADT, and 133–4
US Navy exclusionary regulations 116

values contradiction 233–5
Veterans Affairs services 271–87

Walrod, Ty 79–80
war: physical contest, as 252
warrior ideal 253–5
Warren, Robert Daniel 126–8
wartime contradiction 236–7
Watkins, Perry 141–2
Williams Institute 22–3
Wilson-Buford, Kellie 2–3
Winchell, Barry 97
World War II: women, and 262

Yerke, Adam F. 4